W9-BSX-630

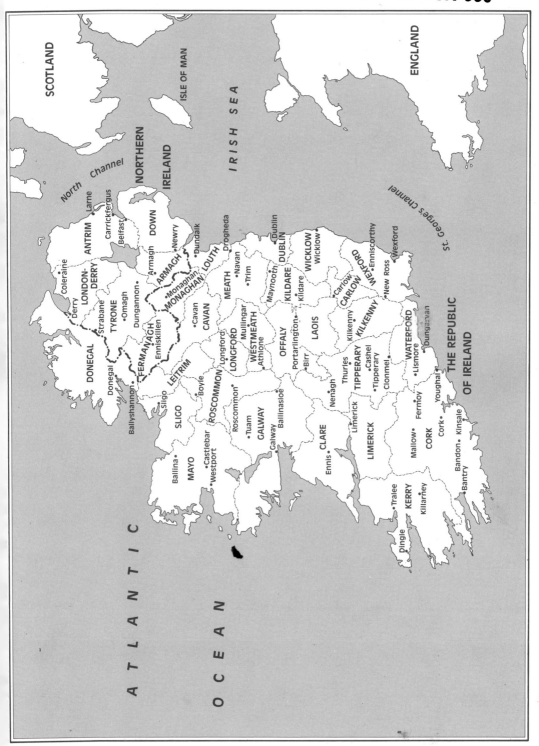

SCOTLAND

ENGLAND

ISLE OF MAN

North Channel

NORTHERN
IRELAND

IRISH SEA

St. George's Channel

Larne
Carrickfergus
ANTRIM
Belfast
DOWN
Newry

coleraine
Derry
LONDON-
DERRY
Armagh
ARMAGH
Dundalk
LOUTH
Drogheda
Strabane
TYRONE
Dungannon
Omagh
Monaghan
MONAGHAN
Navan
MEATH
Trim
Dublin
Dublin

DONEGAL
Donegal
Ballyshannon
FERMANAGH
Enniskillen
Cavan
CAVAN
Mullingar
WESTMEATH
Athlone
Maynooth
KILDARE
Kildare
WICKLOW
Wicklow
Enniscorthy
Wexford

LEITRIM
Longford
LONGFORD
OFFALY
Portarlington
Birr
LAOIS
Carlow
CARLOW
WEXFORD
New Ross

Sligo
SLIGO
Boyle
ROSCOMMON
Roscommon
Tuam
GALWAY
Ballinasloe
Thurles
TIPPERARY
Tipperary
Cashel
Clonmel
Kilkenny
KILKENNY
WATERFORD
Dungarvan
THE REPUBLIC
OF IRELAND

Ballina
MAYO
Castlebar
Westport
Galway
CLARE
Ennis
Nenagh
Limerick
LIMERICK
Mallow
Fermoy
CORK
Cork
Youghal
Lismore

ATLANTIC

OCEAN

Tralee
KERRY
Killarney
Bandon
Kinsale
Bantry
Dingle

T · H · E
INTELLIGENT
TRAVELLER'S
GUIDE TO
HISTORIC
IRELAND

PHILIP · A · CROWL

CB
CONTEMPORARY
BOOKS
CHICAGO

Library of Congress Cataloging-in-Publication Data

Crowl, Philip Axtell, 1914–
 The intelligent traveller's guide to historic Ireland / Philip A. Crowl.
  p. cm.
 Includes bibliographical references and index.
 ISBN 0-8092-4062-9 : $35.00
 1. Ireland—Description and travel—1981—Guide-books. 2. Northern
Ireland—Description and travel—1981—Guide books. 3. Historic
buildings—Northern Ireland—Guide-books. 4. Historic sites—Northern
Ireland—Guide-books. 5. Historic buildings—Ireland—Guide-
books. 6. Historic sites—Ireland—Guide-books. 7. Northern Ireland—
History—1969 8. Ireland—History. I. Title.
DA980.C78 1990
914.1504'824—dc20   90-1959
                                 CIP

Published by Contemporary Books, Inc.
180 North Michigan Avenue, Chicago, Illinois 60601
Manufactured in the United States of America
International Standard Book Number: 0-8092-4062-9

To my grandchildren:
Michael Denton O'Neil
and
Christina Margaret O'Neil

Contents

Acknowledgments

For their indispensable assistance, I am deeply indebted to Dr. Peter Harbison, archaeologist and editor of *Ireland of the Welcomes*, and Professor Aidan Clarke, Department of Modern History, Trinity College, Dublin. Both of them scrutinized large portions of the manuscript, called my attention to numerous errors of fact, and shared with me their profound learning in their respective fields of Irish archaeology and history. Neither, of course, is to be held accountable for any residual flaws in the final product or for any idiosyncrasies of interpretation. These are the sole responsibility of the author.

To the staffs of the Milton Eisenhower Library of the Johns Hopkins University and the Chester W. Nimitz Library of the United States Naval Academy I am indebted for their unfailing courtesy and cooperation. Mr. Robert Tower of Fred Hanna Ltd., Dublin, was most helpful in keeping me currently advised of recent Irish publications in relevant fields of archaeology and history that might otherwise have escaped my attention. Bill Clipson of Annapolis, Maryland, prepared the endpaper maps. Tom Ryan of San Francisco took time off from his own travels in Ireland to investigate sites I had overlooked. Finally, many thanks are owed to numerous Irish friends, casual acquaintances, and even total strangers for facilitating my extensive field trips and for enhancing the pleasure of my visits to both sides of the border.

Introduction

Not long after the close of the Second World War, with the rebirth of serious archaeological research in Ireland, the National Monuments branch of the Office of Public Works in Dublin undertook to clean up the country's famous High Crosses. Over the centuries moss and lichen had gradually encrusted these splendid monuments of sculpted stone—relics of the "Age of the Saints," when Irish Christianity shone like a beacon to all of western Europe. So, chemicals were sprayed, organic growths removed, stone restored to its original color, and the intricate carvings beneath the vegetation once more became legible to those who understood the symbolism of Early Christian iconography.

Yet not everyone was pleased with the results. "Romantic Ireland" may be, as William Butler Yeats put it, "dead and gone," and "with O'Leary in the grave," but Irish romanticists live on. To such as these the destruction of the mossy patina that overlay these ancient monuments was an act of desecration. Better it would be, in their view, to honor antiquity for its own sake than to expose the past to the harsh light of scientific inquiry. The covering layer of vegetation did not so much disfigure the crosses as endow them with a mysterious aura more precious than the precise meaning of the inscriptions thus concealed.

The author of this volume takes his stand squarely alongside the Office of Public Works. Historical accuracy, to the extent that it can be achieved, is deemed preferable to romantic fiction, no matter how endearing the latter may be. This is, therefore, not a book about the legendary Emerald Isle of song and story. The Sorrows of Deirdre receive no mention here, nor does "The Harp that Once through Tara's Halls." The vast treasury of Irish folklore goes largely untapped. Absent too are references to St. Patrick's homily on the shamrock, or to the inflammatory beauty of Queen Dervorgilla of Bréifne, or to the host of other myths, sacred and profane, that have so long obscured the realities of Irish history. Nor is this yet another exercise in retrospective Anglophobia. There is much more to Irish history than the oft-told tale of English perfidy.

This is, rather, a book about Ireland's solid achievements, in the literal sense of both words. It is about buildings and artifacts: dolmens, stone circles, sculptures, castles, towers, monasteries, stately homes, gardens, metalwork, tools, weapons, decorated manuscripts, paintings, books, etc. It is also about the history of Ireland, that is, the political, social, and economic conditions under which these sundry objects were created. Indeed it can be argued that Irish history can best be measured by these physical relics of its troubled past. The plenitude of Irish ruins and the wealth of Irish museum holdings make up in part for the relative sparseness of the documentary record—sadly depleted by long years of neglect, conquest, and internecine warfare. To catalog these relics, to describe their functions, to explain the historical context in which they were produced, used, and abused, and to assist the intelligent traveller in finding and understanding them—these are the major purposes of this book.

This is a companion volume to the author's previous publications, *The Intelligent Traveller's Guide to Historic Britain* (1983) and *The Intelligent Traveller's Guide to Historic Scotland* (1986). Like them, the present book is part narrative history and part gazetteer, the two parts knit together by cross-references. It can be read, therefore, either as a short textbook of Irish history or as a guidebook to Irish historical sites—or, preferably, as both.

PART I: NARRATIVE HISTORY

This is a chronological account of Ireland's past, with emphasis on its visible and visitable remains. It is divided into eight chapters, each covering a period of Irish prehistory and history from the arrival of the first Mesolithic immigrants in about 8500 B.C. to the official birth of the Republic of Ireland on Easter Monday, A.D. 1949. Wherever the name of a prehistoric or historic site appears—or of a museum, monument, church, garden, or distinguished piece of architecture—it is typed in **bold print**, followed by a page reference to Part II.

PART II: GAZETTEER

Here the same sites mentioned in Part I in chronological order are listed in the order of their geographical distribution. The Gazetteer is divided into six geographic regions, starting in the southeastern corner of the Republic of Ireland and ending with the northwesternmost corner of Northern

Ireland.* Each region is subdivided into counties, also arranged in geographic order from east to west and south to north. Within each county the Gazetteer lists in alphabetical order the names of the population centers (cities, towns, or villages) in which, or near which, are situated the sites mentioned in Part I. In general, the sites under each population center are listed in the order of their proximity from that center, in each direction, so as you drive north, for example, from a city, the sites are listed in the order you encounter them.

READING THE GAZETTEER

Here is the heading of a typical Gazetteer entry (actually the first one to appear):

SOUTHEASTERN IRELAND
County Wexford
BALLYHACK

*** **Dunbrody Abbey** *(117, 127, 140)*, 2½ mi N; W side of R 733 (to New Ross); signposted and visible from road; OS ½ 23S 71 15; key at house across road

---

This heading is to be read as follows:

County Wexford is the southeasternmost county in the southeastern region of Ireland. Ballyhack is a village within the county, which, though small, appears on any good road map.

Asterisks: The number of asterisks indicates the author's evaluation of the site's historic or architectural significance and of its attractiveness to travellers. Attractiveness is measured in terms of the intrinsic interest or beauty of the site and of its convenience to visitors measured by such factors

---

*In recent years many travellers have avoided the six counties of Northern Ireland because of the distressing sectarian violence so alarmingly reported by the media. This is a pity, since the region holds many attractions, both scenic and historic. As the Irish writer Dervla Murphy put it, in urging her own countrymen to cross the border more frequently: "Visitors from the South . . . would find the people as welcoming, the scenery as good, the roads better, and the weather no worse." Nor would American visitors likely suffer any greater risk to life and limb than if they stayed at home. On this point, statistics speak clearly: many, if not most, large American cities regularly show a much higher homicide rate than does Belfast or any other part of Northern Ireland.

as accessibility by car, boat, or public transport, the sufficiency and clarity of roadside signposts, and the frequency and duration of visiting hours. (Stately homes, churches, and museums not open to the public at least three days a week during the summer months are downgraded irrespective of their other merits.) The rating of three asterisks (***) means "outstanding" and not to be missed if possible; two asterisks (**) means "very good"; and one asterisk (*) means "good." No asterisks means that the site in question, though of sufficient historic interest to warrant inclusion in the narrative, is either too difficult of access or not attractive enough to warrant most travellers making any great effort to search it out.

Site Name: The name of the site always appears in **bold print**. The parenthesized digits following the site name indicate the page number or numbers where the site is mentioned in Part I.

Mileage and Direction: In the example cited above, the next entry (2½ mi N) means that the site in question is about 2½ miles in a northerly direction from the base population center—in this case, Ballyhack.

Route Numbers and Signposts: R 733 is the number of the road leading north from Ballyhack, on the west side of which Dunbrody Abbey lies. This, and comparable route numbers for other sites, will be found on any modern road map or atlas. Unfortunately, the Irish Republic has been dilatory in updating its road signs, so these map numbers are often different from those posted along the roadsides. In this particular case the route number appearing on the road signs leading to Dunbrody will read "L 159." But also appearing on the same signs will be the name of New Ross, the next town beyond the site itself. In the Gazetteer, therefore, the words "to New Ross" appear in parentheses immediately following the given route number—as in all other cases where route numbers are cited. Thus, by paying attention to towns and villages designated on the road signs, motorists will know where they are heading, even though the route numbers they are reading on the signs are different from those they will have seen on the road map.

In the Republic the signposting of most prehistoric and historic sites is even more erratic. In this regard not much has changed since the close of the last century, when the authors Somerville and Ross (in *The Irish R.M.*) reported that in Western Cork road signs did not exist because "the residents, very reasonably, consider them to be superfluous, even ridiculous, in view of the fact that everyone knows the way, and as for strangers, 'haven't they got tongues in their heads as well as another?' " In other words, the foreign motorist in southern Ireland had best be prepared frequently to STOP AND ASK! In Northern Ireland, on the other hand, accurate and frequent signposts are the rule, and navigation by auto is much less complicated.

Map Coordinates: The entry "OS ½ 23S 71 15" in the example cited refers to Map Number 23 in the Half Inch Maps of Ireland Series, published by the Ordnance Survey of the Republic of Ireland. There are twenty-five maps in the series, and they are available from the Ordnance Survey, Phoenix Park, Dublin, and at most bookshops throughout the country. The first digit or two digits (in this case "23") indicate the number of the appropriate OS map. The capital letter ("S") identifies the grid of the National Grid System in which the site lies and can be disregarded. The next four digits represent distances in kilometers measured from the southwest corner of the map to the site in question. In locating a site on any of these Ordnance Survey Maps, start at the lower left (southwest) corner and read to the right along the bottom edge to the figure indicated by the first two digits. From this point north is your longitude line. Starting again at the lower left corner, read up the left edge of the map to the figure indicated by the third and fourth digits. From this point eastward is your latitude. Where longitude and latitude lines intersect is the approximate location of the site you are looking for.

Like the road signs, unfortunately, the Irish Ordnance Survey maps are somewhat obsolete. They are, furthermore, drawn on too small a scale (1:126,720) to be altogether satisfactory. Many sites do not appear at all, and some that do are identified in such small print as to be illegible without a magnifying glass. Nevertheless, any traveller wanting to visit many field sites in the remote regions of the countryside will find them useful, if not indispensable.

In respect to maps, Northern Ireland is much better endowed than the Republic. Specifically, the eighteen Ordnance Survey maps for these six Irish counties that remain part of the United Kingdom are more up-to-date and much larger in scale (1:50,000). Site identifications are marked clearly, often with a distinguishing light-blue bar. Coordinates are indicated in the same way as for the half-inch maps, except that they are given in six digits instead of four. The third and sixth digits represent tenths of kilometers, thus making possible a more precise pinpointing of the site in question.

One further aid to the traveller, if not indispensable, is at least eminently useful: an ordinary pocket compass. It is not hard to get lost in the remote regions where many Irish field sites are located. Nor is it always easy to make sense of many of the country's ruins without proper compass orientation.

Opening Hours: Where none is stated, as in the example, the site can normally be visited at any time of the day or night. If entry is barred, a key is usually available at some nearby house, identified where possible in the Gazetteer. Protestant churches on both sides of the border (except for cathedrals and some other large houses of worship) are almost always locked when not in use for services. Local inquiry, however, will frequently reveal the location of the necessary keys. Roman Catholic churches are almost always open during daytime hours, although those situated in the outskirts of Dublin sometimes are not. For museums, stately homes, and the like, the hours given in the Gazetteer apply to the summer months only. They are, however, subject to change. For the most up-to-date information concerning stately homes, readers are advised to obtain the current edition of the Historic Irish Tourist Houses & Gardens Association's *Historic Houses, Castles & Gardens*. This pamphlet is published annually and is available at many bookshops and most Tourist Information Offices.

Site Descriptions: Underneath the heading comes a description of the site— one or more paragraphs explaining its historic origins and significance and describing its present appearance. These descriptions may duplicate some of the information contained in Part I, though usually they are more detailed and aimed more specifically at guiding the traveller through and around the site in question. They are not, of course, as detailed as the guidebooks that are sometimes available for on-site purchase. For most travellers, however, they should provide all the guidance needed.

ROAD MAPS AND TOURIST INFORMATION

The only maps provided in this book are those on the endpapers, front and back. They are intended to do no more than orient travellers unfamiliar with Irish geography and particularly to acquaint them with the location and boundaries of the separate counties. Therefore, good road maps, or a road atlas, are essential to the motorist in Ireland. The author prefers the Ordnance Survey's *Road Atlas of Ireland*, which covers the whole island, north and south. There are, however, others equally good and easily available at almost any bookshop. An atlas is preferable to a collection of road maps because it is more easily managed in the front seat of a car. In either case the essential ingredient for serious travellers is a good index to whichever map or atlas they use. *Really* serious travellers will, of course, equip themselves also with the relevant half-inch or 1:50,000 Ordnance Survey maps.

In addition to the above, detailed local maps are often available at the Tourist Information Office run by the Irish Tourist Board (*Bord Fáilte*). There are altogether about eighty of these in the Republic, plus another fifty "Tourist Information Points," usually located in post offices, private shops, etc. Easily identifiable by their signposts showing the small letter *i* on a green background, the Tourist Information Offices are normally open from 9:00 A.M. to 6:00 P.M. Monday through Friday and from 9:00 A.M. to 1:00 P.M. on Saturday. These places are mines of information, courteously offered, about local sites, hotels, lodgings, restaurants, tourist attractions, and more. The North, too, has a proportionate number of Tourist Information Offices providing the same kinds of service as those in the Republic.

APPENDIX A: THE BEST OF IRELAND

This section lists, under a number of categories (e.g., ecclesiastical ruins, stately homes, etc.) those Irish sites considered by the author to be the most attractive and interesting and therefore worthy of three asterisks (***) in the rating system described above.

APPENDIX B: GENEALOGICAL RESEARCH

Because so many North American travellers to Ireland are interested in tracing their family roots, this section offers some basic information about how to find and make use of the major repositories of genealogical records in both the Irish Republic and Northern Ireland. It is intended only as an introduction to this difficult and complicated subject. It will not tell the reader how to compose his or her family tree, only how and where to get started.

APPENDIX C: SELECTED READINGS

This is not a complete bibliography, but rather a guide to further readings for those travellers interested in delving more deeply into the subject of Ireland and its history. Two types of books are included: (1) travel literature, including other guidebooks; and (2) general histories of Ireland, as well as scholarly monographs of special interest.

INDEX

Page references in the index appear in two types of print. Those in **bold print** refer to Part II (the Gazetteer); all others refer to Part I (Narrative History) or to Appendixes A and B.

HOW TO PREPARE AN ITINERARY

Some travellers prefer not to plan ahead, to wander at random through the countryside, stopping and starting as the mood dictates. Others, more frugal perhaps of time and money, believe that advance planning for a journey of any length can eliminate the wastage of both. It is to the latter category that these suggestions are addressed.

1. Study the county map on the endpapers. Without a fairly good understanding of which counties lie where, any reader or traveller is likely soon to get lost.

2. Read Part I as needed. Irish history can be confusing, and few strangers to it will be able to place the sites they visit in proper historical context without studying this narrative account.

3. After reading Part I, make a list of those sites or types of sites you most want to see. Appendix A (The Best of Ireland) should be helpful here. Then decide on which areas of the country you most want to visit. This is the place to begin exercising self-restraint. Ireland is not a big country, but road travel can be slow, and some places of interest require transport by boat, which is even slower. You can't see it all in three or four weeks.

4. Using the index and Gazetteer, match your preferred list of sites with your preference for areas to be visited. Eliminate those sites falling outside the areas chosen. They can await another visit.

5. Using the Gazetteer, check the other sites in the general area of those you have chosen. Though not included in your preferred list, you may want to visit some of them anyway while in the neighborhood.

6. Use the Gazetteer in conjunction with a road map or an atlas for the general location of the sites you are seeking and the shortest route by which they can be reached. Once in the area, consult the appropriate Ordnance Survey map, especially when searching for archaeological field sites. Again, be prepared to STOP AND ASK!

7. Do not crowd your itinerary excessively. A good rule of thumb for the motoring traveller is no more than six sites and no more than seventy-

five miles per day. Even this may prove too much for those who prefer long lunch breaks, early arrival at their evening's destination, and frequent stops to admire the magnificent scenery.

8. Finally, allow time for rest, recreation, and conversation. Play a round of golf. Go to the races. Visit a pub that features group singing. Hoist a Guinness or two. Search out your distant relatives if you know what part of Ireland your great-grandmother came from. And best of all, stop and talk. Nowhere in the world are people more universally friendly than in Ireland. And nowhere in the English-speaking world is the spoken language more deftly or more lovingly handled. The Irish worship words. As a stranger, you are more than welcome to join in the celebration.

Part One

Narrative History

Chapter One
Prehistoric Ireland

"Who first took Ireland in the beginning after the Creation of the World?" Thus begins one of the early prose poems of the *Lebor Gabála Erenn (The Book of the Takings of Ireland)*, a compilation of manuscripts completed in the twelfth century and purporting to narrate the history of the successive colonizations of the country before the coming of Christianity. More commonly known as "The Book of Invasions," it was the handiwork of several generations of Irish monks, whose apparent intention was to weave the oral traditions of their fellow countrymen into the fabric of Old Testament chronology and thereby lend Christian sanctity to long-cherished pagan beliefs. Accordingly, the answer to the question as to who founded the first human settlement in Ireland was "Cessair, daughter of Bith, son of Noah." This lady, in anticipation of the Great Flood, persuaded her father to build an ark in which a party of fifty women and three men escaped to Ireland—"a place where men had never come till then, where no evil or sin had been committed, and which was free from the reptiles and monsters of the world." On arrival, Ladra, the pilot of the ark, died "of an excess of women," and all the rest were overwhelmed by the deluge—save for the youth Fintan, who survived to tell the tale. "In this wise, then," concludes the account, "The Taking of Cessair came to an end."

But this was only the first of seven "takings." After the Flood came one Partholon from Greece, but the colony he founded was eventually destroyed by plague. Next, from Scythia, appeared the followers of Nemed, who were in turn subdued or driven back to the European continent by the Fomorians, a savage race of seafarers. Some of Nemed's descendants settled in Greece, where they were enslaved and became known as the Fír Bolg. Out of their captivity these dark-haired, dark-skinned people subsequently escaped back to Ireland, where they were later set upon and driven westward into Connacht and onto the islands of Aran by the Tuatha De Danann. In contrast to the primitive Fír Bolg, these people (the tribe of the goddess Danu) were a civilized folk, skilled in the arts, and endowed with supernatural powers. But they in their turn were overcome by the last of the invaders of Ireland. These were the Milesians, the sons of Míl. They

14

came from Spain, though their roots lay in Egypt, where Moses had promised Gaedhuil, a remote ancestor, that his posterity would one day inhabit a land free of serpents and other poisonous things. In fulfillment of this prophecy the three sons of Míl—Eber, Eremon, and Ir—made their way to Ireland. Though Ir died en route, Eber and Eremon settled there, to become the forebears of all that country's many native kings and royal clans—a breed that in due time would make up a sizable fraction of the total population.

This account, which for centuries was accepted as more or less factually correct, is unfortunately pure fiction. "Unfortunately" because none of the efforts of latter-day prehistorians has succeeded in producing nearly so dramatic or coherent an explanation of Ireland's pre-Christian past. Advances of fairly recent date in the fields of archaeology, geology, paleobotany, macrophotography, microphotography, comparative anthropology, and linguistics have indeed vastly added to modern man's store of knowledge about his most remote ancestors. Archaeologists have unearthed (often literally) a huge number of artifacts produced by Ireland's ancient peoples. Prehistoric tombs and religious shrines have been mapped and measured in detail. Since its development in 1949, the technique of dating fossils and other organic remains by measuring their radiocarbon (C 14) content has made possible the development of a reasonably accurate prehistoric chronology. Of more recent vintage, the science of dendrochronology (tree-ring dating) has allowed an even greater precision.

Yet bones and stones and all the other objects that together form the grist of the archaeologist's mill are, sad to say, incurably mute. If they have a story to tell, it is one that can be drawn from them only by inference. And inferences are not facts. Nor is there any necessary agreement among the experts who draw them. Thus, though archaeology may be a "hard" science, prehistorical scholarship based on archaeological data is not. All conclusions drawn from such data therefore must perforce be considered tentative. And readers of this chapter are advised to note that, while Ireland's legendary past is largely mythical, the true picture of her actual prehistoric past is but dimly understood.

THE STONE AGE: CIRCA 8500–2000 B.C.

During the hundreds of thousands of years comprising what is known as the Ice Age, no human being is believed to have set foot on Ireland. Four times during that long era, mighty ice sheets moved south from the Arctic Circle to encase most of northern Europe. Between the periods of thick glaciation occurred episodes of rising temperatures known as *interglacials* and *interstadials*. During these intervals of climatic amelioration, nomadic hunters in pursuit of big game moved westward from modern France into the plains and forests of England—not yet separated from the Continent by water. There is no evidence, however, that any of these wanderers penetrated any farther north in Britain than the Highland Line. Thus neither the northern counties of modern England nor any part of Scotland witnessed the advent of these hardy adventurers of the Paleolithic (Old Stone) Age. Nor did Ireland, though it was still connected with northern Britain by one or more land bridges over which passed numerous species of flora and fauna.

Then, in about 14,000 B.C., the last of the great glaciers (called the Devensian) began to thaw, and by about 8500 B.C. the thick layer of ice had disappeared entirely. As the glaciers melted, the surrounding seas rose, and Ireland eventually became an island. With the disappearance of the land bridges, the migration of plants and animals came to an end, so that the number of species native to Ireland was less than two-thirds the figure for Britain. (Among those not making the passage was the snake, whose absence later generations were to attribute to the miraculous intervention of St. Patrick.) But before the encroaching seas inundated the land bridges, a sizable number of animals did make it across. So too did man-the-hunter.

Thus, sometime in the ninth millennium before the Christian Era, members of the species *Homo sapiens* first set foot on Irish soil. These people had reached a stage of culture classified by archaeologists as "Mesolithic"; that is, of the Middle Stone Age between the Paleolithic (Old Stone) era of nomadic big-game hunters and the Neolithic (New Stone) Age of agriculturalists and herdsmen. They were primarily small-game hunters, fishers, and food gatherers. But where these people came from and where they first landed is a matter of endless dispute.

Until quite recently Irish prehistorians agreed that the first arrivals must have settled in modern County Antrim, only twelve miles from the Kintyre peninsula of Scotland. This hypothesis seemed to be confirmed by the discovery in the far northeast of Ireland of Mesolithic settlement sites dating (by radiocarbon analysis) to the first half of the ninth millennium (i.e, 9000–8001 B.C.). The most notable of these is at Mount Sandel on the eastern shore of the river Bann. Among the finds here and elsewhere were numerous tiny microliths of chert and flint, of the type that can be seen today in the display cases of several Irish museums, notably the **National Museum of Ireland** in Dublin *(355)* and the **Limerick Museum** *(337)* in the city of that name. These normally measure less than two inches long and a half inch wide and are not implements in their own right, but parts of composite implements such as barbs for arrows, edgings of knives, and points of borers, awls, and picks, as well as the flakes or nodules from which they were struck.

It is noteworthy, however, that artifacts of the same approximate date and with the same characteristics have not yet been discovered in that region of Scotland lying opposite the Antrim coast. On the other hand they have been found farther south in Britain in the present English counties of Cumbria and Lancashire opposite the Irish coast between County Down and County Dublin. This suggests that the first settlers in Ireland may have crossed not from Scotland but by one or more of the land bridges from northwest England or perhaps from the Isle of Man. This hypothesis of an eastern, versus northeastern, first entry is confirmed to some extent by discoveries, since 1978, of a number of early Mesolithic sites in the south of Ireland; for example, on the shore of Lough Boora, near Kilcormac, County Offaly, 125 miles southwest of the settlement at Mount Sandel, and on the banks of the river Blackwater near Mallow, County Cork, another seventy-five miles south. Thus it would appear that the entire east coast north of Dublin may have served as the passageway of Ireland's first settlers and that they, or their Mesolithic descendants, spread widely throughout the island.

It also appears that in the course of time a new set of implements was contrived—broader and longer than the early Mesolithic finds. Classified as Larnian (after the late Mesolithic site at Larne in County Antrim), these utensils include awls, scrapers, double-pointed implements, elongated pebbles with bevelled ends (thought to be limpet scoops), and picks and axes up to four and five inches long. (Samples are on view at the two museums previously mentioned.) These are heavy-duty implements, some apparently used in hunting, others for cutting and chopping. The uniqueness of this tool kit, along with the absence of a comparable industry of the same date in England, suggests that late Mesolithic culture in Ireland developed more or less in isolation. In short, after the early colonization, further migration from across the sea may have discontinued until about the year 4000 B.C. If so, it was the last long period of time that Ireland was to be free of incursions from abroad.

Sometime early in the fourth millennium before the Christian Era a new set of immigrants began to arrive on Irish shores. Long before this time the sea had covered the land bridges, so these people must have come by boat. The type of vessel they used was probably not dissimilar to the native Irish curragh of a later date—a small round-bottomed craft of bent willow framework covered with hides and waterproofed with animal fat. (There are models of such boats on display at the **National Maritime Museum** *[374]* in Dun Laoghaire, County Dublin, and, of these, the

"Dingle curragh" and the "Boyne coracle" probably bear a close resemblance to the earliest of these prehistoric craft.)

These new immigrants were the precursors of the New Stone Age—farmers and herdsmen spawned by what archaeologists refer to as "the Neolithic revolution"—so named after only one of its significant innovations: the polished and hafted stone ax used for clearing forest. It had taken up to four thousand years for this new culture to reach Ireland from its birthplace in the Fertile Crescent between the Tigris and the Euphrates. There, perhaps ten thousand years ago, men and women began to grow cereal crops, maintain herds of domesticated sheep and goats, weave textiles, mold and bake clay into pots, build permanent houses in nucleated villages, and exchange their nomadic way of life for the more settled occupations of farming and herding. Slowly the techniques of mixed farming spread westward, reaching Britain in about 4000 B.C. and Ireland not much later. Where exactly these immigrants came from is unknown, though it is a good guess that some must have set out from western Britain and some from the Continent, probably by way of the Irish Sea.

While a number of the newcomers apparently established themselves in already-settled Mesolithic communities along the coast, the majority of Neolithic farmers seem to have pushed inland to clear the forest with their polished stone axes and to establish mixed farming communities, where they raised wheat and barley and herded cattle, sheep, pigs, and goats. One such settlement (of late Neolithic date) was situated on the light limestone soils neighboring Lough Gur in County Limerick. Excavations here from the 1930s to the 1950s revealed traces of two small houses dating to Neolithic times. These have been reproduced imaginatively in the form of the connected thatched stone buildings that now house the **Lough Gur Interpretive Centre** *(339)*, where instructive films are shown regularly, and a small collection of stone-age and bronze-age artifacts is on display.

Among the artifacts found at Lough Gur were polished ax heads of porcellanite rock that could only have come from Tievebulliagh Mountain overlooking Cushendall in County Antrim or from Rathlin Island off the northeast coast, both more than two hundred miles from Lough Gur as the crow flies. These were the sites of Neolithic "ax factories," where rocks were mined and shaped into rough ax heads. From both these places the unfinished product was shipped all over Ireland for further polishing and grinding, and, from Tievebulliagh, even into Britain as far south as Kent and Cornwall.

Other implements, also widely distributed, were made of flint, a crystalline, almost glasslike rock, easily hammered or punched into sharp objects useful for cutting, piercing, scraping, and boring. In Ireland the major supply of fresh flint is embedded in the chalk deposits of Counties Antrim, Londonderry, and Down. The wide distribution of flint artifacts throughout the country indicates an active trading network comparable to that for the products of the ax factories. Flint implements of Neolithic provenance, as well as those of chert, come in a great variety of shapes and sizes. Besides ax heads there are leaf- and lozenge-shaped arrowheads, kite-shaped spearheads, knives, scrapers, picks, burins, etc. Samples of this tool kit, as well as of Neolithic round-bottomed clay pots for storing food and of heavier flat-bottomed cooking pots, abound in Ireland's museums. In addition to the two already mentioned—the **National Museum of Ireland** *(355)* in Dublin and the **Limerick Museum** *(337)*—displays of Neolithic artifacts can be seen at the **Hunt Museum** *(338)* on the outskirts of Limerick; **Wexford County Museum, Enniscorthy Castle** *(287)*; the **County Tipperary Museum** *(303)* in Clonmel; the **Monaghan County Museum** *(400)* in Monaghan town; the **Donegal Historical Society Museum** *(427)* in Rossnowlagh; the **Armagh County Museum** *(442)* in the city of that name; the **Fermanagh County Museum, Enniskillen Castle** *(449)*, Enniskillen; and the **Ulster Museum** *(457–458)* in Belfast.

Most of the Neolithic artifacts to be found today in these repositories can be classified as grave goods, that is, tools, hunting gear, pottery, and, more rarely, items of personal adornment originally deposited along with the dead, presumably to accompany them into the next world. The deceased, or at least those whose social and economic status so warranted, were normally buried in great tombs of stone covered with mounds of earth and gravel called *cairns*. Modern archaeologists call these mausoleums *megalithic*, a term derived from the classical Greek words for large (*megas*) and stone (*lithos*). There are at least twelve hundred megalithic tombs extant in Ireland, more than the combined total for England, Wales, and Scotland. They were communal places of interment, used over a period of time for a number of burials. Sometimes the bodies were cremated, sometimes inhumed, that is, buried in an unburned condition.

Probably the oldest of these tombs date from the later fourth millennium B.C. and are classified as "court cairns," so named from the open courts that stood outside the mausoleums and from the mounds or cairns of stone and gravel that had been piled over them. The tombs themselves consisted of long, narrow, stone-walled galleries, normally segmented into chambers, each separated from the others either by a low sill or by septal stones rising to the height of the walls on either side. Occasionally side chambers led off the main gallery, thus creating a transepted or cruciform ground plan. The gallery was entered from the adjacent court (or courts) through two jambstones of equal height across which a lintel stone was laid. Matching vertical jambstones and horizontal lintels also marked the division between the separate chambers. The roof was normally flat, but side chambers might be vaulted by a process known as *corbelling*, which was to have a long life in the history of Irish architecture. Corbelling was achieved by the simple device of laying each course of flat stones on top of the one below so that the upper course projected slightly inward. As the process was repeated, the space between the walls gradually narrowed until the aperture between them at the top could be covered by a single slab.

The court, unlike the burial chambers, was open to the sky and flanked by standing stones (orthostats). In plan it might be either oval or semicircular. Some of these tombs had a court at only one end, some at both ends, and some at or close to the center of the long gallery. Presumably it was within these courts that mourners gathered to participate in some kind of funeral rite incident to the actual burial of the dead, although it is possible that they were the scenes of religious ceremonies unconnected with interments. The covering cairn was usually broader at the front than at the back and was held in place (revetted) by upright stones (kerbstones) at the edges.

Altogether there are more than three hundred known court cairns in Ireland, almost all of them scattered throughout the northern half of the island. In County Sligo **Creevykeel** *(418)*, north of Sligo town, is one of the longest in Ireland, the mound measuring up to 120 feet. This is a "full-court" cairn, so called because, in plan, the single court is a complete oval except for a narrow entranceway on the east. The two-chambered gallery extends from the west end of the court, and west of this are two separate burial chambers entered from the side of the mound and possibly of a later date than the main tomb. **Cohaw** *(401)* in County Cavan, a few miles southeast of Cootehill, is a "double-court" cairn with a semicircular forecourt at each end of a five-chambered galleried tomb. In County Donegal, near Glencolumbkille, are two center-court cairns—**Farranmac-bride (Mannernamortee)** *(427)* north of the village, and **Cloghanamore (Malin More)** *(428)* to the south. The former is now in a tumbled condition; the latter, with its unusually large east-facing court, is partially restored.

Northern Ireland too is rich in court cairns. The most accessible of these now stands outside the main entrance to the **Ulster Museum** *(457)* in Belfast, brought here, stone by stone, from Ballintaggart, County Armagh, and reconstructed. **Audleystown Cairn** *(441)*, west of Strangford, County Down, and overlooking Strangford Lough, is another double-court cairn, which has the distinction of having yielded the largest number (thirty-four) of unburned skeletons yet found in any tomb of this type. In County Armagh, near Crossmaglen, is **Annaghmare Cairn** *(443)*, a good specimen with three burial chambers in line behind the court and a pair of extra chambers placed on opposite sides of the mound behind the main gallery. In County Tyrone, near Pomeroy, **Creggandevesky Court Grave** *(449)*, on the shore of tiny Lough Mallon, is another three-chambered tomb, this one with its semicircular forecourt facing east. The forecourt of the less well-preserved **Ossian's Grave** *(462)* near Cushendall, County Antrim, also faces eastward toward the Scottish shore not many miles away, but **Dooey's Cairn** *(454)*, in the same county near Dunloy, opens to the southwest, as do others among this category of tombs. These differences in orientation would appear to cast serious doubt on one widely held hypothesis that Neolithic burial mounds invariably opened toward the rising sun.

The same variety of orientation is evident in the case of a second class of Irish megalithic monument called *portal dolmens*. These may be of a somewhat later date than the court cairns and are perhaps derived from them, though there is no agreement among archaeologists on this point. *Dolmen* is a Breton word, meaning "stone table," and this is precisely what many of these monuments appear to be. In fact, they are single-chambered megalithic tombs, denuded of their original cairns so that they now stand entirely above ground, often majestically silhouetted against the sky. Dolmens are normally composed of three or more standing stones covered by a large capstone (or capstones). The two tallest of the uprights are usually set near each other and appear to form the portal to the tomb. Sometimes a tall door slab or blocker stands between the portal stones, and sometimes they are connected by a low sill. In either case, it is presumed that these additional stones were meant to bar entry into the tomb after the final burial. The backstone on which the rear of the capstone normally rests is usually, though not always, lower than the two supporting portal stones, so that the roof of the tomb tilts downward from front to back. How capstones as huge as these could be raised so as to rest on the high portals is a puzzle. Possibly they were hauled on rollers up an inclined earthen plane that initially covered the uprights but was subsequently dug away to allow the stone roof to settle.

There are about 160 portal dolmens in Ireland, and although the majority lie in the same northern sector as the court cairns, a significant number are also to be seen in the south. About four miles southwest of the city of Waterford is **Knockeen** *(288)*, an imposing monument with portal stones nine feet high and two capstones, the one in front resting on the one behind, which covers the burial chamber. The portals face southeast, and the capstones are almost horizontal. Not far away is **Gaulstown Dolmen** *(288)* with a single capstone, its portals also facing southeast. Across the border, in County Kilkenny, near Callan, lies **Kilmogue** *(291)*, known locally as *Leac an Scáil*, one of the tallest portal dolmens in Ireland, this one facing northeast. Here also is a double capstone, the one in front resting on the twelve-foot-high portals at an unusually steep backward angle. County Carlow boasts two fine examples: **Haroldstown Dolmen** *(290)* northeast of Tullow, and **Browneshill Dolmen** *(289)*, not far from the city of Carlow. The former has two capstones, and the portals face north with a blocker in between. The latter has but a single capstone, though it weighs approximately a hundred tons and is thought to be the heaviest of its kind in Europe.

Across the country in County Clare, in the center of the rocky region known as The Burren, stands **Poulnabrone** *(342)*, about eight miles northwest of Kilfenora and five miles south of Ballyvaughan. This is a most dramatic sight—or will be when current repair work is finished and the scaffolding removed. Poulnabrone's portals face south, and its capstone rests almost horizontally on only two high flagstones, thus looking more like a table than do many other Irish dolmens, the literal meaning of the word notwithstanding. Coming northeast into County Louth, the traveller can view the more typical "tripod" arrangement at **Proleek Dolmen** *(399)*, north of Dundalk. Here is another enormous capstone (about forty tons), seemingly precariously balanced on three legs about twelve feet high. In County Donegal, in the vicinity of Glencolumbkille, lie a number of Neolithic grave sites, including the **Malin More Portal Dolmens** *(428)*—six in a row, none in a very good state of preservation.

Northern Ireland too is well endowed with dolmens. In County Down, five miles southeast of Rostrevor, stands **Kilfeaghan Dolmen** *(440)*. Its huge, irregularly shaped capstone lies very close to the ground and at a distance looks like nothing more than a solitary boulder lying in a field. In the same county, near Hilltown, is **Goward Dolmen** *(436)*, known locally as Cloughmore Cromlech (the Welsh term for this type of monument). It has a fifty-ton capstone that has slipped sideways on its supporting uprights. Also in Down is **Legananny Dolmen** *(433)*, about five miles southeast of Dromara. Here the thick granite capstone rests, with only a slight backward downtilt, on three uprights—an almost perfect example of the tripod type. The two portal stones face south. **Ballykeel Dolmen** *(443)* at the western foot of Slieve Gullion northeast of Crossmaglen, County Armagh, is another fine south-facing tripod dolmen. And a final example from Ulster is **Ballylumford Dolmen** *(462)* in County Antrim in the front yard of a private house on Island Magee across the harbor from the town of Larne.

Many visitors to Ireland are more attracted to dolmens than to any other type of prehistoric funerary monument. Certainly the stark beauty of their skeletal remains has an aesthetic appeal that is hard to match among prehistoric sites. Yet in fact the dolmen builders were far less sophisticated in both architecture and engineering than their Neolithic successors, who were responsible for a new and different type of megalithic tomb—the so-called "passage grave." Irish passage graves number around three hundred and date also from the late fourth and third milennia B.C. Typically they were built in clusters, forming cemeteries usually in hilltop positions. Their distinctive features are (1) a round, rectangular, or polygonal tomb often roofed by a high corbelled vault and endowed with side chambers leading off the central area; (2) a long, tunnellike passageway leading into the tomb; (3) a massive round mound or cairn covering both tomb and passage, the entry to which opens from one side of the mound; (4) a revetment of kerbstones edging the mound; and (5) a multitude of abstract designs such as spirals, chevrons, concentric circles, lozenges, triangles, serpentine lines, and sometimes shadowy human figures and faces, engraved (picked out) on walls, roofs, and other stone surfaces inside and outside the tomb.

Most archaeologists believe that these passage graves were the product of a new wave of immigrants coming from Brittany and landing first on the east coast of Ireland near the mouth of the river Boyne. Strong architectural and artistic similarities between the Irish graves of this type and those found in considerable number in the Morbihan district of southern Brittany certainly favor such a deduction. Comparable likenesses, however, can be found among prehistoric tombs in the Channel Islands, Scandinavia, the Iberian peninsula, Wales, the Outer Hebrides, and the Orkney Islands. So the case for a Breton origin is not conclusive. Also, there is a possibility that the peculiar architecture of these graves was an indigenous insular development. If so, however, it must have been influenced by overseas contacts, possibly made by Neolithic Irish fishermen or traders.

Whatever their source of inspiration, it is reasonably clear that the earliest of the passage graves were built around 3100 B.C. along the bend of the river Boyne (*Brugh na Boinne*) between modern Drogheda and Slane in County Meath. Here, set on three knolls about a mile apart, are the most celebrated of these tombs: **Newgrange** *(388)*, **Dowth** *(389)*, and **Knowth** *(388)*.

Newgrange *(388)* is now a major tourist attraction, surrounded by a fence and endowed with an on-site information center and museum. Here the covering mound, 280 feet in diameter, rises to a height of about thirty-six feet. A kerb of large flat stones holds the mound in place, but the outer circle of standing stones (now reduced to twelve) is a bronze-age intrusion (see pages 388–389). The passageway is sixty-two feet long, and above its entrance is a slitted stone through whose aperture rays from the rising sun penetrate the interior during the few days before and after the winter solstice (21 December)—at least on the rare days when the winter skies are not cloud-covered. This main chamber is a round, high, vaulted room with three side chambers projecting outward to form a ground plan shaped like a cross. In all three side chambers there are shallow stone basins, probably associated with burial rites. Numerous engravings adorn the stones, both inside and out.

The covering mound at nearby **Dowth** *(389)* is about the same size as at Newgrange and, like it, is kerbed at the edges. Inside are two separate tombs, both roofed with capstones. Unfortunately, however, they have recently been declared unsafe, and visitors are no longer permitted to enter. **Knowth** *(388)*, the third major tomb in the Boyne cemetery, is of approximately the same dimensions as the other two, and as at Dowth, the kerbed mound here covers two long, narrow passageways leading to separate tombs, one cruciform in shape and endowed with a corbelled roof, the other rectangular and covered with a flat capstone. Here too the interior is barred to the public, at least pending the completion of current excavations.

Although the Boyne cemetery is the most impressive single grouping of passage graves, it is not unique. Similar tombs are to be found elsewhere in County Meath, to the northwest in County Sligo, to the south and southwest in Counties Wicklow and Limerick, and in the northern counties of Tyrone and Antrim. At the hill of **Tara** *(385)*, a dozen miles to the southwest of Newgrange as the crow flies, a small passage grave, anachronistically called the Mound of the Hostages, is the most ancient site on what was centuries later to become the royal seat of the kings of Meath and, later still, of the high kings of Ireland. **Fourknocks** *(383)* in County Meath, south of Drogheda, County Louth, has a fine cruciform chamber, much decorated with engravings and now illuminated by natural light coming through shafts in a concrete dome. Also in County Meath is the **Loughcrew** or **Slieve na Calliagh Cemetery** *(387)*, southeast of Oldcastle. Here are more than thirty tombs, of which the most interesting are Carnbane East and Carnbane West, situated on the hilltops lying respectively east and west of the car park. The former has a cruciform burial chamber and is much decorated with concentric circles, zigzags, etc.; the latter has a large central chamber with five side chambers.

To the northwest, in County Sligo, are two more large megalithic cemeteries, both in the Boyne tradition. At **Carrowkeel** *(419)*, on the slope of the Bricklieve Mountain just west of Lough Arrow, are more than a dozen passage graves, though none bears any decorative artwork. To the north, and very close to Sligo town, is **Carrowmore** *(419)*, the largest cemetery of megalithic tombs in Ireland, many of the passage grave variety. These graves are relatively small, none seems to have been corbelled, and many have been denuded of their original covering cairns. In fact, modern gravel quarrying has so disturbed the cemetery that it is difficult for any but the most practiced archaeological eye to make much sense out of this widely scattered agglomeration of megaliths. About a mile westward, on the summit of a mountain, is **Knocknarea**, also known as **Queen Maeve's Grave** *(419)*. This is a huge cairn, thirty-five feet high and two hundred feet in diameter. It has not been opened, but it is probable that underneath lies a large Neolithic passage grave of the Boyne variety. East of here, across the border in Northern Ireland, is **Knockmany Cairn** *(446)*, near Clogher, County Tyrone. It too is a passage grave, but the passage is missing. What is remarkable here—aside from the splendid view of the Clogher valley— are the fine engravings of concentric circles, spirals, serpentine lines, and chevrons with which the stones are decorated.

Excavations at these sites (and others not mentioned here) indicate clearly that the passage graves were communal tombs that served the funerary requirements of sizable communities over many generations. Cremation was the preferred burial rite, and over time the ash piles rose from the floor up to the stone sills that separated the side chambers from the central room. Probably the shallow stone basins, found in so many tombs, served as temporary receptacles for the ashes while the funeral rites were being performed. That such rites were occasions for great feastings is indicated by the large number of unburned seashells and meat bones of large animals found on some of the sites. Unlike their Neolithic predecessors, these people did not bury flint or stone artifacts with their dead. Instead, before putting the bodies of the deceased to the torch, they adorned them with personal ornaments of a great variety: ornamental pins of antler; necklaces of soapstone, limestone, and semiprecious materials fashioned in the shape of miniature axes or miners' mauls; beads of cylindrical, flat, and round designs. All these were found almost invariably in a burned condition, as were accompanying balls of chalk or stone about the size of a child's marble, which may have served as some kind of talisman. Burned also were numerous open hemispherical decorated bowls of a type of pottery known as Carrowkeel Ware.

Examples of all these grave goods can be seen today in Ireland's museums: the **National Museum of Ireland** *(355)* in Dublin, the **Ulster Museum** *(457)*, Belfast, and the others mentioned earlier. What this diverse repertoire demonstrates is that the passage grave builders, wherever they came from, had a higher degree of sophistication (one is tempted to say of civilization) than any of their forerunners in Ireland. The tombs themselves were prodigies of engineering, requiring a huge work force and presumably some kind of managerial talent and authority to supervise it. The artwork adorning these graves, though primitive, is skilled. And all this is the more remarkable when one considers that the only tools available to the builders and artists were mauls and picks and axes of stone and flint. The introduction to Ireland of metal mining and metalwork late in the third millennium B.C. would vastly expand the range of human technological capabilities.

THE BRONZE AGE: CIRCA 2000–600 B.C.

Bronze is an alloy comprised of about nine parts copper and one part tin. Sometime early in the third millennium B.C. natives of the Near and Middle East discovered that these two metals could be smelted together and, in a molten condition, poured into molds of clay or stone to produce tools and weapons superior to, and longer-lasting than, those of stone. Gradually these newfound metallurgical skills spread westward, and the search for deposits of both metals grew apace. Sometime early in the second millennium B.C. prospectors arrived in Ireland, either from the Continent or from Britain or from both. There they found copper in some abundance, especially in western County Cork. Tin, to be sure, was probably not as plentiful, but it could be readily imported from Cornwall, and there was gold to pay for it in the river bottoms of County Wicklow.

Most archaeologists attribute the introduction of metallurgy and metal mining in Ireland to the "Beaker People"—so called because of the pottery they left behind. These "Bell Beakers" are ovoid containers, rust-colored, flat-bottomed, wide-mouthed, often incised with geometric designs or imprinted with cords, and, in profile, S-shaped, more or less in the manner of inverted bells. Examples are to be found in most of the Irish museums already mentioned.

Beakers of this description have been discovered in Ireland in communal tombs known as "wedge graves." Not nearly so splendid as the great Neolithic mausoleums of the passage grave variety, these are small, low, relatively narrow stone galleries, broader and higher at the entry than at the rear. Usually the entrance faces in a southwesterly direction. Some are single-chambered, though in many an antechamber at the western end precedes the main chamber from which it is separated by a large septal stone. Sometimes there is an additional small chamber at the eastern end. Occasionally a short second wall surrounds the gallery, which was originally roofed with one or more flat slabs. The covering cairn, when still in place, is usually D-shaped and edged by kerbstones.

There are, altogether, almost four hundred wedge graves on record in Ireland, with a heavier concentration in the Southwest than elsewhere. Compared to other megalithic tombs, they tend to be poorly marked, hard to locate, and of little or no aesthetic appeal. Hence only a small number need be noted as being of sufficient interest or accessibility to warrant the trouble involved in finding them. **Labbacallee** *(321)*, northwest of Fermoy, County Cork, is larger than the average. It is two-chambered and carries three capstones, the largest weighing twelve tons. The cairn partially survives and is surrounded by a kerb of standing stones. In County Limerick, about a mile southwest of the **Lough Gur Interpretive Centre** *(339)*, is a wedge tomb called **Giant's Grave** *(340)*, with the upright stones of the antechamber still standing, as well as the main chamber, supporting four large capstones. Probably the greatest concentration of wedge graves is in County Clare, especially in that vast expanse of fissured limestone surface rock called The Burren, where about 120 have been identified. Most of these are small in size, unmarked, and unnamed except for the general designation of *leaba* (capstone), which occasionally appears on roadside signposts. Travellers intent on discovering them are advised first to visit the **Burren Display Centre** *(346)* in Kilfenora, where detailed maps of the area, as well as other useful information, can be obtained. The best signposted and most accessible is **Gleninsheen Wedge Tomb** *(341)*, lying close to the road south of Ballyvaughan.

Still another variation of bronze-age megalithic funerary monument, although of a later date than the wedge tomb, is the Tramore passage grave, of which only five have been located—all in the vicinity of the town of Tramore, County Waterford. By contrast there are about fifty of these communal graves in the Isles of Scilly off the coast of Cornwall, which suggests that the Tramore area had been colonized by seagoing metallurgists sailing from the southeast in search of copper. If so, they seem to have penetrated no farther into Ireland than the coastline, and their remaining grave sites are hardly worth the trouble of a visit. They are significant, however, as representing the last phase of prehistoric communal tomb building in Ireland.

Thereafter, burials were individual, often in crowded cemeteries, some flat, some mounded. In eastern and northeastern Ireland a new type of pottery, known to archaeologists as *food vessels*, was often placed inside the graves. Some of these pots were vase-shaped, with thick bodies and narrow necks; others were formed like bowls, ridged and decorated with lozenge and chevron patterns. Some cemeteries from the same period are known as "urnfields" because the cremated remains of the dead were usually covered by inverted "collared" urns, which are large, almost cylindrical pots with overhanging rims. Other urns are encrusted around the edges of the mouth; still others "cordoned." Another typical urnfield grave find is the so-called "pygmy cup," a delicately crafted miniature bowl.

Food vessels, collared urns, encrusted urns, cordoned urns, and pygmy cups are all to be found in abundance in the Irish museums mentioned earlier as well as in the **Cork Public Museum** *(318)*. So are barbed and tanged arrowheads of flint, wrist guards worn by archers, stone battle axes, bronze daggers, and faïence beads from the same grave sites. Other weapons and implements of the early Bronze Age included rapiers and dirks, halberd blades that were mounted at right angles to wooden shafts, decorated flat bronze ax heads cast in open stone molds, socketed spearheads, and palstaves (a type of ribbed ax head). But the most attractive of all early bronze-age artifacts were the ornaments of hammered sheet gold, in the manufacture of which Irish craftsmen seem to have surpassed all others, judging from the number of their products that were exported to Britain and the Continent. These included small gold disks often decorated with a cross motif hammered (*répoussé*) from the back; basket-shaped gold earrings; bracelets and necklaces in the form of torcs, made by twisting bars or strips of gold; and, best of all, crescentic pendants hung around the neck, now known as *lunulae*. The **National Museum of Ireland** *(355)* in Dublin and the **Ulster Museum** *(457)* in Belfast have the best collections of these splendid artifacts, though several of the other museums mentioned earlier are also well endowed with a great variety of bronze-age finds, both from grave sites and from hoards where smiths stockpiled their wares or owners buried them for security's sake. Nor does the repertory stop here. During the late Bronze Age (roughly 1200–600 B.C.) goldsmiths achieved new heights of elegance with bracelets of heavy sheet gold, gold breast ornaments known as *gorgets* (unique to Ireland), earrings of twisted gold wire, dress fasteners, and ornaments of twisted ribbon gold ranging in size from earrings to waist torcs. Bronze smiths were equally prolific in producing a vast array of tools and weapons: socketed hammers and sickles, awls, chisels, gouges, hammered-bronze buckets and cauldrons, horns, leaf-shaped arrowheads and spearheads, and flanged slashing swords. An especially attractive item is the embossed circular shield discovered at Lough Gur and now on display in the **National Museum of Ireland** *(355)* in Dublin. There is another of much the same design in the **Hunt Museum** *(338)* in Limerick. And of equal interest are the bronze-age horse trappings to be seen in numerous Irish museums, including the **Irish Horse Museum** *(377)* in County Kildare.

All this finery and all these accoutrements of war, dating from the late Bronze Age, bespeak the presence in Ireland, beginning perhaps as early as 1000 B.C., of an aristocracy of horse-riding, sword-wielding warriors, luxury-loving and powerful enough to establish control over a significant portion of the island's economic resources and technical skills. Where these people came from and in what numbers they arrived on Irish shores, or over how long a period of time, are matters of great dispute among prehistorians. Also in dispute is whether these new arrivals spoke the Indo-European language called Celtic, which had originated in eastern or central Europe probably before the second millennium B.C.

The Celts, it must be emphasized in view of widespread misconceptions about the origins of the Irish "race," were not a discrete ethnic group. They were Europeans from different parts of the Continent who shared a common language. In time (probably subsequent to the Celtic immigrations to Britain and Ireland) that language became differentiated into two branches which modern linguists call Goidelic (or Gaelic) and Brythonic.

Since the Brythonic dialect substituted the sound "P" for the Goidelic sound "Q," the former is also known as "P-Celtic" and the latter as "Q-Celtic." Brythonic is considered to have developed as a British insular offshoot of Goidelic and is therefore the younger of the two. It is the source of modern Welsh and of the now almost-dead languages of Breton and Cornish. Goidelic established itself in Ireland, the Isle of Man, and the western islands and highlands of Scotland and is the root of the modern Irish Gaelic, Manx, and Scottish Gaelic tongues.

These bronze-age newcomers, whatever language they spoke, from the time of their earliest presence in Ireland left their mark not only on today's museums, so richly supplied with their artifacts, but also on the Irish landscape. Their sacred sites abound, even though the exact nature of the rituals practiced in these places is still a mystery. The most mysterious of their monuments are the *gallans*—solitary pillars of stone. The tallest of these is the easternmost of the **Punchestown Standing Stones** *(379)*, next to the racecourse of the same name in County Kildare. It rises nineteen feet above ground and may have marked a burial site or served some unknown religious purpose.

More certainly religious in character is another type of prehistoric monument of which Ireland abounds in examples. These are circular areas delimited either by a ditched earthen bank or by a ring of standing stones. In the first category the largest in Ireland is the **Giant's Ring** *(458)*, in County Down just southeast of Belfast. Here a great earthen bank, averaging fifteen feet high and about sixty feet wide at its base, encloses a round area, six hundred feet in diameter, at the center of which is a small Neolithic dolmen. Of greater interest to the traveller will be the multitude of stone circles that adorn the Irish countryside—about two hundred altogether. By definition a stone circle is a ringlike arrangement of upright stones that was originally associated with some kind of religious observance. (Not to be confused with stone circles, though somewhat similar in appearance, are the denuded kerbstones of Neolithic burial mounds.) Some of the stones in the circles are high, some low; some cut, some merely rough boulders.

Although the chronological evidence is scanty, what there is points to a bronze-age provenance for most of the circles, though some are probably of later construction. That they served a religious purpose of some sort is hardly questionable. Probably they were the scenes of rites associated with sun worship, and this may account for their usual orientation, with the two tallest stones facing the northeast. It is doubtful, however, that they were used as observatories, as is popularly believed and fervently argued today by a small brotherhood of "astro-archaeologists." These heavy boulders and rough-cut stones could hardly have served as precision instruments for measuring the movements of celestial bodies. This is not to say, however, that the customary northeast-southwest alignment was not deliberate. It doubtless served some ritualistic purpose connected with the rising and setting of the sun. But no more than a countryman's general knowledge of the cardinal points of the compass would have been required to devise such an arrangement, and it is farfetched to impute sophisticated mathematical or astronomical skills to their primitive builders.

The major concentrations of stone circles in Ireland are in the southern counties and in Ulster. A distinguishing feature of some of the stone circles in County Cork is the presence of a horizontal stone in the southwest corner opposite the two tallest vertical stones. Curiously, similar arrangements exist in northeastern Scotland, but there are significant differences in the patterns of each, and the geographic distance between the two types of monuments seems to belie any connection between them. A good example of the Irish variety—and one of the most accessible—is **Drombeg** *(324)*, west of Ross Carbery, County Cork. Here are sixteen standing stones and one recumbent stone in the southwest quadrant. Excavations reveal that the site was in use as late as the second century A.D., but an original bronze-age date is likely.

County Wicklow has two stone circles fairly accessible to the interested traveller. One, known as the **Piper's Stones** or **Athgreany Circle** *(309)*, south of Blessington, consists of thirteen granite stones and a single outlier, the largest measuring more than six feet in height. A much smaller example is **Castleruddery** *(309)*, about four miles northeast of Baltinglass. Here is a double circle of uncut boulders with an earthen bank in between, the arrangement measuring only about one hundred feet in diameter. Westward, in County Limerick, is the largest and most impressive of all of Ireland's circular settings of stone. This is **The Grange** *(340)* or **The Lios**, standing near the western shore of Lough Gur about two miles west of the **Lough Gur Interpretive Centre** *(339)*. The circle is surrounded by an earthen bank, contains more than a hundred boulders and cut stones, and encloses an area 150 feet in diameter. The largest of the orthostats stands some eight feet above ground and is situated in the northeast quadrant. The discovery on the site of a bell beaker and a food vessel clearly indicates an early bronze-age date of construction.

Northward from Limerick, stone circles thin out. At **Newgrange** *(388)*, County Meath, only twelve stones remain out of an original circle of twenty-four, which Beaker People apparently erected around the circumference of the Neolithic passage grave. Of the stone circles of Northern Ireland three sites are especially noteworthy and reasonably accessible. The **Beaghmore Stone Circles** *(447)*, northwest of Cookstown, County Tyrone, comprise an elaborate complex of circles, stone alignments, and denuded cairns. At **Drumskinny** *(452)*, north of Kesh, County Fermanagh, there is a circle of thirty-nine stones with a tangential alignment and a cairn.

Ballynoe *(434)*, south of Downpatrick, County Down, has fifty-five standing stones, set close together in a circle, some standing, some fallen, the highest rising to about six feet. Late Neolithic finds on the site indicate that this may have been one of the earliest of Irish monuments of this type.

Nineteenth-century visitors to these starkly romantic monuments tended to look on them as sites of sacrificial rites of unspeakable grisliness, performed by druids robed in white and garlanded with mistletoe. Today, as already indicated, there is general agreement that they were in all probability sacred enclosures dedicated to some kind of sun worship. But to associate druids with these ceremonies is anachronistic. The druids, according to all contemporary classical sources, were a priestly caste, not of the Bronze Age, but of a later phase of Celtic culture known as the Iron Age. In Ireland this phase was to last for almost a thousand years.

THE IRON AGE: CIRCA 600 B.C.–430 A.D.

Owing to a long hiatus in the archaeological record, fixing a date for the beginning of the Iron Age in Ireland is highly conjectural. As with most prehistoric technological innovations, the smelting and forging of iron began in the Middle East, specifically among the Hittites of Asia Minor. Thence knowledge of the process spread gradually westward and by 700 B.C. had reached central Europe, where a warlike, Celtic-speaking aristocracy, wielding weapons of hammered iron, succeeded in establishing dominance over the indigenous Urnfield population. These were the "Hallstatt Celts," so named after the village in northern Austria where archaeological evidence of the new culture first came to light. Within the space of two or three centuries these fearful chariot-driving warriors and the tribes they led had penetrated into western and southern Germany, the middle and upper Danube, Spain, France, the Low Countries, and across the Channel into Britain. By that time these people, whom contemporary Greeks and Romans called barbarians, had developed a fairly sophisticated (though illiterate) culture known to archaeologists as "La Tène"—from an excavated site in Switzerland. The La Tène culture is distinguished chiefly for its art—largely abstract and nonrepresentational in form and curvilinear in style, that is, dominated by such motifs as spirals, roundels (circles), triskeles (three curved lines radiating from a center), asymmetrical serpentine lines, trumpet patterns, etc.

It was probably the La Tène Celts (and not their Hallstatt predecessors) who came to Ireland in sizable numbers sometime between the sixth and third centuries B.C. Again it is a matter of speculation as to where they came *from*, though it is likely that the Iberian peninsula, France (Gaul), the Low Countries, and Britain were the chief points of origin. It is also likely that immigration accelerated in the first century B.C. with Julius Caesar's invasion of Gaul and with the subsequent Roman conquest of Britain after A.D. 43. Hotly disputed among Irish prehistorians is the question of whether the immigrants came in waves as invaders or in small groups as more or less peaceful colonists. Neither hypothesis is implausible, but in any case it is clear that by the beginning of the Christian Era the newcomers and their descendants had established themselves as a ruling caste in Ireland.

Unlike their stone-age and bronze-age predecessors, these iron-age conquerors and settlers left no great funerary monuments or stone circles for the edification of today's archaeologists. But they did erect a number of still-extant decorated stones that appear to have been cult totems of some sort. The **Turoe Stone** *(413)*, north of Loughrea, County Galway, is a domelike block of granite about four feet high, its top half carved with a profusion of curvilinear ornamentation in low relief, a typical example of La Tène art. Others of the same genre are the **Castlestrange Stone** *(403)*, south of the town of Roscommon, and the Mullaghmast Stone from County Kildare, now in the **National Museum of Ireland** *(355)* in Dublin.

In the same museum are a few examples of La Tène artwork in gold, notably two tubular collars decorated with repoussé ornament—one from Clonmacnoise, County Offaly, the other from Broighter, County Londonderry. The **Ulster Museum** *(457–458)* in Belfast boasts six bronze scabbards engraved with elegant curvilinear patterns from Lisnacroghera and Toome, County Antrim, and Coleraine, County Londonderry. These would have housed swords forged of iron, short and double-edged, possibly with hilts of decorated bronze as in the case of one example in the National Museum. The warriors who wielded them probably rode into battle on horseback or in two-wheeled chariots, their mounts accoutred with bronze trappings like those to be seen in the **Irish Horse Museum** *(377)*, County Kildare, and the **Cork Public Museum** *(318)*. Some would have worn helmets decorated with bronze horns like those on display in the same museum in Cork.

These iron-age Celts, even more than their Urnfield predecessors, were notorious for their warlike disposition. It was of their distant kinsmen on the Continent that the Roman historian Strabo wrote: "The whole race . . . is madly fond of war, high spirited and quick to battle . . . ." The testimony of other classical writers, including Posidonius and Julius Caesar, confirms this judgment. So too does the great native Irish epic, the *Táin Bó Cuailnge (The Cattle Raid of Cooley)*, which offers today's reader, if dimly, a "window" into the Irish Iron Age.

The *Táin*, to use its short title, has survived in monastic manuscripts dating from the twelfth and fourteenth centuries A.D., though the oral bardic traditions on which the tale is based go back perhaps to the fourth century A.D., if not earlier. The society it purports to describe dates probably to the time of the birth of Christ or perhaps a century earlier. But the events it depicts are purely mythical, the leading characters simply eheumerizations (human personifications) of pagan deities. In the words of one of the monks who transcribed it, parts of the *Táin* "are the figments of demons, some of them poetic imaginings, some true, some not, some for the delight of fools [*ad delectionem stultorum*]."

It is in fact an epic saga, often compared with Homer's *Iliad*, although the prize in the war it describes is a brown bull of prodigious size and strength rather than a woman of unparalleled beauty. The Irish Achilles is Cúchulainn, who stands alone at a river ford and single-handedly holds off the invasion of Ulster by the "Men of Ireland," a great army from the south under the leadership of Ailill and Medb, king and queen of Connacht. Notwithstanding the fact that Cúchulainn prevails in every battle, the great bull is ultimately captured, though only to escape to wander over Ireland until he dies within sight of his native Ulster.

However improbable the story, the *Táin* does provide insights into life among the rich and powerful in early iron-age Ireland. The few artifacts that survive, as well as classical accounts of the Continental Celts of an earlier era, confirm, in a general way, the saga's portrait of a heroic age: kings living in state among entourages of boastful and bellicose young warriors; an aristocracy adorned with neck-pieces and bracelets of gold and silver; Amazon-type females (specifically Queen Medb of Connacht) holding positions of high leadership in war and peace; javelin-wielding heroes riding into battle in two-wheeled chariots, then leaping down to engage their foes with sword and spear in deadly single combat, the prize often being their adversary's severed head.

But stripped of all its heroic trappings, the heart of the matter is nothing more glorious than a cattle raid on a neighboring province—which in itself says much about the essential nature of Irish society in the Iron Age. It was a pastoral economy ruled loosely by feuding cattle lords who themselves were bound together loosely in networks of shifting alliances and tribal loyalties. Yet the polity of iron-age Ireland was not totally anarchic. There were recognized gradations of rank and authority and ties of lordship and clientship bearing the earmarks of an embryonic feudal system. And there were indications of a trend toward the concentration of power in the hands of a small number of overlords who, in George Orwell's phrase, were "more equal than others."

The *Táin* mentions four provinces of Ireland: Ulster in the north, Connacht in the west, Leinster in the east, and Munster in the south. There probably was some such rough division of the island at the beginning of the Christian Era, and the same fourfold partition was to receive something like official recognition in the Middle Ages. Each province had its head chief or king, a *rí ruirech*, meaning "king of over-kings," and each provincial king had his royal seat, a hilltop of sacred character that served as the site of his inauguration and meeting place for the assembly of his chief followers for purposes of consultation or of war. Among these "capitals" was Cruachan, seat of the royal house of Connacht, from which, according to the *Táin*, the army of King Ailill and Queen Medb went forth to battle against the Ulstermen. The site has been identified as **Rath Croghan** *(404)*, in the modern county of Roscommon, northwest of the village of Tulsk. Ulster's capital was Emain Macha, today called **Navan Fort** *(443)*, just outside the city of Armagh. At neither of these places are there signs of strong fortifications. Rath Croghan has a number of earthworks, chief among them being a great flat earthen mound, while Navan Fort has a ditch *inside* its circular earthen ramparts, a feature not explicable in military terms. These places were, in short, probably not defensible hill-forts like those mentioned below, but primarily places of inauguration and assembly.

Subordinate to these provincial kings stood graduated ranks of lesser kings or chieftains, about 150 in all at any given time in iron-age Ireland. At the lowest level was the *rí tuaithe*, that is, "king of the *tuath*," a term roughly translatable as "tribal territory." Next up the ladder stood the *rí ríg* or "king of kings." And finally, above all, as already indicated, was the provincial "king of over-kings," the *rí ruirech*. In theory all those descended from a previous king to the fourth generation were eligible for kingship, and the strongest and ablest among them was elected to the office by his peers. A king's fealty to his superior was supposed to be assured by the former's surrendering to the latter a number of hostages, often his own sons. If a superior went to war with another king, his subordinates were expected to come to his aid. Such intertribal wars, though probably frequent, were neither long in duration nor very lethal. Casualties there doubtless were, but these brief forays would normally involve no loss of territory, only the seizure of cattle and a certain amount of plundering.

In the face of such ever-present danger, nonetheless, it was only prudent to take defensive measures. These ranged from elaborate fortifications that took advantage of such natural features as hilltops, cliffs, and coastal promontories, to simple rings of earth around a farming homestead. At the upper level of such defensive works were the great hill-forts and promontory forts. By definition a hill-fort consists of an enclosure surrounded by one or more ramparts of earth, or of mixed earth and stone, each rampart in turn surrounded by a ditch. More or less circular in character, the ramparts usually follow the contours of the hilltop they were built to defend. A promontory fort is protected by ditch and rampart only on one side, the other sides being guarded by surrounding water or by the sheer drop of the cliffs on which they were sited. If a fort has but one rampart with its accompanying ditch, it is called *univallate*; if more than one, *multivallate*.

Iron-age fortifications of either type are less numerous in Ireland than in contemporary Britain. This suggests perhaps that the former was less subject to foreign invasion and internal tribal warfare than was the latter before the Roman conquest. Of the known Irish hill-forts, one of the most accessible today is **Rathgall** *(312)* in County Wicklow, east of Tullow, County Carlow. This is a multivallate fort of two stone walls with exterior ditches enclosing an area of about 18½ acres. An iron-age (or possibly late-bronze-age) date is ascribed to the site, or at least to its outer ring of stone. **Moghane Hill-Fort** *(349)*, south of Ennis, County Clare, is more than twice as large (44½ acres). It too is multivallate, with three great stone walls with exterior ditches running around the top of the hill. It dates also to the early Iron Age, and close by was found the greatest hoard of prehistoric gold ornaments to have been discovered in Europe. (See, for example, the gold collar on exhibit in Dublin's **National Museum of Ireland** *[355]*.)

Of the coastal promontory forts, **Dunbeg** *(329)* in County Kerry stands on a tongue of land jutting into the Atlantic Ocean near the western tip of the Dingle peninsula. Across this narrow strip stretches a high stone wall with a covered entrance passage and two guard chambers. On the landward side, guarding the approach, is a series of banks and ditches. An even more impressive sight is **Dún Dubh Cathair (The Black Fort)** *(411)* on the southeast coast of Inishmore, the main island of the Aran group off the Galway coast. Here a great stone wall, 220 feet long, stretches across the base of a cliff-girt promontory. On the approach side are pointed stone stakes, a defensive device known as *chevaux de frise* whose purpose was the same as a modern tank trap's. Not far up the coast in a westerly direction lies **Dún Aenghus** *(412)*, also guarded by a *chevaux de frise*. This magnificent fort stands on the edge of a sheer cliff dropping off almost two hundred feet into the Atlantic. It is guarded by a triple set of stone walls around the semicircular enclosure. Partially restored, this is certainly one of the most dramatic sights in Ireland. Not far northwest of Dún Aenghus is another stone fort called **Dún Eóganachta** *(412)*, its thick stone walls (restored) with interior terraces enclosing an area about seventy-five feet in diameter. East of here is still another of about the same size, though oval in plan and with a second exterior rampart. This is **Dún Eóchla** or **Oghil Fort** *(411)*, which stands on the brow of the central hill of Inishmore and commands a spectacular view.

There is some doubt as to whether these latter two sites should be classified as hill-forts or ring-forts. The distinction is not always easy to draw and will make little difference anyway to the great majority of travellers. The term *ring-fort*—unique to Ireland—is usually applied to relatively small circular enclosures, from sixty to two hundred feet in diameter, surrounded by a bank or rampart, usually ditched on the outside, and interrupted by a causeway at the entrance. They were hardly forts in the strict sense of the word, since most were not defended strongly enough to withstand sustained military attack. Inside were domestic buildings made of wood and wattle. Essentially they were single, protected farmsteads, whose ramparts were just high and sound enough to keep out wolves and thieves and to keep unguarded cattle from wandering at will. They were in short the ordinary homesteads of prosperous farmers and cattlemen—which accounts for the fact that about forty thousand of these sites have been discovered in Ireland. The most common verifiable dates of construction and occupation seem to lie within the Early Christian period (from the fifth to the twelfth centuries), but there is evidence to support the view that some at least were built by iron-age herdsmen and agriculturalists. Given the fact that the economy and settlement pattern of rural Ireland remained basically unchanged for the entire first millennium A.D., it is not unreasonable to ascribe an early date to these protected homesteads—at least in the absence of any verifiable evidence to the contrary.

Of the many, many sites identified as ring-forts, by far the greatest proportion are bounded by banks of earth faced outside with a ditch. They are called *raths*, and one reason for their survival in such great numbers is that for centuries superstitious peasants regarded them as "fairy forts" and left them undisturbed. Today, plow and bulldozer notwithstanding, they still dot the Irish countryside, though almost always obscured by vegetal growth. For the interested traveller, it is safe to assume that almost any rural circular copse of trees or thornbushes could well conceal a ring-fort—a much eroded circular bank of earth, slightly depressed at the base where the surrounding ditch once lay. The discovery, however, will prove unexciting, as there is really not much to see.

It is otherwise with ring-forts made of stone. These go by the name of *caiseal* or *cathair*, though more commonly they are called "cashels." Smaller than most hill-forts or promontory forts, and often situated on low ground, many are equally impressive to the eye of the modern traveller. Some, or possibly all, of those mentioned below may date from the Early Christian period of Irish history (after A.D. 431). But no firm dates for their construction are available, and since they conform architecturally to known iron-age prototypes, it does not seem inappropriate or anachronistic to include them here.

The ramparts of these ring-forts are of drystone construction; that is, they are made by piling flat rocks on top of each other without benefit of mortar. The heaviest concentration of cashels is in the barren, rocky regions of the west of Ireland. **Knockdrum** *(325)*, near Skibbereen, County

Cork, is a good example, with the added attraction of a glorious view of the southern coastline. It is a circular enclosure surrounded by a drystone wall (repaired) about ninety feet in diameter, with a small mural chamber to the right of the narrow entrance. More impressive still, though no larger in diameter, is **Staigue Fort** *(333)* near Sneem in County Kerry. Here the enclosing walls—thirteen feet thick—rise to a height of eighteen feet and are in turn ringed by a ditch and earthen bank. Internal stone steps lead to the top of the rampart, and there are two mural chambers, one to the left of the lintelled entranceway, the other in the wall opposite. Also in County Kerry, just outside of Caherciveen, are two substantial stone forts within sight of each other. The closest to town is **Cahergal** *(328)*, with a high drystone circular wall enclosing an area about ninety feet in diameter in which are the remains of two small stone buildings, one circular, the other rectangular. Here too internal steps lead to the top of the rampart. A few hundred yards to the west is **Leacanabuaile** *(328)*—very similar in size and appearance.

County Clare also is rich in stone ring-forts, especially in the rock-strewn region known as The Burren. Within about a five-mile radius of the village of Kilfenora are three of note. **Ballykinvarga** *(346)*, about two miles to the northeast, has the distinction of being surrounded by a *chevaux de frise* of sharp stones extending about fifty yards out from the cashel. The fort itself is oval in plan, measuring about 150 by thirty feet, and the surrounding wall rises in places to a height of about twelve feet. North of here lies **Cahermacnaghten** *(342)*, round in plan and about a hundred feet in diameter. The gateway and the interior ruins of a medieval date derive from the fort's occupation by the O'Davorens, who maintained a law school here as late as the seventeenth century. Still farther north is **Caherconnell** *(342)*, about 120 feet in diameter with surviving walls as high as ten feet. To the southeast is **Cahercommaun** *(344)*, which might be classified as a hill-fort except that its interior diameter is only about a hundred feet in length. It sits on the edge of a steep cliff, and around it stand three concentric drystone walls, the innermost and strongest forming almost a circle, the other two semicircles ending at the cliffside. Here too are mural chambers and the remains of interior buildings, two of which had souter-rains—low, underground, stone-walled, and stone-lintelled passages that can also be seen at **Knockdrum** *(325)*, **Dunbeg** *(329)*, and **Leacanabuaile** *(328)*. What purpose they served is disputable. Some were large enough to have been used as places of refuge for the fort's inhabitants in times of danger, though one is tempted to agree with the French archaeologist who said that a people clever enough to have built these underground shelters must certainly have been clever enough to stay outside them. Probably their primary use was to shelter cattle in bad weather or perhaps to store dairy products and grain.

One final type of protected dwelling place deserves mention, though mostly inaccessible today to the ordinary traveller. This is the crannog, a primitive homestead built on an artificial island in the shallows of a lake. The island was constructed of stones, peat, brushwood, and timber, and on it sat a wooden house surrounded by a palisade. In all probability the earliest of the Irish crannogs date to the Iron Age, or possibly even to the Bronze Age, although most of those still standing have been dated by dendrochronology to the seventh century A.D. The site of one such dwelling place can be observed today in **Lough Gur**, looking south toward the opposite shore from the **Interpretative Centre** *(339)*. A better idea of the looks of a crannog, however, can be obtained by visiting the **Craggaunowen Project** *(349)*, near Quin, County Clare, where a fine replica is on view, as well as imaginative reconstructions of a ring-fort, a primitive outdoor cooking place (*fulacht fiadh*), and an iron-age bog roadway.

There remains to be considered, at last, that most famous iron-age site of song and story: the hill of **Tara** *(385)* in County Meath, southeast of Navan. Visitors coming to this fabled spot for the first time are likely to be disappointed initially. Approached from the road to Dublin on the east, the low-lying ridge seems remarkably undistinguished until the summit is reached and long vistas of Irish countryside come into view. In the immediate vicinity the skyline is interrupted by an ugly statue of St. Patrick and a pillar stone commemorating the insurgents of 1798 (see Chapter Six). For the rest, all that is visible are mounds of grass-covered earth. The most distinctive of these (miscalled the Mound of the Hostages) covers the Neolithic passage grave described earlier. It stands in the northern part of an enclosure surrounded by a bank with an internal ditch, inside of which (to the south of the Mound of the Hostages) are the scant remains of two circular earthen ring-forts. To the north of the enclosure (just beyond the Mound of the Hostages) are the much eroded remains of a third ring-fort, the so-called Rath of the Synods.

Sometime in the early years of the Christian Era, probably within a century or two after the saga of the *Táin* was first composed, Tara became the royal center of Mide or Meath, the Middle Kingdom. The coming into being of this discrete provincial kingdom brought the number of such entities in Ireland to five—which no doubt accounts for the fact that the old Irish word for royal province was *cóiced*, meaning "a fifth part." Meath's rise in political status seems to have coincided with that of a new tribal dynasty, the Uí Néill, the founder of which was Niall Noígíallach, "Niall of the Nine Hostages." Here at last appears the first personage in Irish history whose name and accomplishments, in spite of the legendary gloss that overlies them, can be authenticated with reasonable certainty.

Niall was a warrior of Connacht, born in the early years of the fifth century A.D., the son, according to tradition, of one Eochu and a captive British "princess" named Cairenn. Father and son alike probably rose to wealth and power by leading piratical raids against Britain in the years when Rome was relinquishing its grasp on that island before finally abandoning it altogether in A.D. 410. Back in Ireland, Niall and his followers (like the legendary Connachtmen of the *Táin*) waged constant warfare against Ulster, driving its tribal leaders, the Ulaid, out of their "capital" at Emain Macha, which was then destroyed. Hostages were then taken from the confederated tribes of south-central Ulster (Airgialla), thus accounting for the cognomen "Noígíallach." The conquerors pressed on into Donegal, where two of Niall's sons, Eógan and Conall, founded a new kingdom called Ailech. There, on a high hill overlooking Lough Foyle and Lough Swilly, they or their successors built (or occupied) a mighty circular stone fortress, the **Grianán of Ailech** *(428)*, today a splendid ruin, though much of it is a nineteenth-century reconstruction. Subsequently one branch of the Uí Néill, the Cenél Eógain, occupied the present county of Tyrone, where the triple-ramparted earthen ring-fort of **Tullaghoge** *(446)*, still to be seen on a hilltop southeast of Cookstown, may have served as one of their ceremonial places of assembly. But it was Tara that became the preeminently sacred site of the Uí Néill dynasty and remained so for centuries to come. And it was Tara too that became the symbol of sovereignty for later claimants to the title of high king (*ard rí*) of Ireland (see Chapter Two). Here from time to time was held the *feis*, an inauguration ceremony in which the king was ritually married to the goddess of sovereignty, probably the same Medb who had been earlier eheumerized in the *Táin* as the queen of Connacht. The sacred stone, the *lia fáil* where the ceremony took place, is believed to be the same monument that now commemorates the fallen heroes of 1798, though not in its original position. (This stone, it should be noted, is Ireland's most obvious prehistoric phallic symbol.)

Meanwhile in southern Ireland there appears to have been a similar consolidation of power in the hands of a single dynasty that became acknowledged kings of the province of Munster. These were the Eóganachta, who originated perhaps in western Kerry but who in time established their royal seat and ceremonial center on **Cashel Rock** *(301)* in modern county Tipperary. The Eóganachta were probably aided in their ascent to preeminence by tribes known as the Dési, who had settled in the modern counties of Waterford and Clare.

There is some evidence that Dési warriors may have served as auxiliary troops or *foederati* in the armies of imperial Rome in its declining years.

If so, this would have been only one of many contacts between Ireland and the westernmost reaches of the Roman Empire, chiefly Britain. Peaceful trade in luxury products, piratical raids by Irish chiefs bringing back booty and slaves, possibly the voluntary immigration of romanized Britons—all helped to bring Ireland within the fringes of the Roman cultural orbit, in spite of the fact no Roman conqueror had ever ventured across the Irish Sea. But it was not until *after* the departure of the last of the Roman governors from Britain that Ireland fell finally under the sway of the imperial city. And that was the handiwork not of legions of soldiers but of peace-loving missionaries bearing the gospel of the risen Christ.

Chapter Two
Early Christian, Viking, and Post-Viking Ireland: 431–1171

THE EARLY CHRISTIAN ERA

Irish history, properly speaking, begins with the year A.D. 431. Before that time no event in Ireland can be dated precisely or even verified by contemporary documentary evidence. But in that year, or shortly thereafter, Prosper of Aquitaine, chronicler of the fifth-century papacy, recorded the arrival in Ireland of one Palladius, named by Pope Celestine to be "the first bishop to the Irish who believed in Christ."

This much is fact, but this is the only known fact about Palladius or about the advent of Christianity to Ireland. Where the bishop went, how long he stayed, and how successful was his mission are not recorded. But it can be inferred from the wording of Prosper's entry that there were Christians in the country before Palladius's arrival. And other evidence, though scanty, suggests that they probably lived in the south (that is, Munster) where contacts with British converts were most likely. Possibly it is to such as these that the use of the Ogham alphabet in Ireland can be attributed.

Ogham (so called after Ogmios, the Celtic god of writing) is an archaic form of Irish script, derived from the Latin alphabet. It probably evolved during the fourth century and remained in use at least until the ninth, and so far as is known, it was confined largely to inscriptions on memorial monuments, many of them of a Christian character. The Ogham alphabet consists of fifteen consonants and five vowels that appear as linear incisions cut either horizontally or diagonally across, or away from, a vertical stem line, usually the edge of a stone. There are about 350 examples on record, the great majority in the South. (There are also about forty in Wales, where many Irish had settled in the fourth century.)

Of the Irish Ogham stones, the most easily accessible to today's visitor are the stone pillars from Aglish, County Kerry, now in the **National Museum of Ireland** *(355)*, Dublin; several stones from County Kerry in the **Cork Public Museum** *(318)*; the Drumconwell Stone in the **Armagh Public Library** *(442)*; and the example in the **Fermanagh County Museum** *(449)* in Enniskillen Castle. On the side of the road to Dunloe Glen, west of Killarney, County Kerry, is a fine collection of eight, called the **Dunloe Ogham Stones** *(332)*, brought here from their original sites nearby and rearranged in a semicircle. Another group can be seen in situ in a field about two miles east of Dingle. These are the **Ballintaggart Ogham Stones** *(329)*—unusual in that they are mostly prone and are rounded in shape, thus lacking the usual edges that normally served as stem lines for Ogham markings. Another two stones stand inside the ruined **Ardmore Cathedral** *(326)*, southwest of Dungarvan, County Waterford. Single examples still to be seen in situ are the stone outside **Kilmalkedar Church** *(330)* near Ballyferriter, County Kerry; **Derrynane Stone** *(328)* near Derrynane House, County Kerry; a stone outside **Ardfert Cathedral** *(326)*, County Kerry; the stone outside **Tullaherin Church** *(293)*, north of Thomastown, County Kilkenny; the **Castle Keeran Ogham Stone** *(385)*, west of Ceannannas (Kells), County Meath; and the **Breastagh Ogham Stone** *(420)*, north of Ballina, County Mayo.

Sometime after the arrival of Palladius, though the exact year is very much disputed, there appeared in northern Ireland another Christian missionary who is given major credit for the conversion of the country from paganism. This was of course St. Patrick, who, by his own testimony, baptized "thousands of people" and thus rescued the Irish from "the worship of idols and filthy things." So many legends have been spun around this illustrious name that the truth about his career is not easily come by. But most historians will accept as authentic the bare autobiographical details set forth in the saint's *Confessio*, written in his old age, and in an extant letter of protest and excommunication sent by him to one Coroticus, a North British chieftain who had massacred or enslaved a number of Christian converts. Both are written in rustic Latin and are preserved in the *Book of Armagh*, now in **Trinity College Library** *(353)*, Dublin.

Son of a romanized British Christian, Patrick, at the age of sixteen, was seized by a raiding party of *Scotti* (Latin for Irish) and carried off from his father's estate to be consigned to slavery in Ireland. After six years of servitude, mostly tending sheep, he escaped and made his way back to Britain. There, in a dream, he received a divine call to return to the land of his captivity as a Christian missionary. After being ordained as a priest, he did so and, along with a number of companions, spent the rest of his life proselytizing in Ireland, founding churches, and ordaining clergymen— probably mostly or altogether in the northern half of the island. Though he was sometimes harassed, and on one occasion put in irons, no serious obstacles seem to have been put in his path by the various kings and chieftains he encountered. On the contrary, many of their sons and daughters were among his converts. Thus he set the country on the clear path to Christianity, though it was at least another century before the process was completed. In this effort he was aided greatly by other missionaries, some acting under his direction, others independently. Nevertheless, most historians today would agree that it was St. Patrick who played the leading role in the Christianization of pagan Ireland.

Patrick, according to his own testimony, was a bishop (*episcopus*), though by whom he was ordained, or where, is not made clear. According to the usages of the fifth-century Roman Church, this means that he would have had jurisdiction, subject to papal approval, over a specific geographic territory, known as a *diocese*. Ecclesiastical organization was modelled on that of the civil service of the late Roman Empire. That is, like provincial Roman governors, bishops maintained their residences in cities and from these centers exercised control over the churches and their clergy in the surrounding territories. The fact that Ireland had no towns or cities would have made it difficult for Patrick to copy this formula, and in any case he was always on the move. Nevertheless it is apparent that he considered himself an orthodox representative of the Roman Church, and certainly his immediate successors tried to impose a conventional episcopal organization on the Church in Ireland. Thus the earliest known Irish ecclesiastical legislation, dating from the sixth century, indicates an established Christian community with clearly defined dioceses, each under a bishop.

But in addition to founding churches and ordaining clerics, St. Patrick also set up separate Christian communities of men and women; that is, in effect, monasteries and nunneries. The monastic movement had had its origins in the Middle East, where it was not unusual for Christian ascetics to seek solitude in the desert, only to attract the company of like-minded escapees from the corruptions of civilization. Thus the fourth century saw the foundation in Egypt and Syria of numerous isolated Christian communities dedicated to contemplation, worship, and work, each subject to the authority of a superior who, in time, would come to be known as an abbot. By the beginning of the fifth century the movement had spread to Gaul and thence to Britain. Not long thereafter it took root in Ireland, where it soon flourished as nowhere else in western Europe.

Geography alone favored such a development. The myriad tiny islands within visible distance of the west coast of Ireland offered ideal sanctuaries for holy men seeking solitude and ascetic privation. Indeed it would be hard to name a single one of these rocky offshore outcrops where an Early Christian monastic community was *not* established. It may be that St. Brendan's legendary voyage in the sixth century was nothing more than a search for an even more distant oceanic refuge. In any case, it is believed he and his companions sailed as far as North America in an open curragh. (To prove that Brendan might have been that continent's first discoverer, in 1976 a group of intrepid navigators made the voyage from Ireland to Newfoundland in a leather-hulled curragh of their own construction. The boat is now on display at the **Craggaunowen Project** *[349]* in County Clare.)

But most monastic founders were content to settle for less remote locations, and the lightly populated mainland of Ireland offered ample wilderness for those seeking isolation. The Irish Ordnance Survey Map of Monastic Sites pinpoints more than 180 such places known to have been in existence before the end of the tenth century, as well as a much larger number of "other or supposed early Celtic establishments."

Ireland was, in short, a natural breeding ground for monasteries, and it was in these isolated and autonomous communities that early Christianity put down its deepest roots. Thus, no matter what may have been the intentions of St. Patrick, and no matter how hard his successors tried to impose a Roman episcopal system on Ireland, the fact is that this was a country with no tradition of centralized organization that would accommodate a hierarchy of urban and provincial bishops. Here was a society with no fixed centers of political power and not even any clear-cut boundaries separating one *tuath* from another. Irish political organization, such as it was, was not hierarchical but familial. The primary unit of society was the family or *fine*, and the *tuath* was essentially a constellation of families in uneasy occupation of the tribal territory. Property could not be alienated outside the family unit, not even to the Church. But a monastery could be thus endowed if its abbot and his successors were members of the kin. Thus monasteries came to be regarded in many instances as family monopolies, and abbeys grew rich in land and chattels, while bishoprics withered on the vine. To be sure, the episcopal office survived, but by the seventh century the function of the bishop was confined largely to the ordination of priests and the consecration of churches and cemeteries. Within the Irish Church at large, real power had shifted to the abbots, who were usually priests but in some cases might be lay members of the family that had originally founded their monastery.

Among Ireland's many abbots (most of whom, though not officially canonized, were subsequently awarded the titular rank of sainthood) none was more illustrious than St. Columcille, also known as St. Columba. A great-great-grandson, on his father's side, of Niall of the Nine Hostages, and on his mother's a descendant of the royal house of Leinster, Columcille withdrew from the fierce and bloody family rivalries to which his noble birth might naturally have inclined him, to choose instead the life of a monk. Like others of his rank and station, he soon became an abbot. From his monastery at Derry he then founded, in effect, a monastic empire, setting up daughterhouses in Durrow and Kells. About the year 562 he was accused of surreptitiously making an unauthorized copy of St. Jerome's Psalter, a manuscript whose possession would have greatly enhanced the prestige of his own foundations. (This copy is believed by some to be the manuscript called *The Cathach*, now in the possession of the **Royal Irish Academy** *[356]* in Dublin.) Judged guilty of the act by the incumbent Uí Néill king of Tara, Columcille was ordered to hand over the copy to St. Finian, owner of the original, on the grounds that "to every cow its calf and to every book its copy." His response to the judgment was to incite his immediate kinsmen to wage war against the king. Though successful in battle, the accused abbot was persuaded to quiet the scandal by leaving the country. Thus in 563, with a dozen companions, he sailed for Scotland, where he founded still another monastery at Iona, a tiny island off the coast of Mull.

After Columcille's death in 597 he was succeeded by a cousin, and indeed all but two of the first twelve abbots of Iona were members of his family. In time this foundation became the motherhouse not only of the Columban monasteries in Ireland but also of Lindisfarne in Northumbria. Indeed missionary monks from Iona became so influential in England as to incite the jealousy of St. Augustine's monastic establishment at Canterbury. The rivalry came to a head in a famous controversy over the proper dating of Easter, which was settled in favor of Canterbury (and Rome) at the Synod of Whitby in 664. Thereafter in England the influence of the so-called Celtic Church began to wane.

In Ireland, all churches eventually accepted the Roman calculation of the Easter date, but the adverse decision at Whitby in no way diminished the luster of the sainted Columcille. In the seventh century the Columban monasteries, however, did suffer a setback at the hands of the church at Armagh, which by this time had also become monastic. Claiming (without much solid evidence) that St. Patrick had established his episcopal seat at Armagh, the monastery's abbots demanded recognition of the suzerainty of their church over all other churches and monasteries in Ireland and proclaimed their right to levy tribute therefrom. It was to buttress this claim that two monks of Armagh, Muirchu and Tirechán, wrote hagiographies of Patrick purporting to demonstrate that he alone had been responsible for the original conversion of the Irish. (These manuscripts are enclosed within the *Book of Armagh* now in **Trinity College Library** *[353]*, Dublin.) They were on the whole successful works of propaganda, and thus the still-flourishing cult of Patrick owes as much to the hegemoniac designs of Armagh in the seventh century as to the accomplishments of the saint himself in the fifth.

But rivalry between monasteries took more sinister form than the mere purloining of precious manuscripts or the distortion of the historical record. Increasingly in the seventh and eighth centuries these religious establishments came under lay control and thus became embroiled in the incessant intertribal warfare, described so nicely by the historian Liam de

Paor as "a prolonged tedium of ferocious family quarrels." It was not unknown, indeed, for pitched battles to break out between religious establishments, and on one occasion the household of the abbey of Clonmacnoise took credit for killing a hundred men from Durrow in an intermonastic fracas.

Also, with wealth and power came corruption in various guises, and the spiritual fervor that had inspired the monastic communities of the fifth and sixth centuries began to give out in the seventh. But a century later reaction set in by way of a reform movement led by a group of monks calling themselves Céli De, "companions or vassals of God," who laid great stress on contemplation, study, and worship. Some of these men became hermits; others remained within the established religious houses, both part of and separate from the communities where they resided.

Nonconformity of this sort accounts for a significant difference between the Irish monasteries and most of those of the Continent and England, where the rule established by St. Benedict in the sixth century was becoming widespread. Benedictine monks lived under a strict and uniform discipline of daily work and prayer from which no deviation was allowed. Irish monastic life, on the other hand, tended toward diversity. The differences were reflected too in the physical layout of the respective communities. Benedictine monasteries were more or less uniform in plan, with church, chapter house, communal dormitory, communal refectory, and abbot's lodging set out in a square around a central cloister. In Irish establishments, on the contrary, the monks mostly lived in small cells scattered throughout the grounds; there might be more than one church; and separate buildings for eating, study, and work stood at random within an enclosure surrounded by a *vallum*—a wall of wood or stone, or an earthen bank and ditch, or even a mere hedge of thorn trees. (An extant example of a triple-stone *vallum* can be seen at **Nendrum** *[433]* on Mahee Island, County Down, south of Comber.)

Most of the buildings inside the enclosure would have been constructed of timber or of interwoven saplings (wickerwork) coated with clay ("wattle and daub"). All of course have long since disappeared. But even as early as the eighth century some few apparently were built of stone—at least in the rocky coastal regions of the west. Whether any of the extant Early Christian sites date as far back as the eighth century is debatable, but even if not, it is safe to assume that at least a few bear close resemblance to the original monastic settlements.

The most famous of these is **Skellig Michael** *(333)*, situated on a rocky island peak rising more than seven hundred feet above the sea eight miles off the southwestern coast of County Kerry. On a ledge high up on the western face of the rock are the scant ruins of a medieval chapel and, more importantly, the substantial remains of two drystone (mortarless) oratories,

where the monks prayed and worshipped, and six "beehive cells" or
clocháin, which would have served as their living quarters. The oratories
are rectangular in ground plan, and the larger and better preserved of the
two has the appearance of an upturned boat. The beehive cells, also
rectangular at the base, are rounded at the top. In each instance the shape
of the roof was achieved by corbelling, whereby each course of stones was
laid so as to overlap the one beneath on the inside wall, thus creating the
effect of a dome or vault.

As mentioned in Chapter One, corbelling was well known to Irish
stone-age tomb builders. In the Early Christian period and later it continued to be used not only in ecclesiastical buildings but in ordinary
domestic construction as well. A well-preserved cluster of "beehive huts"
(though undatable) stands just north of the coastal road west of Dingle in
County Kerry. Known locally as **Cahir Murphy (Cathair na Martíneach)**
(329), it includes the substantial remains of three *clocháin*, plus the foundations of two others. A few miles to the north is **Caherdorgan** *(330)*, with
the circular stone foundations of five *clocháin* enclosed by a stone wall. Not
far away is perhaps the best known of Early Christian oratories (although
again not precisely datable), known as **Gallarus Oratory** *(329)*. Better built
than its counterparts on Skellig Michael, this little chapel has a rectangular ground plan measuring ten by fifteen feet internally; the east and west
gables lean slightly inward in a curved batter; and the side walls and roof
are corbelled upward into the form of a vault.

Along with corbelling, antae are among the architectural features
peculiar to Irish churches of the Early Christian period. The word *antae*
can be defined simply as the projections of the side walls of a stone
building beyond the face of the end or gable walls. The depth of the
projection is usually slight, but enough to give both front and rear a
slightly recessed appearance. They are thought to be conscious reproductions in stone of earlier timber-built structures. If they had any functional
purpose at all, it would have been to support bargeboards laid laterally
across them to shelter the front and back faces of the church. Though found
only in Ireland, they are not universal among the early stone churches, and
their presence does not necessarily indicate an eighth- or even a ninth-
century date of construction. However, when they are found alongside
other distinguishing features, an early date is suggested. These other
features, common to Early Christian churches, include (1) single-chambered rectangular ground plans of such small dimensions as to exclude the
possibility of more than a few people entering the building at any one
time; (2) exterior mortared walls of massive stones interspersed with small
pieces of stone called *spalls*; (3) low side walls abutted by high end walls or
gables, indicating a very high-pitched roof; (4) stone roofs propped from
below by single arches above which might be installed an upper chamber

called a *croft*; (5) inward sloping or "battered" walls; (6) a single narrow doorway at the west end, with jambs inclining inward, supporting a flat stone lintel; and (7) few windows (sometimes no more than one in the east gable wall), very narrow, round- or triangle-headed, and splayed inward.

Examples of early small, single-chambered churches with antae and some or all of the other features listed above are to be found all over Ireland. Those listed here are representative. **St. Begnet's Church** *(373)* on Dalkey Island, County Dublin, has high-pitched gables, a flat-lintelled western doorway with inward-leaning jambs, and small flat-headed windows. **Killoughternane Church** *(288)*, near Borris, County Carlow, has a small, round-headed east window. The much restored **Labbamolaga Church** *(324)*, north of Mitchelstown, County Cork, is distinguished for its unique western doorway constructed of only three stones. The much mutilated **Teampull Chiárain, Clonmacnoise** *(382)*, County Offaly, is the smallest of the several churches within this famous monastic precinct. **St. Fechin's Church** *(393)* in Fore, County Westmeath, has a cross inside a circle carved in low relief above the doorway and a chancel added probably in the thirteenth century. The partially reconstructed church of **St. Mel's, Ardagh** *(395)*, County Longford, is unusually broad in plan but otherwise typically Early Christian. **St. MacDara's Church** *(415)* on the island of the same name off the Connemara coast, County Galway, has a very short chamber with unique antae extending all the way up the exceptionally high-pitched gable walls. **St. John's Point Church** *(432)*, southwest of Ardglass, County Down, has a flat-lintelled doorway with inward-leaning jambs and a small triangular east window. In the same county, the southernmost of the two **Derry Churches** *(439)* near Portaferry has few remaining features to distinguish it as an Early Christian church beyond the small flat-headed windows and its antae.

Early single-chambered churches of approximately the same dates as the above, but without antae, include the restored **St. Mary's Church, Glendalough** *(311)*, County Wicklow (possibly the nuns' church since it stands outside the abbey grounds); **St. Kevin's Church, Glendalough** *(311)*, also known as St. Kevin's Kitchen, with a belfry, chancel, and sacristy added to the original single-celled church, which has an exceptionally high-pitched stone roof with a croft beneath; **St. Molua's Oratory, Killaloe** *(347)*, County Clare; **St. Columb's House, Kells** *(384)*, County Meath, much modified since its construction possibly as early as 814, also with a very high-pitched stone roof and a croft; and **St. Benen's** *(411)*, on Inishmore, Aran Islands, County Galway, allegedly the smallest church in Ireland and uniquely built along a north–south axis. All of the above are possibly of an eighth- or early-ninth-century date, although such early origins are by no means undisputed among church historians and archaeologists. What cannot be disputed is that none of these churches would have been large enough to hold more than two or three people in addition to priest and acolytes. If larger congregations were to be allowed to observe the celebration of the Mass, they would have had to convene outdoors.

It would be surprising if the pagan tradition of decorative stonework had died out with the coming of Christianity to Ireland, and it did not. Since cremation was forbidden by the Church, early monasteries buried their dead in cemeteries of individual graves. Probably serving as grave markers were the numerous extant stone slabs, inscribed with crosses and sometimes with the words "OR DO," meaning "a prayer for." The crosses vary in form—some simply equal-armed, others framed in boxes, still others with ornamental ends. There are about eight or nine hundred slabs of this sort, the heaviest concentration being in County Offaly, where good collections can be seen at **Durrow Abbey** *(383)*, **Gallen Priory** *(381)*, and **Clonmacnoise Monastery** *(381)*. At **Tullylease Church** *(322)*, north of Kanturk, County Cork, a number of grave slabs are incorporated into the walls. The same is true of **Toureen Peakaun Church** *(299)*, northwest of Cahir, County Tipperary. Leaning against the north wall of ruined **Tully Church** *(372)*, north of Bray, County Dublin, are several Early Christian slabs. Nearby are the **Rathmichael Cross Slabs** *(372)*, built into the south wall of a much-ruined sixteenth-century church. A single slab can be seen standing against the east wall of the westernmost of the **Killevy Churches** *(438)*, south of Camlough, County Armagh.

Christian symbols were also incised or carved in low relief on pillar stones and standing stones. The **Ballyvourney Cross** *(323)*, west of Macroom, County Cork, is a solitary upright slab inscribed with a cross of arcs and, in the upper left corner, the small figure of a man, presumably a priest, bearing a staff or crosier. A cross of the same design decorates a fine ornamented pillar stone within the walls of an Early Christian monastic enclosure at **Reask** *(330)*, near Ballyferriter on the Dingle peninsula, County Kerry. In County Donegal on the site of an Early Christian monastery at **Fahan Mura** *(425)*, south of Buncrana, is a standing slab with crosses carved on each side in an elaborate interlace design in low relief. In the same county, in the graveyard of **Glencolumbkille (Church of Ireland) Church** *(427)*, are several pillars decorated with crosses and geometric designs. In County Armagh, south of Newry, County Down, the **Kilnassagart Stone** *(438)* is covered on both sides with disks enclosing crosses carved in very low relief.

In addition to slabs and pillars, rough crosses were also sculpted to serve the same commemorative (or other) purposes. **Carndonagh Cross** *(425)* in County Donegal is the best example of what might be considered transitional between cross slabs and Ireland's famous High Crosses. Now standing along the roadside just north of the town of Carndonagh, it reaches a height of about ten feet. One face is covered with broad interlace in low relief, while on the shaft below is a full-length figure presumably representing Christ; on the opposite side is an interlaced head. Although the date is disputed, it might be as early as the seventh or eighth century, which places this monument at the beginning of a new phase in the development of stone sculpture in Ireland. Possibly the same dates could be ascribed to the plainer **Carrowmore Crosses** *(426)*, south of here by a few miles, and to the stone cross in the foyer of **Clogher (C of I) Cathedral,** *(444)*, County Tyrone.

Together with the Round Towers (described later in this chapter), the Early Christian High Crosses constitute perhaps the most distinctive (and certainly the most photographed) man-made adornment of the Irish countryside. There are over a hundred surviving examples, of which thirty-four remain substantially intact. They are freestanding stone monuments between eight and twenty-three feet high, rising from cubic or pyramidal bases. To the average observer their most striking characteristic is the open stone ring normally encircling the crossing between shaft and arms. Custom has decreed that monuments with this feature are to be designated "Celtic crosses," although in fact the same technique was used by stonecutters in parts of Britain where the artistic traditions were primarily Germanic or Scandinavian. The ring served a functional as well as an artistic purpose; that is, the four arcs of the circle gave structural support to the arms, which may account for the high survival rate.

Nearly all the High Crosses are covered, in whole or in part, with stone carvings in high or low relief, some purely abstract and ornamental, others representational and religious. Since these monuments were clearly not grave markers, their exact purpose is in doubt. Perhaps they served as centers for congregational assembly outside the churches, which, as mentioned earlier, were usually too small to house many of the faithful at any given time. Perhaps they were sacred totems to ward off evil spirits. Probably the later crosses, carved profusely with scriptural scenes (see below), were meant to be "sermons in stone." All that is really known about them is that they were part of the monastic scenery.

Many scholars believe that the earliest of the High Crosses date to the mid–eighth century, though a ninth-century provenance seems more likely. One group is concentrated in the southern part of modern County Kilkenny and adjacent County Tipperary, north of Carrick-on-Suir. It includes the two **Ahenny Crosses** *(400)*, the westernmost of the **Kilkeeran Crosses** *(300)*, the **Killamery Cross** *(291)*, and the **Kilree Cross** *(291)*. Related to these is the **South Cross** at **Clonmacnoise Monastery** *(383)*, County Offaly. Although all display some representational figure carving, partly scriptural in origin, they are distinguished chiefly for their abstract ornamentation—protruding round bosses, spirals, interlace, and the like. The full development of a Christian iconography translated into stone would not take place until the mid- to late-ninth century (discussed later).

No close observer of the Ahenny Crosses can fail to note the similarity of their sculptured designs to the exquisite metalwork on display at the **National Museum of Ireland** *(355)* in Dublin. The high-relief stone bosses look very much like the typical enamel studs of Irish jewelry usually assigned to the eighth century; the interlacings and spiral designs could well have been wrought in imitation of the chip-carving (*kerbschnitt*) techniques commonly applied to gilt bronze objects by Irish metalsmiths. If so, then the stone carvers of Ahenny could not have found superior models.

Beginning probably in the eighth century and continuing for more than two hundred years thereafter, Irish metalwork achieved a degree of virtuosity and refinement unequalled before or since. Inspiration for this outburst of artistic activity derived from a variety of sources: from native La Tène culture, from Roman influences, from contacts with contemporary Anglo-Saxon craftsmen, and (after the arrival of the Vikings) from current Scandinavian fashions. Cast bronze was the basic raw material, but the embellishments applied to it were many and varied: gilding and silvering; chip carving; engraving; metal grilles filled with molten glass (cloisonné enamelling); filigree in gold and silver, etc. To the modern observer the chief characteristic of all this handiwork is the profusion of design, the closely packed ornamentation, and the absence of bare spaces. It appears that these metalsmiths, like their iron-age predecessors, suffered from a *horror vacui*, an aversion to leaving any inch undecorated. In general, three types of finished products were thus fabricated: reliquaries to enclose and protect sacred objects, liturgical vessels for church services, and personal jewelry, especially pins and brooches.

Of the reliquaries in the National Museum dating from the eighth and ninth centuries, the most interesting is the Moylough Belt Shrine. (St. Patrick's Bell is possibly of even earlier date, but its splendid shrine was made in the eleventh century.) Of the liturgical vessels, two in particular are noteworthy. The first, and possibly the most admired of all the museum's holdings, is the eighth-century Ardagh Chalice, a marvelously ornamented silver bowl with a large subconical foot and handles. Especially worthy of close attention are the polychrome glass studs and gold filigree work. It will be noted that this piece is unusual in that much of the silver surface is unadorned—a departure from the conventional decorative profusion mentioned. The more recently discovered Derrynaflan Chalice is of similar construction and only slightly less elegant. It too is a silver, footed bowl with gold filigree ornamentation of remarkable delicacy. As to personal jewelry, the museum houses a fine collection of brooches, both penannular (broken-ring) and pseudo-penannular (unbroken ring) in form. Of these the most famous, and justifiably so, is the Tara Brooch, an eighth-century piece discovered not at Tara but at Bettystown, County Meath. It is pseudo-penannular, about 3½ inches in diameter, and is made of gilded bronze with added amber, gold, glass, silver, and copper. Unlike the Ardagh Chalice, it is crowded with detailed decoration front and back. Again the gold filigree is of an astonishing intricacy, and the underside reveals an abundance of spirals, triskeles, and other motifs of undoubted La Tène inspiration.

Brooches such as this could well have adorned high-ranking Irish clergy as well as rich and powerful nobles. Whoever owned and wore them, some at least would have been fabricated in the workshops of one or another of the great monastic cities of the Early Christian period. So too were the many manuscripts of the same era—another of Ireland's great contributions to the enrichment of Western arts and letters.

It was undoubtedly the early Christian missionaries who first brought Latin literature to Ireland in the form of gospel books and other religious tracts. St. Patrick, to be sure, wrote in a corrupt version of the language, for which he was constantly apologizing. But as his successors became familiar with St. Jerome's version of the Bible, the *editio vulgata*, the quality of writing improved. In time Irish monks earned an international reputation for the high quality of their scholarship. Even the Venerable Bede, writing in Northumberland in the eighth century, commented on their devotion to learning and their generosity to English students who were attracted to Ireland because of its known superiority in theological studies. On the Continent, Irish missionaries were famous for their scholarly attainments, and the monastic foundations of St. Columbanus at Annegray, Luxeuil, and Bobbio, and of his disciple, St. Gall, in Switzerland exercised a major influence on the intellectual development of western Europe in the early Middle Ages.

It was partly in support of such missionary activity abroad that Irish monastic scriptoria were so prolific in the production of Bibles, missals, Psalters, copies of works of the Church fathers, commentaries of biblical texts, and the like. They also kept records of current events, chronologies of happenings in the secular world preserved as yearly "annals." Even the *Táin* and other bardic poems and tales, hitherto circulated only in oral Gaelic, were reduced to written form by these tireless monks. Gradually Gaelic words began to work their way into monastic writings, and in the seventh century a Gaelic grammar appeared. Thus Christian monasteries came to be the repositories of a vast store of pagan literature, and the Gaelic language, unlike that of the Picts of Scotland for example, was saved from oblivion.

But Latin continued to be the official language of the Church, and from the sixth century onward Irish monks became especially adept in the reproduction of Latin texts. Specifically they developed a highly legible insular script known as *uncial,* in which the majuscules were clear and rounded and the minuscules were cursive, or almost so. The earliest of the Irish manuscripts thus written is *The Cathach,* a copy of St. Jerome's Psalter possibly produced in the later sixth century and believed by some to have been the handiwork of St. Columcille himself and the cause of his disgrace and exile. It is now the property of the **Royal Irish Academy** *(356)* in Dublin and is occasionally on display.

The Cathach is embellished here and there with simple scrollwork and trumpet patterns in the La Tène tradition. Also, at the beginning of each Psalm are large capitals surrounded by red dots—a convention originating in the Coptic monasteries of Egypt. Not until the seventh century would manuscript illumination reach its full development, probably thanks to the scriptoria of the abbey of Iona and especially of its daughterhouse at Lindisfarne, Northumbria, where Irish monks perfected an eclectic style, combining Anglo-Saxon, Roman, and La Tène motifs to produce prodigies of decorative art. This Early Christian Anglo-Irish repertoire included spirals, scrolls, triskeles, trumpet curves, *peltae* (shields), bird's heads, vines, elongated and intertwined animal forms, and ribbon interlace. Designs such as these adorned margins, capital letters, ends of sentences, spaces between lines, and even entire pages (which were called "carpet pages").

The first major monument to the new style was the *Book of Durrow,* now in the **Trinity College Library** *(353),* Dublin. Produced probably in the seventh century, it is a small (9½- by 6½-inch) edition of the four gospels, written on vellum (calfskin) and illustrated lavishly in bright colors derived from natural pigments: green from acetate of copper, bright yellow from orpiment, and vermilion from red lead. Even more ornate (and more famous) is the *Book of Kells,* also on display at Trinity College Library. Originally it measured fifteen by eleven inches, but in the nineteenth century it was trimmed to its present dimensions of thirteen by 9½. It dates probably to the late eighth or early ninth century and may have been the handiwork of the Columban monastery of Iona, although possibly produced at the monastery of Kells itself. Here is a still greater variety of colors and of decorative plants and animals; also sumptuous carpet pages (especially the one introducing the narrative portion of the Gospel of Matthew); also repetitive use of the four symbols of the Evangelists (the man for Matthew, the lion for Mark, the calf for Luke, the eagle for John); also representational portraits of the Virgin and Child, Christ, and of the two Evangelists, Matthew and John.

Two other manuscripts in the Trinity College Library likewise deserve mention. The *Book of Armagh* is a composite manuscript of the ninth century and contains a complete New Testament, the *Confessio* of St. Patrick, the hagiographies of Patrick compiled in the seventh century by Muirchu and Tirechán, and Sulpicius Severus's *Life of St. Martin*. It is fairly small (7¾ by 5½ inches), and its decoration is simple, consisting of a few initials and drawings of the Evangelists' symbols. The *Book of Dimma*, of uncertain date, is smaller still, but the illustrations are colorful and typical. Finally worth mentioning is the little *Stowe Missal* in the **Royal Irish Academy** *(356)*, Dublin, probably dating to the eighth century. These last two manuscripts were probably meant to be carried by monks on pilgrimage or missionary enterprises, whereas the larger examples mentioned earlier were undoubtedly designed as altar books.

Of these great and now priceless manuscripts, two (*The Cathach* and *The Book of Kells*) were possibly brought from Iona to the Columban monastery at Kells in the early ninth century. If so, there was good reason for the transfer to an inland location. Three times in little more than a decade (in 795, 803, and 806) the island of Iona and its monastery had been raided and sacked by seaborne Vikings bent on plunder. It would not be long before the coast of Ireland too would feel the full brunt of these fierce Scandinavian invaders.

THE VIKING ERA

In the very year of the first attack on Iona (795), Viking ships (perhaps the same ones) appeared off the coast of Ireland, either at Lambay Island, County Dublin, or Rathlin Island, County Antrim. This was their first appearance in Ireland proper. Given the nature of Scandinavian expansionism in the eighth century, it was no doubt inevitable. Land hunger and political unrest had driven farmers from western Norway to settle in Orkney and Shetland only about two hundred to 250 miles away. Then came the long ships—some bearing peaceful traders, but others carrying fighting men bent on plunder. Not only were these Norsemen well armed and greedy, but, more significantly, they were by far the most skillful shipbuilders of western Europe. Their clinker-built vessels, about eighty feet in length, combined light draft with heavy keels and were propelled by both oars and sails. They were thus eminently seaworthy in deep waters, capable of penetrating shallow bays and rivers, fast enough to make a landfall without detection, and maneuverable enough to make a quick getaway safe from pursuit. Against such odds, their land-bound victims were defenseless. Especially so were coastal and island monasteries, rich in goods and cattle and well peopled with potential slaves, their claims to sanctity no proof against the pagan greed of these ferocious foreigners.

Inishmurray off the Galway coast was burned and plundered in 807, Skellig Michael in 812, Bangor in 820, Skellig Michael again in 823, Downpatrick in 825, Clonmore in 828. And others besides. But these were sporadic hit-and-run raids. Then, in 832, a Viking chief called Thorgestr (latinized to Turgesius) brought a fleet far up the Shannon to Lough Ree, and from that date on the Norse invasion of Ireland began in earnest. Burned and plundered were all the great monasteries, inland as well as coastal: Armagh, Birr, Clonmacnoise, Lorrha, Terryglass, Inishcaltra, and Emly to name but a few. Permanent Scandinavian outposts were established along the coasts, and these developed into colonies and eventually into petty Viking kingdoms. Among the first was a fortified settlement founded in 841 called Dubh Linn, the Black Pool, near an ancient ford of the Liffey—Ath Cliath, the ford of the wattles. This was followed eventually by the establishment of seaport towns at Wicklow, Wexford, Waterford, Cork, and Limerick. Having come to plunder, the Vikings stayed to colonize and trade.

Meanwhile the native Irish could hardly be described as passive. The Vikings were not the only plunderers of churches, notwithstanding the impressions given by contemporary monastic chroniclers, whose bias in this connection is understandable. Indeed, according to the historian Donncha O'Corráin, the Norsemen, in the first quarter of the ninth century, committed only twenty-six recorded acts of violence as against some eighty-seven perpetrated by the Irish themselves. And, in the words of Peter Somerville-Large: "Beside the 309 recorded occasions when the pagan Vikings robbed ecclesiastical sites can be listed an almost equal number of similar raids by Irishmen." The fact is that long before the first Viking set foot in Ireland Irish kings and chieftains had become notorious for their sacrilegious depredations of ecclesiastical properties. The greatest of the church burners was Feidlimid mac Crimthainn, king of Munster, who is credited with having set fire to the monasteries of Kildare, Clonfert, Durrow, and Clonmacnoise, among others. Feidlimid was himself in holy orders, probably of episcopal rank. As such, his sympathies lay with the Céli De, and he justified his attacks on the monasteries as part of a crusade to stamp out corruption in the Church. A more likely explanation, however, is that he chose his victims because of their affiliations with the Uí Néill kings of the North.

The number of petty kingdoms in Ireland seems to have declined by the beginning of the ninth century, although the country was still a patchwork quilt of independent or semi-independent *tuatha*. Yet by this time two major dynasties had emerged. The northern half of the island (Leth Cuinn) was clearly dominated by the two branches of the Uí Néill (southern and northern) from whom were chosen the kings of Tara, while in the southern half (Leth Moga) the Eóganachta kings of Cashel held uneasy sway. Feidlimid was the first of the Eóganachta to challenge the Uí Néills, in an apparent effort to win recognition as high king (*ard rí*) of Ireland, a title having no legal sanction but signifying a claim to superiority over other provincial kings.

Whether the king-bishop of Cashel won out over his northern rivals is not altogether clear, but in any case, whatever successes he may have had were short-lived. After Feidlimid's death in 846, Munster was overrun by the forces of Máel Sechnaill, king of Tara and head of the southern Uí Néill. He had already waged successful war against the Vikings, captured their leader Turgesius and had him drowned in Lough Owel, defeated their hosts in a battle at Skreen, and ravaged the Norse settlement of Dublin.

On his death in 862 Máel Sechnaill was called *ard rí* of Ireland by the annalists. But nothing was permanent in this turbulent country, and the political scene for the next hundred years and more was a kaleidoscope of shifting alliances and recurring wars between Irish provincial kings, between Irish and Norse, between Norse and incoming Danes vying for a share of trade and booty, between Norse or Danes allied to Irish against other Irish sometimes allied to other Scandinavians. During the first half of the tenth century two kings of Cashel, Cormac mac Cuillenáin and Cellaha, successively challenged the supremacy of the Uí Néill and again failed. Then, toward the end of the century, there appeared out of the west, in the country of the Dál Cais, an upstart dynasty that, for a while, threatened to overwhelm all the ancient royal families of Ireland as well as the Scandinavian invaders in their urban strongholds.

The Dál Cais were a minor tribe of Munstermen who had in the eighth century settled in eastern County Clare, where the inauguration place of their kings has been identified as **Magh Adhair** *(350)*—today a flat-topped mound surrounded by bank and ditch lying southeast of Ennis. Their first king of note was one Mathgamain mac Cennétig, who in 964 seized Cashel from the weakened Eóganacht dynasty and then proceeded to plunder the Viking stronghold at Limerick before being captured by treachery and executed by a rival Munster chieftain. Mathgamain was succeeded by his brother Brian, who took vengeance on his brother's killers, slew the Norse king of Limerick, invaded the neighboring provinces of Osraige (Ossory) and Leinster, and established himself as ruler of the southern half of Ireland. This meant not that he governed these conquered territories in the modern sense but that he enforced compliance to his will by taking hostages from their kings and chiefs and exacting tribute from them. Thus he became known as Brian Boroimhe (Boromha), meaning Brian of the Tributes or, in its short form, Brian Boru.

Having consolidated his power in the South, Brian next turned his attention to the Uí Néill king of Tara. This was Máel Sechnaill II, himself a warrior of no mean mettle, who in 980–81 had soundly beaten the Dublin Norse and temporarily occupied their city. In the year 1002, however, Máel, without a battle, yielded to Brian at Tara. And with the subsequent submissions of the northern Uí Néill kings, Brian Boru could justifiably claim to be *ard rí Erenn*, the high king of Ireland—or, as he called himself during a state visit to Armagh, *imperator Scottorum*, emperor of the Irish.

But *imperium* in Ireland was a sometime thing, and by 1014 the king of Leinster, joined this time by the Dublin Norse and Scandinavian allies from Orkney and the Isle of Man, raised the standard of rebellion. At Clontarf, near Dublin, on Good Friday (24 April) 1014, battle was joined. By the end of a hard day's fighting Leinstermen and Vikings were routed, with many dead left on the field. Dead also was the high king, Brian Boru. His body was carried to Armagh to be buried in state on the grounds of the present **St. Patrick's (C of I) Cathedral** *(442)* in Armagh.

This great battle, celebrated in Viking saga as well as Irish legend, is commonly regarded as a decisive turning point in Irish history: the end of Scandinavian hopes to conquer Ireland as Normandy had been conquered and, with Brian's death, the end of Ireland's opportunity to form itself into a single nation under the rule of a single Irish king. Both hypotheses must be viewed with skepticism. The Norse in fact played a secondary role at Clontarf. Brian's primary adversary was the king of Leinster, to whom the "Ostmen" of Dublin were temporarily allied. The battle was, in other words, merely another incident in the dreary succession of Irish internecine warfare. Moreover, nothing in the known history of Ireland up to Clontarf would seem to indicate that the country was yet capable of unification under either a native ruler or a foreign conqueror.

THE VIKING IMPACT

Though the Ostmen were on the losing side of the Battle of Clontarf, Dublin survived and flourished as a center of trade with Britain and the Continent and as the home of a busy shipbuilding industry and of numerous crafts, including metalwork, comb making, carpentry, the manufacture of leather goods, the minting of coins, etc. Excavations there in 1962 brought to light some thirty thousand objects ranging in date from the late ninth to the early fourteenth century. Among the most significant of these now housed in the **National Museum of Ireland** *(355)* are miscellaneous carved wooden objects and "trial pieces" of bone and stone, believed to have served as patterns for casting ornamental metalwork. The style of the trial pieces is late-eleventh-century Hiberno-Norse Ringerike, which is based on the combination of the motifs of interlaced snakes and animals and scrolls and lobed tendrils. Similar motifs are to be seen on sundry reliquaries of local saints whose cults were much encouraged by monasteries competing for prestige and wealth. Among these, in the Ringerike style, is the Clonmacnoise Crosier, also in the National Museum. In the same repository are to be found several reliquaries in the Scandinavian Urnes style, an elaboration of the Ringerike, with looser animal interlace, quadrupeds with attenuated jaws and interlocking manes and mustaches, and threadlike snakes with protruding eyes. Examples include the Shrine of St. Lachtin's Arm, the Shrine of St. Patrick's Bell, the Lismore Crosier, and, best of all, the Cross of Cong, made in 1123 at the behest of Turlogh O'Connor, king of Connacht, to contain at its center, under a rock-crystal disk, a splinter of the True Cross.

Viking attacks on the monasteries, along with those of native Irish kings, chieftains, and rival religious houses, may also have been responsible for the first appearance in the tenth century of an almost uniquely Irish architectural phenomenon: the Round Tower. About sixty-five of these tall, round, slender buildings are left in Ireland, many of them complete or almost so. All were originally constructed on monastic grounds, although in some cases the associated buildings have disappeared. Sometimes they are now attached to churches, but originally they were freestanding, and most of them still are. Dates of construction probably range from about 900 to as late as 1300, although most fall within the tenth, eleventh, and twelfth centuries. They were multipurpose buildings. The Old Irish word for them is *cloigtheach*, meaning "bell-house," and they were in fact belfries from the top of which hand-bells were rung to announce the canonical hours and summon the monks to prayer. Also, they undoubtedly served as watchtowers from which unfriendly visitors could be spotted from afar. Finally they were strongholds in which monastic records and treasures could be preserved and to which the monks themselves might repair in times of trouble.

In short, although today the Round Towers are admired mostly for aesthetic and romantic reasons, their original design was eminently functional. Circular in plan, their walls of mortared stone rose to heights sometimes in excess of a hundred feet, tapering slightly inward as the thickness of the lower courses diminished. The single doorway normally stood about ten or fifteen feet above ground and was accessible only by a retrievable ladder. Inside there were five or more stories, each with a wooden floor and each with a single narrow window, except for the top story, which had four windows looking out in that many directions. The interior floors were connected with each other by movable ladders. The roof was usually conical, although some of the later towers had battlements, either originally or added during the Middle Ages.

So many of these buildings have survived in whole or in part that the interested traveller is hard put to choose among them. At least two have had their interior floors and ladders restored and can therefore be climbed to the top: the **Kilkenny Round Tower** on the grounds of **St. Canice's (C of I) Cathedral** *(295)* in that city and the **Kildare Round Tower** next to **St. Brigid's (C of I) Cathedral** *(377)*, Kildare.

Several are of interest because of unusual features. Carved and molded doorways (indicating probably a late date of construction) are observable at **Taghadoe** *(379)*, south of Maynooth, County Kildare; **Timahoe** *(314)*, southeast of Port Laoise, County Laois; **Roscrea** *(306)*, County Tipperary; **Dysert Oenghusa** *(336)*, near Croom, County Limerick; **Donaghmore** *(387)*, north of Navan, County Meath; **Kells** *(384)*, in Ceanannas (Kells), County Meath; **Drumlane** *(401)*, near Belturbet, County Cavan; **Devenish** *(450)*, in Lough Erne, County Fermanagh; as well as **Kildare** *(377)*, already mentioned. **Kilmacduagh** *(409)*, County Galway, is the highest of the Round Towers in Ireland, and, like the Tower of Pisa, has a decided list. **Kinneagh** *(316)*, north of Clonakilty, County Cork, is hexagonal at the base and round at the top. **Dromiskin** *(399)*, near Castlebellingham, County Louth, and **Turlough** *(421)*, east of Castlebar, County Mayo, are unusually squat in shape. The **Scattery Island Round Tower** *(347)* in the mouth of the river Shannon, County Clare, is unique in having its door at ground level rather than in the customary elevated position.

All the rest of those listed as follows are more or less conventional, some with conical roofs, some battlemented, some roofless: **Aghagower** *(424)*, County Mayo; **Ardmore** *(326)*, southwest of Dungarvan, County Waterford; **Glendalough** *(311)*, inside the grounds of the famous monastery in County Wicklow; **Fertagh** *(298)*, north of Urlingford, County Kilkenny; **Kilree** *(291)* and **Aghaviller** *(291)*, near Callan, County Kilkenny; **Cashel** *(302)*, County Tipperary; **Tullaherin** *(293)*, north of Thomastown, County Kilkenny; **Castledermot** *(376)* and **Oughterard** *(380)*, both in County Kildare; **Cloyne** *(317)*, east of Cork city; **Rattoo** *(327)*, south of Ballybunnion, County Kerry; **Drumcliff** *(345)* and **Dysert O'Dea** *(343)*, both north of Ennis, County Clare; **Clondalkin** *(372)*, **Lusk** *(374)*, and **Swords** *(375)*, all in County Dublin; **O'Rourke's Tower, Clonmacnoise** *(382)*, County Offaly; the **Monasterboice Round Tower** *(398)* in County Louth; **Clones Tower** *(400)*, County Monaghan; **Meelick** *(422)*, west of Castlebar, County Mayo; **Killala** *(420)*, north of Ballina, County Mayo; and **Antrim Round Tower**

(452), just north of the city of that name in Northern Ireland.

Contemporaneous with the Round Towers is a second series of High Crosses, dating from the ninth through the eleventh centuries. Unlike the towers, however, these great monuments in sculptured stone may not have been designed specifically with the dangers of Viking or native Irish banditry in mind. If anything, they testify to the resiliency of the Irish monasteries in the face of repeated depredations, and indeed their very existence suggests that the Viking period was not, after all, one of unrelieved turmoil. In any case, their function, like that of medieval stained-glass windows, was to teach by visual imagery the lessons of the Bible, to encourage piety among their beholders, and, in some cases at least, to commemorate the great churchmen and laymen responsible for their erection.

Unlike the freestanding stone crosses of the eighth or ninth centuries (discussed earlier), these are distinguished not for their abstract ornamentation but rather for their figural designs. Around the base and/or the cross itself are sculpted scenes, mostly from the Old and New Testaments and from the lives of St. Anthony of Alexandria, founder of Christian monasticism, and of St. Paul of Thebes, thought to have been the first Christian hermit. The Old Testament scenes are taken mostly from three books only: Genesis, Daniel, and 1 Samuel. Adam and Eve are the favorites, next Abraham preparing to sacrifice his son Isaac, then Daniel in the Lions' Den. Other figures portrayed in stone include Noah and the Ark; Cain and Abel; David, either fighting a lion or engaging Goliath in combat; and the Three Children of Israel in the Fiery Furnace. From the New Testament, aside from the Crucifixion itself and the events leading up to and following from it, the most common themes are the Adoration of the Magi, the Flight of the Holy Family, the Baptism of Christ, the Miracle of the Loaves and Fishes, and the Twelve Apostles.

The earliest of the so-called scriptural crosses may be the group of granite monuments in the Barrow valley in the Southeast. The seventeen-foot-high **Moone Cross** *(376)*, County Kildare, is the most clearly carved of the lot, but the figural scenes are confined to the base. In the two **Castledermot Crosses** *(376)* in the same county, representational figures crowd base, shafts, and arms, although one side of the southernmost of the two is pure ornament. The nearby granite cross at **Old Kilcullen** *(376)* is fragmentary but in the same tradition. In County Carlow, south of Graiguenamanagh, County Kilkenny, the small granite cross at **St. Mullins Abbey** *(288)* has a Crucifixion on the east face and interlacing and wavy motifs elsewhere. The **Ullard Cross** *(293)*, County Kilkenny, also of granite, has an interesting display of biblical scenes but is quite worn.

Probably of about the same date as these granite monuments (ninth century) is the sandstone **South Cross** at **Kells Monastery** *(384)*, Ceanannas

(Kells), County Meath. Base, shaft, and arms are covered with scriptural figures, including a Crucifixion on the west face. On the east side of the base there is an inscription to Sts. Patrick and Columba, suggesting that the monument may have been erected to commemorate a reconciliation between the monks of Armagh and Iona after the latter had moved here in 812. On the monastic grounds are two other crosses, one broken (the **West Cross**) and the other unfinished (the **East Cross**), and in the village is the **Kells Market Cross** *(385)*, with roughly the same iconography, though perhaps of a later date.

Of ninth- or tenth-century provenance are the **Cross of Muiredach (the South Cross)** and the **Tall Cross (the West Cross)** at **Monasterboice** *(397)*, near Drogheda, County Louth. The former is certainly one of the sculptural masterpieces of Ireland. Complete to the top (a finial representing a small single-celled church), this massive monument of white sandstone flecked with black mica stands about eighteen feet above ground and is covered on all sides with sharply cut scenes from the Old Testament and New, including a Crucifixion on the west face. The West Cross (more than twenty-one feet tall) is also heavily carved but more weathered. Similar in style and content, and of approximately the same date, is the **Cross of the Scriptures (the West Cross)**, at **Clonmacnoise Monastery** *(381)* in County Offaly. Nearby is the **South Cross**, of an earlier date with a Crucifixion on the west face and animal scenes on the east. Also in County Offaly, north of Tullamore, is the **Durrow Cross** *(383)*, distinguished for its large figure of Christ on one side and representations of Old Testament figures on the other. A similar dichotomy can be observed on the High Cross on the grounds of **Drumcliffe Church** *(418)*, north of Sligo (where the poet W. B. Yeats is buried), and on **Clones Cross** *(400)*, near the town of that name in County Monaghan.

In general most of the crosses surviving in Northern Ireland are fragmentary, but two at least are worth inspection—both in County Tyrone. **Donaghmore Cross** *(447)*, near Dungannon, is a composite of two, reerected in the eighteenth century. On the east face are the Crucifixion and various scenes from the New Testament; on the west are Adam and Eve, Cain and Abel, and the Sacrifice of Isaac. **Arboe Cross** *(445)*, east of Coagh, overlooking Lough Neagh, is noted for its exceptionally full scheme of biblical carving. Here the New Testament story is told on the west face, with the east face reserved for Old Testament scenes. On the narrow south side is a depiction of Sts. Paul and Anthony in the Egyptian desert.

By the twelfth century biblical scenes appear to have largely gone out of fashion, to be replaced by carved animal interlace in the Scandinavian style and by large representations of Christ on one side of the cross coupled with a figure of a bishop or an abbot on the other. Except for the pieced-together and reerected **Tuam Market Cross** *(415)*, County Galway, all the well-preserved examples of this period come from the South. Inside the Visitors' Centre at **Glendalough** *(310)*, County Wicklow, is a twelfth-century cross with the Crucifixion and the figure of an abbot on one side and interlacing motifs on the other. In the **Hall of the Vicars Choral** on **Cashel Rock** *(301)*, County Tipperary, is a curiously shaped cross with a carved Christ on one side and an ecclesiastic, thought to represent St. Patrick, on the other. A replica stands just outside the door, in front of Cormac's Chapel. Also in County Tipperary is the **Roscrea Cross** *(306)*, similarly adorned, though the churchman on the east face may be St. Cronan. County Clare has three good examples of twelfth-century fashions in cross carving. Two stand within the grounds of **Kilfenora Cathedral** *(345)*, one with the figure of Christ in low relief on a background of engraved ornament, the other (the Doorty Cross) with a much worn Crucifixion on one side and three men, probably bishops, on the other. Finally the ringless **Dysert O'Dea High Cross** *(343)* is deeply cut with interlace and other ornament on one side, while on the other is a Crucifixion somewhat overwhelmed by the large ecclesiastical figure, probably meant to be a bishop, carved beneath it.

As indicated above, there is no obvious connection between the Scandinavian invasions of the ninth century and the proliferation of the High Crosses then and later. On the other hand, the gradual abandonment of wood in favor of stone as the preferred material for church building can probably be attributed to the stepped-up assault on the monasteries by Vikings and native Irish alike. Indeed, some archaeologists are doubtful that *any* of Ireland's early churches of mortared stone predate the tenth century. Be that as it may, it is almost certain that none of those mentioned below were built much before the year 950.

The largest of these post-Viking stone churches was the **Cathedral** at **Glendalough** *(310)*, County Wicklow, of which only the lower part of the nave is original, the rest (including the chancel) having been added in the twelfth century. The **Cathedral** at **Clonmacnoise** *(381)*, County Offaly, may date from about the same period, although the Romanesque west doorway was a later insertion, as were the north doorway and the six-bay vaulted chapel, both fifteenth-century. Of probable tenth-century date are the nave of the ruined church of **Innisfallen Abbey** *(331)* and the little oratory south of it on an island in Lough Leane, County Kerry. The eastern end (chancel) of the church was added in the twelfth century, and the oratory to the east, with its Romanesque doorways, also belongs to the twelfth. The island of Inishmore in the Aran group, County Galway, has two little roofless churches, probably of tenth-century date. The single-chambered building called **Tiglagh Enda (Teillach Einde)** *(411)* is larger than average for this period, although the present west end is probably a later extension. **Teampull MacDuagh** *(412)* was originally a conventional single-chambered building with antae, later extended eastward by the addition of a chancel.

The function of the chancel in the Christian church was (and, except in many Protestant churches, still is) to house the altar, which was the centerpiece of the sacrifice of the Mass. Here the presiding priest blessed and consumed the sacramental bread and wine, believed to be the body and blood of Christ Himself, who at the Last Supper had commanded His disciples to do likewise in remembrance of Him. The laity did not participate in this act of worship, except as witnesses, though its propitiatory effects were believed to flow to all the faithful, both living and dead. Thus the division of a church building into separate compartments (chancel for the priest and his acolytes, nave for the laity or for monks not in holy orders) was nothing other than an architectural realization of the centrality of the Mass in Christian worship and of the special and distinctive role of the ordained clergy as mediators between sinful man and his Creator.

At what point in time church builders in Ireland began the construction of two-chambered buildings is debatable, but according to the architectural historian Harold G. Leask: "It seems not unreasonable to assume that the earliest churches with coeval nave and chancel may belong to the tenth century." Possibly the shift from single-chambered to two-chambered buildings was a response to the growing population of the country or at least of the monastic cities where the development seems first to have taken place. In any case, whether added on to an existing structure or built as part of the original plan, the chancel stood at the eastern end of the church and was rectangular or square in plan, though noticeably smaller in both depth and width than the similarly rectangular nave onto which it opened. Two churches in the great sprawling monastic center at **Glendalough**, County Wicklow, are probably among the earliest to have been thus designed: **Reefert Church** *(310)* and **Trinity Church** *(310)*. In both the opening between nave and chancel is surmounted by a round arch of well-cut granite.

Sometime, probably late in the eleventh century, the starkly functional appearance of Irish churches began to change, as here and there stonemasons commenced to add simple embellishments to surfaces hitherto left plain and unadorned. At **Banagher Church** *(464)*, near Dungiven, County Londonderry, for example, a semicircular molded architrave graces the inside of the west doorway, which, with its sloping jambs and horizontal lintel, is otherwise conventional. In the same county **Maghera Church** *(465)*, probably contemporary, has an even more elaborate west door, now under a tower added later. Carvings cover the architrave and jamb faces and especially the lintel on which appears a Crucifixion scene, two feet in height. A similar, though less elaborate, architrave graces the inside of the west door at **Aghowle Church** *(312)*, County Wicklow, which also displays the added embellishment of two round-headed windows in the east wall with hood moldings flanked by little columns. All three of these examples can be taken as representing a transition to a new style of architecture, called Hiberno-Romanesque, which was to prevail in Ireland for about a hundred years.

In its European and British context the term *Romanesque* describes a style of church architecture prevalent in the eleventh and twelfth centuries and distinguishable by massiveness and roundness—semicircular arches above doors, windows, and interior passageways; very thick exterior walls; heavy cylindrical pillars, if any; and simple decorative carving consisting mostly of chevron and zigzag incisions on the surface of the arches. Irish churches of the same period were less likely to be massive, less endowed with interior pillars since side aisles were lacking, but more profusely decorated than their British and Continental counterparts. The stone carvings in the former included a great variety of motifs such as fantastic animals, human masks with strands of hair intertwined, and a rich repertoire of geometric designs derived alike from Celtic, Anglo-Saxon, and Scandinavian sources. Of these the most common is the zigzag or chevron—either carved on a flat surface or sculpted in the form of a pleated ribbon or of sawteeth pointing either outward or downward. In short, the term *Hiberno-Romanesque* connotes primarily a decorative style, not a structural form. It is, in the words of Harold G. Leask, "the most original and truly national of Irish architectural achievements."

Ireland abounds in churches displaying Hiberno-Romanesque features, of which the following sampling, though not all-inclusive, is representative. Although most are roofless, walls, windows, doorways, and arches are in fairly good shape. They are arranged here in geographic order (east to west and south to north) rather than by date.

St. Saviour's Priory, Glendalough *(311)*, County Wicklow, contains on the abbey grounds, according to the archaeologist Peter Harbison, "the best Romanesque decoration to be seen," especially the geometric, animal, and human-face motifs on the chancel arch and east window. **Killeshin Church** *(289)*, County Laois, has one of the finest Romanesque doorways in Ireland, with intertwining hair flowing from human heads, leaf patterns, birds, fantastic animals, chevrons, spandrels, and lozenges. The west doorway of **Freshford Church** *(296)*, County Kilkenny, is deeply recessed, its outer arch distinguished by outward-pointing sawtooth chevrons and a hood molding above; **Donaghmore Church** *(304)*, near Clonmel, County Tipperary, is two-chambered with a profusion of chevrons, spandrels, zigzags, and interlacings carved on both west doorway and chancel arch. The west gable and doorway of **St. Cronan's Church** *(306)* in Roscrea, County Tipperary, display unusually elaborate and clear-cut Hiberno-Romanesque carving, although the rest of the building has disappeared.

Nearby **Monaincha Church** *(306)*, near Roscrea, County Tipperary, has much the same characteristics and is noteworthy especially for the profuse geometric patterns on the west doorway and on the chancel arch and its supporting pillars. **Kilmalkedar Church** *(330)*, on the Dingle peninsula, County Kerry, only partially roofless, is two-chambered and has antae decorated with animal heads, a fine decorated west doorway surmounted by a tympanum flanked by a human head and an imaginary beast, a decorated chancel arch, and a blind colonnade, that is, a row of decorative columns integrated into the interior walls of the nave. Also in County Kerry, near Killarney, is **Aghadoe Church** *(332)*, whose west doorway is surmounted by a typical Romanesque chevroned arch. More elaborate still is the west doorway of **Ardfert Cathedral** *(326)*, County Kerry. Outward-pointing sawtooth chevrons arch above it, and the adjoining wall is decorated with a row of arch-connected columns, called a blind arcade, also chevroned. The main body of the church was built in the thirteenth century, but next to it, alongside a fifteenth-century chapel, is the tiny Temple-na-Hoe, a Romanesque creation decorated with animal and human heads and the usual sawtooth chevrons. The south doorway of **Killaloe Cathedral** *(347)*, County Clare, shows a profusion of carved heads, animals, zigzags, saw- tooth chevrons, and foliage, and on the innermost jamb on the right are two elongated beasts of Scandinavian type with heads intertwined at the top.

Coming into central Ireland, west of Dublin, there are two **Churches** at **Rahan** *(383)*, County Offaly, both with some twelfth-century features. In the smaller of the two is a good Romanesque doorway with a notched (downward-pointing sawtooth) arch, probably inserted here when the church was rebuilt in the later Middle Ages. The other is roofed and has a good chancel arch decorated with heads and a unique Romanesque round window in the east gable. Four Romanesque churches are also to be found at **Clonmacnoise Monastery** *(381)*, County Offaly. **St. Finghin's Church** (Teampull Finghin), built between 1160 and 1170, is a nave and chancel building, though the nave is now ruined to within a few feet of the ground. The chancel, with a somewhat mutilated decorated arch, stands fairly high and boasts, at its southwest corner, a splendid round belfry, fifty-six feet high. **Teampull Connor** *(382)* and **Teampull Rí** *(382)* both date to the twelfth century. East of the monastic enclosure lies the **Nun's Church** *(382)* about the same vintage, though the piers supporting the elaborately carved chancel arch may be older. **St. Mochta's House** *(398)*, in the village of Louth, also dates to the twelfth century, though it has the appearance of an Early Christian oratory. More typically Romanesque is the north doorway of **Kilmore Cathedral** *(401)*, County Cavan, which was inserted here (incor- rectly) after removal from nearby Trinity Island.

"Quite the grandest of the Irish Romanesque chancel arches," in the opinion of Harold G. Leask, is that of **Tuam Cathedral** *(415)*, County Galway, the bulk of which was built in the nineteenth century, though parts of the chancel itself are as old as the twelfth-century arch. Also in County Galway is **Clonfert Cathedral** *(406)*, whose great west doorway is considered by many to be *the* masterwork of Irish Romanesque art. Though the church itself (now serving as the cathedral church of the Protestant diocese) has been much mutilated and badly restored, its deeply recessed doorway, capped by a steeply pitched triangular false gable, belongs to the twelfth century. This is a sculptural tour de force. Interlace abounds; so do chevrons, beading, zigzags, foliage, hemispherical bosses, animal heads, dragons and other fantastic animals, and human masks with intertwining beards.

Finally, though probably built at an earlier date than some of the churches mentioned above, is **Cormac's Chapel** on **Cashel Rock** *(301)*, County Tipperary. It is in a class by itself. Constructed between 1127 and 1134 by order of Cormac MacCarthy, king of Munster and bishop of Cashel, it is the least characteristic of all Irish Romanesque churches—and also the most impressive. A kinsman of Cormac's was bishop of Regensburg (Ratisbon), and two German stonemasons from that city are known to have worked on the building at Cashel. This is a two-chambered church with a barrel-vaulted nave and a groin-vaulted chancel. Both chambers have high-pitched stone roofs, and beneath that of the nave is a typical Irish croft. Square twin towers (unique in Ireland but common among Romanesque churches in Germany) flank the nave at its east end. The chancel arch, carved with numerous human heads among other decorative features, is distinctly Irish. The tunnellike archway of the north doorway combines Irish, West English, and Germanic features. Inside, at the west end of the nave, is a stone coffin carved with Scandinavian Urnes motifs. In short, Cormac's Chapel is remarkable chiefly for its architectural eclecticism—an illustration in stone of the approaching end of Ireland's ecclesiastical isolation and of the integration of the Irish Church into the mainstream of European Catholicism.

CHURCH AND STATE IN THE TWELFTH CENTURY

Cormac's church on the Rock was consecrated in 1134. About two dozen years earlier and not far away from Cashel at a place called Rath Breasail, a synod of churchmen had divided Ireland into twenty-two territorial sees (dioceses) with more or less precise geographical boundaries, each to be ruled by a bishop from a central cathedral, that is, from his episcopal seat or *cathedra*. (Dublin and Down were added later, thus bringing the number to twenty-four.) Superimposed over the bishops were to be two archbishops, one for each province or metropolitan see. The seat of the northern province was to be at Armagh, while Cashel was named as the archiepiscopal see for the south of Ireland. The archbishop of Armagh, as titular heir of St. Patrick, was to be the primate or principal archbishop.

Eighteen years after the consecration of Cormac's Chapel a second synod was held, this time at Kells, and presided over by the papal legate Cardinal Paparo. Following instructions, the legate installed not two archbishops but four. Armagh retained its primacy, but in addition to Cashel, the dioceses of Dublin and Tuam were awarded archiepiscopal rank. Thus the long domination of abbots over the Irish Church came to an end. And the episcopal office, long relegated to secondary status in Ireland, at last assumed the dignity accorded it in the rest of Western Christendom. Visual evidence of the change can be noted in the appearance on certain twelfth-century High Crosses of the figures of crosier-bearing bishops in juxtaposition with carvings of the Crucifixion. Two examples, both in County Clare, are, as already noted, the Doorty Cross at **Kilfenora** *(345)* and especially the **Dysert O'Dea High Cross** *(343)*, where the representation of a mitered bishop is considerably larger than that of Christ himself.

Primary credit for this radical reorganization of the Church in Ireland belongs to one ecclesiastic above all—Máel Maedoc, known to history as St. Malachy. Born in 1095 in the north of Ireland, he held in succession the prestigious positions of abbot of Bangor, bishop of Connor and Down, archbishop of Armagh, and once more bishop of Down. In time he became the chief Irish negotiator with the Vatican in an effort to bring his country's Church into conformity with Rome. For Ireland the first step in this direction was to gain papal blessing for the elevation of the two sees of Armagh and Cashel to archbishoprics, as recommended by the synod of Rath Breasail. Twice Malachy set off for Rome to obtain the cherished *pallia*, the symbolic vestments of archiepiscopal authority. Success eventually crowned his efforts beyond his expectations (or perhaps his wishes) when Ireland was awarded not two, but four, archbishoprics at the synod of Kells. By that time, however, Malachy was four years dead—having expired in the arms of St. Bernard in the abbey of Clairvaux in Burgundy on his second trip to Rome.

Clairvaux was a daughterhouse of the abbey of Citeaux, where the Cistercian Order had originated in 1099, deriving its name from that of the founding monastery. The Cistercians, or "white monks," were distinguished from other monastic orders by their unusually strict observance of the Rule laid down by St. Benedict at Monte Cassino in Italy more than five centuries before. (The Latin word for *rule* is *regula*; hence all monks and other clerics living in monastic seclusion were called "regular" clergy, as distinct from parish priests and cathedral canons, who were termed "secular.") St. Benedict's Rule required that a monastery be a self-contained community and that its residents, isolated from the world, take vows of poverty, chastity, and obedience; engage in prescribed manual or intellectual labor; and, above all, devote their time to the worship of God and to prayers for forgiveness of their own sins and those of their benefactors. Worship took the form of prescribed choral services conducted within the monastic church seven or eight times daily, from midnight until about nine o'clock in the evening. Collectively these were known as the Opus Dei; sequentially, they were designated Vigils (or Nocturns), Matins (or Lauds), Prime, Terce, Sext, Nones, Vespers, and Compline. High Mass was celebrated in the morning, and special masses might be said at other times of the day.

Monastic architecture throughout western Europe was designed primarily to suit these requirements; that is, it was, above all, functional. All the principal buildings were constructed of stone. Of these the church was, of course, the most important and the largest. It was inevitably cruciform in plan. The east end (choir, chancel, or presbytery) behind the high altar was the place where the Opus Dei was sung. In each of the transepts (cross arms, pointing north and south), were two or more chapels along the east walls. West of the crossing (where the transepts intersected the main axis of the church) was the aisled nave where the monks and others gathered to witness High Mass or to attend sermons.

In all these respects the monastic church did not differ greatly in plan from any other large medieval house of worship. The difference lay in the adjacent buildings, which were constructed to meet the special needs of communal living. These normally lay south of the church and were arranged in a square or rectangle around a central plot of land called a *garth*, bordered by a covered walkway or arcade. Together the ensemble constituted the cloister, the north side of which was the south wall of the church itself. The normal arrangement of buildings on the other three sides was as follows (proceeding clockwise from the south transept of the church): along the east range were the sacristy, the chapter house, and the calefactory (warming room), with the monks' dormitory (dorter) above and their latrine (reredorter or *necessarium*) to the rear; in the south range were the dining room (refectory or frater), with a wash-trough (lavabo) in front and the kitchen; the west range contained storage cellars, sometimes guest rooms and, in the case of the Cistercians, living and eating quarters for the lay brothers.

The presence of lay brothers (*conversi*) within the community was the most distinctive feature of the Cistercian Order. The Cistercian ideal called not only for physical isolation and rigid conformance to the Rule but also for economic self-sufficiency. This meant that fields had to be tilled, planted, and harvested by members of the community, sheep raised, fleece spun and cloth woven, grain ground, bread baked, beer brewed, buildings erected and repaired, and so on. Such were the tasks assigned to the *conversi*, while the monks themselves chanted, prayed, worshipped, performed sundry administrative and intellectual labors, and meditated in silence.

Accommodating the lay brothers required certain modifications in the conventional monastic architectural plan. First, they had to be housed in the west range of the cloister; second, the west end of the church's nave was reserved for their use; third, a single or double transverse wall was put up across the nave to separate the *conversi* from the monks; and finally, in some abbeys the refectory ran at right angles to the south cloister-walk so as to allow more space for the enlarged kitchen required to serve both monks and lay brothers. In all other respects, however, there was no significant difference between the ground plans of Cistercian monasteries and those of other monastic orders.

Nor did their buildings differ greatly in elevation, although the founders of the order had stressed the need for a simplicity of design bordering on starkness. Basically, at the time of St. Malachy's visits to Clairvaux, monastic and other large churches in western Europe were being built in the style known to architectural historians as Transitional, that is, somewhere between Romanesque and thirteenth-century Gothic. The heavy round pillars, semicircular barrel vaults, and round arches of the former were still in evidence, but interspersed among them were pointed arches, pointed barrel vaults, and triplets of narrow round-headed windows in the east end—all typical of a later (Gothic) stage of architectural design, except that truly Gothic windows were pointed at the top.

This ordered sequence of stone buildings placed around an enclosed cloister garth that Malachy observed in Burgundy stood in marked contrast to the random arrangement of oratories and individual cells typical of contemporary monasteries in Ireland. Equally striking was the contrast between the rigorous discipline of these Continental houses and the lax supervision normally exercised by Irish abbots, some of them laymen, some absentees, many holding their abbacies solely by right of hereditary succession. Also, Irish monasteries were far more tolerant of idiosyncrasy than their European and English counterparts: ascetic Culdees might live side by side with married monks, biblical scholars with semiliterates, holy recluses with men of the world in clerical garb. Small wonder that St. Malachy, former abbot, bishop, and archbishop, should have been so impressed with the strict conformity and orderliness of Clairvaux that he left a handful of his companions there to be trained as novices in the hope that they might found a Cistercian house in Ireland.

In 1142 that hope was realized with the establishment of the first such abbey at **Mellifont** *(397)* in present County Louth on land granted by Donogh O'Carroll, king of Oriel. From Mellifont soon sprang a number of daughterhouses—ten or eleven altogether in the twenty-eight years before the Anglo-Norman invasion. Of these, portions of the following (along with Mellifont itself) still stand: **Bective Abbey** *(391)*, County Meath, founded about 1147 on land granted by Murchad O'Melaglin, king of Meath; **Baltinglass Abbey** *(308)*, County Wicklow, founded in 1148 by Dermot MacMurrough, king of Leinster; **Monasternenagh Abbey** *(336)*, County Limerick, founded between 1148 and 1151 by Turlough O'Brien, king of Limerick; and **Boyle Abbey** *(402)*, County Roscommon. Along with these must be numbered **St. Mary's Abbey** *(368)*, Dublin, originally belonging to another reformed Benedictine Order—the Savignacs—but becoming Cistercian in 1147. Its sole existing remains consist of the chapter house, embedded in, and almost hidden by, a cluster of shabby warehouses. The others, of course, are in various states of ruination, but none so much so as not to be worth a visit.

Clairvaux was not the only Continental monastery visited by St. Malachy on his first trip to Rome. In France he also spent some time at the abbey of Arrouaise, founded for canons regular of the Order of St. Augustine of Hippo. The Rule of St. Augustine was a statement of general principles rather than a set of precise detailed regulations. Hence Augustinian canons were allowed greater freedom of action than were the monks of the Cistercian or other Benedictine orders. Specifically they were encouraged to mingle among laymen, administer to their spiritual needs, form cathedral chapters, found hospitals, and provide accommodation for travellers. Yet within their own houses, as at Arrouaise, they were normally subject to the standard monastic rules of poverty, chastity, and obedience. Thus these canons too won St. Malachy's admiration. He made copies of the Arrouasian rules and observances and on his return home succeeded in introducing them to a fair number of existing Irish monasteries, whose abbots preferred the flexibility of the Augustinian Order to the more rigid Cistercian.

Before his death in 1148 Malachy saw some twenty Augustinian houses established in Ireland, and by the time of the Anglo-Norman invasion there were perhaps as many as sixty-two, not counting an unknown number of nunneries of the same order. Included in these numbers are the following establishments whose ruined buildings can still be observed: **Annaghdown Priory** *(408)* in modern County Galway and **Cong Abbey** *(422)*, County Mayo, both founded in about 1140 by Turlough O'Connor, king of Connacht, under the persuasion of St. Malachy; **Clontuskert Abbey** *(405)*, County Galway, founded at about the same time probably by the O'Kellys; **St. Mary's Priory** *(390)*, Trim, County Meath (of which the sole remnant is the so-called "Yellow Steeple"); **Dungiven Priory** *(464)*, County Londonderry, founded by the O'Cahans; **St. Mary's Priory, Devenish** *(451)*, in County Fermanagh; **Monaincha Abbey** *(306)*, County Tipperary; **Molana Abbey** *(325)* in County Waterford; and **Ferns Abbey** *(281)*, County Wexford, established by Dermot MacMurrough, king of Leinster. To this list must be added two of the greatest pre-Conquest Augustinian houses, both founded by St. Laurence O'Toole, who shared with Malachy the distinction of later canonization by Rome. As abbot of **Glendalough** *(310)*, he brought Augustinian canons to **St. Saviour's Priory** *(311)* in 1162 and a year later, as the second archbishop of Dublin, persuaded the secular canons of **Christ Church Cathedral** *(360)* to become regular canons under the Rule of St. Augustine.

Laurence O'Toole was brother-in-law to the king of Leinster, Dermot MacMurrough—commonly and reproachfully known as "Dermot of the Foreigners" (Diarmaid na nGall) because it was he who first opened the door to the English (or Anglo-Norman) invaders of Ireland. His motives for doing so, ignominious as they might seem to later generations, are understandable enough if viewed in the context of contemporary Irish politics.

For a little more than a hundred years after the Battle of Clontarf, Brian Boru's descendants, the O'Brien kings of Munster, maintained an uneasy primacy over the country's six other major provinces: Leinster, Connacht, Meath, and the three Ulster kingdoms of Ailech, Airgialla (Oriel), and Ulaid. But ascendancy over all of Ireland, even to the limited extent achieved by Brian Boru, proved impossible. A new term came into common usage: *rí cofresabra* or "king with opposition." Neither the O'Briens nor any of their rival claimants to the high kingship could rise to any higher status.

By the time King Murtagh O'Brien died in 1119, Munster had already lost its preeminence in the ever-shifting interprovincial balance of power. This time the ascending star was the king of Connacht, Turlough O'Connor, who the year before had driven the O'Brien dynasty into northwestern Munster (Thomond) and replaced it with the MacCarthys as kings of Cashel (Desmond). Turlough was less successful, however, in dealing with two other rival kings, Murtagh MacLoughlin of Ailech and Dermot MacMurrough of Leinster. And by the time of Turlough's death in 1156, the king of Ailech had won general, though not universal, acknowledgment of his claim to the high kingship.

Within a decade Murtagh MacLoughlin too was dead, leaving Rory O'Connor, Turlough's successor as king of Connacht, without a serious rival in the North. Promptly he laid claim to the high kingship and proceeded by force majeure to compel the Ostmen of Dublin and the kings of Meath, Oriel, Desmond, and Cashel to do homage. The king of Bréifne, Tighernan O'Rourke, was already a longtime ally and client. Of all the Irish potentates, this left only Dermot MacMurrough of Leinster unreconciled to the hegemony of Connacht.

Then, in 1166, the kings of Meath and Bréifne (O'Rourke), along with a contingent of Dubliners, invaded the territory of Leinster. Whether they did so at the prompting of O'Connor is unclear, but it is unlikely that they would have acted thus without his concurrence. Tighernan O'Rourke, to be sure, had his own personal ax to grind. Some years previously, his wife, Dervorgilla, along with her dowry, had been abducted by the king of Leinster (McMurrough). And although both lady and dowry had meanwhile been returned undamaged, the grievous wound to Tighernan's pride still festered. In any case, O'Rourke and his allies easily overcame what little resistance Dermot could offer, drove him out of his "capital" at Ferns (County Wexford), and in effect expelled him from the kingship.

Normally MacMurrough would have retaliated by forming an alliance with another provincial Irish king against the victors. But this time there was none to turn to; all had been reduced to submission to the king of Connacht. So, *faute de mieux*, he sailed to England on 16 August 1166 in search of foreign allies who might restore him to his kingdom. The deed was not altogether unprecedented. Irish provincial kings had in times past frequently welcomed foreign (that is, Norse) aid in their incessant wars against each other. Only in its long-term consequences was Dermot's ploy to prove unique.

After a brief stay in Bristol, MacMurrough crossed the English Channel and proceeded to Aquitaine (southern France) to get permission from King Henry II of England to recruit mercenaries among his restless and land-hungry Anglo-Norman knights of the Welsh Marches. Henry, though not enthusiastic, gave his consent. Dermot then returned to Wales, where he succeeded in landing a bigger fish than either he or King Henry had probably anticipated. This was Richard fitz Gilbert de Clare, lord of Striguil and claimant to the earldom of Pembroke, known to history as "Strongbow." Out of favor with his own king and generally down on his luck, the earl offered to lead a military expedition across the Irish Sea and help restore MacMurrough to his kingdom. In return he was promised the hand of Dermot's daughter Eva (Aoife) in marriage and the right to succession as king of Leinster on the death of his father-in-law—a gift, incidentally, that Dermot had no legal right to bestow. Lesser, but equally persuasive, offers were made to a number of other Norman-Welsh knights and barons, chiefly sons and grandsons, legitimate and illegitimate, of Nesta, daughter of the native Welsh king, Rhys ap Tewdwr. These doughty warriors are known to history as the Geraldines (because Nesta was married to

Gerald of Windsor), although their paternal ancestry was in fact mixed. Among them were Maurice fitz (that is, *fils de* or son of) Gerald, Robert fitz Stephen, Meiler fitz Henry, and Raymond le Gros.

Dermot then, in the summer of 1167, returned to Leinster with a small bodyguard of retainers, there to await for almost two years the arrival at Bannow Bay on 1 May 1169 of the first contingent of the adventurers recruited in Wales—a body of some ninety mounted knights, sixty men at arms, and about three hundred infantrymen and archers led by Robert fitz Stephen. A few days later they were joined by a neighbor from Pembrokeshire of Flemish descent—Maurice de Prendergast—with two more shiploads of fighting men. In short order, the Normans captured the nearby Norse town of Wexford. Soon thereafter Maurice fitz Gerald landed with another contingent of troops that, early in the following year, joined Dermot in a march on Dublin, where the Ostmen (men of the East, i.e., Scandinavians) readily submitted. In May Raymond le Gros came over with still another fighting force, landing near Baginbun Head, also in modern County Wexford. Then, in August of 1170, Strongbow himself arrived with about two hundred cavalry and a thousand infantry. He proceeded to capture the town of Waterford, where he was promptly married to Eva as previously agreed to. Father-in-law and son-in-law then marched on to Dublin, which was invested and captured, this time with heavy casualties among the inhabitants. Less than eight months later, in May 1171, Dermot died at Ferns, leaving Strongbow as his designated heir to the kingdom of Leinster.

But earlier that spring the Anglo-Norman adventurers had received a shock. King Henry II forbade any more ships to leave his kingdom for Ireland and ordered all his subjects already in that country to return home by Easter. The English king had finally awakened to the danger of an independent Norman kingdom growing up at his back door. An underdeveloped, fragmented Ireland, torn apart by endless warfare among its numerous native kings, was no threat to the security of England. An Ireland united and led by members of Europe's most aggressive and efficient military caste might be. If nothing else, the lure of land and booty would inevitably siphon off scarce military manpower needed by Henry to consolidate and defend his vast Angevin empire stretching from the Scottish borders to the Pyrenees.

So it was that at a council held in Argentan in July 1171, King Henry II announced his intention to cross over in person to the Irish coast. It was to prove a critical turning point in the history of Ireland. Left to their own devices, the Anglo-Norman adventurers, like the Vikings before them, might eventually have accommodated themselves to Irish culture and to

Irish politics, perhaps carving out independent petty kingdoms of their own but not permanently disturbing the status quo. Active intervention by the most powerful feudal monarch of the age was another matter altogether. Now, at long last, Ireland's isolation from English and European politics was coming to an abrupt end.

Chapter Three

Medieval Ireland: War and Politics, 1171–1534

THE ANGLO-NORMAN OCCUPATION:
1171–1315

On 16 October 1171 King Henry II set sail from the Welsh port of Milford Haven to land the following day at Crook on the western shore of Waterford Harbor, about five miles south of the old Viking city. With him he brought some four thousand troops—five hundred armored knights, the remainder archers and foot soldiers. Among the royal entourage was Strongbow himself. The next day at Waterford the lord of Striguil formally surrendered the city to his overlord, the king. In return Strongbow received the province of Leinster to be held in exchange for the service of a hundred knights. Waterford, Wexford, Dublin, and their adjacent territories were retained as royal demesne. Thus did Henry, king of England, duke of Normandy and Aquitaine, and count of Anjou, introduce feudalism into Ireland.

The term *feudalism* is a seventeenth-century invention, coined to describe the military organization prevalent throughout western Europe in the Middle Ages and the economic, social, and political arrangements that derived from it. Ultimate ownership of all land, held by either conquest or inheritance, was vested in the ruler alone, whether king, duke, or count. He then allotted (i.e., enfeoffed) portions of it to his vassals (tenants-in-chief) in return for past services or in expectation of services to come. The tenants-in-chief, in turn, parcelled out (subinfeudated) portions of their holdings to subordinate knights, again in exchange for past or future services. All these grants of land were conditional, the chief, though not necessarily the only, condition being the obligation of military service by the grantee (the vassal) to the grantor (the lord). The bargain was sealed by the former's paying homage and swearing fealty (that is, fidelity) to the latter. Once formalized by charter, the grants became hereditary by primogeniture or, in the case of church lands, permanent. As time passed, military services were often commuted; that is, payments in money or kind were substituted for the provision of military service. The system, entrenched in England for more than a century, was a novelty in Ireland, where wealth was reckoned not in land but in cattle, where proprietary rights to real estate were vague and ill defined, and where inheritance was partible. The differences were to have a profound and disruptive effect on future relations between newcomers and natives.

While the English king was in Waterford, and later at various places in Munster and in Dublin, a succession of Irish kings and chieftains came into his presence and formally submitted. Included among them were Dermot MacCarthy, king of Cork (Desmond); Donal Mór O'Brien, king of Limerick (Thomond); Tighernan O'Rourke of Bréifne; and many others. In so doing they were acting not only out of a prudent consideration for Henry's military superiority but also from their perception of him as a prospective guardian of their rights. His purpose in coming to Ireland, after all, had been to put a curb on Strongbow and his band of land-hungry Welsh adventurers. Submission to a foreign king, then, seemed a small price to pay for such protection as he seemed to offer not only against the Anglo-Normans but against the territorial ambitions of the high king, Rory O'Connor, or other Irish rivals. But it is doubtful that they considered themselves thenceforth to be vassals of the English king or that they understood the feudal meaning of that term. And it is certain that King Henry did not consider himself inhibited by the formalities of their submission from making further disposition of his newly "conquered" territories in Ireland.

The winter of 1171–72 Henry spent in Dublin—in a "palace" of wattles (wickerwork) built in the Irish fashion somewhere in the vicinity of the present site of Trinity College. Before he returned to England and the Continent in the spring, he had granted a charter of the city to "my men of Bristol" and had begun the displacement of the native Hiberno-Norse to a suburb north of the river Liffey, later known as Villa Ostmannorum or Oxmantown. He also granted the "land of Meath" (roughly modern Counties Meath, Westmeath, and Longford) to one of his barons, Hugh de Lacy, whom he left in command of the garrison at Dublin with the title of justiciar and whom he expected to serve as a counterpoise to Strongbow. Other garrisons were billeted in Wexford and Waterford, as they had earlier been in Cork and Limerick. Such was the extent of King Henry's personal "conquest" of Ireland. He was never to return.

Warfare was a seasonal occupation in Ireland, and soon after Easter 1172 both Anglo-Normans and native Irish took up arms again. Next year Raymond le Gros led a raid against MacCarthy territory in Desmond (roughly modern Counties Kerry and western Cork); in 1174 Donal Mór O'Brien defeated Strongbow in a pitched battle near Thurles, in modern County Tipperary; in the same year Rory O'Connor, king of Connacht and titular high king, crossed the Shannon into Meath with a sizable force. The next year Rory, who had not previously submitted to King Henry, came to terms. At Windsor the representatives of each signed a treaty that, in effect, divided Ireland into two distinct spheres of influence: (1) the Anglo-Norman area, under the direct rule of Henry II, comprised of Leinster, Meath, Dublin, Wexford, and Waterford and their adjacent lands; and (2) the Irish area, comprised of all the rest, to be held by Rory O'Connor, as king of Connacht, but only as "liege king" under Henry and subject to an annual tribute payable in hides. Rory was, moreover, bound to collect and remit to the English Crown all tribute owed to it by the many subkings of Ireland and to compel all refugees from Anglo-Norman Ireland to return to their baronial lords.

But the Treaty of Windsor notwithstanding, there was to be no peace. Few if any of the Irish petty kings and chieftains regarded themselves bound to honor an obligation assumed by the king of Connacht, in spite of his claim to be high king of Ireland. As for the Anglo-Normans, they too proved uncontrollable once Henry II had absented himself from the country.

Early in 1177 a young Somerset knight named John de Courcy led an unauthorized expedition of fellow adventurers into Ulster, where he drove out the local king, Rory MacDunleavy, and later overwhelmed an army led by Malachy MacLoughlin, king of Cenél Eóghain (roughly modern Counties Armagh, Tyrone, and Monaghan). The fact is that, in spite of occasional victories such as Donal Mór O'Brien's at Thurles, lightly clad Irish foot soldiers, armed only with ax and dart or sling, were grossly mismatched against heavily armored Anglo-Norman mounted knights, wielding lances and swords and supported by battle-tested archers, many of them Welsh.

At Downpatrick, near the site of his victory over the Ulstermen, de Courcy raised the first of his several fortifications at a place now known as **Downpatrick Mound** or **The Mound of Down** *(434)*. Though built on the site of an iron-age hill-fort, this was otherwise a typical Norman motte-and-bailey castle of the type first introduced to England by William the Conqueror and his followers. It normally consisted of a high truncated cone of earth, flat on the top and surrounded by a deep ditch. On the summit stood a wooden tower; inside the ditch was a palisade of heavy timber. Adjacent to the mound was another ditched and palisaded enclosure—the bailey, containing stables, smithy, and housing for the garrison.

These motte-and-bailey castles served as the major instruments, and most conspicuous symbols, of military occupation in a hostile land. Defensible enough against the primitive arms of the Irish, their chief advantage, from the Norman point of view, was that they could be thrown up quickly. And so they were. Out of Downpatrick, de Courcy gradually extended his influence over eastern Ulster, building castles as he went. A fair number remain in evidence—either his handiwork or that of his followers and successors. Now reduced to grass-covered mounds and ditches, the following sites are typical: **Dromore Mound** *(435)*, **Duneight Motte and Bailey** *(436)*, and **Clough Castle** *(433)*—all in County Down—and **Harryville Motte and Bailey** *(453)* in Ballymena, County Antrim.

But it was on the Antrim coast, overlooking Belfast Lough, that de Courcy raised his most impressive monument—probably the first of the medieval stone castles in Ireland. This was **Carrickfergus Castle** *(460)*, today one of Northern Ireland's most visited tourist attractions. Although now the product of several centuries of rebuilding, its earliest portions are the polygonal inner ward and the great high rectangular tower or keep, both almost certainly begun by John de Courcy. The keep stands about ninety feet in height and measures sixty by fifty-five feet in plan. Only a few narrow windows pierce its thick upper storeys; the roof is enclosed by a battlemented or crenellated parapet (from the Latin *crena*, meaning notch). Behind solid lengths of stone (merlons) lying between the open notches (crenels) the defending garrison could take shelter while dropping heavy stones or shooting arrows against attackers pressing close against the castle walls. Until the thirteenth century the typical form of castle construction did not depart much from that of the keep at Carrickfergus. Its essential defensive features were thick stone walls impervious to fire and difficult to breach, an elevation too high to be reached by projectiles launched from siege engines, and crenellated parapets to protect its rooftop defenders as they opened fire against attackers on the ground below.

While de Courcy and his cohorts were making themselves masters of Ulidia (roughly modern Counties Down and Antrim), Hugh de Lacy was undertaking to do the same in Meath. There, according to the Irish annalist, "from the Shannon to the sea was full of castles and of Foreigners [i.e., Anglo-Normans]." De Lacy built his most important motte at the site of **Trim Castle** *(390)*, County Meath, on the south bank of the river Shannon. The place was promptly overrun by Rory O'Connor but rebuilt about 1190 and subsequently replaced with the stone castle that was to be one of the most strategically important of all the Anglo-Norman fortresses. Near the outermost limit of de Lacy's domain another of his tenants, Richard de Tuit, raised **Granard Motte** *(394)*, County Longford, now a high grass-covered mound with a deep ditch and bank enclosing both motte and bailey. At Durrow, closer to the center of his power, the lord of Meath in 1186 set about to construct another castle on the site of the ancient Columban monastery. Presumably in protest against the sacrilege, one of his Irish workmen put an end to the enterprise by suddenly decapitating de Lacy with an ax.

The year before this ominous event, Prince John, the fourth and youngest son of Henry II, had landed at Waterford in the company of about three hundred knights and two or three thousand soldiers. His father, in 1177, had named him lord of Ireland. With the prince came a Welsh cleric,

Gerald de Barry (Giraldus Cambrensis), a relative of the Geraldines who was to achieve lasting renown as author of *Expugnatio Hibernica (The Conquest of Ireland)*, a colorful chronicle of the early years of the Anglo-Norman occupation.

Also in Prince John's retinue was an important handful of newcomers to Ireland—English, not Welsh; courtiers, not hard-bitten marcher lords like the early Geraldines. To the native chieftains who had come to Waterford to greet the prince, these frivolous young men gave great offense, according to Giraldus, pulling at their long beards and otherwise treating them with derision and contempt. Frivolous these court favorites may have been, but certainly not indifferent to the exploitability of this vast newly opened frontier. To them John made extensive grants of land, thus introducing an entirely new set of feudal masters, more alien even than Strongbow and the Geraldines to Irish culture and traditions.

In modern County Louth, near Dundalk, he gave two baronies to Bertram de Verdun, who raised **Dún Dealgan Motte** *(398)* on the site traditionally held to be the birthplace of Cúchulainn. Another grant in County Louth was **Greenmount Motte** (399), still observable on the roadside south of Dunleer. Still another, though its history is obscure, was **Millmount** *(396)*, now lying within the present city limits of Drogheda.

In Munster the lord of Ireland was even more lavish. To the royal butler, Theobald Walter, went scattered estates in modern Counties Clare and Limerick as well as in northern Tipperary, where he built a motte-and-bailey on the site of **Nenagh Castle** *(305)*, later to be replaced by the still-standing cylindrical stone keep. This became the *caput* or headquarters of Theobald's descendants, the Butler family, one of four great Anglo-Irish dynasties of the later Middle Ages. Unlike Carrickfergus, the keep at Nenagh is round instead of rectangular. It represents therefore an advance in castle architecture, brought about by the recognition that square corners were particularly susceptible to destruction by the impact of missiles (usually stone balls launched from siege engines) and by mining operations—that is, digging a trench beneath the juncture of the two walls and laying a brushfire underneath so as to cause them to collapse. Another probable Butler stronghold is **Terryglass Castle** *(414)*, also in County Tipperary, of which only the bottom storey still stands. Here the vulnerability of square corners was mitigated by covering them with circular towers. The architectural historian Harold G. Leask classifies castles of this type as "towered or turreted keeps" and claims that "this form seems to be peculiar to Ireland in the first half of the thirteenth century," having had "no forerunners in England or France."

In southeastern Tipperary, near the present town of Cahir, is **Knock-graffon Motte** *(299)*, built by another of John's favorites—Philip de Worcester. To William de Burgh (or Burgo), ancestor of a second great medieval family that included the earls of Ulster and the lords of Connacht, went a huge property on the southern shore of the river Shannon, where he built a castle called Eskelon, probably on the high volcanic rock where now stands the much ruined fifteenth-century tower house **Carrigogunnel Castle** *(339)*. Also to de Burgh John granted two baronies in western County Limerick, where, on a rocky islet in the river Deel, was built **Askeaton Castle** *(334)*—probably of stone from the outset since it would have been impossible in this place to dig the earth required for throwing up a motte.

Nor did the prince overlook the original Anglo-Norman invaders. To Maurice fitz Gerald went a large estate south of the river Shannon in modern County Limerick. There either he or his third son, Thomas, raised a thirty-five-foot-high motte on which still stands the present stone ruin of **Shanid Castle** *(335)*—circular in plan as at Nenagh. This Thomas fitz Maurice was the ancestor of another of the great late medieval dynasties, headed by the Geraldine earls of Desmond. Their even more powerful relatives, and occasional rivals, were the earls of Kildare, descended from Gerald, baron of Offaly, the second son of the invader, Maurice. Strongbow had subinfeudated to this Maurice most of present County Kildare along with parts of Counties Offaly, Laois, and Wicklow. Prince John confirmed these grants, and Maurice's son, Gerald, built two strongholds—one, **Lea Castle** *(313)*, in modern County Laois, the other on the site of the present ruin of **Maynooth Castle** *(377)* in County Kildare. In the same county is **Ardscull Motte** *(375)*, probably also built by a FitzGerald or one of the family's dependents. Another FitzGerald property was **Black Castle** *(312)* on a rocky promontory jutting into Wicklow harbor—today a spectacular if scanty ruin. As at Askeaton, there was no earth here from which to build a mound, so the castle was probably originally constructed of stone and may be one of the oldest of this type in Ireland.

Large feudal estates enriched their holders, as well as their superior lords, including the king or, in the case of Ireland, Prince John. Another important source of royal revenue derived from rents imposed on towns in return for their chartered privileges to levy tolls and other charges on merchants and the goods they traded. Like other medieval rulers, the lord of Ireland was eager to tap this potential gold mine. After he left the country in 1185, John renewed his father's charter to Dublin and granted new charters to Drogheda, Dungarvan, Cork, Waterford, and Limerick. The last-named place had had a checkered history since the first arrival of the Anglo-Normans. It had been garrisoned in 1172 by Henry II; then retaken by Donal Mór O'Brien, king of Thomond, soon after the English monarch's departure; recaptured by Raymond le Gros; then occupied again by O'Brien, who held it until his death in 1194. Soon thereafter the Anglo-

Normans were back and at some time around the year 1200 commenced building **King John's Castle** *(337)*, the great stone fortress on the Shannon that still dominates the city. Probably about the same time the citizens of Waterford erected the high round keep of mortared stone known as **Reginald's Tower** *(285)*. Giraldus Cambrensis mentions a Viking fortress in this place and identifies it as Raghnall's Tower (turris Raghnaldi), built allegedly in 1003 by Raghnall (or Ragnaud) the Dane. It is unlikely, however, that the Vikings erected any buildings of mortared stone in Ireland, and all the archaeological evidence points to this one's having been put up in the early thirteenth century. (The city fathers of Waterford, naturally enough, claim a greater antiquity for their prime tourist attraction.)

Not all medieval towns in Ireland originated with royal charters. In Leinster William Marshal (the hereditary marshal of England) was responsible for founding New Ross on the river Barrow. Under his tutelage this became southeastern Ireland's busiest port, soon overshadowing Wexford, some sixteen miles downstream. No early medieval buildings, however, survive here except for those few portions of St. Mary's Church not totally obscured by subsequent rebuilding.

William, marshal of England, probably the grandest of that country's grandees of the late twelfth and early thirteenth centuries, did not come to Ireland until 1207, and only then because he had been deprived of his estates in Normandy by King Philip Augustus of France. He came to look after the vast holdings, mainly in modern Counties Kilkenny, Wexford, Laois, and Carlow, inherited by his wife, Isabel de Clare, from her father, Strongbow, who had died in 1176 without male issue. (The great Richard de Clare, lord of Striguil, was buried in state at **Christ Church** *[360]*, Dublin, though the monument known as "Strongbow's tomb" is in fact that of another medieval armored knight.)

The marshal (from whose office the family name of Marshal was derived) was also a great castle builder. His *caput* was **Kilkenny Castle** *(294)*, built on the site of Strongbow's earlier motte-and-bailey, although the present building here is mostly of nineteenth-century construction. Also in County Kilkenny, the high grass- and tree-covered mound called **Callan Motte** *(290)* was probably a Marshal stronghold. He built another at **Dunamase** *(314)*, County Laois, where the ruined keep may date to Marshal's time, though most of the castle is of later construction. **Carlow Castle** *(289)* in the town of that name, also first chartered by Marshal, was a great square stone keep with rounded corner towers (now badly ruined) built either by him or by his son William Marshal the younger. This, like Terryglass, can be classified as a "towered or turreted keep." Another is **Ferns Castle** *(282)*, County Wexford, probably a Marshal stronghold, today in a bad state of ruination. Also in Marshal territory, and possibly raised by one of the family's tenants, are the remains of a motte-and-bailey in the vicinity of **St. Mullins Abbey** *(288)*, County Carlow—now a small grass-covered mound outside the monastery wall.

Marshal's stay in Ireland coincided with the middle years of the reign of King John (1199–1216). To the surprise of all and the consternation of many, this, the fourth son of Henry II, outlived all his brothers to succeed to the throne of England. The event was fateful for the future of Ireland. It had clearly been Henry's intention to establish some kind of autonomous feudal monarchy there, with his youngest son, John, at its head. Had that happened, England and Ireland might well have developed as separate feudal monarchies more or less independently of each other. But when the Irish lordship was merged with the English Crown, Ireland's dependent and subordinate status was fixed. For the next seven centuries and more it would remain a colony.

King John came back to Ireland in 1210, the last of the English monarchs to do so for 180 years. He came for much the same reason as had his father in 1171—to reassert control over that country's unruly Anglo-Norman barons. The king had already driven John de Courcy into exile, replacing him with Hugh de Lacy II, whom he named earl of Ulster. It was probably he who built the upper ward and great round keep at **Dundrum Castle** *(437)*, County Down. De Lacy is also the likely builder of the oldest surviving portion of the polygonal keep of **Carlingford Castle** *(395)*, otherwise known as **King John's Castle**, in County Louth on the southwest shore of Carlingford Lough. By the year 1210 he too—along with his brother Walter, lord of Meath—had fallen into royal disfavor.

King John arrived at Crook near Waterford on 10 June with an army of about eight thousand men. Marching through Leinster to Dublin, he forced a reluctant William Marshal to join his expedition and extracted from him the castle at **Dunamase** *(314)* as surety. From Dublin, where he reportedly received the submission of twenty Irish kings, John moved into Meath and took **Trim Castle** *(390)*, Walter de Lacy's principal fortress. He then proceeded into Ulster. By 8 July he was at Dundalk, which Hugh de Lacy had evacuated, probably burning **Dún Dealgan** *(398)* before leaving. The next day the king was at **Carlingford Castle** *(395)*, which promptly surrendered. After occupying **Dundrum Castle** *(437)*, he marched through Downpatrick to **Carrickfergus Castle** *(461)*, which held out for nine days before capitulation. De Lacy fled overseas. By 8 August John was at Drogheda and four days later at **Granard Motte** *(394)* in present County Longford. By the 18th he was back in Dublin and on the 24th or 25th left Ireland. Altogether he had spent no more than nine weeks in the country, but in that short time he had dispelled all opposition, Anglo-Norman and native Irish alike. As his biographer, W. L. Warren, was to put it, John was "the most successful high king Ireland had ever seen."

Before he left Dublin, the king had appointed John de Gray to be justiciar. It was probably he who began the construction of **Dublin Castle** *(358)*, although the first phase was to be completed by his successor, Archbishop Henri de Londres. The king's requirement for such a building had been explained in a directive issued in August 1204 to Gray's predecessor, Meiler fitz Henry: "You have given us to understand that you have no safe place for the custody of our treasure and . . . for this reason and for many others we are in need of a strong fortress in Dublin . . . ." Once completed, the castle was to serve for seven centuries as the center and symbol of English rule in Ireland. Very little, however, remains today of the original building: only the so-called Record Tower at the southeast corner of the inner court, the battered base of the Bermingham Tower, a portion near the northwest corner, and about a hundred feet of the old south curtain wall. The rest is mostly the product of a wholesale "Gothick" reconstruction carried out in the eighteenth century.

Dublin Castle was not the only one to be constructed by order of John de Gray. Shortly after the king had left, he raised another at **Clones** *(400)* in County Monaghan—probably a motte-and-bailey now marked by the high mound on the northwest side of the town. More importantly he led an expedition to the Shannon and built the great stone **Castle** of **Athlone** *(391)*, County Westmeath, to guard a newly installed bridge across the river. Raised on the site of an earlier motte, Gray's tower collapsed the following year, probably because the artificial earthen mound was packed too loosely to support it. It was promptly rebuilt. Here the ground plan of the keep is polygonal—a compromise designed to be less vulnerable than the rectangular form but easier to build than the circular and better adapted to internal walling.

After Archbishop Henri de Londres succeeded to the justiciarship in 1213, one of his first acts was to build or complete **Roscrea Castle** *(305)*, County Tipperary, on the main route from Dublin to Limerick. Here is a tall rectangular tower incorporated into a polygonal curtain wall with two additional D-shaped towers. What portion of this complex belongs to the original building is unclear. At **Clonmacnoise** *(383)* in County Offaly, the archbishop put up another tower outside the great monastic enclosure. As at Athlone, the stone castle was built on top of an earlier motte, this one apparently solid enough to bear the additional weight.

Thus was completed a long triangular string of royal castles: running north from Dublin through Drogheda, Carlingford, and Dundrum to Carrickfergus; thence southwest through Clones, Athlone, Clonmacnoise, and Roscrea to Limerick; and thence in an easterly direction back to Dublin. Within the triangle and south of it, the land was studded with the strongholds built by the first and second generations of Anglo-Norman adventurers. West of it the conquerors had made some few inroads, as in the FitzGerald territory south of the river Shannon and the coastal band north and west of Carrickfergus that King John had granted to Duncan, earl of Carrick. But Thomond (modern County Clare), Connacht (modern Counties Galway, Mayo, Sligo, Leitrim, and Roscommon), and most of Ulster west of the river Bann (modern Counties Armagh, Tyrone, Londonderry, and Donegal) were still occupied by the native Irish. In English eyes, however, their ownership was less than absolute. In 1210 King John had forced Cathal Crovderg O'Connor, king of Connacht, to do homage and to acknowledge that he held his kingdom as tenant-in-chief of the English monarch. At the same time Donnchad O'Brien had made a like submission for his kingdom of Thomond.

After his triumphant march through Ireland King John went home to become embroiled in the famous controversy with his English barons that ended in June 1215 with the signing of the Magna Carta on the field of Runnymede. Except for William Marshal, who stood by the king, none of his barons in Ireland played any part in the affair. The colony did, however, feel some repercussions. Short of funds after his humiliation, John extracted a huge fine from Cathal Crovderg O'Connor in return for confirming his feudal charter to the kingdom of Connacht. He also allowed Walter de Lacy to buy back his earldom of Meath.

It may have been about this time that de Lacy had **Trim Castle** *(390)*, County Meath, rebuilt in stone. It is today perhaps the most impressive Norman fortress to be seen in Ireland. The earliest building here is the great high square keep, unusual only in having smaller square towers projecting from its sides (three of which survive). Sometime later—probably by Walter Peppard, lord of Tabor—a high curtain wall was put up to surround the keep. At regular intervals along its face were D-shaped turrets (five of which survive); on the south side is a huge round gatehouse tower (the Dublin Gate) with an outer defensive courtyard and gate, called a *barbican*; a smaller, rectangular gate with a portcullis intersects the west wall; and there are two sally ports, north and south. The river Boyne runs along one side, and the others were originally bordered by a water-filled moat over which a drawbridge led to the Dublin Gate. Trim Castle, then, exemplifies most of the features characteristic of early-, middle-, and late-thirteenth-century military architecture. The keep, being square and therefore especially vulnerable at the corners, was old-fashioned, even at the time of its construction. By the mid–thirteenth century the main burden of defense, as at most castles of the period, had been shifted to the outer wall. Hence the moat, the drawbridge, the barbican, and the wall turrets. Sally ports were installed against the possibility that the garrison might want to escape or to permit them to exit the enclosure and engage an attacker outside the walls. The portcullis is a great grilled gate capable of being raised and lowered by pulleys operated from a room above. The main gatehouse served both a residential and a defensive purpose. By the end of the thirteenth century, in England and to a lesser extent in Ireland, buildings like this had come to serve as the sole residence of the castellan and to displace the central keep altogether. Trim, therefore, can be viewed as a splendid example of medieval castle architecture in transition.

More typical of the mid-thirteenth century is **Castleroche** *(399)* in County Louth. Probably built by John de Verdon, this is a keepless court- yard castle whose main defensive feature was the double-towered gatehouse in the middle of the north wall of the triangular crenellated curtain. Adjoining the gatehouse to the south was another building that probably served as the great hall. **Liscarrol Castle** *(316)*, County Cork, probably built by the de Barrys (heirs of the Geraldine family to which Giraldus Cam- brensis belonged), is also a keepless courtyard castle, this one square in plan, with a strong gate tower in the center of the south wall. Another high mural tower stands in the opposite wall, and three of the original four corner towers survive as well. **Granagh Castle** *(287)*, County Kilkenny, is a thirteenth-century courtyard castle to which a tall square keep was added later—probably in the fourteenth century. Of the original structure, prob- ably built by the le Poers, all that remains is the curtain wall with three round turrets overlooking the river Suir. Even less remains of **Clonmore Castle** *(290)* in County Carlow. Its courtyard is also square in plan, with rectangular towers at each corner, but there is not much else to be seen today. Also in County Carlow is **Ballymoon Castle** *(290)*, probably built by the Anglo-Norman Roger Bigod. This too is a keepless square courtyard, here surrounded by walls exceptionally high and thick. From the center of three of these project small oblong towers; on the fourth side is the arched gatehouse with the grooves for a portcullis still visible.

In Connacht, King Cathal Crovderg O'Connor continued, until his death in 1224, to hold his kingdom against both rival Irish dynasts and encroachments by his Anglo-Norman neighbors to the east. His sons and successors, Aedh and Felim O'Connor, were not so fortunate. An infant king—Henry III—was on the English throne, and more importantly for Ireland, the reins of government were in the hands of the justiciar, Hubert de Burgh. Hubert's nephew was Richard de Burgh of the Anglo-Norman family already ensconced in County Limerick and elsewhere in Munster. To him, in 1226, was granted the kingdom of Connacht, save for Athlone and the region roughly equivalent to modern County Roscommon, which were reserved to the Crown. That the gift was in breach of King John's previous agreement with Cathal Crovderg was undeniable. Yet the latter's sons, at war with their own kinsmen over the right of succession, were in no position to contest it.

In 1235 de Burgh, with some five hundred knights, led a hosting into southern Connacht and drove Felim O'Connor and his people north into County Leitrim and the adjacent parts of County Roscommon. There they are credited with the construction of **Ballintober Castle** *(404)*—a splendid keepless courtyard castle with polygonal turrets at the corners of the curtain wall and a twin-towered gatehouse on the east side, the whole surrounded by a moat. If this is indeed an O'Connor stronghold—and not, as some authorities believe, another Anglo-Norman building—it is the only surviving thirteenth-century castle of a Gaelic Irish ruler. Most Irish chieftains of this period seem to have been content to reside—in conditions considered barbaric by the Anglo-Normans—in raths or cashels of the traditional Irish type.

As to the Anglo-Normans who came to Connacht in the train of Richard de Burgh, they proceeded to occupy most of the western parts of modern Counties Galway, Mayo, and Sligo. Among de Burgh's tenants were the de Berminghams, who built **Athenry Castle** *(404)* and **Dunmore Castle** *(406)*, both in County Galway. The former was a three-storey keep surrounded by a high battlemented wall; the exact form of the latter is unknown since it was subsequently burned and replaced by the massive rectangular tower and curtain whose ruins are still to be seen. Another de Burgh vassal was Jordan of Exeter, who constructed **Ballylahan Castle** *(422)* in County Mayo—a polygonal courtyard castle with a twin circular towered gatehouse, of which the ruin of only one tower now remains.

Notwithstanding their progress in overrunning large segments of hitherto unconquered Gaelic Ireland, the Anglo-Normans were beginning to suffer military setbacks. Indeed the third quarter of the thirteenth century witnessed the beginnings of a sort of Gaelic resurgence—a turning of the tide that was to reach full flood in the following century. The balance of military power was beginning to shift, the main reason being the appearance in Ireland at about the mid–thirteenth century of a species of professional soldiers called *gallowglasses*. These were mercenaries from the western highlands and islands of Scotland who sold their services to Gaelic kings. Some—like the MacSwineys, MacDonnells, and MacDowells—settled on lands granted by their patrons to become themselves petty chieftains of a sort. They fought on foot but were well accoutred with iron helmets and shirts of mail over quilted jackets and were armed with long-handled double-edged poleaxes, called *spars*. With their assistance Gaelic leaders could for the first time risk pitched battles with their Anglo-Norman foes.

In 1257 Godfrey O'Donnell of Tyr Connell (County Donegal) crossed the river Erne and, with the help of a contingent of these mercenaries, routed an Anglo-Norman army at Credran in County Sligo. The following year Aedh O'Connor, younger son of Felim, came together with Tadgh O'Brien, son of the king of Thomond, and Brian O'Neill, king of Tyrone, at Caeluisce on the river Erne. There the three Gaelic leaders agreed to revive the high kingship of Ireland with Brian as king. Two years later

O'Neill, with a sizable army of Ulstermen, Connachtmen, and gallow-glasses, marched against the English settlement at Downpatrick. At about the same time Irish insurgents destroyed **Greencastle** *(436)*, County Down, so that it had to be rebuilt in the form now represented by the substantial ruin overlooking Strangford Lough. Brian O'Neill's army was overwhelmingly defeated by the colonists at Down, and he himself was killed, his severed head dispatched to London. But Aedh O'Connor escaped the field and ten years later defeated a royal army at Athankip near Carrick-on-Shannon. He then proceeded to throw down the new English stronghold of **Roscommon Castle** *(403)*, but in 1280 the justiciar, Robert de Ufford, recaptured and rebuilt it. Today its substantial ruins provide the finest example in Ireland of a thirteenth-century keepless courtyard castle. Rectangular in shape, the court is enclosed within thick battlemented curtain walls with D-shaped turrets at each of the four corners. At the center of the east wall is a high twin-towered gatehouse, and in the opposite wall is a second gate tower, rectangular in shape.

At about the same time as the royal castle of Roscommon was being rebuilt, Thomas de Clare, to whom King Henry III had made a large grant of land in Thomond (modern County Clare), was putting up a courtyard castle with rounded corner towers, later to be incorporated into **Quin Friary** *(348)*. But while the Anglo-Normans thus succeeded at last in pushing north of the river Shannon, their progress into western Munster had been checked. In July 1261 at a place called Callan (near Kenmare in modern county Kerry), an Irish force led by Fineen MacCarthy overthrew an army sent from Dublin to the aid of John fitz Thomas (FitzGerald) of Shanid. Eight Anglo-Norman barons and twenty-five knights lost their lives in this single engagement. And though Fineen was himself killed shortly thereafter, the Irish victory in effect secured western Counties Kerry and Cork from further penetration.

In Ulster, however, the third decade of the thirteenth century witnessed a significant extension of Anglo-Norman power west of the river Bann. In 1264 Walter de Burgh, son of Richard, lord of Connacht, was given the earldom of Ulster. He was succeeded by his son Richard, the so-called "Red Earl," whose vast holdings as earl of Ulster and lord of Connacht amounted, in theory at least, to virtually half of Ireland. To consolidate his position he occupied or built a chain of castles from which his authority spread into the Gaelic interior as far as the O'Neill territory of County Tyrone. One of these may have been **Dunluce Castle** *(460)*, County Antrim, whose earliest portions—the northeast and southeast cylindrical towers and the south curtain wall—date to about the year 1300. More certainly attributable to the Red Earl is **Greencastle** or **Northburgh Castle** *(429)* on the Inishowen peninsula, County Donegal, overlooking the mouth of the river Foyle. Now a badly neglected ruin, the stronghold seems to have been built as a rectangular keep within a quadrilateral courtyard enclosed by curtain walls with a twin polygon-towered gatehouse on the western side. Finally, near the northern end of his domain in Connacht, Richard de Burgh erected **Ballymote Castle** *(417)*, County Sligo. Now in ruins, it was a fine keepless courtyard castle, almost square in plan, with massive round towers at all four corners, a twin-towered gatehouse in the north wall, a rectangular sally port opposite it, and a smaller D-shaped tower in the center of each of the side walls.

Thus, with the spread of the earl of Ulster's power from Carlingford Lough around the coast as far as Galway Bay, almost three-quarters of Ireland was brought under the sway of Anglo-Norman lords. As it turned out, however, this was to be the high-water mark of their occupation of the country. Thenceforth the tide of conquest (or "half conquest" as some historians put it) began to recede.

IRELAND AT THE END OF THE THIRTEENTH CENTURY

As of the close of the thirteenth century the term "Anglo-Norman" becomes less appropriate than formerly as a description of the intrusive conquerors, or semiconquerors, of Ireland. Though still presumably French-speaking—as were their baronial counterparts in England and Scotland—these men were English in attitude and outlook, sworn vassals of the English king. Many, however, had been born in Ireland, often of Irish mothers or grandmothers. Intermarriage between the two "races" had commenced early—with Strongbow's taking Eva, daughter of the king of Leinster, as his wife. Hugh de Lacy married Rory O'Connor's daughter, William de Burgh the daughter of Donal Mór O'Brien. And this was not the end of it. "Many, perhaps most, of the Anglo-Normans of the 13th and 14th centuries," according to the historian Kenneth Nicholls, "belonged by birth as much to one race as to the other." From this point on, therefore, it will be more accurate to speak of the feudal aristocracy, their dependents, and the town dwellers in the settled parts of the island as "Anglo-Irish"—a term still in use though no longer nearly so inclusive.

Yet within the colonized areas, prevailing legal and political institutions were all of purely English origin. The chief governor of the country, the king of England's alter ego in Ireland, was the justiciar, later styled lieutenant or deputy to the lieutenant if the latter was an absentee. This official was commander-in-chief of the armed forces, supreme judge, and chief executive, subject of course to the king's overriding veto. He was assisted by a council of Anglo-Irish magnates and high churchmen, modelled on the king's council in England. And though Dublin was the fixed seat of the exchequer and of the highest stationary law court, both justiciar and council were, in the words of the historian A. J. Otway-Ruthven, "endlessly itinerant."

Neither did parliament have any permanent meeting place. The first assembly to be so called met at the town of Castledermot, County Kildare, in 1264. It was in essence an expanded council, with a few lesser barons added to the usual gathering of magnates and prelates. From such modest beginnings the Irish parliament, following the English precedent, gradually developed into a genuine legislative body. Never in the Middle Ages, however, did it attain the independence sometimes successfully asserted by its counterpart at Westminster. Nor did it have the exclusive right to legislate for Ireland, where English ordinances and statutes had the force of law. But most significantly, by the end of the thirteenth century the Irish parliament had become a representative body. In 1297 two knights from each of the colony's counties and liberties were summoned to meet with the magnates. Two years later two burgesses were summoned from each town. In the year 1300 both counties and boroughs were ordered to elect delegates who would have full power (*plena potestas*) to speak and act on their behalf. Thus was the principle of representation established. "Its appearance in Ireland at such an early date," suggests the historian James Lydon, "is one of the major constructive achievements of the English settlement." But it did not apply to Gaelic Ireland. Except for the occasional high churchman, no native Irishman—not even the greatest of the chieftains— was ever invited to attend a council or parliament until the sixteenth century.

Nor were the native Irish living within the English settlement entitled, except by special license, to access to the courts of common law. Though not entirely without legal rights, they could not personally bring civil action against an Anglo-Norman defendant. Nor were they afforded equal protection of the criminal law. It was not a capital offense, for example, for an Englishman to kill an Irishman. In the years 1276–80 a group of churchmen led by David MacCarvill, archbishop of Cashel, offered King Edward I the sum of eight thousand marks for the grant of English law to all Irishmen outside of Ulster. The offer was declined. Just how many Gaelic-speaking Irish people were affected by such discrimination is impossible to determine because there is no way to know what proportion of the native population remained within the settled parts of the colony.

The towns seem to have been peopled mostly by English and Welsh immigrants. Trade flourished in the thirteenth century, and kings and magnates alike were liberal in granting civic charters to old communities and new. In the first category were the five ancient Viking cities—Dublin, Wexford, Waterford, Cork, and Limerick. Among the latter were Carrick-fergus, Drogheda, Dundalk, New Ross, Clonmel, Dungarvan, Youghal, Mallow, Killmallock, Galway, Trim, and Athenry. All the larger towns were defended at first by ditched banks of earth and timber palisades, later by stone walls with mural towers and gates. A fair number of these survive, though most are probably of a later medieval date. The most complete today is the **Youghal Town Wall** *(325)*, County Cork; the second best preserved are the **City Walls of Waterford** *(286)*. Fragments of **Town Walls** are to be seen in **Dublin** *(361)*; **Limerick** *(337)*; **Carrickfergus** *(401)*, County Antrim; **Clonmel** *(304)* and **Fethard** *(304)*, County Tipperary; **Trim** *(390)*, County Meath; and **Galway** city *(407)* and **Athenry** *(405)*, County Galway. In Drogheda, County Louth, **St. Laurence's Gate** *(396)* is the barbican (forward fortification) defending a long-gone city gate. And at Kilmallock, County Limerick, **Blossom Gate** *(336)* is the only one of the original five that in the Middle Ages gave entry into the town. Nearby are also fragments of the wall itself.

In the countryside probably all the good arable land was taken up by the conquerors and the large number of peasants they imported from England and Wales. There they introduced the English three-field system of agriculture and succeeded so well that in the thirteenth century Ireland produced a surplus of grain for export. Except for an indeterminate number of serfs (called *betagh* in Gaelic), most of the native Irish seem to have been displaced to the mountains and bog lands adjacent to the English settlements.

For purposes of local government, the colony was divided into English-style administrative units called *shires* or *counties*—twelve in all by the year 1307. Within the shire the sheriff was the chief agent of the king, collecting revenues, administering justice, and presiding over the county court. At the end of the thirteenth century there were also four "liberties" (Kilkenny, Wexford, Trim, and Ulster) whose lords enjoyed quasi-regal rights of government, subject, however, to royal taxation. Here seneschals performed the same duties as the royal sheriffs.

Such, in brief, were the conditions prevailing in what the settlers called "the land of peace." Matters were very different in Gaelic Ireland, the so-called "land of war." Geographically this area included, as of the year 1300, (1) most of Ulster except for the present Counties Down and Antrim, northern County Londonderry, and the Inishowen peninsula of County Donegal; (2) northeastern Connacht, that is, Counties Longford, and Leitrim and parts of County Roscommon; (3) northern County Clare; and (4) most of Desmond, that is, County Kerry and western County Cork. In addition, islands of virtual Irish autonomy remained inside the English colony. Such were the Wicklow Mountains south of Dublin and a large tract centering around Slieve Bloom, including the western parts of Counties Offaly and Laois.

Here, to the extent that any law prevailed, it was the ancient "brehon law." The word *brehon* is an anglicization of the Gaelic *breitheamh*, meaning "judge," and every Irish provincial king or chieftain had his own brehon or brehons drawn from a hereditary caste of lawyers. Disputes over property, as well as settlements for criminal acts, were resolved by the payment of compensation to the aggrieved party or his kinfolk, as determined by the brehons serving as arbitrators. They would sit and give their decisions in public, usually in some ancient assembly place, such as the ring-fort of **Cahermacnaghten** *(342)* in County Clare, where the O'Davorens, hereditary brehons of Thomond, performed their judicial duties and also maintained a school for the study of the ancient brehon texts. In the eyes of the English, the substitution of private compensatory payments for criminal punishment in such cases as homicide, theft, and arson served only to exacerbate native Irish tendencies to lawlessness and disorder. King Edward I himself denounced brehon law as "detestable to God, and so contrary to all law that they ought not to be deemed laws." In this, as in other respects, the cultural divide between the "land of peace" and the "land of war" appeared unbridgeable.

Gaelic Ireland, in contrast to the Anglo-Irish colony, remained predominantly pastoral. Oats were the standard cereal crop for men and horses, but cattle was the primary element in the Irish economy, providing meat, milk, butter, cheese, and curds. Cattle also provided the primary *casus belli* for the incessant low-intensity warfare that continued to be endemic in the mountains and forests of the North and West. "Creaching" or cattle raiding, in the words of the historian Art Cosgrove, "always remained a favorite recreation of the Gaelic ruling classes."

Dynastic wars, for higher stakes than a neighbor's herds, also continued unabated. Election, not primogeniture, still governed succession to kingship or lordship and was a constant source of intrafamilial feuding. Between 1274 and 1315, for example, there were thirteen kings of Connacht, of whom nine were killed by their own brothers or cousins and two deposed.

And finally there were the Anglo-Irish intruders, coming with fire and sword and studding the land with castles. Of these the most formidable was Richard de Burgh, the Red Earl of Ulster. Among his many Irish enemies was Donal O'Neill of Tyrone, who claimed to have inherited from his father, Brian, the high kingship of Ireland. Though the title was by this time almost meaningless, he agreed to surrender it to the king of Scotland in return for that monarch's armed intervention in behalf of Gaeldom. To this proposition Robert the Bruce readily agreed. In June 1314 he had decisively beaten an English army at Bannockburn in central Scotland, but the "War for Scottish Independence" was by no means over. Hoping to open up a second front, King Robert decided to send his brother Edward with a large expeditionary force across the North Channel from Scotland. Ireland might prove to be the chink in England's armor. Thus was born a strategic concept that was to recur many times to England's foreign enemies.

THE IRISH RESURGENCE: 1315–1399

On 26 May 1315 Edward Bruce landed at Larne, County Antrim, with an army of about six thousand Scots, soon to be joined by Donal O'Neill and a number of lesser Irish chieftains and their followers. Burning and pillaging as he went, he reached Dundalk on 29 June and then marched north to besiege the earl of Ulster's **Greencastle (Northburgh Castle)** *(429)* on the Inishowen peninsula, then east again to **Carrickfergus** *(460)*, where he laid siege to the castle. From Carrickfergus the Scots and their Irish allies proceeded south and west as far as **Granard Motte** *(394)*, County Longford, which they burned. By February 1316 they were in County Laois, where they set fire to **Lea Castle** *(313)* before retreating back to Ulster. Near-starvation, rather than hostile action, dictated this course. Bruce's invasion coincided with the worst famine of the Middle Ages, caused by excessive rainfall and consequent spoilage of the grain crop. In Ulster the Scots finally took the earl's castle in Inishowen and proceeded to capture the other **Greencastle** *(436)*, on Carlingford Lough in County Down. In May Edward had himself crowned high king of Ireland at Dundalk. That autumn, after receiving the surrender of the garrison at **Carrickfergus** *(460)*, he returned to Scotland to recruit more troops. Soon he was back in Ireland, this time in the company of his brother, King Robert.

Again the invaders headed south. In February 1317 they drew up before Dublin but turned away in the face of the city's formidable defenses. After heading west almost as far as Limerick, the Scots once more retreated back to Ulster. Robert Bruce went home. Not until October of 1318 did Edward head south again, this time reaching the neighborhood of Dundalk near the site of the old Norman motte of **Dún Dealgan** *(398)*. There he was killed in battle, his forces routed by an English and Anglo-Irish army under John de Bermingham. Famine, however, more than enemy action, was the major cause of the Bruces' ultimate defeat. Another reason was the failure of any significant number of the native Irish to rally to their banner. Some even opposed their passage through the country, preferring the foreigners who had long lived among them to this latest influx of robbers and plunderers. Small wonder, considering the dreadful devastation left in the wake of the invasion. "No better deed was performed since the beginning of the world," wrote a contemporary Irish annalist, than the slaying of Edward Bruce, "the destroyer of all Erinn in general, both English and Gael."

But if Gaelic and Anglo-Irish suffered alike from the depredations of the Bruces, it was the former who in the long run benefited. For the remainder of the Middle Ages, royal government in Ireland never fully recovered the control of the country it had held before the invasion. In hundreds of local battles native victories were won against the colonists, and for a century and more after the departure of the Scots, the English settlement gradually contracted.

Even before the death of Edward Bruce, the O'Briens of Thomond (County Clare), in May 1318 at a place called Dysert O'Dea, had overwhelmed an Anglo-Irish contingent led by Richard de Clare, killing both him and his son, driving his widow and remaining supporters out of the country, overthrowing **Quin Castle** *(348)*, and eventually taking over his stronghold of **Bunratty Castle** *(350)*. For about two centuries the Anglo-Irish never came back to County Clare. Elsewhere in Munster, the MacCarthys gradually expanded their holdings eastward to include the lordship of Muskerry in County Cork.

West and north of MacCarthy territory, in modern County Limerick, the FitzGeralds of Shanid still held sway. In 1329 Maurice fitz Thomas (FitzGerald) was created first earl of Desmond, and, though he expanded his territory, he failed to recover from the MacCarthys the lands in the extreme southwest of County Cork. **Askeaton Castle** *(334)*, County Limerick, originally a stronghold of William de Burgh, came into Desmond's possession before 1344. Often at odds with the government in Dublin, he raised and maintained a private army by imposing "coign and livery" (forced hospitality and billeting of troops), and, in league with his Mac-Carthy neighbors, terrorized Munster, town and country. His grandson Gerald fitz Maurice (FitzGerald), the third earl, became thoroughly hibernicized to the extent of composing poetry in Gaelic and fostering his son with the O'Briens.

In 1328 most of modern County Tipperary was confirmed to James Butler, who in that year was created first earl of Ormond. He and his successors proved more loyal to the English Crown and its representatives in Dublin than did their Desmond neighbors. The *caput* of the earldom was at first **Nenagh Castle** *(305)*, but near the close of the fourteenth century the third earl transferred his seat to **Kilkenny Castle** *(294)*, which the family retained until 1935. Another Butler stronghold, acquired in about 1375, was **Cahir Castle** *(298)* on the river Suir in County Tipperary—a high rectangular keep enclosed by a multitowered perimeter wall and a gated outer court guarded by a barbican. Built originally in the thirteenth century, it was greatly enlarged in the fifteenth and sixteenth and restored in the nineteenth to achieve its present form as one of the largest and most impressive medieval castles in Ireland.

Richard de Burgh, the Red Earl, died in Ulster in 1326. His grandson and successor, William, the "Brown Earl," was murdered (by fellow Anglo-Irish) seven years later. Thereafter the earldom, as well as the lordship of Connacht, fell apart. **Greencastle (Northburgh Castle)** *(429)*, on the Inishowen peninsula, fell into the hands of the O'Dohertys. The rest of present County Donegal was dominated by the O'Donnells, kings of Tyr Connell. **Dunluce** *(460)* became the property of the MacQuillans. Late in the century the O'Neills destroyed the royal castles of **Carlingford** *(395)* and **Greencastle** *(436)* on opposite shores of Carlingford Lough. Of all the royal castles in Ulster, **Carrickfergus** *(460)* alone remained in the hands of the English king, while on the Ards peninsula of County Down and in neighboring Lecale small colonies of Anglo-Irish retained but a precarious foothold. Meanwhile in central Ulster the Clandeboy O'Neills established a kind of local hegemony. One of their number, Henry Aimreidh O'Neill, built a fine twin-towered stone castle near the present town of Newtown Stewart, County Tyrone. Today called **Harry Avery's Castle** *(448)*, it was, with the possible exception of Ballintober Castle, the only stone castle to have been built by a medieval Gaelic leader. To the east of here, in modern County Fermanagh, the Maguires became the predominant family; to the south, in County Monaghan, the MacMahons.

In Connacht the surviving de Burghs, hibernicized to the extent of adopting the surname Burke, split into two clans (Clan MacWilliam and Clan Rickard), which between them gained control of most of modern Counties Galway and Mayo, while County Sligo fell to the O'Connors. The royal castle of **Roscommon** *(403)* succumbed to the Gaelic Irish, as did the earl of Ulster's stronghold of **Ballymote** *(417)*. The Midlands became once more a patchwork of petty semiautonomous principalities, each dominated by a locally powerful clan: the O'Reillys and O'Rourkes in Bréifne (roughly modern Counties Cavan and east Leitrim), the O'Farrels in County Longford, the O'Carrolls of Ely in County Offaly, and to the west of them, in the ancient kingdom of Uí Maine, the O'Kellys.

Finally, even in Leinster, heartland of the original Anglo-Norman settlement, the Anglo-Irish community suffered serious setbacks. In 1327 Donal MacMurrough, distant descendant of Dermot of the Foreigners, was elected king of Leinster by the Gaelic survivors of the conquest. By the end of the century the MacMurrough kings had recovered control over much of the old province. From the Wicklow Mountains south of Dublin, the O'Byrnes and O'Tooles constantly raided the Anglo-Irish settlement, demanding and receiving "black rent" as the price of temporary immunity from arson and theft. West of Dublin was the domain of the FitzGerald earls of Kildare, consisting of most of the county that now bears their name. The *caput* of the earldom was **Maynooth Castle** *(377)*, probably begun in the early thirteenth century by Gerald fitz Maurice (FitzGerald), first baron of Offaly. The first earl of Kildare was John fitz Thomas (FitzGerald), who achieved that rank in 1316. His son Thomas, the second earl, like his cousin of Desmond, maintained a large private army, with Gaelic as well as Anglo-Irish retainers. Maurice, the fourth earl, did the same and was much engaged with fending off raids by the neighboring Gaelic clans of O'Dempsey and O'More. Dublin itself, pressed by these two tribes from the West and the MacMurroughs, O'Tooles, and O'Byrnes from the South, was less than safe. Most of the other cities of the South—Carlow, Wexford, Waterford, Cork—were isolated, surrounded by enemy territory and subject always to extortion and attack.

Contemporaneous with the military resurgence of Gaeldom, and to some extent perhaps inspiring it, was an upsurge of Gaelic nationalism throughout the country. *Nationalism* in the modern sense is perhaps too strong a word to describe the fourteenth-century burgeoning of anti-English sentiment, not only among the Irish but also among the Scots who followed Bruce. Yet no other term can quite describe the Declaration of Arbroath sent to Pope John XXII in 1320 by the leading earls and barons of Scotland, declaring they "would never in any wise consent to submit to the rule of the English." Nor of the like-worded Remonstrance dispatched to the same pope in 1317 by Donal O'Neill, king of Ulster, denouncing English misrule under which the Irish had been "violently reduced to the deep abyss of miserable bondage."

A related phenomenon was the cultural and literary revival of fourteenth-century Gaelic Ireland. National bardic festivals commemorated Irish traditions and history. In 1351 William O'Kelly of Uí Maine held a great feast, inviting to it all the poets of the country. Thirty-five years later Nial O'Neill built a house for the entertainment of the region's scholars and poets on the site of the ancient center of the kings of Ulster at Emain Macha (**Navan Fort** *[443]*), County Armagh. Not surprisingly, then, there survive from the late fourteenth and early fifteenth centuries a significant number of the great compilations of Gaelic literature, history, and law:

anthologies of the traditional learning of bards and brehons and annalists. Among these still to be found at the **Royal Irish Academy** *(356)*, Dublin, are *The Speckled Book (Leabhar Breac)*, containing lives of Saints Patrick and Brigid; *The Book of the Dun Cow (Leabhar na huidre)*, which includes, among other things, the oldest version of the *Táin*; *The Book of Lecan (Leabhar Mór Leacain)*, full of miscellaneous genealogical, historical, biblical, and hagiographical materials; the *Book of Fermoy*, which contains part of *The Book of Invasions (Lebor Gabála)*; and the *Book of Ballymote*, with the remainder of the *Lebor Gabála* plus a great miscellany of genealogies and hagiographies. Another such compilation is *The Yellow Book of Lecan* in the **Trinity College Library** *(353)*, Dublin.

The expansion of Gaeldom (or the shrinkage of the Anglo-Irish colony) proved to be a self-perpetuating phenomenon, aggravated by the precipitous decline in the royal revenues required to put a stop to it. As the "land of peace" shrank in size, so did the central government's income from the profits of justice in the royal courts, taxes, customs, etc. The bare figures tell the story. The average annual revenue received by the Irish exchequer in the years 1278–1299 was £6,300, for the period 1368–1384 it had fallen to £2,512, and for the rest of the century to no more than £2,000. This meant, among other things, that royal castles could not be maintained and soldiers could not be paid. And this in turn meant further Gaelic encroachments on Anglo-Irish territory.

Had the government in England chosen to mount a large and sustained military operation to defend the colony, perhaps the trend might have been reversed. But other military and fiscal demands on the Crown's revenues precluded such a solution. The war with Scotland dragged on. Then, in 1338, King Edward III sailed for France in an attempt to make good his claim to that country's throne. The Hundred Years' War thus began, and the defense of Ireland sank further on the list of English priorities.

Finally, another cause of the decline of the colony was the Black Death, a plague carried by rats and fleas that struck Ireland first in the summer of 1348. Naturally enough the epidemic hit hardest among the more thickly populated areas, that is, among the Anglo-Irish in the South and East. Towns were decimated, nearby manors abandoned. "A general malaise," in the words of the historian James Lydon, "descended on the land."

In the usual manner of shaky regimes beset by outside dangers, the English Crown and its representatives in Dublin sought to identify and punish internal enemies as the source of their troubles. Subversion from within was the charge brought against the Anglo-Irish community itself. The fault lay with the "degenerate English," more Irish than the Irish themselves *(Hibernis ipsis Hiberniores)*, who, in going native, had sold their birthright. Such was the reasoning behind the famous Statute of Kilkenny, passed by a parliament held in that city in 1366 under the aegis of Lionel, duke of Clarence, second son of King Edward III. It was intended to solve the problem of "degeneracy," which, according to its preamble, had led to the decay of good government and of "the allegiance due our lord the king." Specifically the statute forbade (1) marriage or concubinage between the Anglo-Irish and the Gaelic Irish; (2) the fosterage of Anglo-Irish children with Gaelic Irish families; (3) the use of the Irish language within the Anglo-Irish settlement or of the Irish mode of dress or style of riding (without saddle, bridle, or spurs); (4) the employment by the Anglo-Irish of Irish bards, musicians, etc.; and (5) playing the Irish game of "hurlings" (hurley) within the Anglo-Irish colony. Furthermore, to curtail Irish influences within the Church no Irishman was to serve on the chapter of any collegiate church or cathedral or be admitted into any religious house "amongst the English of that land," that is, within the present Counties Louth, Meath, Westmeath, Dublin, Kildare, Carlow, Kilkenny, Wexford, Waterford, and Tipperary.

Although often cited as a unique and particularly reprehensible example of English intolerance and racism, the Statute of Kilkenny was aimed primarily not at the native Irish but at the "degenerate English." Nor did it contain much that was new. Rather it was a codification of existing laws and ordinances, passed within the previous two generations. Also the law set up machinery for licensing exceptions to its rules and in any case proved impossible to enforce. It soon became, for most practical purposes, a dead letter.

Lionel, duke of Clarence, spent almost five years in Ireland, broken by an eight-month visit home. He had been sent over with a small but well-equipped army, during a lull in the French wars, to pacify the country and recover lost lands for the Crown. In neither respect was he successful. No more so was his successor, William of Windsor, who, as lieutenant from 1369 to 1371 and again between 1374 and 1376, waged intermittent warfare against the country's chronic "rebels," both Gaelic Irish and Anglo-Irish. Then, in October 1394, King Richard II himself, with an army of some five thousand, landed at Waterford—the first English monarch since King John to visit Ireland. Within the space of seven months most of the rebellious chiefs, north and south, had made formal submission to him. The king in turn promised concessions, including an acknowledgment of the right of Gaelic leaders to sit in parliament. No sooner had he left the country in May 1395 than the Gaelic Irish took up arms again. Richard returned in June 1399 with another army. A month later his cousin, Henry Bolingbroke, landed in the north of England, shortly to lay claim to the English throne. On 27 July Richard sailed away again, this time to face deposition in favor of his rival (Henry IV) and eventual death. The Irish problem remained unsolved.

THE FIFTEENTH AND EARLY SIXTEENTH CENTURIES: 1399–1534

After the departure of Richard II in 1399, Ireland was to suffer (or enjoy) the better part of a century of neglect by the English Crown. The three Lancastrian kings had other problems. Henry IV (1399–1413) was occupied by rebellions in Wales and the North; Henry V (1413–22) with the renewal of the Hundred Years' War with France; Henry VI (1422–61) with the loss of most of France, followed by the internal dynastic struggle known as the Wars of the Roses. All this left Ireland, Anglo- and Gaelic, largely free to fend for itself. Everywhere independent lords, great and not so great, pursued their own ends, often in conflict with each other. Local warfare of low intensity continued. Yet notwithstanding superficial appearances of anarchy, the country enjoyed a relative degree of stability and prosperity, once full recovery from the Bruce invasion and the Black Death had taken place. Indicative of this was the remarkable revival of building activity, which had come to a virtual standstill in the last half of the fourteenth century. Starting sometime before the mid–fifteenth century and continuing well into the sixteenth, a veritable boom took place in the construction of tall residential buildings called *tower houses*. They could be counted in the thousands: 325 in County Cork alone, more than 250 in Tipperary, and about 120 in Clare.

The tower house is best defined as "a manor-house with the accommodation extending vertically rather than horizontally for reasons of security" (J. Forde-Johnston). Strictly speaking they are not castles, though often bearing that name (e.g., Blarney Castle). The difference consists of both size and defensibility. Tower houses cover less ground, are less commodious, less massive, and less well equipped with defensive features. Built of stone, they stand, typically, three to five storeys high from a battered (inward-inclining) base to a crenellated parapet. The merlons (solid pieces) of the parapet are often "stepped," that is, shaped like a thick, inverted T. (This is an Irish characteristic not found in Britain, though occasionally in the south of France.) A small turret at one corner, usually above the staircase, rises above the twin-gabled roof. Often a small machicolation projects from the parapet over the entrance doorway below. Resting on corbels (stone braces secured to the wall), these projecting platforms had open spaces through which lethal objects such as stones, quicklime, and burning oil could be dropped on unfriendly folk below. The walls were pierced with narrow slits, now mostly referred to as *arrow-loops*, although their primary purpose was interior illumination rather than defense. Sometimes a pair of towers might be joined together, at right angles to each other, forming an L. Another variation was the U-plan tower with the two arms projecting forward of the main block. Though usually rectangular in plan, circular towers are not unknown. The interior arrangement normally consisted of two main vertical divisions separated by a wall. In front were the entrance, the winding stair, and a number of small chambers. In back were the large rooms, the principal one of which (the hall) was on one of the upper storeys. Adjoining the tower was a small courtyard or bawn enclosed by stone walls.

These places were designed to protect their owners from small raiding parties of the type that might be expected almost anywhere in the Irish countryside. They would have been incapable of resisting prolonged sieges by professional armies. Thus many of the features typical of the early medieval castle were normally missing: the moat, the barbican, the gate-house, the sally port, the heavy mural towers, etc.

In the northwestern corner of Ireland lies the ancient kingdom of Tyr Connell (County Donegal), where the chiefs of the O'Donnells held sway. Their *caput* was **Donegal Castle** *(426)* on the river Esk (now in Donegal town center), built probably in 1474 by Aedh Rua O'Donnell. Here today is the partially restored ruin of their high-standing tower house; also the remains of a fine manor house built beside the tower in the seventeenth century. On the northern coast of the same county, overlooking Sheep Haven Bay, is **Doe Castle** *(426)*, built in the early sixteenth century by one of the MacSweeneys (MacSwineys), originally a gallowglass family serving the O'Donnells. The high square battlemented tower is original; the other buildings were added later. **Enniskillen Castle** *(449)*, County Fermanagh, was erected originally by Hugh Maguire early in the fifteenth century. Of his handiwork only the vaulted ground floor remains; the rest of the tower (now housing the county museum) is of later construction. On the other (eastern) side of Ulster is the Lecale region of County Down (south of Strangford Lough), where an Anglo-Irish enclave still maintained its integrity in spite of the Gaelic resurgence of the fifteenth century. Here are the remains of three substantial fifteenth-century tower houses, with architectural features rare in Ireland and probably derived from Scottish models. These are the much restored **Jordan's Castle** *(432)* in Ardglass; **Kilclief Castle** *(440)*, about six miles to the north and erected sometime after 1413; and **Audley's Castle** *(441)*, overlooking Strangford Lough, built at about the same time and unusual in retaining much of its original bawn wall. The ground plan of all three is a shallow U. At the base is the main rectangular tower containing most of the residential rooms superimposed on top of each other. In front of this at one corner is a small wing enclosing the circular staircase. It is matched on the other side by a wing of small chambers on top of each other. Stretching between the two wings at roof level is an arched machicolation protecting the main entrance door underneath. The effect is not unlike that of some late-thirteenth-century castle gatehouses, although in other respects these buildings are not so well defended.

Connacht too has its share of late medieval tower houses. In County Mayo two examples of the conventional rectangular type are **Aghalard Castle** *(423)*, belonging to the gallowglass family of MacDonnells who served as mercenaries to the gaelicized Anglo-Norman Burkes, and **Rockfleet Castle** *(423)*, originally a Burke property but in the sixteeenth century occupied by Grace O'Malley, who commanded a fleet of galleys and dominated (some would say terrorized) Clew Bay. Others of the same ground plan and general appearance are to be found in County Galway. **Pallas Castle** *(415)* was a Burke stronghold. Five storeys high and surrounded by a well-preserved bawn, it is, in the opinion of the archaeologist Peter Harbison, "possibly the best preserved tower house" in the county. **Aughnanure Castle** *(408)*, on the southwest shore of Lough Corrib, is a double-bawned five-storey tower house that belonged to the O'Flahertys of Connemara. **Dunguaire (Dungory) Castle** *(410)*, a three-storey rectangular tower, was built by the O'Heynes, probably tenants of the Clanrickard Burkes, but has been restored radically and is now one of the Shannon Free Airport Development Company's tourist attractions. **Ardamullivon Castle** *(409)*, close to the County Clare border, was an O'Shaughnessy stronghold that still stands five storeys high, with wickerwork markings on the ground-floor vaulting.

Munster had a greater concentration of fifteenth- and sixteenth-century tower houses than any other region of Ireland. County Clare is especially well represented in surviving examples. **Gleninagh Castle** *(341)* is an L-plan tower built by the O'Loughlins on the south shore of Galway Bay. Nearby, **Newtown Castle** *(341)*, by an unknown builder, is unusual in having a round tower rising from a square base. Near the extreme southwest corner of the county overlooking the mouth of the river Shannon is **Carrigaholt Castle** *(346)*, a five-storey battlemented tower house standing within a substantial bawn wall. It was originally a MacMahon stronghold, later taken possession of by the O'Briens. Another O'Brien residence was **Leamaneh Castle** *(346)*, five storeys high and later joined by a fine seventeenth-century mansion. **Dysert O'Dea Castle** *(343)*, near the scene of the former battle of that name, was the *caput* of the O'Deas, dependents of the O'Brien kings of Thomond. Recently restored, it stands four storeys high to a battlemented parapet. Another restored tower house, one of those belonging to the MacNamaras, is on the grounds of the **Craggaunowen Project** *(349)*. Still another, also a MacNamara property, is **Knappogue Castle** *(349)*, with a nineteenth-century addition and now lavishly furnished and used for nightly "medieval banquets" during the high tourist season. The same attraction is offered at **Bunratty Castle** *(350)*—one of Ireland's most visited sites because of the attached folk park and also by reason of its proximity to Shannon Airport. It too was built by the MacNamaras in the mid–fifteenth century but was in O'Brien hands by the year 1500. The central rectangular block is three storeys high, and at each corner is a still higher tower, between each pair of which stretches a high machicolated arch. Typically the basement was given over to storage and dungeons, the first floor served as quarters for servants and retainers, on the floor above it was the great hall, and the top floor contained bedrooms and solars (private apartments).

In County Kerry across the Shannon close to the river shoreline is **Carrigafoyle Castle** *(327)*, a rectangular fifteenth-century tower house with one wall now missing, thus providing a sort of dollhouse view of the interior. Built toward the end of the fifteenth century by the O'Connors of Kerry, it is five storeys high and stands within a partially surviving bawn that opens to the water and encloses a dock. Also in County Kerry, on the shore of Lough Leane near Killarney, is **Ross Castle** *(331)*, built in the fifteenth or sixteenth century by O'Donoghue Ross—a high-standing rectangular tower house with rounded turrets surrounded by a bawn. Not far away is the contemporary **Ballymalis Castle** *(332)*, a four-storey tower house with corner turrets diagonally placed. In County Limerick **Castle Matrix** *(340)* on the outskirts of Rathkeale was originally one of the many strongholds of the earls of Desmond. Built as a tower house in the fifteenth century, it was heavily restored and enlarged in the nineteenth and now serves as headquarters for the Irish International Arts Centre and the Heraldry Society of Ireland. In the same county is **Glenquin Castle** *(340)*, thought to be an O'Hallinan stronghold—a seven-storey tower house, now much restored. **Conna Castle** *(321)*, standing high over the river Bride in County Cork, is another Desmond tower house, built in about 1500, five storeys high, battlemented, and with the usual machicolation above the main doorway. Now a substantial ruin, the four-storey **Ballynacarriga Castle** *(314)*, near Clonakilty, belonged to the Hurleys. Closer to Cork city is **Blarney Castle** *(319)*, perhaps the most famous of all of Ireland's tower houses and the most visited. Built in the fifteenth century by Cormac MacCarthy and today partially restored, this is an L-plan tower, four storeys high, with fine battlements stepped in the Irish fashion. These are unusual in that they project more than two feet beyond the wall heads on all four sides, thus forming a continuous machicolation borne by high corbels secured to the walls. In one of these battlements is the famous

"Blarney Stone," and a visitor wanting to kiss it must lie on his back with his head projecting over the hollow space of the machicolation.

In County Tipperary two tower houses built by the Purcell family are noteworthy. **Loughmoe Castle** *(308)* was constructed in the fifteenth or sixteenth century but enlarged and embellished in the seventeenth. The original tower is four storeys high with rounded corners. **Ballynahow Castle** *(307)*, probably of sixteenth-century date judging from the presence of musket-loops, is one of the few round tower houses in Ireland. It is five storeys high and battlemented. The internal vaulting is dome-shaped, and the arrangement of chambers is irregular—structural idiosyncrasies that probably explain why the circular ground plan was not employed more often. In neighboring County Kilkenny **Ballyragget Castle** *(296)* was a Butler stronghold—a four-storey tower house within a high bawn wall most of which still survives. **Burnchurch Castle** *(292)*, near Callan, was a Fitz-Gerald tower rising six storeys to stepped battlements. **Clara Castle** *(292)*, near the town of Kilkenny, is of particular interest because the original oak floors are still in place, thus providing the visitor with an unusually good view of the internal appearance of a fifteenth-century tower house.

The Butlers and FitzGeralds were not the only Anglo-Irish to house themselves and their dependents in towers. John Rosseter, seneschal of the liberty of Wexford in the mid–fifteenth century, is believed to have been the builder of **Rathmacknee Castle** *(284)*, a well-preserved five-storey battle-mented tower house standing in the corner of a walled bawn, complete on three sides. Also in County Wexford is **Slade Castle** *(282)*, a tower house dating to the late fifteenth or early sixteenth century, to which a more spacious residence was added later—both probably built by members of the Laffan family.

In County Offaly stands **Clonony Castle** *(381)*, a sixteenth-century four-storey tower house, now much ruined but conveniently situated on the roadside southwest of Ferbane. Closer to Dublin, within the region known by the mid–fifteenth century as the Pale, other Anglo-Irish families were active in erecting tower houses. Sir Thomas Plunkett, chief justice of the court of common pleas, was responsible for **Dunsoghly Castle** *(371)*, County Dublin. More elaborate than most, it is a four-storey rectangular block with smaller square towers at all four corners rising above the parapet. In County Louth **Roodstown Castle** *(399)* consists of a like-sized central block, but with only two turrets at diagonally opposite corners. In Carlingford is the three-storey, fifteenth-century tower with stepped battle-ments known as **The Mint** *(395)*. The four-storey tower of **Athlumney Castle** *(389)*, County Meath, belongs to the fifteenth century, although the adjoining mansion is later. Finally, also in County Meath, is **Donore Castle** *(391)*, a very simple three-storey tower with rounded corners and a project-ing turret at one. This is the only tower house in Ireland almost certainly attributable to statutes passed in 1429 and later offering a ten-pound subsidy to any "liege-man of our Lord the King" who would build a fortified tower to specified measurements in any part of Counties Dublin, Meath (including present Westmeath), Kildare, and Louth.

These were the counties of the Pale, stretching from Dublin south no farther than Dalkey, north to Carlingford in County Louth, and west and northwest to Naas, Trim, and Kells—an area roughly thirty miles long and slightly less across. Within it lived most of the remnant of the Anglo-Irish colony that had once extended over almost three-quarters of the island. From time to time it was trenched and palisaded, at least in part. Hence the word *Pale* from the Latin *pilium,* meaning "fence" or "stockade." Behind it the loyal colonists lived on the defensive—"depleted in numbers and resources," to quote the historian Art Cosgrove, "and increasingly harried by Irish enemies and English rebels." Yet economically it was the most prosperous region of Ireland. The land was fertile; agriculture predominated; and the flat, lush countryside was dotted with the tower houses of the Anglo-Irish gentry who looked to Dublin for protection and their share of whatever patronage the royal government could provide.

Onto this scene, in 1449, arrived from England a new chief governor (that is, lieutenant)—Richard, duke of York. Senior member of the Yorkist branch of the royal house, he was, at the time of his arrival, next in succession to the then-childless King Henry VI, head of the house of Lancaster. Titular heir, through his mother, to vast lordships in Gaelic Ireland, York was well received, even by most of the Gaelic chiefs, who promptly made their submissions. It made little difference, however, because in 1450 York returned to England. There, after the birth of a son to King Henry's queen, he took up arms against his sovereign. Thus began the protracted dynastic struggle known as the Wars of the Roses. Defeated in battle in October 1459, the duke fled to Ireland, where he was received favorably, except by the Butler family, whose head, the earl of Ormond, was firmly attached to the Lancastrian cause. At a parliament summoned to Drogheda, York was declared lieutenant, in spite of having been convicted of treason at Westminster, and was given legal immunity from being summoned back to England. Parliament, furthermore, denied the applicability of English statutes to Ireland and declared that only such laws as were passed in the Irish council or parliament should have the force of law in Ireland—a revolutionary concept without legal precedent or foundation. The Statute of Drogheda, however, quickly became a dead letter. York soon returned voluntarily to England to be killed in the battle of Wakefield. But when his son succeeded to the throne in 1461 as Edward IV, the new king was not disposed to allow Ireland the measure of home rule envisaged by his father.

One of the first acts of the new government was to execute the earl of

Ormond for his Lancastrian sympathies. His rival, Thomas FitzGerald, earl of Desmond, was elevated to the chief governorship of Ireland. Overstepping himself, he too incurred the disfavor of the new monarch, who replaced him in 1467 with Sir John Tiptoft, soon to become the earl of Worcester. Tiptoft prevailed on another parliament at Drogheda to declare Desmond a traitor and promptly had him beheaded. Thus, within the space of a few years, the house of Ormond suffered eclipse and the Desmond FitzGeralds disappeared from the seat of power in Dublin. These events paved the way for the rise of the FitzGerald earls of Kildare, the third of the great provincial dynasties of Ireland.

In 1478 the eighth earl, Garret Mór FitzGerald (the "Great Earl") succeeded to the chief governorship. For most of the remainder of his life he retained the office under four succeeding kings of England (Edward IV, Edward V, Richard III, and Henry VII). The prime basis of his power was his vast landed wealth, mostly in County Kildare, where stood his *caput*, **Maynooth Castle** *(377)*, rebuilt on its early medieval foundations by his grandfather. Although Anglo-Irish in blood and sympathy, Garret Mór forged strong connections with various Gaelic dynasties by giving sundry female members of his family in marriage to their chiefs. Similarly connected with several important Anglo-Irish families, he managed, by force of arms and by the judicious dispensation of patronage, to win general recognition as "all but king of Ireland."

Even that wily and ambitious Tudor monarch, Henry VII, failed to put an effective curb on the Great Earl, nothwithstanding the latter's open support of Lambert Simnel and failure to act against Perkin Warbeck, two impostors laying claim to the English throne on spurious grounds of royal inheritance. With the concurrence of Kildare, Simnel had himself crowned "King Edward VI" in **Christ Church Cathedral** *(360)*, Dublin, and only the defeat of an army sent from Ireland to England in behalf of the pretender put the quietus on the rebellion. When Perkin Warbeck landed at Cork, claiming to be the younger son of the late King Edward IV, Kildare was more circumspect, but Henry VII suspected him nonetheless of duplicity and temporarily dismissed him from office. In 1494 the king dispatched to Ireland Sir Edward Poynings, who prevailed on the Irish parliament to pass a self-denying statute requiring prior royal approval for any meeting of that assembly or for any bill submitted to it for possible enactment. Parliament then, at Poynings's behest, attainted Kildare and sent him off to England. The attainder, however, was reversed, and king and earl reached a *modus vivendi*. Kildare "must be meet to rule all Ireland," King Henry is reported to have said, "seeing all Ireland cannot rule him." He was then sent back to serve for another seventeen years as the king's chief representative in Dublin.

His son, Garret Óg (the younger), who succeeded in 1513, was less fortunate in his dealings with the new English king, Henry VIII. The ancient FitzGerald–Butler feud was renewed, to the king's displeasure. News reached the king's ear that Kildare had turned a blind eye to a plot by the FitzGerald earl of Desmond to welcome an armed invasion of Ireland by Emperor Charles V. Kildare, fearing his imminent replacement, transferred the royal ordnance from Dublin to Maynooth. He was ordered to England.

Before his departure he named as his surrogate his eldest son, Thomas, Lord Offaly (nicknamed "Silken Thomas" for his sartorial elegance). In May 1534 Sir William Skeffington was appointed the king's lord deputy in Ireland and Kildare forbidden to return. The next month, by prearrangement with his father, Silken Thomas dramatically resigned his office by throwing down the sword of state in the presence of the council and about a thousand of his own retainers at **St. Mary's Abbey** *(368)*, Dublin. Kildare was then imprisoned in the Tower of London (where he later died of natural causes). Offaly openly declared himself a rebel, laid siege to **Dublin Castle** *(358)*, and seized and executed the English archbishop. In October Skeffington arrived with an army of twenty-three hundred men, the largest English force to come to Ireland since the time of Richard II. Silken Thomas held out through the winter of 1534-35, but in March, with the surrender of **Maynooth Castle** *(377)*, the rebellion collapsed. Five months later the now tenth earl of Kildare gave himself up. Despite his captors' assurances to the contrary, he and and his five uncles were subsequently put to death. The Tudor conquest of Ireland had begun.

Chapter Four

Medieval Ireland:
The Church, 1171–1534

THE EARLY MIDDLE AGES: 1171–1315

Two months after Henry II landed at Waterford the bishops of Ireland met at a great synod on Cashel Rock to declare their submission to the English king. They had been summoned there by Christian O'Conarchy, bishop of Lismore and papal legate. In attendance were all but one of the archbishops and most of the bishops of Ireland. The king's own representatives were the abbot of the Cistercian monastery of Buildwas and the archdeacon of the cathedral of Llandaff, both in Wales. Neither they nor their royal master could have been disappointed by the results of the council's deliberations.

As expected, the assembled churchmen swore formal oaths of fealty to King Henry as their overlord. They decreed, moreover, that the Irish Church was to be brought in all respects into conformity with the English Church. Each bishop and archbishop then gave Henry a sealed confirmation of his submission. These submissions were subsequently sent to Pope Alexander III, along with letters deploring the moral and religious failings of the Irish people.

From Rome the pope promptly replied with letters of his own to the bishops, to the lay "princes" of Ireland, and to King Henry himself. All three missives enthusiastically endorsed the decisions made at Cashel. To the bishops he admitted to being "overjoyed" that "our dearest son in Christ, Henry, noble king of the English, prompted by God, has, with his assembled forces, subjected to his rule that barbarous and uncivilised people ignorant of divine law." The lay rulers of Ireland were admonished to remain submissive to Henry II according to their recently sworn oaths of fealty. And to the English king himself the pope expressed his "gladness of heart" that such a "pious prince and magnificent king" had "wonderfully and magnificently triumphed over the disordered and indisciplined Irish, . . . a people unmindful of the fear of God."

All the above was consonant with an earlier papal decree, issued in 1155 by Pope Adrian IV, the only Englishman ever to preside over the Holy See. In his famous bull *Laudabiliter* the pontiff had authorized Henry II to invade and conquer Ireland so as to "enlarge the boundaries of the Church, to proclaim the truths of the Christian religion to a rude and ignorant

people, and to root out the growths of vice from the field of the Lord."
Now, sixteen years later, Henry could cite the authority of not only one
pope, but two, to justify his unprovoked act of aggression.

Considering that, in the winter of 1171-72, the king of England was
under threat of excommunication for his part in the recent murder of
Archbishop Thomas à Becket, this vote of confidence from the Vatican
might seem surprising. Rome seemed to be turning a blind eye to the
accomplishments of St. Malachy and to the church reforms already instituted by the Synods of Cashel (1101), Rath Breasail (1111), and Kells (1152).
The Irish Church had unequivocally subordinated itself to Rome; a new
diocesan structure had been erected; numbers of Augustinian and Cistercian monasteries had been founded; the canon law respecting lay control
and clerical marriage had been reaffirmed. But though much had been
achieved, neither the papacy nor the leading bishops and prelates of Ireland
itself (on whose reports the Vatican relied) were satisfied that the Church in
Ireland could reform itself or, more particularly, could impose a Christian
discipline on the Irish laity.

Of special concern to churchmen both in Ireland and abroad were the
notoriously lax sexual habits of the Irish people. Marriage and cohabita-
tion among relatives, to a degree considered incestuous by the Church, were
the main charges brought against the upper classes. "This people," wrote
Pope Alexander to Henry II, "openly cohabit with their stepmothers and
do not blush to bear children by them; a man will misuse his brother's wife
while his brother is still alive; a man will live in concubinage with two
sisters and many have intercourse with daughters of mothers they have
deserted." To the king's determination "to eradicate the filth of such great
abomination," said the pope, "we show, as we should, our gratitude and
approval in every way." And, to seal his approval of Henry's Irish enterprise, Alexander sent over another legate, Cardinal Vivian, who, at a
council of bishops held in Dublin in 1177, formally proclaimed the right
of the English king to the lordship of Ireland and threatened the excommunication of those who forsook their allegiance to him.

Reform, it was assumed, would have to come from the top. So, in the
years that followed, vacancies in the country's many bishoprics tended to be
filled by Anglo-Norman prelates, who, by 1254, were to occupy about a
third of the Irish dioceses. It was to such as these, and to their compatriot
abbots, that Ireland owed the introduction of the new style of ecclesiastical
architecture now known as Early English Gothic. In general the Gothic
style is distinguished from the earlier Romanesque by the complete substitution of pointed for round arches; by the replacement of semicircular
barrel vaults (ceilings) with steeply pitched vaults supported from below by
ribs with bosses at the intersections; and by the placement of high, thin
shafts around the circumference of the columns so as to create "clustered"

or "compound" piers in lieu of plain barrel-shaped pillars. The most obviously distinctive feature of the Early English variety of Gothic is the lancet window—a narrow pointed opening, sometimes appearing singly, sometimes in groups of three to five.

These novelties began to appear in Ireland as a new generation of English bishops set about to construct cathedral churches befitting their recently acquired rank and status. Among the first of these were John Comyn (Cumin), who succeeded Laurence O'Toole as archbishop of Dublin on the latter's death in 1180, and Henri de Londres, who succeeded Comyn in 1213. One of the two brought stonemasons over from western England to introduce the new fashion at **Christ Church Cathedral** *(360)*. Choir and transepts had been finished in the Romanesque style, but the nave was to be Early English. Though the church was remodelled radically in the nineteenth century, this early-thirteenth-century workmanship can still be seen in the north wall of the nave. Typical are the clustered columns, the pointed-arched arcade between nave and aisle, the lancet windows in the upper level (the clerestory), and the (restored) rib vaulting.

The cathedral chapter of Christ Church was made up of Augustinian canons, first brought to Dublin by Laurence O'Toole. Regular clergy such as these, however, were traditionally less amenable to episcopal control than their secular counterparts. Probably for this reason, Henri de Londres converted his predecessor's collegiate church of St. Patrick to cathedral status, in spite of its near proximity to Christ Church. Thus Dublin's single archbishop gained two archiepiscopal seats—an oddity unknown elsewhere in the British Isles.

Work on the construction of **St. Patrick's Cathedral** *(362)* began in about 1220 and ended (except for the lady chapel and tower) in about 1254, the year of its consecration. In spite of several restorations, including a drastic rebuilding of the fabric in the nineteenth century, the cruciform, aisled cathedral church of St. Patrick is arguably the best example of Early English architecture in Ireland. Surviving sections of the original building include the north and east walls of the choir, the east wall and east aisle (with vaulting) of the south transept, and the three eastern bays of the north aisle of the nave.

St. Patrick's, Dublin, was the longest cathedral church in medieval Ireland. Almost as long was **St. Canice's Cathedral** *(296)* in Kilkenny, begun by Bishop Hugh de Mapilton in the 1250s and finished in about 1285 by Bishop Geoffrey St. Leger, except for the square tower, which was added in the fourteenth century. Though much restored, much remains of the original building. Especially noteworthy are the three sets of high triple lancets in the choir, though those in the south and north walls are round-headed—a not unusual Irish departure from the Gothic norm. Shorter pointed lancets pierce the walls of nave and chapels, making this perhaps the best lighted of all the early medieval churches in Ireland. There are no vaults, however, and the timber hammerbeam roof dates to the nineteenth century. **St. Brigid's Cathedral** *(377)*, Kildare, was begun by Bishop Ralph of Bristol between 1223 and 1230. All the windows are lancets. The original parts of the cruciform, aisleless church include the south transept, the north and south walls of the nave, and about half of the tower. The stepped and machicolated battlements date probably to the late fourteenth century. The rest is the product of a nineteenth-century restoration.

None of the other thirteenth-century Anglo-Norman cathedrals survives to the extent of those named above. The **Newtown Trim Cathedral** *(390)*, County Meath, built by Simon de Rochefort sometime after 1202, is now in a very ruinous condition. Of the original cruciform church only the walls of the choir and a much foreshortened nave survive. The remains of **Kilmacduagh Cathedral** *(409)*, County Galway, are only slightly more extensive. Presently incorporated into the **Ferns (C of I) Church** *(281)*, County Wexford, is the choir of the cathedral built by Bishop John St. John between 1223 and 1243. About all that remains of the original are two lancets in the east wall and pairs of lancets in the side walls near the east end. The fine neo-Gothic **Lismore Cathedral** *(284)*, as it stands today, is mostly a seventeenth-century rebuilding of the church erected on this site by Bishop Robert de Bedford sometime after 1218. Only the chancel arch and the windows in the south transept clearly date to the thirteenth century. Of **Cloyne Cathedral** *(317)*, County Cork, built by Bishop Nicholas of Effingham after 1270, even less remains in evidence. The much-modernized choir now serves as a Church of Ireland parish church, and only the surviving lancets in the vacated transepts indicate the original date of construction.

All of the archbishops and bishops mentioned above were Anglo-Normans, which is not surprising in view of the conscious effort made by the English Crown in the early thirteenth century to exclude Gaelic Irish clergymen from high episcopal office. In 1216 the justiciar, Geoffrey Marsh, was specifically instructed to ensure that no native Irishman be elected to any see in Ireland. Subsequently, however, the Vatican intervened, and Pope Honorius III condemned the principle of ethnic exclusion as iniquitous. Not long afterward, following King Henry III's complaint to Rome of reverse discrimination being practiced by certain Irish clergy, Pope Innocent IV instructed the papal delegate to put a stop to that too. During the reign of Edward I (1272–1307) there is no evidence of royal interference to prevent the elevation of native Irishmen to episcopal rank, and of the hundred bishops holding sees in Ireland, fifty-one were Gaelic Irish. In view of the fact that by the end of the thirteenth century almost

three-quarters of the island was under Anglo-Norman control, these figures alone indicate that, at least within the diocesan Church, the native
Irish were more than holding their own.

The archdiocese of Cashel in the thirteenth century was ruled exclusively by Irish archbishops—three in a row. All three—Marianus O'Brien,
David MacKelly, and David MacCarvill—are responsible for building the
fine Gothic **Cathedral** adjacent to Cormac's Chapel on **Cashel Rock** *(301)*
on the site of an earlier church placed there by Donal Mór O'Brien, king of
Thomond. Here again the prevalence of narrow lancets—in the unusually
long choir, the transepts, the chapels, and the short nave—testify to the
thirteenth-century origin of the now roofless building. The choir, however,
is not vaulted; the low tower over the crossing is of a somewhat later date
than the rest of the fabric; and the massive tower at the west end was put up
in the fifteenth century as the archbishop's palace. An interesting architectural contrast is to be seen at the ruined **Ardmore Cathedral** *(326)* in
western County Waterford. Though finished in the early thirteenth century—by an Irish archbishop named Máel Etain O'Duib Ratha—the style
is predominantly Hiberno-Romanesque, with massive masonry and narrow round-headed windows splayed widely inward. Apparently Early English Gothic fashions had not yet penetrated this still-remote region close
to the border of County Cork. Still farther west, however, in County Kerry,
a Dominican bishop named Christian remodelled the fabric of **Ardfert
Cathedral** *(326)* from Romanesque to Gothic, retaining only the splendid
original western doorway and blind arcades on either side of it. The nave
and choir of this ruined church are Early English, with a triplet of high
lancets in the eastern wall and a row of nine occupying most of the south
wall of the choir.

The same juxtaposition of Romanesque and Gothic styles can be seen
at **St. Mary's Cathedral** *(338)*, Limerick, still in use for Protestant worship.
This was one of the many ecclesiastical foundations of Donal Mór O'Brien,
king of Thomond. Building began in about 1180, and to the first period of
construction can be assigned the doorway and parts of the nave and
chancel. Early in the thirteenth century the chancel was extended, the
transepts rebuilt, and the western tower added. In the fifteenth a number of
chapels were added on either side of the nave, and the whole fabric was
heavily restored in the nineteenth. Another establishment of King Donal's
was **Killaloe Cathedral** *(347)*, County Clare, now a Protestant church. Its
builders were probably two Irish bishops, Cornelius O h-Enna and Dom-
nall O h-Enna, the latter having succeeded to the see in 1216 only after
papal intervention had prevented the forceful intrusion of an English
candidate. Again this is an architectural medley: the doorway in the
southwest corner is a Hiberno-Romanesque insertion taken from an earlier
building on this site, but the rest of the church belongs to the thirteenth

century, and the high triple lancets in the east wall are unmistakably Gothic. Another probable O'Brien foundation in County Clare is **Kilfenora Cathedral** *(345)*. The early-thirteenth-century choir is now roofless, and the much restored nave serves as a Protestant parish church. The most distinctive architectural feature here is the triple-lancet fenestration of the east gable of the choir—round-headed, not pointed—an architectural anomaly fairly common in Ireland, especially in the West, where native masons were more conservative and probably less skilled than their English counterparts. The late-thirteenth- (or early-fourteenth-) century choir of **Tuam Cathedral** *(415)*, County Galway, is, by contrast, very English—perhaps because the archbishop was William de Bermingham of that great Anglo-Norman family. Though the rest of the original fabric has been replaced by a nineteenth-century church, the eastern end survives. Its most distinguished feature is the fine window in the east gable—five lancets in a row under a pair of quatrefoil windows surmounted by a larger octafoil—all under a spreading pointed arch. This may be the earliest example in Ireland of the Decorated style of Gothic architecture, which in the fourteenth century began to replace the simpler Early English forms.

Although the division of Ireland into episcopal dioceses preceded the coming of the Anglo-Normans, the subdivision of dioceses into parishes did not. The prerequisite for a parochial system was the regular collection of tithes from each locality for the support of the local parish church. Not until the Synod of Cashel in 1171 were such payments made mandatory by Church decree. Thereafter the establishment of fixed parish boundaries seems to have been fairly rapid, and by the end of the thirteenth century both Anglo-Norman and Gaelic Ireland (except for modern Counties Longford and Leitrim) were covered by a network of parishes.

But Irish parishes, compared to those in England, were poor, and the number of substantial thirteenth-century churches is therefore small. In Dublin, to be sure, there were seven altogether, though only one survives. This is **St. Audeon's (C of I) Church** *(361)*, of which only the west doorway, a part of the nave, and the ruined choir still stand today. More or less contemporary with it are a few ruined parish churches in other parts of the country. Among these are **Ballylarkin Church** *(296)*, County Kilkenny; **St. Mary's Church** *(293)*, Gowran, County Kilkenny (nave only); **Thomastown Church** *(296)*, County Kilkenny (on the grounds of C of I parish church); the **Church of Saints Peter and Paul** *(336)*, Kilmallock, County Limerick; **St. Finghin's Church** *(349)*, Quin, County Clare; **Drumacoo Church** *(407–408)*, County Galway; and **Layd Church** *(462)*, County Antrim.

In addition to these, Ireland boasts a few fine parish churches built originally in the thirteenth century, but since restored and still in use for Protestant (Church of Ireland) services. The largest of these is **St. Mary's Church** *(325)*, Youghal, County Cork. It is cruciform in plan, with an aisled nave and short aisle in the north transept. In the west wall are the original three-light lancet windows and in the transepts pointed triple and double-light windows. The base of the square tower at the northwest corner is original, but the choir is a heavily restored sixteenth-century addition. **St. Multose's Church** *(322)*, Kinsale, County Cork, was first built in the early thirteenth century and displays both Romanesque and Early English features. The high tower at the northwest corner, with its round-headed doors and windows, is Romanesque in style; the lancets in both east and west gables are, of course, Early English. **St. Mary's Church** *(304)*, Clonmel, County Tipperary, is also of thirteenth-century construction, but restorations in the fifteenth century and again in the nineteenth have all but obscured its Early English origins.

If parish churches of medieval foundation are sparse on the ground in Ireland, ruined monasteries are not. As in Britain itself, the Anglo-Normans were liberal benefactors of these religious houses, filling them mostly with monks and canons of their own nationality. The Cistercian and Augustinian orders were the most favored, although there are two noteworthy exceptions among those whose remains are still to be seen. The first is the **Trinitarian Friary** *(334)* in Adare, County Limerick, now incorporated within the Roman Catholic parish church, restored in the nineteenth century by the great neo-Gothicist Augustus W. N. Pugin. It is the only house of the Trinitarian Canons of the Order of the Redemption of Captives to have been established in Ireland. The founder is unknown, but in 1272 the priory was rebuilt by Thomas fitz Maurice (FitzGerald), father of the first earl of Kildare. The second exception is **Fore Abbey** *(392)* in County Westmeath, founded probably by Hugh de Lacy, lord of Meath, in the late twelfth or early thirteenth century. It is the only one of the nine Benedictine monasteries founded in the thirteenth century by Anglo-Normans to have survived to any significant degree. Although modified in the fifteenth century, the three Romanesque round-headed windows in the east wall indicate a late-twelfth- or early-thirteenth-century date of original construction.

An even earlier monastery—**Duleek Abbey** *(389)* in County Meath—was also founded by Hugh de Lacy in 1182. This was a house for canons of the Order of St. Augustine, the first of the Continental orders to have been imported to Ireland. Most of the existing church here is of later construction, but parts of the south wall may be of thirteenth-century provenance. In Ulster de Lacy's contemporary, John de Courcy, is responsible for the two most impressive Cistercian abbeys to be found in Northern Ireland. The first is **Inch Abbey** *(434)*, near Downpatrick, colonized by monks from Furness Abbey in Lancashire. The surviving choir of what was once a typically Cistercian cruciform church boasts seven tall early Gothic lancets, the central one in the east wall being twenty-three feet high. The other is **Grey Abbey** *(435)*, County Down, founded by de Courcy's wife, Affreca, daughter of the king of the Isle of Man. Lancets also pierce the walls of the choir of this very well-preserved church; the handsome west doorway is virtually intact; a portion of the chapter house in the east claustral range survives; and the frater (refectory) in the south range stands high.

In the Southeast two surviving religious houses owe their charters to William Marshal. **Tintern Abbey** *(283)*, County Wexford, was founded in about 1200 and colonized by Cistercian monks from the house of the same name in Wales. Here the thirteenth-century cruciform church forms the infrastructure of a post-Reformation private residence, but current restoration promises to reveal its original thirteenth-century features. **Graiguenamanagh (Duiske) Abbey** *(293)*, County Kilkenny, originally Cistercian, was twice restored in the nineteenth century for use as the local Roman Catholic parish church. The doorway to the baptistry and the narrow windows, some pointed, some round-headed, some trefoil-headed, all point to an early-thirteenth-century construction, as do the remains of the frater south of the church. Another Marshal foundation, though initiated by William the younger, was **St. John's Priory** *(295)* in the town of Kilkenny. This was an establishment of Augustinian canons. Though mostly demolished in the eighteenth century, the ruined choir remains, as does the rebuilt lady chapel to the south of it—now in use for Protestant (Church of Ireland) services.

Another of the early Anglo-Norman adventurers was Hervé de Montmorency, son-in-law of Maurice fitz Gerald and Strongbow's paternal uncle. Though described by Giraldus Cambrensis as thoroughly debauched and "addicted to venery from youth," he founded the largest of the Cistercian monasteries in Ireland before himself retiring to Canterbury to follow the monastic life, though not "to lay aside his evil disposition along with his layman's habit." His legacy to Ireland was **Dunbrody Abbey** *(280)*, County Wexford, today a stately and well-preserved ruin at the confluence of the rivers Suir and Barrow. Its Early English features include the fine tall lancets in the choir and the north wall with five pointed arches borne by square piers. Another pious benefactor was Geoffrey de Marisco, Archbishop John Comyn's nephew and himself justiciar of Ireland. He founded two Augustinian houses—**Kells Priory** *(292)* in County Kilkenny and **Killagha Abbey** *(333)*, County Kerry. The extensive remains of the former belong probably to the fourteenth or fifteenth century, but at the latter the lancet windows, doors, and niches of the abbey church are clearly of a thirteenth-century date.

Three more Augustinian houses and one Cistercian complete the list of early-thirteenth-century Anglo-Norman foundations whose ruins are still standing. William de Burgh was the patron of **Athassel Abbey** *(303)* in

County Tipperary. It is considered by the architectural historian Harold G. Leask to be "still the most impressive of the Augustinian achievements," especially with respect to its claustral remains, which are more extensive than most. Here the most distinctive thirteenth-century features are the five tall lancet windows in each of the opposite walls of the choir, the vaulted dorter (dormitory) in the east range of the cloister, and the fine doorway leading into the refectory in the south range. Alexander FitzHugh Roche was the founder of **Bridgetown Priory** *(321)* in County Cork. Today untended and overgrown, the ruins here are hard to interpret, but the lancet windows in both church and frater (refectory) are doubtless part of the original construction. **Ballybeg Priory** *(315)*, also in County Cork, was founded in 1229 or thereabouts by another Geraldine—Philip de Barry. Little remains of the east end, though the west wall displays two high lancets. In modern County Longford in the farthest reaches of the Anglo-Norman settlement in Meath, Richard de Tuit founded **Abbeylara Abbey** *(394)* in 1211—a Cistercian house close to his castle of Granard. Little remains here, however, of the early church except for the crossing.

Pious generosity among the great and powerful in late-twelfth- and early-thirteenth-century Ireland was not confined to the Anglo-Norman community. Native Irish kings and chieftains were equally lavish in their endowments, none more so than Donal Mór O'Brien, king of Thomond— already mentioned as patron of the cathedrals of Limerick, Killaloe, and Kilfenora. In 1180 King Donal brought to **Holy Cross Abbey** *(307)* in County Tipperary a band of Cistercians from Monasteranenagh in County Limerick. There they built a new monastery, complete with a church to house a supposed fragment of the True Cross that had somehow found its way to Ireland. The remnants of this building are now mostly embedded within, and concealed by, a drastic fifteenth-century reconstruction of the abbey. Still visible on the recently restored premises, however, are the west wall of the church with traces of the original lancet windows, portions of the nave, the rib vaulting in the choir and crossing, and the round-arched doorway leading from the east end of the church to the cloister-walk. Even less of the original construction remains at **Kilcooly Abbey** *(297)*, County Tipperary, another Cistercian foundation of the king of Thomond. Badly ravaged by armed men in 1444–45, it too was rebuilt before being allowed to fall to ruin after the Reformation. Donal MacGilapatrick, king of Ossory, is credited with bringing Cistercians from Baltinglass to establish **Jerpoint Abbey** *(297)* in County Kilkenny—today one of the finest and best preserved monastic ruins in Ireland. Though its tower dates to the fifteenth century, most of the church and the remaining parts of the cloister belong to the original period of construction in the late twelfth or early thirteenth century.

Farther west, in modern County Clare—the heart of the O'Brien territory—are four more abbeys founded by Donal Mór. The best preserved today is **Corcomroe Abbey** *(342)*, a Cistercian house founded in 1194. Here a fair amount survives of the thirteenth century construction—the rib vaulting and lancet windows of the choir, the chapel arches in both transepts, and the lancets in the west wall. **Clare Abbey** *(344)* was an Augustinian house, established in about 1189. As at Holy Cross, most of the present attractive ruins date to a fifteenth-century rebuilding. In an islet in the river Shannon **Canon Island Abbey** *(347)*, another Augustinian foundation of 1189, retains more of its early thirteenth-century origins, although the tower and claustral buildings date to the fifteenth. Still another of the king of Thomond's Augustinian establishments was **Killone Abbey** *(345)*—this one to house a community of nuns (canonesses). Very few Irish medieval nunneries have survived at all, so the beautifully situated lakeside ruins of this one have a special appeal. The round-headed windows in the east gable, the chevron-molded arches, and the Gothic wall shafts point to a late-twelfth- or early-thirteenth-century building.

North of the kingdom of Thomond, in Connacht, King Cathal Crovderg O'Connor was responsible for the establishment of two important monasteries whose remains are still to be seen. The first was **Knockmoy Abbey** *(416)*, County Galway, a Cistercian house founded in about 1190. Both church and claustral buildings are in a fair state of preservation. The choir is rib-vaulted; pointed arches lead to the transept chapels; windows are both round-headed and pointed. **Ballintubber Abbey** *(421)* in County Mayo is an Augustinian house dating from 1216—recently restored and again in use for Roman Catholic services. Here too the choir is vaulted, but most of the original windows are round-headed—another indication of a stylistic lag in this remote part of western Ireland.

A lesser Irish chieftain, Owen O'Heyne, is credited with building the Augustinian priory at **Kilmacduagh** *(409)*, County Galway, traditionally referred to as O'Heyne's Church. Here the best surviving features are the fine pair of narrow east windows and the decorated chancel arch. **Abbeyshrule Abbey** *(394)*, County Longford, was Cistercian, founded by the O'Farrels of the kingdom of Oriel and colonized from Mellifont. About all remaining here of the thirteenth-century construction are the tower and the small chapel, which was originally the choir. Much more survives at **Hore Abbey** *(303)* on the outskirts of Cashel, where Cistercians from Mellifont were brought in 1272 by Archbishop MacCarvill, one of the builders of nearby Cashel cathedral. Here, today, the ruins are substantial. The church retains a trio of lancets in the east wall, another pair in the transept gable, and single lancets elsewhere. Of the claustral remains (here, contrary to the usual Cistercian plan, north of the church), part of the chapter house survives, but not much else.

Hore Abbey was the last of the Cistercian houses to have been founded before the Reformation. Its establishment came at the end of a long period of travail within the order. From the beginning, native Irish monks had resisted the efforts of motherhouses on the Continent and in Britain to enforce an unwonted and unwanted conformity. As early as the 1140s the French monks who had joined the original community at Mellifont left in disgust over the poor discipline among their Irish brothers. St. Bernard found it difficult thereafter to find replacements. In 1217 monks from Clairvaux, on an official visit of inspection, were forcefully kept from entering Mellifont. At Jerpoint their appearance was greeted with a riot and at other abbeys with sullen obstructionism. This was the *conspiratio Mellifontis*—a widespread mutiny among the daughterhouses of Ireland's first Cistercian monastery. Ten years later the newly appointed Anglo-Norman abbot of Baltinglass was knocked off his horse and driven out of the abbey. Shortly thereafter the abbot of Citeaux complained to the pope of the "dissipation, dilapidation of property, conspiracies, rebellions, and frequent machinations of death" among all the order's houses in Ireland. Next year Stephen of Lexington, another visitor from Clairvaux, was set upon by robbers near Kilcooly and at Monasteranenagh found the monastery fortified against his arrival. But by the time Stephen left in 1228 he had succeeded in reimposing at least a modicum of control—chiefly by breaking up the Mellifont network and assigning the Irish abbeys to new motherhouses in Britain and Burgundy. Thereafter a fair degree of peace seems to have prevailed—enough so that in 1274 the Irish houses were restored to their former affiliations.

By this time, however, the Cistercian Order, and also apparently the Augustinian, were losing the vitality that had characterized the early days of the reformed monastic movement in Ireland. By the mid-thirteenth century, however, a new wave of religious enthusiasm was sweeping the country—one set into motion by the arrival of bands of mendicant friars. The first to come were the Dominicans, the "Black Friars" or "Friars Preachers," who appeared in Dublin and Drogheda in 1224. Franciscans (Friars Minor) followed in 1230 or 1231, settling first at Youghal and Cork. Carmelite Friars were in Ireland not later than 1272, and Augustinian Friars (the Order of Hermits of St. Augustine) established a house in Dublin in 1282. All four orders expanded, the first two phenomenally. By the end of the thirteenth century the Dominicans had an estimated twenty-four houses in Ireland; the Franciscans, thirty-one; the Carmelites, nine; and the Augustinians, four.

Unlike the Cistercians, who could be self-sustaining on the vast land grants with which they were endowed, the friars, being by definition mendicants, depended on the regular and continuous charity of the laity. Another difference was that, whereas the Cistercians sought seclusion from the world, and occupied themselves mostly with communal prayer and work, the friars thrust themselves into the world where they could best carry out their prime mission of preaching the Word of God. Both considerations naturally gave encouragement to the establishment of friaries in the more densely settled parts of Ireland, which, in effect, meant Anglo-Norman Ireland.

In ground plan the typical friary eventually resembled that of a Cistercian monastery, with the church adjoined by domestic buildings centered around a square cloister garth. There were, however, significant differences, especially in the early days of friary construction. Thirteenth-century friary churches, for example, tended to be long and narrow without transepts or at most with only one on the side opposite the cloister (actually a projecting wing rather than a proper transept since there was no crossing of the nave). The eastern half of the church (the choir or chancel) was reserved for the friars and was normally well illuminated, while the less well-fenestrated western half (the nave) was where the laymen gathered to be preached to. The cloister was, on average, smaller than its monastic counterpart and usually situated on the north side of the church. The reason for this location is obscure, although one can guess that, since the friars spent much of their time outside the friary, they did not share the monks' need for a sunny place to stroll. It is doubtful, however, that any of the thirteenth-century friaries had complete cloisters. Except for a sacristy and chapter house lying north of the choir, the domestic buildings of the earlier friaries were probably made of wood and not necessarily set out in ranges around a square. The many impressive claustral buildings and arcades to be seen today among Ireland's ruined friaries are all products of fifteenth-century rebuilding. Finally, in contradistinction to many Irish abbeys, the friaries are almost uniformly Gothic in style—either Early English or, if built in the fourteenth or fifteenth century, Decorated. The occasional round arch or round-headed windows are anachronisms—attributable to the idiosyncratic conservatism of some Irish masons and not to a pre-Gothic period of construction.

As in the case of the monasteries, any list of the patrons of thirteenth-century friaries reads in part like a roster of the great Anglo-Norman families. And although most of these places were rebuilt or greatly modified in the fourteenth and fifteenth centuries, they usually retain in their present form at least some typical thirteenth-century features.

Black Friars' Church *(295)* in Kilkenny, now serving a Roman Catholic parish, was founded in 1226 for Dominican friars by William Marshal the younger. The nave is of thirteenth-century construction, though the south wing, tower, and traceried windows are later additions. In the same town William's brother Richard was the patron of the **Franciscan Friary** *(295)*, established in 1232. Now within the grounds of a busy brewery, most of the scant remains belong to the fourteenth century, but that portion of the choir just east of the tower seems to be original. In a much better state of preservation is **Castledermot Friary** *(375)*, County Kildare, a Franciscan house founded by Walter de Riddlesford in 1247. It has twin lancets in the west wall and widely spaced lancets on the north side. The so-called **French Church** *(286)* in Waterford, with its fine set of triple lancets in the east wall and single lancets in the north, was originally a Franciscan friary founded in 1240 by Sir Hugh Purcell. **St. Mary's Priory** *(396)*, Drogheda, of which only a remnant now remains, was a house of Augustinian friars founded in the thirteenth century. David de Barry was the patron of **Buttevant Friary** *(315)*, County Cork, a Franciscan house established in 1251. Situated within the grounds of St. Mary's (Roman Catholic) Church, this is today a substantial ruin with a liberal placement of lancets, though some were reshaped at a later date. Also in County Cork is **Castlelyons Friary** *(320)*, a Carmelite foundation sponsored by John de Barry. Though founded in 1309, the fairly extensive ruins of church and cloister date to the fifteenth century. Walter de Burgh was the founder of **Lorrha Friary** *(414)* in County Tipperary, a Dominican house established in about 1269 and built soon thereafter, as indicated by the remaining lancet windows. **Kilmallock Friary** *(336)*, County Limerick, is a substantial ruin with high-standing and unusually well-cared-for remains of the nave, choir, central tower, transept, and claustral north range. The outstanding thirteenth-century feature here is the fine quintuple-lancet window in the east wall. This was a Dominican friary founded in 1291 by King Edward I himself. Thomas fitz Maurice fitz Raymond (FitzGerald), the Geraldine lord of Kerry, founded **Ardfert Friary** *(336)* for Franciscans in about 1253. Although tower and south wing belong to the fifteenth century, the long, slender rectangular nave and choir are distinctly Early English in style, with nine lancets in the south wall and five in the east.

Leinster and Munster were not the only areas of Ireland to be penetrated by friars in the thirteenth century. Although Ulster, for reasons unknown, was host to very few of their establishments, Connacht surprisingly sprouted a great many. And among their patrons were several of the Anglo-Norman adventurers who accompanied or followed Richard de Burgh's expedition in 1235 into that remote and underpopulated country. Maurice FitzGerald, second baron of Offaly, was one of these. To him de Burgh granted most of present County Sligo, where he built a castle around which the town of Sligo grew. Here came Dominican friars in 1252–53 to build **Sligo Friary** *(417)* under FitzGerald's patronage and protection. Although rebuilt and enlarged after a fire in 1414, the ruined friary still reveals many thirteenth-century features: the south wall of the choir with its row of eight lancet windows, the opposite blank north wall, the north wall of the nave with three pairs of shorter lancets, and some parts of the sacristy and chapter house. Another Anglo-Norman patron of the Dominicans was Meiler de Bermingham, who provided the land and funds for **Athenry Friary** *(404)*, County Galway, founded in 1241. Of the original church building, the north wall of the choir with its seven closely grouped lancets is the most distinctive part. **Claregalway Friary** *(408)*, also in County Galway, is a Franciscan establishment, founded before 1252 by John de Cogan. Though, like most friaries, it was later modified, its thirteenth-century origins are attested to by the lancets on both sides of the choir. **Loughrea Friary** *(412)*, a Carmelite house in County Galway, was founded at the end of the thirteenth century by Richard de Burgh, lord of Connacht and earl of Ulster. Here in the renovated church original lancets can still be seen in the south wall of the choir. **Rathfran Friary** *(421)*, a Dominican establishment on the shore of Killala Bay in County Mayo, was founded in 1274, although by whom is uncertain. The names of Stephen de Exeter, Sir Richard Dexter, and William de Burgh have all been suggested. Here the east window retains a trio of lancets—an unusual occurrence since in most friaries the plain narrow windows in the east end were replaced in the fifteenth century with wide traceried apertures. Also in County Mayo is **Strade Friary** *(421)*, originally Franciscan but later taken over by the Dominicans. Its founder was probably Jordan of Exeter and the date of foundation early in the thirteenth century. Again, most of the present ruins date to the fifteenth century, but the choir with six lancets in the north wall is of thirteenth-century provenance.

Although clearly in the majority, Anglo-Normans were not alone in their generosity to the first two generations of Irish friars. Also among their patrons, a few distinctly Irish names stand out. Archbishop David O'Kelly of Cashel, for example, founded **St. Dominic's Friary** *(302)* in 1243 at the foot of the Rock in his archiepiscopal city. The nine regularly spaced lancets in the south wall of the choir attest to the early origins of the church, which was rebuilt after 1480 by Archbishop John Cantwell. **Nenagh Friary** *(305)*, at the other (western) side of County Tipperary, was also Dominican—founded sometime before 1268, probably by Donal O'Kennedy, bishop of Killaloe. In the north wall of the ruined choir are eleven lancets, the longest row in Ireland. A group of three remains in the east wall. The choir at **Timoleague Friary** *(316)*, County Cork, also dates to the thirteenth century. It was founded for Franciscans, probably by MacCarthy Reagh, lord of Carbery, though possibly by William de Barry. Although extended and rebuilt several times, the choir of the church belongs to the thirteenth century. Donough Cairbreach O'Brien, king of Thomond, established **Moor Abbey** *(308)* for Franciscan friars early in the thirteenth century, although the present scant ruins near Galbally, County Limerick, date to a much later (fifteenth-century) rebuilding. Both choir and nave survive at **Roscommon Friary** *(403)*, a Dominican house founded in 1253 by Felim O'Connor, king of Connacht. Here only the lancets in the south wall of the nave attest to the original building. Finally, the noblest survivor of the Franciscan houses in Ireland is undoubtedly **Ennis Friary** *(344)*, County Clare, founded probably before 1242 by Donough Cairbreach O'Brien, king of Thomond. The more elegant features of this building belong to the fifteenth century, but to the earlier period of construction can be assigned the choir with its fine high lancets in the east and south walls.

Whatever the national origins of their patrons, most friaries in the first half century after the arrival of their inhabitants in Ireland seem to have been free of strife between Anglo-Normans and Gaelic Irish. By the close of the thirteenth century, however, any such "interracial" harmony was disappearing. In 1291 at a meeting of the provincial chapter of the Franciscans at Cork, open warfare broke out between Irish and English friars, and many on both sides were killed or wounded. The incident, though exceptional in its violence, was to prove an unhappy harbinger of a widespread split within the Church that grew more pronounced in the fourteenth century.

THE LATER MIDDLE AGES: 1315–1534

It was undoubtedly Edward Bruce's invasion that brought the long-festering sore of Anglo-Gaelic hostility to a head, among both secular and regular clergy. The government in Dublin became convinced that native Irish prelates and friars were openly abetting the Scottish invader, and in 1316 King Edward II sent a mission to Pope John XXII at Avignon to demand papal action against such rebellious activities. From the other side Pope John received even more bitter complaints against the Anglo-Irish clergy. Brian O'Neill's Remonstrance of 1317 charged them with preaching the pernicious doctrine that it was no sin to kill an Irishman. Specifically O'Neill denounced the Cistercians of Abbeylara for hypocritically singing evening Vespers after spending the day hunting the neighboring Irish with spears. As the Gaelic revival spread, the government grew especially nervous about the danger of clerical sedition within the Anglo-Irish colony. Hence the clause in the Statute of Kilkenny (1366) barring native Irish from admission into the chapter of any cathedral or collegiate church or from entering any religious house within the English community.

Civil war within the Church, however, did not take place, owing largely to the gradual geographic segregation of the Gaelic and Anglo-Irish clergy. By the end of the fourteenth century a fairly clear line of demarcation was forming between the Anglo-Irish colony within the Pale and the Gaelic Irish beyond it. For the most part both the diocesan Church and the religious houses (monasteries and friaries) mirrored this partition. In the Dublin archdiocese, which included most of the Pale, there were, for example, no native Irish bishops; in Tuam, no English or Anglo-Irish. In the archdiocese of Cashel, where the Butler family was predominant but not all-powerful, two of the nine dioceses had Gaelic Irish bishops. The province of the primate (the archbishop of Armagh) was split between the Pale and the Gaelic Irish area; consequently half the dioceses normally had Gaelic bishops, the other half English or Anglo-Irish. The English or Anglo-Irish archbishops themselves lived within the Pale—at **Termonfeckin Castle** *(397)*, County Louth; the Gaelic deans of the chapter had their residence on the grounds of the cathedral at Armagh beyond the Pale. The same division along national lines took place among the monasteries. Mellifont, for example, seedbed of Gaelic resistance to English influence in the thirteenth century, became, in the fourteenth, thoroughly anglicized because of its location within the Pale. Conversely, Abbeylara, cited in 1317 by Brian O'Neill for its maltreatment of the native Irish, was, by mid-century, completely Gaelic and under the thumb of the O'Farrell dynasty of Oriel.

Within the Pale, of course, Gaelic Irish clergymen were banned by the Statute of Kilkenny from practicing their profession. Their exclusion, to be sure, was not total, since entrance could be, and frequently was, obtained by special license. Outside the Pale, the gaelicization of the Church was reinforced by a revival (if it had ever died out) of the hereditary principle of succession to bishoprics, deanships, abbacies, and priorships. Vows of celibacy were generally ignored; marriage and concubinage were common among both priests and monks; sons succeeded fathers in the diocesan Church and the religious houses. Cormac MacDavid, for example, followed his father as abbot of Boyle; Dermot O'Heffernan, abbot of Holy Cross in the mid–fifteenth century, was the son of the abbot of the Cistercian monastery of Inishlounaght. In the diocese of Clogher (County Fermanagh) the Maguires and the MacCawells had a virtual monopoly of all important church offices. Murtough O'Kelly, bishop of Clonfert and archbishop of Tuam, was succeeded in both positions by one son, while another became abbot of Knockmoy.

Architecturally, however, the division of the Irish Church along "racial" lines appears to have made little difference. The fourteenth century marks the appearance in Ireland of the Decorated style of Gothic architecture—imported from England, where it had begun to come into fashion around 1250. The most obvious distinction between Decorated and Early English architecture lies in the width and design of the windows. Wide apertures under a wide-angled pointed arch took the place of narrow lancets. Moreover the ample space within the window frames was filled at the top, under the arch, with tracery—narrow strips of stone worked into a variety of designs. Irish tracery took three forms: (1) switch-line tracery (the simplest) in which the mullions (vertical stone bars separating panes of glass) curved at the top and intersected one another; (2) geometric or reticulated tracery in which the window area under the arch was honeycombed with geometric patterns of circles, diamonds, lozenges, trefoils, quatrefoils, and the like; and (3) curvilinear or flamboyant tracery in which the bars of stonework make patterns of flowing curves and the arch is sometimes ogee-shaped, that is, formed of a double curve, one convex, the other concave.

There are three good examples of Irish Decorated churches built in the fourteenth century. First is the **Adare Augustinian Friary** *(334)*, County Limerick, founded by John fitz Thomas (FitzGerald), first earl of Kildare, and now in use as the Church of Ireland parish church. The five-light east window and the narrower windows in the south and west walls are prime examples of switch-line tracery. In the now ruined church of **St. Mary's** *(372)*, Howth, County Dublin, most of the tracery is gone, but the twin-lighted ogee-arched west window is typically Decorated in style. **St. Nicholas Church** *(406)* in Galway—now used for Church of Ireland services—is the second largest parish church in Ireland of medieval foundation. Although enlarged in the fifteenth and sixteenth centuries, it retains its fourteenth-century chancel and switch-line east window, and worked into the south window are some fine geometric and curvilinear patterns.

Not many more than these three in all of Ireland can be attributed to the fourteenth century. Recovery from the devastation caused by Edward Bruce was slow. His invasion was followed in 1348–49 by the first outbreak of the Black Death, during which perhaps as much as a third of the country's population died. The congested religious houses, like the urban centers of population, suffered heavily. Those of the Cistercian Order never recovered. Their lay brothers succumbed or departed, leaving their broad acres uncultivated and their flocks of sheep untended. Since there was no longer any use for the west range of domestic buildings, these were allowed to fall into decay. Hence their almost total absence from the present scene among Ireland's many Cistercian ruins. (The west range at **Holy Cross Abbey** *[307]*, County Tipperary, is a notable exception.) The chapters of choir monks too diminished in size: by the time of Henry VIII's dissolution of the monasteries, Mellifont had only fourteen monks in residence; Jerpoint, five; Kilcooly and Hore, two. At some of the monasteries one response to the departure of the lay brothers was to wall off the now redundant western part of the nave and sometimes even the transepts. This was done, for example, at **Inch Abbey** *(434)*, County Down; **Corcomroe Abbey** *(342)*, County Clare; and **Monasteranenagh Abbey** *(336)*, County Limerick, where parts of the transverse walls can still be seen. (A similar wall can be seen at the Augustinian **Bridgetown Priory** *[321]* in County Cork.) Further structural changes ensued as the number of resident monks diminished. Dormitories were deserted and monastic buildings converted into living apartments with fireplaces and other amenities for those who remained in residence. This is still apparent at **Knockmoy Abbey** *(416)*, County Galway, and at the **Abbeys** of **Holy Cross** *(307)* and **Kilcooly** *(297)*, County Tipperary.

With the disappearance of their lay brothers and the dwindling of their monastic chapters, most Cistercian houses found it impossible to continue the profitable economic exploitation of their vast estates. Hence many rented out large portions, thus deriving income. In some monasteries the abbots were replaced by "commendators"—some of them clerics, others laymen—who had gone to Rome to secure papal appointments. "Rome trotters" they were called, and their primary interest was personal financial gain derived from the monastic revenues they were authorized to control. Yet some of the profits were plowed back into the monasteries themselves. Hence the fifteenth century witnessed a widespread revival of rebuilding and restoration, the results of which are happily still visible today. This mostly took the form of adding tall belfry towers to the churches, restructuring their choirs, substituting wide Decorated windows for the original narrow lancets, and remodelling the cloisters.

All the above and more took place at **Holy Cross Abbey** *(307)*, County Tipperary, which was again restored in the twentieth century to become the most perfect example of a Cistercian monastery in Ireland. At nearby **Kilcooly Abbey** *(297)* a new tower was added and a splendid flamboyant traceried window in the east end. **Mellifont Abbey** *(397)*, County Louth, got a new chapter house, and **Bective Abbey** *(391)*, County Meath, got a new cloister. High belfry towers were built above the churches at **Jerpoint Abbey** *(297)*, County Kilkenny; **Dunbrody Abbey** *(280)* and **Tintern Abbey** *(283)*, County Wexford; **Hore Abbey** *(303)*, County Tipperary; and **Abbeylara Abbey** *(394)*, County Longford. Some of the Augustinian houses were likewise restored. At **Clontuskert Abbey** *(405)*, County Galway, an elaborate new Decorated doorway and a rood gallery between nave and chancel were installed. **Clare Abbey** *(344)*, County Clare, was embellished with a traceried east window and received a new tower and cloister. At **Fore Abbey** *(392)*, County Westmeath, the cloister was reduced in size, and castellated towers were built up above both the west end of the nave and the sacristy south of the choir. At **Kells Priory** *(292)*, County Kilkenny, there seems to have been considerable reconstruction either in the late fourteenth or the fifteenth century. Here are a square belfry tower over the crossing, another at the northwest angle of the church, and two walled enclosures with numerous mural turrets—all very military in appearance.

Many friaries and some parish churches also underwent significant structural changes—some as early as the fourteenth century, more in the fifteenth. These generally took the form of adding south wings (mistakenly called transepts) at right angles to the nave, inserting Decorated traceried windows, completing the claustral buildings around the garth, and raising belfry towers above the church. All the above was accomplished in the fifteenth century at **Sligo Friary** *(417)*, perhaps the best of the country's Dominican ruins. The splendid Franciscan **Ennis Friary** *(344)*, County Clare, underwent a thorough reconstruction during the same period. The reticulated window in the south aisle of **Kilmallock Friary** *(336)*, County Limerick, is probably of fifteenth-century provenance, as is the tower. **Magdalene Tower** *(396)* in Drogheda, County Louth, built in the fifteenth century, is the sole surviving portion of the first Dominican friary church in Ireland. The tower of **Black Friars' Church** *(295)* in Kilkenny is also a fifteenth-century addition. So are the belfry towers atop the Franciscan **Friaries** of **Timoleague** *(316)*, County Cork, and **Claregalway** *(408)*, County Galway, as well as the **French Church** *(286)* in Waterford City. **Skreen Church** *(386)* in County Meath, a fourteenth-century foundation, received its high tower in the fifteenth.

Nor did the fifteenth-century enthusiasm for ecclesiastical restoration and expansion stop here. Many of Ireland's cathedral churches were also rebuilt—some to the extent that their original Early English features are almost submerged by later additions in the Decorated style. A case in point is **St. Mary's Cathedral** *(338)*, Limerick, where the fifteenth-century choir and the two ranges of chapels on either side of the nave mask the cruciform ground plan and obscure the church's early Gothic features. (The famous misericords are also a fifteenth-century addition.) The massive tower over the west end of the nave of **Cashel Cathedral** *(301)*, County Tipperary, was built as a residence for the archbishop between 1406 and 1440. Coeval with it on the same site is the **Hall of the Vicars Choral** *(301)*. The south wing of **Ardfert Cathedral** *(326)*, County Kerry, is a fifteenth-century addition, as indicated by its wide windows. The north doorway at **Clonmacnoise Cathedral** *(382)*, County Offaly, is of the same vintage. So are the west wall at **Newtown Trim Cathedral** *(390)*, in County Meath, the chancel arch and sacristy of **Clonfert Cathedral** *(406)*, and the south doorway, west window, and transepts of **Kilmacduagh Cathedral** *(409)*, the last two in County Galway.

Renovation, rebuilding, and enlargement of existing churches and religious houses were not the sole occupations of Irish stonemasons in the fifteenth century. As indicated in the preceding chapter, new tower houses by the scores were rising from the ground. So were new parish and collegiate churches. Admittedly, at no time in the Middle Ages was Ireland to be as well endowed with small parish churches as England. Nor, as a rule, did Irish stonemasons, glaziers, and woodworkers match the consummate craftsmanship of their English counterparts. Stylistically, ecclesiastical buildings of the fifteenth and early sixteenth centuries were for the most part only marginally different from those of the last half of the fourteenth. That is to say, the Decorated style persisted, though with modifications. As already mentioned, Irish masons, especially those in the West, tended to conservatism and even anachronism. Hence ecclesiastical buildings of the later Middle Ages are likely to contain Romanesquelike features, especially round arches above windows and doorways. On the outside they occasionally assume a fortresslike appearance with stepped battlements in imitation of contemporary secular styles. "Irish Gothic of the late middle ages," to quote Brian de Breffny, is thus "unpredictable . . . [and] defies the normal categories of style, producing unusual combinations which are often refreshingly original."

Meanwhile England was witnessing the development and spread of a new style of Gothic architecture known as Perpendicular. The most characteristic feature here is the large window of rectangular panels of glass underneath a very flattened four-centered arch. Other features include rectangular wall panels, intricate fan vaulting, pinnacled towers, and arched flying buttresses around the outside of the building. The new fashion, however, made little headway in Ireland. In County Meath, to be sure, three parish churches have late Decorated features that some architectural historians label Perpendicular, although most of the characteristic elements of the contemporary English style are missing. These are **Killeen Church** *(386)*, **Dunsany Church** *(386)*, and **Rathmore Church** *(387)*. All were built by members of the Plunkett family; all are rectangular in ground plan (nave and chancel without transepts); and all have square corner turrets on the outside, wide (but not flattened) traceried windows, and pinnacled stonework within.

Other noteworthy fifteenth-century parish churches within the Pale are **Newcastle Church** *(374)*, County Dublin, and **Taghmon Church** *(393)*, County Westmeath. Both are distinguished by their fortresslike towers at the west end. Another example of this genre is **Lusk Tower** *(374)*, County Dublin, where an Early Christian round tower was incorporated into the structure of the western belfry of a fifteenth-century church that has since disappeared. Outside the Pale there is a dearth of fifteenth-century parish churches worth mentioning.

Also missing from Ireland, in any significant number, are collegiate churches, except for those like **St. Mary's Church** *(325)*, Youghal, and **St. Nicholas Church** *(406)*, Galway, which were awarded collegiate status after having been first built as parish churches. In the Middle Ages the term *college* normally referred to a permanent body of secular priests and choristers endowed to celebrate Mass in perpetuity on behalf of their patron and/or anyone else he might designate. The procedure was an insurance policy of sorts, intended primarily to ease the passage of the souls of the donor and his family through purgatory. Such a collegiate body might be assigned to a church already in use. Or a new church or chapel might be built for such purposes. In England collegiate foundations of this sort were common in the later Middle Ages. Not so in Ireland for reasons to be mentioned below. Two, however, are worth noting. The first is the now ruined **Slane College** *(388)*, County Meath, on the grounds of a contemporary Franciscan **Friary** founded in 1512 by Sir Christopher Fleming and his wife for four priests, four clerks, and four choristers. The second, and more significant because of its later associations, is Maynooth College, County Kildare, founded in 1521 by Gerald FitzGerald, the ninth earl of Kildare. The present **Maynooth (C of I) Parish Church** *(378)* stands on the site and probably incorporates portions of the original building.

It should be noted that in Ireland, unlike Britain, no collegiate foundation developed into a center of learning to form the nucleus of a university. Three times efforts were made to form such an institution—in Dublin in 1320 and again in 1358, then in Drogheda in 1465. All three enterprises failed for want of funds.

The apparent reluctance of Irish patrons to invest in collegiate foundations can be explained, at least in part, by the continued, and even growing, popularity of the friars. Between 1400 and 1508 were founded ninety new houses of friars. Not only was the number large, but all three of the major orders underwent a reform process that seems to have contributed signally to the vitality of these religious establishments. This was the "Observant" movement, so called because of its dedication to a stricter observance of the Rule, whether Dominican, Augustinian, or Franciscan. In the case of the first two the Observants remained within the body of the parent order. But the Franciscans in 1517 split into two separate Orders of Minors Conventual and Minors Observant, with the latter gradually taking over the majority of Franciscan houses, old and new. The great strength of the friaries, of no matter what order, rested in their close and continuous contacts with the laity. Even tighter bonds were forged in the fifteenth century by the foundation of the Franciscan Third Order Regular, generally referred to as Tertiary brothers. These were laymen, bound by oaths of poverty, chastity, and obedience, living in separate communities but subject to visitation and correction by Conventual Franciscans. They occupied themselves primarily with pastoral work in the surrounding parishes and with teaching in the boys' schools attached to the monasteries. They were responsible for the construction of about forty of the religious houses built in the late fifteenth and early sixteenth centuries.

Unlike the establishments of the fourteenth century, which tended to concentrate in the more heavily settled areas under Anglo-Irish control, the great preponderance of the new houses was in Gaelic Ireland, where they enjoyed the patronage of numerous Irish chieftains and the favor of the population at large. Architecturally the Decorated style prevailed, with occasional lapses into Romanesque anachronism. As in the past, friary churches tended to be long and narrow, divided into nave and choir. Frequently, however, a south wing was now added to accommodate the growing number of devout laity; also a complete set of claustral buildings centered around the garth, usually lying north of the church. One distinctive feature of a number of friary cloisters of this period was the "integrated" ambulatory or cloister-walk that formed part of the ground floor of the claustral buildings, separated from the garth only by an open arcade. Except for this feature, plus the northern orientation of the cloister and its relatively small size, the ground plan of the typical fifteenth- to sixteenth-century Irish friary mostly duplicated the standard Cistercian arrangement.

The greatest concentration of these houses was in Connacht. Two were founded by the O'Maddens of County Galway—**Portumna Friary** *(413)* for Dominicans and **Meelick Friary** *(415)* for Franciscans. The former is a substantial ruin; the latter is one of the few medieval churches still in use for Catholic services. **Kilconnell Friary** *(405)* and **Dunmore Friary** *(406)*, also in County Galway, were founded respectively by William O'Kelly in 1414 and Walter de Bermingham in 1425. The former is Franciscan and has a fine tower and a series of tomb niches with good Decorated Gothic tracery; of the latter Augustinian establishment, nothing remains but the simple ruined nave-and-chancel church. There are three surviving houses owing their existence to the patronage of members of the Burke family. **Ross Errilly Friary** *(410)*, County Galway, was a Franciscan Observant establishment and is the largest and best preserved of all their houses, having an extra courtyard north of the cloister. Dominican **Burrishoole Friary** *(423)*, on the shore of Clew Bay in County Mayo, is more ruinous. **Moyne Friary** *(420)*, another house of Observant Franciscans, north of Ballina, County Mayo, is extensive and is distinguished by its large chapel lying south of the nave, which it exceeds in size. Not far away, near the mouth of the river Moy, is **Rosserk Friary** *(420)*, built in the mid–fifteenth century for Franciscan Tertiaries and today one of the best preserved of all friary ruins in Ireland. Farther south in County Mayo, on the southern shore of Westport Bay are the remains (church only) of **Murrisk Friary** *(424)*, an Augustinian house founded by Hugh O'Malley. Probably the last of the friaries to have been established before Henry VIII's suppression of the religious houses was **Creevelea Friary** *(416)*, County Leitrim, a Franciscan house founded in 1508 by Owen O'Rourke, where the ruins of both church and cloister are substantial.

Farther north, in sparsely populated Ulster, the friaries thin out. The best of today's ruins is **Donegal Friary** *(426)*, a Franciscan Observant house founded by Red Hugh O'Donnell, his mother, Nuala O'Connor, and his wife, Nuala O'Brien. Though quite fragmentary, this lovely site overlooking the headwaters of Donegal Bay is better tended than most. **Rathmullan Friary** *(429)*, on the Donegal shore of Lough Swilly, is even more ruinous. This was a Carmelite house founded by Owen Roe MacSweeney in 1516 and converted a century later into a residence for the Protestant bishop, Andrew Knox. East of here, in County Antrim, is **Bonamargy Friary** *(453)*, the substantial ruin of a Franciscan house of Tertiary brothers.

In those parts of Munster dominated by Gaelic chiefs in the fifteenth century, the Franciscans seem to have been the most favored Order. Cormac MacCarthy brought them to **Kilcrea Friary** *(319)*, County Cork, where their church is still a high-standing ruin, though the claustral remains are missing. **Sherkin Island Friary** *(314)*, also in County Cork, was a Franciscan Observant house, founded by one of the O'Driscoll chiefs; it is somewhat smaller in size and also lacks any sign of the original cloister. Another establishment of the same order is **Muckross Friary** *(332)* near Killarney, County Kerry, founded by Donal MacCarthy. This is today a splendid and well-tended ruin, with both church and cloister in excellent condition. Much less substantial are the remains of **Lislaughtin Friary** *(327)* near Ballylongford, County Kerry—a Franciscan house founded by O'Connor Kerry. More impressive are the ruins of **Quin Friary** *(348)*, County Clare, a Franciscan house built by Macon MacNamara on the ruins of a thirteenth-century castle of the Anglo-Irish de Clares, who had been evicted from Ireland after the Battle of Dysert O'Dea.

Unlike the de Clares, the great Anglo-Irish families of FitzGerald and Butler still held their own in the south of Ireland in spite of the Gaelic revival. To them can be attributed the establishment of at least three important friaries. James Butler, father of a later earl of Ormond, brought members of the Order of Hermits of St. Augustine (Augustinian friars) to **Callan Friary** *(291)*, County Kilkenny, in 1462. Today only their ruined church survives. Much more remains of both church and cloister at **Askeaton Friary** *(335)*, County Limerick, a Franciscan establishment founded by James FitzGerald, sixth earl of Desmond. Finally, Thomas FitzGerald, seventh earl of Kildare, established for Observants the **Adare Franciscan Friary** *(334)*, County Limerick. It is now a romantic ruin situated on the grounds of the local golf club. Like the others mentioned above, it is a testament in stone to the durability of the religious reforms brought to Ireland by the friars of the later Middle Ages.

According to one observer writing in 1515, "There is no archbishop, no bishop, abbot nor prior, parson nor vicar, nor any other person of the Church, high or low, great or small, English or Irish, that is accustomed to preach the Word of God, saving the poor friars beggars . . . ." The indictment is probably overdrawn, but only to a degree. As indicated above, organized religion had sadly deteriorated by the early sixteenth century. The ancient monastic orders had been depleted, their lands rented out, their houses taken over by wealthy laymen, their Rules forsaken, their services neglected. The diocesan Church was split between Gaelic Irish and Anglo-Irish. Absenteeism was rife within the higher ranks of the prelacy. Even some of the cathedrals (Clonmacnoise and Armagh specifically) were already in ruins. Yet the winds of the Protestant Reformation blew lightly if at all on Ireland. And despite the efforts of three English monarchs in the sixteenth century to impose a new order on the Irish Church, the ancient faith persisted. For this the friars, and especially the reformed orders, bear at least a measure of responsibility.

Chapter Five

Tudor and Stuart Ireland: 1534–1691

THE TUDOR RELIGIOUS SETTLEMENT

Shortly after he renounced his allegiance to the king of England in June 1534, Thomas FitzGerald (Silken Thomas) sent envoys to both Emperor Charles V and the pope seeking their assistance in the name of the Roman Catholic faith. He and his followers, the "Geraldine league," claimed to have taken up arms in support of the papacy against a heretical king. Nothing came of the appeal, to be sure, and in any case the religious issue was not a paramount cause of the rebellion. But this was the first time that relations between England and Ireland would bear the imprint of the deep schism that was dividing Christendom into two warring camps, Catholic and Protestant. It was not to be the last.

As of 1534, Henry VIII's "heresy" consisted chiefly of having divorced his first wife, Catherine of Aragon, despite papal disapproval; of having repudiated papal jurisdiction in England; and of having had himself declared by the English parliament to be "Supreme Head of the Church of England." In 1536 and 1537 the Irish parliament followed suit. Henry was declared "the only supreme head on earth of the whole Church of Ireland"; the king's marriage to Catherine of Aragon was rendered null and void; the children of his second marriage to Anne Boleyn and then of his third marriage to Jane Seymour were successively legitimated; and an oath of supremacy, renouncing papal authority, was required of all officeholders, clergymen, and heirs taking possession of their fathers' estates.

The Church of Ireland thus established, however, was by no means Protestant in doctrine. True, the newly appointed Archbishop of Dublin, George Browne, made an effort to introduce minimal liturgical reforms: the pope's name was expunged from the books of ritual; English versions of the Pater Noster, the Credo, the Ave Maria, and the Ten Commandments were circulated among the clergy; a few venerated relics were burned and a few churches deprived of their statues. But even Browne, the most radical among Ireland's higher clergy, drew up short after the passage by the English parliament in May 1539 of the Act of Six Articles, which reaffirmed most of the articles of faith of the old religion. The Irish Church, though no longer affiliated with Rome, remained essentially Catholic. Not until the accession of the boy-king Edward VI to the throne in 1547 did Protestantism finally come to Ireland.

Beginning in Wittenberg in 1517 with Martin Luther's denunciation of the papal practice of selling indulgences (blanket exemptions from penances required of confessed sinners), the Protestant Reformation had rapidly developed into a total rejection of Roman Catholicism and had rapidly spread throughout central and northwestern Europe and into England and Scotland. The main theological foundation of Protestantism was the doctrine of "justification by faith," which postulated that sinful man might be saved from eternal perdition only by the grace of God; that the mediation of the Church of Rome—its Masses, prayers for the dead, auricular confession, penances, and indeed most of the functions performed by its clergy—were supererogatory. Not by such "works" was man to achieve salvation, nor by his own free will, but by God's grace alone, bestowed on the faithful. Anathema to Protestant theologians was the priestly claim of transmuting the bread and wine into the real body and blood of Christ, in accordance with the Roman doctrine of transubstantiation. In place of this sacrament of the Mass the Protestants substituted the rite of Communion in which the laity, as well as the clergy, partook of both the bread and wine as merely commemorative of the Last Supper. Gone also were such Romish practices as prayers for souls in purgatory, the adoration of the Virgin Mary and of the saints, the veneration of sacred objects, pilgrimages to enshrined holy relics, and even the wearing of ornate vestments by ordained priests. None of the above, according to Protestant doctrine, was sanctioned by the Scriptures, and they alone stood as the ultimate authority for the true Christian believer. Hence it was imperative that Holy Writ be translated into the vernacular for all to read. And the primary role of the clergy was changed from that of mediation to that of preaching and interpreting the Bible and of preparing the laity to receive the free gift of God's grace. Otherwise, in the true Church there was no clear distinction between clergy and laity; it was a priesthood of all believers.

In the brief reign of Edward VI these were the changes that Thomas Cranmer, archbishop of Canterbury, imposed on the Church of England, and George Browne, with less success, tried to impose on the Church of Ireland. But the succession to the throne in 1553 of Edward's eldest sister, Mary, brought an abrupt end to the experiment. Daughter of Catherine of Aragon and wife of King Philip II of Spain, Mary Tudor was passionately devoted to the Catholic faith. The English and Irish acts of supremacy were repealed, and in both countries the old religion was restored. In Ireland, where the Edwardian Reformation had hardly taken root, the restoration proceeded smoothly, and there was no burning of Protestant martyrs as in

England. Even Archbishop Browne reconverted to Catholicism, though he lost the see of Dublin because he had meanwhile married and sired a large brood of children. (It had not been unusual for Irish bishops to produce offspring, but clerical marriage was forbidden by canon law.) Then Queen Mary in turn died after a reign of only five years, leaving the throne to her Protestant sister, Elizabeth.

Now at last the Reformation gathered momentum, and Ireland was no longer to be spared the official establishment of a Protestant Church. Again following the English lead, the Irish parliament in 1560 passed the Act of Supremacy declaring Elizabeth to be the "supreme governor" of the Church of Ireland, and an oath recognizing her supremacy was required of all clergymen, officeholders, judges, mayors, members of universities (still nonexistent in Ireland), and minors before coming into their inheritance. The Act of Uniformity reinstated Archbishop Cranmer's Book of Common Prayer with minor revisions and required its use at all church services. Attendance at such services was mandatory. Refusal (recusancy) to do so was punishable by fine for each absence.

Yet outside of Dublin and some of the coastal cities, plus parts of the Pale and the territories of the earls of Ormond, the Church of Ireland did not flourish. The queen was no zealot, and nonconformity or occasional conformity was tolerated. Recusancy fines were collected only sporadically. Though the medieval churches were expropriated by the Protestant Church of Ireland, many were already in a state of disrepair, and they deteriorated further for lack of funds. The income from tithes on which the resident Protestant clergy depended was depleted. Largely for these reasons, English-speaking parish priests were hard to find. Gaelic-speaking clergymen, even had many been willing to accept the posts, were unsuitable since the Book of Common Prayer had not been translated into Irish, nor had the Bible itself until a Gaelic version of the New Testament appeared in 1603. To make up for the dearth of qualified clergymen the queen established **Trinity College** *(352)*, founded in Dublin in 1592 and opened for students in 1594. Though there were originally some Catholics among its students, the college was a Protestant foundation, intended primarily as a source of trained personnel for the established Church of Ireland. The institution survived but failed to provide the desired catalyst for the spread of the reformed religion.

Meanwhile the disestablished Church of Rome underwent a remarkable recovery. Conservative Ireland had from the beginning offered barren ground for the seeds of religious reformation. Unlike England or Scotland, the country had no medieval universities where humanism flourished and new and radical ideas might find receptive audiences. Nor was there any strong tradition of anticlericalism. Partly owing to the diligence and dedication of the Observant friars, the laity in general felt a strong attachment to their Church. And these dedicated clerics continued to preach illegally and perform the other pastoral duties of their profession, especially in Gaelic Ireland. Even the more visible and therefore more vulnerable diocesan Church survived, at least in form. After 1560 Rome appointed several bishops to vacant sees in Ireland. Richard Creagh served as the Catholic archbishop of Armagh until his arrest and imprisonment in the Tower of London. He and the Limerick-born Jesuit David Wolfe (also eventually imprisoned) were named papal legates. Following the meetings of the Council of Trent between 1545 and 1563, the Church of Rome undertook an institutional housecleaning, eliminated some of the more flagrant abuses with which it had been charged, tightened its internal discipline, and opened new seminaries for the training of priests and missionaries. Now began the exodus of young men of prominent Irish families to the Continent to be trained as priests and to be returned to serve in that capacity in their native land. The Church militant of the Catholic Counter-Reformation was on the march. Nowhere was it to find a more advantageous battleground than Ireland.

Yet if the Protestant government of England failed to seduce the souls of any great number of the Irish, it did manage to lay hold of much of the property of the Catholic Church. Again following the English precedent, the Irish parliament in 1536–37 ordered the suppression of the country's monasteries and nunneries and the confiscation of their lands and buildings. In 1539–40 the friaries were added to the list. By the end of the reign of Henry VIII, about 140 monasteries and nunneries and about eighty friaries (roughly 55 and 40 percent respectively) had been suppressed, mostly in the Pale, County Wexford, the Butler territories, and the seaport towns. Progress in Munster, Connacht, and Ulster was much slower and not even quite completed at the end of Elizabeth's reign. In spite of her ardent Catholicism, Queen Mary made no effort to reverse the process.

The financial rewards to the Crown were disappointing, partly because of the slow progress of the various commissions appointed to carry out the sequestration and partly because so much monastic land had already been alienated to neighboring landowners before the Reformation. Where the Crown did succeed in establishing ownership, it normally sold or leased the properties to wealthy laymen who mostly fell into three categories: (1) English officials in Ireland (the so-called New English), especially members of the lord deputy's entourage; (2) established Anglo-Irish families (henceforth referred to as the Old English), such as the Butlers and the FitzGeralds of Desmond; and, though rarely, (3) favored Gaelic Irish lords, as in the case of the O'Briens of Thomond.

In this redistribution of monastic property the contrast with England is marked. There the Crown's disposition of the rich lands of the religious houses created a new class of landed gentry augmented by town merchants anxious to achieve the social status attached to the possession of rural estates. In Ireland no such social revolution occurred in the countryside. A few of the religious houses, to be sure, were converted to residential uses by the new owners or lessors. Queen Elizabeth's deputy governor, Lord Leonard Grey, took over **St. Mary's Abbey** *(368)* on the outskirts of Dublin as his official residence, though there is now nothing left of the buildings he occupied. **Mellifont** *(397)* went to the vice treasurer, William Brabazon, but was soon transferred to the Moore family, which erected the castellated house (since gone) where the earl of Tyrone later capitulated to Lord Mountjoy (see below). Another New English official, Thomas Agard, collector of the Dublin mint, fashioned a fortified residence out of the tower and cloister court of **Bective Abbey** *(391)*—still visible among today's ruins. An English soldier, Sir Osborne Etchingham (or possibly his son Edward), built a country house on top of the south transept chapels of **Dunbrody Abbey** *(280)*. **Tintern Abbey** *(283)* went to Sir Anthony Colclough, a government official who reconstructed the chancel into a manor house. The Nugent family (Old English) converted the domestic buildings of **Fore Abbey** *(392)* for residential purposes. **Kilcooly Abbey** *(297)* and **Hore Abbey** *(303)* were put to similar uses.

As for the bulk of the postdissolution religious houses, their fate is unclear. **Holy Cross** *(307)* and two other abbeys (Abington and Newry) became secular colleges. **Grey Abbey** *(435)*, **Baltinglass** *(308)*, and **Graiguenamanagh** *(293)* were eventually converted to parish churches. Probably many others were similarly disposed of, sometimes with the former monks serving as curates. On the whole, monks and nuns were treated considerately. It is known that the members of at least thirty-nine monasteries and six nunneries received lifetime pensions, some still being paid in the reign of Queen Elizabeth. It was not so with the mendicant friars. Where possible, they were simply evicted, though many later returned under the protection of the landlords to whom their houses had been let. In any case they seem to have remained active in the performance of their pastoral duties. By the governments in both London and Dublin they were anathematized above all others, except possibly the Jesuits, as the most dangerous of the pope's subversive agents.

THE TUDOR "CONQUEST" OF IRELAND

If the Tudor monarchs failed to convert the mass of their Irish subjects to the reformed religion, the same cannot be said of their efforts to extend and strengthen their temporal sway over Ireland. In June 1541 the Dublin parliament willingly agreed to changing Henry VIII's title from "lord of Ireland" to "king of Ireland." This constitutional amendment served a triple purpose: (1) it invalidated the theory that the lordship established by King Henry II for Prince John derived its sanction from the papal bull *Laudabiliter*; (2) it presumably would impress the sixty-odd native chiefs with the overpowering majesty of the English monarch; and (3) it symbolized the government's intent to remove the *de facto* medieval distinction between the Anglo-Irish colony and Gaelic Ireland by accepting the Irish as subjects and to assume responsibility for governing the entire island as a political unit.

Accordingly the lord deputy, Anthony St. Leger, began the process of introducing throughout Gaelic Ireland the English system of land tenure, based on the feudal principle that all land was held directly or indirectly of the king, subject to payment of rents and/or military service, and that the succession to all such lands would be determined by primogeniture. (King Henry II and King John had tried to accomplish the same thing, but their successors had failed to follow through.) Historians have called St. Leger's policy "surrender and regrant." The agreements he negotiated with about thirty Gaelic chieftains and some of the "degenerate" Anglo-Norman lords included their submission to the king and recognition of his title to their lands; regrant of these lands by the king, in some cases with titles of nobility and the right to be summoned to the Irish house of lords; establishment of the law of primogeniture in determining rights of inheritance; military aid to the king and his deputy in exchange for an implied promise of a royal guarantee of the security of tenure; and renunciation of the papacy and acknowledgment of the king's supremacy over the Church. Pursuant to these agreements a few of the greater Irish chieftains received patents of nobility—notably Conn O'Neill, who became earl of Tyrone, and Murrough O'Brien, who became earl of Thomond. Other, lesser chieftains were made barons or knights.

Conciliatory as it was, the policy of surrender and regrant failed to bring permanent peace to Gaelic Ireland. In the reign of Edward VI the Pale itself came under attack at the hands of the O'Mores and the O'Connors Faly. The Dublin government retaliated by garrisoning soldiers in the rebel territories of Leix and Offaly. Under Queen Mary permanent forts were set up at Maryborough and Philipstown (now Portlaoise and Daingean), and the region was shired into Queen's County and King's County (now County Leix and County Offaly). The native Irish were ordered to remove themselves well to the west of the two forts, and colonies of "Englishmen born in England or Ireland" were to be planted in the lands thus vacated. Thus was born the threefold policy of dealing with recalcitrant natives: forceful repression, evacuation, and replacement by English-speaking subjects. It was to be the dominant policy of the English government in Ireland for the next century and a half.

Lest it be thought, however, that sheer love of conquest was the sole motive for England's treatment of Ireland, it should be pointed out that there were sound strategic reasons for her prolonged effort to force the Irish into submission. During the entire reign of Queen Elizabeth, Protestant England was engaged in intermittent warfare with Catholic Spain. Ireland was the obvious back door through which the Spanish king might invade England or at least engage her armies in an environment friendly to himself. "He that will England win, let him in Ireland begin," said the Jesuit David Wolfe to King Philip II, quoting a well-known jingle. And Spanish opportunities were greatly enhanced by the resistance of the Irish to the Protestant Reformation. A war against England was a war against heresy. In 1570 Pope Gregory XIII made this proposition unmistakably clear in his bull *Regnans in Excelsis* excommunicating the "pretended" Queen Elizabeth and calling on the faithful to withhold their allegiance from her. Small wonder that the monarch and her government tended to equate Catholicism with treason and to regard most of Catholic Ireland as potentially, if not actively, subversive.

Also, to the queen and many of her contemporaries, Ireland presented itself as a likely field for colonial expansion. The famous Elizabethan sea dogs and adventurers were fired alike by hatred of Spain, a militant Protestantism, and a lust for the alleged riches of the underdeveloped regions of the earth. Ireland was not the Indies, but it was close at hand. It is significant that several of the names associated with the early English exploration and settlement of North America served their apprenticeship, so to speak, in Ireland. Among them were Sir Francis Drake, who explored the coast of California en route to the Orient; Sir Richard Grenville, who visited Virginia with a view to establishing a colony there; Sir Humphrey Gilbert, who made two trips to Canada in search of the legendary Northwest Passage; and Gilbert's half brother Sir Walter Raleigh, who founded the first English colony in North America on Roanoke Island.

Munster was the scene of the first Elizabethan attempts at colonization. Grenville and Gilbert were both involved in settling at least 106 Englishmen at Kerrycurrihy on the west Cork coast. Another adventurer was Sir Peter Carew, who laid claim to lands in Counties Cork, Kerry, and Waterford, as well as Meath and Carlow, on the dubious legal basis of his descent from one of the original Norman-Welsh invaders. Both enterprises threatened the security of the region's leading landholders, the MacCarthys, the Butlers, and the Desmond FitzGeralds. In 1569 they took to arms. The queen sent Thomas Butler, earl of Ormond, back to Ireland to represent her interests. He succeeded in pacifying his brothers and other kinsmen and in gaining their allegiance, but James Fitzmaurice FitzGerald, cousin of the then imprisoned earl of Desmond, kept up the fight until 1573, when he surrendered and fled to France. In suppressing the "rebellion," Humphrey Gilbert demonstrated an unprecedented ruthlessness, even lining the pathway to his tent with the severed heads of his Irish enemies, with the deliberate intention of terrorizing the natives—*pour encourager les autres*, as Voltaire would later put it in another connection. Henceforth, atrocity, fired by religious zeal, xenophobia, and tribalism, was to be a major recurring theme in relations between English and Irish.

The queen's alter ego in Munster, the tenth earl of Ormond ("Black Tom Butler"), was also a distant cousin by virtue of the marriage of Elizabeth's maternal great-grandparents, Sir William Boleyn and Margaret Butler. He had been reared a Protestant in the English court during the reign of Edward VI. On returning to his native land (where he stayed until his death in 1614), he set about rebuilding **Ormond Castle** *(299)* in Carrick-on-Suir, County Tipperary. To the ancestral fifteenth-century double tower house he added a long, low palatial Elizabethan manor house, defenseless except for the small gunports on either side of the front door. With its many-gabled frontage, its mullioned windows, elegant stuccowork, and splendid long gallery, it was architecturally unique in Ireland—a Tudor masterpiece, testifying in stone and brick to the lifelong loyalty of its builder to the interests of the English Crown.

Ten years after Ormond's return, James FitzMaurice FitzGerald renewed his insurrection, this time unmistakably under the papal banner. With a band of about seventy-five men paid for by Pope Gregory XIII, he landed at Smerwick Harbor on the Dingle peninsula and built a fortified camp on the site of the iron-age promontory fort called **Dún an Oir (Fort of Gold)** *(330)*. His proclamation absolving the Irish from their allegiance to the queen and exhorting them to rise in support of the Catholic religion met, however, with little response. The English broke up his camp, and FitzMaurice was killed a month after his arrival in a skirmish with the Burkes of Castleconnel.

Gerald FitzGerald, fourteenth earl of Desmond, recently returned to Ireland from imprisonment in London, at first remained uncommitted to his cousin FitzMaurice's rash enterprise. But pressure from his more belligerent brothers and encouragement from the pope himself soon brought the earl into the field, also announcing his commitment to "the defence of our Catholic faith." In Leinster, James Eustace, Viscount Baltinglass, joined the crusade, but after winning one stunning victory against the English at Glenmalure he fled to Scotland and thence to Spain. Desmond had even less success. In September 1580 a force of about six hundred Italians and Spaniards sent by the pope landed at FitzMaurice's former encampment at **Dún an Oir** *(330)*. The English besieged the fort both by land and by sea. When the garrison surrendered, the deputy governor, Lord Grey, dispatched Sir Walter Raleigh to massacre them all. Desmond fought on, but with diminishing support. He was eventually (in 1583) tracked down by native Irish in Kerry and hacked to death, his head cut off and sent to Ormond, who forwarded it to the queen. Lord Grey then proceeded to ravage Munster. His secretary, the poet Edmund Spenser, approvingly recorded the devastation: "In short space, there were none almost left and a most populous and plentiful country suddenly left void of man or beast." Of the survivors, he noted "out of every corner of the woods and glens they came creeping forth upon their hands, for their legs would not bear them. They looked like anatomies of death; they spoke like ghosts crying out of their graves . . . ."

Spenser was one of those to win personal profit out of the miseries he depicted. In 1586 bills of attainder were brought against Desmond and his principal confederates, and their lands were confiscated by the Crown— close to three hundred thousand profitable acres in all. It was then divided into units of regular size (seigniories) and granted to suitable "undertak- ers" who agreed to plant them with a stipulated number of English settlers. Those so favored were mostly soldiers who had fought in the recent wars in Munster, Dublin officials, and English courtiers, merchants, and gentle- men, although the earl of Ormond too received large tracts of land in County Tipperary. Desmond had burned most of his own castles during the rebellion, but some were restorable and taken over by the new colonists. The earl's *caput*, **Askeaton Castle** *(334)* in County Limerick, along with more than five thousand acres, went to Captain Francis Berkeley. Nearby, **Castle Matrix** *(340)* was occupied by Henry Billingsley, who later sold it to Sir John Dowdall, who in turn purveyed it to Edmund Southwell. Sir George Bourchier won the Desmond castle at **Lough Gur** *(339)*, which was appropriately renamed Bourchier Castle. Spenser received **Kilcolman Cas- tle** *(316)*, County Cork. During his sojourn there (until 1598) he wrote the fourth, fifth, and sixth books of *The Faerie Queene*, as well as the *Amoretti* and the *Epithalamion*. Sir Thomas Norris, later president of Munster—an office established by the queen in 1570—commenced the construction of a new house in County Cork, called **Mallow Castle** *(323)*, on the grounds of an earlier Desmond tower. It was a castellated, four-storey, gabled, rectan- gular building with polygonal turrets at the two front corners, projecting wings front and back, and large mullioned windows—architecturally a compromise between defensible castle and Tudor manor house. To Sir Walter Raleigh went the largest grant of all—forty-two thousand acres in Counties Cork and Waterford. But more exciting adventures and later incarceration and execution in the Tower of London precluded his ever residing in Ireland.

Altogether the Munster undertakers planted about four thousand settlers on their properties, far fewer than had been anticipated but still the largest English colony to have been established during the reign of Queen Elizabeth. Their hold was tenuous, however. Their estates were scattered widely throughout five counties otherwise occupied by hostile natives biding their time to rise up against these unwanted foreigners.

In Connacht no such formal plantation was deemed necessary by the government. In Galway city, to be sure, the Gaelic Irish were excluded, and the right to residency was reserved for the "tribes of Galway," hibernicized families of Norman origin, of which the Lynches, Joyces, Blakes, and Frenches were the most prominent. Within the substantial **City Wall** *(407)* their solid houses of stone reflected their growing prosperity, based primarily on trade with Spain but further enhanced by profitable land speculation at the expense of their Gaelic neighbors in the surrounding countryside. One of these town houses still survives—**Lynch's Castle** *(407)*, a much restored tower with interesting gargoyles and decorative stonework, now in use as a bank. The same family was responsible in the sixteenth century for enlarging the **St. Nicholas Church** *(406)* to its present size— extending the south transept and inserting a triplet window, elevating the roof of the north transept, and installing the west window and the three- gabled front.

Like Munster, Connacht (along with Thomond) was placed under the authority of a president, who divided the province into counties (Galway, Mayo, Roscommon, Sligo, Leitrim, and Clare), introduced sheriffs and county courts in the English manner, and negotiated the "composition of Connacht" whereby landowners were confirmed in their estates in return for their agreement to pay yearly rents to the Crown—a logical extension of Henry VIII's policy of surrender and regrant. The first of the presidents was Sir Edward Fitton, who established his headquarters on the east side of the river Shannon at **Athlone Castle** *(391)*. He was succeeded in 1578 by Sir Nicholas Malby, who took over **Roscommon Castle** *(403)* and modernized it to the extent of substituting mullioned windows for the original slitted apertures—a sign of English confidence in their ability to pacify the region. In 1584 Malby was succeeded by Sir Richard Bingham, who carried the process of pacification into the northern part of the province with a heavy hand. Two years after he had taken command, he massacred two thousand Scottish mercenaries in the service of the Mayo Burkes—a deed reported as "the only piece of service, next to Smerwick [i.e., Dún an Oir], that hath been done in this land in many years." It was probably not long thereafter that the government built and garrisoned **Ballinafad Castle** *(402)*, County Sligo, to guard the pass over the Curlew Hills.

Of the three predominantly Gaelic provinces, Ulster proved the most difficult for the Tudors to subdue. During the reign of Henry VIII Lord

Deputy Leonard Grey recaptured **Dundrum Castle** *(437)* from the Magennises of Iveagh, who had occupied it since the previous century. Soon thereafter English soldiers were settled at Newry, County Down, under the leadership of Sir Nicholas Bagenal, later to be appointed marshal of the English forces in Ireland. In about 1560 **Narrow Water Castle** *(437)* was put up to guard the river approach to Newry from Carlingford Lough. This was a small, battlemented, three-storey rectangular tower house, recently restored. Bagenal also gained custody of the medieval stronghold of **Greencastle** *(436)*, County Down, at the mouth of the same lough about a dozen miles farther south.

About the time that Narrow Water Castle was being built, trouble broke out in western Ulster, where Shane O'Neill led an expedition against the O'Donnells of County Donegal. Shane was the second son of Conn O'Neill, earl of Tyrone, and claimed to be his legitimate successor as well as overlord of all Ulster. The government of Queen Elizabeth denied both claims; English troops invaded Ulster; Shane submitted in person to the queen herself; she allowed him to return to Ulster, where he took up arms again, only to be defeated in battle by the O'Donnells. He then sought refuge among the Scottish MacDonnells of Antrim, who promptly murdered him, pickled his head in a barrel, and sent it to Dublin, where it was stuck up over the castle gate.

Five years later (1572) came the first effort to establish an English colony in Ulster. Sir Thomas Smith, former ambassador to France, formed a joint stock company to finance the planting of about a hundred settlers on the Ards peninsula, east of the present city of Belfast. The enterprise failed: Smith's son, the leader of the expedition, was killed by his Irish household servants, who boiled his body and fed it to their dogs. Next to try his hand was Walter Devereux, earl of Essex, who brought twelve hundred soldiers into Antrim to fight against both native Irish and recent Scottish settlers. With him came Sir Francis Drake and Sir Thomas Norris (later president of Munster), who massacred the entire Scottish population of Rathlin Island—six hundred men, women, and children. Essex's enterprise also failed; the queen countermanded the project.

The steady influx of Scottish soldiers and settlers into Ulster so alarmed the government in Dublin that Lord Deputy John Perrot led an expedition north and seized **Dunluce Castle** *(460)* on the north Antrim coast from its owner, Sorley Boy (Somhairle Buide) MacDonnell, who claimed to be a subject of the king of Scotland. The next year (1685) Sorley Boy, with an army of Scots, retook the castle, then made a formal submission to the queen and was confirmed in his possession of that part of County Antrim called the Route, while his kinsman, Angus MacDonnell, received the adjacent territory of the Glens, which included **Kinbane Castle** *(453)*, now a gaunt ruin hugging the seashore.

Between these two MacDonnell properties lies the Giant's Causeway, one of the great natural wonders of the British Isles—a widespread cluster of high basaltic columns rising out of the sea. On this treacherous coast in the autumn of 1588 the Spanish galleass *Girona* ran aground with the loss of almost all hands aboard. Almost three centuries later Belgian divers recovered from the wreck a large miscellany of artifacts now on exhibit at the **Ulster Museum** *(457)* in Belfast—cannons, jewelry, coins, etc. This ship, like others that came to grief on the coasts of Ulster and Connacht, had become separated from the main body of the famous Spanish Armada as it beat its way back to Spain after being so badly mauled in the English Channel. Some of the survivors were looted and killed by the native Irish; more were executed upon capture by English soldiery; perhaps five hundred escaped to Scotland and eventually made their way home. There is no evidence that any number stayed long enough in Ireland to add significantly to the country's genetic bank as is commonly believed.

Meanwhile the process of incorporating Ulster into the kingdom of Ireland marched slowly. In 1585 the province was officially shired—the first step toward the introduction of English courts, English law, and English intrusion into local affairs. (By this date all the other modern Irish counties except Wicklow had already been established, though Coleraine was to be renamed Londonderry.) In 1591 the chief of the MacMahons was executed, and his lordship in southern Ulster, which comprised most of County Monaghan, was split up among the lesser members of his lineage, to be held directly of the Crown. To the west, in Counties Fermanagh and Donegal, the Maguires and O'Donnells came out in open rebellion. Hugh Roe O'Donnell escaped from imprisonment in **Dublin Castle** *(358)*, returned to Donegal, was inaugurated chief of his clan, and helped Hugh Maguire recapture from the English his family's stronghold of **Enniskillen Castle** *(449)*.

At this point English hopes hinged on the continued loyalty of Hugh O'Neill, grandson of Conn, the first earl of Tyrone. Educated in England, he had helped suppress the Desmond rebellion in Munster and had been rewarded with the patent for his grandfather's earldom. Not content to be merely earl of Tyrone, in September 1595 he had himself inaugurated The O'Neill (i.e., chief of the clan)—a title which his grandfather had renounced at the insistence of the English government—at the ancient ancestral royal site of **Tullaghoge** *(446)* near Cookstown. Shortly thereafter Tyrone joined forces with his rebellious sons-in-law, Maguire and O'Donnell.

As in Munster, the war in Ulster (referred to by historians as the Nine Years' War) quickly developed religious and international dimensions. Even before his open break with the English government, O'Neill had offered the crown of Ireland to King Philip II of Spain in return for military assistance. In 1596 a Spanish agent arrived in Ulster along with ships carrying arms and ammunition. The Ulster lords offered the crown to Archduke Albert, Philip's nephew. An expedition set out from Spain for Ireland but was turned back by weather (a "Protestant wind" was the English explanation). In April of 1600 a thousand firearms did at last reach Donegal, and Pope Clement VIII issued a bull granting "plenary pardon and remission of sins" to all who followed or assisted O'Neill.

Meanwhile things went badly for the English. Connacht was overrun. In August 1598 at the Yellow Ford near Armagh, O'Neill and O'Donnell ambushed an army of four thousand sent from Dublin, killing its commander, Henry Bagenal, and about half his men. With Tyrone's encouragement, Owen MacRory O'More of Queens County swept through Munster with fire and sword, driving out most of the recently established English settlers, including Edmund Spenser, whose **Kilcolman Castle** *(316)* was set afire. In great alarm Queen Elizabeth dispatched to Ireland her court favorite Robert Devereux, second earl of Essex, with an army of seventeen thousand. Essex dallied. An eight-week campaign in Munster accomplished little beyond the capture of **Cahir Castle** *(298)* in County Tipperary—a mere "Irish hold," complained the queen, held by "a rabble of rogues." Under heavy royal pressure he finally led his army north from Dublin, held a private horseback parley with Tyrone in the shallows of the river Lagan, concluded a truce, and then fled back to England to disgrace and eventual execution. Meanwhile O'Neill marched triumphantly into Munster.

Essex's successor as the queen's lieutenant was Charles Blount, Lord Mountjoy, who reached Ireland in February 1600. An aggressive soldier, he sent Sir George Carew to suppress the rebellion in Munster and planted a garrison under Sir Henry Dowcra at Tyrone's back door in Derry. He himself, with an army of fourteen thousand men, marched into Ulster, burning crops and reducing the countryside to famine. In May 1601 he returned, this time setting up a small stone fort called **Moyry Castle** *(438)* to guard the vital pass between Dundalk and Newry. Then, in September, came news that a Spanish force, under the command of Don Juan de Aquila, had at last landed in Ireland—at Kinsale in County Cork.

The siege of Kinsale proved to be the climax of the Nine Years' War. O'Neill and O'Donnell marched south by separate routes and joined forces in early December with a total force not much smaller than Mountjoy's. The two armies came together under the walls of Kinsale on Christmas Eve of 1601. The Ulstermen, skilled at guerrilla warfare but undisciplined as a field army, were routed. Tyrone fled back to his native heath. O'Donnell took ship for Spain. A week later Don Juan surrendered the city; he and his troops were sent home on shipping supplied by the English. Mountjoy occupied Kinsale and on the southwest bank of the harbor built a star-shaped fortress, later called **James Fort** *(323)* in honor of Queen Elizabeth's successor to the throne.

The final phase of the war was anticlimactic. In June 1602 Mountjoy again marched into Ulster, though Tyrone succeeded in evading him. At **Tullaghoge** *(446)* the queen's lieutenant proclaimed symbolically the powerlessness of his enemy by smashing the so-called coronation chair of the O'Neills. It was probably about this time that **Mountjoy Castle** *(445)* was erected on the western shore of Lough Neagh—a rectangular tower of stone and brick with four corner turrets and a plethora of gunports.

Tyrone still laid low, avoiding any contact with the invader. Frustrated and weary of the heavy expenses of the war, Queen Elizabeth instructed Mountjoy to offer generous terms. On the latter's invitation Tyrone came to Garret Moore's house at Mellifont in March 1603 and there submitted. The terms imposed were even more generous than the queen had contemplated. Mountjoy felt obliged to be lenient because he had received word that Elizabeth had died—a fact unknown to his adversary, who might otherwise have been more stubborn. As it was, O'Neill was granted absolute ownership over his earldom of Tyrone (except for the territory occupied by two English garrisons) and was awarded, in addition, lordship over his estranged son-in-law Donal O'Cahan. In return the earl reaffirmed his fealty to the queen and renounced the king of Spain. Later, Tyrone went to England to make personal submission to the new king, James I. With him went the younger brother of Hugh Roe O'Donnell, who had died in Spain—Rory O'Donnell, who was now created earl of Tyrconnell with the same rights as those granted to Tyrone. It was, in the words of the historian G. A. Hayes-McCoy, "a brittle settlement, and one that did not match the conquest that had been effected."

THE EARLY STUARTS AND CROMWELL: 1603–1659

Thus the Tudor conquest of Ulster was incomplete when the death of Queen Elizabeth brought an end to the Tudor dynasty. She was succeeded by her kinsman (grandson to her first cousin), James Stuart, the sixth of that name to sit on the throne of Scotland. As King James I of England and Ireland he would preside over Ulster's effective incorporation into the new Great Britain.

With the end of the fighting, eastern Ulster was opened up to a new wave of immigrants from the Scottish lowlands. They were welcomed by such land speculators as James Hamilton and Hugh Montgomery, who had acquired from the chief of the Clandeboye O'Neills huge estates in Counties Down and Antrim, and by Sir Arthur Chichester, lord deputy of Ireland after 1605 and chief colonizer of Carrickfergus and its environs. The colonists themselves were small farmers, graziers, and tradesmen, and in their religious persuasion staunch believers in the advanced Protestant doctrines of John Calvin. As such they rejected absolutely not only the theology, governance, and liturgy of the Roman Catholic Church but also the episcopal organization of the established Churches of England and Ireland. These Scotsmen's churches were governed instead by bodies of presbyters or elders, under the general jurisdiction of a General Assembly of elected clergy and laymen. Finally, in common with those radical English Protestants known as Puritans, they believed in the doctrine of predestination, which asserted that salvation was available, by the preordained will of God, only to a small body of the elect, among whom they naturally numbered themselves. Confident in the ultimate security of their souls, these were a proud, independent, sober, industrious, and God-fearing people, with little tolerance for other Protestant denominations and none at all for Roman Catholicism. The culture they imported, along with their Presbyterian faith, is to this day very much in evidence throughout Northern Ireland.

Meanwhile in the rest of Ulster, the process of anglicization was making rapid headway. English soldiers were garrisoned at strategic points throughout the country. County courts were set up; sheriffs, justices of the peace, coroners, and constables were installed. Under the aegis of Sir John Davies, solicitor general and attorney general for Ireland, assizes were held regularly and Gaelic law was uprooted in favor of English law. Specifically this meant the destruction of the ancient Irish system of landholding based on ownership by extended family groups and partible inheritance and the substitution of individual ownership and inheritance by primogeniture. It also meant the abolition of much of the authority hitherto exercised by Irish landlords over their tenants.

None of this sat well with the great Gaelic chiefs of Ulster, despite the fact that the Treaty of Mellifont had dealt gently with them. Nor were Cuconnaught Maguire of Fermanagh or Rory O'Donnell, earl of Tyrconnel, satisfied with the decisions of English royal commissioners to break up their huge estates in favor of their lesser neighbors. Nor could Hugh O'Neill avoid becoming alarmed when Sir John Davies persuaded Donal O'Cahan to challenge the patent granted to the earl of Tyrone in 1603, especially when the case was remanded to London for adjudication, requiring O'Neill's personal appearance before the king.

Maguire and O'Donnell were the first to take action—laying plans to leave the country to pursue careers in the Spanish army in the Netherlands.

This was tantamount to treason, and though O'Neill opposed the scheme, he was privy to it and therefore possibly liable to prosecution as an accessory before the fact. So, when he received an invitation to join these malcontents, he hastened to Lough Swilly, where a boat awaited. There in early September 1607, from the shore opposite **Rathmullan Friary** *(429)*, the three Gaelic leaders, with about a hundred of their families and retainers, took ship for the Continent, never to return. This was the famous "flight of the earls." Glorified and lamented by the bards, the incident came to be enshrined in the legend and literature of exile. It served, for many years to come, to legitimate and even ennoble the voluntary and involuntary departure of thousands of Irish emigrants to foreign shores.

The flight of the earls was soon followed by the short-lived and unsuccessful revolt of Sir Cahir O'Doherty of Inishowen, supported by some of the O'Hanlons and O'Cahans. Exiles and rebels were alike judged outlaws and their lands confiscated—close to a half million acres in all, comprising most of six counties in central and western Ulster: Cavan, Armagh, Fermanagh, Tyrone, Donegal, and Coleraine. This opened the way for a wholesale plantation scheme, devised chiefly by Sir John Davies and Sir Arthur Chichester. Roughly a quarter of the land was distributed to approximately a hundred English and Scottish undertakers. Another fifth went to servitors—soldiers or officials of the Crown, including Chichester, who received all of the Inishowen peninsula. Still another fifth was awarded to "deserving Irish" landlords. Almost all of County Coleraine (about a tenth of the total area confiscated) became the property of a group of London companies (clothworkers, drapers, ironmongers, etc.), who renamed the county and its principal town Londonderry. The remainder fell mostly to the Church of Ireland and Trinity College.

All of the grantees except the "deserving Irish" were expected to settle their estates with Protestant English and Scottish tenants, much in the manner that eastern Ulster had already been peopled with new arrivals from the lowlands of Scotland. No native Irish were to be permitted to remain on those lands acquired by the undertakers. All other landlords might sublet to natives, though only for higher rents than those charged to British immigrants. Altogether by 1620 about thirteen thousand English and Scottish settlers (not counting children) had migrated into the six escheated counties, almost double the number then settled in counties Antrim and Down. Yet the native Irish were not wholly displaced. There was more than enough land to share, and to avoid being uprooted, Irish occupants were often willing to pay higher rents than the immigrants. Hence even the undertakers were inclined to allow them to stay and were legally permitted to do so after 1628. Thus Ulster became the uneasy host to a hybrid population, part British and Protestant, part Irish and Catholic, a "house divided against itself."

In the Protestant areas new towns took shape, in keeping with the provisions of the plantation scheme. By 1625 over twenty-four had been incorporated, though only four of these (Londonderry, Carrickfergus, Coleraine, and Belfast) had a population of over five hundred even as late as the mid–seventeenth century. Londonderry, settled by the London companies, was the largest. It had a fine stone **City Wall** *(463)* (still standing) with eight projecting artillery bastions and four diametrically opposed gates. Inside was a gridiron of streets around the focal point of the market-place, referred to (as elsewhere in Ulster) as "the diamond." Close by, the Protestant citizens built the finest of Ireland's seventeenth-century churches, **St. Columb's Cathedral** *(464)*, a battlemented, rectangular gray-stone building in the style known as "Jacobean Gothic." (Contemporary with it and similar in appearance is the cruciform **Belturbet Parish Church** *[401]*, County Cavan.)

Carrickfergus too had its **Town Wall** *(461)*, dating from 1611—more than twelve feet high and entered through gates from the north and north-west. Sir Arthur Chichester, lord deputy of Ireland, governor of Carrickfergus, and first lord baron of Belfast, was its builder. He also rebuilt **St. Nicholas' Church** *(461)*, a medieval house of worship taken over by the Church of Ireland after the Reformation. The baptistry and most of the nave date to the seventeenth-century reconstruction. The most noteworthy feature here is the Chichester or Donegall Aisle, a family burial vault of marble and alabaster containing effigies of Sir Arthur; his wife, Lettice; their only child, who died in infancy; and the lord deputy's brother, Sir John Chichester, killed by the MacDonnells in 1597.

In the countryside the equivalent of the town wall was the "planter's castle" and bawn. Memories of the fate of the English settlers in Munster were still green, and all undertakers, servitors, and even the larger Irish grantees were required, by the conditions of the Ulster plantation, to build stone or brick defensible "castles" and/or bawns. The castles might be tower houses, constructed usually in the Scottish style, or fortified English-type manor houses. The bawns were square or rectangular in plan, with walls usually from eight to fourteen feet high, corner flankers, and a gate at the entrance.

Typical of the Scottish variety is **Monea Castle** *(451)*, built by the planter Malcolm Hamilton in County Fermanagh. The round twin towers at the entrance are capped by square chambers with crowstep gables—an architectural feature found elsewhere only at the tower house called Clay-potts near Dundee in Scotland. **Castle Balfour** *(452)*, also in Fermanagh, is a T-plan tower house, constructed by a Scottish settler, Sir James Balfour. In the same county, overlooking Lough Erne, is **Tully Castle** *(451)*, built by Sir John Hume—another T-plan tower, three storeys high, with a fine bawn wall guarded by square corner turrets. An even more impressive bawn wall surrounds **Park's Castle** *(416)*, considered by architectural historians to be a "planter's castle" even though built outside of Ulster in County Leitrim. Overlooking Lough Gill, this is one of the best preserved of the species in Ireland. Another still farther south (in County Meath) is **Robertstown Castle** *(385)*, whose most distinctive features are the two corner turrets corbelled in the Scottish fashion.

Old Castle Archdale *(452)*, near Kesh, County Fermanagh, was built for the English planter John Archdale about 1615. Not much remains, however, of the three-storey T-shaped house and bawn. In a far better state of preservation is **Castle Caulfield** *(447)*, near Dungannon, County Tyrone. It too is English in style, having been built for Sir Toby Caulfield between 1611 and 1619. Here the gatehouse leading into the bawn has "murder holes" and gun-loops, though the house itself lacks defensive features. **Benburb Castle** *(444)*, County Tyrone, consists today of nothing more than a high bawn wall, well defended with gun-loops and flanked by tall rectangular towers. It was built by Sir Richard Wingfield in about 1615. **Brackfield Bawn** *(465)* in County Londonderry was put up on land granted to the Skinners' Company of London. Though there are scant remnants here of a house, the ruins consist chiefly of a rectangular bawn wall with towers at opposite corners.

County Down lay outside the Ulster plantation proper, but conditions there were nevertheless unsettled enough in the early seventeenth century to warrant the fortification of at least two country dwellings. These are **Kirkiston Castle** *(433)* and the **White House of Ballyspurge** *(433)*, both built by members of the Savage family, descendants of one of John de Courcy's original band of adventurers. The former is a three-storey tower house (altered in about 1800) inside a bawn. The latter is a gabled farmhouse that has gun-loops at ground level and is also protected by a bawn wall and gatehouse.

Notwithstanding the defensive features incorporated into the structures mentioned above, the seventeenth century in general was, in the words of the architectural historian Maurice Craig, "a period during which the claims of defence gradually yielded to those of comfort and convenience." Nowhere is this more apparent than in the occasional modification of medieval buildings to render them both more livable and more stylish. When the English planter Sir Basil Brooke took possession of Hugh Roe O'Donnell's **Donegal Castle** *(426)* in 1623, he added a fine Jacobean wing, inserted mullioned windows, crowned the building with about a dozen gables, and installed an ornate Renaissance-style chimneypiece in the main upper room of the original tower. In 1607 Captain Sir William Cole took possession of the Maguire stronghold of **Enniskillen Castle** *(449)*. Although subsequent restorations have largely obscured the substantial modifications he made in the original medieval keep, the water gate he constructed on the grounds is still largely intact. Scottish masons were undoubtedly responsible for the twin corbelled angle turrets with conical roofs. **Dunluce Castle** *(460)*, County Antrim, after the death of Sorley Boy MacDonnell, became the residence of his son Randal (MacSorley), whom James I named first earl of Antrim in 1620. It was he who installed in the upper courtyard of the castle the great hall (now ruined) with its huge bay windows and fine heraldic chimneypiece. (In 1639 part of the cliffside castle fell into the sea, and a few years later the family moved out.)

Reconstruction and modernization of ancient dwelling places was not confined to Ulster. In County Clare, Conor O'Brien and his wife, Maire Ruadh Ni Mahon, built onto the family's fifteenth-century tower called **Leamaneh Castle** *(346)* a four-storey gabled house lighted by rows of large mullioned and transomed windows. This was apparently accomplished in 1643, the date inscribed on the bawn gateway, since removed to Dromoland Castle (now a hotel), where the builder's son, Sir Donogh O'Brien, later established the family seat. A similar renovation took place early in the seventeenth century at **Loughmoe Castle** *(308)*, County Tipperary, residence of the Old English family of Purcells. To the north end of the fifteenth-century tower house they attached a three-storey house with matching tower. The addition had the usual wide mullioned and transomed windows as well as numerous fireplaces.

Also in the early seventeenth century there were a few country houses built *de novo*, usually in a style called "Jacobean" (from *Jacobus*, Latin for James). Typical features were symmetrical ground plans; spacious, well-lighted interiors; an amplitude of large mullioned and transomed windows; ornamental stonework inside and out in the neoclassical style of the English Renaissance; and a minimum of defensive features such as gunports and machicolations. None was so magnificent as the so-called "prodigy houses" of contemporary England, but all represented an advance in comfort and style over the standard Irish tower house of the fifteenth and sixteenth centuries. One of these was **Portumna Castle** *(414)*, County Galway, built sometime before 1618 for Richard Burke, earl of Clanrickard. This tall, handsome four-storey house overlooking Lough Derg is rectangular in plan with square towers at each corner, well fenestrated with mullioned windows, topped by a crenellated parapet interrupted by curvilinear gables, and a facade graced by a fine Renaissance doorway. Provision for defense was confined to machicolation above the main entrance and gunports around the doors. Similar in ground plan was **Kanturk Castle** *(322)*, County Cork, begun by Dermot MacDonagh MacCarthy, lord of Duhallow, in about 1609 but abandoned before completion, allegedly because of the intervention of jealous English neighbors but more probably as a result of foreclosure proceedings brought by Sir Philip Perceval, to whom he had mortgaged the property. Even so, the shell of the house remains impressive—a tall rectangular building with four corner towers, a fine Renaissance doorway, and many two- and three-mullioned windows. The roof was never completed, although there is a legend (of unlikely veracity) that it was originally made of glass, which the owner smashed to pieces before abandoning the project. Another fine Jacobean mansion in County Cork was **Coppinger's Court** *(324)* near Rosscarbery. It was a semifortified gabled U-plan manor house consisting of a central block with two projecting wings and an added wing at the back. Machicolations run along the sides of all three wings, but the many chimney stacks and mullioned windows bespeak comfort and elegance rather than defensibility.

The builder of this attractive residence was Sir Walter Coppinger, scion of a pre-Norman family, a prosperous merchant and prominent member of the Old English community of Cork city. He was one of a sizable number of moneyed men and land speculators—Old English, New English, and native Irish—to amass large properties in Munster in the wake of the exodus of the Elizabethan planters during the Nine Years' War. Some of those planters—or their descendants—held on to their property. The heirs of Edmund Spenser, though converted to Catholicism, recovered **Kilcolman Castle** *(316)*. Francis Berkeley, who had successfully defended **Askeaton Castle** *(334)*, stayed on; Henry Bouchier was reinstalled on his property at **Lough Gur** *(339)*; and, of course, the earl of Ormond suffered no diminution of his extensive estates in County Tipperary. Also, a number of army officers who had fought in the Nine Years' War moved into some of the seigniories vacated by the original planters. John Jephson married the heiress of Sir Thomas Norris and thereby acquired **Mallow Castle** *(323)* and the land around it. Sir John Dowdall bought up Henry Billingsley's estate in County Limerick, including **Castle Matrix** *(340)*, but later sold out to the Southwells, a Suffolk family. Along with these so-called New English landowners came a number of smaller fry to farm the land or populate such new and expanding inland towns as Mallow, Bandonbridge, Tallow, and Tralee. Altogether the English population of Munster rose from about four thousand in 1598 to approximately eighteen thousand in 1630 and twenty-two thousand in 1641. And of all the newcomers none was so successful in the pursuit of wealth and power as Richard Boyle of Canterbury, Kent.

Boyle's was the classic rags-to-riches story. In 1588 he arrived in Ireland penniless; in 1590 he secured appointment as deputy escheater and succeeded in acquiring at ridiculously low rents much valuable Crown property; later in the 1590s he was imprisoned for alleged misconduct in office but was freed on the intervention of Sir George Carew; in 1602 he bought the vast Munster estates of Sir Walter Raleigh for a mere thousand pounds; by 1630 his estimated income from rents was £20,000—which made him one of the richest men in the British Isles. The rewards in status and influence were commensurate: in 1603 he was knighted; in 1607 he became a member of the provincial council in Munster and in 1613 of the Irish privy council; in 1616 he acquired a barony; in 1620 he was made first earl of Cork; in 1629–33 he served as lord justice of Ireland; in 1631 he was appointed lord high treasurer of Ireland; in 1640 he achieved membership in the English privy council. Of his numerous offspring, one daughter was married to George FitzGerald, earl of Kildare; others to Viscount Barrymore, the son of Lord Ranelagh, the earl of Norwich, and the earl of Warwick. His eldest son married the granddaughter of the first earl of Salisbury, another son the daughter of the earl of Denbigh, and a third the daughter of the earl of Suffolk.

For the first of the above-mentioned daughters and her husband, Boyle renovated the Kildare family seat of **Maynooth Castle** *(377)*. For his own use he built **Lismore Castle** *(285)*, County Waterford. The castle itself was later much modified by a descendant, the duke of Devonshire, although the present walled garden and the "riding house" through which it is entered date from Boyle's own occupancy. Nearby he completely renovated **Lismore Cathedral** *(284)*, converting the medieval church into the attractive Jacobean Gothic edifice it is today. Like many another parvenu, Boyle had a penchant for showy funerary monuments. In the south transept of **St. Mary's Church** *(325)* in Youghal, County Cork, he had built an elaborate classical mausoleum with effigies of both wives, his mother-in-law, and his sixteen children gathered in attitudes of prayer around the figure of himself lying recumbent in his peer's robes. Behind the high altar at **St. Patrick's Cathedral** *(362)*, Dublin, he installed another tomb, only slightly less ornate, dedicated to the memory of his second wife, whose effigy is surrounded by others representing her grieving husband, her children, her parents, and her grandfather.

It was this monument in particular that aroused the ire of Thomas, Viscount Wentworth, who arrived in Ireland in 1633 as lord deputy, appointed by Charles I, king of England since 1625. To Wentworth the tomb symbolized the "vanity and insolent novelties of the earl of Cork." He took particular offense at its liturgically incorrect location at the east end of the church, where the congregation could not worship without "crouching to an earl of Cork and his lady." Wentworth had the tomb dismantled stone by stone and packed in boxes (though it was later reerected at the southwest end of the nave, where it now stands). The lord deputy next attacked the earl's appropriation of the revenues formerly adhering to the collegiate chapter of **St. Mary's Church** *(325)* in Youghal, compelling him to surrender his patent and pay a fine of £15,000.

Wentworth's grudge against Boyle was more than personal. It was also an attack against the faction of New English settlers and officials among whom he was the most prominent figure. These, like Boyle, were English-born colonists, recently arrived in Ireland in search of wealth and power. They were also mostly Protestants of a Puritan and Calvinist persuasion, in contrast to the High Church formalism and antipredestinarianism espoused by William Laud, archbishop of Canterbury, and favored by Wentworth himself. Indeed the Church of Ireland, under the leadership of its primate, James Ussher, *was* more Puritan in both theology and order of worship than its counterpart in England. Its first full confession of faith—the Irish Articles of 1615—was more aggressively antipapist than the Thirty-Nine Articles governing the Church of England and more specifically Calvinist than was pleasing to Archbishop Laud. Wentworth moved to change all this. As most of the Irish sees fell vacant, he had them filled with Laudians. Trinity College, formerly a center of Puritan learning, was similarly purged.

In Ulster the Presbyterians fared even worse. In Scotland their coreligionists had promulgated a "national covenant" to defend their church against innovations pressed by Archbishop Laud, especially the new Book of Common Prayer. Wentworth ordered all Ulster Scots over the age of sixteen to take an "oath of abjuration of the abominable covenant" (the so-called "black oath") and dispatched the bulk of the Irish army to the North to enforce subscription. At the same time he levied a fine of £70,000 against the London companies of Londonderry and took steps to void their patent. The Protestant community of Ulster seethed.

If these new Ulster settlers suffered under Wentworth's rule, the Old English elsewhere in Ireland were at even greater risk. Most who fell into that category were descendants of the English colonists who had established themselves in Ireland during the Middle Ages. Most were Roman Catholic. Among their number were many of the greatest landowners in Ireland; indeed about a third of the profitable land in the country was in their hands. Yet because of their religion they were disbarred from high office, and because of King James I's creation of a number of new Protestant boroughs (chiefly in Ulster) they were outnumbered in the Irish parliament.

In matters of conscience, though most Catholic laymen in the reign of James I suffered discrimination and harassment, they were seldom actively persecuted. After 1623, while James I was seeking a Spanish alliance, recriminations against Catholics in Ireland subsided further. Recusancy fines were imposed only intermittently, and even the Catholic clergy, though ordered to quit the realm, managed to survive and grow in number. Priests, monks, and friars, trained in such post-Tridentine seminaries as those at Rome, Salamanca, Louvain, and Douai, returned in large numbers, perhaps as many as forty a year. Many were younger members of the great Old English families who gave them shelter, sustenance, and encouragement. Religious foundations were reestablished; "mass houses" for the conduct of religious services reappeared.

Anticipating this resurgence of the old faith, King James complained to a deputation of Irish Catholics: "Surely I have good reason for saying that you are only half-subjects of mine. For you give your soul to the pope, and to me only the body, and even it, your bodily strength, you divide between me and the king of Spain." But he did nothing drastic to force the issue. So the Old English were inescapably caught on the horns of a dilemma. At a time when all over Europe the indivisibility of the dominion of church and state was largely taken for granted, these people found themselves faced with a logically impossible choice between being simultaneously good Catholics *and* good subjects to a heretic king. King James, no mean logician himself, had correctly diagnosed their problem as well as his own.

Of more immediate concern to Irish Catholics, however, at least to Old English landholders, was the ever-present threat that the government would take legal action against their titles and in effect expropriate their estates. Soon after he came to the throne in 1625, King Charles I, desperate for the grant of an Irish subsidy, promised as a matter of "grace and bounty" not to continue legal proceedings against Irish land titles and to allow certain categories of Catholics to substitute an oath of allegiance for the oath of supremacy that recognized the king, rather than the pope, as supreme head of the Church in Ireland. These concessions were later embodied in fifty-one "graces" for which parliamentary ratification was promised. Then, in 1633, Thomas Wentworth arrived on the scene, determined to increase the king's revenues by asserting royal ownership of as much private property as a rigorous prosecution of the law might allow.

The lord deputy's first move against the Old English was to call a parliament in which he tricked the Catholic members into agreeing to six subsidies, after which he promptly repudiated the most important of the graces. Next, in the spring of 1635, he launched an attack against the Old English landowners of Connacht by resurrecting long-defunct royal claims to their estates. After browbeating juries in Roscommon, Mayo, and Sligo to admit the king's claim to all three counties, he moved on to Galway. There he held hearings at **Portumna Castle** *(414)*, Irish seat of the greatest of the Galway Catholic landlords, Richard Burke, earl of Clanrickard, then resident in London. Wentworth's choice of sites was interpreted as a deliberate affront to the dignity of the earl, as was his spoilage of both castle and grounds. The Galway jurors, however, balked. Wentworth retaliated by subjecting them to heavy fines and even imprisonment. Thus forewarned, a second jury complied. So did their counterparts in County Clare. The lord deputy's scheme to open Connacht to plantation, however, failed for want of willing English settlers.

Meanwhile the attempt by Charles I and Archbishop Laud to impose an alien form of worship on the Scots had provoked an armed rebellion. For the king's protection Wentworth raised an army of eight thousand foot and one thousand horse in Ireland. Though the army was commanded by the Protestant earl of Ormond, a few of the officers and most of the rank and file were Catholics. Subsequently Charles summoned the lord deputy, newly created earl of Strafford, back to England to assist in managing a parliament summoned to meet the Scottish danger. Before he left, Strafford had built a splendid viceregal mansion of stone and brick called **Jigginstown House** *(379)*, near Naas in County Kildare. He was never to occupy it. In London the parliament, dominated by Puritans, brought articles of impeachment against him. One of the most telling charges was that Strafford planned to use the newly raised Irish army to suppress English liberties. His Irish enemies, both Catholic and Protestant, flocked to testify against him. It was of course the latter, including the earl of Cork, who carried the most weight with their fellow Puritans at Westminster. The upshot of these proceedings was the passage of an act of attainder for treason. Strafford was beheaded in May 1641. In August of the following year civil war broke out in England between the royalist forces of King Charles and the army of the English parliament.

Meanwhile England's distractions proved, as usual, to be Ireland's opportunity, and plans were quickly developed to throw off the conqueror's yoke. Rory O'More of County Kildare; Conor, Lord Maguire of Fermanagh; and Phelim O'Neill of Tyrone were the chief instigators. Rebellion was to commence with the capture of Dublin Castle in October 1641. The plot was betrayed, Dublin saved, and Maguire and others were taken prisoner. But in Ulster Phelim O'Neill, claiming to act in the king's name, raised the standard of a revolt that quickly degenerated into a religious war of typical ferocity. Caught by surprise, Protestant settlers were murdered by the thousands, while other thousands were turned out of their villages and homesteads to die of exposure and starvation. Though grossly exaggerated by Puritan propagandists in England (including the poet John Milton), the total number of casualties represented a significant fraction of the entire Protestant population of Ulster. It was enough, at any rate, to fire the hearts of the survivors and their coreligionists in Britain with a lust for bloody revenge, which in due time they took.

Rebellion quickly spread to the other provinces, and at Kilkenny in the summer of 1642 a Catholic confederacy was formed and a provisional government established to govern Ireland in the name of the king. The confederacy, an uneasy alliance between Old English and Gaelic Irish, received the blessing of the Roman Catholic hierarchy and set among its goals a guarantee to Catholic landowners against further encroachments by the government. But unity of purpose soon broke down as the Old English faction persisted in their nominal loyalty to King Charles while the Gaelic Irish rejected compromise with a heretic monarch and insisted on the restoration to the ancient Church of its former privileges and immunities. In their intransigence the latter were supported by the papal legate, Giovanni Battista Rinuccini, who freely employed his power of excommunication against the compromisers. Nor were the military efforts of the confederates any better coordinated. In the North Owen Roe O'Neill, claiming the title of earl of Tyrone, led the Ulster troops; in Leinster another veteran of the Spanish army, Thomas Preston, was in command; in Munster Garret Barry was the confederacy's chief military officer. Little love was shared among these regional commanders, who acted independently of each other.

On the other side there was no less fragmentation of effort. James Butler, earl of Ormond, was commander-in-chief of the royalist army in Ireland, which was too feeble to venture very far outside of Dublin. The English parliament, though at first engaged in more pressing matters at home, eventually sent a contingent of two thousand troops under Colonel Michael Jones to take control of Dublin after the defeat of the king in England. In Munster Murrogh O'Brien, earl of Inchiquin, fighting under the parliamentary banner, ravaged the countryside, sacked Cashel, and captured **Cahir Castle** *(298)* before changing sides to join the royalists. In Ulster parliament's cause was represented by Sir Robert Munroe and his army of Scots. He was badly defeated at Benburb by Owen Roe O'Neill, who then annulled his victory by abandoning Ulster and marching south to lend a hand to Rinuccini against the Old English of the Confederacy.

Then, in January 1649, King Charles was executed, and with him died the royalist cause in Ireland, though Ormond stayed on until December 1650 in a vain effort to organize effective resistance to the now triumphant English parliament. Meanwhile, on 15 August 1649, the redoubtable Puritan general, Oliver Cromwell, with an army of twelve thousand foot and horse, had landed at Ringsend near Dublin. He declared his purpose to be a "great work against the barbarous and blood-thirsty Irish, and the rest of their adherents and confederates, for the propagation of the Gospel of Christ, the establishing of truth and peace, and restoring that bleeding nation to its former happiness and tranquility."

Cromwell's campaign in Ireland was, in the words of the historian Margaret Mac Curtain, "swift, terrible, and decisive." In September he stood before the walls of Drogheda issuing a summons to surrender, which the garrison commander refused. The parliamentary army then breached the walls and stormed the town. The defenders took their final stance on the old Norman motte called the **Millmount**, where today stands a **Museum** *(397)* housing spent cannonballs and other relics of the siege. The Cromwellians massacred priests and soldiers indiscriminately, and probably civilians as well, though the latter point is debatable. Such ruthlessness was not unusual in seventeenth-century warfare on the Continent and was indeed sanctioned by the laws of war as a salutary inducement to the prompt surrender of beleaguered towns and fortresses. But, except for the sack of Aberdeen by Scottish highlanders and Irish mercenaries under the earl of Montrose, the civil war in Britain had been free of such incidents. The fact is, Cromwell's severity was clearly motivated as much by the desire to avenge Catholic atrocities in the 1641 Ulster uprising as by any purely military consideration. As he himself explained the matter: "I am persuaded that this is a righteous judgment of God upon these barbarous wretches, who have imbrued their hands in so much innocent blood . . . ." In fact the Drogheda garrison consisted mostly not of Irish, but of English, Catholics who could have had no hand in the Ulster business. In the seventeenth century, however, such nice distinctions were not considered significant.

Dundalk and Trim capitulated to the invader without hesitation, and after harrying Meath and Westmeath, Cromwell moved next to Wexford. There, while negotiations for surrender were still in progress, his troops broke into the city and once again ran amok, this time apparently without the authorization of their commander. No such episodes, however, were to be repeated. When New Ross surrendered, its soldiers and civilians went unmolested. The siege of Waterford was abandoned because of sickness among the English troops. In January 1650 Fethard opened its gates to the besieging army, and again there was no slaughter or plundering. When Kilkenny did likewise in March, the citizens were spared on their payment of £2,000. Clonmel fell in April after its defending garrison had escaped. Here too no recriminations against civilians took place. In May 1650 Cromwell departed Ireland for good.

Meanwhile in Ulster, Colonel Henry Venables and Sir Charles Coote had moved rapidly to reestablish English control. Their task was made easier by the enthusiastic cooperation of Protestant militia under the leadership of such local citizens as Sir Arthur Hill, who built **Hillsborough Fort** *(436)* in County Down to secure the area against a recurrence of Catholic armed dissent. He also began the construction of **St. Malachy's (C of I) Church** *(435)* on the foundations of an earlier building burned down during the uprising of 1641.

When Cromwell went back to England, his son-in-law Henry Ireton took over command of the parliamentary troops in Ireland and continued the reduction of strong points until his death in November 1651, when he was succeeded by Edmund Ludlow. By that time Carlow, Waterford, and most of Munster, Limerick, and County Clare were in the hands of the Cromwellians, as was the province of Connacht, including Galway city, which had been overrun by Coote. Innumerable castles had fallen to the conquering army, most of them to suffer no worse fate than "slighting," which usually took the form of throwing down the parapets and breaching part of the walls so as to make them indefensible against ordinary assault. Most were later reoccupied, and their present ruined state is attributable to subsequent desertion, neglect, and vandalism rather than to Cromwellian destruction. One—**Burncourt Castle** *(299)*, a newly built fortified manor house in County Tipperary—was reportedly set on fire by the wife of its owner, the royalist Sir Richard Everard, to prevent its falling into Cromwellian hands. Almost the last stronghold to surrender was **Ross Castle** *(331)* on Lough Leane (Lake Killarney), which yielded to Ludlow in May 1652 under threat of amphibious attack from across the lake.

Some of the captured leaders of the defeated armies (e.g., Sir Phelim O'Neill) were executed, but usually both officers and men were allowed safe conduct out of the country to pursue the soldier's trade in the armies of Catholic Europe. An estimated fifteen thousand went to Spain, ten to fifteen thousand to France, and hundreds to Austria. These were the first of the "wild geese" who for the next century and more were to fight so valiantly under foreign flags. North America too received its share of immigrants, though of a different kind. Some were voluntary exiles to Virginia, Maryland, and the West Indies. More were transported there as servants against their will. By 1669 there were reportedly some twelve thousand Irish in the West Indies alone—Barbados, Monserrat, Nevis, St. Christopher, Antigua, and Guadeloupe. A few of these were Catholic priests, forced into exile. Also, perhaps a thousand priests "voluntarily" left the country under threat of execution if they stayed, and the government offered a five-pound reward for the capture of those who declined to go. As to Catholic laymen, they were no longer to be forced to attend Protestant services or pay recusancy fines for nonattendance. Neither were they allowed to attend their own, since "popery" was to be exterminated. As Cromwell himself explained to the governor of New Ross: "I meddle not with any man's conscience, but if by liberty of conscience you mean a liberty to exercise the mass, I judge it best to use plain dealing and to let you know, where the Parliament of England have power, that will not be allowed of."

As threatening as these policies were to the religious life of the vast majority of Irish men and women, they could be and often were evaded, though at great risk to the priests who stayed on or surreptitiously returned and to those laymen who gave them shelter. What could not be evaded was the land settlement, which in the end proved to be Cromwell's most lasting legacy to Ireland.

In 1642, following the Ulster uprising, the English parliament had raised over three hundred thousand pounds from the subscription of about fifteen hundred "adventurers" who were to be repaid with confiscated Irish land. A year later another ordinance was passed allowing English soldiers to receive their pay in Irish lands on the same terms as the adventurers. About thirty-five thousand men eventually qualified. Although about half of the original adventurers and a considerably larger percentage of private soldiers eventually sold their claims to land speculators and army officers, in 1652 Cromwell's government was faced with the problem of redeeming these promises to pay. It did so by confiscating and redistributing virtually all the land owned by Catholics in the three provinces of Leinster, Munster, and Ulster. Most of the province of Connacht, plus County Clare, was reserved for the transplantation of former Catholic landlords from the rest of Ireland. Transportation took place in 1654 and 1655. Approximately forty-four thousand people—Catholic landlords and their families and servants—were thus forcibly removed west of the river Shannon. But most of their former tenants were not touched. They remained behind to work for, pay rents to, and even join the Protestant landlord class to form an enlarged ascendancy—ancestors of the Anglo-Irish gentry of the eighteenth, nineteenth, and twentieth centuries. In the towns the same transformation took place, as Catholic merchants lost their properties to English Protestant newcomers while the laboring class stayed on. Thus the policy of plantation, commenced more than a century before in the reign of Queen Mary, was brought almost to completion. Thus too in all of Ireland outside of Connacht was born a new caste system, with Protestants of English and Scottish birth or heritage in the ascendancy and Catholic and usually Gaelic-speaking Irish natives in a subordinate and dependent status.

THE LATER STUARTS: 1660–1691

Oliver Cromwell, since 1653 lord protector of England, Scotland, and Ireland, died in September 1658, to be succeeded by his son Richard, who held the office for less than a year before being forced into retirement. General George Monck, English military commander in Scotland, promptly engineered the return from the Continent of the late king's eldest son, who was proclaimed in England as King Charles II on 6 May 1660. Six days later the same proclamation was issued in Dublin, largely on the initiative of Sir Charles Coote and Roger Boyle, Lord Broghill, son of the erstwhile earl of Cork. Both, it should be noted, were Protestants, and both had fought on Cromwell's behalf during the recent war in Ireland. Under such leadership the Cromwellian land settlement was not likely to be set aside. And, though modified, it was not.

Whatever may have been the new king's inclinations, it was simply not politic to alienate too many of the New English settlers on whose loyalty the Restoration government depended. Some of them lost as much as a third of their property, though not a number of prominent Cromwellians such as Broghill (now the earl of Orrery) and Coote (earl of Mountrath). The Londonderry planters received royal confirmation of their charters. Some of the great royalist landlords such as the earls of Antrim (MacDonnell), Carlingford (Taafe), Westmeath (Nugent), Clanrickard (Burke), Clancarty (MacCarthy), and Muskerry (MacCarthy) received full restitution. About seven hundred other Catholics recovered all or part of their lost property, but several thousand remained unrewarded. The shift in land-ownership between 1641 (before the Cromwellian settlement) and 1665 (after the Restoration settlement) tells the story. In the former year Catholics owned about three-fifths of Ireland; in the latter, only one-fifth. The worst hit were the Gaelic Irish lords of Ulster, with the exception of the MacDonnell earl of Antrim. In Leinster and Munster Catholic holdings were reduced from about two-thirds of the land to about one-fifth; in Connacht from about four-fifths to one-half. A number of disappointed Catholics who had escaped transportation to Connacht took to the hills and bogs to become outlaws. They were called "tories," a term of opprobrium later applied to the Catholic and High Church faction in England and still later adopted proudly by the conservative party in that country.

Lands and tithes were also restored to the Church of Ireland, which was reestablished as the state church, though attracting no more than two hundred thousand worshippers, as against about eight hundred thousand Roman Catholics and perhaps one hundred thousand Presbyterians in Ulster, where migration from Scotland continued unabated. Despite the efforts of the primate, Archbishop John Bramhall of Armagh, the established church remained underendowed, ill served by an underpaid clergy, and incapable of repairing much of the damage to its buildings incurred during the years of war and Cromwellian neglect. The Presbyterians fared better on all counts partly because of an annual royal grant to their clergy of £600, the so-called *regium donum*.

As to the Catholics, their expectations of religious tolerance from the new king were to be disappointed. For most of the reign, to be sure, they were not actively persecuted, and a vigorous hierarchy was reestablished, with Oliver Plunkett as Catholic archbishop of Armagh and Peter Talbot as archbishop of Dublin. Then, in 1678, came the so-called Popish Plot— a totally fictitious English Catholic conspiracy to kill the king, concocted in the warped minds of two shady characters named Titus Oates and Israel

Tongue. In the mass hysteria that followed, thirty-five innocent English priests and Catholic laymen were put to death. In Ireland Archbishop Talbot was imprisoned in Dublin Castle, where he soon died. Archbishop Plunkett fared worse. Accused of abetting a scheme for a French landing in Carlingford Lough, he was tried in Dundalk, acquitted, retried in London, convicted of treason, and executed at Tyburn in 1681. Though King Charles was convinced of the archbishop's innocence, he sadly admitted, "I cannot pardon him because I dare not." Plunkett was later canonized and a shrine erected to his memory in the north aisle of **St. Peter's (RC) Church** *(396)* in Drogheda. It contains the severed and embalmed head of the Blessed Saint Oliver as well as the door of his cell in Newgate prison.

For most of Charles II's reign, Ireland was governed by that long-faithful royalist, James Butler, elevated in 1662 from earl to duke of Ormond. From 1660 to 1685 Dublin's population trebled (from about twenty thousand to sixty thousand) to become Great Britain's second city. Ormond set out to create there a physical setting suitable to his viceregal rank and his own great personal fortune, which was by far the largest in Ireland. Close to his residence he walled off two thousand acres of deer park, called **Phoenix Park** *(370)*, still one of the glories of the city. Closer to town, **St. Stephen's Green** *(357)* was laid out as a city square, twenty-seven acres in extent. During his term of office the area north of the river Liffey called Oxmantown expanded so rapidly that four new bridges had to be built within twenty years. To serve the new suburb's Protestant population **St. Michan's (C of I) Church** *(369)* rose on the foundations of an earlier house of worship. Across the river and west of the city, in **Kilmainham**, Ormond authorized the building of the **Royal Hospital** *(364)* for retired soldiers. Inspired by Louis XIV's Les Invalides in Paris, he appointed William Robinson as architect to design what is today Ireland's oldest truly neoclassical building and one of Dublin's showpieces.

Ormond's other residence was at Kilkenny, an ailing inland market town that the duke was largely responsible for revitalizing. There today in the upper floor of **Shee's Alms House** *(294)*, a late-sixteenth-century building, can be seen the "cityscope exhibit" consisting of a large contour map of the town and its buildings as they stood in Ormond's time. The most impressive of these still standing is **Rothe House** *(294)*, consisting of a main block built by the local merchant John Rothe in 1594, behind which are two courtyards and two additional houses added in the seventeenth century. Ormond's personal architectural contribution to the city's glory in the seventeenth century was the reconstruction of the Butler family seat of **Kilkenny Castle** *(294)*, which he converted into a magnificent French-style chateau. Unfortunately, later renovations here have altered and concealed almost all of the great duke's handiwork, which was undoubtedly more tasteful than the nineteenth-century neo-Gothic pile now masking it.

More durable was the viceroy's great fortification on the bank of Kinsale harbor, called **Charles Fort** *(323)* in honor of the reigning sovereign. This was a star-shaped fortress, designed by the Kilmainham Hospital's architect, Sir William Robinson, in the fashion made popular in the seventeenth century by the great French military engineer Sébastien le Prestre de Vauban. The contemporary remodelling of the ancient **Athlone Castle** *(391)*, County Westmeath, followed the same style. Ormond's concern for Ireland's defense led also to a restructuring of the army's organization. Following the English precedent, a new regimental system was adopted, which resulted in the creation of three regiments of horse and seven of foot. It was almost entirely a Protestant force, with all ranks required to take the sacrament according to the established Church of Ireland's Book of Common Prayer. When King Charles's Catholic brother came to the throne as James II in 1685, he took great pains to break this Protestant monopoly of the Irish army. In doing so he set himself on a course that was to lead to revolution in England, the loss of his throne to a Protestant Dutchman, a three-year war in Ireland, and the commencement of the "second hundred years' war" between Great Britain and France.

Shortly after coming to the throne, James II recalled the duke of Ormond, replacing him with Henry Hyde, second earl of Clarendon. The real power, however, lay with Richard Talbot, brother of the late Catholic archbishop who had died in Dublin Castle, a victim of the Popish Plot. Talbot advanced rapidly from regimental commander, to the rank of earl of Tyrconnel, to lieutenant general of the army, and finally in August 1686 to lord deputy of Ireland. In three years' time he retired from the Irish army 90 percent of its Protestant officers and men, replacing them with Catholics; created Catholic majorities in all three common law courts; appointed an English Catholic as lord chancellor of Ireland; replaced all county sheriffs but one with Catholics; voided most of the country's borough charters; and issued new charters giving Catholics and dissenters substantial majorities in town councils. In the autumn of 1687 Tyrconnel proposed, and the king approved, a bill to be submitted to the Irish parliament that would have returned to the heirs of the original Catholic owners a substantial fraction of the lands confiscated by Cromwell. Then, in June 1688, a male heir was born to James II, thus promising a Catholic succession to the throne of England. The event precipitated the so-called Glorious Revolution. Invitations were issued to the king's Protestant son-in-law, Prince William of Orange, to seize the English crown; the prince landed in Devon in November 1688 and moved on to London; the next month King James escaped to the Continent. The Protestant minority in Ireland rejoiced.

Having lost one kingdom, James II decided to regain another. In March 1689 he landed at Kinsale with French money and arms and moved on to Dublin, where a "patriot parliament" of Catholics acknowledged his sovereignty, declared its independence of the English parliament, formally invalidated the Cromwellian and Restoration land settlements, and proceeded to legalize the confiscation of the estates of about twenty-four hundred named persons, all Protestants.

Meanwhile the citizens of Londonderry had proclaimed Prince William and his wife, Mary, as king and queen. Then, thanks to the prompt action of a small band of apprentice-boys, they closed the gates of their **City Wall** *(463)* against the Jacobite troops sent from Dublin to garrison it. The town of Enniskillen followed suit. King James himself appeared in April before the Londonderry walls to offer terms. Led by a Protestant minister, George Walker, the citizens refused surrender, and a long siege ensued. Starvation gripped the town, which now harbored some thirty thousand people, including Protestant refugees from the countryside. Not until late July did an English fleet break the Jacobite boom emplaced across the river Foyle and bring relief; two days later the besieging army marched away. (On display in the chapter house museum of **St. Columb's Cathedral** *[464]*, Derry, are numerous relics of the siege.) Meanwhile at Newtown-butler the Protestants of Enniskillen had routed another besieging army under Justin MacCarthy, Viscount Mountcashel, taken the viscount prisoner, and slaughtered a large number of his Catholic troops from Munster.

These events in Ulster marked the beginning of what in Ireland is called "the War of the Two Kings" (*Cogadh an Dá Rí*), though in fact it was but one phase of a much larger war fought between England, Holland, and their allies and King Louis XIV of France, who was King James's patron. The only occasion when the two kings actually confronted each other on the field was at the river Boyne in County Louth, where James, with a force of about twenty-five thousand mixed Irish and French, faced William's army of thirty-seven thousand English, Dutch, Germans, Danes, French Huguenots (Protestants), and Ulstermen from Londonderry and Enniskillen. On 1 July 1690 (12 July by the present calendar), King William forced a passage across the river and routed the Catholic army. James fled to Dublin and thence to France. William of Orange moved south and occupied Dublin, but at the end of August he left for England and the war on the Continent, transferring command of his forces in Ireland to the Dutch general, Goddard van Reede, Baron von Ginkel.

The Battle of the Boyne, though strategically decisive, left most of the Jacobite army intact. The war went on. In the autumn of 1690 Cork fell to John Churchill, earl of Marlborough, as did Kinsale after the siege and capture of **James Fort** *(323)* and **Charles Fort** *(323)*. In May 1691 a sizable body of French reinforcements arrived under the command of Charles Chalmont, marquis de St. Ruth. On 30 June Ginkel took Athlone and on 12 July badly mauled St. Ruth's army at Aughrim Hill in County Galway sixteen miles south. St. Ruth himself was killed, along with about seven thousand of his troops—the largest casualty list from any battle ever fought on Irish soil. Galway city surrendered on generous terms on 21 July, and Ginkel moved on to the city of Limerick, the last of the Jacobite strongholds, now held by a largely Irish army under Sir Patrick Sarsfield. After a siege of more than two months Sarsfield capitulated, and on 3 October he and Ginkel signed a treaty of surrender, probably on the site of the **Treaty Stone** *(338)* now standing at the west end of the Thomond Bridge in Limerick city. The clauses of the treaty affecting Sarsfield and his troops were generous. They were allowed to sail to France to serve in the armies of King Louis XIV. About twelve thousand did so, many on ships provided by the English. Thus occurred the second massive exodus of "wild geese."

As to the Catholic civilians who remained, the first article of the treaty promised freedom of worship "consistent with the laws of Ireland or as they did enjoy in the reign of King Charles II." The second article offered pardon and a guarantee of property rights to those soldiers and civilians of Limerick, as well as of those parts of western Ireland still under Jacobite control, who remained in Ireland and took an oath of allegiance to William III. Since the existing laws of Ireland did not allow freedom of worship to Catholics, and since enforcement of those laws in the reign of Charles II had at times been strict and at other times lax, the meaning of the first article of the treaty was ambiguous at best. It is probable, however, that Ginkel and King William, in their anxiety to transfer their troops from Ireland to the Continent, meant to offer at least tacit religious toleration as an inducement to Sarsfield to surrender. In any event, the promise was to be repudiated by the Protestant Irish parliament. So was the treaty guarantee of property rights to those Jacobites who surrendered and swore allegiance after the end of hostilities. (See Chapter Six.)

The "betrayal" of Limerick, then, was to be added to the list of Irish Catholic grievances against the English and their Irish Protestant cohorts. The list was already long: the Ulster plantation, the Cromwellian sack of Drogheda and Wexford, the forcible transplantation of Catholic landlords to Connacht, the martyrdom of St. Oliver Plunkett, etc. On their side, the Protestants could point accusingly to the massacre of 1641 in Ulster, to Tyrconnel's attempted confiscations of 1687, boastfully to the heroic resistance of the apprentice boys of Londonderry, and to "King Billy's" glorious victory at the Boyne. Later generations too would draw selectively from the history of seventeenth-century Ireland to compose a sort of antiphonal chorus of recrimination: "hatred answering hatred," in the words of Lady Augusta Gregory, "death answering death through the generations like clerks at the mass."

Chapter Six

The Protestant Ascendancy: 1691–1801

Anxious to write *finis* to the Irish distraction and get on with the war on the Continent, King William and Queen Mary were quick to ratify the civil articles of the Treaty of Limerick. Not so the Protestant-controlled Irish parliament. Not until 1697 was the treaty confirmed, and then not in its original form. The first article concerning the religious rights of Roman Catholics was simply ignored. From the second the clause guaranteeing the property rights of Jacobites in the five counties of western Ireland was omitted entirely. Of these two deletions from the negotiated treaty, the latter was the less serious. By 1697 the Irish privy council had already heard the claims of 491 former Jacobites and accepted 483; after 1697 another 783 claims—out of 792 submitted—were granted by a panel of high-court judges. In the end nearly a quarter million profitable Irish acres were restored to their former owners, many of them among the leading Jacobite families, that is, those chiefly Roman Catholic nobles and gentry who had backed King James against the victorious King William III. The proportion of land owned by Catholics was thus reduced only from 22 percent in 1688 to 14 percent in 1703. But the assurance Catholics had received at Limerick of some kind of religious toleration was another matter. The now firmly entrenched "Protestant ascendancy" was not disposed to make the slightest concession to "popery" or to run the least risk that Roman Catholics might ever reassert themselves in Ireland.

CHURCH AND STATE

Roman Catholicism

Between 1691 and 1745 the Irish parliament enacted a series of anti-Catholic laws, known collectively as the "penal code." Their objectives were fourfold: (1) to break up the estates still in the hands of Catholic landlords and simultaneously prevent them from acquiring any additional real property; (2) to exclude Catholics from any role in government, either national or local; (3) to bar them from any professions, civil or military; and (4) to raise serious impediments to Catholic worship so that eventually Catholicism in Ireland would wither away.

Specifically the following measures were enacted: Catholics could not purchase land, acquire any by marriage, or obtain any by lease running for more than thirty-one years. The law of primogeniture no longer applied to Catholic estates, which, on the death of the owner, were to be divided among all male heirs unless the eldest conformed to the established Protestant Church, in which case he inherited in entirety. If the eldest son converted to the established Church during the lifetime of his father, he came into possession immediately. Catholics could neither vote for nor sit in parliament, nor could they sit on the bench, hold county offices, or be members of municipal corporations. They could not enter the legal profession or the university (Trinity College), act as school masters, bear arms, own a horse worth more than £5, or serve in the army or navy. Archbishops, bishops, and other prelates exercising ecclesiastical jurisdiction, as well as regular clergy (monks, friars, etc.), were to be banished from Ireland with severe penalties for returning. All other priests were compelled to register their names and to take oaths abjuring the exiled King James II and his son. No priests could enter the country from abroad. No Irish children could be educated in Catholic schools abroad. To enhance enforcement, "discoverers" of illegally held property were to be rewarded with the gift of the same, and comparable inducements were offered to "priest catchers," informers who exposed the presence of friars or other outlawed Catholic clergymen.

Draconian as these measures were, they appeared justified in the eyes of Ireland's political leadership as necessary (1) to protect the lives and property of the Protestant interest against the possible resurgence of the Catholic population, which constituted a majority of at least three or four to one; (2) to safeguard the Protestant succession to the throne of Ireland and Britain against the rival claims of the exiled Stuarts, James II and his son and grandson (James III, the "Old Pretender," and Charles Edward Stuart, the "Young Pretender"); and (3) to forestall a potential "fifth column" of Irish Catholics presumed to be in sympathy with France during the Anglo-French wars waged intermittently throughout the eighteenth century.

Nor were these fears entirely illusory. After 1714 Jacobite schemes for the return of the Stuart pretenders did indeed constitute an ongoing challenge to the Protestant Hanoverian dynasty, whose legitimacy was questionable anyway under the rule of primogeniture. Ireland's particular susceptibility to the appeal of Jacobitism had been demonstrated amply when James Butler, second duke of Ormond, though not himself Catholic, defected to the Old Pretender in 1715 and four years later led an abortive invasion of Britain. (The duke's portrait by Geoffrey Kneller still hangs in the picture gallery of **Kilkenny Castle** *[294]*, which he deserted after expending considerable sums on its restoration.) How widespread Jacobite sentiment was throughout the country is unknown. Among the dispossessed, disinherited, and deprived Catholics, there is certainly no reason to believe that it was not. On the basis of literary evidence alone, sympathy for the Stuart cause and hopes for its success may have been general among the Gaelic-speaking Irish. Typical spokesmen for such hopes were the Gaelic poets Eoghan Rua O'Suilleabháin and Aogan O'Rathaille, who had perfected a unique poetic genre—the *aisling*, an elegy to Ireland's past glories coupled with a vision of future rescue from the "Saxon" usurpers by the return of a Stuart prince from overseas. Even Brian Merryman, in his well-known ribald *The Midnight Court (Cúirt an Mhea Oiche)*, paused briefly from his reflections on female lasciviousness and male impotence to lament "the king himself, that in his reign/Such unimaginable disaster/Should follow your people, man and master/Old stock uprooted on every hand/Without claim to rent or law or land . . . ."

The "king himself" was of course James II, who had fled to St. Germain in France, only to play the part of perpetual pawn in the wars of King Louis XIV against England—as did his son and grandson in the reign of Louis XV. In support of the Stuarts were thousands of Irish soldiers in French pay—"wild geese *(geanna)*" who fought bravely against the British at Blenheim and Fontenoy and elsewhere on the Continent and would presumably form the nucleus of any expeditionary force launched by the French king against the British Isles. Also to France came hundreds of Irish students (contrary to law) to study for the priesthood with the intention of returning to their homeland. That they were Jacobites to the man could be inferred from the fact that until 1760 the papacy recognized the Stuart claim to the throne of Britain and Ireland and furthermore allowed the Old Pretender to recommend candidates for vacant Irish bishoprics.

Thus Protestants in Ireland found it easy to believe that their Catholic fellow countrymen were all potential traitors eagerly waiting the day when a Stuart prince, with French and papal assistance, should appear on Irish shores to free the land of British and Protestant rule. But no such deliverance ever occurred, nor was there any Jacobite uprising, even in the years 1708, 1715, and 1745, when the two Pretenders successively led expeditions to Scotland. And when, in 1760, a French admiral, François Thurot, did succeed in capturing and briefly occupying **Carrickfergus Castle** *(460)* on the Antrim coast, no Catholics rose in his support; indeed many signed petitions of loyalty to King George. By that time, in any case, enforcement of the penal laws against the Catholic religion, as such, had slackened almost to the point of disappearance. Those affecting the distribution of land had, to be sure, accomplished their purpose. By the 1770s the share owned by Catholics had shrunk from about 14 percent to an estimated 5 percent—largely owing to conversions (nominal or otherwise) to the established Church. Also the laws barring Catholics from political office and from the professions had succeeded in their intent—with the unexpected result of driving many Catholics into trade and thus creating a substantial "papist" middle class.

But, except during the early years, the laws against clerics and religious observances were enforced only intermittently, with the result that Catholicism not only survived but flourished. In a report of 1731 to the Irish house of lords it was estimated that there were altogether in Ireland 1,440 priests, sixty religious houses, and 890 Catholic houses of worship (called "mass-houses"). "Popery" obviously was not about to wither away.

By mid-century the Catholic hierarchy had been restored to full strength, meaning that there were resident bishops in all dioceses and that all four Irish archiepiscopal sees were filled. Almost eight hundred friars, half of them Franciscans, were active in both town and countryside. Registered parish priests were free to say mass, administer the sacraments, officiate at marriages, bury the dead, etc. At first services were commonly held in private houses, barns, warehouses, and the like, or sometimes in open fields at places marked by "mass rocks." As the century progressed, however, more substantial places of worship came to be constructed, though often sited as unobtrusively as possible and lacking church bells or steeples so as not to attract the attention of unfriendly Protestant magistrates. The oldest and best preserved of these is **St. Patrick's Church** *(286)*, now incorporated within the Christian Brothers school in Waterford. Approachable by an alleyway leading off George Street, this building's modesty belies its elegant galleried interior of neoclassic design. Even more modest is **St. Finbarr's South (South Chapel)** *(318)* in Cork, built in 1766 but since restored after a fire. Far more numerous than the surviving eighteenth-century Catholic churches are the collections of so-called "penal crosses" now on view in numerous museums; among others, the **Maynooth College Ecclesiological Museum** *(378)*, County Kildare; the **Mullingar Cathedral Museum** *(393)*, County Westmeath; the **Hunt Museum** *(338-339)*, Limerick; the **Donegal Historical Society Museum** *(427)* in Rossnowlagh; and the **Armagh County Museum** *(442)* in Armagh city. Miniature in size, they were once thought to have been thus made so that outlawed clerics could conceal them on their persons. More probably they were distributed as souvenirs of pilgrimages to Lough Derg and other holy places. Forbidden by law, pilgrimages were nonetheless popular among the laity, though generally frowned upon by French-trained bishops, who deemed such manifestations of native piety to be archaic superstitions and occasions for unseemly and even riotous behavior.

The last four decades of the eighteenth century saw a steady erosion of the penal code, ending in its all but total repeal. Many factors led to this conclusion. In the Treaty of Paris of 1763, ending the Seven Years' War with France, the British government acknowledged the right of Catholics in the newly acquired province of Canada to worship according to their own conscience. Consistency seemed to demand similar concessions to Ireland, and the fact that Irish Catholics (unlike many Presbyterians) were demonstrably loyal to the Crown during the American and French Revolutions served as a further inducement. With the death of the Old Pretender in 1766 and the refusal of the pope to recognize the claim of his son Charles Edward ("Bonnie Prince Charlie") to the throne of Britain, the specter of a Jacobite succession evaporated. The need for Irish recruits to fight in Britain's wars persuaded the government in Westminster to bring pressure on a reluctant parliament in Dublin to remove the penal laws, one by one, from the statute book. Within the Irish Protestant community itself, enlightened thinkers emerged to question century-old assumptions about the incompatibility of Catholicism and loyal citizenship. Among these were such disparate figures as the liberal parliamentarian Henry Grattan, the radical republican Theobald Wolfe Tone, the Francophobe conservative Edmund Burke, and the wealthy Church of Ireland bishop Frederick Augustus Hervey.

Finally prominent members of the Irish Catholic community itself took heart and organized themselves into a political pressure group, the Catholic Committee of Dublin. In December 1792 a convention of two hundred Catholic representatives from most of the towns and counties of Ireland met at the **Tailors' Hall** *(361)* on Back Lane in Dublin to petition King George himself for relief. The king in fact received in person the convention's chosen delegation—a gesture inconceivable even a decade earlier. The following January the British home secretary, Henry Dundas, prepared a relief bill, subsequently passed by the Irish parliament. Except for the privilege of parliamentary membership, full citizenship was virtually restored to Irish Roman Catholics, their religious freedom assured, and their rights to property reinstated. Only two years later (in 1795) the Irish parliament, in response to the closing of the Irish colleges in France by the revolutionary government, authorized and endowed a national seminary for the training of Catholic priests—**Maynooth (St. Patrick's) College** *(378)* in County Kildare. In the following year the first of the post-Reformation Catholic cathedrals opened its doors—**Holy Trinity Cathedral** *(286)* in Waterford, a handsome neoclassic edifice built to the design of the architect John Roberts.

But if a new spirit of religious tolerance (coupled with considerations of expediency) undermined the Protestant zeal of political leaders in both Britain and Ireland, it cannot be said that such enlightenment was widespread among the Irish people at large. Religious animosities were too deep-seated to be exorcised by mere acts of parliament. In Ulster especially, sectarian strife was rampant in the 1790s. Bands of Protestant laborers and small farmers, calling themselves "Peep o'Day Boys," took to terrorizing local Catholics, who in turn formed themselves into societies of "Defenders" to take retaliatory measures. In 1795 a skirmish between two such gangs took place at a spot called "the Diamond" near Loughgall in County Armagh. The Protestants won and celebrated their victory by founding the first of Ireland's "Orange Societies" in a house in Loughall now home to the **Orange Order Museum** *(443)*, named grandiosely after William of Orange, paramount deity in the Irish Protestant pantheon. Thus a seemingly insignificant roadside brawl rang up the curtain on the long-lasting sectarian vendetta with which the name of Ulster is still unhappily identified.

The Church of Ireland

Protestant in form of worship, episcopalian in organization, and established by law, the Church of Ireland after 1691 was, legally speaking, without serious rival. It was also without a sufficient number of communicants to justify its titular claim to being *the* national church. Membership probably included no more than an eighth to a tenth of the total population of Ireland. The weakness of the established Church was, in the words of Anthony Dopping, bishop of Meath, "the want of Protestants." Financially, however, this was no major handicap, since almost all of the agrarian population, of no matter what religious persuasion, had to pay tithes to the established Church—theoretically computed at one-tenth of the fruits of the earth, payable either in kind or in money equivalents. Notwithstanding this guaranteed source of income, the Irish Church was poor—compared at least to its sister establishment in England. It was of course the lower clergy—vicars and curates of the parish churches—who suffered most. In many cases church revenues had long since been alienated to lay patrons. In others, where the collection of tithes had been assigned to "tithe proctors" or "tithe farmers," only a fraction of these revenues passed ultimately into the hands of the parish clergymen themselves. This led inevitably to pluralism and absenteeism on the parish level—several parishes being ministered to by a single clergyman.

Church fabrics also suffered for want of upkeep and repairs. The Protestants of course had taken over all medieval churches at the time of the Reformation, but two centuries of intermittent warfare, along with general neglect, had taken a grievous toll. Some were in ruins; more were in a state of severe disrepair—especially in rural districts. In the towns, however, and in many villages bordering the demesnes of great landlords, the eighteenth century witnessed a building boom of Protestant churches—many of them still in use, though their congregations have shrunk significantly. Some were built *de novo*; others were the product of radical restorations of existing structures. In some instances the chunky neo-Gothic architectural style of the Jacobean period (sometimes called "planters' gothic") persisted. But in most cases church builders adhered to the fashionable canons of Palladian or neoclassic design. Standard Protestant interiors were rectangular, flat-ceilinged, with galleries on three sides, a shallow chancel at the east end, a high pulpit with sounding board, and box pews in the nave. Windows were usually capacious, round-headed, and clear, although nineteenth-century "restorers" often inappropriately substituted stained glass. Classical motifs were common to both exteriors and interiors: pedimented doorways, columns and pilasters reminiscent of ancient Greece or Rome, rectangular wall panels, carved or molded swags of flowers and fruits, etc.

Erected sometime beween 1697 and 1702, to a design by Thomas Burgh, the surveyor general of Ireland, **St. Mary's Church** *(368)* on Mary Street, Dublin, was probably modelled on one or more of Christopher Wren's London churches built after the great fire of 1666. Burgh was also the architect of **St. Werburgh's Church** *(359)* in Dublin, built in 1715 as the chapel royal for nearby Dublin Castle. Though the tower was later removed, the extant neoclassical west front is original. Also in Dublin are **St. Anne's** *(356)* on Dawson Street and **St. Catherine's** *(363)*, Thomas Street, both built in the eighteenth century. The former is still a Protestant house of worship, but the latter, designed by John Smyth, has been converted into a concert hall.

In County Laois stands the only church designed by the great James Gandon. This is **Coolbanagher Church** *(313)*, an architectural gem, as might be expected of such a master of classicism. Recently restored, it has a narrow rectangular nave, a gallery at the west end, and classical urns in niches lining the side walls. There is no prettier small church in Ireland. Less attractive is **Cashel (C of I) Cathedral** *(302)*, County Tipperary, built in 1763 when the Protestant archbishop decided to move his seat from the decrepit medieval cathedral on the nearby Rock. He chose the outdated neo-Gothic style, and the church's appearance was not improved by heavy-handed restoration in the nineteenth century. More typical of the age is **St. Iberius Church** *(283)* in Wexford, with its serenely classical galleried interior and pews untypically arranged along the long axis of the building facing an altar flanked by twin Corinthian pillars. **Christ Church Cathedral** *(287)* in Waterford was built in the 1770s to the design of a local architect, John Roberts, who was also responsible for the Roman Catholic cathedral in the same city, described earlier. Like St. Mary's, Dublin, this was apparently modelled on one of Wren's churches, probably St. James, Piccadilly. The church is an aisled rectangle, very classical in appearance, though the subsequent removal of the original side galleries rendered the interior somewhat out of proportion. In Cork the neoclassical **St. Anne Shandon Church** *(319)*, with its tall western domed tower, is one of the prominent landmarks of the city. Reputedly designed by the local architect John Coltsman, it was begun in 1722, though the tower, with its famous set of bells, was not raised to its present height until 1749. More elegant is **St. Peter's (C of I) Church** *(396)*, Drogheda, erected in 1753 on the site of an earlier church burned down by Cromwell's soldiers during the famous siege. The tower and steeple by Francis Johnston were added toward the end of the century. Inside is to be found the usual rectangular arrangement, with galleries resting on Corinthian columns, ornate stuccowork on the walls, and fine plasterwork and woodwork throughout.

In Northern Ireland **Holy Trinity Cathedral** *(434)*, Downpatrick, is a handsome eighteenth-century rebuilding of the medieval church first established here by John de Courcy. More handsome still is **St. Malachy's Church** *(435)* in Hillsborough, also in County Down. Begun in the seventeenth century, this neo-Gothic cruciform church is mostly the product of a rebuilding in 1774 financed by Wills Hills, marquess of Hillsborough. Also cruciform, though otherwise neoclassic in design, is tiny **Clogher Cathedral** *(444)*, County Tyrone, built about 1744, though later remodelled. Finally, and more typical of the scores of "landlord churches" put up in villages all over Ireland in the eighteenth century, is **Holy Trinity Church** *(453)* in Ballycastle, County Antrim. This is a simple rectangular building with a classical pedimented west doorway and tower, unpretentious but well proportioned—a testimonial to the good taste that informed even the most modest essays in Georgian architecture.

Protestant in creed and liturgy, the Church of Ireland, like its English counterpart, was episcopalian in structure—meaning that it was ruled by bishops *(episcopi)*. The primate, as in the medieval church and the revived Roman Catholic Church, was the archbishop of Armagh. Second in rank was the archbishop of Dublin. Both archiepiscopal sees were normally filled by Englishmen, as were the bishoprics of most of the important dioceses in Ireland. Preferment to high office in the Church depended more on patronage than either piety or talent. One could almost say, as did Lord Melbourne of the Order of the Garter, that there "was no damned merit in it."

Nonetheless, the Church of Ireland in the eighteenth century produced a number of able and enlightened prelates who left their mark on the country's cultural landscape. Narcissus Marsh, archbishop of Armagh, founded the country's first public library in Dublin—**Marsh's Library**

(362)—a building designed by Sir William Robinson and still in use. Another primate, Richard P. Robinson, founded the **Public Library** *(442)* in the city of Armagh and engaged Thomas Cooley to design this fine neoclassical building. In Cashel Archbishop Theophilus Bolton donated eight thousand books to the diocesan library (now the **GPA-Bolton Library** *[303]*) on the grounds of the Protestant cathedral church. Frederick Augustus Hervey, bishop of Derry and earl of Bristol, commissioned the construction of **Mussenden Temple** *(463)* adjacent to his great country house **Downhill** *(463)*, now a romantic ruin overlooking the sea on the rugged northern coast near Coleraine, County Londonderry. The rotunda-shaped temple was originally planned as a library and a repository for objets d'art picked up by this indefatigable traveller on the Continent, after whom were named the many Bristol Hotels in Europe. It is thought to have been modelled on the Temple of Vesta at Tivoli and is a splendid example of neoclassicism in its purest form. More ecumenical than most of his peers, the earl/bishop allowed mass to be said for his Roman Catholic tenants in the temple's crypt. Another enlightened bishop, though of a different stripe, was George Berkeley, whose recumbent effigy is still to be seen in **Cloyne Cathedral** *(317)*, his episcopal seat in County Cork. A philosopher of international reputation best known today for his *Treatise Concerning the Principles of Human Knowledge* (1710) and *Alciphron, or the Minute Philosopher* (1732), he was also an astute observer of the contemporary scene, as demonstrated in the *Querist* (1735-37), three volumes addressed to Ireland's myriad social and economic problems.

Finally, at the head of the roster of distinguished eighteenth-century Irish churchmen stands the name of Jonathan Swift, dean of **St. Patrick's Cathedral** *(362)*, Dublin, for more than thirty years (1713-45). Dublin-born and Trinity College–educated, Swift hoped vainly for ecclesiastical preferment in England and only grudgingly accepted the deanship of St. Patrick's. Out of political favor after the Whigs came to power in 1715, he remained in Ireland *faute de mieux*, nursing his grievances and plying an acid pen against the world's injustices and follies. Best remembered today for *Gulliver's Travels*, his most popular writings during his own lifetime were those denouncing the maltreatment of Ireland by the English parliament.

Afflicted with Ménière's disease, he suffered a debilitating stroke in 1742 and was judged mad by his contemporaries. The judgment, though incorrect by the standards of modern medicine, seemed confirmed when it was revealed that he had bequeathed the bulk of his fortune to the establishment in Dublin of a hospital for the insane ("of aged lunaticks and other diseased persons"). The product of his generosity was **St. Patrick's (Swift's) Hospital** *(363)*, which still serves as the city's leading institution for psychiatric care. On display inside is a good collection of Swift's publications and personal memorabilia. (His death mask, desk, and other mementos are to be seen in **Marsh's Library** *[362].*) The dean lies buried, alongside his dear friend "Stella" (Esther Johnson), in **St. Patrick's Cathedral** *(362),* where his bust stands against the south wall and sundry memorabilia are to be found in the north transept.

Swift's reputation as a satirist has tended to obscure the fact that he was above all a churchman—a powerful and popular preacher, lavish in his personal gifts to the Dublin poor, diligent in the preservation and restoration of his cathedral. He was also an ardent defender of the privileges and prerogatives of the established Church of Ireland. And in that connection he was a bitter enemy to Protestant dissenters, especially the Presbyterians of Ulster, among whom he had briefly and unhappily sojourned while pastor of the parish church at Kilroot near Carrickfergus, County Antrim.

The Dissenters

Stepchildren of the Ascendancy were those Protestants who declined to conform to the established Church. In numbers they almost equalled the communicants of the Church of Ireland. Economically, socially, and above all politically, their status was inferior.

The least objectionable of the dissenting sects, in the eyes of the establishment, were the French Huguenots. About ten thousand of these people had emigrated to Ireland soon after Louis XIV's revocation of the Edict of Nantes in 1685; at least as many fought with King William III and stayed on after the Treaty of Limerick; and more were still to come. In religious persuasion and form of worship they were Calvinist, and an act of parliament of 1692 allowed them to worship "in their own several rites used in their own countries." But pressures to conform to the usages of the Church of Ireland were strong, and many of the Huguenot congregations eventually did so, although those who did remain faithful to the religion of their forebears were tolerated.

The earliest and largest settlement of French Protestants was in Dublin, where the Huguenot La Touche family eventually became the city's most prominent bankers. Another colony (veterans of King William's army) made their homes in Portarlington, County Laois, under the protection of one of the king's generals, Henri de Ruvigny, earl of Galway. The French church there did not close its doors until 1841, when the site was taken over by **St. Paul's Church** *(313),* which still proclaims itself as "the Huguenot Church." In Waterford the settlers were allowed to worship in the now-ruined Franciscan friary, still known as the **French Church** *(286).* In 1698, by royal invitation, Louis Crommelin, a Dutch Huguenot, settled in Lisburn with seventy-five French families and a thousand looms for the production of linen cloth. Relics of the enterprise are still to be seen in the **Lisburn Museum** *(462)*, County Antrim.

Far greater in number, and far less welcome to the established Church, were the Presbyterians. In the fifteen years after the Battle of the Boyne approximately fifty thousand Scots emigrated to Ireland, mostly to Ulster, where the total number of so-called Scotch-Irish rose to about two hundred thousand, or roughly one-third of the population of the province. With few exceptions these people were Presbyterians, worshipping according to the precepts of the Church of Scotland and organizing themselves into a religious community ruled by joint committees of clergymen and laymen called *presbyteries* and (on a higher level of authority) *synods*. In Scotland, with the concurrence of King William and Queen Mary, they had succeeded in abolishing episcopacy in favor of their own preferred form of church government. Lest they attempt the same in Ireland, the hierarchy of the established Church and its lay supporters among the Ascendancy imposed severe restraints on their political power as well as other discriminatory disabilities.

In the so-called Popery Act of 1704, the Dublin parliament required that none but communicants of the established Church hold any office, civil or military, or receive any pay or salary from the Crown, or have "command of any place of trust from the sovereign." This in effect barred Presbyterians from the municipal corporations that ruled the towns and elected members to the Irish house of commons, from magistracies and other county offices, and from commissions in the army and the militia. It did not, surprisingly, bar them from sitting in parliament, although very few ever did so. After 1719, to be sure, the act was nullified substantially by the periodic grant of indemnities to Presbyterians who had failed to pass the sacramental test, but it was not until 1780 that it was finally repealed, and then only under heavy pressure from the government in Westminster. The second major Presbyterian grievance was the nonrecognition of the validity of their marriages by the ecclesiastical courts that had the power to levy charges of fornication against men and women joined in matrimony by a Presbyterian minister and thus to bastardize their children. Not until 1782 was this disability completely removed by act of parliament. Finally Presbyterians were compelled by law to pay tithes for the support of the established Church. In this respect they were fellow sufferers with Roman Catholics, though not until the last decade of the century did sectarian hostility between the two denominations abate to the extent of allowing some cooperation against their common oppressor.

Notwithstanding these handicaps, Presbyterianism flourished, especially in Ulster, where their congregations numbered about 120 in the early years of the century. One reason was that their ministers, except during the final years of the reign of Queen Anne, received a regular stipend from the

Crown. This was the *regium donum*, first granted in 1672 and by 1784 amounting to £2,600 per annum. On the other hand their position was weakened somewhat by internal strife on the issue of whether or not to subscribe to the Westminster Confession of Faith, which, since the mid–seventeenth century, had been the doctrinal cornerstone of the Church of Scotland. In 1726 the matter was more or less settled when all nonsubscribing congregations seceded to form the presbytery of Antrim, leaving the majority in the Synod of Ulster. It was one of these seceding congregations that built the **First Presbyterian Church** *(456)* on Rosemary Street in Belfast. Completed in 1783 to the design of a local architect, Roger Mulholland, it is still in operation, though now holding Unitarian services. It is a charming red brick building, oval in shape, though somewhat marred by alterations to the front in the nineteenth century. The interior is also oval, with curving galleries supported by Corinthian columns, box pews, and a fine high pulpit with a curving staircase. Among the still-standing "subscribing" churches of about the same date are two worth mentioning. The **First Presbyterian Church** *(463)*, Randalstown, County Antrim, also oval in shape, built in 1780 but later modified by the addition of a polygonal front porch. The second is the **First Presbyterian Church** *(432)* of Banbridge, County Down, a very pretty neoclassic building with Ionic pillars in front, galleries on three sides, and a fine panelled ceiling.

Despite these evidences of growth and increasing prosperity, the Presbyterians of Ireland remained second-class citizens. Thus the term "Protestant Ascendancy" is something of a misnomer. Defined by the Dublin corporation in 1792 as consisting of "a protestant king in Ireland, a protestant parliament, a protestant hierarchy, protestant electors and government, the benches of justices, the army, the revenue through all their branches and details protestant," the Ascendancy in fact represented only half of the Protestant population and therefore no more than one-eighth of the total population of Ireland. And of that proportion only a fraction, consisting of landed families and a small number of lawyers and prosperous merchants, actively participated in the business of government.

GOVERNMENT AND POLITICS, 1691–1789

The king of England was also king of Ireland, and his viceroy in that country was the lord lieutenant. This office was filled by a succession of prominent English noblemen who, until 1767, resided in Dublin only when the Irish parliament was in session but after that date took up permanent official residence in **Dublin Castle** *(358)*. This complex of buildings underwent drastic remodelling in the first half of the eighteenth century, and to this period belongs most of the construction to be seen today around the Upper Yard, including the luxuriously appointed State Apartments that stretch along the entire south side of the yard.

Before 1767, during the lord lieutenants' frequent absences, their executive duties were performed by the chief justices of Ireland, who were normally the primate, the lord chancellor, and the speaker of the house of commons. The lord lieutenant's primary responsibility was to maintain British interests in Ireland, especially to ensure that revenue measures were carried through parliament. In this respect he had the tremendous advantage of Poynings's Law of 1494, which in effect subordinated the Irish government to the English king and privy council (see Chapter Three). "The Castle," to use the popular sobriquet for the executive branch of the Irish government, also had at its disposal a considerable amount of patronage—positions or "places" in the civil service, the Church, and the military—which it employed unabashedly to buy votes in parliament. This species of corruption, common also in contemporary Britain, was euphemistically called "management" and was conducted with the cooperation of "undertakers," that is, members of parliament in league with the Castle. The lord lieutenant, and the chief justices during his absences, were assisted by a privy council, most of whose business stemmed from Poynings's Law. That is, it prepared government bills; transmitted them to the English privy council before they could be submitted to the Irish parliament; approved or disapproved measures initiated in the Irish parliament (called "heads of bills"), then sent them on to the English privy council for acceptance, rejection, or alteration; and finally resubmitted them to the Irish parliament for approval or disapproval without further alteration.

Parliament, as in Britain, consisted of a house of lords and a house of commons. The former contained twenty-two spiritual peers (archbishops and bishops of the Church of Ireland) and a varying number of temporal peers. The commons (an all-Protestant body) had three hundred members, two from each of the thirty-two counties, two from each of 117 boroughs, and two from Trinity College. Parliaments were in session once every two years for about six months. Elections were infrequent since, until the passage of the Octennial Act of 1768, the life of any single parliament lasted for the entire length of the reign of the monarch under which it was first called. The franchise was extremely restricted, first by religious qualifications and second by property qualifications, but most of all by the pervasive power and influence of the great Protestant landlord families, not only in the counties but in most of the boroughs as well. Only in Dublin and Cork was there anything approaching popular election of members of parliament. As already indicated, the legislative powers of the Irish parliament were severely limited by Poynings's Law, which in effect denied it the authority to alter bills submitted by the government or to prevent the alteration of "heads of bills" initiated by itself. Moreover, matters touching the British Empire or Britain's foreign policy were considered reserved subjects that the Irish parliament was not allowed to touch. And to banish any doubt on the matter, in 1720 the Westminster parliament passed the so-called Declaratory Act, asserting that it had full authority to make laws binding the kingdom and people of Ireland and that the Irish house of lords had no appellate jurisdiction.

Until 1728 parliamentary sessions were held in Chichester House, just northwest of the entrance to Trinity College. In that year the cornerstone was laid for the splendid new neoclassic edifice with its facade of Ionic columns that now houses the **Bank of Ireland** *(353)*. The building came into being on the initiative of William Conolly, powerful speaker of the house of commons (1715–29), son of a Donegal publican, successful speculator in forfeited Jacobite property, and fabulously rich by Irish standards. The original architect was himself a member of parliament—Sir Edward Lovett Pearce—who died before the job was finished, to be replaced by Arthur Dodds, another member. In 1780 the English traveller Arthur Young judged the building to be far superior "to that heap of confusion at Westminster." And this was before the architect James Gandon added the handsome portico that was to contain the house of lords.

Another of Gandon's neoclassic masterpieces was the magnificent domed **Four Courts** *(368)*, upriver from the town center. The original architect was Thomas Cooley, but after his death in 1774 Gandon took over and completed the building twenty years later. Here (and before 1796 in more crowded quarters near Christ Church Cathedral) sat the court of chancery and the three common law courts of king's bench, common pleas, and exchequer. From 1720 to 1782 (during the operation of the Declaratory Act) appeals from their decisions could be taken only to the British house of lords. The Irish legal profession (exclusively Protestant for most of the century) was organized into a body called the Honourable Society of King's Inns, modelled on the English inns of court. Until 1795 it was housed in a building on the site turned over to the Four Courts; after that date it had a new home on the north side of the river—**King's Inns** *(369)*, another great neoclassic structure, built to the design, again, of James Gandon.

Although the Ascendancy's privileged position and its security from internal and external foes depended largely on British protection, the Anglo-Irish Protestant community chafed from time to time under the restrictions imposed by Westminster. Most of their complaints stemmed from the economic subordination of Ireland to Britain and from their country's being force-fitted into an imperial pattern deliberately designed, in accordance with mercantilist principles, for the primary benefit of the "mother country." Economic historians today differ as to whether the costs to Ireland under Britain's "old colonial system" outweighed the benefits, or vice versa. Few such doubts seem to have occurred to contemporary Irishmen, or at least those who saw fit to express themselves in writing on the subject. They strenuously protested the constitutional arrangements that subjected Ireland to British parliamentary rule, and they urged Irish economic reprisals in self-defense. In general their arguments anticipated those of the American colonists from 1763 to 1776, although not until the final decade of the century did the most radical among them contemplate secession from the British Empire.

Earliest among the complainants was William Molyneux, member of parliament from Trinity College and friend of the English political philosopher John Locke, from whom came many of his ideas. Anticipating the English parliament's passage of the Woollens Act of 1699, which forbade the export of Irish woolen textiles except to England, where they faced prohibitive duties, Molyneux published *The case of Ireland's being bound by acts of parliament in England stated*. Arguing the constitutional right of Ireland to be subject to no laws except those passed by its own parliament, he concluded (drawing on Locke) that "the right of being subject only to such laws to which men give their own consent is . . . inherent to all mankind." Some two decades later Jonathan Swift echoed the same sentiment, questioning "whether a law to bind men without their own consent" was valid. In his first appearance as a popular pamphleteer, Swift, in *A proposal for the universal use of Irish manufacture*, urged his fellow countrymen to boycott British goods and burn "every Thing that came from England, except their People and their Coals." Two years later (in 1722), in response to a grant by the king to one Thomas Wood of a monopoly to mint debased copper coinage in Ireland, Swift published his *Drapier's Letters*. In the fourth of these, addressed "to the whole People of Ireland" (by which he meant the Anglo-Irish Protestant community), he claimed that "all Government without the consent of the Governed is the very Definition of Slavery." Four years later his anger and bitterness toward British rule drove him to suggest in *A Modest Proposal* that Ireland's poverty could be resolved only by marketing small children to be butchered and then "roasted, baked or boiled."

The constitutional arguments of Molyneux and Swift were soon taken up by a faction in the Irish parliament calling themselves the "Patriot Party." Prominent among them were Henry Flood and Henry Grattan in the house of commons and, in the house of lords, James Caulfield, earl of Charlemont. But not until the outbreak of the American Revolution did they make much headway. Denuded of her regular troops, Ireland was exposed to a serious risk of invasion when France and Spain entered the war on the American side. In response to the emergency Irish Protestants all over the country organized themselves into corps of "volunteers," procured uniforms and weapons, drilled and paraded, formed social and political clubs, and in the course of time began to demand constitutional reform and an end to the long-established commercial restrictions. Grattan and Flood sounded the same note in the Irish house of commons. Anxious to avoid a second war of independence so close to home, the British government gave way. In 1778 and 1779 most of the commercial restrictions were removed, in effect establishing free trade. In August 1781 Lord Cornwallis surrendered to General Washington at Yorktown, thus ending hostilities in America. The following March the Tory government in Westminster was forced to resign, In June 1782 a newly elected British parliament repealed the Declaratory Act of 1720; in July Poynings's Law was amended radically and the Irish judiciary declared independent. Finally an act was passed declaring the right of the people of Ireland to be bound only by laws enacted by the parliament of Ireland.

"Ireland," announced Grattan in the Dublin house of commons, "is now a nation." And for the next eighteen years "Grattan's parliament," though still the preserve of the Ascendancy, enjoyed legislative independence of Great Britain. True, the lord lieutenant and the Castle remained answerable to the British government alone. Yet to a degree the Protestant Ascendancy had won Home Rule, although the term itself would not come into general use for years to come. And Dublin for the first time could be called a national capital—at least of the "Protestant nation."

THE URBAN SCENE

In the first seven decades of the eighteenth century Dublin's population rose from about fifty thousand in 1700 to an estimated 129,000 in 1771, making it the second largest city in the British Isles. It was of course Ireland's major seaport. By 1728 artificial walls, constructed of oak staves and sunken boats loaded with stones, had been extended on both sides of the Liffey as far as Ringsend, thus clearing the harbor of its silted sand barriers and enabling seagoing ships to sail into the city's quays. Dublin's hinterland too began to open up. By mid-century roads leading out of the city had been sufficiently improved to allow regular coach services to Athlone, Cork, Kilkenny, Drogheda, and Belfast. In 1756 work began on the **Grand Canal** *(380)*, an ambitious project designed to link Dublin with the river Shannon. By 1779 the first stretch of water was opened as far as Robertstown, County Kildare, which is today a good place to get a view of it. In the

1790s digging began on the Royal Canal, running north of the Liffey, but by the end of the century it had advanced only about twenty miles west of Dublin.

The capital city was not, however, a manufacturing center of any significance. Most industrial activity was concentrated in the Liberties—west of St. Patrick's Cathedral—and consisted chiefly of linen weaving, furniture making, glass manufacture, and brewing. Here in 1759 Arthur Guinness, a brewer of Leixslip, obtained the lease on a brewery on James's Street to brew ale and porter. After 1799 he stopped producing ale, but by that time his dark porter (so called because it had proven a popular drink among London's porters) was already a much sought-after commodity in Ireland, and Guinness's was one of the biggest employers in Dublin. Today the museum and showroom of the **Guinness Brewery** *(363)* on the original, though much-extended, grounds are open to the public, though tours through the plant itself have been suspended. (They are still conducted at **Smithwick's Brewery** *[295]*, in Kilkenny, another eighteenth-century establishment, founded in 1710.)

As Dublin grew in numbers, it expanded in geographic scope—mostly downriver (eastward) of the old city, which had been centered around the two cathedrals south of the Liffey and Oxmantown to the north. Early in the century Joshua Dawson and Viscount Robert Molesworth began the development of a new residential area south of Trinity College. They enlarged Grafton Street and opened Anne, Duke, and Molesworth streets as well as Dawson Street, where the developer built his own house (now called the **Mansion House** *[356]*), which he later gave to Dublin corporation as a permanent residence for the lord mayor. East of here, the Fitzwilliam estate was opened up in the 1760s, and the architect John Ensor developed **Merrion Square** *(354)*, the first, and still perhaps the finest, of the Georgian residential areas that so elegantly grace the city. Here and elsewhere the streets are lined with rows (terraces) of tall, parapeted, red brick houses, somewhat plain in appearance but distinguished by their panelled doorways flanked with neoclassic pillars and surmounted by lacy fanlights of almost infinite variety. North of the river the banker Luke Gardiner built Henrietta Street (also lined with Georgian houses, some of them now being restored after years of neglect) and, with his son Charles, laid down the unusually wide boulevard (150 feet) called Gardiner's Mall, later to be renamed Sackville Street and still later O'Connell Street.

In 1757 the Irish parliament appointed the "commission for making wide and convenient streets," giving the commissioners (all members of parliament except for the lord mayor) authority to raze houses in the path of the new thoroughfares they planned. Their first endeavor was Parliament Street, which extends from the Castle down to the river at the new Essex (now Grattan) Bridge. Later they widened Dame Street and linked

Gardiner's Mall with the Parliament House by extending the mall to the Liffey and building Carlisle (now O'Connell) Bridge and Westmoreland Street, which ran in front of the portico Gandon built for the house of lords. All of this expansion was accompanied by a boom in the construction of both residential and public buildings, which fortunately coincided with one of the most felicitous of all phases in the history of British (and therefore Irish) architecture. Actually there were two overlapping phases, Palladian and neoclassic, not always easily distinguishable as both derived ultimately from ancient Greece and Rome. The seventeenth-century English architect Inigo Jones had first introduced Palladianism to Britain, but in the eighteenth century it was reintroduced by the Scot Colen Campbell and made fashionable by the third earl of Burlington. The style was imitative of the Roman architect Vitruvius as interpreted in the sixteenth century by Andrea Palladio, who, in his *I Quattro Libri dell' Architettura*, laid down precise rules of harmonic proportions and was profuse in his employment of certain stereotyped classical motifs, among them the temple-front portico of columns of the five classical orders (Ionic, Doric, Corinthian, Tuscan, and Composite) supporting a huge triangular pediment, heavy pediments over doors and windows, and the Venetian window consisting of a central round-arched light flanked by two smaller rectangular lights. British neoclassicism, largely a late-eighteenth-century development, is associated chiefly with the architectural designs of Robert Adam and his brothers, Sir William Chambers, and James Wyatt. Deriving from study of the sites of ancient Rome, or from the published illustrations of Giambattista Piranesi, the neoclassicists were somewhat more purist than the Palladians in their strict interpretation of the classical canon. In Ireland, however, Palladian elements lingered, and the distinction between the two styles is not so easily discernible. Among stuccodores who applied decorative plasterwork to interior walls a similar progression is evident—from the curvaceous and exuberant naturalism of the baroque and rococo to the cool and restrained symmetry typified by the work of the Adam brothers.

In Dublin the leading Palladian architect was Richard Cassels, German-born, who came to Ireland in the 1720s and anglicized his name to Richard Castle. En route he seems to have spent some time in England and there fallen under the influence of Lord Burlington and his school. For a while he worked with Sir Edward Lovett Pearce, original architect for Parliament House (now the **Bank of Ireland** *[353]*), and inherited his practice. About 1744 he was commissioned by James Fitzgerald, twentieth earl of Kildare, to build Kildare House, later called **Leinster House** *(355)* when the earl was elevated to the dukedom of that name and now the seat of the Irish national parliament (Oireachtas). Castle also designed **Tyrone House** *(365)* in Marlborough Street for Sir Marcus Beresford, later earl of

Tyrone. His masterpiece, however, was the **Rotunda Hospital** *(367)*, designed (more or less in imitation of Leinster House) before his death in 1751 and later completed by John Ensor. This was the first maternity hospital in the British Isles, opened in 1745 by Dr. Bartholomew Mosse, who planned to finance the project from the proceeds of the adjacent pleasure garden and the round assembly room (now the Ambassador Theatre) from which the hospital derives its name. Inside, the most interesting feature is the chapel with its spectacular baroque plasterwork by Bartholomew Cramillion, a French or Huguenot stuccodore. This is his only known handiwork in Dublin. An Irish artist of equal skill, Michael Stapleton, was responsible for the intricate designs in plaster applied to the walls of Belvedere House (now **Belvedere College** *[393]*), Great Denmark Street, and Powerscourt House (now **Powerscourt Townhouse Centre** *[357]*), South William Street.

The transition from Palladian to the purer form of neoclassic architecture is best illustrated in the work of Sir William Chambers, an English architect of established reputation who received several commissions for Irish buildings though he never himself visited the country. For the earl of Charlemont he designed two houses. The first, Charlemont House in Parnell Square (formerly Rutland Square), is now the **Hugh Lane Municipal Art Gallery** *(367)*, distinguished for both its style and its fine collection of paintings. The second, built as a garden house on the earl's country estate three miles outside of Dublin, is the **Casino Marino** *(370)*, arguably the most authentic replica of a Roman temple in Ireland. Another Englishman, Thomas Cooley, won the open competition for the commission to design Dublin's Royal Exchange. This splendid building on Dame Street, domed in the manner of Rome's Pantheon, now serves as the **City Hall** *(359)*. The interior plasterwork, by the Dublin alderman Charles Thorp, is purely classical, in contrast to the lively baroque style favored by Cramillion and Stapleton. Cooley also entered the competition for the commission to build the **Blue Coat (King's Hospital) School** *(369)* for boys, but it was won by Thomas Ivory, the Cork-born master of architectural drawing in the Dublin Society schools, described later in this chapter. This fine neoclassic (arguably Palladian) edifice still stands on Blackhall Place, though now it houses the law school and offices of the Incorporated Law Society of Dublin.

Finally the architectural landscape of late-eighteenth-century Dublin owed perhaps its biggest debt to the English Palladian/neoclassicist James Gandon, one-time student of Sir William Chambers, who settled in Ireland in 1781 at the behest of John Beresford, member of parliament and wide-streets commissioner. Two of his architectural masterpieces (the **Four Courts** *[368]* and the **King's Inns** *[369]*) have already been mentioned, as well as his addition to Parliament House (the **Bank of Ireland** *[353]*). His most magnificent building undoubtedly is the **Custom House** *(365)*, built on a reclaimed mud bank downriver from Carlisle (O'Connell) Bridge, near which its predecessor had stood. Although Grattan denounced it as "a building of the sixth rank in architecture but of first rate in extravagance," few then would have agreed, and none now. This monumental building, with its long facade and high dome, dominates the seaward (eastern) side of the central city of Dublin, just as Gandon's **Four Courts** *(368)* does on the west.

Dublin was not only the seat of government but the cultural center of Ireland as well. In this respect the heart of the city was **Trinity College** *(352)*, alma mater of Ireland's most distinguished lawyers, members of parliament, clergymen, and writers. In the last category are to be included Dean Swift, Bishop Berkeley, the conservative philosopher Edmund Burke, the poet Oliver Goldsmith, and the playwrights Thomas Southerne and William Congreve. The college grew substantially in numbers during the last half of the eighteenth century and, under the provostship of John Hely-Hutchinson, expanded its curriculum to include the teaching of physical science as well as modern languages. It also expanded architecturally. The **Library** *(353)* was begun in 1712 to the design of Thomas Burgh. Richard Castle is responsible for the little Doric printing house at the entrance to New Square. The splendid Palladian west front on College Green was put up in the 1750s, as was the like-styled Provost's House, copied from General Wade's residence in London, designed by Lord Burlington himself. Sir William Chambers was chosen as the architect for the chapel and the Examination Hall, both gems of neoclassic style with fine ceiling plasterwork by Michael Stapleton.

Trinity College was not the only center of intellectual activity in Georgian Dublin. In 1786 the **Royal Irish Academy** *(356)* received its charter, though not its present home on Dawson Street, which is of mid-nineteenth-century date. Its first president was the earl of Charlemont, and its purpose was to collect ancient Irish manuscripts and promote the knowledge of Irish history and literature. More immediate and practical were the concerns of the Dublin Society, founded in 1731 with the objective of "improving husbandry, manufacture and the useful arts and sciences." Dedicated to "improvement," an eighteenth-century enthusiasm widespread among enlightened thinkers and doers throughout the British Isles, it set up a model farm, provided instruction, encouraged tillage, imported agricultural machinery, and in general encouraged modernization in agriculture and industry. And in the 1740s the society took over the operation of a drawing school founded by Robert West, a Dublin artist and stuccodore. This was to be the beginning of a new era of professionalism in Irish graphic art.

Prior to the establishment of the Dublin Society Drawing Schools, professional painters in Ireland were few in number. In the last decade of the seventeenth century the native-born Garret Morphey had painted portraits, chiefly of Jacobite families. Early in the eighteenth century Charles Jervis, Irish-born but London-based, made several trips home to paint the likenesses of Irish sitters. Other popular contemporary portraitists were the Englishman Stephen Slaughter and James Latham of County Tipperary, the latter being the most accomplished of the lot. In the second half of the century the influence of the Dublin Society Drawing Schools is reflected in the native portraitists Hugh Douglas Hamilton, Nathaniel Hone the elder, his son Horace Hone (a miniaturist), James Barry, and Robert Hunter.

Landscape painting too was becoming popular, influenced not only by the school, but also by the publication in 1756 of Edmund Burke's tract *A Philosophical Enquiry into the Origin of our Ideas of the Sublime and Beautiful*. Burke was a patron of James Barry and also of George Barrett, whom he encouraged to paint the wild scenery of Counties Dublin and Wicklow. Other Irish landscapists of the Romantic school inspired by Burke were Robert Carver, Thomas Roberts and his younger brother Thomas Sautell Roberts, Susannah Drury, Joseph Tudor, and William Ashford.

In a category by himself is James Malton, an architectural draftsman and watercolorist, whose twenty-five *Views of Dublin* were drawn in 1790–91, published during the following eight years, and reprinted many times since. They constitute a unique pictorial record of the architectural glories of the Georgian city before it was partially submerged under the heavy hand of Victorian builders in the nineteenth century and all but overwhelmed by neglect, demolition, and ugly new construction in the twentieth. Examples of the work of all of the above-named artists (and others) are to be found hanging today in the **National Gallery of Ireland** *(354)* in Dublin; **Malahide Castle** *(371)*, County Dublin; **Fota House** *(320)*, County Cork; and the **Ulster Museum** *(457)* in Belfast.

The city of Cork too produced one fine local landscapist in the person of Nathaniel Grogan, whose works can be seen in the **Crawford Municipal Gallery** *(318)* in that city and at **Fota House** *(320)* a few miles outside. Cork's population, like Dublin's, mounted rapidly in the eighteenth century, reaching about eighty thousand in 1800, making it the second largest city of Ireland. By mid-century it had become a vital seaport, especially in the trade to the British colonies of North America and the West Indies, where Irish exporters of servants, horses, linen textiles, and provisions enjoyed a privileged market under the Acts of Trade and Navigation. Cork harbor, also, was an important rendezvous for convoys during times of war, and here the Royal Navy and the vessels it was escorting regularly took aboard large supplies of salted beef. Even French ships, during the intervals of peace, put into Cork to take on beef and other supplies. Catholic merchants, not barred by the penal code from commercial activities, shared the town's prosperity. Civic improvements came in due order. The city fathers widened the streets, built bridges, and laid out the Mardyke, the South Mall, and the Grand Parade. They also built handsome houses and public buildings, but few of these have survived except for the Customs House, which forms the center of the **Crawford Art Gallery** *(318)*.

Limerick was the third largest city in Ireland, with a population of close to sixty thousand in 1800. Here more eighteenth-century construction survives than in Cork. In 1751 Edmund Sexton Pery built New Square (now John's Square), an enclave of stone-built "Queen Anne style" houses, recently restored to very good effect. In the 1760s Pery, then speaker of the Irish house of commons, laid out Newton Pery south of the old city—a gridiron of wide, straight streets lined with Georgian buildings, some of which still stand. Pery's architect was Davis Ducart (or Daviso de Arcort), an Italian, who also designed Limerick's **Custom House** *(338)*, a fine Palladian edifice, still standing.

Waterford at the end of the century could claim about twenty thousand inhabitants. Its primary export was butter, and it dominated Ireland's trade with Newfoundland to which it shipped both provisions and men during the fishing season. The city also had a glass factory, opened in 1783 by George and William Penrose after the British parliament had eased restrictions on glass making in Ireland. These works continued in operation until 1851, when they were shut down, but in 1947 the present world-famous **Waterford Glass Factory** *(287)* reopened, claiming lineal descent from the Penrose brothers' original enterprise.

Belfast was about the same size as Waterford and growing, thanks in part to the enthusiastic town planning of Arthur Chichester, fifth earl and first marquess of Donegall, who owned all the real estate. Among his other contributions was the donation of a parcel of land for the erection of a poorhouse in 1774. This handsome red brick building, known as **Clifton House** *(456)*, still stands and is used as a retirement home. Belfast was already a busy seaport in 1792, when William Ritchie started the shipyard that was to mark the beginning of the development of the city's shipbuilding industry in the nineteenth century. But in the eighteenth the town's chief commercial activity was the linen trade. It boasted two linen halls where finished cloth was brought in from the countryside for resale. One of these, the White (that is, bleached) Linen Hall, provided space for the Belfast Reading Society, whose collection of books was later transferred to the **Linen Hall Library** *(456)*—a former warehouse on Donegall Square, North.

THE COUNTRYSIDE

The manufacture of linens was Ireland's major industry in the eighteenth century, encouraged by an act of the English parliament in 1696 that removed duties on imports into that country of Irish linen yarn and cloth at a time when tariff barriers against Continental linen remained high. Two years later the English government financed the Huguenot Louis Crommelin to import French weavers and set up looms in Lisburn, County Antrim—a development commemorated in the **Lisburn Museum** *(462)*. In 1711 the Irish parliament established the Linen Board to regulate the industry and subsidize various projects, while in 1731 the British Acts of Trade and Navigation were amended to allow Irish linen cloth to be exported directly to the American colonies. As a result of all these measures, Irish linen exports rose from little more than 305,000 yards in 1700 to more than 18,700,000 yards in 1780.

Most, though by no means all, linen manufacture was concentrated in the nine northern counties of Ulster. It was essentially a cottage industry; that is, the spinning and weaving were done largely in the homes of cottiers and small tenant farmers who grew and processed their own flax. Women and children spun; men worked the looms. Merchandising was chiefly in the hands of the owners of the bleaching fields. Here and there water-powered mills were set up to finish the cloth, especially the fine damasks and other luxury items. These were called "beetling" mills, the process of beetling (as explained by Arthur Young) consisting of "a continued system of perpendicular strokes upon the cloth wound round a cylinder for the purpose of smoothing it and giving it a gloss." One such establishment—the **Welbrook Beetling Mill** *(446)* near Cookstown, County Tyrone—has been restored by the National Trust, its machinery still activated by a giant exterior wheel turned by the pressure of water running through a sluice.

Though the linen industry provided more than welcome supplemental income to an impoverished peasantry, it also exposed them to the vagaries and fluctuations of an international market. Depressions were not infrequent, the worst occurring in the early 1770s, when perhaps a third of the weavers were unemployed. Faced with such hardships, exacerbated by rising rents and tithes and occasionally by serious crop failures, many a hard-pressed Irish tenant or cottier chose to emigrate to British North America. Most of them left from Ulster. This mass movement began in 1718, when approximately a thousand disembarked from ten vessels in Boston. By the 1730s it had swollen to about three to four thousand a year, bound mostly for the middle colonies of Pennsylvania and Delaware, with another stream of emigrants headed for South Carolina. In the early 1770s it swelled to about eight thousand annually, then abated during the War of American Independence, then picked up again after peace was declared in 1783, and continued, though at a somewhat diminished rate, into the 1820s.

Most of these people were Protestants, and a high proportion were Ulster Scots ("Scotch-Irish") of the Presbyterian persuasion. As such they were subject to a rankling discrimination at the hands of the Church of Ireland establishment, though economic distress was the more compelling reason for their departure. Also, in contrast to the native Irish, they were a rootless folk to whom the prospects of another dislocation posed no novel anxieties. In any case, leave they did, and in numbers sufficient to distress the government in Westminster, even though Ulster landlords assured the English traveller Arthur Young that "the emigrations, which made so much noise in the north of Ireland, were principally [of] idle people, who, far from being missed, left the country the better for their absence." Be that as it may, after their arrival in America many of them prospered, and their descendants often climbed the ladder of success to the very top.

Today in Northern Ireland, accordingly, the Ulster-American connection is pointed to with pride, and the ancestral homes of several famous Americans have been restored and refurbished to serve as popular tourist attractions. The most elaborate of these is the **Ulster-American Folk Park** *(448)* near Omagh, County Tyrone. Here, among other relevant exhibits, is a reconstructed farmhouse, birthplace of Thomas Mellon, who left Ireland as a child in 1818 to become a judge in western Pennsylvania and father of the great Pittsburgh financier Andrew Mellon. Another emigrant born in these parts was John Hughes, who later became first Roman Catholic archbishop of New York. His part-time boyhood home is also to be seen here—a cottage transported from County Monaghan across the border. Hughes was not the only Irish Catholic to emigrate to America in the late eighteenth or early nineteenth century, but neither was he typical. Tradition-bound, impervious to the seductions of the propaganda printed in a foreign language (English) by owners of emigrant ships, and not likely to be attracted anyway to Protestant colonies where the practice of their religion was seriously handicapped, Irish Catholics in general remained rooted in their native soil.

Not so the Presbyterian Jacksons, who left Bonybefore, near Carrickfergus, County Antrim, for North Carolina in 1765. Parents of the seventh president of the United States, their Irish homestead now boasts a newly constructed whitewashed stone cottage housing the **Andrew Jackson Centre** *(461)*, a small museum devoted to the history of the Ulster-American migration. The **Grant Ancestral House and Simpson Farm** *(444)* near Ballygawley, County Tyrone, contains a two-room cottage and adjoining farm belonging to the emigrant John Simpson, maternal great-grandfather of General Ulysses S. Grant. The **Arthur Ancestral Home** *(461)* near Cullybackey, County Antrim, is the farmhouse (restored) from which President Chester Arthur's father left for America in 1815. **"President Wilson's House"** *(465)* near Strabane, County Tyrone, was the birthplace of President Woodrow Wilson's grandfather, Judge James Wilson, who emigrated in 1807. It is a more substantial house than those previously mentioned, and members of the Wilson family still occupy the modern farmhouse next door and farm the land.

Despite exodus to America, the population of Ireland grew at an accelerating pace during the eighteenth century—from an estimated 2½ million in 1700 to about 5½ million in 1800 and still mounting. This took place in spite of periodic famines caused by bad weather and resultant crop failures. Famine struck in 1728-29 and more severely in the early 1740s, when about three hundred thousand died—a rate of mortality comparable to that of the "great hunger" a hundred years later. Also a long run of bad harvests brought near famine in 1756-57. Yet the population curve kept ascending. Increased fertility among the mass of the population, brought on in part by early marriages, is half the explanation. The other half is the decline in the death rate, which can be attributed largely to the increasing cultivation of the potato—a dependable crop (until hit by the mid-nineteenth-century blight), easily grown and providing far more nutriment per unit of measurement than either oats or barley. It rapidly became the basic food staple, and in the winter months almost the sole sustenance, of the poor—a category that included the majority of the rural population.

The endemic poverty of Ireland was a constant object of comment among social critics of the eighteenth century. Swift's bitter animadversions on the subject in *A Modest Proposal* are well known. Edmund Burke in 1747 noted that "whoever travels through this kingdom will see such Poverty as few Nations in Europe can equal." Yet the picture was probably overdrawn. When the English agricultural reformer Arthur Young toured the length and breadth of Ireland in the years 1776-79, he remarked that the "lower classes" generally had "such plenty of potatoes as always to command a bellyfull," to say nothing of a cow or two, a pig, and numbers of poultry. And, if their crowded, windowless, chimneyless, smoke-filled, mud-walled cabins were mere hovels, they at least were warm and dry—a matter of no small consequence considering Irish weather. Moreover, some supplemental income was usually available in the form of the proceeds from the domestic textile industry. The spinning of flax and the weaving of linen cloth were widespread in the North and in a few regions elsewhere; in the Midlands and the South spun woolen yarn found a ready market, especially after 1739, when English import duties on Irish yarn were repealed.

Yet withal, the Irish peasant was a deprived and downtrodden species, an easy target of exploitation, victimized by a system of landlordism he was powerless to contest. A common and recurring grievance was rack-renting—jacking up a tenant's rent each time his lease expired. Middlemen seem to have been the most culpable of this practice. These were those substantial farmers, merchants, or lawyers who held long leases of landlords (often absentees) and who in turn relet their holdings in subdivided lots to small cultivators on short tenure at ever-rising rents. Arthur Young described them as "the most oppressive species of tyrant that ever lent assistance to the destruction of a country." But landlords themselves were not above such practices. At least that is the only conclusion to be drawn from Maria Edgeworth's novella *Castle Rackrent* (published in 1801), a harsh picture of rural life drawn from the author's study of the neighboring gentry around her father's estate in County Longford.

Yet not all landlords were either as grasping or as irresponsible as those depicted by Miss Edgeworth. "Improvement" was in the air, especially after the founding of the Dublin Society in 1731. Modernizing landlords enclosed open fields and put them to productive uses, drained ditches, fertilized their lands, gave long leases to tenants on condition that they do the same, introduced green crops, invested heavily in turnpike roads, and financed the digging of canals. They also built whole villages on their estates, sometimes installed linen bleacheries, and erected houses for imported textile workers. In fact most Irish villages today are late-seventeenth- or eighteenth-century landlord creations. Among the latter are Portarlington, Birr, Tullamore, Mitchelstown, Doneraile, Cootehill, and Monaghan. And of course, for their own use, enjoyment, and self-advertisement, these provincial grandees also put up houses.

The first of the great palatial country mansions was **Castletown** *(379)*, County Kildare, built for Speaker William Conolly, reputedly the richest commoner in Ireland. Begun in 1722 to the design of an Italian architect, Allesandro Galilei, it was constructed mostly under the supervision of Sir Edward Lovett Pearce, the architect of the new Parliament House (**Bank of Ireland** *[353]*) in Dublin. The style is pure Palladian, with a large central block flanked by twin pavilions linked to the main house by colonnaded curtain walls—imitative of some of the Tuscan villas designed by Palladio himself. Pearce also designed **Cashel Palace** *(302)*, County Tipperary (now a hotel), for Archbishop Theophilus Bolton—a well-proportioned brick house with an elaborate entrance front (front facade) flanked by Venetian windows—a typical Palladian feature. After the speaker's grandnephew, Thomas Conolly, inherited Castletown, he had the interior embellished with a fine staircase and the walls decorated with intricate plasterwork by the Italian stuccodores Paul and Philip Francini. Later the Francini brothers decorated the rooms of the bishop of Cork's much more modest **Riverstown House** *(320)* with a stunning variety of classical figures and motifs. They also were responsible for the marvelous plasterwork at **Russborough** *(309)*, County Wicklow, built between 1741 and about 1750.

Russborough *(309)* was the grandest of the great houses designed by the German architect Richard Castle. The owner was Joseph Leeson, who had inherited a fortune from his father, a Dublin brewer, and was later to be named viscount and then earl of Milltown. Here is another huge Palladian masterpiece, with central block and curving colonnades of Doric columns connecting to flanking pavilions. **Powerscourt** *(309)*, County Wicklow, is another of Castle's creations, unhappily burned out in 1974, though the magnificent gardens remain intact. It too is Palladian, but without flanking wings and pavilions. Less distinctly so is **Westport House** *(424)*, County Mayo, built by Castle in the 1730s for John Browne, later earl of Altamont, subsequently enlarged and reroofed probably by Thomas Ivory, and still later redecorated by James Wyatt for the third earl, afterward first marquess of Sligo. Castle was also commissioned to rebuild **Strokestown Park House** *(404)* in County Roscommon for Thomas Mahon, whose father had put up a much simpler dwelling place here in the 1680s, of which only one room remains intact. The much enlarged mansion was again Palladian, the two connecting wings in this case serving respectively as kitchen and stable. **Belvedere House** *(393)* in County Westmeath is alleged also to have been designed by Castle, though, except for the two Venetian windows on the front, there is little here to suggest a Palladian inspiration.

Another distinguished architect was the English-born George Ensor, who, with his brother John, came to Dublin in about 1730. While John was responsible for laying out Merrion Square and, after Castle's death, for completing Dr. Mosse's **Rotunda Hospital** *(367)*, George worked on the remodelling of the upper yard of **Dublin Castle** *(358)*. In 1760 he married Sarah Clarke of County Armagh and thus came into possession of her family home, called **Ardress** *(444)*, a seventeenth-century house that he proceeded to remake into a Georgian mansion. For the interior decoration he called in the fashionable Irish stuccodore Michael Stapleton, whose elegant neoclassical plasterwork in the drawing room is among the finest in the country. Another Irish stuccodore of note was Robert West, also the master of the drawing school taken over by the Dublin Society as well as an architect of some distinction. He is credited with having been both builder and decorator of **Newbridge House** *(375)* near Donabate in County Dublin, though it seems likely that the plasterwork was actually executed by one of his assistants. The exterior is conventionally Georgian, but the ornate plastered ceiling of the red drawing room is purely rococo after the manner of West. James Gandon, famous for his public buildings in Dublin, won only one commission for a private residence, and this he did not complete, owing to the death of the owner, James Dawson, earl of Arlington. This was **Emo Court** *(313)*, County Laois, designed in the Palladian manner with a high central block flanked by twin single-storey pavilions. Gandon also designed the elegant stable at **Carriglas Manor** *(394)*, County Longford, though the house itself is of early-nineteenth-century construction. Equal to Gandon and Castle in elegance and grandeur was James Wyatt, an Englishman who designed **Castle Coole** *(450)*, County Fermanagh, in absentia, leaving its actual construction to local builders. It too is Palladian in essence, with a splendid central block connected to twin flanking pavilions by colonnaded wings, and Venetian windows on the rear facade. The house was built for Armar Lowry Corry, viscount, and later first earl, of Belmore.

Also, throughout Ireland are a number of impressive eighteenth-century houses designed in the classical manner but by architects whose names are now unknown. Possibly the owners themselves drew up the plans with the aid of local master builders. Recently restored by the Georgian Society, **Damer House** *(306)*, built in about 1726 on the grounds of **Roscrea Castle** *(306)*, County Tipperary (see Chapter Three), is considered "pre-Palladian." In about 1770 Richard White bought the small Georgian house at the head of Bantry Bay in County Kerry, added a wing, and renamed it Seafield House and later **Bantry House** *(315)*; it is a mansion of neoclassic appearance to which a fourteen-bay front with red brick Corinthian pilasters was added in the early nineteenth century. **Springhill** *(446)*, County Londonderry (near Cookstown, County Tyrone), is another eighteenth-century enlargement of an earlier house built, in this case, in the late seventeenth century. The original construction is represented by the central block of the present house; the two wings were added by Colonel William Conyngham about 1765. Much grander is **Florence Court** *(450)*, County Fermanagh, a Palladian mansion with the usual large central block linked by shallow arcades to two flanking pavilions. The main house was built probably in 1760 by John Cole; the pavilions about 1770 by his son William, first earl of Enniskillen. The rococo plasterwork was probably designed by Robert West.

In about the middle of the century in England a minor revolt against the rigidities of the neoclassical canon came into fashion. It took the form of a Gothic revival, which, to distinguish it from the heavy neo-Gothicism of the late Victorians, is spelled *Gothick*, in the eighteenth-century manner. The originator of the style was Sir Horace Walpole, who converted his plain Georgian house at Strawberry Hill into a fantasy of towers, cloisters, fan vaults, pinnacles, and crockets. But one of the leading Gothick practitioners was James Wyatt, despite his reputation as a Palladian and neoclassical virtuoso. In 1785 he was commissioned by the second baron Conyngham to build **Slane Castle** *(388)* in County Meath, though the project was completed under the direction of Francis Johnston. This is a typical Gothick exercise: the pointed arches, turrets, and battlements of the exterior tend to disguise the fact that the ground plan is classically symmetrical; inside, the great hall (by Johnston) contains fluted Corinthian columns, but the two-storey ballroom with its traceried domed ceiling is a Gothick delight. Another Gothick exercise was the restoration of **Malahide Castle** *(371)*, County Dublin, in the 1760s, when the insertion of ogee windows in the turret room and the addition of Irish crowstep battlements to the roof served to embellish what must have been a somber medieval fortalice. The most interesting example of the Gothick style in Ireland, however, is the northeast front of **Castle Ward** *(440)* in County Down. Here Lady Anne, wife of the owner, Sir Bernard Ward, instructed the architect (unknown) to install a Gothick facade and to design and decorate the facing rooms in the same manner. Her husband preferred a more conventional classicism; accordingly the southwest front is pure Palladian, as are the hall and front staircase. The contrast offers a nice study of the history of architectural style in the eighteenth century.

An even greater contrast lay, of course, between these great private palaces and the rural slums that often surrounded them. During his brief visit to Ireland in 1771 Ben Franklin compared "the most sordid wretchedness" of peasant living conditions to his own country, "where the Cultivator works for himself, and supports his family in decent Plenty." Arthur Young was somewhat less censorious, even noting that the well-thatched mud cabins of the Irish poor were "far warmer than the thin clay walls in England." What shocked Young more than outward signs of poverty was the Irish peasantry's subjection to the unbridled tyranny of the landlord class. "The landlord of an Irish estate, inhabited by Roman Catholics," he wrote, "is a sort of despot who yields obedience, in whatever concerns the poor to no law but that of his will." "A long series of oppressions," he added, "have brought landlords into a habit of exerting a very lofty superiority, and their vassals into an almost unlimited submission; speaking a language that is despised, professing a religion that is abhorred, and being disarmed, the poor find themselves in many cases slaves . . . ."

These remarks were published in 1780. They overlooked the fact, though Young was aware of it, that Irish peasants were not universally docile. Agrarian unrest, to use the conventional euphemism, cropped up recurrently in the second half of the eighteenth century. In Ulster in 1763 bands of peasants, calling themselves "Oakboys," organized to resist forced labor on the private roads of landlords and to prevent the collection of tithes, obnoxious to Presbyterians and Catholics alike. Trouble broke out again in 1770, when groups of "Steelboys" forcefully protested rack-renting and evictions on the estates of Lord Donegall. Meanwhile in Munster and parts of Leinster organized bodies of men, garbed in linen smocks and therefore called "Whiteboys," took to terrorizing the countryside, throwing down fences, killing or crippling cattle, burning houses, and occasionally resorting to murder. Their chief complaints were rack-renting, land enclosures, and, again, the payment of tithes to the established Church. The government in Dublin responded with repressive legislation, and in 1766 a parish priest, Father Nicholas Sheehy, was hanged for his alleged Whiteboy sympathies. After the outbreak of the French Revolution, rumors spread among the propertied classes that French Jacobin conspirators were at loose in the Irish countryside urging insurrection. The word "Croppies" now entered into the vocabulary of the frightened establishment—a term applied to rebellious peasants who allegedly cut their hair short in imitation of the French republicans. And out of this fear was born a new ballad popular in some Protestant circles—each stanza closing with the words "Down, down, Croppies lie down."

IRELAND AND THE FRENCH REVOLUTION: 1789-1801

Not many Irish Catholic peasants, however, were in fact stirred to action by the fall of the Bastille in July 1789 and the subsequent overthrow of France's ancien régime. Rather it was the mostly Protestant urban tradesmen, lawyers, and journalists, along with a handful of liberal-minded aristocrats, to whom the slogan "Liberté, Egalité, Fraternité" made its greatest appeal. Edmund Burke's conservative manifesto, *Reflections on the French Revolution*, won him an honorary degree from his alma mater Trinity College, but Tom Paine's rebuttal, *The Rights of Man*, was a bestseller in Dublin and Belfast. In October 1791 a group of Ulster Presbyterians, with the help of the Dublin Protestant barrister Theobald Wolfe Tone, founded the first Society of United Irishmen. In November Tone and the merchant James Napper Tandy organized its counterpart in Dublin, with headquarters in **Tailors' Hall** *(361)* on Back Lane. Within a few months branches had been formed in Armagh, Clonmel, Gorey, Limerick, Lisburn, Nenagh, and Tullamore.

The stated aims of the United Irishmen were at first reformist rather than revolutionary. They included demands for annual parliaments, pay for members of parliament, disqualification of pensioners and placemen (considered to be corrupt tools of the English government), the division of the country into three hundred electoral districts, election by ballot, and universal manhood suffrage—*including Catholics*. Tone and his followers were conscientiously nonsectarian, hoping thereby to win the support of the Catholic middle class. To some extent they were successful, and in some areas United Irishmen and Catholic Defenders in fact joined forces. But the Defenders' first order of business remained self-protection against Orangemen and other Protestant extremists, and devout Roman Catholics were naturally skittish about reforms inspired by the anticlerical revolutionary government of France. This was particularly true of the Irish Roman Catholic hierarchy, which expressly renounced Defenderism and prudently pinned its hopes for Catholic relief on the intervention of the government in Westminster.

In February 1793 the French Directory declared war against Great Britain. Francophile radicals in Ireland thus became automatically suspect of treason. On their side, the United Irishmen soon abandoned their goals of parliamentary reform in exchange for republicanism and secession from the British empire. Repression followed in due course. The regular army forces in Ireland were increased by five thousand men; an Irish militia (to include Roman Catholics in the ranks) was formed for home defense; the Irish parliament passed an act against conventions, declaring unlawful any unauthorized assemblies, such as the recent meeting in Dungannon of the United Irish Societies of Ulster. Two Dublin radicals, Napper Tandy and Hamilton Rowan, were prosecuted; Tandy escaped to the United States, Rowan to France. Wolfe Tone, in the face of unmistakable proof of his dealings with a French spy in Dublin, fled to the United States and then to Paris, where he set about to persuade the French director, Lazare Carnot, to launch a military expedition to Ireland, promising a general uprising of the Irish people to break the shackles of British rule.

Carnot at last succumbed to Tone's importunities. On 16 December 1796 an Armada of forty-three French ships sailed from Brest for Ireland. Aboard were fourteen thousand troops commanded by General Lazare Hoche; sailing in the *Indomitable* was Wolfe Tone himself, now a general officer in the French army. Owing to foul weather and navigational difficulties, only thirty-four of the fleet reached Bantry Bay on the southwestern coast five days later. An Atlantic gale made landings impossible. One lone French lieutenant, trying to move from one anchored ship to another, was swept ashore and captured. (His longboat is on view at the **National Maritime Museum** *[374]* in Dun Laoghaire.) He and his crew were brought for interrogation to **Bantry House** *(315)*, headquarters of the British garrison. Except for a few foragers, they were the only Frenchmen to set foot on Ireland. By 31 December the amphibious operation had been called off and those few vessels still in Bantry Bay weighed anchor and set sail for France.

Inevitably the government resorted to even more severe repressive measures. Late in 1796 corps of volunteer yeomanry (mostly Protestant) were formed, under the command of officers commissioned by the lord lieutenant. The habeas corpus act was suspended. Justices of the peace were authorized to "proclaim" their counties as being in a state of disturbance, search houses for concealed weapons, and enforce curfews. More troops were brought from England to enforce law and order. Ulster was proclaimed, and General Gerard Lake was dispatched to put down incipient rebellion. Parts of Leinster were proclaimed, as was all of County Sligo. In the search for rebel arms, houses were burned, suspects flogged unmercifully, their heads sometimes crowned with caps of molten pitch. Few efforts were made to restrain the troops in this campaign of state terrorism, especially after General Lake replaced commander-in-chief Sir Ralph Abercromby, who had reported that the army was "in a state of licentiousness which must render it formidable to everyone but the enemy."

On 12 March 1798 the government moved in on the Dublin headquarters of the Leinster Provincial Committee of the United Irishmen, thought to be the focal point of sedition. Fifteen of its directors were arrested, and another, Lord Edward Fitzgerald, was later mortally wounded while resisting capture. Their removal did nothing to stop the spread of insurrection. Toward the end of May a sizable contingent of armed United Irishmen encamped on the hill of **Tara** *(385)* in defiance of the local yeomanry. They were promptly routed, thus bringing an end to effective rebellion in the Midlands. (Among Tara's prehistoric remains still stands a solitary monolith commemorating the battle.) In early June two more outbreaks occurred in Ulster, to be put down after brief encounters with government troops at Antrim and Ballynahinch, County Down.

It was in County Wexford, however, that popular resistance to authority achieved the level of a truly widespread peasants' revolt. Though vaguely, and vainly, hoping for French intervention, the rebels here were inspired mostly by local grievances unconnected with United Irish dreams of an independent republic on the model of revolutionary France. The Insurrection of 1798 in Wexford defies easy explanation. Long-standing Whiteboy grievances—rack-renting, enclosures, tithes, etc.—had never been resolved. Protestants comprised between 15 and 20 percent of Wexford's population, and "Orangeism" was apparently stronger here than in any county outside Ulster. In any case, sectarian animosity was a driving force among the Catholic rebels. At least three priests emerged as leaders: Father John Murphy, Father Patrick Murphy, and Father Roche. Yet the rebellion was publicly denounced by three Catholic archbishops as well as the president and faculty of Maynooth College. Protestants indeed did suffer terrible atrocities—the most notorious being the shooting and burning of about two hundred prisoners in Scullabogue barn outside New Ross. On the other hand one band of rebels chose a Protestant landlord, Beauchamp Bagenal Harvey, as their commander. And on still another it was Catholic militiamen who were responsible for many of the atrocities committed *against* the insurrectionists. Unambiguous religious animosity, therefore, does not fully account for the insurrection and the civil war that it provoked. Less ambiguous was the bitter resentment of the poor against long-standing oppression, matched by the determination of the propertied class to defend its vested interests at all costs.

After capturing Enniscorthy in late May, the rebels moved on to Wexford, which fell after a short fight. They then failed to take New Ross and on 21 June fell back on **Vinegar Hill** *(281)*, outside Enniscorthy, where they set up camp in the vicinity of the windmill whose stump still stands. General Lake then charged the hill, routed its occupants, killed many, and set fire to the adjacent town. (Relics of the battle are on display at the **Wexford County Museum** *[281]* in Enniscorthy Castle.) By 21 July the last of the rebel bands surrendered at Timahoe, County Laois, and the rebellion was over. Reprisals were vicious. When Lord Cornwallis arrived as commander-in-chief and lord lieutenant in June, he bemoaned the "violence of our friends and their folly in making it a religious war, added to the ferocity of our troops who delight in murder, [which] most powerfully counteract all plans of conciliation." The rebellion, which had lasted only three months, cost altogether about twenty-five thousand lives, most of them among the defeated peasantry. Poorly organized and armed mostly with pikes, scythes, and a few muskets, they stood no chance against the well-equipped regulars, yeomanry, and militiamen who opposed them. (Weapons, equipment, and other mementos of the insurrection are on display at the **Cork Public Museum** *[318]* and the **Mullingar Military Museum** *[393]*, County Westmeath.)

The long-awaited French, when they finally did come, came too late. On 22 August General Joseph Humbert, with a thousand officers and men, landed at the head of Killala Bay in County Mayo, distributed fifty-five thousand muskets to the local peasants, and marched with them to rout a detachment of government forces under General Lake at Castlebar but was subsequently overwhelmed by Cornwallis at Ballinamuck in County Longford on 8 August 1798. After the Battle of Ballinamuck, Humbert's "Mayo Legion Flag," brought from France to help rally the native Irish to his cause, came into the possession of John Browne, Lord Altamount, and is on display at **Westport House** *(424)*, County Mayo. Meanwhile a French corvette with a large supply of arms and a few men, including Napper Tandy, landed briefly at Rutland Island off County Donegal. Despairing of success, the party returned promptly to its ship and sailed for home. (Relics of this expedition can be seen at the **Donegal Historical Society Museum** *[427]* in the Franciscan Friary at Rossnowlagh.) Finally, in October, a third naval expedition of six ships was intercepted and captured off the Donegal coast by a British squadron. On board the *Hoche* was Wolfe Tone, again in

French uniform. He was taken to Dublin, tried for treason, convicted, and died in prison of self-administered wounds. Thus ended "the year of the French," to borrow the title of a splendid novel on the subject by the American author Thomas Flanagan.

To British eyes the year's events proved beyond doubt that Ireland was the Achilles' heel of the empire and that radical corrective measures must be taken. Prime Minister William Pitt's solution was to consolidate the two kingdoms into one by a legislative union similar to that which had united Scotland with England in 1707. This would necessarily involve the abolition of Ireland's separate parliament and the enlargement of the British parliament to include Irish representatives.

Appropriate measures to accomplish this end easily won the approval of the majority of both houses at Westminster. Dublin was another matter. On the first legislative trial union was defeated in the Irish house of commons by five votes. Cornwallis, the lord lieutenant, and his chief secretary, Robert Stewart, Viscount Castlereagh, then set about to reverse the decision. Though no money bribes may have been tendered, new peerages were promised; pensions and ecclesiastical preferments were granted lavishly; the proprietors of boroughs threatened with disfranchisement were assured compensation for their losses; antiunion members were persuaded to vacate their seats. Added to these material inducements was the persuasive argument that Irish Protestant interests would be better protected at Westminster than in the Dublin legislature, which sooner or later would have to yield to the inexorable pressures to give Catholics full political rights. Contrariwise, Roman Catholics were led to believe that they would no longer be barred from membership in a new United Kingdom parliament. In the event, when the Act of Union was again presented to the Irish house of commons in January 1800, it passed by a majority of forty-three. The house of lords followed suit, royal assent was given, and the act became law on 1 January 1801.

By this measure the Irish parliament was dissolved. Ireland was to be represented in the new house of commons of the United Kingdom of Great Britain and Ireland by a hundred members, only a third of the number that had sat in the Dublin parliament. To achieve this reduction almost two hundred Irish boroughs lost or suffered a diminution of their right of representation. The real losers in these instances were the great Protestant landed families who had owned or controlled the boroughs. Representation of the Irish peerage underwent even further curtailment in the British house of lords, where only thirty-two seats were allocated to Ireland. The Church of Ireland and the Church of England were to be united as the established church. Free trade was to be allowed between the two countries.

Ireland was to contribute two-seventeenths to the budget of the United Kingdom. Each country was to retain its own legal system.

In 1802 the parliament house on College Green, Dublin, was sold to the **Bank of Ireland** *(353)*, which still occupies it. The directors hired the architect Francis Johnston to convert the commons' chamber into a banking facility. The chamber of the house of lords, however, remained intact, although some of its furnishings were moved to the **Royal Irish Academy** *(356)*, where they are now on display. The year before, immediately after the passage of the Act of Union, Pitt, as promised, raised the issue of Catholic entry into the British parliament. George III refused to sanction the proposal, claiming that it ran counter to his coronation oath. Pitt and Castlereagh, accordingly, resigned. Catholic Emancipation, as the concession of full political rights came to be called, would have to await another day.

Chapter Seven

The Nineteenth
Century: 1801–1891

While Irish legislators were proceeding to vacate Gandon's splendid edifice on College Green, new plans were being hatched nearby to destroy the union they had created. One center of this clandestine activity was the **Brazen Head Hotel** *(361)* on Bridge Street, Dublin, an early-eighteenth-century inn, even today in operation though in a sorry state of dilapidation. Here in the 1790s sundry United Irishmen had spun their seditious plots, and here another Irish patriot, Robert Emmet, set about to reverse the verdict of 1801. Like Wolfe Tone, Emmet was a Trinity College–educated Protestant, inspired by the heady idealism of the French Revolution and self-deluded about the imminence of large-scale French armed intervention in Ireland. With about a hundred fellow conspirators, on the night of 23 July 1803 he launched an attack on Dublin Castle with the object of establishing "a free and independent republic." The outbreak was easily suppressed, with the loss of about thirty lives. Emmet himself escaped but was soon captured, imprisoned in **Kilmainham Jail** *(364)* in Dublin, tried, convicted, and hanged in front of **St. Catherine's Church** *(363)* on Thomas Street, where a plaque now marks the site of the execution. This pitiful and doomed foray might well have been relegated to a mere footnote in the history of Irish nationalism but for Emmet's speech from the scaffold. "My race is run," he announced, "the grave opens to receive me, and I sink into its bosom. I have but one request to ask at my departure from this world; it is the charity of its silence. Let no man write my epitaph," he begged, "for as no man who knows my motives dare now vindicate them, let not prejudice or ignorance asperse them. Let them rest in obscurity and peace, my memory to be left in oblivion and my tomb remain uninscribed . . . . When my country takes her place among the nations of the earth, then and not till then, let my epitaph be written."

A year after Emmet's death the French, now under the leadership of Napoleon Bonaparte, did indeed renew plans for an invasion of Ireland. An army of eighteen thousand was to be landed on the west coast in conjunction with a massive amphibious operation against England to be mounted from Boulogne. Nothing came of the scheme. Napoleon broke up the camp at Boulougne and sent his army of a quarter-million men into central

Europe. Then, to bring an end to all prospects of an invasion of the British Isles, the Royal Navy overwhelmed the combined fleet of France and Spain at Trafalgar in October 1805. Chief credit for the victory went to the British admiral-in-command, Horatio Nelson, who died during the battle. So grateful were the Protestant citizens of Dublin that they promptly raised a high monument to the fallen hero, with 134 spiral steps leading up to a viewing platform below the larger-than-life-sized statue of Lord Nelson. Looming over Sackville (O'Connell) Street, Nelson's Pillar became one of the Dublin cityscape's most prominent features until 1966, when it was blown up, presumably by members of the IRA (Irish Republican Army). Fragments of the monument, including portions of the admiral's sculpted head, are today on view at the **Civic Museum** *(358)* on South William Street.

If the Royal Navy was Britain's first line of defense, the second was a string of coastal fortresses erected quickly in the first decade of the nineteenth century along the shorelines of both England and Ireland. These were the martello towers, so named after a French fortification on Mortella Point in Corsica, which had successfully resisted an English bombardment in 1794. With walls eight feet thick, they were round or oval in plan, about thirty feet high and thirty-six feet in exterior diameter, with a single doorway ten feet above the ground and a parapeted roof on which rested a twenty-four-pound cannon. Today the best known of these fortalices is **Joyce's Tower** *(373)* at Sandycove, near Dun Laoghaire, though its fame derives not from any historic military significance but rather from its later association with the writer James Joyce (see Chapter Eight). Like the nearby **Dalkey Island Martello Tower** *(373)*, it was built in 1804, one of sixteen erected to guard Dublin Bay. On the southeast coast the approach to Bannow Bay (where Normans had landed in 1167) was guarded now by the **Baginbun Head Martello Tower** *(282)*, while farther along the coast two **Duncannon Martello Towers** *(280)* stood watch over Waterford Harbor. All three are now in private possession and, though visible, are not visitable. Five towers were built along the shoreline of Cork harbor and another two to guard the Shannon estuary, but none is sufficiently accessible today to warrant attention. In the far North Lough Foyle was bracketed by two towers—**Greencastle Martello Tower** *(429)* in County Donegal on the west coast and **Magilligan Martello Tower** *(465)* on the opposite shore in County Londonderry.

The third line of defense was the British army, which maintained a large force in Ireland, numbering, as of 1800, about twenty-nine thousand, not counting militia and yeomanry. Their mission was twofold: to protect the country against foreign invaders and to quell native disorder of whatever origin or to whatever purpose. There was no such thing as an Irish army, but, since the close of the seventeenth century, there had been a number of British regiments of foot and horse paid and equipped at Irish expense and forming what was called the "Irish establishment." Although these units often served overseas, their regimental headquarters were in Ireland and, in addition to their numerical designations, were known by names of Irish origin. Some of them are still commemorated in regimental museums—all, not surprisingly, situated in Northern Ireland. Thus mementos of the Sixth Inniskilling Dragoons and the Royal Inniskilling Fusiliers are housed in **Enniskillen Castle** *(449)*, County Fermanagh; the **Royal Irish Fusiliers Museum** *(442)* in Armagh city contains those of the 87th or Prince of Wales's Irish Regiment and the 89th Foot as well as three regiments of Irish militia; **Carrickfergus Castle** *(460)*, County Antrim, is the home of the regimental museum of the Fifth Royal Inniskilling Dragoon Guards and the Queen's Royal Irish Hussars; and the **Royal Ulster Rifle Regimental Museum** *(454)* in Belfast is dedicated exclusively to the distinguished history of that unit. The contents of all these museums are much alike—uniforms, weapons, medals, honors, regimental plate, paintings, photographs, etc., dating from all the wars in which the British army was engaged from the eighteenth century through the twentieth.

It must not be thought that these regiments were exclusively Irish in personnel or that all Irish soldiers in British service served in Irish regiments. In fact by the time the Napoleonic wars were ended, almost a third of the entire personnel of the British army consisted of native Irishmen. (So were about a quarter of the Royal Navy.) They were mostly in the enlisted ranks and mostly Catholics. Until 1793 no Catholic could lawfully hold an officer's commission, and until 1829 none could aspire to the rank of general. Anglo-Irish Protestants, on the other hand, were prominent among the officer ranks. Best known of all, of course, was Arthur Wellesley, duke of Wellington. Younger son of the Irish earl of Mornington, he was born in a house on **Merrion Square** *(354)* in Dublin. Not far away, in Phoenix Park, still stands the **Wellington Monument** *(370)*, a huge granite obelisk raised in 1817 in commemoration of the victories of the city's most famous soldier.

The future "iron duke," however, was to spend little of his childhood in Dublin. In 1778 Lord Mornington moved to London, thus anticipating, by about a quarter of a century, a general exodus of Irish nobility from Dublin following the Act of Union. With the demise of the Irish parliament there was no further need for them to maintain residences in the city. Powerscourt House (recently converted to the **Powerscourt Townhouse Centre** *[357]*) was bought by the commissioners of stamp duties in 1807. The most magnificent of the great town houses, **Leinster House** *(355)*, was sold to the Royal Dublin Society. Later **Tyrone House** *(365)* in Marlborough Street became headquarters of the board of national education. Later still Lord Belvedere sold his residence on Great Denmark Street to the

Society of Jesus, which converted it into **Belvedere College** *(367)*, where the young James Joyce was to attend classes (see Chapter Eight). As to public building in Dublin, the only construction of any significance during the early nineteenth century (except for churches) was on Sackville (O'Connell) Street, where the **General Post Office** *(366)* was erected in 1815. Designed by Francis Johnston, it is a mammoth neoclassic edifice, 223 feet wide, 150 feet deep, and fifty feet tall, with a huge portico of Ionic pillars topped by a pediment.

In the countryside, however, great houses continued to be built and established residences to be enlarged and "modernized" in accordance with the latest architectural fashions. The most magnificent of these was **Mount Stewart** *(438)* in County Down, begun in 1804 by Robert Stewart, first marquess of Londonderry, to the design of the London architect George Dance, and mostly completed in the 1830s by Charles Stewart, the third marquess, and his Irish architect, William Vitruvius Morrison, who were responsible for the splendid Greek Revival edifice that stands today. It is surrounded by superbly planted gardens and grounds that include the "Temple of the Winds," an exquisite two-storey hexagonal neoclassic garden house by James "Athenian" Stuart that predates the earliest part of the main residence by twenty years. The most famous occupant of Mount Stewart was Robert Stewart, second marquess, better known by his earlier title, Lord Castlereagh. It was he, along with Prince Clemens von Metternich of Austria, who negotiated the long-lasting peace that brought an end to the Napoleonic wars. From his labors at the Congress of Vienna in 1815 he brought back to Mount Stewart (where they are still on view) the chairs used by the delegates, embroidered with their personal arms and those of the countries they represented. Seven years later he died a suicide—much honored by European statesmen but not by Irish nationalists, who blamed him for the demise of their parliament in 1801 (see Chapter Six).

Unlike Mount Stewart, most of the great Irish houses dating to the first two decades of the nineteenth century are the product of rebuilding and restoration. **Shane's Castle** *(452)*, County Antrim (now a ruin), was a sixteenth-century tower house later incorporated into a castellated palatial residence with a conservatory (the Camellia House), designed by John Nash and added in 1815. **Tullynally Castle** *(392)*, County Westmeath, seat of the Pakenham family, is a seventeenth-century tower "Gothicized" in 1801–06 for the second earl of Longford by the Dublin architect Francis Johnston and again in the 1820s by James Shiel. This earl's daughter was Kitty Pakenham, who married Arthur Wellesley, later first duke of Wellington. A son, major general Sir Edward Pakenham, was killed in 1815 at New Orleans in the battle that launched the victorious Andrew Jackson toward the presidency of the United States. Another son, the third earl, engaged the Irish architect Richard Morrison to add the two wings that make up the sides of the present court. Pakenhams still occupy the house and show it to the public for about a month during the summer. Not on public view, though visible from their surrounding gardens, are **Birr Castle** *(380)*, County Offaly, and **Lismore Castle** *(285)*, County Waterford. The former, originally a medieval stronghold of the O'Carrolls, was "Gothicized" by William Parsons, first earl of Rosse, in the first decade of the nineteenth century. A local architect, John Johnston, directed the work, which consisted mainly of adding Irish-style stepped battlements to the roofline, refacing the front, and installing a handsome vaulted Gothick reception room on the side overlooking the river Camcor. At Lismore the same sort of face-lifting was applied in the early nineteenth century to the seventeenth-century castle of Richard Boyle, earl of Cork, by a descendant, William Spencer Cavendish, sixth duke of Devonshire. The Gothick facade of the present building is mostly the work of the architect William Atkinson, although the battlements were added later by Joseph Paxton, designer of the Crystal Palace in London. **Killeen Castle** *(386)*, County Meath, is currently neither occupied nor open to view, although in a good state of repair and visible from the outside. The eighth earl of Fingall had it remodelled in the Gothick manner by Francis Johnston in the first decade of the nineteenth century. **Glin Castle** *(341)*, County Limerick, is another Gothick restoration dating to about 1820—the handiwork of John FitzGerald, twenty-fifth knight of Glin, who also built the pepper-pot gatehouse lodge that now houses a restaurant and shop. **Johnstown Castle** *(283)*, County Wexford, is more accessible. This is a splendid example of the Gothick style, produced in the second decade of the nineteenth century when the owner, John Knox Grogan, added the battlemented south front and flanking cylindrical and octagonal towers to an existing medieval tower house incorporated into a seventeenth-century mansion. The pseudo-Gothic porte cochere was a still later addition, and subsequently the premises were converted into a state-run agricultural institute and museum.

All this building and rebuilding reflected an unprecedented prosperity in rural Ireland during the war years. From 1760 on, agricultural prices rose steadily, and from 1793 to 1815 sharply, as the volume of Irish exports increased by some 40 percent. Ireland of course benefitted from the frequent interruptions of trade between England and the Continent. Cereal grains and flour were especially in high demand. Starting in about 1770, there was a marked tendency among Irish agriculturalists to convert pastureland to tillage—an abnormal development in a country endowed by nature with lush grasslands particularly suitable to the grazing of cattle. Landlords of course were the prime beneficiaries of the economic boom. But tenant farmers too reaped their rewards, especially since rents rose more slowly than prices and, owing to a surge in population, farm labor was cheap.

There were, however, ominous signs—mostly unnoticed at the time. As the population grew, the practice of subletting into parcels of ever-decreasing size became more commonplace. Subtenants became increasingly dependent on the potato as their major source of subsistence. Agricultural prosperity became more and more linked to the vagaries of the international market as an ever-growing percentage of Irish grain and cattle products was shipped abroad, chiefly to Britain. Outside of Ulster, there was no widespread growth of native industry to absorb either the surplus agricultural produce or the surplus population. Ireland, which had never had a well-balanced economy, was becoming less and less capable of sustaining itself in an era of industrial revolution, rapid capitalist expansion, and unbridled economic rivalry on an international scale.

THE LAND: 1815–1891

The first warning signals came with the outbreak of peace in 1815 following Napoleon's final downfall at Waterloo. By the early 1820s the price of wheat had fallen to two-thirds of its wartime level. Oats, barley, butter, beef, mutton, and bacon followed suit. The depression in Irish agriculture lasted until about 1835, in spite of the Corn Laws, which effectively excluded foreign grain from both the Irish and British markets. Then recovery set in, and for about twenty years Irish agriculture and cattle raising prospered. Primary beneficiaries were the strong farmers, that is, leaseholders of more than thirty acres. Landlords, naturally, took their share of the increase, even though for the most part rents lagged behind prices. In consequence great houses continued to spring up, some even before the end of the agricultural depression.

At **Fota House** *(320)* in County Cork, John Smith-Barry employed the services of the fashionable Irish architect William Vitruvius Morrison to convert the family's hunting lodge into a stately mansion. He raised the central block by a storey, added projecting wings, and faced it with a neoclassic portico of Doric columns to create a Regency masterpiece, unexcelled in the elegance of its interior decoration and furnishings. The nearly contemporary (1820–24) house in County Armagh called **The Argory** *(447)* is a somewhat less successful exercise in the neoclassic manner. The main part of the building is a single massive block from one side of which extends a wing ending in an octagonal pavilion. The owner was one Walter McGeogh (who later changed his name to Bond), and the architects were Arthur and John Williamson, formerly apprenticed to Francis Johnston. To design **Lissadell House** *(418)* in County Sligo, Sir

Robert Gore-Booth commissioned the London architect Francis Goodwin. This is a rather plain two-storeyed building over a basement with a neo-classic entrance front. The classical theme is most pronounced in the interior, especially the roof-high gallery with its Ionic columns. When it later served as the home of the famous Gore-Booth sisters, Eva and Constance (Countess Markievicz), William Butler Yeats was a frequent visitor here and penned a charming poem in honor of the house and his hostesses (see Chapter Eight). Built in the 1830s, this is one of the last of Ireland's great houses to be modelled on classical precedents. Thereafter architectural fashion, inspired by nineteenth-century Romanticism, moved again toward the Gothic. **Muckross House** *(331)*, County Kerry, is essentially neo-Tudor. The architect was William Burn of Edinburgh, who was commissioned by Henry Arthur Herbert in 1843 to raise this sprawling, many-gabled, many-chimneyed mansion overlooking lower Lake Killarney. Finally, though strictly speaking not a country house, **Kilkenny Castle** *(294)*, as restored in the late 1820s, stands as the supreme example of early-nineteenth-century neo-Gothicism. Employing a local architect named William Robertson, James, nineteenth earl and second marquess of Ormond, rebuilt the ancient Butler stronghold to achieve its present appearance—raising and castellating the towers and adding sundry mock machicolations and battlements. Architectural pseudo-medievalism reached no greater heights in nineteenth-century Ireland, even in the heavy baronial fashion of the late Victorian era.

All these stately homes and palaces stood in stark contrast to the far more numerous hovels of the poor. According to the census of 1841, some 40 percent of the houses in all of Ireland, and close to 60 percent in Connacht, were one-room mud cabins. Their floors were normally earthen; their roofs consisted of sods covered with straw or heather thatch. Many had neither windows nor chimneys, so that the smoke from their open hearths escaped through the thatch or through the single open door. Not much had changed since Arthur Young had reported on the living conditions of the Irish peasantry in the 1770s. In fact, they had grown quantitatively worse as the number of peasants had multiplied in the intervening decades.

From something less than 5.5 million in 1800, total population rose to 6.8 million in 1821, to 7.7 million in 1831, and to 8.175 million in 1841. The proportion of increase was even greater in the poorer areas of the West and among the poorer classes of the rural proletariat—small landholders of less than five acres, cottiers who exchanged their labor for the right to occupy a cabin and a small plot of ground, and farm laborers hired on a seasonal basis. With an average population of 335 persons per square mile of arable land, Ireland had become probably the most densely peopled country of Europe.

Emigration, to be sure, siphoned off some of the surplus. Between 1815 and 1845 approximately eight hundred thousand people abandoned their homes to set up permanent residence abroad. In the early 1820s the major flow of emigrants had been to Britain; by the end of the decade it had shifted to North America. And whereas the vast majority of Irish emigrants in the eighteenth century had been Ulster Scots, by 1835 Ulster and Leinster were exporting people in about equal numbers, while the percentage leaving from Connacht was growing.

Impressive as these figures are, they did not remotely equal the natural increase in population. Most of those who did not leave were simply compelled to eke out meager livings on lots of ground of ever-decreasing size. Farmers sublet parcels of land to tenants, who in turn split off still smaller lots to *their* subtenants—more often than not their married children in both cases. Early marriages accelerated the process of both subdivision and population increase. The ubiquitous potato made these developments possible. Even a quarter of an acre thickly planted with this nutritious tuber was, in good years, sufficient to feed a family at least at a minimum level of subsistence. Of course, given the vagaries of Irish weather, not all years were good years. There were partial and local failures of the potato crop in 1817 and again in 1822. Famine ensued in parts of the country but was more or less contained, chiefly by the intervention of the British government and private charities. Thousands of pounds of public moneys were distributed through relief committees, and between 1823 and 1828 about £2,500,000 was advanced for public works, mainly road construction, to provide employment. Thus, when the crop failed again in the autumn of 1845, there appeared to be no obvious reason why yet more heroic measures of famine relief need be applied.

The fungus *phythopthera infestans*, originating in South America, reached England in the summer of 1845 and first hit southeastern Ireland in September. Its effects on potatoes still in the ground were immediate and devastating, reducing them overnight to rotten and stinking pulp. Luckily, before it spread widely, the early potatoes had been lifted so that probably no more than a third of the crop was destroyed. The British government reacted promptly and, on the whole, effectively. The prime minister, Sir Robert Peel, had been Irish chief secretary during the famine of 1817, and this experience bore fruit. He ordered huge purchases of maize (Indian corn) on the American market and arranged for its distribution in Ireland. Simultaneously public works were set into operation to enable the destitute to buy the corn at controlled prices. Approximately 140,000 people were thus employed. Peel, however, was voted out of office in June 1846, to be replaced by a Whig government led by Lord John Russell. Day-to-day management of the Irish problem was assigned to his chancellor of the exchequer, Charles Wood, and to the permanent assistant secretary of the treasury, Charles Trevelyan. All three men were ill prepared to handle the ongoing emergency, partly because of their blind adherence to prevailing economic theories opposing government intervention in the self-corrective "natural" operation of the law of supply and demand. Poverty and distress, according to the accepted wisdom of the so-called Manchester School, were but temporary and necessary by-products of the business cycle, best handled by being left alone (*laissez-faire*).

Nevertheless, when the blight returned in full force in the fall of 1846, the new government resorted again to public works, though with the stipulation that the main financial burden be borne by Irish landlords and farmers. By the spring of 1847 the total number thus employed reached 750,000. That year the blight abated somewhat, but the crop was small, chiefly because so many of the seed potatoes had been eaten. Meanwhile the government decided to abandon public works as too costly and substitute direct relief in the form of soup kitchens. There was a delay in setting them up, and in the interval between the stoppage of the works program and the dispensation of free food there was great, and sometimes fatal, hunger. Finally the main burden of relief was shifted to the Irish workhouses, which were authorized to provide "outdoor relief" in exchange for labor—breaking stones for the men, sewing and laundry for the women. By mid-1848, with no abatement of the blight, some eight hundred thousand people were thus employed. Many (those who had held more than a quarter of an acre) were forced by law (the "Gregory Clause") to abandon their holdings to become eligible for relief. Many more had been evicted not only because they were in arrears in rent but also because their continued occupation of unproductive holdings increased the liability of Irish farmers and landlords responsible for the payment of poor-law rates (that is, taxes to support relief). Thus, from the combined forces of blight, evictions, and abandonment of the land, potato production in Ireland fell from about ten thousand tons in 1845 to two thousand in 1847, rising again to four thousand in 1849, the last year of the Great Famine.

Estimates of the number of people who died as a direct result of the potato blight approach a million. Probably the majority of fatalities are ascribable not to outright starvation but to scurvy, dysentery, typhus, and relapsing fever. These last two ailments were carried by lice, and their high incidence was no doubt due to overcrowding in workhouses and food depots. No mere statistics, to be sure, can approximate the horror of these years, when death and desolation, homelessness and despair were the common lot of the Irish peasantry. Few visible reminders of the disaster remain to be seen in Ireland today. A famine exhibit is on display at the **Clare Heritage Centre** *(343)* in Corofin. On the grounds of the **Glencolumbkille Folk Museum** *(427)*, County Donegal, is a "famine pot" purportedly used in a soup kitchen. At **Strokestown House** *(404)*, County Roscommon, is a room devoted to the story of the assassination of Dennis Mahon in 1847 in retaliation for his evicting tenants and forcing them to emigrate. For the most part, however, time has erased all visible traces of the disaster.

But the national trauma remains embedded in the Irish folk memory, both at home and abroad. Bitterness at the failure of the British government to cope with the crisis still survives after almost a century and a half. "Genocide" is the strongest accusation brought to bear, "callousness" the most charitable. Yet neither term exactly fits the bill. Parsimony, dilatoriness, bureaucratic incompetence, excessive legalism, ideological rigidity— all these can legitimately be ascribed to the administration of Lord John Russell. Yet these men should not be judged by the criteria of performance demanded of the modern welfare state. The only way disaster could have been averted after the return of the potato blight in 1846 was by a prompt and massive infusion of public funds administered efficiently by an army of social workers, managers, doctors, nurses, transport experts, and other technicians. No mid-nineteenth-century government, English or otherwise, would have been able or willing to go so far.

As many people as died, or possibly more, took to the emigrant ships, bound chiefly for America—more than a hundred thousand in 1846, more than two hundred thousand in 1847, and by 1851 a quarter of a million. Attracted by quick profits, shipowners overloaded their vessels with panic-stricken refugees. These were the so-called "coffin ships" aboard which many more died or fell fatally ill. On arrival the survivors more often than not were greeted with undisguised hostility inspired mostly by native American anti-Catholicism combined with the legitimate fear that their influx into the labor market would drive down wages. Yet, in spite of overt discrimination, most of the newcomers found jobs—the men as manual laborers and the women as domestic servants. In time the melting pot absorbed them—if not in the first generation, then in the second or third. Upward social and economic mobility was not forever to be denied to Irish-Americans. The career of John F. Kennedy and his immediate forebears bears ample witness to generational progress. His great-grandfather emigrated from the little village of Dunganstown, County Wexford, where the **Kennedy Homestead** *(283)* is still to be seen—a tiny stone cottage, now on private property. Nearby is the **Kennedy Memorial Park** *(283)*—620 acres of woodland dedicated to the memory of the late president of the United States, more esteemed in Ireland even than in his own country. At Ballyporeen, in the neighboring county of Tipperary, the **President Reagan Centre** *(299)* honors still another American president whose great-grandfather left these parts for the United States.

The central sociological fact of post-Famine Ireland—overriding all other social, political, and economic developments—was the rapid reduction of the country's population. From over eight million in 1841, the numbers declined to 6½ million in 1851, with a further attrition of from six to eight hundred thousand each succeeding decade until 1900, when the figure stabilized at about 4½ million. Famine deaths and emigration caused the initial drop; thereafter continuing emigration and a fall in the birthrate were the operative factors. Birthrates declined largely because of delayed marriages and increased celibacy. Until the Famine the Irish were probably the earliest-marrying people in Europe; afterward they were the latest and most rarely marrying. Famine-induced dread of economic insecurity was the obvious reason.

As the population declined, the typical landholding increased in size through the process of consolidation. Between 1841 and 1851 the percentage of holdings under five acres fell from 44 to 15, and those between five and fifteen acres from 37 to 33, while farms from fifteen to thirty acres rose in number to comprise 25 percent of the land and those above thirty acres 26 percent. These numbers remained relatively stable for the remainder of the century, chiefly because farmers tended to desist from the age-old Irish practice of dividing their property among their heirs. Normally one son alone inherited; the others emigrated *en masse*. Consolidation also encouraged a widespread shift from tillage to cattle raising. By the 1870s livestock accounted for three-fourths of Ireland's agricultural output and an even greater proportion by the end of the century.

With depopulation, consolidation, and the expansion of pasturage, coupled with improved market conditions at home and abroad (until 1877 at least), came a general rise in per-capita income and, except in Connacht, a marked improvement in the standard of living. Housing conditions especially mirrored the change. Whereas about 40 percent of all Irish houses in 1841 were one-room cabins, by 1861 they constituted less than 10 percent. By 1901 56 percent of the population lived in houses with five or more rooms. Three model cottages (one pre-Famine and two post-Famine) on the grounds of the **Glencolumbkille Folk Museum** *(427)*, County Donegal, illustrate the change dramatically. Other cottages and farmhouses from both before and after the Famine have been reconstructed on the grounds of the **Bunratty Castle Folk Park** *(350)* in County Clare and the **Ulster Folk and Transport Museum** *(459)* at Cultra Manor, Holywood, County Down. A photographic exhibit of vernacular domestic architecture at **Muckross House** *(331)*, County Kerry, is equally enlightening.

As to the landlord class, most survived the harsh years of the late 1840s to share in the ensuing general prosperity. But some did not. Already burdened by debts and mortgages, taxed heavily during the Famine years to help finance relief, and unable to collect arrears of rent, many went to the wall. By acts of parliament in 1848 and 1849, an encumbered estates court was established to facilitate the transfer of such debt-ridden properties to new owners. In ten years' time the court disposed of over three thousand estates, often to native Irish merchants and speculators (so-called "gombeen men") who, in the words of the historian Gearoid O'Tuathaigh, "adopted the old vices and made them worse."

The "old vices" of Irish landlordism were chiefly rack-renting and eviction. The most notorious case of postfamine eviction occurred in 1861, when forty-seven families were driven out of their homes in the district of Derryveagh in Donegal. The landlord responsible was John George Adair, who had acquired the estate in 1859 and subsequently (in the 1870s) improved it by building **Glenveagh Castle** *(428)*, a splendid neo-Gothic pile in the Scottish baronial style made fashionable by Queen Victoria's consort, Prince Albert, at Balmoral in Scotland. Adair claimed to have acted in retaliation for the recent murder of his steward, but mixed with righteous anger was his firm determination to clear the land for raising sheep. This particular case, however, was exceptional in late-nineteenth-century Ireland. Between 1855 and 1880 there were 17,775 recorded evictions resulting in tenants being permanently forced to leave their homes. Out of a total of about 506,000 holdings this represents an eviction rate of only slightly more than 3 percent for the entire sixteen years. As to rents, in spite of the fact that most tenants now held on very short leases or from year to year, most landlords raised rents very infrequently. A survey of thirteen hundred estates in 1880 showed that 40 percent of the rents had been fixed before 1850, in spite of the fact that agricultural prices had risen considerably in the meantime.

Yet statistics such as these, even had they been generally known at the time, could have made little impression on those tenants who *did* suffer, or feared they *might* suffer, under a system of land tenure that guaranteed them no security and tipped the legal scales against them. Hence the forty years after the Famine were marked by recurring and well-organized agitation among Irish tenants and their journalistic, clerical, and political supporters to modify the law so as to secure the rights of tenants in the possession and disposal of their properties, to lower rents, and to facilitate the transfer of ownership from landlords to peasant occupiers of the soil.

In 1850 the Tenant Right League was founded by Charles Gavan Duffy, editor of a Dublin journal called *The Nation*. Its objective was to legalize and extend to the whole country the so-called "Ulster custom," which recognized the tenant's right of occupancy subject to an agreed rent and the right to sell his interest at a price that would compensate him for his improvements to the property. In spite of early success in mobilizing the support of some Irish members of parliament, nothing substantial was accomplished until 1870, when the Liberal government of William Ewart Gladstone belatedly conceded some of the demands put forth by the Tenant Right League.

Then, in the late 1870s, severe agricultural depression set in—the result of three successive bad harvests plus increased competition on the British market from American grain exports. Unrest became general throughout the countryside as tenants fell into arrears and evictions followed. In 1879 Michael Davitt returned from England to County Mayo to organize protest meetings. A former convict, imprisoned for his association with the Fenian uprising of 1867, Davitt's own family had been evicted during the Famine. (The **Michael Davitt Memorial Museum** *[422]* in Straide, County Mayo, contains a collection of mementos pertaining to his life and career.) In October 1879 he founded the National Land League of Ireland and persuaded a rising young Protestant politician to assume its presidency. This was Charles Stewart Parnell of County Wicklow, where his country home, called **Avondale** *(310)*, is still preserved as a memorial to his distinguished career in Irish politics. Between them Parnell and Davitt launched a "land war" against Irish landlords and their agents. Mass meetings were held, rent strikes fomented, and individual malefactors singled out for economic and social ostracism. The most publicized of such cases was that of Captain Charles Boycott, a land agent on an estate near Lough Mask, who was eventually driven out of County Mayo, but not before his name had become a synonym for discriminatory economic coercion. Typically the government tried to quell these disturbances by forceful repression but eventually gave way. A new land act, passed by parliament in 1881, was to serve as the Magna Carta of Irish tenants' rights.

The major innovation of this law (and of a supplementary act of parliament passed the following year) was to set up land courts to adjudicate disputes between landlords and tenants over rent. As a result average rentals were reduced almost immediately by nearly 20 percent. The act of 1881 also provided financial assistance to tenants wanting to purchase their holdings outright. The drop in rents of course made landlords amenable to such arrangements. Then, in 1885, the Ashbourne Act so liberalized the terms of purchase that within five years over nineteen thousand tenants had been able to buy out their landlords. Still more liberal measures were to follow, and still more acreage came into the possession of former tenants (see Chapter Eight). The end of Irish landlordism was in sight.

Contrary to the conventional wisdom of the time, however, peasant proprietorship was not to solve the problem of low agricultural productivity. Barren lands such as those in the west of Ireland yielded no more to peasant owners than they had to landlords. Nor was Irish agriculture any less subject than before to price fluctuations on the international market, changes in consumer habits, and competition from other countries. The long, drawn-out battle between landlords and tenants had tended to obscure the realities of Ireland's economic predicament. The country's overdependence on farming and grazing and its retarded industrial development had produced a functional imbalance that boded ill as Ireland entered the twentieth century.

INDUSTRIAL AND URBAN DEVELOPMENT: 1815–1891

The reasons for Ireland's failure to keep pace with the industrial revolution of the nineteenth century are many and varied, and there is no agreement among economic historians as to their relative weight and significance. Certainly foremost among them was the country's paucity of natural deposits of coal and iron—the two ingredients essential to progress in the age of steam. The proximity of British factories to the iron and coal fields of the Midlands, Wales, and southern Scotland reduced unit costs sufficiently to give them a competitive edge over any Irish industries that might have developed had waterpower remained the prime source of industrial energy. Venture capital was scarce in Ireland, and savings tended to be invested in land and livestock or to be siphoned off into the construction of churches, which, though providing temporary employment and a market for building materials, was ultimately unproductive, at least in the material sense. Nor was foreign capital likely to flow into a country where population was rapidly declining, poverty widespread, and rural disorder endemic. Free trade between Britain and Ireland, institutionalized by the Act of Union, undoubtedly facilitated the penetration of Irish markets by English goods, as did the rapid advance of steam transportation by both ship and rail. Most woolen and cotton textiles and household wares consumed in Ireland were of English manufacture. Even the predecessor of the **Waterford Glass Factory** *(287)* went out of business in 1851. The production of fancy earthenware at the **Belleek Pottery** *(449)* in County Fermanagh was a minor exception to the rule. Major exceptions, however, were the manufacture of drink, the construction of railroads, and the linen textile and shipbuilding industries centered around Belfast.

Whiskey drinking had become popular in the eighteenth century, and by the nineteenth there was an abundance of distilleries throughout the country. One of these, still operating and visitable, was the **Old Bushmills Distillery** *(459)* in County Antrim. The officially recorded consumption of spirits rose from 8.7 million gallons in 1831 to 12.2 million in 1843, and these figures do not take into account the illicit manufacture of poteen made in private stills from partly fermented grain. After 1838 consumption fell to 6.5 million in 1841 and 5.5 million in 1844, partly as a result of a countrywide temperance campaign launched in 1838 by Father Theobald Mathew, a Capuchin friar from Cork, where the **Church of the Most Holy Trinity** *(318)* and the larger-than-life-sized **Father Mathew Monument** *(318)* memorialize his remarkable career. He is credited with having given the pledge to 2½ million people.

But though Father Mathew advocated total abstention from alcoholic beverages, the chief target of his preaching was hard liquor, and his crusade does not appear to have had much effect on the consumption of beer. Certainly the **Guinness Brewery** *(363)* continued to prosper in the nineteenth century and, in terms of capital investment, was Dublin's leading industry. By 1868 the plant at James's Gate was the largest porter brewery in the world and, five years later, expanded to the Liffey, where, between 1870 and 1876, the brewhouse was almost completely reconstructed. Some of the profits from this vast enterprise were to be plowed into the construction of **Ashford Castle** *(422)* by Sir Arthur Edward Guinness, later Lord Ardilaun. This noble, sprawling, baronial-style palace on the banks of Lough Corrib, County Mayo (now Ireland's most luxurious hotel), was built to the design of Joseph Franklin Fuller and completed in 1870—a suitable testament to the country's greatest industry and to the family that had brought it into being. By this date, too, whiskey production had recovered from the effects of Father Mathew, and by the turn of the century the Irish industry accounted for a quarter of the United Kingdom's output, exporting even a higher proportion of its product than did Scotland. There was no dearth either of domestic consumers, and no want of public houses for the slaking of their thirst. One of these, the **Crown Liquor Saloon** *(457)* on Great Victoria Street in Belfast, has been restored by the National Trust of Northern Ireland—a splendidly gaudy emporium elegantly furnished in the High Victorian manner. More typical, especially in the rural areas, were the many "shebeens"—private unlicensed drinking houses dispensing poteen. One of these has been reproduced on the grounds of the **Glencolumbkille Folk Museum** *(427)* in County Donegal.

In 1834, only six years after the opening of the pioneer Stockton and Darlington railway line in England, Ireland's first steam-powered locomotive pulled out of Westland Row Station, Dublin, headed for Kingston (now Dun Laoghaire), six miles south. The railway boom began in earnest in 1844–45, half of the capital coming from England. By the end of 1860 there were thirty companies operating 1,364 miles of line with 324 locomotives and about fifty-five hundred carriages and wagons. (A representative collection of this equipment can be seen at the **Witham Street Depot** of the **Belfast Transport Museum** *[458]*.) Eventually five major trunk lines absorbed most of the business, each with a passenger/freight station in Dublin that served as the hub of a radiating network. Among the four still standing, **Connolly (Amiens Street) Station** *(366),* which opened in 1844, is a granite Italianate building serving the Dublin and Drogheda Railway. The same year the Great Southern and Western Railway began operating out of **Heuston (Kingsbridge) Station** *(363),* a huge neoclassic building more or less in the Renaissance manner. **Broadstone Station** *(369)* was built in 1850 as headquarters of the Midland Great Western Railway. This is a portentous edifice in the style Victorians called "Graeco-Egyptian." It is now used as a freight depot and bus station. **Harcourt Street Station** *(356),* opened in 1859, was the terminus of the Dublin and Wicklow Railway. The passenger waiting room now houses a branch of Barclay's Bank.

In 1861 Dublin had a population of just over a quarter of a million. In twenty years' time it had grown by approximately twenty-five thousand chiefly from the influx of Famine refugees from the countryside. Overcrowding was rife, especially in that part of the central city bounded by the Royal and Grand canals, where decaying tenements literally reeked of poverty. Dublin had the worst slum conditions in the British Isles, worse even than Glasgow's. In the ancient parishes of the Liberties the average number of persons per room was 3.49, and per bed 2.71.

Yet east of here, in the area between College Green, Merrion Square, and St. Stephen's Green, were pleasant vistas and enough elegant new buildings to remind visitors today that old Dublin is as much a nineteenth-century as a Georgian city. New construction in **Trinity College** *(352)* included the late-nineteenth-century Graduate Memorial Building by Sir Thomas Drew and the Museum Building, built in 1854 to the design of Thomas Deane and Benjamin Woodward in the Lombardo-Venetian style popularized by the English art historian John Ruskin. **St. Stephen's Green** *(357)* was landscaped at the expense of Lord Ardilaun (Arthur Edward Guinness) and opened to the public in 1880. West of the green stands the **Royal College of Surgeons** *(357),* a handsome neoclassical building by William Murray, built between 1825 and 1827. To the north is the **Shelbourne Hotel** *(357),* "a high Victorian interloper in a Georgian neighborhood," to quote the city historian, Adrian MacLoughlin. It was opened for business by William Jury in January 1867. At the corner of Kildare and Nassau streets stands the building that once housed the Kildare Street Club, bastion of Dublin's Protestant elite. It is a fine Venetian-style red brick palazzo by Deane and Woodward with fascinating stone carvings of monkeys, birds, etc., by James and John O'Shea and Charles W. Harrison. The premises are now occupied by the Alliance Française and the **Irish Genealogical Museum** *(358).* Also on Kildare Street is the **Royal College of Physicians** *(358),* another neoclassical essay built between 1860 and 1864 to the design of William G. Murray, son of the architect of the Royal College of Surgeons. Nearby is the **National Library** *(358)* and, facing it, the

National Museum *(355)*, both heavily neoclassic in the Victorian manner and both completed before 1890 to the designs of Sir Thomas Newenham Deane and his son Sir Thomas Manley Deane.

The third of Dublin's great cultural repositories, the **National Gallery of Ireland** *(354)*, was raised in Merrion Square between 1859 and 1864 and designed by Francis Fowke. Here are housed, among other things, most of the major works of Ireland's leading nineteenth-century artists. Included are landscapes by Thomas James Mulvaney (first director of the gallery), Roderick O'Conor, Walter Frederick Osborne, and (best of all) Nathaniel Hone the younger; portraits by Nicholas Crowley and Martin Arthur Shee; and genre and narrative paintings by Matthew James Lawless, William Mulready, and Daniel Maclise. Dublin's primacy in the field of Irish painting had been assured by the founding of the Royal Hibernian Academy in 1823. No other city in Ireland could thereafter rival it, although the **Crawford Municipal Art Gallery** *(318)* in Cork and the **Limerick Municipal Art Gallery** *(338)* both contain respectable collections of the above-named and other artists. So does the **Ulster Museum** *(457)* in Belfast, though the building itself is of a much later date—begun in 1924 and not completed until 1971.

Belfast, alone of Irish cities in the nineteenth century, developed into a modern, industrialized, urban agglomeration. The metamorphosis was rapid. In 1800 the town's population was not much more than twenty thousand; by 1831 it had reached fifty thousand; by 1861, 120,000; and by 1891, 350,000—a number higher than Dublin's. In the first two decades of the century cotton-spinning factories accounted for—and absorbed—much of the growth. Fierce competition from the mills of Manchester, however, led to a wholesale shift to linen manufacture—providentially as it proved to be when the American Civil War produced a shortage in the supply of raw cotton. The region's necessary reliance on imported coal to drive steam-powered machinery was offset by low labor costs, the plenitude of local flax, and especially by the lack of English competition. Then, in the 1850s, a Clydesman, Edward Harland, bought out a struggling shipyard on Queen's Island and, with the help of his partners William James Pirrie and G. W. Wolff, converted it into one of the world's major builders of iron ships, specializing in passenger liners. By 1891 the yards of Harland and Wolff and Workman and Clark and Company (founded in 1879) were producing a total annual tonnage of more than a hundred thousand and still growing. Ancillary industries—ropeworks, marine engines, etc.— sprang up in consequence, and Belfast was to become one of the major industrial centers of the British Isles.

With industrial growth, naturally, came urban sprawl, facilitated in this case by the bankruptcy of the second marquess of Donegall, whose family had owned all the land on which the city stood until most of it was sold out to former urban tenants by the encumbered estates court to satisfy the claims of creditors. According to the contemporary economist John Stuart Mill, the consequent "creation of innumerable freehold owners of building ground did more to promote the rise and progress of Belfast than any other fact or circumstance in its history." The result was the creation within a very few decades of the modern city that still stands as the greatest single achievement of Victorian architecture to be found anywhere in Great Britain. The most successful of these architects was Charles Lanyon, who came from England to serve as surveyor of Antrim in 1835 and stayed to oversee the construction of a major part of the nineteenth-century city.

Among Lanyon's early achievements was the reconstruction of the **Belfast Bank** *(454)* on Waring Street—an elaborate Italianate palazzo, still one of the city's handsomest buildings. Nearby is the **Ulster Bank** *(454)*, completed in 1860 to the design of another architect, James Hamilton of Glasgow. It is another neoclassical exercise in the Italianate manner and, in the words of the architectural historian C. E. B. Brett, one of Belfast's "most magnificently exuberant buildings." Lanyon's masterpiece is the **Custom House** *(454)* on Queen's Square—a Palladian-style building of golden stone that dominates the city's waterfront. **Richardson Sons and Owden Warehouse** *(456)* at 1 Donegall Square, North, is, like the Museum at Trinity College, Dublin, a splendid exercise in the Venetian style favored by John Ruskin. The architect was W. H. Lynn, Lanyon's junior partner. In an entirely different style is **Belfast Castle** *(459)*, built in 1870 to the design of the architectural firm Lanyon, Lynn and Lanyon for the third marquess of Donegall, who had restored the family fortunes by marrying an English heiress. This great pseudomedieval pile on Cave Hill overlooking the city is a masterpiece of the Scots baronial style, with details copied from the prototype designed by the prince consort for the royal family at Balmoral.

Belfast's rapid growth was not trouble-free. With new industry came new jobs, and thousands flocked into the city from the countryside to fill them, especially during the Famine years and those immediately following. Among these urban immigrants was a large number of Roman Catholics, amounting to about 40 percent of the population by 1850, as against a mere 6 percent in 1800. Protestant and Catholic workers settled in separate sections of West Belfast: Sandy Row, built in the 1840s, was largely Episcopalian (i.e., Church of Ireland) and inhabited mostly by linen workers. (A terrace [row] of workmen's houses from Tea Lane, running west from Sandy Row, has been rebuilt on the grounds of the **Ulster Folk and Transport Museum** *[459]* in Cultra Manor, County Down.) Close by, the area along Falls Road was Catholic territory. The Shankill was the home of shipyard workers, mostly Presbyterian and fiercely anti-Catholic. Proximity did not breed mutual tolerance, and ancient rural animosities drew new vigor from the urban soil. Sectarian riots broke out in 1835, 1843, 1852, 1864, 1872, 1884, and 1886. The twelfth of July, anniversary of the Battle of the Boyne, became a regular occasion for mob violence. The Orange Order, suppressed by the British government in 1835, soon revived and from 1850 onward moved from strength to strength as the chief organizer of Protestant militancy. Modern sectarianism in Northern Ireland, for all its seventeenth- and eighteenth-century antecedents, has its strongest roots in the crowded proletarian quarters of Victorian Belfast.

CHURCH AND STATE: 1801–1891

By the Act of Union the Church of Ireland was amalgamated with the Church of England to become the established church of the United Kingdom. Its Irish communicants, as in the past, comprised a small minority of the population—no more than 12 percent according to the census of 1861. The 12 percent, however, included the majority of landowners, about half the lawyers, doctors, architects, and bankers, and 80 percent of the Irish officers in the British army.

Also included were most of the top government officials and civil servants, who administered the country from their headquarters in **Dublin Castle** *(358)*. There, in 1814, the city's most distinguished architect, Francis Johnston, built the neo-Gothic Chapel Royal—an architectural symbol of the marriage of church and state and of the survival of the Protestant Ascendancy. Johnston's next commission in Dublin was to build **St. George's (C of I) Church** *(366)* on Hardwicke Place—a fine Greek Revival exercise with a pedimented portico faced with Ionic columns and a tiered tower and spire resembling James Gibbs's Church of St. Martin's-in-the-Field on Trafalgar Square in London. A rival Dublin architect of the Greek Revival school was John Bowden, who built **St. Stephen's (C of I) Church** *(354)* on Mount Street Crescent in 1824–25, again with an Ionic portico and a clock tower, this one graciously topped by a cupola supported by Corinthian columns. Nine years earlier he had incorporated into his otherwise rather plain **St. George's (C of I) Church** *(455)* in Belfast a grandiose Corinthian portico transported here intact from the earl-bishop of Derry's great house in Ballyscullion. Still another early-nineteenth-century Dublin church builder was John Semple. His now deconsecrated, high-spired St. Mary's Chapel of Ease was erected in 1830 at the corner of Upper Dorset Street and St. Mary's Place and is known as the **Black Church** *(367)* because of the dark-hued building material used. Another of his contributions was **St. Mary's (C of I) Church** *(374)* in suburban Monkstown—an extravagantly designed neo-Gothic cruciform building, more or less Lusitanian in inspiration.

Notwithstanding the flurry of building in the first three decades of the nineteenth century, the Church of Ireland suffered severely from underattendance at its services and from overstaffing at the top. Of its more than two thousand benefices in 1830, 425 had fewer than a hundred parishioners, twenty-three fewer than ten, and forty none. Yet its hierarchy included four archbishops and eighteen bishops to preside over some two thousand clergymen, many of whom were pluralists and/or absentees. Reform came with the passage by parliament in 1833 of the Irish Temporalities Act, which suppressed ten bishoprics and established a board of ecclesiastical commissioners to reorganize and revitalize the establishment at the parish level.

The commissioners were also authorized to build new churches and repair old ones. The first to undergo a much needed restoration was **St. Patrick's (C of I) Cathedral** *(441)* in Armagh, seat of the Episcopalian primate. An English architect, Lewis Cottingham, was commissioned to do the job, and though he restored the church to usability, he obliterated most of its medieval features, including the fine west doorway. **Tuam Cathedral** *(415)* underwent an equally drastic restoration at the hands of Sir Thomas Deane in 1863, though the Romanesque chancel arch was preserved more or less intact. **St. Patrick's Cathedral** *(362)*, Dublin, was rebuilt at about the same time at the expense of Sir Benjamin Lee Guinness, but with somewhat greater consideration for the original plan. As to new construction, the most ambitious undertaking of the established church was the erection of **St. Fin Barr's Cathedral** *(317)* in Cork. Begun in 1863, the cathedral had as architect the great English Gothicist William Burges. Completed in 1878, this magnificent three-spired cruciform building, with its fine west rose window and multitude of stone carvings, was consciously modelled on French thirteenth-century prototypes, though the interior is closer to the Early English style.

By the time St. Fin Barr's was finished, the Church of Ireland had been legally disestablished. An act of parliament, passed in 1869 at the instance of Prime Minister Gladstone, had completely severed the legal connection between church and state in Ireland. This brought to an end the long-standing and often violent controversy over the payment of tithes. Thirty years before (1838), the Tithe Commutation Act had transferred the obligation for payment from occupiers to owners of the land (from tenants to landlords). This, in effect, removed the hated tithe proctor from the Irish scene but did nothing to relieve the country's economy of the burden of supporting an established Church to which only a small minority of the population belonged. With the passage of the Act of Disestablishment, the Church of Ireland would henceforth be an entirely voluntary body. Thereafter its building activity inevitably dwindled, confined mostly to repairs of existing churches. One of these was **St. Brigid's Cathedral** *(337)* in Kildare, restored by the London architect George Edmund Street in 1875. Another of Street's restorations was **Christ Church Cathedral** *(360)*, Dublin, completed in 1878. Both retain much of their original medieval form and style.

Disestablishment was no more pleasing to the Roman Catholic majority than to the Presbyterians of Ulster. In the six counties now comprising Northern Ireland, Presbyterians in 1861 made up 33 percent of the population. Since 23 percent belonged to the Church of Ireland, Protestants of the two major denominations constituted a clear majority. Friction between the two had already abated with the commutation of tithes in 1838. Even before that event, the Reverend Henry Cooke, Presbyterian minister at Killyleagh, County Down, had publicly proclaimed "the banns of sacred marriage" between the Presbyterian Church and the established Church of Ireland. The "marriage" of his imagination was in fact a mutual defense pact against encroaching "papism." Times had changed since the 1790s, when Ulster Protestants and Catholics had found common cause in the ranks of the United Irishmen. Wolfe Tone's dream of an interdenominational community of interest among all native Irishmen was fast evaporating. (See Chapter Six.)

Cooke was the leader of the "old light" faction among Presbyterians—evangelical, fundamentalist, and virulently anti-Catholic. In 1822 he had driven out of the Synod of Ulster a more moderate group, called "new lights" and led by Dr. Henry Montgomery. The rift was partially healed in 1840 with the establishment of the General Assembly of the Church of Ireland, although a smaller Non-Subscribing Presbyterian Association of clergymen and churches remained unreconciled. Factionalism of this sort, however, did not deter the proliferation of new Presbyterian churches, especially in Belfast. Two are especially noteworthy. The **May Street Presbyterian Church** *(455)*, dating from 1829, is a handsome Palladian building with a brick and stucco facade faced with Ionic columns and pilasters. The other is the **Sinclair Seamen's Church** *(454)* in Corporation Square, a neo-Gothic structure with a high Lombardic tower. The interior was (and is) furnished with miscellaneous nautical artifacts in keeping with the church's original mission to "watch over the spiritual interest of seamen frequenting the port of Belfast."

Elsewhere in Ireland religious affiliations were overwhelmingly Roman Catholic—86 percent in Leinster and more than 90 percent in Munster and Connacht, according to the census of 1861. Abolition of the penal laws in the 1790s had set in motion a wave of church building that continued into the first two decades of the nineteenth century. In Dublin work began on **St. Mary's Pro-Cathedral** *(366)* in 1816. The original site chosen was on Sackville (O'Connell) Street, where the General Post Office now stands, but discretion persuaded the sponsors to place the building on a less visible location on Marlborough Street. The style is neoclassical, with a pedimented front portico of six heavy fluted Doric columns, matched on the inside with a colonnade of twenty-two columns of the same order under a handsome coffered dome. Although the architect, John Sweetman, was an amateur and the exterior is somewhat overwhelmed by adjacent buildings, the pro-cathedral's elegant interior is one of the prettiest in Dublin. In an altogether different style, but almost as attractive, is Carlow's cruciform **Cathedral of the Assumption** *(289)*, begun in 1820 to the design of Thomas Cobden. With its high tower crowned by an octagonal lantern, its slender clustered columns, triple lancets, and diagonal rib vaulting, this is a very successful exercise in the still modish Gothick manner.

Both these substantial and well-accoutred churches were, in a sense, emblematic of the growing prosperity and self-confidence of the Catholic middle class. Since 1793 they had been allowed to maintain schools, join the professions, and vote in parliamentary elections. But, in spite of Pitt's implied promises during the controversy over the Act of Union, they were still barred from judgeships, from ministerial positions in the government, from the higher ranks of either the armed services or the civil service, and, most galling of all, from sitting as members of parliament. For more than two decades pressures on the British government to remedy the situation proved unavailing. Then, in 1823, a powerful political pressure group— the Catholic Association—was organized by a prominent Irish Catholic barrister, Daniel O'Connell. Its objective was "Catholic emanicipation," that is, the removal of the remaining legal disabilities mentioned above.

O'Connell was the scion of a County Kerry family that had survived the penal laws to enjoy a moderate prosperity. His father had been a landlord; an uncle a general in the French army; an aunt, Ellen O'Leary (Eibhlin Dubh ni Laoghaire), the well-known author of one of the greatest poems in the Gaelic language, the *Lament for Art O'Leary*, an elegy to her late husband, killed by an English sheriff. The family home near Caherdaniel, called **Derrynane** *(328)*, was (and still is) a substantial, if modest, country mansion.

O'Connell's plan was to promote the election to parliament only of members pledged to "Catholic emancipation." His political genius consisted of mobilizing popular support by offering association membership to all who would subscribe a mere penny a month. Moreover, the Catholic clergy were declared *ex officio* members. In a single stroke he thus brought into being for the first time in Ireland a broad-based political machine capable of organizing and giving direction to the sentiments of the entire Catholic population. By March 1825 over £19,000 had been amassed. Parish priests recruited members, collected the "Catholic rent" on Sundays, addressed political meetings, and marched voters to the polls. In 1826 pro-

Emancipation Protestant candidates were chosen at parliamentary elections in Waterford, Louth, Monaghan, and Westmeath. Then, in 1828, O'Connell, though disqualified as a Catholic to sit in the house of commons, presented himself as a candidate. He won easily and duly appeared at Westminster to claim his seat.

Fearing widespread civil disorder in Ireland, the government of Sir Robert Peel gave way. A Catholic emancipation bill was pushed through both houses and became law in 1829. By a change in the wording of the oath of allegiance, Catholics were now made eligible for all offices of state, except those of regent, lord lieutenant, and lord chancellor of either Britain or Ireland. To be sure, the number of potential beneficiaries was small. Moreover, the government promptly procured the passage of a second bill that drastically reduced the size of the Irish electorate by raising the property qualification. O'Connell made no effective protest, thereby tacitly accepting the automatic disfranchisement of the majority of his own supporters. His was no victory for democracy in Ireland, but the manner in which it had been achieved set a precedent for Catholic political activism that was to have significant consequences in the years to come.

The post-Emancipation years were to witness a rapid advance in the economic and social status of Irish Catholics, especially in the cities. By 1861 28 percent of all barristers were Catholic, as were 35 percent of solicitors, 32 percent of physicians and surgeons, 50 percent of apothecaries, and 33 percent of all other professions. The surge of church building both paralleled and reflected this advance. Until about mid-century the great majority of new Catholic churches were neoclassical in design. In Dublin work on the Franciscan **Church of the Immaculate Conception** *(363)* on Merchant's Quay began in 1832. Behind an undistinguished facade decorated with both Corinthian and Doric pilasters lies a handsome cruciform interior with good plasterwork in the ceilings and a glassed bull's-eye dome over the crossing. The building was erected on the site of a tavern called "Adam and Eve," used surreptitiously for services during penal days. The name stuck, and the church continues to be called "Adam and Eve's." Close by, on John Dillon Street, **St. Nicholas of Myra Church** *(362)*, also built in 1832, has an Ionic portico, a clock tower, and a copper cupola. The best feature of its somewhat gaudy interior is the fine altarpiece with eight fluted Ionic columns. **St. Andrew's (RC) Church** *(351)* in Westland Row, completed in 1837, has a fine Doric facade and a high altar screen of Corinthian pillars. North of the Liffey, on Arran Quay, stands **St. Paul's (RC) Church** *(369)*, built the same year, with an Ionic portico, clock tower, and cupola not unlike St. Nicholas of Myra's. Facing it, on the opposite side of the river, stands **St. Audeon's (RC) Church** *(361)*—erected in 1846 to the neoclassic design of Patrick Byrne—a monumental building with a facade of Corinthian columns supporting a pediment topped by three huge statues. Other Irish cities could boast a similar outburst of architectural classicism in the design of new Catholic church construction in the 1830s and 1840s.

One interesting exception to the current fashion was **St. Malachy's Church** *(455)* in Belfast, completed in 1844 by Thomas Jackson. Here the style is Tudor Gothic or Perpendicular. The interior, modelled on the Henry VII Chapel in Westminster Abbey, is a visual delight—intricate fan vaulting of lacy plasterwork, crockets and pendants galore, and an elegant Italianate altarpiece of superb delicacy of design. St. Malachy's was, in a sense, the forerunner of a new wave of neo-Gothicism that was to dominate ecclesiastical architecture in the second half of the nineteenth century.

Nowhere is this more evident than in St. Mary's Square, the great quadrangle designed in 1842 by England's foremost Gothicist, Augustus Welby Northmore Pugin, as an enlargement to **Maynooth (St. Patrick's) College** *(378)*. The quadrangle was completed in 1879 by his disciple James J. McCarthy, with the erection of the college chapel on the north side. With its great rose window, figure-painted ceiling, intricately carved stalls, and rose-marble altarpiece, there is no finer example in Ireland of the Victorian Gothic revival.

By mid-century Maynooth boasted an enrollment of about five hundred seminary students and an alumni body making up more than half the priests of Ireland. It was the seat of a rejuvenated Church, the seedbed of an aggressive and self-confident clergy, determined to reestablish the centrality of Catholic worship in the lives of a people grown ignorant and careless of their religious obligations. In the pre-Famine years it was the faculty of Maynooth that spearheaded what the historian Emmet Larkin has labelled the "devotional revolution." After the Famine leadership in the movement was assumed by Paul Cullen, archbishop of Armagh and Dublin and, from 1866 to 1878, the country's first native cardinal. If Ireland today is remarkable among European nations for the conspicuousness of its religiosity, the origins of this state of affairs need be traced back no further than to the devotional revolution of the nineteenth century.

Before the Church could strengthen its control over the spiritual lives of its communicants, the clergy had first to extirpate a host of popular superstitions and folk customs, many of them rooted in pre-Christian antiquity. These included festivals of pagan origin, festive (and often drunken) wakes held over the bodies of the recently dead, and "patterns" or pilgrimages to holy wells or to the presumed burial sites of local saints. The Lough Derg pilgrimage, to be sure, was left untouched, though subject to stricter clerical control. The Church also gave approval to a new pilgrimage to Knock, County Mayo, where in August 1879 a group of villagers claimed to have seen an apparition of the Virgin Mary accompanied by St. Joseph and St. John the Evangelist. (Today the **Knock Shrine** and Folk Museum *[423]* rivals Lourdes and St. Anne de Beaupré in the huge number of the faithful it regularly attracts.) But most traditional, unsanctioned exercises of religious fervor were curbed or forbidden altogether.

Religion became more church-centered than it had ever been. Marriages, baptisms, and funerals in private homes were discountenanced. New devotions, mainly of Roman origin, were introduced and encouraged. These included the rosary, novenas, perpetual adoration, benedictions, Stations of the Cross, Vespers, etc. Sodalities and confraternities such as the Society of St. Vincent de Paul sprang up with clerical blessing. Devotional aids such as beads, scapulars, medals, missals, and holy pictures came into common use. Vestments and altar furnishings became more magnificent. Regular attendance at Sunday Mass rose from about 33 percent at the beginning of the nineteenth century to more than 90 at the end. Thus, in the words of Emmet Larkin, "the great mass of the Irish people became practicing Catholics, which they have uniquely and essentially remained both at home and abroad down to the present day."

A natural and necessary corollary to the devotional revolution was an even greater proliferation of new Catholic churches in the last half of the century. Providentially, the architects of the Gothic revival were uniquely gifted to supply the new demand for grandeur dictated by this resurgence of faith and reemphasis on public worship. Foremost among the pioneers of the revival was Augustus Welby Northmore Pugin, an English convert to Catholicism who had resolutely rejected classicism as pagan, Protestant, and decadent and had affirmed that only the medieval Gothic style of building was truly Christian and Catholic. Pugin first came to Ireland in 1839 and between that date and his death in 1852 designed twelve or thirteen churches and chapels and five monastic-type structures, including the quadrangle at Maynooth mentioned earlier.

Among these buildings, Pugin's own personal favorite was **St. Mary's Cathedral** *(331)*, Killarney, a magnificent high, cruciform church in the Early English style, though its architect would probably have disapproved of the bareness of its present interior walls from which all ornamentation has recently been removed. More authentically Puginesque is **St. Aidan's Cathedral** *(281)*, Enniscorthy, a fine exercise in the English Decorated style with good Victorian stained glass in both east and west windows. After the architect's death, his son Edward Welby founded the firm of Pugin and Ashlin, which carried on in the same tradition. Their best work was **St. Colman's Cathedral** *(317)* in Cobh (formerly Queenstown), County Cork. Begun in 1868, but not completed until 1912, this is a huge cruciform church overlooking the harbor, with a fine western rose window, handsome red marble columns, and elaborate stone carvings.

Pugin's most productive successor, however, was not his son, but the

Irish-born architect James Joseph McCarthy. Three of Ireland's most magnificent neo-Gothic cathedrals are his handiwork. Arguably the greatest is **St. Patrick's (RC) Cathedral** *(442)*, perched on a hilltop overlooking the city of Armagh across the valley from the less impressive Church of Ireland cathedral dedicated to the same saint. The foundation stone of this new church was laid in 1840, but construction was interrupted by the Famine, and McCarthy took over the work in 1848, though the cathedral was not dedicated until 1872. This is a huge neo-Gothic building in the Curvilinear Decorated style, with lofty twin spires above the west door, on either side of which are statues of St. Malachy and St. Patrick. The walls are decorated with mosaics; the ceiling of the nave is painted with scenes from the lives of Irish saints; the main altar, reredos, side altars, and statuary are of Italian marble—a fitting seat for the Catholic primate of Ireland. The foundation stone for McCarthy's **St. Eugene's Cathedral** *(464)*, Derry, was laid in 1853, and the church was completed twenty years later. Not so grand as St. Patrick's, it too is in the Decorated style. The east window is especially fine. **St. Macartan's Cathedral** *(400)*, Monaghan, was begun in 1861 and not quite complete at the time of McCarthy's death in 1882. Also Decorated in style, this is a cruciform church with shallow transepts and a deep rounded apse. There is some excellent Victorian stained glass in the windows; the nave is very high, with a hammerbeam roof. Curiously, the interior pillars are classical in design with Corinthian capitals. A more drastic departure from the strict neo-Gothic canon can be observed at McCarthy's **Cathedral of the Assumption** *(307)* in Thurles, County Tipperary. Completed in 1872, the style is Lombardo-Romanesque, with three storeys of blind arcading on the facade and a rose window. A circular domed baptistry stands on one side of the west front and a four-storey rectangular tower on the other. The basilical interior has a distinctly baroque appearance. The effect is not altogether pleasing.

Of the architect's parish churches, two are particularly worth mentioning. **St. Saviour's Church** *(368)* in Dublin, begun in 1848 and finished in 1861, is conventionally neo-Gothic with a splendid rose window in the west wall and a handsome vaulted ceiling. The **Church of Saints Peter and Paul** *(336)* in Kilmallock, County Limerick, has an Early English east window of quintuple lancets, a rose window in the west gable, and a crocketed Gothic altarpiece, but again the pillars (red marble) are topped with Corinthian capitals.

In Limerick city **St. John's Cathedral** *(337)*, another essay in Early English Gothic, was designed by the English architect Philip C. Hardwick, though the tower and spire (the highest in Ireland) were the work of a local architect, Maurice Hennessey. Hardwick also designed **St. Alphonsus Redemptorist Church** *(338)* in the same city—another Early English exercise. In Belfast **St. Patrick's Church** *(456)* on Donegall Street was completed in 1877 to designs by Timothy Hevey and Mortimer Thompson. A large neo-Romanesque building of red sandstone, it is distinguished chiefly for its fine triptych in the Pre-Raphaelite style by Sir John Lavery. Thompson was also responsible for the twin spires on the west front of Belfast's **St. Peter's Pro-Cathedral** *(458)*, whose chief architect was John O'Neill. Conventionally neo-Gothic, with a somewhat gloomy interior, the church stands on Derby Street near the Catholic enclave of Falls Road, scene of some of the worst sectarian disturbances in Belfast's unhappy past and present.

Sectarianism in nineteenth-century Ireland, however, was not confined to Belfast or to those other parts of Ulster with a Protestant majority. Elsewhere as well, the two communities, Catholic and Protestant, drew further apart as the nineteenth century progressed. "They lived," writes the historian Sean Connolly, "in their own separate circles, supported their own educational, medical and charitable institutions, and took opposite sides in politics—no longer warring but still very much separate peoples." Efforts by representatives of the Church of Ireland to convert the natives to the Protestant faith exacerbated the rift. Proselytizing by such organizations as the Hibernian Bible Society and the Irish Society for Promoting the Education of the Native Irish through the Medium of Their Own Language met with little success except to infuriate the Catholic clergy. During and after the Famine, charges were rife that Protestants had commonly refused relief to hungry Catholics who refused to convert. Specific incidents of this so-called "souperism" are difficult to substantiate, but belief in their authenticity was, and to an extent remains, fixed in the folk memory of those dreadful years.

Distrust of Protestants permeated the Catholic clergy up to the highest level. Archbishop Paul Cullen once boasted that he had never dined with a Protestant. In a letter from Rome he admonished the more ecumenically minded Father Mathew: "We should entertain most expansive sentiments of charity towards Protestants but at the same time we should let them know that there is but one true Church and that they are strayed sheep from the one fold . . . . otherwise we might lull them into a false security in their errors and by doing so we should really violate charity."

Clergymen on both sides of the religious divide were particularly concerned lest education should be used by the other as a tool for proselytization. When, in 1831, parliament set up an endowment for free primary-level national schools, Protestant and Catholic hierarchies alike objected both to absence of church control over appointments and curricula and to the mixing of Catholic and Protestant children. None was more vehement than John MacHale, Catholic archbishop of Tuam, although his province in western Ireland stood in greater need than any other of the tools to combat illiteracy. After Paul Cullen came back to Ireland in 1850 from his

sojourn in Rome, he too joined the battle, although neither he nor Mac-
Hale was able to persuade the papacy to take a strong stand against the
national schools. Self-segregation, however, and the gradual extension of
clerical influence over the schools eventually undermined the state's efforts
to secularize public elementary education. By 1885 nearly half of all
national schools were in effect denominational, and by 1900 a synod of
Irish Catholic bishops could declare with satisfaction that "the system of
National education . . . in a great deal of Ireland is now in fact, whatever
it is in name, as denominational almost as we could desire."

An even more substantial victory attended the efforts of the Catholic
hierarchy to resist the establishment of interdenominational and strictly
secular state-endowed education at the university level. At the beginning of
the nineteenth century there was still but one university in Ireland, the
University of Dublin, better known as Trinity College. After 1793 Catholics
had been admitted as undergraduates, but relatively few applied as they
were still excluded from scholarships and fellowships. In 1845 prime
minister Sir Robert Peel pushed through parliament a bill to establish
three provincial colleges in Cork, Galway, and Belfast respectively, under
the general administrative umbrella of a "Queen's University" in Dublin.
Again Archbishops MacHale and Cullen joined forces in opposition to
these "godless colleges," chiefly because of the government's refusal to
allow clerical control over the teaching of such subjects as philosophy and
history. This time Rome cooperated with the Irish hierarchy by prohibit-
ing Catholic clergy from accepting teaching appointments and by urging
the bishops to discourage students from enrolling. In 1850 the Synod of
Thurles, under Cullen's leadership, officially condemned the colleges and
decreed that no bishop was to cooperate in their administration, that the
clergy were prohibited from holding any office therein, and that the laity
was to shun them as "dangerous to faith and morals."

Notwithstanding this formidable opposition, all three colleges opened
their doors in 1849. On University Road in Belfast rose a fine red brick
Tudor Gothic building with a tower modelled on that of Magdalen College, Oxford, designed by the city's most eminent architect, Charles Lanyon. It remains the central architectural feature of the much expanded
Queen's University *(457)*, which today has a student body of some seven
thousand. In Cork the original building on the grounds of what is now
called **University College, Cork** *(319)*, was designed by the architects
Thomas Deane and Benjamin Woodward. Laid out on an open courtyard
plan facing Western Road, it was described by the historian Thomas
Babington Macauley (a Cambridge graduate) as "a Gothic college worthy
to take its place in the High Street of Oxford." The same remark might
have been made of its counterpart in Galway. The original building on the
grounds of what is now **University College, Galway** *(407)*, as designed by

Joseph B. Keane, has a clock tower copied from Tom Tower, Christ Church, Oxford. Enrollments at Belfast in the first ten years of the college's life averaged 189, rising to four hundred in its second decade. The lower figures for Cork (147 and 253) and Galway (85 and 153) are probably to be explained by the Catholic hierarchy's opposition.

At Thurles in 1850 the bishops, having registered their disapproval of Peel's "godless colleges," agreed to establish a purely Catholic university on the model of Louvain. John Henry Newman, that most famous of English converts, was invited to be rector. The university opened its doors in 1854 in a house (Number 86) on St. Stephen's Green, South, in Dublin. Four years later Newman gave up the rectorship to return to England, but not before he had supervised the building of the **University Church** *(357)* next door. Designed by the English architect John Hungerford Pollen, this was to be a radical departure from the neo-Gothic canon of Pugin, whom Newman considered to be an architectural bigot. The interior of this tiny chapel is essentially Byzantine—a narrow single chamber with a rounded apse, walls covered with gold leaf, and a flat ceiling of painted panels. The Catholic University, except for its medical school, had only moderate success. It held no charter and received no financial support from the government. After 1879, when the Queen's University was abolished and replaced by a purely degree-granting examining body called the Royal University of Ireland, qualified graduates of the Catholic University were at last entitled to receive degrees. The same opportunity was opened to those of University College, Dublin, the name adopted by the Catholic University when the Jesuits took over the premises in 1883. Finally, in 1908 parliament established the National University of Ireland, to consist of two separate universities, one in Belfast (Queen's University) and one in Dublin with three constituent colleges—University College, Cork; University College, Galway; and University College, Dublin. Though religious tests for admission to any of these newly chartered institutions were forbidden, the governing bodies of each was to be so constituted as to ensure that Queen's University, Belfast, would remain under Protestant control, while the three colleges in the South would be predominantly Catholic. Thus the British government's prolonged effort to secularize higher education in Ireland was, for all intents and purposes, at last abandoned.

If the majority of Catholic bishops (and after 1850 all of them) opposed the government on the matter of denominational education, the hierarchy took no such clear-cut position on questions relating to the fundamental constitutional relationship between Ireland and Britain. Agitation for greater self-government for Ireland than allowed for under the Act of Union was the central theme of Irish politics from the 1840s to the end of the nineteenth century and beyond. On such issues as repeal of the union, Irish Home Rule, and Irish separatism, the Church's position was ambivalent and divided. Instinctively conservative and opposed to civil disobedience—especially of the extreme nationalist variety—the episcopate in general and Paul Cullen in particular were wary of committing the Church unreservedly to any political program that might subvert established law and order. Notwithstanding the political activism of many individual clergymen, low and high (John MacHale among them), the Church's attitude toward relations between England and Ireland was essentially pragmatic. Irish birth and upbringing may have inclined most priests to sympathize with Irish nationalism in its several forms, but the official position of their Church was dictated primarily by concern for its own institutional needs, which transcended purely political considerations.

IRELAND AND ENGLAND: 1815-1901

The Act of Union, which had abolished the Irish parliament, made no other significant change in the country's internal government. The lord lieutenant remained the titular head of the Irish administration, but it was the chief secretary, normally a cabinet member in Whitehall, along with his appointed undersecretary in Dublin, who actually administered Ireland's domestic affairs. Below the undersecretary, whose headquarters was in Dublin Castle, stood a sizable army of civil servants on whom fell the day-to-day burdens of administration. Until the Emancipation Act of 1829, Catholics were legally barred from the higher ranks of the civil service and were informally excluded from most of the lower ranks as well. From 1835 to 1840, during the undersecretaryship of Thomas Drummond, some Catholics were appointed to important posts in the central government, others to judgeships and local magistracies. Drummond also procured the passage of an act of parliament in 1836 that established a national Irish police force to be recruited on a nonsectarian basis. Another piece of legislation—the Corporations Act of 1840—gave elective councils to the country's nine largest towns, thus helping to break the Protestant stranglehold over municipal affairs. These measures, however, marked the highwater mark of reform, so far as concerned the officially sponsored intrusion of Catholics into the machinery of government. For the most part both the castle and local administration remained the province of the Protestant Anglo-Irish elite.

Ireland did benefit, however, from a series of paternalistic measures passed by parliament, even before the Famine, to ameliorate the most grievous consequences of the country's endemic poverty. Far more than it was willing to do for England itself, the government doled out public assistance in recognition that Ireland was a special case, requiring special treatment. During the early nineteenth century state-aided dispensaries were set up to provide free medicine and medical attention to the poor; six hundred were in existence by 1840. In 1817 a central loan fund for Irish public works began to finance buildings, roads, bridges, fisheries, etc. In 1831 a board of works was set up to administer these programs. Over the next five years it spent more than £1 million in outright grants as well as loans.

Publicly endowed charity, on the other hand, was more than matched by repression when the poor dared to take matters into their own hands. Outbreaks of rural disorder were as common in the nineteenth century as they had been in the 1790s. Secret societies, known variously as "Rockites," "Whiteboys," "Terryalts," and "Ribbonmen," periodically committed "outrages" such as arson, cattle maiming, assault and battery, and occasionally murder. Their grievances were mostly the old ones—tithes, rack-renting, evictions, the conversion of tillage to grassland, and so forth. Their victims were occasionally landlords or their agents, but mostly they were farmers or fellow subtenants who had moved into properties from which former occupiers had been evicted. The government's answer to these disturbances was the traditional one of coercion. In this it was assisted by the army, the militia, and the police, stationed in barracks throughout the country to the number, altogether, of almost thirty-five thousand as of 1828. Legal warrant for extraordinary measures of law enforcement was obtained by regular suspensions of the Habeas Corpus Act or by the passage of emergency measures such as the Crimes and Outrages Act and the Peace Preservation Act. In only sixteen years of the nineteenth century was Ireland considered peaceful enough to allow the ordinary processes of the criminal law to operate unaided.

On a higher level protest against the status quo took the form mostly of demanding repeal of the Act of Union and the reestablishment of an Irish parliament and some measure of local autonomy. Daniel O'Connell, "the Liberator," fresh from his victory on the issue of Catholic Emancipation, took the lead. In 1840 he founded the National Repeal Association and began to use the same techniques perfected by the Catholic Association—"repeal rents," mass meetings, etc., all designed to elect pro-repeal members to parliament and intimidate the British government into conceding a fundamental revision of the constitutional relationship between England and Ireland. In the summer of 1843, at a "monster meeting" called by O'Connell to assemble on the Hill of Tara, more than half a million people forgathered. Denouement followed quickly. In October another such meeting was scheduled for Clontarf, scene of Brian Boru's famous battle. This time the government acted decisively and declared the assembly illegal. Fearing bloodshed, O'Connell backed down, never again to pose a serious threat to the established order. He died on a pilgrimage to Rome in 1847. Seven years later the citizens of Dublin raised the elaborate **O'Connell Monument** *(366)* at the foot of Sackville Street, which was later to be renamed in his honor, as was Carlisle Bridge, leading thence across the Liffey. The Liberator's failure to repeat the success of 1829 can be attributed in part to his inability to win the wholehearted support of the Catholic Church. Archbishop John MacHale, to be sure, and about half of the episcopate and an even higher percentage of parish priests were on his side. But a large minority of the bishops was not, and in 1844 the Vatican itself condemned the clergy's excessive political activism on behalf of repeal. Even more significantly, O'Connell could find no effective allies in England, as he had on the issue of emancipation. Prime minister Sir Robert Peel could therefore be confident of full public support in his own country when he declared that no power his government possessed would *not* be used "for the purpose of maintaining the union; the dissolution of which would involve . . . the dismemberment of this great empire."

Meanwhile a small faction of radical Nationalists, contemptuous of the Liberator's respect for law and order, had broken off from the main body of repealers. These were the Young Irelanders, who chose as their model Guiseppe Mazzini's Young Italy, a conspiratorial organization of patriots aimed at violent overthrow of all the monarchical governments in the fragmented Italian peninsula and their replacement by a single democratic republic. In February 1848 revolution broke out in Rome, followed by republican uprisings in Paris and Vienna, which succeeded in driving both King Louis Philippe and Prince Clemens von Metternich out of power. Fearful of the possible spread of the revolutionary virus to Irish shores, the British government moved quickly against the Young Irelanders. One of their leaders, John Mitchel, was arrested, tried for conspiracy, convicted, and sentenced to fourteen years' transportation, first to Bermuda, then to Tasmania, whence he later escaped to America. Minor uprisings broke out in Counties Waterford, Kilkenny, and Tipperary. All were put down. Among the conspirators, James Stephens escaped to France, but William Smith O'Brien, Terence Bellew McManus, and Thomas Francis Meagher all suffered capture and transportation to Tasmania. Meagher and McManus eventually made their way to America, where the former achieved fame as a Union army general in the Civil War before falling to his death from a Missouri River steamboat. A collection of Meagher memorabilia can be seen today on the ground floor of **Reginald's Tower** *(285)* in his hometown of Waterford. Other mementos of the Irish uprisings of 1848 are to be found in the **National Museum of Ireland** *(355)* in Dublin and the **Cork Public Museum** *(318)*.

In the same two museums are sundry artifacts associated with a second Irish uprising, better organized and more widespread than that of 1848 but essentially a sequel to it. This was the Fenian insurrection of 1867. Eleven years before it took place, the exiled James Stephens had returned to Ireland and on St. Patrick's Day 1858 had helped to found the Irish Republican Brotherhood, dedicated to the forceful overthrow of British rule in Ireland and the establishment of a democratic republic based on universal manhood suffrage. Simultaneously in New York City other veteran forty-eighters established a sister organization that, together with the Irish branch, assumed the cognomen of "Fenians"—after the Fianna, the war band of the legendary Celtic hero Fiona MacCumhail (Finn MacCool). In November 1861 Stephens arranged for the reburial of another forty-eighter, Terence Bellew McManus. After his death in San Francisco McManus's body, attended by much publicity, was brought back to Ireland, with stops in New York, Cork, and Tipperary, before arrival in Dublin—where it lay in state in the Mechanics Institute because Archbishop Cullen had refused to allow the pro-cathedral to be used as a setting for this carefully staged Fenian *coup de théatre*. The final reinterment took place in **Glasnevin Cemetery** *(370)* with some fifty thousand mourners in attendance. It was to be the first of several "political burials" that were to convert this lovely graveyard into an Irish Nationalist shrine.

After the end of the American Civil War Irishmen who had served in both the Union and Confederate armies began to make their way back home to swell the Fenian ranks and kindle hopes for a successful revolution to be carried out with arms and money supplied by sympathizers in the United States. Revolution did break out in March 1867 but soon degenerated into a series of inconclusive clashes with the police in Counties Dublin, Cork, Tipperary, Limerick, and Clare. The few Fenians killed in these fracases were soon to be immortalized in song and story, as were four of their cohorts, the "Manchester Martyrs," later hanged in that city for their participation in a prison rescue attempt resulting in the death of an English policeman. Otherwise the uprising of '67 produced no substantial results except to embitter relations further on both sides of the Irish Sea and to deepen the estrangement between Irish Nationalists and the Roman Catholic Church, whose bishops, led by Paul Cullen, denounced all secret societies and declared the Fenians excommunicate.

After 1867 hopes for some form of Irish constitutional autonomy centered not on revolution but on the ballot box and British parliamentary concessions. Home Rule—an updated version of O'Connell's repeal movement—became the watchword of the greater part of the politically conscious Irish nation. Impetus was supplied, ironically, by the British parliament itself in a series of laws that gradually expanded the Irish electorate. In 1829, as the price of Catholic Emancipation, the number of Irish voters eligible for participation in parliamentary elections had been reduced drastically. The Electoral Reform Act of 1832 raised the figure to about 121,000—still small compared to England's. By mid-century the number had fallen again to a mere forty-five thousand, largely as a result of Famine depopulation. Then, in 1850, parliament passed the Irish Franchise Act, deemed by the historian K. T. Hoppen to have been "the single most important legislative influence upon the makeup of the electorate and the course of electoral politics in nineteenth century Ireland." Specifically it increased the total number of parliamentary electors to more than 163,000. In 1868 the Irish Reform Act added another fifteen thousand borough voters to the rolls, and four years later the secret ballot was introduced. Finally the Electoral Reform Act of 1884 trebled the size of the Irish electorate, bringing it in line with England's for the first time.

The first leader of the new movement for reestablishing an Irish parliament with jurisdiction over domestic affairs was Isaac Butt, a Protestant barrister who founded the Home Government Association in 1870, which three years later was renamed the Home Rule League. In the election of 1874, the first held by secret ballot, fifty-nine of the 103 Irish seats in parliament were won by Home Rulers, who promptly constituted themselves a separate party in the house of commons. In 1877, two years before Butt's death, he was replaced as leader of the Irish parliamentary bloc by the far more aggressive Charles Stewart Parnell, who was soon to become involved with the agitation inspired by Michael Davitt and the Land League.

Parnell, a calculating, taciturn Protestant landlord from County Wicklow, was surprisingly effective as a public speaker and even more so as a master of obstructionist parliamentary tactics. By these means he succeeded in holding the balance of power between the two almost evenly divided British political parties, Liberal and Conservative. The leader of the former was William Ewart Gladstone, who in the parliamentary election of 1885 ran for office on a Home Rule platform. Among the Protestants of Ulster, convinced that Home Rule was an invitation to "Rome rule," Gladstone's name promptly became anathema—as illustrated by the chamber pot with the Liberal leader's portrait printed on the inside, still on view at **Florence Court** *(450)*, County Fermanagh. Elsewhere in Ireland the Liberal/Home Rule ticket was overwhelmingly victorious—thanks in part to the support of most of the Roman Catholic clergy on the one side and the remnants of the Fenian brotherhood on the other.

In January 1886 Gladstone introduced a Home Rule bill that contemplated the establishment of a separate Irish parliament and executive branch to legislate and administer domestic affairs (though not on matters touching foreign affairs, the army and navy, or even customs and excises). The Conservative party sent Lord Randolph Churchill to Belfast, where he stirred a largely Protestant audience to fever pitch with the pronouncement that, rather than accept Home Rule, "Ulster will fight, and Ulster will be right." In the political parlance of the day, this was known as "playing the Orange card," that is, luring Ulster Protestants into the thinning ranks of the Conservative party by promising total resistance to Irish Home Rule. It worked. Thanks to the combined opposition of British Conservatives, Ulster Protestants, and a faction of Unionists defecting from his own party, Gladstone's Home Rule bill was defeated in the house of commons. The prime minister resigned, and the Conservatives under Lord Salisbury took office. Parnell fought on. When, in 1887, the conservative *London Times* charged him with condoning the May 1882 murders in Phoenix Park of the newly appointed chief secretary and undersecretary (Lord Frederick Cavendish and T. H. Burke, respectively) he was able to prove the newspaper's evidence to be forgeries. His popularity and credibility outside Ulster reached a new zenith.

Then, in 1889, Captain W. H. O'Shea, a former Irish member of parliament, brought divorce proceedings against his wife Katherine, citing Parnell as corespondent. The charge was accurate enough, as the liaison had been going on for several years. Victorian Britain was scandalized, especially the Protestant nonconformists who comprised an important element of the Liberal Party. Gladstone thus felt compelled to repudiate the Irish leader. Parnell's own bloc of parliamentary members, meeting in committee room 15 of the house of commons, voted forty-three to twenty-seven in favor of his resignation. Parnell returned to Ireland to plead with the electors in three by-elections to vindicate him by returning his supporters to office. Shocked by the divorce scandal (though Parnell had subsequently married Mrs. O'Shea), the Catholic bishops and most of the clergy turned against him. Worn out by his unsuccessful campaigning, he fell sick and, in October 1891, died at Brighton. With him died the chances for Irish Home Rule for another twenty years.

Death brought Parnell resurrection as a national hero. His burial at **Glasnevin Cemetery** *(370)* was the biggest seen to date in Dublin—a city not unfamiliar with extravagant funerary rites. Later the citizens would erect the tall **Parnell Monument** *(367)* at the top of O'Connell Street, a fine piece of sculpture by the Dublin-born American Augustus Saint-Gaudens.

Yet notwithstanding these outward signs of mourning and respect, the circumstances of Parnell's downfall left a bitter and divisive legacy not soon to be forgotten. Years later (1935), Ireland's greatest poet, William Butler Yeats, reflecting on Parnell's funeral, was to indict the entire Irish nation for the fallen leader's disgrace and premature death:

> . . . But popular rage,
> *Hysterica passio* dragged this quarry down.
> None shared our guilt; nor did we play a part
> Upon a painted stage when we devoured his heart.
> Come, fix upon me that accusing eye.
> I thirst for accusation. All that was sung,
> All that was said in Ireland is a lie
> Bred out of the contagion of the throng,
> Saving the rhyme rats hear before they die . . . .

Chapter Eight
The Early Twentieth Century: 1891–1949

THE IRISH RENAISSANCE

The year Parnell was buried the young James Joyce, who was to become Ireland's most distinguished prose writer, was only nine years of age. Later, in his autobiographical novel *Portrait of the Artist as a Young Man* (1916), he recaptured some of the bitterness of the controversy engendered by the national hero's downfall. Writing of a family Christmas dinner, he recalled the angry words of two of his parents' guests, spoken in the presence of the young boy he then was:

> O he'll remember all this when he grows up, said Dante hotly—the language he heard against God and religion and priests in his own home.—Let him remember too, cried Mr. Casey to her across the table, the language with which the priests and the priests' pawns broke Parnell's heart and hounded him into his grave. Let him remember that too when he grows up.

Joyce did indeed remember, and throughout much of his literary opus the theme of betrayal (of Parnell, of himself, and of his fictitious characters) was to remain a constant. Dublin-born, the eldest son of a spendthrift, bibulous petty civil servant, James Augustine Joyce received a Jesuit education at Clongowes, **Belvedere College** *(367)*, and University College, Dublin, before leaving Ireland for the Continent in 1904. There, except for two brief visits home, he remained until his death in Zurich in 1941. His "exile" was self-inflicted—the product of an abiding sense of alienation from the philistinism and religiosity of his native land. Yet Ireland—and in particular Dublin—remained at the center of all his literary works. These included, in addition to the *Portrait*, a collection of short stories published under the title of *Dubliners* (1914), *Ulysses* (1922), and *Finnegan's Wake* (1939).

Of these the best known, though perhaps not the most widely read, is *Ulysses*, a lengthy (780 pages), rambling work of fiction covering a single day (16 June 1904) in the lives of its two leading characters—Stephen Dedalus and Leopold Bloom. Their wanderings through the streets of Dublin and its environs are traced meticulously in the novel—so much so

244

that it is still possible, though not easy, to replicate their itineraries (eighteen miles by foot, tram, train, and horse-drawn vehicle for Bloom; even more for Stephen Dedalus). And though the celebration of "Blooms-day" has become something of a subspecies of Irish tourism, devotees of Joyce who make the effort to retrace the steps of his fictitious characters need to be reminded that much has changed in Dublin since June 1904, and much has vanished. Gone are the cobbled streets, the gaslights, the trams and horse-drawn vehicles, and of course the omnipresent horse manure. Gone too are Bloom's house at 7 Eccles Street, Barney Kiernan's pub on Little Britain Street, and Bella Cohen's brothel on Railway (now Tyrone) Street. Yet much remains, and the following sites featured in *Ulysses* can be visited fairly easily today by Joyce enthusiasts:

1. **Joyce's Tower** *(357)* at Sandycove, a martello tower built in 1804 where the author lived for a few days in September 1904 after it had been leased by his friend Oliver St. John Gogarty, whom Joyce fictionalized as Buck Mulligan. This is the locus of the opening scene of Ulysses and the beginning of Stephen Dedalus's (that is, Joyce's) personal odyssey through the city of Dublin and its suburbs. It now serves as a museum of Joyceana, including manuscripts, books, photographs, articles of clothing, etc.

2. **Glasnevin Cemetery** *(370)*, where Leopold Bloom, a middle-aged salesman of advertising copy for the *Freeman's Journal* (now defunct), attends the funeral of his recently deceased friend Paddy Dignam.

3. **St. Andrew's (RC) Church** *(351)* on Westland Row, called "All Hallow's" in *Ulysses*, where Bloom interrupts his own odyssey long enough to observe the celebration of the Mass and from which he departs before the collection plate is passed.

4. **Sweney's Chemist's Shop** *(351)* on Lincoln Place, where Bloom buys a bar of lemon soap (still on sale) and where he orders lotion for his wife, Molly.

5. **Ormond Hotel** *(365)* on Upper Ormond Quay, where Bloom stops for a drink and meets up with Simon Dedalus, Stephen's father. The bar and dining room have been recently restored and redecorated in the Edwardian manner.

6. **Davy Byrne's Pub** *(356)* on Duke Street, labelled the "moral pub" in *Ulysses*, where Bloom lunches on a Gorgonzola cheese sandwich and burgundy—still on the bill of fare and very popular on "Bloomsday."

In May 1899, while Joyce was still a student at University College, Dublin, he had attended the opening of a play, *The Countess Cathleen*, by the already-distinguished poet William Butler Yeats. While his fellow students hissed and booed the performance as blasphemous, Joyce clapped loudly—presumably to show his contempt for the Church authorities who had condemned the play in advance of its production. Years later, Yeats would return the favor by pronouncing *Ulysses* to be "perhaps a work of genius" and its author to have "certainly surpassed in intensity any novelist of our time."

William Butler Yeats, born in Sandymount, Dublin, in 1865, eldest son of John Butler Yeats, Ireland's most distinguished portraitist, published his first book of poetry (entitled simply *Poems*) in 1895. Inclined toward mysticism and *fin-de-siècle* European occultism, he was converted to Irish nationalism under the combined influence of the Fenian John O'Leary and the actress Maud Gonne, with whom he fell deeply in love and to whom he dedicated that most charming of love lyrics, beginning with the lines:

> When you are old and grey and full of sleep,
> And nodding by the fire, take down this book,
> And slowly read, and dream of the soft look
> Your eyes had once, and of their shadows deep . . . .

Yeats's nationalism, however, was more cultural than political, and in 1896 he met up with a kindred spirit, Lady Augusta Gregory, who promptly became his friend, patroness, and collaborator, as together they probed the rich resources of Irish folklore with a view to developing a uniquely Irish national consciousness and a literary idiom to match it.

Lady Gregory, widowed at the age of forty-four, was the owner of **Coole Park** *(409)* in County Galway—a conventional Georgian country home set in the midst of extensive parkland with an adjoining lake whose "nine and fifty swans" Yeats was to immortalize in his poem "The Wild Swans at Coole." Here the poet, in the company of the writer Edward Martyn of nearby Tullira Castle, first came in the summer of 1896, and here he returned many times until his hostess's death in 1932. Other guests, at what was in effect the unofficial headquarters of the Irish intelligentsia, included the novelist George Moore, the poet and artist George Russell (known as AE), the playwrights George Bernard Shaw and John Middleton Synge, the Gaelic scholar Douglas Hyde, the patron of the arts Hugh Lane (Lady Gregory's nephew), and Yeats's brother Jack, who was to become Ireland's most talented painter. The house at Coole was unfortunately torn down after Lady Gregory's death, but the park and lake are well preserved and open to the public. Here can still be seen the famous "autograph tree," a stately beech with the carved initials of many of the estate's distinguished visitors, including most of those mentioned above.

It was Yeats and Lady Gregory, with the financial backing of Edward Martyn, who founded a new Irish theater, which in 1902 developed into the Irish National Theatre Society, with Yeats as president and George Russell (AE) and Douglas Hyde as vice presidents. The society's first production was Yeats's *Cathleen ni Houlihan*, with Maud Gonne in the leading role. A stirring patriotic drama based on the landing of the French army at Killala in 1798, the play met with an enthusiastic reception from its Dublin audience. Two years later a generous Englishwoman, Miss Annie Horniman, bought the building in Dublin that became the Abbey Theatre and provided it with an annual subsidy. It opened with another presentation of *Cathleen ni Houlihan*, but the second night was given over to a new play, *Shadow of the Glen*, by John Middleton Synge. Three years later, when the same author's *Playboy of the Western World* was presented at the Abbey, the attending crowd objected so vociferously to the author's alleged slurs on the fair name of Irish womanhood that Yeats had to call in the police. The Abbey survived, however, to become the centerpiece of Dublin's still-thriving legitimate theater. And although the original building was destroyed by fire in 1951, it has been replaced on the same site on Lower Abbey Street by the present **Abbey Theatre** *(365)*, where paintings by John Butler Yeats of Lady Gregory, George Russell, Annie Horniman, et al., and a fine portrait of William Butler Yeats by Sean O'Sullivan are still on display.

Among Yeats's fellow guests at Coole Park was Douglas Hyde, son of a Church of Ireland minister, graduate of Trinity College, and translator and publisher of several collections of Gaelic folk stories, legends, and songs. In 1893, in collaboration with a young law clerk, Eoin MacNeill, Hyde founded the Gaelic League, whose aims were (1) to preserve the ancient Irish language and extend its use as a spoken tongue and (2) to encourage the study and publication of existing Gaelic literature. The league was, in a sense, merely the culmination of a century-long effort by Irish antiquarians and writers (mostly Anglo-Irish) to revive the country's native culture and to protect the still sizable corpus of Gaelic manuscripts from further loss and destruction. Chiefly to this end the **Royal Irish Academy** *(356)* was founded in Dublin in 1785. A comparable collection was organized by the antiquarian Charles O'Conor of Balinagare and later housed, along with the harp of the blind Turlough O'Carolan, in **Clonalis House** *(402)*, a mid-Victorian mansion built by Charles Owen O'Conor in County Roscommon, where some five thousand books, manuscripts, and other Gaelic documents are still on display. Other special organizations for the study of the ancient language and history were established throughout the nineteenth century: the Gaelic Society of Dublin in 1806, the Hiberno-Celtic Society in 1818, the Ulster Gaelic Society in 1830, the Irish Archaeological Society in 1840, the Celtic Society in 1845, the Ossianic Society in 1853, and the Society for the Preservation of the Irish Language in 1877. Among the writers who translated and published Gaelic legends, poems, etc., were Samuel Ferguson of Belfast (1816–86); Thomas Davis (1814–45), cofounder of *The Nation*; James Clarence Mangan (1803–49), whom Joyce considered "the most significant poet of the modern Celtic world"; and Standish O'Grady (1846–1928), author of *History of Ireland's Heroic Period* and *Cuchulain and His Contemporaries* and usually considered to be "the father of the Irish Revival."

More than any of its predecessors, in the 1890s the Gaelic League captured the popular imagination with its adult classes and social gatherings, all propagating national self-reliance and self-respect. By 1903 there were six hundred Gaelic League branches, and instruction in the Irish language had been introduced in nearly thirteen hundred national schools. This was insufficient, however, to reverse the decline in the popular use of the Gaelic language, which had begun in about 1750 and had accelerated abruptly during the Famine and post-Famine years as the population of Connacht and west Munster fell off so precipitously. Whereas about half the population of Ireland was monolingually Irish-speaking in 1801, the proportion had fallen to a mere 5 percent by 1851 and stood at only half of one percent by 1901. By that time too only 14 percent of the population could speak any Irish at all, even as a second language.

In the beginning Hyde had insisted that the organization be nonpolitical. But with its commitment to cultural separatism and its campaign against "west-Britonism," this proved impossible. By the first decade of the twentieth century the league had become a haven for extreme Nationalists—so much so that Hyde resigned the presidency in 1915.

Even more self-consciously nationalistic was the Gaelic Athletic Association, founded in Tipperary in 1884 by Michael Cusack, whom Joyce later caricatured in *Ulysses* as that surly xenophobe known simply as "The Citizen." Its purpose was to discourage the playing of such English games as lawn tennis, cricket, and rugby and to replace them with Gaelic football and a modernized version of the ancient sport of hurling, played with large implements of ash shaped like a cross between a hockey stick and a golf club. (A fine collection of hurley sticks, antique and modern, is on view at the **Wexford County Museum** *[281]* in Enniscorthy Castle.) The GAA from the outset made no pretense at being anything but anti-English. Soldiers from the numerous garrison towns were excluded from play, and "foreign games" were expressly banned. Under the cover of athletics the association shortly became, in effect, a highly politicized organization dedicated to separation, peaceful or otherwise, from British rule.

Parallel to these developments was a movement among certain Irish artists and craftsmen to develop a purely "Celtic" art form. Its leading figure was Sarah Purser (1849-1943), a highly talented painter who in 1903 founded a stained-glass studio in Dublin called An Túr Gloine (the Tower of Glass). Among her associates were Evie Hone, Ethel Mary Rhind, A. E. Childe, Hubert McGoldrick, Harry Clarke, and Michael Healy. All are represented in the murals, ironwork, and stained-glass windows of **St. Brendan's (RC) Cathedral** *(413)* in Loughrea, County Galway, built between 1897 and 1903—a veritable museum of early-twentieth-century Irish art and artisanship. Another example of the fine workmanship of this school can be seen at the **Honan Chapel** on the grounds of **University College, Cork** *(319)*, begun in 1915. The style of this nave-and-chancel church is neo-Hiberno-Romanesque, and the west front is copied from the ruined facade of St. Cronan's in Roscrea. Several of the same artists who worked at Loughrea were responsible for the splendid stained-glass windows. Of all the several cultural movements that so enlivened the scene of early-twentieth-century Ireland, only this so-called "Celtic Art Revival" remained for the most part nonpolitical. As such it was a rarity in a country otherwise obsessed with the politics of constitutional reform, that is, with the issue of redefining the legal relationship between Ireland and Great Britain.

THE ROAD TO INDEPENDENCE AND PARTITION: 1891–1922

Parnell's downfall signalled the breakup of his party into three warring factions, and not until 1900 was John Redmond, political heir to the fallen leader, able to reestablish a kind of unity among the Irish members of parliament pledged to support Home Rule. Not included in this group, of course, were the Unionists of the northeast counties who, encouraged by "Orange card" players in the Conservative party, formed an "Ulster Defence Union" and began to collect arms and offers of armed support from England. "I do not come here to preach any doctrines of passive obedience or non-violence," proclaimed the Conservative leader Arthur J. Balfour to an audience of eighty thousand in Belfast. "You have had to fight for your liberties before. I pray God you may never have to fight for them again." Delivered at this time and in this place, these words were little short of an open invitation to sedition. None of this, however—neither the split within the Home Rule party nor the intransigence of the Ulster Unionists— prevented the aging Gladstone from pushing through the house of commons a second Home Rule bill. Inevitably, it too was defeated overwhelmingly in the house of lords; Gladstone retired from office to be replaced as Liberal prime minister by Lord Roseberry; then, at a general election held in 1895, the Conservatives won by a large majority and remained in office for another decade.

Convinced that the fundamental cause of Irish discontent was not political but economic, the newly elected government set about to "kill Home Rule with kindness" by attacking the twin evils of extreme rural poverty and landlordism. In 1891 the congested districts board was established to deal with the special problems of the five counties of Connacht plus parts of Kerry, Cork, Clare, and Donegal—an area containing a half-million inhabitants, a large portion of whom were not much better off than before the Famine. The board was authorized to buy land and distribute it among tenants, consolidate scattered strips into compact holdings, erect better farm buildings, build harbors, encourage fisheries, and establish cottage industries. Between the date of its founding and 1923, when it was dissolved, the board spent some £9 million on the purchase and distribution of land and an additional £2 million on improvements. Moreover special state subsidies led to the construction of 605 miles of light railway in the West. The leading spirit implementing these reforms was Sir Horace Plunkett, also founder of the Irish Agricultural Wholesale Society, a cooperative movement centered around local creameries (dairies) whose aim was to eliminate the toll exacted by middlemen and to make Irish butter more competitive on the English market by improving its quality.

As to landlordism, long thought—mistakenly it would appear—to be the principal cause of Ireland's economic backwardness, the Conservatives enacted a series of laws designed to transfer most of the country's arable and grazing acreage from landlords to peasant proprietors (formerly tenant farmers). This legislative program culminated in the Wyndham Act of 1903, which (1) offered land-purchase loans to tenants at a mere $3\frac{1}{4}$ percent interest payable over $68\frac{1}{2}$ years and (2) encouraged landlords to sell their entire estates by giving them a substantial down payment as a bonus for doing so. By 1909 some 250,000 purchases had thus been negotiated and a further forty-three thousand were pending; and by 1922, in the newly established Free State, only seventy thousand holdings remained unpurchased.

Inevitably this wholesale transfer of landownership led to some consolidation of holdings and some enlargement of farms—though not as much as might have been expected. Between 1891 and 1910 farms of more than fifteen acres but fewer than thirty increased in number from 133,947 to 136,681, and those of more than thirty acres rose from 162,940 to 166,848. This modest trend toward larger-scale agriculture and grazing was accompanied by an equally modest advance in mechanization. Ireland, it is true, lagged behind most other Western countries in this respect, and even as late as the 1930s the scythe, the spade, and the single-horse-drawn plow remained the staple implements on a significant proportion of Irish farms. Still, the early decades of the twentieth century saw a marked increase in the number of agricultural machines: between 1908 and 1912 the number of harrows rose from 185,342 to 204,270; reapers and mowers from 61,956 to 96,777; self-binders from 6,210 to 9,394; gas, oil, and steam engines from 402 to 1,542. Representative collections of such machinery are to be seen today at the **Fethard Folk Farm and Transport Museum** *(305)*, County Tipperary, in the Irish Agricultural Museum at **Johnston Castle** *(283)*, County Wexford, and in the Talbot Collection at the **Bunratty Folk Park** *(351)*, County Clare.

Although the Conservatives had succeeded in dealing a mortal blow to Irish landlordism, they failed to "kill Home Rule with kindness." The movement, backed strongly by a reunited Parnellite party under the leadership of John Redmond, gathered new strength after the return to office of the Liberal party in 1906. Not until 1912, however, did a new prime minister, Herbert Henry Asquith, find it politic to introduce a third Home Rule bill—this one setting up a two-chamber Irish parliament to legislate for domestic affairs, while reserving imperial matters such as defense, foreign policy, customs, and excise to the jurisdiction of the Westminster parliament, to which forty-two Irish members would be elected. Meanwhile, by the Parliament Act of 1911, the absolute veto power of the house of lords had been abolished and its power to obstruct the enactment of bills duly passed in the commons reduced to a mere two-year delay. Thus, when Asquith's measure, having received the assent of the commons, was rejected by the lords, its eventual passage into law by no later than the summer of 1914 still seemed to be assured.

Ulster, in the meantime, reacted to this new and most serious threat in the manner by now to be expected. Local leadership in the fight against Home Rule was assumed by Sir Edward Carson, a Protestant lawyer from Dublin, and James Craig, a stockbroker and member of parliament from County Down. "We must be prepared," announced Craig, ". . . the moment Home Rule passes, ourselves to become responsible for the government of the Protestant Province of Ulster." And from across the Irish Sea came the echoing voice of the Conservative leader Bonar Law: "I can imagine no length of resistance to which Ulster will go, in which I shall not be ready to support them." On 28 December 1912, at Belfast's newly built **City Hall** *(455)*, Carson was the first of over two hundred thousand signatories to append his name to a "solemn league and covenant" pledging to "use all means which may be found necessary to defeat the present conspiracy to set up a home rule parliament in Ireland." Next month the Ulster Volunteer Force was established and soon enrolled one hundred thousand members. In April 1914 Ulster volunteers succeeded in clandestinely bringing ashore at Bangor, Larne, and Donaghadee 24,600 illegal guns and three million rounds of ammunition purchased in Germany. The month before, the commanding officer of the British army contingent at Curragh Camp in County Kildare had offered his subordinates the option of resigning in the event they were ordered to assist in putting down Ulster resistance to Home Rule. About sixty officers signified their preference for dismissal from the service. This was the so-called "Curragh Mutiny"—a misnomer since no orders had been issued or disobeyed, yet a clear enough indication of the unreliability of the British army as a potential instrument for forcing Home Rule down the throats of the northeastern counties.

In the south of Ireland, meanwhile, ardent Home Rule advocates and others of more extreme Nationalist inclinations organized the "Irish Volunteers," to which recruits were drawn from the Gaelic League, the Gaelic Athletic Association, and the Irish Republican Brotherhood (IRB), total membership swelling to about two hundred thousand. They too undertook to smuggle into Ireland firearms from Germany. In July 1914 one of the volunteers, Erskine Childers, brought his yacht *Asgard* into Howth and landed a shipment of guns and ammunition. (The hull of this vessel is now on display at **Kilmainham Jail** *[364]*, Dublin.) British soldiers failed to seize the contraband weapons, but on their return to Dublin they fired into a jeering crowd at Bachelor's Walk, killing three civilians and wounding thirty-eight.

Britain's dilemma in the late summer of 1914 thus appeared to be inescapable: if Home Rule came into operation, Ulster seemed prepared to take up arms in open rebellion; if it did not, the rest of Ireland might do likewise. Then, on 4 August, the German army marched into Belgium; the next day Britain was at war. Redmond and Carson both promised full support for the war effort and agreed to a compromise by which the Home Rule Act (which received the royal assent in September) would be suspended for twelve months or the duration of the war, whichever was longer. Carson promptly offered the services of the Ulster Volunteers to the British cause, and as many as twenty-nine thousand joined early, most of them to be formed into the 36th (Ulster) Division, which later fought with particular distinction at the Battle of the Somme. At Woodenbridge, County Wicklow, on 20 September, Redmond called on the Irish Volunteers not to shrink "from the duty of proving on the field of battle that gallantry and courage which has distinguished our race through its history." About eighty thousand from the South did in fact volunteer immediately to join the British army. Before the end of the war, perhaps as many as two hundred thousand Irishmen, North and South, were serving in His Majesty's armed forces.

But there were others in the South who did not forget the ancient adage that "England's difficulty is Ireland's opportunity" and were prepared to assert the nation's independence without waiting for constitutional Home Rule to take effect. One such was Arthur Griffith, founder of a newspaper and of an embryo political party, both called *Sinn Féin (Ourselves)*. Griffith advocated a program of civil disobedience and passive resistance to British rule, to be initiated by the withdrawal from Westminster of all Irish members of parliament and their reconstitution in Ireland as a native legislative body that would assume full responsibility for the country's government. Among those early attracted to Sinn Féin were two fiery female revolutionaries, Constance Gore-Booth and Maud Gonne, both well known to William Butler Yeats. Constance Gore-Booth (later Countess Markievicz) of **Lissadell House** *(418)*, County Sligo, was one of the two sisters immortalized in the poet's lines "Two girls in silk kimonos, both/ Beautiful, one a gazelle." The actress Maud Gonne had been Yeats's lover before her marriage to Major John MacBride, who had fought against the British during the Boer War before returning to Ireland to join the IRB. Of a different stripe was James Connolly, Socialist and labor leader, who had cofounded the tiny Irish Citizen Army in 1913 to protect Dublin workers against the strong-arm tactics of strikebreakers and who advocated an armed insurrection against England as the opening gambit of a workers' revolution. Among the early members of the radical wing of the Irish Volunteers (which had seceded from the main body when Redmond promised support for Britain's war effort) was Eamon de Valera, a mathematics teacher, born in the United States of a Spanish father and Irish mother but reared in the village of Bruree, County Limerick, present site of the **De Valera Cottage** *(335)* and **De Valera Museum** *(335)*. At the center of all this revolutionary activity was the IRB, direct heirs of the nineteenth-century Fenians and, like them, dedicated to the creation of an independent Irish republic by force of arms. Within the brotherhood none was more zealous than Patrick (Padraic) Pearse, Gaelic linguist and founder of St. Enda's School (now housing the **Pearse Museum** *[370]* in the outskirts of Dublin)—an ardent Nationalist who believed that "bloodshed is a cleansing and sanctifying thing, and that the nation which regards it as the final horror has lost its manhood."

Another member of this oddly assorted company of visionaries was Sir Roger Casement, an Irish-born British civil servant, recently knighted for humanitarian services in Africa. In 1914 he had been commissioned by the IRB to procure arms in Germany, where he was to spend a year and a half before completing negotiations for the dispatch in mid-April 1916 of twenty thousand rifles, ten machine guns, and matching ammunition aboard the steamer *Aud*, disguised as a Norwegian fishing vessel. Intercepted by the Royal Navy, the *Aud* was scuttled in Cork harbor, but not before Casement himself had been landed from a German submarine on Banna Strand near Ardfert, County Kerry, where today stands the **Casement Memorial** *(327)*, a simple obelisk commemorating the event. Promptly taken into custody by the Royal Irish Constabulary (RIC), he was later executed for treason.

Meanwhile, banking on the timely arrival of arms from Germany, Casement's fellow conspirators had set Easter Sunday 1916 as the date for an uprising. Countermanding orders from the head of the Irish Volunteers resulted in a day's postponement so that it was not until the following

Monday, 24 April, that about two thousand Irish Volunteers, IRB men, and Connolly's Citizen Army, mostly in Dublin, came out in open revolt against His Majesty's government. Thus took place the "Easter Rising," concerning which Yeats later wrote: "All changed, changed utterly/A terrible beauty is born."

One contingent of rebels, including Pearse and Connolly, seized the **General Post Office** *(366)* on Sackville (O'Connell) Street, from the steps of which Pearse proclaimed the birth of "the Irish Republic as a Sovereign Independent State," pledging "our lives and the lives of our comrades-in-arms to the cause of its freedom, of its welfare and of its exaltation among the nations." Another, under Eamon de Valera, took possession of Boland's Flour Mills on the road to Kingstown (Dun Laoghaire), from which direction British reinforcements were bound to come. Still another, to which the uniformed, pistol-wielding Countess Markievicz was attached, occupied **St. Stephen's Green** *(357)* until gunfire from the Shelbourne Hotel drove them into the nearby **College of Surgeons** *(357)*.

The Dublin rising lasted five days. On Friday the GPO caught fire and had to be evacuated. On Saturday Pearse, as "Commander-in-Chief of the Irish Republican Army" (IRA) and provisional president of the Irish Republic, surrendered unconditionally. None of the rebels had been killed, and only sixteen wounded, including Connolly, who was taken to **Dublin Castle** *(358)* before being housed in **Kilmainham Jail** *(364)* with the rest of the prisoners. Retribution was quick. Within twelve days in May, in groups of twos and threes, fourteen of the rebels, including Pearse, Connolly, and MacBride, were taken from their cells to Kilmainham's courtyard and shot. Over fifteen hundred were interned in Britain, including Eamon de Valera, whose death sentence had been commuted because of his American birth, and Countess Markievicz, spared because of her sex. (Her prison dress is on view at the **Sligo County Museum and Art Gallery** *[417]*.)

In the eyes of the British authorities the rising had all the earmarks of a German plot—a not unreasonable deduction in view of Casement's negotiations in Berlin and the specific mention in Pearse's Easter Monday proclamation of expected support from "gallant allies in Europe." Hence the severity of the reprisals. But given the long history of martyr worship in Ireland, the executions were, at best, impolitic. Irish public opinion, at first indifferent or even hostile to the rebels, soon "changed utterly." Ironically the chief beneficiary of this shift was Sinn Féin, although Arthur Griffith had not taken part in the rising, and his party had officially advocated only nonviolent resistance. By October 1917, when Griffith yielded the party presidency to de Valera (recently released from prison), Sinn Féin could claim close to a quarter-million members. The following spring it acquired an even larger following when the new prime minister, Lloyd George, pushed through an act of parliament empowering the

British government to extend conscription to Ireland. Everywhere outside the Northeast, the Irish response was unmitigated outrage. The Irish MPs (since Redmond's death led by John Dillon) walked out of the house of commons in protest. The Catholic hierarchy, cautiously quiescent during and after the rising, now denounced "forced levies" as "oppressive and inhuman." A one-day general strike was called on 23 April 1918. An anticonscription pledge was drawn up by de Valera, calling on "all true Irishmen to resist by the most effective means at their disposal." Fortunately for the government, before a showdown could take place, the Allied victory at the second Battle of the Marne removed the necessity for another major draft of troops, and in November the Germans sued for an armistice, thus bringing about an end to the war.

A month later the first postwar general election was called. Under the new Electoral Reform Act of 1918 the size of the Irish electorate had been almost trebled—from 698,098 to 1,931,588—a development distinctly favoring Sinn Féin. When the ballots were counted, de Valera's party had won seventy-three out of Ireland's 105 parliamentary seats on a platform that promised nonrecognition of the Westminster legislature and the convening of a national assembly in Dublin. In January 1919 those elected Sinn Féin members not in prison or in hiding met at the **Mansion House** (356) in Dublin as the first parliament of the Irish Republic (*Dáil Eireann*). There they affirmed Pearse's proclamation of 1916, asserted the "inalienable right of the Irish Nation to sovereign independence," demanded the "evacuation of our country by the English garrison," elected Eamon de Valera as president, set up "Republican courts" to administer justice throughout the country, and announced their intention to appeal to the Paris Peace Conference for recognition (a vain hope as it turned out, thanks in part to President Woodrow Wilson's hostility).

Simultaneously with the meeting of the first Dáil the country drifted into what was to become known as the Anglo-Irish War, or the War of Irish Independence, or, euphemistically, as "The Troubles." It began, even before the Dáil assembled, with the shooting of two policemen in Soloheadbeg, County Tipperary. For the next year hostilities took the form chiefly of murderous attacks on other members of the Royal Irish Constabulary (RIC), themselves native Irishmen in almost every instance. Leadership in this low-intensity conflict (to the extent that it had any central direction) was assumed, in the absence of de Valera, who went to America to solicit funds, by Michael Collins, finance minister of the newly proclaimed republic, but, more importantly, director of intelligence of the Irish Republican Army (IRA). Genial, charismatic, ruthless, and efficient, this giant of a man from County Cork, with no previous military training, proved to be one of the twentieth century's great guerrilla fighters. According to the historian J. C. Beckett, "more perhaps than any other man

Collins has a claim to be regarded as the creator of the Irish Free State."

After March 1920 the war assumed a deadlier aspect when the British government began to resort to counterterrorism, reinforcing the declining ranks of the RIC with an "auxiliary division" of the constabulary, consisting mostly of young ex-army officers, and with ill-disciplined recruits from England, called "Black-and-Tans" because of their half-military/half-constabulary uniforms. Atrocities on both sides mounted. Thomas MacCurtain, lord mayor of Cork, was shot dead in his home by masked men presumed to be members of the RIC. His successor, Terence McSwiney, died in Brixton prison after a hunger strike of seventy-four days. (McSwiney memorabilia are on display at the **Cork Public Museum** *[318]* along with other mementos of "The Troubles.") In November 1920 Collins ordered the murder of eleven unarmed English civilians believed to be intelligence agents. That afternoon, in reprisal, Black-and-Tans fired into a football crowd at Croke Park, killing twelve of the spectators. In May 1921 a band of IRA soldiers set fire to the Dublin **Custom House** *(365)*, burning out the entire interior. Finally, in response to British overtures, a truce was arranged in July. Thus began the tortuous negotiations that led to the peace treaty of December 1921.

(Irish museums are generously supplied with uniforms, weapons, flags, photographs, and other mementos of the Easter Rising, the Anglo-Irish War, and the subsequent civil war. The most complete collection is in the **National Museum of Ireland** *[355]* in Dublin. Others are to be found at **Kilmainham Jail** *[364]*, Dublin; the **Wexford County Museum** *[281]* in Enniscorthy Castle; the **Cashel Folk Village** *[302]*, County Tipperary; the **Cork Public Museum** *[318]*; the **Limerick Museum** *[337]*; the **De Valera Museum** *[335]*, Bruree, County Limerick; the **Dysert O'Dea Castle and Archaeological Centre** *[343]* in County Clare; the **Millmount Museum** *[397]* in Drogheda; the **Mullingar Military Museum** *[393]*, County Westmeath; and the **Donegal Historical Society Museum** *[427]* in Rossnowlagh.)

Meanwhile in Westminster, Lloyd George, who had become prime minister of a coalition government of Liberals and Conservatives, had to deal with the fact that the Home Rule Act of 1914 had, in effect, been nullified, not only by the War of Independence but also by the unmistakable determination of the Protestants of the Northeast *not* to be governed from Dublin. Trying to ride two horses running in opposite directions, the prime minister declared his Irish policy to be committed to (1) honoring the commitment to Home Rule, already on the statute book; and (2) refraining from coercing Ulster into accepting the rule of a Dublin parliament. The upshot was the Government of Ireland Act, passed in December 1920, which partitioned the island into Northern Ireland and Southern Ireland, both to be given bicameral legislatures with complete power over most internal matters and each entitled to continued, though greatly reduced, representation in the imperial parliament at Westminster. Northern Ireland was to consist of the six counties of Antrim, Down, Londonderry, Armagh, Tyrone, and Fermanagh. This was the maximum territory in Ulster with a Protestant population of sufficient size to assure continued Unionist domination. The preponderantly Catholic counties of Ulster—Cavan, Monaghan, and Donegal—were thus reluctantly ceded to the South, which was to consist of twenty-six counties in all. Elections were held for both parliaments in May 1921. In the North the Unionists naturally won overwhelmingly at the polls and chose a provincial government headed by James Craig. In the South Sinn Féin denied the applicability of the act of 1920 to independent Ireland but used the electoral machinery it provided to elect a second Dáil Eirrean, which again chose as its president Eamon de Valera, recently returned from America with a promised loan of $5 million. It was this body that began negotiations with the British government following the truce.

De Valera did not join the delegation sent to London, where the Dáil was represented by a team consisting of Arthur Griffith, Michael Collins, and three others, all of whom were named as plenipotentiaries, though their actual instructions were worded ambiguously. In any case, on 6 December 1921 the Irish delegates, under Lloyd George's threat of "war within three days," affixed their signatures to the Anglo-Irish treaty under the terms of which the Irish Free State (of twenty-six counties) was created, with the same constitutional status in the British empire as Canada, Australia, New Zealand, and South Africa; that is, it was allowed self-government in all matters not affecting foreign policy or imperial affairs. Members of the Free State parliament were required to take an oath of allegiance to the new constitution and swear to be faithful to "King George V, his heirs and successors." Three naval and air bases in the South were reserved for British use—Queenstown (Cobh), Cork harbor; Bearhaven, Bantry Bay, County Cork; and **Fort Dunree** *(425)*, Lough Swilly, County Donegal, the last of which now contains a fine military museum. Finally, on the question of the partition of the island, the treaty promised the creation of a three-man boundary commission to "determine in accordance with the wishes of the inhabitants, so far as may be compatible with economic and geographic conditions, the boundaries between Northern Ireland and the rest of Ireland."

When the Dáil met on 14 December 1921 to consider the treaty draft, de Valera and a minority of his cabinet argued strongly for rejection. Oddly enough in the light of later events, it was not the partition clause that bothered them. Their chief objections, rather, were to the oath of allegiance to the king and the prospects of the continued presence of a British governor-general, both considered contrary to the pure republican principles for which the recent war had been fought. In the event, when put to a vote on 7 January 1922, the treaty passed by a majority of sixty-four to fifty seven. De Valera resigned, and Griffith took office as president of the Dáil. The following June, when elections were held for a new Dáil, fewer than a third of the candidates returned were opposed to the treaty. The election was, in effect, a popular referendum, and the results were unmistakably pro-treaty. But by that time, with civil war engulfing the Free State, the will of the people, as expressed at the polls, was no longer relevant.

NATION BUILDING: 1922–1939

The Civil War

Eager to go home once the Westminster parliament had ratified the Anglo-Irish treaty, British troops in short order commenced the evacuation of their Irish barracks. By the end of March, all those in Connacht and Munster (except for Cork) had been abandoned; in May so were Cork and the major British army base at **Curragh Camp**, County Kildare, where today a **Military Museum** *(380)* contains a complete photographic record of the formal change of command. In this case an army unit loyal to the pro-treaty provisional government took charge. Elsewhere, in many instances, the Irish Republican Army officers who relieved the British opposed the treaty and were prepared forcibly to resist the government that had signed it. Thus former companions in arms found themselves at war with each other. So did their political leaders, with de Valera, Erskine Childers, and other staunch republicans pitted against Griffith, Collins, and their colleagues in the newly constituted Free State government.

The ensuing civil war lasted for ten months. In Dublin contingents of antitreaty forces (referred to as "irregulars") occupied the **Four Courts** *(368)* and other buildings. With artillery borrowed from the not-yet-departed British garrison in Dublin, government troops opened fire on the Four Courts on 28 June and forced the occupants to surrender, but not before they had fired the building and destroyed the public records office with its irreplaceable collection of historic documents. Elsewhere in the country, by the end of July, the irregulars had been mostly driven back to the "Munster Republic" between the sea and a line running roughly from Waterford to the Shannon. Waterford, Tipperary, Carrick-on-Suir, Clonmel, Tralee, and Cork fell in that order. On 22 August Michael Collins, on an inspection tour, was ambushed and murdered at the tiny village of Béal na mBláth, County Cork, only a short distance from his birthplace at Sam's Cross. The site of his assassination is marked today by the **Michael Collins Monument**

(323), a high stone roadside crucifix. In nearby Clonakilty the **West Cork Museum** *(316)* houses sundry memorabilia of the "Big Fellow's" remarkable career as guerrilla fighter and embryo statesman. (He died just short of his thirty-second birthday.) Ten days earlier Arthur Griffith had suffered a fatal stroke; William T. Cosgrave now inherited the mantle of leadership in the Free State government.

Not until 23 May 1923 did the leaders of the IRA and of the "republic" they claimed to represent decide to stop fighting—though not to surrender unconditionally. De Valera announced simply that "military victory must be allowed to rest for the moment with those who have destroyed the republic." In the previous ten months the government had executed seventy-seven republicans, among them Erskine Childers. This was more than three times the number thus put to death by the British between the date of the Easter Rising and the close of the Anglo-Irish War. The number of other Irish casualties on both sides is incalculable. Material damage was immense, especially to railways. Rails were torn up, bridges and viaducts destroyed, locomotives burned. Also, an estimated total of 162 great houses went up in flames between December 1921 and March 1923, and this does not include those similarly destroyed during the Anglo-Irish War. Most, but not all, had been the homes of the Protestant gentry, whose power had already been totally eclipsed and whose lands had already been mostly distributed among their former tenant farmers. In her novel *The Last September*, the Anglo-Irish writer Elizabeth Bowen vividly describes one such incident as symbolic of the finality of the collapse of a once-powerful ruling class:

> At Danielstown, half way up the avenue under the beeches, the thin iron gate twanged (missed its latch, remained swinging aghast) as the last unlit car slid out with the executioners bland from accomplished duty. . . . Then the first wave of a silence that was to be ultimate flowed back confidently to the steps. The door stood open hospitably upon a furnace.

Government and Politics

Given the bitter discord that attended the birth of the Irish Free State, it is remarkable that the transition from colonial status to quasi-independent statehood was so smooth. The provisional government led by Collins and Griffith promulgated in 1922 a written constitution that established a responsible government closely modelled, except for terminology, on that of Britain. The executive council and its president were the equivalent of the Westminster cabinet and prime minister; the *oireachtas* served as parliament; its house of lords (with minimal powers) was the senate; its house of commons the Dáil. True, in contrast to Britain, members of the latter were to be chosen by proportional representation, which militated against the development of a two-party system, though not sufficiently to encourage a frequent turnover of governments as was to occur in postwar Europe. (President William Cosgrave's party, the Cumann na nGaedheal, held office without interruption from 1922 to 1932.) British law became for the most part Irish law, and the judicial system was a close replica of its British prototype—even to the point of judges and barristers wearing gowns and wigs. Finally—and most significantly—the colonial civil service remained virtually intact, with 98 percent of all government employees in the Free State keeping the jobs they had held under the British regime.

During Cosgrave's administration, under the tight control of Ernest Blythe's department of finance, public expenditures were kept to a minimum, budgets were balanced, income taxes maintained at a low level, and borrowing, especially from abroad, mostly avoided. One result was a strict curtailment of social expenditures. Old-age pensions were cut; unemployment and health insurance was minimal. As to agriculture, the government continued the established policy of transferring landownership and accelerated the process by making it compulsory. Owner occupancy rose from 64 percent of all land under pasture and tillage in 1916 to 97 percent by 1930. Some progress was made toward agricultural diversification when the government subsidized the establishment of a beet-sugar factory in Carlow, which was later taken over by the Irish Sugar Company. This semi–state corporation, along with the Electricity Supply Board set up in 1927 to harness the river Shannon and provide cheap electricity, was a highly successful innovation and established an important precedent for subsequent economic development in Ireland. Yet during the interwar years little significant progress was made toward the diversification of the economy through greater industrialization. Ireland remained not exactly an underdeveloped country in the sense the term is used today but rather the dependent agrarian hinterland of an advanced industrial metropolis—in this case England. Standards of living, to be sure, improved somewhat before the onslaught of worldwide depression in the 1930s, but not enough to stop the flow of emigration, now tending to move toward England rather than to the United States. As in the period just before the First World War, the years 1921 to 1926 saw the permanent departure from the twenty-six counties now comprising the Free State of over twenty-seven thousand each year or slightly less than 1 percent per annum of the total population; after that date it fell to an annual exodus of about 16,700.

Yet independent Ireland's poor economic performance did not feature prominently in the country's domestic politics. Whereas Britain and other countries of western Europe were split along class lines—socialists versus free-enterprise conservatives, rich versus poor, left versus right—Ireland remained, in the words of Friedrich Engels a half-century earlier, "the Holy Isle whose aspirations must on no account be mixed with the profane class struggles of the rest of the sinful world." Instead, *the* single most divisive issue continued to be the English connection, now focused, as during the civil war, on the Anglo-Irish treaty. That focus was further sharpened when it began to appear that partition between North and South might become permanent.

The outbreak of war between pro- and antitreaty factions in the South had delayed for several years the convening of the boundary commission promised by Article 12 of the treaty. This was just long enough for the Protestant majority in the North to consolidate itself behind the "what we have we hold" position of Sir James Craig's government. When the commission was in fact ready in 1924 to commence deliberations, Craig refused to nominate a member. Hence the British government named a Belfast Unionist, J. R. Fisher, to represent the North, while the Free State chose Eoin MacNeill; the third, supposedly neutral, commissioner was Justice Richard Feetham of South Africa. In fact the dice were loaded against MacNeill, as was clearly shown when a London paper, the *Morning Post*, published a leaked report to the effect that the boundary established in 1920 would remain the same, except for minor adjustments that would still leave predominantly Catholic areas in Counties Down, Armagh, Tyrone, Fermanagh, and Londonderry under the jurisdiction of Belfast. MacNeill promptly resigned. Cosgrave, fearing that the publication of the report by the other two commissioners would do more harm to the Free State's claim than no report at all, then joined an Irish delegation to London to meet with Craig. There, in December 1925, it was agreed that the established boundary was to remain unchanged. And unchanged it stayed, thus providing substantial grist to the antitreaty faction's mill and exposing the Cosgrave government still further to the charge of truckling to the British.

Until 1926 veterans of the IRA and other die-hard republicans, even when elected to the Dáil, had boycotted the Free State government, some of them (including de Valera) going to prison rather than desist from seditious efforts to overthrow it. In May of that year, however, de Valera broke with the intransigents and founded a new political party, the Fianna Fail (Soldiers of Destiny), which put up candidates in the election of 1927. Those chosen at the polls, including de Valera himself, then took their seats in the Dáil, having salved their republican consciences by merely signing their names to the hated oath of allegiance instead of taking it orally. By 1932 the new party was strong enough to win a plurality of the popular votes and, with Labour and three other independent parties, to form a Fianna Fail government under the leadership of de Valera, who was to remain head of government without interruption for sixteen years. Having broken with his former companions of the IRA, he embarked on a program of draconian suppression of their organization, including internment without trial. Similar measures were taken in the early 1930s against a quasi-fascist movement, popularly called the "Blue Shirts," led by Eoin O'Duffy, formerly chief of the national police (Gardai Siochána). O'Duffy left Ireland for Spain in 1936 to fight for General Franco, but not before helping to found a new political party called Fine Gael (United Ireland), the major components of which were the remnants of Cumann na nGaedhael and the National Centre Party. Under Cosgrave's moderate leadership, this became the major parliamentary party in opposition to Fianna Fail and remains so to this day.

Once in office de Valera, as promised in the election, set about to nullify the treaty without actually repealing it. The governor-general was stripped of the power to delay passage of bills by withholding his consent. The right of appeal from Irish courts to the British privy council was abolished. So was the oath of allegiance to the Crown, along with the senate, which had defied de Valera by delaying passage for two years of a bill to accomplish that end. In 1936, without going quite so far as to declare Ireland a republic, the External Relations Act reduced the role of the British monarch to that of validating the accreditation of Irish diplomatic representatives abroad. In 1937 a new constitution was promulgated. The name of the Irish Free State was changed to Eire or Ireland. The chief of state was no longer to be the king, but a popularly elected president, whose duties were to be largely ceremonial. The government was to be headed by the *taoiseach* or prime minister, chosen by the majority of the Dáil. The upper house (the *seanad*) of the legislature *(oireachtas)* was restored, though with its power again restricted to delaying legislation. Notwithstanding the boundary agreement of 1925, the "national territory" was declared to consist of "the whole island of Ireland, its islands and the territorial seas," including, that is, Northern Ireland.

Meanwhile, beginning in 1932, de Valera had refused to transfer to the British treasury the annual payments due on loans made to tenants under the various land-purchase acts passed before independence. The British government retaliated by imposing a duty of about 20 percent on almost two-thirds of Irish exports to the United Kingdom. The Irish government replied in kind, and for six years a tariff war ensued. The economies of both countries suffered, but the Irish cattle industry was particularly hard hit. (This was not altogether unwelcome to de Valera, whose economic program for Ireland envisaged a self-sufficient nation of sturdy peasants devoted to tilling their own small holdings rather than a land of huge cattle ranches with a much reduced labor force.) In the event, the economic war was finally ended in 1938 by a negotiated agreement between de Valera and Prime Minister Neville Chamberlain. Under this arrangement the British claim of £104 million for the land annuities was reduced to a £10 million settlement, and both countries agreed to reopen their markets to the other's products. As an additional concession, de Valera won from Chamberlain the promise to relinquish the three naval bases (the "treaty ports") at Cobh, Bearhaven, and Lough Swilly—a sacrifice that a later British government would deeply regret when a second war with Germany broke out in 1939.

Church and State

Although Ireland had always been predominantly Roman Catholic in religious affiliation, the new state that came into being in 1921 was overwhelmingly so. After the six counties of Ulster had been excluded from Free State jurisdiction, only 10.4 percent of the remaining twenty-six counties' population was Protestant. Intermarriage, lower birth rates, and above all emigration reduced this number to 7.4 percent in 1926; it was 6.6 percent in 1946; and is still falling. Somerville and Ross, authors of *The Irish R.M.*, had jokingly predicted that "if Home Rule comes, there won't be a fox or a Protestant left in Ireland in ten years' time." On the latter score at least, they were not too far off the mark.

Yet the Constitution of 1922, in conformance with the Anglo-Irish treaty, had been strictly neutral with respect to all organized religion. It guaranteed freedom of worship and declared expressly that "no law may be made either directly or indirectly to endow any religion, or prohibit or restrict the free exercise thereof or give any preference, or impose any disability on account of religious belief or religious status." Notwithstanding these provisions, the Catholic Church from the beginning enjoyed, unofficially at least, a privileged position; its hierarchy could always expect reverential deference in the corridors of government; and its views on any question pertaining to public or private morality almost inevitably prevailed.

During the civil war, to be sure, antitreaty forces had defied the hierarchy, which had unequivocally sided with the Free State government. A joint pastoral letter of 10 October 1922 declared that "the guerilla warfare now being carried on by the irregulars is without moral sanction." The killing of soldiers of the national army was labelled "murder," the seizing of public and private property by the antitreaty forces "robbery," the breaking up of roads, railways, etc., "criminal destruction." After the shooting died out, the Church remained supportive of the Cosgrave government. And the Cosgrave government supported the Church. Irish primary and secondary education remained not merely denominational but clerically controlled. Divorce, previously obtainable in Ireland by way of private bills in the Westminster parliament, was in effect outlawed when Cosgrave forbade the introduction of such bills in the Dáil. In 1923 censorship of films "subversive of public [meaning Catholic] morality" was authorized by law. In 1929 the Censorship of Publications Act provided for a board of five persons (headed by a Catholic priest) with power to prohibit the sale or distribution of any book considered to be "in its general tendency indecent or obscene." By the same act it became a criminal offense to advertise methods and materials of birth control.

Secular-minded libertarians (including most Irish intellectuals) who hoped for a modification of this strict code by the Fianna Fail government were to be grievously disappointed. Indeed de Valera was, if anything, more placatory than his predecessors toward the views of the Roman Catholic hierarchy. Thus, while the censorship act of 1929 had made it illegal to promote the use of contraceptives, the Criminal Law Amendment Act of 1935 prohibited their sale and importation. The same year, the Church's campaign against public dance halls as "traps for the innocent" was rewarded with the passage of a law requiring all such establishments to obtain special licenses from their local district courts. Censorship was stepped up; between 1930 and 1939 some twelve hundred books and 140 periodicals were banned on the advice of the censorship board. (Not until 1956 was there any marked liberalization of the board's attitude toward new publications, and not until 1964 was the ban removed from books in print for at least twelve years.) Finally the new Constitution, promulgated by de Valera and endorsed by 57 percent of the voting electorate in 1937, though reasserting established guarantees of religious freedom and nondiscrimination, formally recognized "the special position of the Holy Catholic Apostolic and Roman Church as the guardian of the Faith professed by the great majority of the citizens." (This clause was repealed by popular referendum in 1972.) The new constitution also forbade the passage of any law authorizing divorce, declared the family to be "a moral institution possessing inalienable and imprescriptible rights," and acknowledged the role of woman "within the home" to be essential to the common good of the state. Thus the religious faith of the great majority of Irish men and women and the traditional moral values of the Catholic Church in Ireland were given the full sanction of fundamental law.

Language, Literature, and the Arts

As with respect to relations between Church and State, there was no fundamental difference between the two major political parties in their attitudes toward the Irish (that is, Gaelic) language and in their efforts to restore it to general use. The Constitution of 1922, while acknowledging that English was *an* "official language," declared that "the national language of the Irish Free State is the Irish language." The means by which this statement of principle was to be realized in practice were threefold: (1) making the teaching of Irish compulsory in the schools; (2) requiring competence in the language as a prerequisite for civil service and other government jobs; and (3) providing special educational and economic facilities for the population of the Gaeltacht, that is, those isolated pockets in the West where Gaelic was still the vernacular tongue.

In 1922 the provisional government ordered that "the Irish language be taught, or used as a medium of instruction for not less than one full hour each day in national schools." Four years later the Cosgrave government ordered that all instruction in infant classes (that is, grades one and two) be conducted in Irish. After de Valera came into office, Irish became a compulsory subject in secondary schools. All schoolteachers were required to have some competence in the language; all undergraduates of the National University had to pass an examination in Irish before they could proceed to their degrees; so did all civil servants and members of the Garda Síochána; all law students were supposed to be able to cross-examine in Irish before they could be called to the bar. As to the Gaeltacht, in addition to special economic assistance not unlike that previously provided by the congested districts board, a policy of reverse discrimination was introduced to facilitate the entry of the region's younger generation into the universities, the teaching profession, the army, the police, and the civil service.

None of the above was eminently successful. Teachers in the national schools objected to the policy of giving language competence priority over mastery of the subject matter being taught. Parents, as in the past, recognized the disadvantage, in terms of material and social progress, of their children's not being fluent in English. Children, especially in the lower grades, suffered from the double burden of being forced to learn unfamiliar subjects through the medium of what to most of them was a foreign language. As a result, in the words of the historian Oliver MacDonagh, "a condition of semi-Gaelicization settled down on the country, while leaving large tracts of ordinary life untouched." While there was a significant increase in the number of those who could claim some knowledge of the Irish language, there was also a marked decline in the number of exclusively Irish speakers, even in the Gaeltacht. English remained the working language of the great majority of people. As of 1950, the number who used Gaelic as their ordinary medium of speech probably did not exceed thirty-five thousand—fewer than in the highlands and islands of western Scotland. Otherwise the use of the "national language" was confined mostly to street and road signs, stamps and postmarks, the beginning and end of official letters otherwise written in English, and official titles such as *taoiseach, garda siochána, Dáil,* etc.

True, the interwar years witnessed a spate of Irish-language publications of which the most novel, and uniquely Irish, were reminiscences of natives of the Blasket Islands, a bleak, rocky archipelago off the Kerry coast, since depopulated. Tomás O' Criomhthan's (O' Crohan's) *An tOileánach* appeared in 1929 and in English translation as *The Islandman* in 1934; Muiris O' Súileabháin (Maurice O'Sullivan) published *Fiche Blian ag Fás* in 1933, the English version of which *(Twenty Years A-Growing)* appeared the same year; and *Peig* by Peig Sayres, the Irish version of which was published in 1936, appeared in an English translation three years later.

But English was the language of most of the serious literary works for which postwar Ireland was justly world-famous. After the publication of *Ulysses* Joyce spent most of his life in Paris in painstaking labor over his "work in progress," not to be published until 1939 as *Finnegan's Wake.* There he was joined and assisted by the young Samuel Beckett, whose novel *Murphy* came out in 1938, after which its author took up permanent residence in Paris and commenced writing in French. (His most famous play was to appear in 1953 under the title *En Attendant Godot.*)

In Ireland Yeats towered above the literary scene, his established reputation further enhanced by his receipt of the Nobel prize in 1923. After the rejection of his proposal of marriage by Maud Gonne (widowed by virtue of John MacBride's execution following the Easter Rising), he was wedded to Georgie Hyde-Lees, a fellow mystic especially gifted in the occult art of automatic writing. He brought her home to **Thoor Ballylee** *(410)* near Gort, County Galway, a sixteenth-century tower house that the couple assiduously set about restoring. Now serving as a Yeats museum, this four-story building displays a tablet on the wall inscribed with the owner's commemorative lines:

> I, the poet William Yeats,
> With old millboards and sea-green slates,
> And smith work from the Gort forge,
> Restored this tower for my wife George . . . .

Some of the poet's best work dates from the first two decades of Ireland's independent statehood—*Michael Robartes and the Dancer* (1923), *The Tower* (1928), *The Winding Stair and Other Poems* (1933), *A Full Moon in March* (1935), and *Last Poems* (1936–39). During these years he maintained, as well, an active connection with the Abbey Theatre and was responsible for introducing to its audiences the works of the young playwright Sean O'Casey, arguably the greatest Irish dramatist of them all.

The country's recent history provided the subject matter of O'Casey's best-known plays: *The Shadow of the Gunman* (1923), set against the background of the Anglo-Irish war; *Juno and the Paycock* (1924), with an Irish civil war setting; and *The Plough and the Stars* (1926), the scene of which was Dublin at the time of the Easter Rising. At the opening night performance of the last of these the Abbey audience rioted, ostensibly outraged by the appearance onstage of an actress representing a prostitute. Three nights later, in the midst of another uproar, the Abbey's management rang down the curtain and called the police. Yeats himself walked onto the stage to quell the disturbance. "You have disgraced yourselves again," he scolded. Referring to a similar outbreak on the occasion of the production of J. M. Synge's *Playboy of the Western World*, he demanded of his obstreperous listeners: "Is this going to be a recurring celebration of Irish genius: Synge first, then O'Casey? . . . Dublin has again rocked the cradle of a reputation. . . ." As one of the actors present at the scene reported: "Yeats was like a lion that night. No one could have withstood him, the lower lip sticking out like a fighter, his body trembling with suppressed rage."

The incident at the Abbey served to confirm Yeats's growing disillusionment with the Free State and with Irish politics in general. In "The Second Coming," written during "The Troubles," he had given voice to this pessimism:

> Things fall apart; the centre cannot hold;
> Mere anarchy is loosed upon the world,
> The blood-dimmed tide is loosed, and everywhere
> The ceremony of innocence is drowned. . . .

Again, in 1925, he had risen in the senate to protest Cosgrave's Church-approved proposal to ban divorce in Ireland, seeing it as an affront to the Protestant community to which he himself belonged. "I think it is tragic," he declaimed, "that within three years of this country gaining its independence we should be discussing a measure which a minority in this nation considers to be grossly oppressive. I am proud to consider myself a typical man of that minority. We against whom you have done this thing are no petty people; we are the people of Grattan; we are the people of Swift, the people of Emmet, the people of Parnell. . . ." He was, of course, voted down. Thereafter, except for a brief and ill-advised dalliance with O'Duffy's Blue Shirts, Yeats mostly abjured Irish politics. He even began to entertain second thoughts about the "terrible beauty" of the Easter Rising—lying awake "night after night," he wrote in 1938, wondering, "Did that play of mine [*Cathleen ni Houlihan*] send out/Certain men the English shot?"

O'Casey's disillusionment with the new Ireland had different roots. In 1928 he left home permanently, like Joyce a voluntary exile from his own country. As a Marxist and former member of Connolly's Irish Citizen Army, the playwright found himself thoroughly disgusted with the triumph of Catholic and bourgeois values under the Free State dispensation. Almost equally repelled by the course of events since the civil war was a group of young fiction writers whose sympathies lay with the extreme republicans whom they considered to have been betrayed, not only by Cosgrave but by de Valera as well. Among them were Sean O'Faolain, Liam O'Flaherty, and Michael O'Donovan (writing under the *nom de plume* of Frank O'Connor). Their complaint against contemporary Ireland was best summarized by O'Connor in 1942: "Every year that has passed, particularly since de Valera's rise to power, has strengthened the grip of the gombeen man, of the religious secret societies, . . . of illiterate censorships." Needless to say, all of the above-named, plus numerous others among their contemporaries, suffered under the heavy hand of the board of censors for one or more of their works. Indeed, not to have been so singled out was considered something of a disgrace in Irish literary circles.

Irish graphic artists in the 1920s and 1930s fared better, no doubt because of the noncontroversial nature of their usual choice of subject matter: landscapes, bleak but dramatic in their grandeur; thatched cottages against the backdrop of majestic mountains; turf stacks under lowering rain clouds; fishermen plying their dangerous trade; sturdy peasants, pious villagers, etc. Representative titles from the palettes of Ireland's best-known painters of the interwar years include Jack B. Yeats's *The Man from Arranmore* in the **National Gallery of Ireland** *(355)*, *Empty Creels* in the **Hugh Lane Municipal Gallery of Modern Art** *(367)*, Dublin, and *An Island Funeral* in the **Sligo County Museum and Art Gallery** *(417)*; Paul Henry's *Dawn, Killary Bay* in the **Ulster Museum** *(457)*, Belfast; James Humbert Craig's *Cloud Shadows, Connemara* in the **Hugh Lane Municipal Gallery of Modern Art** *(367)* and *Going to Mass* in the **Crawford Municipal Art Gallery** *(318)*, Cork; *The Potato Gatherers* by George Russell (AE) in the **Armagh County Museum** *(442)*; Sean Keating's *Men of the West* and *An Aran Fisherman and His Wife*, both in the **Hugh Lane Municipal Gallery of Modern Art** *(367)*; *The Quaint Couple* by Charles Lamb in the **Crawford Municipal Gallery** *(318)*; and *The Jaunting Car* by William Conor in the

Ulster Museum *(457)*, Belfast. Naturalistic in style, these painters comprised what the art historian Bruce Arnold has called the "school of Irish academic realism." Most of their handiwork seemed to confirm de Valera's idealized image of the new Ireland as "the home of a people who valued material wealth only as a basis of right living, of a people who were satisfied with frugal comfort and devoted their leisure to the things of the spirit."

Of the so-called domestic arts, gardening in Ireland, as elsewhere in the British Isles, enjoyed unchallenged preeminence, at least in terms of money, labor, and enthusiasm invested. Many of the splendid gardens to be seen today are survivals of the great age of the Anglo-Irish country houses; others have been developed *de novo* since the end of the First World War. At **Malahide Castle** *(371)*, County Dublin, the magnificent grounds with their rare plants from all over the world are mostly the work of Lord Milo Talbot between 1948 and 1973. The nearby **Howth Castle Garden** *(371)*, with its spectacular cliffside massing of rhododendrons, was begun in about 1850. The great formal gardens at the **Powerscourt Estate** *(309)*, County Wicklow, were first laid out by the landscape architect Daniel Robertson between 1843 and 1875 but have been much expanded and rearranged in the twentieth century. At **Mount Usher** *(308)*, County Wicklow, the precepts of the great English gardener William Robinson were followed strictly by George and Edward Walpole in their creation of a riverside "wild garden," beginning in 1875 and continued by two later generations of Walpoles into the 1970s. At **Birr Castle** *(380)*, County Offaly, most of the present magnificent formal garden, though originating as early as the eighteenth century, owes its appearance to the horticultural enthusiasm of the sixth earl of Rosse, who inherited the estate in 1918. **Anne's Grove** *(321)* in County Cork is another fine riverside woodland garden and dates to the years 1900 to 1966, when the property belonged to Richard Grove Annesley. In County Donegal the formal gardens adjacent to **Glenveagh Castle** *(428)* were installed by Henry McIlhenny of Philadelphia, who bought the estate in 1937, although much of the surrounding woodland park was laid out in the late 1850s, when the owner was J. G. Adair, famous for his role in the Derryveagh evictions (see Chapter Seven). In Northern Ireland, **Rowallane Garden** *(440)*, County Down, now headquarters of the National Trust for Northern Ireland and noted especially for its azaleas and rhododendrons, is the handiwork of Hugh Armytage Moore, who inherited the property in 1903. Finally the exquisite gardens of **Mount Stewart** *(438)*, County Down, were laid out chiefly by Edith, seventh marchioness of Londonderry, and her daughter Lady Mairi Bury, beginning in 1921. Here one of the most unusual features is the Red Hand of Ulster set out in red begonias in the middle of the "shamrock garden." This symbol of Ulster's belligerency serves as a reminder that this part of the Emerald Isle is a distinct province, separate from the rest, and determined, in the view of the majority of its inhabitants, to remain so.

NORTHERN IRELAND: 1921–1939

The geographic boundaries of the province were determined by the Government of Ireland Act of 1920 as confirmed by the agreement among Craig, Cosgrave, and the British government in 1925. Six counties of the Northeast were thus assigned to the jurisdiction of the parliament of Northern Ireland, formally opened by King George V in Belfast's **City Hall** *(455)* in June 1921. Contrary to the expectations of Collins, Griffith, and the other members of the Irish delegation at the London peace talks of 1921, a large number of Catholics found themselves permanently consigned to the alien and unfriendly rule of a Protestant majority. Indeed roughly one-third of the population of Northern Ireland was, and still is, Catholic. Moreover, Catholics from the beginning slightly outnumbered Protestants in Counties Fermanagh and Tyrone and in the cities of Newry and Derry (officially Londonderry, but more commonly called by its original name).

Thus the Protestants of Northern Ireland, though constituting a majority of roughly two to one, found themselves saddled with a sizable dissident minority, for the most part anxious to be reunited with the predominantly Catholic state south of the line of partition. In the face of this internal threat and of the openly declared irredentism of the Free State (Eire after 1937), Protestants clung desperately to the British connection while at the same time taking every feasible step to reduce the minority to a condition of impotence.

In 1922 the Northern Ireland parliament abolished proportional representation in the elections for local government offices. This measure in effect reduced by half the number of county and city councils that might otherwise have been controlled by Catholics. Further to consolidate Unionist domination of local government, electoral districts were repeatedly gerrymandered. The most flagrant example was the 1930 reconstruction of electoral boundaries in Derry so that 9,961 Nationalist (that is, Catholic) voters could choose only eight city councillors, while 7,444 Unionists were assured a representation of twelve. Altogether, Unionists, who represented about two-thirds of Northern Ireland's population, controlled 84.6 percent of all local authorities, including many areas with large Catholic, and therefore Nationalist, populations. And along with this virtual monopoly of political power on the local level went the authority to bestow contracts for public works, distribute jobs, assign public housing, etc. Although difficult to prove conclusively, there can be little doubt that, in such matters, discrimination in favor of Protestant coreligionists was the rule.

The same imbalance of representation obtained in the Northern Ireland parliament, which after 1932 (and until 1972) met in the enormous neoclassical building erected for that purpose at **Stormont** *(459)* on the outskirts of Belfast. "All I boast of," declared Sir James Craig in 1934, "is that we are a Protestant Parliament in a Protestant state." It was no idle boast, as Craig knew well enough, having himself served uninterruptedly as prime minister since 1921 (and as he continued to do until his death in 1940). One-party domination too was further assured after 1929, when members of the Stormont, as well as Northern Ireland representatives at Westminster, were no longer elected by proportional representation. Actually it made little difference since, for the most part, Catholic Nationalists, even when chosen, abstained from attendance.

Belfast's great, sprawling **City Hall** *(455)* was another bastion of unionism. Nearby it rose two great "temples of Protestantism," so designated by the architectural historian W. C. Brett—each representing respectively the major Protestant denominations. On Great Victoria Street was the Presbyterian **General Assembly Hall** *(457)*, a neo-Tudor pile with an open-crown spire copied from St. Giles's Church in Edinburgh. On the other side of the town center, facing Donegall Street, was the Church of Ireland's **St. Anne's Cathedral** *(456)*, largely neo-Romanesque in style, with a mixed classical/Romanesque/Gothic west front dedicated in 1927 as a World War I memorial.

West Belfast, as before, was one of the worst slum districts of the British Isles, with Catholics and Protestants living cheek by jowl in their respective ghettos. Here the economic consequences of postwar depression were especially severe. The linen industry and shipbuilding were especially hard hit. Employment in the former fell by a factor of one-third by 1930. By 1933 the work force in the shipyards had shrunk to a tenth of its 1924 total of seventy-nine thousand. By the late 1930s unemployment in Northern Ireland stood at 29.5 percent, thus superseding even Wales as the most job-scarce region of Britain.

One by-product of this prolonged slump was a resurgence of sectarian violence, especially in Belfast. Riots had already been severe in 1920-22, chiefly in response to "The Troubles" in the South. The year 1935 was even worse, especially in July, after the annual Orange Day parade. Although both sides of the sectarian divide suffered serious property losses, bodily injuries, and even deaths, Catholic casualties exceeded those of the Protestants. This was due partly to the former's being outnumbered but is also attributable in part to the less-than-equal protection afforded them by those responsible for the enforcement of law and order. Although the Royal Ulster Constabulary, established in 1922, was supposed to recruit among the Catholic community, a combination of Protestant discrimination and Catholic abstention had kept minority membership low. Even more Protestant-dominated was the Special Constabulary, a paramilitary body heavily infiltrated by the Orange Order. As to the British government, through the better part of two decades it pursued a hands-off policy with respect to Northern Ireland's domestic problems while at the same time maintaining sovereignty over the region. Given the strategic problems facing the United Kingdom after 1939, this proved to have been the prudent course to follow.

THE SECOND WORLD WAR AND AFTER: 1939–1949

Northern Ireland

The words "Ulster is British" (frequently displayed today on signs and banners throughout the North) were never so explicitly confirmed as after 1 September 1939, when the United Kingdom again found itself at war with Germany. The imperial government, to be sure, made no attempt to apply conscription to Northern Ireland, partly out of deference to the warnings of the Catholic bishops and partly to placate Unionist opposition to arming Irish Nationalists. Nevertheless, recruitment in the six northeastern counties brought thousands of volunteers into the British armed services, many to serve under the commands of the distinguished Ulster-born soldiers Generals Bernard Montgomery, Harold Alexander, and Alan F. Brooke.

More vital to the Allied military effort was the conversion of Northern Ireland's failing industry into full-time production of war matériel. Belfast shipyards produced over 170 warships and 511 merchant vessels; aircraft manufacturers supplied fifteen hundred bombers; linen mills turned to the fabrication of uniforms and parachutes; munitions plants worked overtime. Of still greater significance, in view of Neville Chamberlain's previous surrender of the southern Irish treaty ports, was the buildup in Northern

Ireland of Allied ground, air, and naval bases. Thousands of British troops received their basic training in Ulster camps. Convoy protection against German U-boats relied heavily on RAF antisubmarine and long-range fighter planes stationed at Aldergrove, Limavady, and Lough Erne and on Royal Navy escort vessels based in Belfast and Derry. In February 1942 Derry was turned over to the U.S. Atlantic Fleet Command and thereafter played a vital role in the Battle of the Atlantic. A month earlier American forces had first landed in Northern Ireland, eliciting thereby a formal protest from Eire's prime minister, de Valera—which went unheeded. By the autumn of 1943 over a hundred thousand American troops were in Ulster, being readied for the invasion of the European continent. Belfast became one of the principal staging areas for U.S. naval forces assigned to the invasion of Normandy in June 1944.

None of this activity, of course, passed unnoticed in Berlin, and retaliation was inevitable. On the night of 7/8 April 1941, a half dozen enemy bombers destroyed the Harland and Wolff fuselage factory. One week later a force of more than 150 German planes dropped over a hundred tons of bombs on Belfast, killing 745 civilians, seriously injuring 420, and forcing the evacuation from the city of about one hundred thousand persons. In the first week of May, in two separate raids, Harland and Wolff was struck again, while much of Belfast harbor was set afire by incendiaries and oil bombs. (A register of the civilians killed by enemy action in World War II is on view in the now all but deserted parliament house at **Stormont** [459].)

After the coming of peace, Northern Ireland was to receive considerable compensation for its sacrifices by virtue of its inclusion in the newly emerging British welfare state. In 1948 a general health services board supervised the same kind of comprehensive medical care that British citizens were to enjoy. The Housing Acts of 1945 and 1946 provided subsidies for slum clearance, public housing, and new construction of private homes. Insurance against unemployment was guaranteed. All this public money, coupled with British subsidies in both the private and public sectors, contributed enormously to the rapid growth of the Northern Irish economy. And, whereas living standards on both sides of the border in 1930 had been much the same, by the late 1940s income per head in Northern Ireland was nearly 75 percent above the average in Eire. But it was the war experience itself, more than any other factor, that sank the wedge between North and South more deeply than ever. The effect of Northern Ireland's significant contribution to the Allied war effort and of the sacrifices her people endured was, in the words of the historian John A. Murphy, "to strengthen the link with Britain, buttress Unionism, and place the North on a still more divergent path from the neutral South."

Eire: 1939–1949

On 1 September 1939, the day Germany invaded Poland, the Dáil declared itself unequivocally in favor of neutrality for the duration of the conflict, which, in Ireland, was euphemistically designated "the Emergency." And although thousands of Irish citizens later volunteered for service in the British armed forces, there is no doubt that the overwhelming majority of the people endorsed the decision. Throughout the war de Valera was scrupulously correct in observing a neutral stance vis-à-vis all belligerents, even going so far as to pay a formal visit of condolence to the German legation on the occasion of Hitler's death. Steadfastly he resisted the urgings of Prime Minister Churchill to allow the Royal Navy access to its former base at Bearhaven in the desperate campaign Britain was waging against German U-boats in the Atlantic. To the even more persistent importunities of President Roosevelt and his minister to Dublin, David Gray, the taoiseach also turned a deaf ear. Yet Irish neutrality was unquestionably tilted in favor of the Allies. When German aviators came down in Eire, they were interned. Under the same circumstances their British and American counterparts were dispatched to Northern Ireland. Privately Irish army officers shared military intelligence with their opposite numbers in the Allied armed forces. The United Kingdom's representative in Dublin promptly received reports of submarine sightings by the Irish coast-watching service. Members of the IRA suspected of clandestine dealings with the Germans were interned summarily. Had Hitler been looking for a *casus belli* with Eire, it would not have been too hard to find.

Though southern Ireland as such escaped direct damage (outside of a few German bombs dropped by mistake on Dublin), the economic consequences of "the Emergency" were considerable. Shortages of both consumer and capital goods were severe: coal, fertilizer, oil, petrol (gasoline), spare parts, and tea in particular. Meat, milk, butter, and eggs, however, were plentiful enough—far more so than in Britain. Compulsory tillage of wheat kept the supply of bread about equal to the demand. Prices, naturally enough, rose to 70 percent above the 1940 level, while wages lagged far behind.

In the immediate aftermath of the war conditions were not much improved. A wet summer in 1946 diminished grain production to the point where bread had to be rationed. The severe winter of 1947 produced a fuel crisis. One result of the postwar depression was the defeat of de Valera and Fianna Fail in the election of 1948—after sixteen uninterrupted years in office. For the first time since its foundation, Fine Gael took over the reins of power, with John A. Costello as taoiseach. It was, however, a coalition government, dependent for its majorities on a number of smaller parties, the most important being the recently founded Clann na Poblachta (Children of the Republic), led by Seán MacBride, whose father had been executed after the Easter Rising and whose mother was Maud Gonne.

MacBride became minister of external affairs in the new government, and it was he, probably, who took the initiative to sever the last formal connection between Eire and Great Britain. A public announcement to that effect was made by Costello during a visit to Canada in September 1948. After his return the Dáil passed two measures, the Executive Power of the State (International Relations) Act and the Republic of Ireland Act, which respectively abolished the residual power of the Crown in regard to Irish foreign affairs and renamed Eire "the Republic of Ireland." Appropriately, Easter Monday 1949 was selected as the birth date of the newly designated state. One unexpected result was to induce the British parliament to pass an act declaring that "in no event will Northern Ireland or any part thereof cease to be part of His Majesty's dominions and of the United Kingdom without the consent of the parliament of Northern Ireland."

The year before, MacBride, as foreign minister, had arranged for the shipment back to Ireland of the body of his mother's former lover, William Butler Yeats, who had died in southern France in 1939. As the poet himself had requested, he was reinterred "under bare Ben Bulben's head" in the grounds of **Drumcliffe Church** *(418)*, County Sligo, where one of his forebears had been rector. The stone above his grave carried the epitaph he himself had written:

> Cast a cold eye
> On life, on death.
> Horseman, pass by!

A large crowd gathered at Drumcliffe for the ceremony. They came to pay tribute to Ireland's greatest man of letters, the poet who had expressly announced his desire to "accounted be/True brother of a company/That sang to sweeten Ireland's wrong,/Ballad and story, rann and song." But the man they so honored had been no mere Irish bard or patriotic rhymester. He was a literary giant of universal appeal and international renown, Nobel laureate, and citizen of the world. It would be absurd, of course, to say that Yeats "put Ireland on the map." But in one sense he, more than any of his contemporaries, prepared the way for his country—in Robert Emmet's famous words—to take "her place among the nations of the earth."

Part Two

Gazetteer

The Republic

SOUTHEASTERN IRELAND

County Wexford

BALLYHACK

*** **Dunbrody Abbey** *(117, 127, 140)*, 2½ mi N; W side of R 733 (to New Ross); signposted and visible from road; OS ½ 23S 71 15; key at house across road

Beautifully situated on the eastern shore of Waterford harbor, these are the substantial ruins of a Cistercian house founded in about 1178 by Hervé de Montmorency, Strongbow's uncle. The buildings date mostly to the early thirteenth century. They consist of a long nave (south wall mostly missing), a choir lighted by Early English lancets, a fifteenth-century central tower, a north transept with three chapels along the east wall, and a south transept with one chapel similarly placed. From the south transept an unusually well-preserved set of night stairs leads up to what was once the monks' dormitory. From the north transept a spiral staircase mounts to the transept wall head. Of the claustral remains there are traces of the sacristy, chapter house, parlor, and dormitory undercroft in the east range, while in the south range the frater (refectory) stands almost to full height. After Henry VIII's dissolution of the abbeys, the place was bought by Sir Osborne Etchingham, who converted the south transept into a private residence.

DUNCANNON

Duncannon Martello Towers *(207)*, N of village center, E of coastal road to Ballyhack

These two squat round towers were built in 1804 against the presumed danger of a Napoleonic invasion of Ireland by way of Waterford harbor. Both have been converted to private use, and neither is easily accessible.

ENNISCORTHY

** Wexford County Museum, Enniscorthy Castle *(19, 202, 248, 256)*, town center; open June–Sept, daily, 10:00 A.M.–6:00 P.M.

Raised on the foundations of a thirteenth-century Prendergast castle, this late-sixteenth-century tower house (restored) was built by Sir Henry Wallop and briefly leased by the poet Edmund Spenser. Today it houses the local museum, an interesting miscellany of items illustrating the history of County Wexford. On the top floor are ship models, figureheads, farm tools, pottery, lace, hardware, and hurley sticks. The first floor displays memorabilia of the War of Irish Independence and civil war (1916–22); muskets, cannonballs and other items found on the nearby site of the Battle of Vinegar Hill (1798); church vestments; and cross slabs. On the ground floor are neolithic ax heads and numerous medieval and later weapons; also nineteenth-century kitchen and dairy equipment; and finally a nineteenth-century "jaunting car."

** St. Aidan's Cathedral *(230)*, town center

Designed by A. W. N. Pugin, begun in 1843, and consecrated in 1860, this is a handsome neo-Gothic church in the Decorated style. It is an aisled cruciform building with high ceilings, a deep, square-ended choir with chapels on each side, shallow transepts, and fine Victorian stained glass in both the east and west windows.

Vinegar Hill *(202)*, 2 mi NE; signposted

At the summit of this steep hill is the stump of the windmill where a band of Wexford peasants took their final stand on 21 June 1798 to be mowed down by the troops of General Gerard Lake, thus bringing an end to all effective resistance in the insurrection of that year.

FERNS

Ferns (C of I) Church and Abbey *(72, 113)*, E of village center, E of N 11 (to Gorey); cathedral church closed except for services

The present C of I church incorporates the choir of the Early English cathedral built between 1223 and 1243. The two lancets in the east gable wall and those on the side walls near the east end are original. About seventy-five yards to the east are the scant ruins of a detached building the same width as the church. Its purpose, according to the historian Harold G. Leask, "is an enigma." From its position one might guess it to have been a retrochoir (behind the high altar), except that such eastward extensions of the choir were rare in Ireland.

In a field still farther to the east is the ruined abbey—a foundation of Augustinian canons brought here in about 1158 by Dermot MacMurrough, king of Leinster. Still to be seen are the tower (square at the bottom and round at the top) at the west end of the abbey church, the remains of the north wall of the nave, those of a sacristy north of the choir, and the scattered foundations of the cloister to the south.

Ferns Castle *(84)*, N of village center, E of N 11 (to Gorey), S of cathedral and abbey grounds; no admission

Here are the scant remains of a thirteenth-century "towered or turreted keep," that is, a rectangular building with round towers affixed to each corner. It was probably built either by William Marshal or his son, called William Marshal the younger. The castle exchanged hands many times until its surrender to Cromwell in 1649, sometime after which it came into the possession of the Donovan family.

Two of the original round towers with the wall between survive to some height. The latter is pierced with good trefoil-headed windows, two of which give on to a vaulted chapel inside.

FETHARD

Baginbun Head Martello Tower *(207)*, 5 mi S, at end of unmarked road continuing from R 734

This well-preserved martello tower, built in 1804, is now a private dwelling but is clearly visible from the road. Round in shape with a slightly convex conical roof, it has four corbelled machicolations built out from the walls. Close to the site where Normans landed in 1167, it was designed to ward off an anticipated invasion by Napoleonic troops.

* Slade Castle *(105)*, 5 mi SW; 1 mi NE of Hook Head lighthouse; not signposted but clearly visible from road; OS ½ 23X 75 98; no entry to interior

Picturesquely situated beside a fishing harbor on the eastern side of Hook Head, this is a high-standing sixteenth-century tower house with a seventeenth-century residence attached—both built apparently by the Laffan family. The tower is fifty-six feet high, the residence somewhat lower. Both are battlemented. Although entry is barred, parts of the interior are visible through iron grilles. A fine view of the south coast extends eastward to Baginbun Head, where the Normans landed in 1170.

** **Tintern Abbey** *(117, 127, 140)*, 4 mi N; E of R 734 (to New Ross); signposted; OS ½ 23S 79 10

The earliest parts of this Cistercian abbey, founded by William Marshal in about 1200, date to the thirteenth century, but they are mostly concealed by the fifteenth-century reconstruction, which was in turn modified when the tower and chancel were converted into a private residence in the 1550s by Sir Anthony Colclough, whose descendants lived here until fairly recently. The wide east window of the choir is in the Decorated style but has lost its tracery. The mullioned windows in the tower were part of the sixteenth-century conversion. Nothing is left of the claustral buildings. The site is currently undergoing restoration.

NEW ROSS

** **Kennedy Memorial Park** *(215)*, 4 mi S; S of R 733 (to Ballyhack); signposted

Dedicated to the memory of President John F. Kennedy, here, on the lower slopes of Slieve Coilte, are 620 acres of parkland planted with over four thousand varieties of trees and shrubs. The site was chosen partly because of its proximity to Dunganstown, ancestral home of this branch of the Kennedys. At the eastern end of this village is the **Kennedy Homestead** *(215)*, a tiny stone building on private property (not signposted), which President Kennedy's great-grandfather left when he emigrated to America.

WEXFORD

* **St. Iberius (C of I) Church** *(176)*, Main Street, city center; open for services only

Drab on the outside, this church, built in 1760, has an interior of elegant neoclassic design—galleried on three sides, with pews arranged along the long axis facing an altar flanked by twin Corinthian pillars and lit by bay windows from above.

*** **Johnstown Castle and Agricultural Museum** *(210, 251)*, 3 mi S; signposted; open May-June, M-F, 9:00 A.M.-12:30 P.M., 1:30-5:00 P.M., Sa-Su, 2:00-5:00 P.M.; July-Aug, M-F, 9:00 A.M.-5:00 P.M., Sa-Su, 2:00-5:00 P.M.

Underneath the battlements and pseudomachicolations of this sprawling nineteenth-century Gothic Revival castle are the foundations of a medieval tower house incorporated within a seventeenth-century mansion. The present structure owes its appearance mostly to John Knox Grogan's Gothick rebuilding in the second decade of the nineteenth century and to subsequent additions by Hamilton K. Grogan-Morgan in the heavier baronial style of the mid-century. The castle proper is now headquarters of the Irish Agricultural Institute and is used chiefly as a soils research center. The agricultural museum is housed in a nearby block of neo-Gothic farm buildings. Its many rooms, very well arranged, contain exhibits of farm carts and traps, power-driven barn machines, a hunting-horse stable, carpenter and wheelwright workshops, a smithy, a harness maker and shoemaker shop, dairy equipment, a great variety of farm machinery, a collection of Irish country furniture, and much else besides. Situated at the edge of an artificial lake and surrounded by fifty acres of well-planted parkland, this place is not only highly instructive, but remarkable for its natural beauty.

** **Rathmacknee Castle** *(105)*, 6 mi S; ¼ mi W of R 739 (to Tenacre Crossroads); obscurely signposted; OS ½ 23T 03 14

Built in the mid–fifteenth century, probably by John Rosseter, seneschal of the Liberty of Wexford, this is an unusually well-preserved late medieval tower house and bawn. The house (locked) stands five storeys high to stepped battlements. The twenty-four-foot-high bawn wall is complete on three sides, the fourth being taken up by a modern farmhouse. A flight of steps inside the wall leads to a machicolated round turret in the northeast corner of the bawn, and another smaller square turret stands at the northwest. In the words of the archaeologist Peter Harbison, this place "gives a very good idea of what the tower-houses and bawns of the 15th and 16th centuries in Ireland looked like."

County Waterford

Lismore

** **Lismore Cathedral** *(113, 156)*, town center; open daytime hours

Now used for Protestant (Church of Ireland) services, the original cruciform cathedral church on this site was built by Bishop Robert de Bedford sometime after 1218. The only remnants of this period of construction are the chancel arch (between nave and choir) and the windows in the south transept. Most of the church was built by Richard Boyle, first earl of Cork, in the seventeenth century and is a fine example of the neo-Gothic style of that era. An elegant crocketed doorway leads from the nave to the west porch; several Early Christian grave slabs are embedded in the west wall; an elaborate carved oak screen divides the choir from the nave and another the nave from the north transept; the stone carving on the sixteenth-century McGrath tomb is excellent. Interior walls are whitewashed, and most of the windows are filled with clear glass, which gives the church an unusually bright and cheerful appearance.

** **Lismore Castle and Gardens** *(210)*, town center; signposted; open Su–F, 1:45–4:45 P.M.; no entry to castle

Visible only from the outside, this is a nineteenth-century neo-Gothic castle erected on the foundations of the original building built by Richard Boyle, earl of Cork. The "restoration" was accomplished by the earl's descendant, William Spencer Cavendish, sixth duke of Devonshire, in two stages, the first under the architectural direction of William Atkinson, the second under that of Joseph Paxton. The adjacent gardens are open to the public. They are entered through the "riding house," built in 1631 by Boyle, who was also responsible for laying out the gardens themselves, more or less on the plan that still exists. The upper garden contains a remarkable collection of yew hedges and topiary, though the herbaceous borders are undistinguished. The lower garden consists mostly of woodland trails, heavy with rhododendrons, camellias, magnolias, and the like.

WATERFORD

*** **Reginald's Tower and Waterford Civic Museum** *(84, 237)*, Parade Quay; open M–F, 9:30 A.M.–12:30 P.M., 2:00–5:30 P.M.; Sa, 9:30 A.M.–12:30 P.M.

Tradition, reinforced by local pride, ascribes the building of this three-storey circular tower to the Viking chief Ragnvald, son of Sygrygg, in the year 1003. Archaeological evidence, however, points to the Anglo-Normans of the thirteenth century as the probable builders. In the fifteenth century it was used as a mint; in the mid-seventeenth it was captured by Cromwellian troops under General Henry Ireton; in the nineteenth it became a prison; and today it serves as a museum housing numerous items of local interest, such as:

Ground Floor: Maritime paintings and artifacts illustrating the history of this busy harbor.

First Floor: Memorabilia of Thomas Francis Meagher, leader of the Young Ireland movement. He was transported to Australia in 1848, escaped to America, and became commanding general of the "Irish Brigade" in the Union Army during the Civil War. Appointed governor of the territory of Montana, he died as a result of falling off a steamboat in the Missouri River.

Second Floor: Medieval and Tudor royal charters of the city; ceremonial swords of King John and King Henry VIII; other regalia.

Third Floor: Models and photographs of the city and county bridges.

* City Wall *(93)*, Spring Garden Alley, Castle Street, Jenkins Lane

Waterford claims to have the longest surviving stretch of medieval city wall in Ireland with the exception of nearby Youghal. Reginald's Tower stands at the northeast corner of the original enclosure. Fairly high segments of the wall can be seen along Spring Garden Alley; along Castle Street, where three mural towers are still standing; and at the end of Jenkins Lane, where there is still another tower. All the above is within fairly easy walking distance from the tower.

* French Church *(122, 128, 179)*, Greyfriars Street, city center; key at No. 5 (across street)

This is a high-standing ruin of a Franciscan friary church built in about 1240. Nave, north aisle, and choir of the thirteenth-century building survive, the best feature being the triple lancets in the east wall. The massive battlemented tower is a fifteenth-century addition. Along the north wall of the choir is an interesting collection of medieval grave slabs. In 1693, following the revocation of the Edict of Nantes by King Louis XIV, Protestant refugees from France were given the use of the building—whence its present name.

** St. Patrick's (Christian Brothers) Church *(173)*, off George's Street, city center; not signposted and not visible from street

Incorporated into the Christian Brothers' School, this small L-plan chapel has a charming neoclassical interior, painted white, with a panelled barrel-vaulted ceiling, galleries supported by fluted Doric pillars around three sides of the nave, and an altar surmounted by a neoclassical pediment. Built in 1764, this is the oldest intact post-Reformation Roman Catholic church in any Irish city. The present approach down an alley off a busy street is not easy to find, but originally it was even more concealed behind a cluster of shops, so as not to give offense to unfriendly Protestant magistrates and townspeople.

*** Holy Trinity Cathedral *(174)*, Barron Strand Street, city center

The first post-Reformation Roman Catholic cathedral, this splendid house of worship was built in 1792–96 to the design of a local architect, John Roberts. The apse was added in 1854 and the front in 1893, but the basic neoclassic plan was unaltered by these modifications. Laid out along the lines of a Greek cross, the church has comparatively shallow transepts, curved galleries supported by fluted Ionic pillars, a bow-fronted organ loft in the rear, and blue and gold Corinthian columns rising to the roof. An elegant Italianate baldachin surmounts the altar.

** **Christ Church Cathedral** *(176)*, corner of Henrietta Street and Cathedral Square, city center; open only for (C of I) services, though admission at other times can be arranged by application to the Tourist Information Office on Merchant's Quay

Designed by the local architect, John Roberts, and built in 1773–79, this fine building was apparently modelled on the works of Christopher Wren, particularly St. James, Piccadilly, in London. The church is an aisled rectangle with raised Corinthian and Ionic pillars and handsome plasterwork in the ceiling. The altar is flanked by a high pediment supported by white and gold fluted Corinthian columns. The cylindrical stone pulpit is encircled by Ionic columnettes. The interior architectural purity has been marred somewhat by the removal of the original side galleries.

*** **Waterford Glass Factory** *(191, 219)*, 1½ mi SW, N side of N 25 (to Cork); 40-minute mandatory guided tours, weekdays at 10:15, 11:00, and 11:45 A.M.; 1:45 and 2:30 P.M.; advance booking required—tel (051) 73311 or arrange through Tourist Information Office, Merchant's Quay

Moved in 1967 to its present spacious premises in the Kilbarry district of Waterford, this fascinating factory claims to be the lineal descendant of the glassworks opened by George and William Penrose in 1783. In 1799 the Penrose brothers sold their plant to the Gatchell family, which continued operations until 1851, when glass making in Waterford ceased. It was revived on a small scale in 1947 and has expanded ever since, now employing more than three thousand people. The guided tour covers most of the stages in the manufacture of this fine ware, and visitors can observe at close quarters the highly trained and superbly skilled craftsmen at work. The display room *cum* shop is unsurpassed for elegance.

* **Granagh Castle** *(88)*, 2 mi NW; S side of N 24 (to Carrick-on-Suir); in County Kilkenny; not signposted but visible from road; OS ½ 23S 57 14

The original castle here, probably built by the Le Poers in the thirteenth century, was of the keepless courtyard type. It is represented by the three round turrets and adjoining curtain wall overlooking the river Suir. The tall square keep was added in the fourteenth century by James Butler, second earl of Ormond, though it was modified in the fifteenth. West of the keep stands a two-storeyed hall, probably of fifteenth- or sixteenth-century date. Over one of the upper windows is a sculpted representation of the Butler arms. The circular building outside the southwest corner of the courtyard has gunports facing the river and probably dates to the sixteenth century. In 1650 the castle was captured and slighted by Cromwellian troops under Major Daniel Axtell (that is, the soldiers threw down the parapets and breached part of the walls to make them indefensible against ordinary assault). Its present ruinous condition, however, postdates that event.

** **Knockeen** *(21)*, 4½ mi SW; 3 mi S of N 25 (to Cork) from just E of Waterford Glass Factory, across field in copse; signposted but not visible from road; OS ½ 23S 57 07

This imposing Neolithic portal dolmen is twelve feet high overall. The two portal stones, facing southeast, have a door stone between them, though somewhat to the rear. An immense front capstone rests on high side stones and a smaller rear capstone covering the burial chamber. The top is almost horizontal; ergo, this is a true "tabletop" or dolmen in the literal sense of the Breton word.

* **Gaulstown Dolmen** *(21)*, 7 mi SW, 5 mi NW of Tramore, through iron gate and up private lane; poorly signposted; OS ½ 23S 54 06

The single large capstone of this portal dolmen rests on five uprights. The two portal stones face southeast, with the broken blocker stone slightly to their rear.

County Carlow

BORRIS

Killoughternane Church *(49)*, 4 mi NE; on minor roads; not signposted; OS ½ 19S 77 54

Not easy to find, this small (twenty- by twelve-foot) ruined Early Christian church has slightly projecting antae, east and west, and a small round-headed east window. It dates to the ninth century or later. There is a square baptismal font inside.

St. Mullin's Abbey *(61, 85)*, 8 mi S; 1 mi SW of R 729 (to New Ross, County Wexford); signposted; OS ½ 19S 73 38

At the back of the graveyard and behind the modern church are the remains of a monastery founded by St. Moling in the seventh century. The largest of these ruins is that of a medieval church. Outside its northeast corner, on a stone pedestal, is a badly eroded Early Christian High Cross with the Crucifixion carved on the east side and interlace on the west. Near the southwest corner of the church is the stump of a round tower. Outside the northwest corner of the graveyard is a small Anglo-Norman motte. The other ruins here are difficult to interpret.

CARLOW

* Carlow Castle *(84)*, town center; behind Corcoran Mineral Water Factory; not signposted; key at office

This very ruinous castle was built early in the thirteenth century either by William Marshal or by his son William Marshal the younger. It is the first of a type of keep peculiar to Ireland—the so-called "towered or turreted keep," distinguished by the four round towers at each corner of the central rectangular block. Parts of three of the towers still stand high, as well as the crenellated walls between them. The castle changed hands many times throughout the Middle Ages and was captured by Cromwell in 1650. The English general, however, was not responsible for the castle's ruination. That was accomplished in 1814, when about half the building was deliberately blown up to make room for a lunatic asylum.

** Cathedral of the Assumption *(277)*, town center

This very pretty Gothick building was designed by Thomas Cobden and begun in 1820. Its high Perpendicular tower is crowned by an octagonal lantern. Aisleless and with shallow transepts, the interior is graced with slender clustered columns, triple lancets, and diagonal rib vaulting.

*** Browneshill Dolmen *(21, 467)*, 1 mi E; S of R 725 (to Tullow); signposted; OS ½ 19S 75 77

Here is one of the best cared for and most accessible portal dolmens in Ireland. The huge heart-shaped capstone, weighing about a hundred tons, is supported at the front end by three uprights. A fourth upright stands nearby. The rear of the uptilted capstone rests on the ground.

** Killeshin Church *(65)*, 3 mi W in County Laois; S of R 430 (to Abbeyleix); signposted; OS ½ 19S 67 78

This ruined twelfth-century church (with a chancel of later date) is noted for its Hiberno-Romanesque west doorway, one of the most attractive of its kind in Ireland. The receding entryway of four orders has columns carved with foliage scroll patterns, capitals with human heads of inter-twined hair, and a hooded round arch decorated profusely with chevrons and floral and zoomorphic designs. The site is grass-grown and untended, deserving better treatment from the commissioners of public works than it receives.

LEIGHLINBRIDGE

* Ballymoon Castle *(88)*, 5 mi SE; 2 mi E of N 705 (to Borris) through Muine Bheac (Bagenalstown), N of R 724 (to Fennagh), across wooden footbridge into field; not signposted but visible from road; OS ½ 19S 74 61

Here, in the midst of a cow pasture, are the extensive ruins of a large keepless courtyard castle probably built by Roger Bigod late in the thir-teenth century. Square towers project from three sides of the high walls, and on the fourth is the arched gate with grooves for a portcullis.

TULLOW

** Haroldstown Dolmen *(21)*, 5 mi NE; S of R 727 (to Hacketstown), 2½ mi E of N 81 (to Baltinglass) on Hacketstown Road; signposted and visible from road just after crossing stone bridge; OS ½ 19S 90 78

This is a fine Neolithic portal dolmen. The two portal stones face north with a blocker in between. They support a large capstone resting on side stones and a second smaller capstone to the rear.

Clonmore Castle *(88)*, 12 mi E; 2 mi S of Hacketstown; not signposted; OS ½ 19S 96 76

This romantic ivy-covered pile is the ruin of a keepless courtyard castle built in the thirteenth century. Remains of the turrets at the four corners of the curtain wall are still fairly substantial, although the buildings inside are barely distinguishable. The castle changed hands numerous times and in 1650 fell to Cromwell's forces under Colonel John Hewson.

County Kilkenny

CALLAN

Callan Motte *(84)*, N of town center, W of N 76 (to Kilkenny) by short lane and through gate; not signposted; OS ½ 18S 41 44

Here is a high grass- and tree-covered mound, the remains of a motte-and-bailey castle probably built around 1217 by William Marshal.

* Callan Friary *(132)*, N of town center, E side of N 76 (to Kilkenny); signposted and visible from road; OS ½ 18S 42 44

This ruined Augustinian friary was founded in 1462 by James Butler of the Polestown branch of that powerful Anglo-Irish family. It is rectangular in plan, with walls still mostly complete to the tops, a square tower, and curvilinear tracery in the west window. The most remarkable feature here is the elegantly carved sedilia in the south wall of the choir. The claustral buildings have disappeared.

** Killamery High Cross *(51)*, 6 mi S; ¼ mi E of N 76 (to Clonmel), in graveyard N of ruined modern church; signposted; OS ½ 18S 38 36

This is a well-preserved High Cross, probably dating to the ninth century, with a complete ring and a house-shrine capstone. The west face is covered mostly with interlace and geometric motifs; marigold and serpent motifs cover the east face, which also has a prominent boss at the crossing. At the end of the north arm are four biblical scenes arranged in a square. The base of the cross is also decorated. Nearby is an incised cross slab with a Gaelic inscription, translatable as "a prayer for Maelsechnaill."

** Kilree Church, High Cross, and Round Tower *(51, 60)*, 7 mi SE; 1½ mi NE of R 699 (to Thomastown) from Dunamaggan village, over two stiles and into copse; not signposted; OS ½ 18S 49 41

The small ruined Early Christian church has a flat-headed west doorway and antae projecting from the west gable wall. Chancel and rounded arch are later additions. Nearby is a ninety-six-foot-high Round Tower without its original top. In a field west of the church, within a fenced enclosure, is a fine High Cross, decorated mostly with interlace and prominent circular bosses on each face. Other carvings, hard to interpret, are to be found on the end of the south arm of the cross.

Aghaviller Church and Round Tower *(60)*, 8 mi SE; S of Kilmaganny–Knocktopher road; not signposted; OS ½ 19S 50 35

The only remnant of the twelfth- or thirteenth-century church on this site is the large rectangular tower that appears to have been heightened and fortified in the sixteenth century. Nearby is the forty-foot-high stump of a Round Tower with a modern doorway at ground level.

** Kilmogue *(21)*, 13 mi SE; 3½ mi S of Hugginstown, W of Harristown; signposted "Leac an Scáil"; OS ½ 19S 50 28

Known locally as Leac an Scáil, this is one of the tallest portal dolmens in Ireland, the two portal stones rising to a height of more than twelve feet with a blocker in between. The huge main capstone slants sharply backward to rest on a secondary capstone to the rear, which in turn rests on a low upright. Both are supported by uprights along the sides.

* Burnchurch Castle *(105)*, 5 mi NE; 2 mi E of N 76 (to Kilkenny) on road to Bennettsbridge; not signposted but visible from road; OS ½ 18S 48 47; no entry into interior

Originally a FitzGerald residence, this fifteenth- or sixteenth-century ruined tower house stands six storeys high to stepped battlements above the roofline. It displays an unusual number of arrow-loops. Just north of the house is a high round tower, originally part of the bawn wall.

** Kells Priory *(117, 127)*, 6½ mi E; ½ mi E of Kells village on N side of road to Stonyford; signposted and visible from road; OS ½ 18S 50 43

These very military-looking ruins are those of an Augustinian priory founded in 1193 by Geoffrey de Marisco, justiciar of Ireland. Most of the buildings, however, date to the fourteenth and fifteenth centuries. South of the church and cloister is a double enclosure surrounded by two sets of walls. The outer wall is protected by four square mural towers pierced with arrow-loops, while a fifth, machicolated tower in the southeast sector served as the gatehouse. The inner wall (entered from the east) has two mural towers. The church has a long nave, a high central tower, a choir at the east end, a chapel south of the choir, and a north transept opening into another chapel. Near the northwest corner of the nave is another tower— probably the prior's residence. The ruins of the claustral buildings south of the church are hard to interpret. The site is currently undergoing restoration.

** Clara Castle *(195)*, 6 mi NE; 2 mi N of N 10 (to Leighlinbridge), W of road to Ballyfoyle; not signposted; key hangs on gatepost at M. Murphy's house across lane

Untended and not easy to find, this is nevertheless one of the best-preserved unrestored fifteenth-century tower houses in Ireland. A small bawn with numerous gunports lies in front of the main doorway. High above it is a machicolation through which missiles could be dropped on unwelcome intruders. The ceiling immediately inside is pierced with a "murder hole" serving the same purpose. Most remarkably, the oak beams of the floors are still in place, and the tower can be climbed to its battle-mented rooftop.

GOWRAN

St. Mary's Church *(115)*, village center; W of N 9 (to Thomastown)

The ruined nave of this thirteenth-century church has fine triple lancets with trefoil heads and at each end of the aisles twin lancets, also trefoil-pointed, surmounted by a quatrefoil window. The tower dates to the fourteenth or fifteenth century. The site of the original choir is now occupied by a nineteenth-century church, since closed down and boarded up.

* Tullaherin Church and Round Tower *(43, 60)*, 4 mi SW, ¾ mi SW of N 9 (to Thomastown); signposted; OS ½ 19S 59 48

The nave of this little church probably dates to the tenth or eleventh century, the chancel to the fifteenth. There are antae east and west. Outside, near the southwest corner of the church, is a small Ogham stone with faint markings. Nearby is a six-storey Round Tower, almost seventy feet high, the ruined upper portion of which is probably a later addition.

GRAIGUENAMANAGH

** Graiguenamanagh (Duiske) Abbey *(117, 140)*, village center; open daytime hours

Founded by William Marshal in 1207, this Cistercian abbey once boasted the largest church of any monastery of this order in Ireland. Most of it was rebuilt in the late eighteenth and early nineteenth centuries and is now in use for Roman Catholic services. An abundance of lancet windows—pointed, round, and trefoil-headed—however, attest to its thirteenth-century origins, as do two of the crossing piers and the doorway to the baptistry in the south wall. In the graveyard south of the choir are two High Crosses brought here from elsewhere.

Ullard Church and High Cross *(61)*, 3½ mi N; ½ mi E of R 705 (to Leighlinbridge, County Carlow); not signposted; OS ½ 19S 72 48

This is a much restored twelfth-century church with a Romanesque west doorway radically altered in the sixteenth century. Behind the church, at the southeast corner of a handball court, is a High Cross with a Crucifixion on the east face with very eroded biblical scenes underneath.

KILKENNY

** Kilkenny Castle *(84, 97, 166, 172, 212)*, Castle Road; open daily, 10:00 A.M.–7:00 P.M.

Strongbow built a castle on this site in about 1172, probably a motte-and-bailey of which no trace remains. Around 1192 his son-in-law William Marshal began the construction of a stone castle of the keepless courtyard variety, the ground plan of which seems to have closely resembled that of the present building. In 1391–92 the place passed to the ownership of James Butler, third earl of Ormond, and remained in the Butler family until 1935. In 1650 castle and town were taken by Cromwell's forces, and James Butler, twelfth earl and first duke of Ormond, went into exile on the Continent in the company of King Charles II. After the Restoration Ormond remodelled the castle in the French style, and his son, the second duke, continued the work, adding a splendid neoclassical gatehouse, of which the pedimented facade survives as the present entrance to the courtyard. But it was not until 1826 that the castle began to assume its present appearance, with a major rebuilding instituted by James Butler, second marquess of Ormond, with the professional assistance of the architect William Robertson.

Open to the public are the Picture Gallery, the former first-floor dining room, and the basement. Not much furniture was left when the Butlers departed in 1935, but there is a fine collection of tapestries on the walls, and in the Picture Gallery are priceless portraits by Lely, Kneller, Wissing, and others.

* Shee's Alms House *(165)*, town center, Rose Inn Street; signposted "i"

Built in the 1580s by Sir Richard Shee as an almshouse for twelve paupers, this restored building now houses the Irish Tourist Information Centre. Upstairs is the "cityscope exhibit," where a large contour map of seventeenth-century Kilkenny and its buildings is on exhibit and an excellent audiovisual presentation describes the layout of the city at that time.

*** Rothe House *(165)*, town center, Parliament Street; signposted; open M-Sa, 10:30 A.M.–12:30 P.M., 3:00–5:00 P.M.; Su, 3:00–5:00 P.M.

Begun by the merchant John Rothe at the end of the sixteenth century and enlarged in the early seventeenth, this is a well-restored Tudor-style house with two courtyards, each with an additional house, to the rear. It now houses the museum of the Kilkenny Archaeological Society. Among the contents are a costume gallery, a collection of penal crosses and rosaries, Charles Stewart Parnell memorabilia, eighteenth- and nineteenth-century weapons, nineteenth-century craftsmen's tools, and a small exhibit of prehistoric artifacts, including Mesolithic microliths, Neolithic axes, bronze-age axes and ax molds, etc. An audiovisual show explains the history of the house and of the people associated with it.

St. John's Priory *(117)*, Lower John Street, NE of town center; closed except during services

A house for Augustinian canons was founded on this site in 1220 by William Marshal the younger. A Protestant (C of I) church occupies the much restored thirteenth- or fourteenth-century lady chapel. The adjacent ruins are those of the choir of the original church, built about the time of the founding. There are no claustral remains.

* Black Friars' Church *(121, 128)*, Abbey Street, town center; signposted "Black Abbey"

Now used for Roman Catholic services, this was the church of a Dominican friary founded in about 1226. The original choir has disappeared, but the present church occupies the site of the thirteenth-century nave and fourteenth-century south wing. The tower was added in the fifteenth century at about the same time as the fine Decorated windows were inserted, the one in the east wall being filled with attractive modern blue and orange stained glass. In the south wing is a fine medieval alabaster statue of the Holy Trinity to whom the friary was dedicated.

* Smithwick's Brewery and Franciscan Friary *(112, 186)*, E of Parliament Street, town center; guided tours M–F, 3:00 P.M.

This still-active brewery was founded by the Smithwick family in 1710. The guided tour includes an audiovisual show and a free drink. On the grounds are the ruins of a Franciscan friary founded by Richard Marshal in 1232. Of the thirteenth-century building only the choir remains, and it was extended eastward in the early fourteenth, when the seven beautiful lancets were inserted in the east window. The tower was added at about the same time. The sacristy south of the church now serves as a chapel for employees of the brewery.

*** St. Canice's (C of I) Cathedral and Kilkenny Round Tower *(60, 112)*, Irishtown, N of town center; signposted; open daytime hours

This much restored thirteenth-century cathedral with a fourteenth-century tower is a cruciform aisled church with chapels on either side of the choir and at the extremities of the transepts. The west door is simple but attractive; the chancel is lit by three sets of lancets, some of them round-headed; the nave by shorter lancets and quatrefoil windows. The hammer-beam roof is a nineteenth-century reproduction. The aisles abound in fine effigies and tombstones, mostly of the sixteenth and seventeenth centuries. A thirteenth-century baptismal font stands near the west end.

Outside the church, near its southeast corner, is a ninety-five-foot-high Round Tower, which can be climbed to the top. (Key is available from cathedral custodian.)

Freshford Church (65), 9 mi W on R 693 (to Freshford), in Freshford village center; not signposted but visible from road; OS ½ 18S 41 65

Here is a fine twelfth-century Hiberno-Romanesque doorway incorporated into the west wall of an undistinguished, small eighteenth-century church. The doorway is recessed in three orders (i.e., triple arched), with outward-pointing sawtooth chevrons.

Ballylarkin Church (115), 11 mi W; 2 mi SW of Freshford; not signposted but visible from road

This small, very ruinous nave-and-chancel parish church dates probably to the thirteenth century. Its most unusual features are its narrow single door in the north wall and its comparative lack of windows (two only). Inside, carved piscina (for washing sacred vessels), aumbrey (recessed space for storing them), and triple sedilia (seats for bishops and other dignitaries) are remarkably well done for such a tiny and undistinguished church.

* Ballyragget Castle (105), 10 mi N; W of N 77 (to Durrow), through red brick arch on N side of Ballyragget village square; not signposted; OS ½ 18S 45 71

Though derelict, this is a high-standing fifteenth- or sixteenth-century four-storey rectangular tower house within a well-preserved high bawn wall. It was the residence of the Ballyragget branch of the Butler family. On private property and now used as a storehouse, it is nonetheless open and can be climbed to the top.

THOMASTOWN

Thomastown Church (115), town center; grounds open only during C of I services

On the premises of the modern C of I parish church are the sparse ruins of a thirteenth-century aisled nave-and-chancel church. The best features are the north arcade and the clerestory windows in the north wall. Some of the west wall still stands, but the rest of the church is reduced to foundations.

*** **Jerpoint Abbey** *(118, 127)*, 1½ mi S; E side of N 9 (to Waterford); signposted and visible from road; custodian on duty; OS ½ 19S 57 40

This is one of the best preserved and best tended of Ireland's abbey ruins. It was colonized in 1180 by Cistercians from Baltinglass under the patronage of Donal MacGillapatrick, king of Ossory. Choir, transepts, and nave date to the late twelfth and early thirteenth centuries. The three-light west window is original, but the present east window is of fourteenth-century provenance. A row of six arches separates the nave from the north aisle, but only one arch survives on the south side. The remains of the wall separating the monks' choir from the area used by the lay brothers can still be seen. The tower over the crossing is of fifteenth-century date. There are two eastward-facing chapels in each transept. A wooden ladder replaces the original night stair connecting the south transept with the monks' dorter in the upper storey of the east range. Of the claustral remains the chapter house has been restored completely and now serves as a reception center. Portions of the remainder of the east range still stand, as does one wall of the refectory in the south range. The west range has disappeared, as is the case with most Irish Cistercian abbeys. Inside the church are sedilia and a double piscina as well as some fine thirteenth-century effigies and sixteenth-century tombs.

URLINGFORD

** **Kilcooley Abbey** *(118, 127, 140)*, 3 mi S in County Tipperary; E of R 689 (to Fethard), at end of lane off road to private residence; signposted; gates sometimes locked; OS ½ 18S 29 58

Here is a fine ruin of the Cistercian monastery founded in 1182 by Donal Mór O'Brien, king of Thomond, and largely rebuilt after its almost complete destruction in 1445. Most of the remains, therefore, date to the late fifteenth century. Noteworthy are the traceried Decorated east window, the vaulting in the north transept, the decorated wall between the south transept and sacristy, the night stair to the now-missing monks' dorter, the two sedilia, and the sixteenth-century tomb of Piers Fitz Oge Butler. The claustral buildings are gone, but still standing are a columbarium and a two-storey structure that may have been the infirmary. After the dissolution of the monastery in 1540, it passed first to James Butler, earl of Ormond, and eventually to the Barker family, which used it as a residence.

* Fertagh Round Tower *(60)*, 4 mi NE; ¼ mi W of N 8 (to Durrow); not signposted; OS ½ 18S 31 70

This is an unusually high (one-hundred-foot) tower of eight storeys.

County Tipperary

Cahir

*** Cahir Castle *(97, 148, 160)*, town center; signposted; open daily, 10:00 A.M.–8:00 P.M.

Situated on a rocky islet in the river Suir, this is one of the largest and best-preserved medieval castles in Ireland. It was first built, probably sometime in the thirteenth century, as a keepless courtyard castle, but in the fifteenth the high rectangular gatehouse tower was converted into a keep by walling up the arched entryway. At the same time the curtain wall was extended so that the ground plan consisted of an inner ward around the keep, a middle ward to the south, and an outer ward still farther south. Considerable restorations and additions were also made in the mid–nineteenth century. Today's visitor proceeds up a path along the riverside, through a small gate into the outer ward, thence into the middle ward and the sparsely furnished keep, and finally into the outer ward with its two square corner towers and great hall.

Other than the keep, the thirteenth-century remains include most of the curtain walls of the inner ward, part of the square tower at the northwest corner of the inner ward, and the foundation of the thick wall in the middle ward. The fifteenth- and sixteenth-century additions include the small round tower with the conical roof and the adjacent barbican wall to the left (south) of the present entrance, the gateway between outer and inner wards, the curtain walls of the outer ward, and the lower part of the small square northeast corner tower of the inner ward. In the nineteenth century were added the lower barbican wall on the river side of the path leading up to the castle entrance, the gateway to the outer ward, and the house at the south end of the outer ward, the curtain wall west of the keep, the great hall in the inner ward, the battlements, and the upper parts of several of the buildings.

From 1375 until the eighteenth century the castle was occupied by a junior branch of the Butler family. Considered impregnable, it was in fact captured in 1599 by Queen Elizabeth's favorite, Robert Devereux, earl of Essex. In 1647 it was again taken by parliamentary forces under Murrough O'Brien, Lord Inchiquin, and after Inchiquin's defection to the royalists it was retaken by Cromwell in 1650.

Toureen Peakaun Church *(50)*, 4 mi NW, S of N 24 (to Tipperary), by footpath 100 yd beyond railway gate; not signposted; OS ½ 18S 01 28

This is a twelfth-century roofless church with a Romanesque round-headed narrow window at the east end. Two cross slabs are built into the east wall, and several others are in the graveyard farther east. To the west of the church is an Early Christian pillar stone.

Knockgraffon Motte *(82)*, 3½ mi N; 1½ mi NW of N 8 (to Cashel), W of Boystown Farm; poorly signposted; OS ½ 18S 04 29

Close to the east bank of the river Suir, this high grass-covered mound was the motte-and-bailey of Philip de Worcester, vassal of King John. It dates probably to the early thirteenth century.

* Burncourt Castle *(162)*, 8½ mi SW; 1½ mi SW of N 2 (to Mitchelstown), N side of minor road behind private farmhouse; not signposted but visible from road; OS ½ 22R 95 18

Built in 1641 by Sir Richard Everard, this ruin, untended and overrun by weeds, consists of a long rectangular block with a square tower at each corner, many mullioned windows, and numerous fireplaces. Some of the original twenty-six gables and seven chimneys survive. The house has been abandoned since it was set on fire in 1650, either by Cromwellian troops or, more probably, by Lady Everard on their approach.

President Reagan Centre *(215)*, 12 mi SW; 4 mi W of Clogheen on R 665 (to Mitchelstown), in Ballyporeen village center; open Tu–F, 10:30 A.M.–12:30 P.M., 2:30–4:30 P.M.; Su, 1:30–5:00 P.M.

This building was dedicated by President Ronald Reagan in June 1984 in commemoration of his great-grandfather, Michael Regan *(sic)*, who emigrated to America from nearby. A copy of the parish baptismal register recording Michael Regan's baptism is on display, as are numerous photographs of the visit of the American president and Mrs. Reagan. A fifteen-minute audiovisual show covers the event.

CARRICK-ON-SUIR

*** Ormond Castle *(143)*, E of town center; signposted; open mid-June–mid-Sept, daily, 10:00 A.M.–6:00 P.M.; mandatory 30-minute guided tour

This fine castle-*cum*-mansion, now mostly restored, consists of three parts: (1) the large walled courtyard of mid-fifteenth-century date on the south side; (2) the twin-towered castle of approximately the same date, built by Sir Edward MacRichard, grandson of James Butler, third earl of Ormond; and (3) the Elizabethan manor house erected in front of the towers by Thomas Butler, tenth earl of Ormond ("Black Tom"), kinsman and loyal supporter of Queen Elizabeth I.

The manor house is the chief attraction. It was unusual when built in that it lacked any defensive features other than two gun-loops on either side of the front door. Its high-pitched gables, pinnacles, and mullioned windows are typical of English Tudor architecture, but rare in Ireland and nowhere else to be found in such an elegant combination. The interior rooms are especially distinguished for the fine plasterwork on walls and ceilings, including high-relief medallions of Queen Elizabeth with the letters "E.R." and the royal arms. At the end of the splendid long gallery is an ornate fireplace with a mantel depicting the Butler coat of arms.

*** Kilkeeran Crosses (51), 4 mi N, in County Kilkenny; ½ mi E of R 697 (to Kilkenny); signposted; OS ½ 18S 42 27

On this site are three High Crosses and the shaft of another, possibly of ninth-century date, and an Early Christian pillar stone. The west cross is complete with ring and conical cap. It is covered with interlace and geometric motifs on all four sides and with circular bosses on the east and west faces. The base too is decorated, mostly with geometric motifs but also with eight horsemen on its east face. The east cross is complete to its conical top but is undecorated. Between the two is the reconstructed cross shaft. The north cross is ringless and short-armed and is only faintly decorated. All three crosses belong to the Ahenny group.

*** Ahenny Crosses (51), 5 mi N; ½ mi W of R 697 (to Kilkenny); signposted; OS ½ 18S 41 29

In the graveyard east of the hamlet of Ahenny stand two well-preserved High Crosses, possibly among the earliest to have been carved. The north cross, minus one quadrant of its ring, has interlace and geometrical motifs on both faces; also four bosses on each face and a conical cap. Its base is carved with figures on all sides, including one of Christ flanked on each side by three apostles bearing staffs. The south cross, with a complete ring but an incomplete conical cap, has the same type of geometric designs and the same number of bosses on each side. Its base displays badly worn carvings of humans and animals.

CASHEL

*** **Cashel (St. Patrick's) Rock** *(39, 63, 67, 114, 128)*, town center

Rising some ninety feet above the surrounding plain, this high limestone protuberance became the seat of the Eóganacht kings of Munster, probably early in the fifth century. When the Dál Cais of west Munster ousted the Eóganachta from the kingship, Cashel remained their principal seat, and Brian Boru and his dynasty continued to rule as kings of Cashel. In 1101 Muirchertach O'Brien handed Cashel over to the church, and in 1152 the Rock became the seat of the archbishop of Cashel. All the present buildings therefore are ecclesiastical. They are four in number, listed below in the sequence that today's visitor will want to observe them.

1. **Hall of the Vicars Choral** *(128)*: This is a fifteenth-century building. At the far end of the undercroft is "St. Patrick's Cross," probably of twelfth-century date. On the west face is the Crucifixion, with Christ wearing a long robe; on the east face is an ecclesiastic holding a crosier, possibly meant to represent a bishop, probably St. Patrick. The base is decorated with interlaced beasts and sundry geometric patterns. A cast of the cross stands just outside the north door.

2. **Cormac's Chapel** *(67)*: Begun in 1127 by order of King/Bishop Cormac MacCarthy and consecrated in 1134, this two-chambered church with steep roofs over each chamber is, in the opinion of many, the finest, though by no means the most typical, example of Hiberno-Romanesque architecture in Ireland. Atypically, there is no west door; two high square towers flank the nave at its east end; the chancel is groin-vaulted and the nave barrel-vaulted. More typically Irish are the high-pitched roofs, the sculpted chancel arch, the croft above the nave, and the round-headed, recessed south and north doors. Both these entryways, and especially the latter, are profusely decorated with carved chevrons, geometric motifs, human heads, and, on the tympanum of the north door, a centaur shooting a lion. There are good blind arcades (columns connected by arches, both integrated into the wall) both outside and in, and in the northwest corner is a stone coffin carved with interlaced beasts in the Scandinavian Urnes style.

3. **Cathedral** *(128)*: This fine cruciform aisleless church was begun probably soon after 1224, when Archbishop Marianus O'Brien was appointed to the see of Cashel. Work was continued throughout the thirteenth century by Archbishops David MacKelly and David MacCarvill. The fine lancets of the choir (longer than the nave) are typically Early English in style, though

the tiny windows above them are atypical. Also of this period is the southwest porch, though its doorway belongs to the fifteenth century. The nave was built largely between 1406 and 1440, kept unusually short so as to accommodate the fortified episcopal residence (the Archbishop's Castle) at the west end. The tower above the crossing was raised in the fourteenth century. In the north transept are three beautifully carved sixteenth-century altar tombs. The lancets in both transepts are connected by mural passages. The church was reportedly burned in the late fifteenth century by Gerald FitzGerald, eighth earl of Kildare, "because the archbishop was inside," as he is said to have explained to King Henry VII. The present state of ruination, however, apparently began in the seventeenth century and continued until the late nineteenth, when the site was taken over by the commissioners of public works.

4. **Round Tower** *(60)*: This is the oldest building on St. Patrick's Rock, dating probably to the early twelfth century. It now stands at the northeast corner of the cathedral and can be entered through a passage leading from the north transept.

* **St. Dominic's Friary** *(123)*, town center, at foot of Cashel Rock; no admittance but visible from street

Founded by Archbishop David O'Kelly in 1243, the church of this Dominican friary was rebuilt in the fifteenth century, except for the south wing, which dates to about 1270. Although a number of lancet windows date from the original building, the Decorated traceried windows are insertions of the fifteenth century.

* **Cashel Folk Village** *(256)*, town center, at foot of Cashel Rock

Here are four small buildings full of a miscellany of homely nine-teenth- and early-twentieth-century artifacts and memorabilia, a black-smith's shop, a butcher's shop, and many photos, clippings, and other mementos associated with the Anglo-Irish War of 1916–22 and the ensuing Irish civil war. A most unusual item is an original blue shirt worn by a member of Eoin O'Duffy's quasi-fascist organization in the 1930s.

Cashel Palace *(195)*, town center

Now serving as a luxury hotel, this pleasant Georgian house was designed sometime before 1729 by Sir Edward Pearce as the archiepiscopal palace for the see of Cashel. Theophilus Bolton was the first occupant.

Cashel (C of I) Cathedral *(176)*, town center

This rather undistinguished neo-Gothic church was built in 1784 on the site of the parish church to which the Protestant archbishop, Arthur P. Price, had twenty years earlier removed his episcopal seat from the decaying medieval cathedral on the Rock. Tower and spire were added some years later; the interior was remodelled in the nineteenth century, at which time stained glass was inserted in the eastern window.

* GPA-Bolton Library *(178)*, on grounds of Cashel (C of I) Cathedral, town center; open Su, 2:30–5:30 P.M.; W, 9:30 A.M.–5:30 P.M.

Housed in a nineteenth-century building formerly used as the cathedral chapter house, this diocesan library contains a precious collection of over eleven thousand books and manuscripts, of which eight thousand were originally donated in 1744 by Archbishop Theophilus Bolton.

** Hore Abbey *(119, 127, 140)*, 1 mi NW; S of R 505 (to Dundrum); signposted; OS ½ 18S 09 41

Founded by Archbishop David MacCarvill in 1272, this was the last of the Cistercian monasteries established in Ireland. Architecturally it is unique in that the cloister lay north of the church. Nave, choir, and transepts all date to the thirteenth century. The lancet windows are typically Early English. The tower is a fifteenth-century addition. Of the claustral buildings only the chapter house survives to any extent. After the dissolution of the monastery in 1540, the lands passed to James Butler, earl of Ormond. Subsequently the nave, south transept, and chapter house were converted into private residences.

** Athassel Abbey *(117)*, 6 mi W; 1¼ mi S of N 74 (to Tipperary); signposted from main road but not at site; OS ½ 18S 01 36

This once-magnificent Augustinian monastery, founded in about 1200 by William de Burgh, is now a substantial but poorly tended ruin lying in the midst of a cow pasture with access only through a hole in the stone wall surrounding the monastic precinct. Nave, transepts, and choir were built in the thirteenth century. The east window, however, is a later insertion, though the lancets in the side walls of the choir are original Early English. The tower over the crossing dates to the fifteenth century and is a replacement of an earlier one in the same location. In the east end is a fine standing effigy of a thirteenth-century knight. All three ranges of the cloister stand high enough to be discerned easily.

CLONMEL

** County Tipperary Museum and Art Gallery *(19)*, Parnell Street; open Tu-Sa, 10:00 A.M.–1:00 P.M., 2:00–5:00 P.M.

This is a well-organized local museum whose holdings include Neolithic microliths; bronze-age swords and ax heads; Roman coins; Early Christian ring pins; seventeenth-century coins minted in Cork, Kinsale, and Youghal by refugees from the 1641 Catholic rebellion; eighteenth-century muskets; and memorabilia of the founding of the Irish Labour party in Clonmel in 1912.

The art gallery includes prints of Bianconi carriages (originating in this town) and paintings by Charles Lamb, John Butler Yeats, William Leech, Sarah Purser, Nathaniel Hone, and other Irish artists.

* St. Mary's Church *(116)*, town center; key at Morgan's Furniture Store, Main Street, W of Westgate

Not much is left of the original thirteenth-century building, currently in use for Church of Ireland services, but the fine Decorated east window dates to the fifteenth century, as do the chancel arch, west window, aisle walls, and lower portion of the tower.

* Clonmel Town Wall *(93)*, NW of town center, behind St. Mary's Church

At the northwest corner of St. Mary's churchyard is a well-preserved section of the medieval town wall, including a square tower at the northwest angle and two others flanking it. (Westgate in O'Connell Street is an early-nineteenth-century imitation, though erected on the probable site of one of the town's original gates.)

* Donaghmore Church *(65)*, 5 mi N; 1 mi W of R 689 (to Fethard); not signposted; OS ½ 18S 19 29

Here is the roofless ruin of a two-chambered church built probably in the twelfth century. The original gable walls stand high, but the north and south walls are probably restorations. The west doorway is a fine, though badly eroded, example of Hiberno-Romanesque stone carving, with a profusion of outward-pointing sawtooth chevrons, interlace, beading, zigzags, and foliage. Most of the carving on the chancel arch is gone, but the flanking engaged columns have survived. Above the arch is the entry to the loft—typical of pre-Norman Irish churches but seldom found elsewhere. Numerous round-headed narrow windows pierce the walls.

FETHARD

Town Wall *(93)*, town center

Here are fragments of the medieval stone wall, including a gate at the northwest end of town on the road to Moyglass.

* Fethard Folk Farm and Transport Museum *(251)*, ½ mi W; S of R 692 (to Cashel)

This is a tidily arranged folk museum containing, among other items of interest, horse-drawn carriages, farm carts, and hearses; household and kitchen wares; a blacksmith forge, bellows, and tools; sewing machines; a jockey-weighing scale; butter churns; and miscellaneous farm machinery—all from the late nineteenth and early twentieth centuries.

NENAGH

** Nenagh Castle *(82, 97)*, town center, behind Roman Catholic parish church; signposted; key from Liam White, 40 Rahilly Street

Built sometime after 1200 by Theobald Walter, progenitor of the Butler family, this is perhaps the finest medieval cylindrical keep in Ireland. It remained the *caput* of the Butler earls of Ormond until late in the fourteenth century. Thereafter it changed hands several times until it was taken possession of by General Ginckel in 1690 and slighted.

Fifty-five feet in external diameter, it is about a hundred feet high, although originally only seventy-five, the top portion with its anachronistic stepped battlements having been added in the nineteenth century. The base is battered (leaning inward), and a machicolation protrudes above the original doorway (now walled up) on the first floor above ground level. Unroofed, the keep can be climbed almost to the top.

* Nenagh Friary *(127)*, S of town center

The best features of this well-preserved ruin of the Dominican friary church, founded probably by Bishop Donal O'Kennedy before 1268, are the fine Early English lancet windows—eight in the north wall of the choir and three huge apertures taking up most of the east gable wall. There are no claustral remains.

ROSCREA

*** Roscrea Heritage Centre: Roscrea Castle and Damer House *(85, 197)*, town center; open M–F, 10:00 A.M.–5:00 P.M.; Sa, 11:00 A.M.–5:00 P.M.; Su, 2:00–5:00 P.M.; optional 45-minute guided tour

Attributed to Archbishop Henri de Londres, this well-preserved ruin was originally a thirteenth-century keepless castle consisting of a polygonal courtyard enclosed by a curtain wall with two D-shaped mural towers and one rectangular, the latter of which served as both gatehouse and residence and was rebuilt in the sixteenth or seventeenth century. It is three storeys high, and the slots for the portcullis can still be seen. In 1315 the castle was granted to Edmund Butler and remained in the hands of the Butler family for nearly four hundred years, until it was sold by the duke of Ormond in 1703.

Damer House *(306)* was built on the castle grounds in 1726, probably by John Damer, a local merchant. After 1798 it and the adjacent buildings were converted into military barracks. Now restored, it is a handsome three-storey Georgian mansion with a particularly fine wooden staircase of hand-carved red pine. On display on the ground floor is the "Kelly Collection," a diverse miscellany of implements and domestic furnishings brought here from a nearby farm.

* St. Cronan's Church and Roscrea Cross *(63, 65)*, town center

All that remains of this twelfth-century church is the west gable, but this is a particularly fine example of Hiberno-Romanesque stone carving. The recessed round-arched doorway is decorated with outward-pointing sawtooth chevrons, surmounted by a steeply pitched false gable (tympanum) with the figure of a cleric, probably meant to represent St. Cronan. On either side of the door are twin blind arcades, also with false gables and outward-pointing sawtooth chevrons. Just to the north stands a badly damaged stone cross of about the same date. On the west face, on a network of animal interlace, appears the figure of Christ wearing a long garment; on the east is a bishop or possibly St. Cronan, reputed founder of the monastery here.

* Roscrea Round Tower *(60)*, town center

As it now stands, the tower is about twenty feet shorter than its original, having been reduced to its present height during the Insurrection of 1798. Its most noteworthy feature is the ship carved on the inner face of the second-storey window (north window jamb), although it is barely discernible from the street below.

* Monaincha Abbey Church *(66, 72)*, 2½ mi E; 1½ mi S of N 7 (to Dublin); signposted; OS ½ 15S 17 88

This is a ruined late-twelfth-century nave-and-chancel church of red sandstone in which canons regular of the Order of St. Augustine were installed sometime before Giraldus Cambrensis mentioned the place in

1185. Especially fine are the Hiberno-Romanesque stone carvings on the west doorway and the chancel arch. Vine scroll and chevrons cover both in profusion. The windows on the south side and the eastern window are thirteenth-century insertions; the ogee light in the western window belongs to the fifteenth, the small sacristy on the north side of the chancel to the fifteenth or sixteenth. Outside the church is a High Cross, consisting of broken fragments cemented together and reerected.

THURLES

* Cathedral of the Assumption (231), town center

Designed by James J. McCarthy and completed in 1872, this building represents a departure from the architect's customary neo-Gothicism. It is Lombardo-Romanesque in style, with a circular domed baptistry on one side of the entrance and a four-storey rectangular tower on the other. The interior is basilical, with massive marble columns, inlaid polychrome mosaics, a painted ceiling, and a heavy baroque altarpiece. The total effect is somewhat oppressive.

* Ballynahow Castle (105), 3½ mi W; N of R 503 (to Rosnult), on grounds of farmhouse; signposted; OS ½ 18S 08 60

Here is a sixteenth-century tower house, unusual in having a circular ground plan. Built by the Purcells, it has five storeys with internal domical vaults. Musket-loops are to be found beside the principal windows. Circular stairs can be climbed to the top.

*** Holy Cross Abbey (118, 126, 127, 140), 4 mi SW; E of R 660 (to Cashel); signposted; OS ½ 18S 09 54; open daytime hours

This Cistercian abbey, founded in 1180 by Donal Mór O'Brien, king of Thomond, and recently restored, offers the visitor a chance to see what a late medieval monastery actually looked like. The original thirteenth-century construction is mostly covered up by a fifteenth-century rebuilding, but the original west wall of the church survives, with traces of lancet windows, as do portions of the nave, the rib vaulting in choir and crossing, and the round-arched doorway from the east end of the church to the cloister-walk. The rest of the church and cloister are of fifteenth-century provenance or twentieth-century rebuilding. Noteworthy features are the Decorated windows, both Flamboyant and reticulated; the sedilia, curiously called "the tomb of the Good Woman's son"; the tomblike stone structure called "the Monks' Waking Place" (of uncertain function); the central tower; and the east and west ranges of the cloister. The cloister arcade has been reconstructed from fragments of the original. The south range is missing. For a while after the dissolution of the monastery in 1540 the abbey was transformed into a secular college.

* **Loughmoe Castle** *(105, 154)*, 6 mi N; 2 mi E of N 62 (to Templemore) through Loughmoe village, through farmyard; signposted; OS ½ 18S 12 67

The south end of this building is a fifteenth- or sixteenth-century tower house with rounded corners. Attached to it on the north side is the ruin of a fine residence, with fireplaces and mullioned windows, built by the Purcells in the seventeenth century.

TIPPERARY

Moor Abbey *(123)*, 9 mi SW; ¾ mi E of Galbally village; N side of R 663 (to Newtown); signposted and visible from road; OS ½ 18R 81 28

Of the Franciscan friary founded in the thirteenth century by Donough Cairbreach O'Brien the only remnant is the fairly high-standing ruined fifteenth-century church consisting of nave, choir, and slender tower. The church was burned by Humphrey Gilbert in 1569, and when the friars returned the following year they were massacred by English troops.

County Wicklow

ASHFORD

** **Mount Usher** *(269)*, S of village center; E side of N 11 (to Wicklow); open M-Sa, 10:30 A.M.-6:00 P.M.; Su, 11:00 A.M.-6:00 P.M.

This pleasant woodland garden of some twenty acres set astride the river Vartry was begun in 1875 and has since been expanded and improved by various members of the Walpole family. Here are over four thousand species of trees, shrubs, and plants collected from all over the world.

BALTINGLASS

* **Baltinglass Abbey** *(71, 140)*, N of town center; on grounds of C of I parish church; gate locked, but interior of ruined church clearly visible

Founded by Dermot MacMurrough, king of Leinster, in 1148, this was the second Cistercian monastery to have been colonized from Mellifont. It was built in the Transitional style between 1148 and 1180. After Henry VIII's dissolution of the Irish monasteries the choir was used for Protestant services, but the church was abandoned and allowed to fall into ruin after 1883. Its most noteworthy features are the square-ended choir with its well-preserved sedilia, the low round arches that separated the choir from the long-gone transepts, the alternate square and cylindrical piers of the roofless nave, and the modest stone carvings on the pier capitals. There are no claustral remains.

Castleruddery *(30)*, 3½ mi NE; ½ mi E of N 81 (to Dublin); about 100 yards from road behind locked gates; signposted; OS ½ 16S 91 94

This circle of boulders set in a low bank is about a hundred feet in diameter.

BLESSINGTON

*** **Russborough** *(196)*, 2 mi S; W of N 81 (to Baltinglass); open June, Sept, Oct, Su, 2:30–5:30 P.M.; July–Aug, daily, 2:30–5:30 P.M.; mandatory 1-hour guided tour

Built in the 1740s for the rich brewer's son, Joseph Leeson, later earl of Milltown, to the design of Richard Castle, this great Palladian mansion consists of a three-storey central block connected to flanking pavilions by curving colonnades of Doric columns. High walls lead out from the pavilions to baroque archways surmounted by cupolas. Inside, all the principal rooms are decorated with plasterwork by the Francini brothers, the great Italian stuccodores of the eighteenth century. After Castle's death in 1751 Francis Bindon completed the interior decoration. The house also contains the splendid Beit collection of Dutch, Spanish, and British paintings, including works by Frans Hals, Jan Vermeer, Jacob Ruisdael, B. E. Murillo, Goya, Thomas Gainsborough, and Sir Henry Raeburn.

* **Athgreany Stone Circle (Piper's Stones)** *(30)*, 8 mi S; E of N 81 (to Baltinglass), through field to brow of hill; signposted "Pipers' Stones"); OS ½ 16N 93 03

Here is a circle of fourteen granite boulders, some standing, some prone, the tallest measuring more than six feet high. About forty yards to the northeast is a single stone (an outlier), which, in local lore, represents the piper to the circle of dancers—all ossified for breaking the sabbath with their revels.

ENNISKERRY

*** **Powerscourt Estate and Gardens** *(196, 269)*, W of village center; open daily, 9:00 A.M.–5:30 P.M.

The fine rectangular Palladian house, built here in the 1730s to the design of Richard Castle, was seriously damaged by fire in 1974 and is now a shell. The gardens, however, remain intact and are magnificent. Especially so are the upper terrace and the Italian garden laid out in the 1840s by Daniel Robertson for the sixth Viscount Powerscourt, who was responsible for collecting most of the statuary scattered throughout. The eighth viscount installed the Japanese Gardens in 1908. Four miles from the house is the spectacular Powerscourt Waterfall, almost four hundred feet high and one of the great scenic wonders of Ireland.

RATHDRUM

** **Avondale** *(218)*, 2 mi S, in Avondale Forest; signposted; open May-June, F-M, 2:00-6:00 P.M.; July-Aug, daily, 2:00-6:00 P.M.

Built before 1779 by Samuel Hayes, this pleasant country house was the home of Charles Stewart Parnell during his childhood and young manhood. It is agreeably, though not sumptuously, furnished, and the walls are replete with placards describing the statesman's career and its collapse.

*** **Glendalough** *(41, 63, 64, 65, 72)*, 7 mi NW, S side of R 756 (to Holywood); OS ½ 16T 10-13 96

This Early Christian and medieval monastic site extends for about two miles along the "Glen of the Two Lakes" from which it takes its name. The monastery was founded by St. Kevin in the sixth century and continued to prosper until early in the thirteenth under the rule of many abbots, the best known of whom was St. Laurence O'Toole, who left here in 1163 to become archbishop of Dublin. Today the ruins are clustered around two separate sites, each endowed with a car park. The easternmost of these is close to the Lower Lake, the westernmost to the Upper Lake. If both are to be visited, at least three hours should be allowed.

Lower Lake

1. **Vistors' Centre**, next to car park: This is the place to start. Recently opened, it offers all kinds of information about the history of the monastery, including a seventeen-minute audiovisual show. Here also are a model of the reconstructed monastery, a twelfth-century High Cross, and some Early Christian grave slabs.

2. **Trinity Church** *(64)*, 100 yards E of Visitors' Centre: This is a nave-and-chancel church dating to the eleventh or twelfth century, with a west porch added later. Windows are both round-headed and pointed. The corbel

stones on the outside corners held wooden rafters, thus performing the same function as antae.

3. St. Saviour's Priory *(65)*, by footpath about ½ mi E of Visitors' Centre, then N (left) into forest past signpost: This is a fine Hiberno-Romanesque nave-and-chancel church dating probably to the mid–twelfth century, when Abbot Laurence O'Toole brought canons regular of the Order of St. Augustine to Glendalough. Note especially the narrow round-headed east windows and the chancel arch with carved sawtooth chevrons and human and animal masks. The north wing of the church is a late medieval addition, and some reconstruction took place in the nineteenth century.

4. The Cathedral *(63)*, 100 yd W of Visitors' Centre, through monastery gateway: The lower parts of the nave of this ruined church date to the eleventh century, as do the antae at each end and the flat-lintelled west doorway. The sacristy to the north of the nave and the chancel to the east (with its Romanesque arched entry) were added in the twelfth century. Along the south wall of the chancel are some Early Christian grave slabs.

5. Round Tower *(60)*, W of Cathedral: Standing about a hundred feet high and with a door in the usual position about ten feet above ground, this is a fine example of a post-Viking monastic bell tower. The conical cap is a restoration.

6. St. Kevin's Church *(49)*, S of Cathedral: This small Early Christian church still boasts its original stone roof, underneath which is a walled loft that keeps the roof from sagging. The belfry at the west end is a later addition, and the west doorway to the nave is blocked. The chancel to the east has been reduced to foundations, but the chancel arch remains above the present entry. The small stone-roofed room next to it is the sacristy.

7. The Priest's House, SW of cathedral: This tiny building with the remains of a Romanesque arch dates probably to the twelfth century and may have been a shrine covering the tomb of St. Kevin.

8. St. Mary's Church *(49)*, 100 yd W of cathedral, over roadside stile and down footpath through field: This is an Early Christian church, perhaps a nunnery. Its flat-headed west doorway has a saltire carved on the underside of the lintel. The nave probably dates to the eleventh century, the chancel to the twelfth or thirteenth. On the outside of the east window is a good example of Romanesque molding.

Upper Lake

1. Reefert Church *(64)*, 200 yd S of car park by signposted footpath: This small ruined nave-and-chancel church dates probably to the eleventh century, though perhaps earlier. The west doorway is covered with a flat lintel; the chancel is small and narrow; the windows are small and round-headed. Projecting corbels on the outside corners once supported rafters. In the churchyard are several rough-hewn cross slabs.

2. St. Kevin's Cell, 100 yd W of Reefert Church, up steep signposted footpath: Only the bare foundations remain of a beehive hut, reputed to have been the saint's dwelling place. The climb would not be worth it except for the glorious view of the Upper Lake from this spot.

SHILLELAGH

* **Rathgall** *(35)*, 6 mi NW, ½ mi N of R 725 (to Tullow, County Carlow); signposted to "Ring of the Rath" and "Rath Geal"; OS ½ 19S 90 73

The outer of these concentric circular drystone walls is seven to ten feet high and encloses an area of more than eighteen acres. It is of iron-age date and, according to tradition, was the seat of the kings of south Leinster. The inner wall is of no earlier provenance than the Middle Ages.

* **Aghowle Church** *(64)*, 5 mi W; 2 mi S of R 725 (to Tullow, County Carlow), by single-track lane through two iron gates; signposted; OS ½ 19S 93 69

This is an unusually long and narrow, high-walled building of the twelfth century, when Romanesque decorative effects were just beginning to appear in Ireland. The two round-headed east windows have chevron carvings on the outside hooded moldings and are flanked externally by little columns projecting from the wall, supported by corbels with animal heads. There is a single window of the same sort in the north wall. The lintelled west doorway has a Romanesque molding on the outside and is arched within. There is a plain granite ringed High Cross northwest of the church.

WICKLOW

* **Black Castle** *(83)*, Wicklow harbor

Poised dramatically on a small rocky promontory jutting into the sea, this is the ruin of a late-twelfth-century castle built probably by Maurice fitz Gerald on land granted him by Strongbow. The remains are too fragmentary to allow deductions as to the size and shape of the solitary keep, but it may have been among the earliest to have been built in stone by the Anglo-Norman invaders.

County Laois

PORTARLINGTON

St. Paul's Church *(179)*, town center; open only for C of I services

This undistinguished nineteenth-century Gothic Revival parish church stands on the site of an earlier building erected in 1696 for the Huguenot settlers brought here by Henri Massue, Marquis de Ruvigny and Lord Galway, one of William III's generals in the War of the Two Kings (1689–91).

Lea Castle *(83, 95)*, 2½ mi W; ½ mi N of R 420 (to Monasterevin); not signposted; access difficult, over locked gate, through abandoned farmyard, and across pasture; OS ½ 16N 57 12

The oldest part of this ruined castle dates to the early thirteenth century and was probably built by Gerald fitz Maurice (FitzGerald), although the large window on the north side may have been a later insertion. In 1316 the castle was burned by Scots under Edward Bruce. In 1650 it was captured by Cromwell's army.

The high-standing but very ruinous keep is rectangular in plan with round corner towers of which only the one at the north corner is still fairly complete. The curtain wall and twin-towered gatehouse (blocked) to the east of the keep are late-thirteenth-century additions. Another gateway, much ruined, is situated between the outer and inner wards.

** Emo Court and Gardens *(197)*, 5½ mi S; ½ mi E of R 419 (to Port Laoise); gardens open daily, 2:30–5:30 P.M.; house open M, 2:00–6:00 P.M.; mandatory 30-minute guided tour through house

Here is a handsome Palladian mansion designed by James Gandon in about 1790 for John Dawson, later first earl of Portarlington, but not completed (by Richard Morrison) until the 1830s. The house consists of a domed central block with Ionic porticos front and back, flanked by twin pavilions. Over the entrance hall is a splendid central domed ceiling, painted blue and gold; the plasterwork throughout is elegant; the furnishings are mostly Regency and early Victorian. The gardens are of the woodland variety with extensive plantings of rhododendrons, laurel, etc. The walled garden unfortunately is closed to the public owing to recent vandalism.

** Coolbanagher (St. John the Evangelist) Church *(176)*, 6 mi S; E side of R 419 (to Port Laoise); open weekdays and for C of I services

This very attractive little church is the only one designed by the great

James Gandon, who was also architect for nearby Emo Court, both built for John Dawson, first earl of Portarlington. The church was completed in 1786. The rectangular nave is small and narrow, with a rounded apse and a gallery at the rear. Large plaster classical urns adorn niches on either side of the nave. The tall steeple is a later addition.

PORTLAOISE

* Dunamase Castle *(84, 85)*, 4 mi E; NE of N 80 (to Stradbally), by single track road, thence by steep footpath from church; not signposted but visible from road; OS ½ 16S 53 98

The castle here is an Anglo-Norman successor to an ancient fortress held by the kings of Leinster. Strongbow inherited it from his father-in-law, King Dermot MacMurrough, and in turn passed it on to his son-in-law William Marshal. The present fragmentary ruins, however, may date to a somewhat later (mid-thirteenth-century) occupation. In 1651 it was taken and slighted by the Cromwellian generals John Hewson and Sir John Reynolds.

The much ruined rectangular keep stands on the highest part of the rock that doubtless was the center of the pre-Norman fortification. It lies within a courtyard entered through a gatehouse, now very ruinous. East of this is another, triangular courtyard with another gatehouse, and still farther east is a D-shaped bailey through which today's visitor approaches the castle. The view in all directions is splendid.

** Timahoe Round Tower *(60)*, 6 mi SE; W of R 426 (to Castlecomer); signposted; OS ½ 16S 54 90

The tower stands ninety-six feet high to the peak of its conical top. Its Romanesque doorway, about ten feet above ground, is unusually ornate for this type of monument. The window in the third storey is also Romanesque. Nearby are the scant remains of a fifteenth-century church.

SOUTHWESTERN IRELAND
County Cork

BALTIMORE

* Sherkin Island Friary *(132)*, 2 mi S, by ferry from Baltimore pier (10 minutes); not signposted but visible from road leading from boat landing; OS ½ 24W 03 26; no entry to interior

This now-ruined church belonged to an Observant Franciscan friary founded in about 1460 by one of the O'Driscolls. Nave, choir, south wing, and tower stand fairly high, and part of the eastern range of the cloister survives. Most of the tracery is missing from the Decorated east window. The grounds are untended.

BANTRY

*** Bantry House *(197, 200)*, W of town center; S of N 71 (to Skibbereen); signposted; open daily, 9:00 A.M.–6:00 P.M.

The original construction here dates to about 1750; a wing was added by Richard White in 1770; the front with its red brick Corinthian pilasters was the result of an early-nineteenth-century remodelling that also included the balustraded roof parapet. The house served as army headquarters during the abortive French landing in Bantry Bay in 1796. The elegant and exotic furnishings were collected mostly by a succeeding Richard White, Viscount Berehaven, who filled the house with *objets d'art* collected during his extensive European travels in the 1840s. The surrounding gardens are gorgeous, and the view of the bay is glorious.

BUTTEVANT

* Buttevant Friary *(122)*, town center; signposted; no entry to interior

Lying within the grounds of St. Mary's (Roman Catholic) Church are the ruins of a Franciscan friary founded in about 1250. Although entry to the ruined friary church is barred, the interior is clearly visible through the west doorway. It is a long, rectangular building with a south wing. Throughout are numerous Early English lancets, some of them blocked up when new windows were inserted in the fifteenth century. There are no claustral remains.

Ballybeg Priory *(118)*, ½ mi S; E of N 20 (to Mallow), across road from large quarry; signposted and visible from road; OS ½ 21B 54 08

Here are the rather scant remains of a priory of Augustinian canons founded by Philip de Barry in 1229 or 1237. Of the thirteenth-century church little is left of the east end, though the west gable is standing and is pierced by two high lancets. The tower dates to the fifteenth century. The claustral buildings have mostly disappeared. Southeast of the church stands a fine beehive-shaped dovecote, its interior still lined with compartments for nesting fowl.

** **Liscarroll Castle** *(88)*, 6½ mi NW; E of R 522 (to Newcastle West); not signposted but visible from road; OS ½ 21R 45 12; entry barred, but inner court clearly visible through the gatehouse archway

This is the substantial ruin of a thirteenth-century keepless courtyard castle built by the de Barrys. Three of the four original corner towers are still standing, as is the twin-towered gatehouse (modified in the fifteenth century) with traces of the portcullis. Opposite stands another square tower. The curtain wall (uncrenellated) stands high on all four sides.

Kilcolman Castle *(144, 148, 155)*, 7 mi NE; 3 mi N of R 522 (to Mitchelstown) from Doneraile, in grounds of wildfowl refuge; poorly signposted to "Spenser's Castle" and not visible from road; OS ½ 21R 42 21

This fragmentary ivy-covered ruin, probably built by the sixth earl of Desmond in the fifteenth century, was for nine years (1588 and 1591–98) the home of the Elizabethan poet Edmund Spenser. It was here he wrote three books of *The Faerie Queen* as well as other works. So little remains of the castle, and it is so hard to locate, that only the most avid Spenser enthusiast will consider it worth the effort.

CLONAKILTY

* **West Cork Museum** *(259)*, town center

This is a fairly typical local museum, distinguished for its collection of memorabilia associated with Michael Collins and other west Cork soldiers of the Anglo-Irish and Irish civil wars.

** **Timoleague Friary** *(123, 128)*, 6 mi E; in Timoleague village center; signposted and visible from road

Here are the substantial ruins of a late-thirteenth-century Franciscan friary. The choir dates from about the time of the friary's foundation, but the nave was extended westward in the fifteenth century, at which time the tower and south wing were also added. The claustral buildings are unusually well preserved. Remains of the sacristy and chapter house in the east range are still visible, as is the well-lighted frater in the north range. On the west a large walled courtyard still survives.

* **Kinneagh Round Tower** *(60)*, 12 mi N; S side of R 688 (to Cappeen) at W end of churchyard; signposted; OS ½ 24W 33 57

About sixty-five feet high, this tower is unique in having a hexagonal base and a round top. The doorway is square-headed, indicating perhaps a tenth-century date. The tower can be climbed to the top.

* **Ballynacarriga Castle** *(104)*, 10½ mi NW; 2 mi S of R 586 (to Dunmanway from Ballineen); signposted and visible from road; OS ½ 24W 29 51; key available at The Castle Bar next door

Here are the substantial ruins of a four-storey square tower house, built probably in the sixteenth century by Randal Hurley. Machicolated turrets are placed at diagonally opposite corners, and remnants of a round corner bawn tower survive. The circular steps can be climbed to the top storey, entry to which is barred.

CLOYNE

* **Cloyne Cathedral and Round Tower** *(60, 113, 178)*, village center; interior to tower closed pending building repairs

The foundations of this cruciform church are of thirteenth-century date, but except for the surviving lancet windows the superstructure is modern. The chancel serves as the Church of Ireland parish church. In the foyer is a fine alabaster recumbent statue of Bishop George Berkeley, who held this see from 1734 to 1753 after his return from Rhode Island.

Standing opposite the cathedral, the Round Tower rises about ninety-five feet to its battlemented top (presumably a replacement for the original conical roof).

COBH

** **St. Colman's Cathedral** *(230)*, town center

Designed by the firm of Pugin and Ashlin and opened in 1879 (though not completed until 1919), this huge neo-Gothic building with a single tower at the southwest corner and a hexagonal apse stands on a steep hill overlooking Cobh harbor. It is more or less Early English in style, with slender clustered columns, lancet windows, elaborate stone carving, and a fine rose window in the west gable.

CORK

** **St. Fin Barre's (C of I) Cathedral** *(225)*, O'Sullivan's Quay

Begun in 1863 and completed in 1878 to the design of the English architect William Burges, this is a splendid neo-Gothic cruciform building in the French style on the outside but with an essentially Early English interior. Its three high spires dominate the Cork cityscape; the rose window in the western gable and the multitude of stone carvings are especially noteworthy.

* St. Finbarr's, South (South Chapel) *(173)*, Dunbar Street, city center

This is one of the earlier of the surviving post-Reformation Roman Catholic churches in Ireland. Built in 1766, its interior is typically Georgian in style and very pretty. The south chapel was added in 1809. The figure of *The Dead Christ* is by John Hogan, a mid-nineteenth-century sculptor.

* Crawford Municipal Art Gallery *(190, 191, 222, 268)*, Emmet Place, city center; open M–F, 10:00 A.M.–5:00 P.M.; Sa, 9:00 A.M.–1:00 P.M.

The central portion of this building was originally the Cork Custom House, erected in 1724. The rest is of early-twentieth-century provenance. It now houses a good, but not very well displayed, selection of Irish paintings, including those by James Barry, Nathaniel Grogan, James Sleator, Daniel Maclise, Sir William Orpen, Maurice MacGonigal, William John Leech, Paul Henry, Sean Keating, Walter Osborne, James Humbert Craig, Charles Lamb, George Russell (AE), and Jack B. Yeats.

* Church of the Most Holy Trinity *(220)*, Father Mathew Quay

Designed by George Richard Pain and begun in 1832, this otherwise undistinguished neo-Gothic building is noteworthy for its association with Father Theobold Mathew, OSFC, the "Apostle of Temperance" and superior of the Capuchin monastery for which it was built. The tower and spire, as well as the sanctuary, are later additions. It is usually referred to locally as "Father Mathew's Church."

Father Mathew Monument *(220)*, S end of Patrick Street Bridge

Erected in 1864, this is a more-than-life-sized statue of Father Theobold Mathew (1790–1856), founder of the Irish temperance movement.

*** Cork Public Museum *(27, 32, 42, 202, 238, 256)*, Fitzgerald Park

This small building, situated within a very pretty public park, is replete with materials illustrative of Irish prehistory and history down to the 1920s. On the ground floor are exhibits of Cork silver and glass and memorabilia of the insurrection of 1798, the Young Ireland insurrection of 1848, the Fenian uprising of 1867, and the Anglo-Irish War and Civil War of 1916–22 (including a display of mementos of Terence McSwiney, mayor of Cork, who died as the result of a seventy-four-day hunger strike). On the first floor are bronze-age axes and palstaves, urns and food vessels, finds from nearby ring-forts, iron-age horse trappings and brooches, model bronze-age houses, a rare runic (Viking) inscribed stone, Ogham stones from County Kerry, a facsimile of the *Book of Kells*, and numerous artifacts from medieval Cork.

* University College, Cork *(233, 249)*, Western Road

The earliest building in one of Sir Robert Peel's "godless colleges" was the open courtyard facing Western Road, built in 1846–49 to the design of Thomas Deane and Benjamin Woodward. The most interesting structure on the grounds, however, is the **** Honan Chapel** *(249)*, built in 1915. It is Hiberno-Romanesque in style, with round-arched narrow stained-glass windows by Sarah Purser and Harry Clarke, a fine floor mosaic representing the River of Life, and wall mosaics of the Stations of the Cross. Other noteworthy features are the tapestry reredos, the modernistic wood-carved lectern, the president's chair, and the bride and groom chairs to accommodate the many weddings held here each year.

** St. Anne Shandon (C of I) Church *(177)*, Church Street, north of city center; open weekdays and for services

This is an attractive small church with a handsome barrel-vaulted ceiling over the nave. It was begun in 1722, probably to the design of the local builder, John Coltsman. The high west tower was added later. Visitors may climb its steps and ring the bells for which the church is famous.

*** Blarney Castle *(104)*, 4 mi NW; S side of R 617 in Blarney village center; signposted; open M–Sa, 9:00 A.M.–6:30 P.M.; Su, 9:30 A.M.–5:30 P.M.

This well-known and well-preserved, though partially ruined, "castle" is in fact a tower house built by Cormac MacCarthy of Muskerry in about 1446. It is L-shaped in plan, four storeys (eighty-five feet) high, rising to a stepped-battlemented parapet. It is the last-named feature that is the most interesting, partly because of its structural uniqueness and partly because of the legend of the Blarney stone, the kissing of which is supposed to endow eloquence. Here the stepped battlements project more than two feet beyond the wall heads, thus forming a continuous machicolation borne by corbels on the outside of the building. The Blarney stone is the base of one of these battlements. To kiss it the visitor lies on his back with his head positioned downward over the open space of the machicolation. The origin of the tradition is uncertain.

** Kilcrea Friary *(132)*, 7 mi W; ½ mi S of N 22 (to Macroom), E of Farran; signposted; OS ½ 21W 51 68

Here is a high-standing ruin of a fifteenth-century friary founded by Cormac Laídir MacCarthy for Franciscan Observants. Nave, choir, south wing, and tower are all well preserved, as are the claustral buildings north of the church, though the ambulatory itself has disappeared.

* **Riverstown House** *(195)*, 8½ mi NE, in Glanmire; ¼ mi E of N 8 (to Fermoy); open by appointment only; tel (021) 821-205; mandatory 30-minute guided tour

Built in the eighteenth century for Jemmet Browne, bishop of Cork, this is a plain, moderately sized country house of no particular distinction except for the elegant interior plasterwork by Paul and Philip Francini, comparable to their masterpieces at Castletown and Russborough.

*** **Fota House** *(190, 191, 211)*, 10 mi E; 1½ mi S of N 25 (to Midleton) from Carrigtohill via R 625 and R 624 (to Cobh); open M–Sa, 11:00 A.M.–6:00 P.M.; Su, 2:00–6:00 P.M.

This fine Regency mansion with its Doric portico and elegant rooms was originally a hunting lodge but was expanded in the 1820s by Richard Morrison for the owner, John Smith-Barry. In 1975 the estate was purchased by University College, Cork. In addition to its superb early-nineteenth-century furnishings, the house contains numerous Irish paintings (especially landscapes), arguably the best collection outside the National Gallery in Dublin. Included among the artists represented are Charles Jervis, Nathaniel Grogan, Robert Carver, Thomas Sautell Roberts, James Latham, George Barret, Hugh Douglas Hamilton, William Ashford, Daniel Maclise, James Arthur O'Connor, Francis Danby, Nicholas Crowley, Edwin Hayes, and George Petrie. On the grounds are magnificent gardens, an arboretum started in the 1820s, and a seventy-acre wildlife park installed by the Royal Zoological Society.

FERMOY

* **Castlelyons Friary** *(122)*, 3½ mi SE by minor roads to Castlelyons village; OS ½ 22W 84 93

These extensive ruins are those of a Carmelite friary founded in the early fourteenth century by John de Barry. Three walls remain of the nave-and-chancel church, as do the square central tower and a recessed west doorway topped by twin cusped lancets. Both east and west ranges of the cloister stand fairly high. All this was probably not built until about a century after the friary's foundation.

** **Labbacallee Tomb** (26), 4 mi NW; 1 mi NW of R 512 (to Kilmallock), E side of E fork of road to Glanworth; signposted from junction of 2 roads, both leading to Glanworth, and visible from road; OS ½ 22R 78 02

Known locally as the "Hag's Bed," this very large wedge-shaped tomb (perhaps the largest of its kind in Ireland) has three capstones sloping backward and resting on numerous uprights tending to converge at the rear. (Hence the term *wedge grave*.) Underneath the capstones are two burial chambers, the larger in front. The tomb is surrounded by a kerbed cairn with some of the stones still in place.

** **Bridgetown Priory** (118, 127), 10 mi W; 1¾ mi S of N 72 (to Mallow) from Castletownroche; signposted; OS ½ 22W 69 00

Here is a ruined priory of Augustinian canons founded in the early thirteenth century by Alexander FitzHugh Roche. Good Early English lancets light the choir. The nave is intersected by a transverse wall, probably installed in the later Middle Ages to shorten the nave after the number of canons had diminished. At the west end is a square tower with a fireplace in the upper storey. This may have been the prior's or commendator's lodging and was probably installed in the fifteenth century. Remains of the east and south ranges of the cloister stand fairly high, with a well-preserved integrated ambulatory in the former and a substantial portion of the frater (with Early English lancets) in the latter. The tower next to it was possibly the canons' dayroom. Unfortunately the grounds are untended, and there are no historic markers to guide the visitor around these somewhat confusing buildings.

*** **Anne's Grove** (269), 11 mi W; 1½ mi N of N 72 (to Mallow) from Castletownroche; signposted; open M-F, 10:00 A.M.-5:00 P.M.; Su, 1:00-7:00 P.M.

Although the eighteenth-century house here is not open to the public, the extensive gardens beyond it are a delight. The woodland garden has a fine collection of rhododendrons, magnolias, etc., and along the river Awbeg a variety of exotic water plants flourishes on one side of the path, while a cliffside rock garden graces the other. Best of all is the walled garden with its lush and variegated herbaceous borders.

* **Conna Castle** (104), 10 mi SE; 2 mi S of N 72 (to Lismore) through Knockmourney to E end of Conna village; OS ½ 22W 93 94; entry is normally (but not always) barred

Standing on a high bluff overlooking the river Bride, this tower house was built in about 1500 by the earl of Desmond. In the early seventeenth century it was granted to Richard Boyle, earl of Cork. Assaulted but not taken by Cromwell in 1650, it was burned three years later. The building is five storeys high and battlemented. The usual machicolation protrudes from the east wall high over the doorway.

KANTURK

** Kanturk Castle *(154)*, 1 mi S; W side of R 579 (to Cork); signposted; OS ½ 21W 18 02

This roofless ruin is rectangular in plan and four storeys high with massive five-storey square towers at each corner. It was begun by Dermot MacDonagh MacCarthy, lord of Duhallow, about 1609, but never completed, probably owing to the builder's financial difficulties. It is well fenestrated with mullioned windows in the Jacobean manner and has numerous fireplaces and a fine Renaissance doorway on the north side.

* Tullylease Church *(50)*, 12 mi N; 1 mi E of R 579 (to Broadford); signposted to Tullylease village; OS ½ 21R 38 18

The nave of this monastic church dates to the twelfth and thirteenth centuries, the chancel to the fifteenth. The most interesting feature of the site is the collection of Early Christian grave slabs incorporated into the wall. Of these the best is the very early (probably eighth-century) stone enjoining "whoever read this inscription, pray for [Saint] Berichter [QUICUMQUE LEGERIT HUNC TITULUM ORAT PRO BERECHTUIRE]," presumably the missionary founder of the monastery here.

KINSALE

*** St. Multose Church *(116)*, town center; open daily

Built in the early thirteenth century in the Transitional style between Romanesque and Early English, this fine aisled church with a north wing now serves as a Protestant (Church of Ireland) parish church. The Romanesque square tower at the northeast corner is probably the oldest part of the building. The lancet windows are Early English, though not all necessarily belonging to the original period of construction. There is a piscina in the south wall of the choir, an interesting collection of seventeenth-century grave slabs and a stone reredos in the south wall of the nave, and a set of eighteenth-century stocks in the foyer.

*** Charles Fort *(166, 167)*, 1 mi SE of town center, on southeast bank of harbor; signposted; open daily

Designed by the architect William Robinson, built in 1678-81 under the auspices of Roger Boyle, earl of Orrery, and dedicated to the reigning monarch, Charles II, by the duke of Ormond, this fortress is modelled on those erected for King Louis XIV of France by the great military engineer Sebastien de Vauban. The grounds are enclosed by a star-shaped wall with five major bastions, each with gun embrasures inside as well as on top of the walls. Outside the main ramparts is a dry moat protected by a counter-scarp (exterior) wall. Inside are the original magazine, guard house, and governor's house as well as ruins of nineteenth-century barracks. During the War of the Two Kings, the fort fell to John Churchill, earl of Marlborough, in October 1690 after a thirteen-day siege.

* James Fort *(149, 167)*, 1 mi S of town center, on southwest bank of harbor; signposted; open daily

Built by Lord Mountjoy in 1601, this ruined complex of stone buildings lies within a modified star-shaped enclosing wall surrounded by an earthen ditch and moat. Grounds are well tended, and the view of the harbor is impressive. Like Charles Fort (above), James Fort was captured by the earl of Marlborough in October 1890 during the War of the Two Kings.

MACROOM

Michael Collins Monument *(258)*, 10 mi SE; W end of Beal na mBlath, S side of R 585 (to Cappean), 3½ mi SW of Crookstown

This high stone roadside crucifix has the name Micael O'Coileam (Michael Collins) as well as the date of his assassination (22 August 1922) inscribed at the base.

Ballyvourney Cross *(50)*, 10 mi W; ½ mi N of N 22 (to Killarney) from E end of Ballyvourney village; not signposted; OS ½ 21R 21 78

Within a fenced enclosure in a field on the east side of the minor road from Ballyvourney village is this Early Christian pillar inscribed with a cross of arcs and a small figure bearing a cross in the upper left corner.

MALLOW

** Mallow Castle *(144, 145)*, town center

Begun by Sir Thomas Norris, president of Munster, in the late sixteenth century and probably completed by his son-in-law Sir John Jephson, this is the well-preserved ruin of a four-storey, gabled, castellated house with polygonal turrets at the two front corners and square turrets at the center, back, and front. The multitude of mullioned windows indicates that it was built for comfort as well as defense. On the well-groomed grounds also are the stump of a thirteenth-century castle and an early-nineteenth-century manor house (not open to the public).

MITCHELSTOWN

Labbamolaga Church *(49)*, 6 mi NW; ½ mi N of R 517 (to Kilfinane), in churchyard on E side of road; not signposted; OS ½ 22R 76 18

Of the two church ruins on this site only the smaller dates to the Early Christian period. It has a flat-lintelled west doorway of only three stones and antae projecting from the west gable wall. On the south side of the church is an Early Christian grave slab; also the remains of a small stone cross, presumably another grave marker.

ROSS CARBERY

*** Drombeg *(30)*, 3 mi W; ½ mi S of B 597 (to Glandore); signposted; OS ½ 24W 25 35

This is a small circle of sixteen standing stones and one horizontal (recumbent). The two tallest are in the northeast quadrant; the recumbent stone is in the southwest. Radiocarbon testing indicates that the site was in use as late as the eighth century A.D., but this does not preclude a bronze-age date of construction, which would be the normal provenance for this type of stone circle. To the southwest of the circle itself are the foundation stones of two circular huts and a communal cooking pit and hearth (*fulacht fiadh*) of probable iron-age date. These were used to cook meat by first dropping preheated stones into the stone trough until the water therein was brought to a boil.

** Coppinger's Court *(155)*, 3 mi W; ½ mi S of Glandore Road from W end of S-curved stone bridge; not signposted; OS ½ 24W 26 36

Built in the early seventeenth century by the Cork city merchant Sir Walter Coppinger, this is the substantial, now-ivy-covered ruin of a U-plan Jacobean manor house with an added wing at the back. It was defended by machicolations at the sides of each wing, is well fenestrated with mullioned windows, and is well supplied with elegant tall chimney stacks.

SKIBBEREEN

** **Knockdrum** *(36)*, 3 mi E; S of R 596 from 1 mi W of Castletownshend, by footpath to hilltop; signposted; OS ½ 24W 17 31

This ring-fort measures about eighty-five yards in diameter and is encircled by a drystone wall, now only three feet high. Inside is the entrance to a souterrain.

YOUGHAL

*** **St. Mary's Church** *(115, 129, 156)*, top of Church Street, town center; open daily

Now in use for Protestant (Church of Ireland) services, this is the second largest medieval Irish parish church still standing, though it was converted to collegiate status in 1468. It was built in the thirteenth century, modified in the fourteenth and fifteenth, and rebuilt in the nineteenth. It is cruciform in plan, with an aisled nave and a fine Decorated (fifteenth-century) east window. In the nave is a fourteenth-century octagonal baptismal font, and in the north transept is a fine effigy of Thomas Parish holding a falcon. In the south transept is the enormous and elaborately carved tomb of Richard Boyle, first earl of Cork, who died in the mid–seventeenth century. Along with the effigy of the earl himself are carved representations of his two wives, one mother-in-law, and sixteen children.

** **Town Wall** *(93)*, town center; up steps from Clock Gate in Main Street and then east as far as the Collegiate Church of St. Mary; not signposted but clearly visible from street and from St. Mary's churchyard

This is the best-preserved medieval town wall in Ireland, dating probably from the fifteenth century but refortified in 1642. At the top of the steps leading up from the Clock Gate is the "Banshee Tower," one of the thirteen original mural turrets. East of it are the "Montmorency Tower" and the "Half Moon Tower," also original. At the end, behind the church, is a fourth tower erected in the nineteenth century.

* **Molana Abbey** *(72)*, 4½ mi N in County Waterford; 2 mi N of N 25 (to Dungarvan) from W end of Blackwater Bridge; through twin gatehouses on E side of minor road to Glendine Church (signposted), then about ¼ mi by private road and footpath along Blackwater riverbank; not signposted; OS ½ 15X 08 83

In a setting of unsurpassed sylvan beauty, this much ruined and untended ivy-clad Augustinian abbey, founded in about 1170 on the site of an Early Christian monastery, stands close to the edge of the slow-flowing river Blackwater. The rectangular church is lighted by ten lancets; all four cloister walls to the south are still visible; so are the remains of the chapter house in the east range and the refectory and kitchen in the south. North of the choir is a high building that was probably the abbot's lodging.

*** **Ardmore Cathedral and Round Tower** *(43, 60, 114)*, 9 mi E, in County Waterford; 3 mi SE of N 25 (to Dungarvan); signposted; entry barred; OS ½ 22X 19 77

The ruined cathedral church dates to the late twelfth or early thirteenth century and is a fine example of Irish Romanesque architecture. Inside, the round-headed west window is recessed, and a blind arcade stretches along the north wall. In the chancel are two Ogham stones. The best feature here, however, is on the exterior west wall, where sculptured figures appear under two tiers of arches. In the upper row the archangel Michael can be seen weighing the souls of the dead; in the lower are representations of Adam and Eve, King Solomon's judgment in the dispute between the two mothers, and the Adoration of the Magi.

Nearby St. Declan's Oratory is a small rectangular drystone building with antae east and west, a lintelled flat-headed west doorway, and a modern north doorway and roof. (St. Declan is traditionally believed to have preceded St. Patrick in this part of Ireland—a not implausible hypothesis.)

The Round Tower is more than ninety feet high and has a conical top. It is one of the best preserved of its species in Ireland, though unusual in having three offset string courses, above each of which the tower narrows slightly in circumference, and a roll molding high above the door.

The tower was the scene of the capture by an English army in 1642 of about 150 Irish Confederates, most of whom were hanged on the spot.

County Kerry

Ardfert

*** **Ardfert Cathedral** *(43, 66, 114, 128)*, N of town center

Chancel, nave, and south chapel of this high-standing ruin were built in the thirteenth century. Noteworthy are the triple lancet windows in the east gable of the chancel, the pair of twin lancets in the north wall of the nave, the row of nine in the south wall, the effigy (probably of a bishop) in the northwest corner, and the remains of a triple-sedilia in the south wall. The stepped battlements and the south wing of the church are fifteenth-century additions. The oldest and most interesting part of the church is the

Romanesque west doorway, surmounted by a semicircular arch carved with deep outward-pointing sawtooth chevrons. On the west wall, flanking the doorway, are delicately carved blind arcades. West of here are two small chapels with typically Irish high-pitched roofs. The nearest is Temple-na-Hoe, a small two-chambered church, also Romanesque. The building next to it is of fifteenth-century date.

** Ardfert Friary *(122)*, NE of town center; signposted

These substantial ruins are those of a Franciscan friary founded in about 1253 by Thomas fitz Maurice fitz Raymond (FitzGerald), lord of Kerry. Nave and choir of the church date to the thirteenth century, as indicated by the large number of Early English lancet windows. The south wing of the church, the tower at the west end, and the well-preserved claustral buildings date to the fifteenth century.

Casement Memorial *(253)*, 3 mi N, on Banna Strand; signposted

This simple obelisk with Sir Roger Casement's profile in low relief stands close to the spot where he was landed from a German submarine on Good Friday (21 April) 1916. The wooded ring-fort where he was taken prisoner shortly afterward lies about four miles to the north.

BALLYBUNNION

** Rattoo Round Tower *(60)*, 6 mi S; ¼ mi E of R 551 (to Bellyheige) from ½ mi S of Ballyduff; not signposted but visible from road; OS ½ 17Q 88 33

More than eighty feet high, this is a very well-preserved tower with a round-headed doorway. Nearby is a fifteenth-century church.

BALLYLONGFORD

Lislaughtin Friary *(132)*, 1 mi N; signposted; OS ½ 17R 00 46

Founded for Franciscans in 1478 by John O'Connor Kerry, this is now a badly ruined relic, consisting of nave, choir, and south wing plus scanty remains of the claustral buildings to the north. The windows nevertheless display some fine Decorated tracery, and there is a good triple sedilia in the south wall of the choir.

** Carrigafoyle Castle *(104)*, 3 mi N; N of R 551 (to Ballybunnion) from W end of Ballylongford village; not signposted; OS ½ 17Q 99 48

At the edge of the south bank of the Shannon estuary, this ruined five-storey tower house was built by O'Connor Kerry in the fifteenth or sixteenth century. Three sides are complete to the parapets, but the fourth is totally demolished, leaving the interior open—much in the manner of a dollhouse. The northwest corner of the bawn wall still stands. Originally it enclosed a dock that allowed boats to tie up close to the tower. Beautiful views of the Shannon are afforded from the parapets to which the well-preserved circular staircase still leads.

CAHERDANIEL

* Derrynane Stone *(43)*, 2 mi W; ½ mi S of N 70 (to Waterville), E of road to Derrynane House; not signposted but visible from road; OS ½ 24V 54 59

Along one edge of this upright pillar, about eight feet high, are clearly incised Ogham markings.

*** Derrynane *(227)*, 6 mi W; 2 mi SW of N 70 (to Waterville); signposted; open M–Sa, 9:00 A.M.–6:00 P.M., Su, 11:00 A.M.–7:00 P.M.

Rebuilt in 1825 by Daniel O'Connell, this house was his country seat for most of his active political career. Well preserved and authentically furnished, it now serves as an O'Connell museum, with numerous portraits of "the Liberator" and his family and sundry memorabilia, including a handbill typically urging his followers to behave peacefully.

CAHIRCIVEEN

** Cahergal *(37)*, 2½ mi NW; N of road leading left (west) after crossing bridge; signposted; OS ½ 20V 45 81

This well-preserved but untended drystone ring-fort (cashel) is about ninety feet in diameter. Interior stone staircases mount the inside walls to the high ramparts. Inside are the remains of a rectangular drystone house and a beehive hut *(clochán)*. Date of construction is estimated to be between A.D. 500 and 900, but it could have been earlier, during the Iron Age.

** Leacanabuaile *(37)*, 3½ mi NW; N of road leading left (west) after crossing bridge; signposted; OS ½ 20V 44 82

Currently undergoing restoration, this drystone ring-fort has an interior diameter of about eighty feet and walls about six feet high at the most. The interior face of the wall has steps leading upward, and there are two mural chambers. Inside are foundations of a *clochán* (beehive hut) and another building; also the entrance to a souterrain. An estimated date of A.D. 500 to 900 has been posted, but an Iron-Age date is possible.

DINGLE

* **Ballintaggart Ogham Stones** *(43)*, 2 mi E; ½ mi S of R 559 (to Tralee) from red brick nursing home to T-junction and then ¼ mi E (left), in fenced field on left of minor road; not signposted; OS ½ 20V 49 01

Inside a circular stone wall are nine stones with Ogham markings. They are unusual in that most are recumbent and rounded, thus lacking the usual sharp edge, which normally served as stem line for Ogham incisions.

*** **Dunbeg** *(35, 37)*, 7½ mi W; S of R 559 (to Slea Head); signposted; OS ½ 20Q 35 97

This is one the best preserved and most accessible of Ireland's Iron-Age promontory forts. Hugging a coastal cliff falling off into the Atlantic, the fort is guarded on the landward side by a series of earthen banks with intervening ditches and a massive drystone wall almost 150 feet long. A lintelled doorway cuts through the wall, and just inside the entrance are flanking mural chambers, presumably used as sentry boxes. Within the enclosure are the remains of a *clochán* (beehive hut) still standing to a height of about six feet. A souterrain lies underneath the wall, with openings on either side of it.

* **Cahir Murphy (Cathair na Mairtineach) Clocháin (Beehive Huts)** *(48)*, 8 mi W, N of R 559 (to Sleahead), ¼ mi E of ford; signposted; OS ½ 20V 34 97; on private property, small fee charged

Here, within a stone-fenced enclosure, are three drystone corbelled beehive huts, one completely roofed, one almost complete to the top, and the third unroofed but rising about ten feet above ground. Also on the grounds is a souterrain. Mural chambers can be seen within the enclosing wall.

*** **Gallarus Oratory** *(48)*, 5 mi NW; E of road to Ballydavid; signposted; OS ½ 20V 41 05

This is the best preserved of all Early Christian oratories, possibly dating to the seventh or eighth century, though perhaps later. It is rectangular in plan, measuring ten by fifteen feet internally, with walls 3½ feet thick, corbelled upward to form a vault. In appearance the building thus resembles an upturned boat. In the east gable is a small round-headed window; in the west, a doorway with inward-leaning jambs supporting a horizontal lintel. Over the lintel on the inside are two jutting stones pierced with holes, from which probably a door was hung. A cross-inscribed stone stands nearby.

* Caherdorgan Fort *(48)*, 5½ mi NW; W of road to Ballydavid; not signposted; OS ½ 20V 40 05

Here, within a single outer stone wall, is a cluster of five *clocháin* (beehive huts) with walls reaching as high as six feet. Inside one hut is a souterrain. The word *fort* is a misnomer; this was probably nothing more than a walled village.

** Kilmalkedar Church *(43, 66)*, 6 mi NW; E of road to Ballydavid; signposted; OS ½ 20V 40 06

This is a mostly roofless two-chambered stone church with antae and a finial on the west gable, built in the mid–twelfth century. Good Romanesque carvings adorn the west doorway and the chancel arch, and animal heads are to be seen on top of the antae. Around the interior walls of the nave runs a blind (i.e., integrated into the wall) colonnade. Inside the church is a stone carved with the letters of the Latin alphabet. In the churchyard are an early sundial, a stone cross, and an Ogham stone.

** Reask (Riasc) *(50)*, 7 mi NW; S of road to Ballyferriter and about ½ mi E of that village; signposted; OS ½ 20Q 37 04

These low drystone foundations are the remains of an Early Christian settlement. Here are the lower courses of several *clocháin* (beehive huts) and of an oratory inside a low wall of unmortared stone (a cashel). The outstanding feature of the site is the pillar stone inscribed with a cross enclosed in a circle, beneath which are spiral decorations.

Dún an Oir *(143)*, 9 mi NW; 3 mi N of Ballyferriter; signposted "Fort del Oro"; OS ½ 20A 35 08

Here, overlooking Smerwick harbor, on the site of an Iron-Age promontory fort, James Fitzmaurice FitzGerald landed with a tiny band of mercenary soldiers in papal pay in July 1579 in the hope of inciting rebellion against the Protestant queen of England (Elizabeth I). The effort failed, and Fitzmaurice was killed in a skirmish. The following year a larger contingent of Spanish and Italian troops, recruited by the pope to assist the earl of Desmond in his rebellion, established a fort at the same place. The English besieged it by land and sea, the foreigners surrendered, and the lord deputy, Leonard Grey, delegated to Sir Walter Raleigh the task of massacring all six hundred of its defenders.

KILLARNEY

*** St. Mary's Cathedral *(230)*, town center

Consecrated in 1855, this is a splendid cruciform Roman Catholic cathedral church in the Early English style, designed by the great English Gothicist Augustus Welby Northmore Pugin. In the 1970s the plasterwork was removed from the interior and the brickwork replaced with stone, giving it an austere appearance, which, though appealing to the modern eye, would probably not have met the approval of the original architect, with his Victorian propensity for heavy ornamentation.

* Ross Castle *(104, 162)*, 1½ mi S; W of N 71 (to Kenmare); signposted; OS ½ 20V 94 89

Situated at the edge of Lough Leane, this is a high-standing fifteenth- or sixteenth-century ruined tower house built by O'Donoghue Ross. It stands inside a bawn wall, two of whose corner towers survive. The lower annex was added in the eighteenth century. In 1651 the stronghold was threatened by an amphibious attack from the lake by the Cromwellian general Ludlow and surrendered. Magnificent view of the lower lake and surrounding hills.

* Innisfallen Abbey *(63)*, 2 mi SW, in Lough Leane; access by boat from Ross Castle; OS ½ 20V 93 89

The largest of the three ruined buildings on this island is the tenth-century abbey church with antae and a lintelled doorway (restored) in the west gable wall. The eastern third of the church, however, is a later addition. Of a later date still (probably twelfth century) is the little oratory close to the landing pier. This has a small round-headed east window and a good Romanesque west doorway decorated with animal heads and saw-tooth chevrons. North of the abbey church are buildings of an even later, medieval, date. The view from here of Ireland's most famous lake is alone worth the boat trip.

*** Muckross House *(212, 216)*, 6 mi S; W side of N 71 (to Kenmare); open 17 Mar–30 June, Sept–Oct, M–Sa, 9:00 A.M.–6:00 P.M., Su, 10:00 A.M.–6:00 P.M.; July–Aug, M–Sa, 9:00 A.M.–7:00 P.M., Su, 10:00 A.M.–7:00 P.M.

This splendid many-gabled, many-chimneyed, neo-Tudor mansion was built in 1843 for Henry Arthur Herbert to the design of William Burn of Edinburgh. The porte cochere was a later (1870) addition. The grounds overlooking lower Lake Killarney are laid out beautifully with extensive plantings of rhododendrons, azaleas, etc. "Jaunting cars" for trips through the grounds are available at the roadside.

The house contains the Museum of Kerry Life, with excellent photos and placards describing the history and prehistory of southwestern Ireland; the development of vernacular housing in the nineteenth century; and numerous workshops, including a creamery, bookbindery, looms, printing shop, etc.

*** **Muckross Friary** *(132)*, 3 mi S; ¼ mi W of N 71 (to Kenmare); signposted; OS ½ 21V 98 87

Here are the splendid and unusually well-maintained ruins of a fifteenth-century Franciscan Observant friary, founded by Donal MacCarthy. Nave, choir, south chapel, and tower stand high. The windows show a fine display of switch-line tracery. North of the church lies an unusually well-preserved cloister. The ambulatory is integrated into the adjacent ranges of buildings and hence covered. Dormitory, kitchen, and refectory are well fenestrated, and between the latter two are the remains of a massive double fireplace. The surrounding grounds are kept beautifully, and the site may be reached by a horse-drawn "jaunting car" for hire at the roadside.

* **Aghadoe Church** *(66)*, 4 mi NW; 1 mi N of R 562 (to Killorglin) at E end of Aghadoe village; signposted; OS ½ 20V 93 93

The western doorway of this ruined church is decorated with Romanesque carvings dating to the twelfth century, but the eastern portion dates to at least a century later. Outside is a much restored Round Tower, about twenty feet high. In a field southwest of the church are the ruins of a thirteenth-century round castle standing in an enclosure surrounded by wall and moat. The best feature of the site is the splendid view of lower Lough Leane.

*** **Dunloe Ogham Stones** *(42)*, 8 mi W; 1½ mi S of R 562 (to Killorglin), S of Beaufort; E side of road; signposted; OS ½ 20V 88 91

Here is a fine collection of eight Ogham stones brought here from their original sites nearby and rearranged in a semicircle.

* **Ballymalis Castle** *(104)*, 9 mi W; 1 mi S of R 562 (to Kilorglin); signposted; OS ½ 20V 84 94

Here is the well-preserved ruin of a four-storey fifteenth- or sixteenth-century tower house on the bank of the river Laune. It has small turrets projecting from diagonally opposite corners and can be climbed to the parapet.

KILLORGLIN

Killagha Abbey *(117)*, 8 mi N; W of N 70 (to Tralee); signposted; OS ½ 21Q 82 01

This ruined thirteenth-century nave-and-chancel church belonged to the house of Augustinian canons founded here in about 1216 by Geoffrey de Marisco. The splendid Flamboyant Decorated east window is a fifteenth-century insertion.

SKELLIG ISLANDS

*** Skellig Michael *(47)*, on Great Skellig, 8 mi offshore; boats available, weather permitting, from Ballinskelligs and Port Magee; for boat hire, call Sean O'Shea, Bunavalla Pier, Caherdaniel; Des Lavelle, Ballinskelligs; Dermot Walsh, Valentia; or Joe Roddy, Waterville. For additional information about transportation, inquire at J. Harrington's Tourist Information Point, Sneem; OS ½ 20V 25 61

Here on the western face of this high rough pyramid of bare rock are the extensive remains of an Early Christian monastery, though the exact dating of the ruins is in doubt. Ascending from the boat landing up the steep path, the first building to be encountered is a ruined twelfth-century chapel. Beyond this is the early monastery, consisting now of the remains of six drystone *clocháin* (beehive huts) and two oratories, all corbelled. Adjoining the larger of the oratories (resembling an upturned boat) is a walled patch of ground with a standing slab incised with a cross. To the rear, in an area called the Monks' Graveyard, is a row of cross-inscribed slabs. There are two wells on the premises.

The location of the monastery and the physical contours of the precipitous island on which it stands make this one of the more spectacular sights in Ireland, though reaching it is a problem and, in rough weather, an impossibility.

SNEEM

*** Staigue Fort *(37)*, 11 mi SW; 2 mi NW of N 70 (Ring of Kerry) from 9 mi W of Sneem; signposted; OS ½ 24V 61 63

This is one of the best preserved and most impressive of Ireland's stone ring-forts or cashels. The circular drystone wall is thirteen feet thick and rises to a maximum height of eighteen feet. Stone steps rise to the ramparts from the inside face of the wall. The lintelled entrance lies on the south side. Opposite it and to the left are mural chambers. A ditch and earthen bank, obviously part of the defensive works, encircle the wall. Date of construction is unknown but probably lies within the Iron Age. Some restoration was done in the nineteenth century.

County Limerick

ADARE

Trinitarian Friary Church *(116)*, town center

Now serving as a Roman Catholic parish church, the tower, south wall, and the adjacent building to the north (now a museum) are relics of the Trinitarian Friary founded here in the thirteenth century. It is the only surviving medieval house of this order in Ireland. The rest of the church is the product of a nineteenth-century restoration by Philip C. Hardwick of London.

**** Adare Franciscan Friary** *(132)*, S of town center on grounds of Adare Golf Club behind the ninth tee; permission to visit from office

This romantic ruin is that of the friary founded for Franciscan Observants in 1464 by Thomas FitzGerald, seventh earl of Kildare. The remains consist of church, choir, south chapel, and a tower added later in the center to separate nave and choir. Decorated windows with switch-line tracery are in a fair state of preservation. So are the claustral buildings to the north, including parts of the arcade.

**** Adare Augustinian Friary** *(126)*, E of town center, N of N 21 (to Limerick); open daytime hours; OS ½ 17R 47 47; no entry into cloister

Now serving as a Protestant (Church of Ireland) parish church, this building belonged originally to the Augustinian friary founded in about 1325 by John fitz Thomas (FitzGerald), first earl of Kildare. It is one of the few surviving fourteenth-century churches in Ireland. Nave and choir were built soon after the foundation; the wide south aisle and the tower were added sometime afterward. Several of the windows show fine examples of switch-line tracery, an early form of the Decorated Gothic style. The domestic buildings have been restored, but entry into the cloister is barred.

ASKEATON

**** Askeaton Castle** *(83, 96, 144, 155)*, town center

Situated on an islet in the river Deel, this was the *caput* of the FitzGerald earls of Desmond from the fourteenth century until the close of the Desmond Rebellion in 1579, when it was granted to Sir Francis Berkeley. It stands on the site of an early-thirteenth-century stronghold of William de Burgh. The existing ruined tower and the fine hall adjoining it date to the fifteenth century. It was slighted by Cromwellian soldiers in 1652.

*** **Askeaton Friary** *(132)*, N of town center, on bank of river Deel; signposted; OS ½ 17R 34 50

On untended grounds stand the substantial ruins of this Franciscan friary founded by James FitzGerald, sixth earl of Desmond, in about 1420. Nave, choir, and north wing survive, and there is some good switch-line tracery in the windows. The best feature of the site, however, is the cloister, which is unique among fifteenth-century Irish friaries in lying south of the church. The east and west ambulatories are integrated into the ranges, while those on the north and south have passagelike upper storeys. The refectory projects south of the south range, in the manner of Cistercian abbeys, and retains its original reader's niche.

* **Shanid Castle** *(83)*, 8 mi W; W of R 521 (to Ardagh), 4 mi S of Foynes; not signposted but visible from road; OS ½ 17R 24 45

This thirty-five-foot high motte (mound) was probably raised by Thomas fitz Maurice (FitzGerald), ancestor of the earls of Desmond, in the early thirteenth century. It would have been the site of a motte-and-bailey castle of timber. The ruined circular stone keep and curtain wall probably belong to a somewhat later date. From this seat derived the battle cry of the Desmond FitzGeralds ("Shanid Aboo").

BRUREE

* **De Valera Museum** *(253, 256)*, village center; open Th, Su, 2:00–5:00 P.M.

In this disused schoolhouse is a small museum dedicated to the life and career of Eamon de Valera. Contents consist of photos and sundry mementos, including his rosary, his spectacles, and a suit of clothes. Also on view are memorabilia of the Anglo-Irish War, such as weapons, spent bullets, and photos of Irish soldiers.

De Valera Cottage *(253)*, 1 mi N; signposted; key from Mrs. O'Gorman, 200 yd north of cottage (first house on right)

In this small, sparsely furnished cottage de Valera lived as a boy.

CROOM

* Monasteranenagh Abbey *(71, 126)*, 2½ mi E; N of minor road to Fedamore; signposted; OS ½ 17R 55 41

This Cistercian abbey was founded by Turlough O'Brien, king of Thomond, and colonized from Mellifont in about 1150. The ruined buildings date from about 1170–1200 and are Transitional in style. In the west gable of the long church are twin round-arched windows; the pointed arched windows in the eastern wall all but disappeared with the collapse of the roof in the nineteenth century. In the fifteenth century the nave was divided by a high wall—a not unusual practice in Cistercian churches after the decline in the number of lay brothers. Claustral remains south of the church are scanty.

* Dysert Oenghusa Round Tower *(60)*, 2½ mi NW; 1 mi N of minor road to Ballingarry; not signposted; OS ½ 17R 49 41

This is a late (probably twelfth-century) tower, sixty-five feet high and roofed. An unusual feature is the molding around the round-headed doorway. The adjacent church ruins date to the fifteenth or sixteenth century.

KILMALLOCK

* Blossom Gate and Town Wall *(93)*, Emmet Street and Sheares Avenue, respectively, town center

Here is the substantial ruin of the only remaining medieval town gate out of the original five. A segment (about two hundred yards long) of the town wall stands at the foot of Sheares Avenue in a modern housing estate.

Church of Saints Peter and Paul *(115, 231)*, town center; key from Cyril O'Brien, 43 Millmount Street

Here is the substantial ruin of an aisled thirteenth-century church consisting of nave, choir, and south wing. Five lancets pierce the east wall, three the west. A pre-Norman round tower is incorporated into the fabric at the northwest corner.

** Kilmallock Friary *(122, 128)*, N of town center; signposted

Here are the substantial and unusually well-tended ruins of a Dominican friary founded in 1291 by King Edward I. The nave and choir of the church are probably of late-thirteenth-century provenance, as indicated by the quintuplet of Early English lancet windows in the east wall. The south wing was added in the fourteenth century, though its fine curvilinear

Decorated window is probably a fifteenth-century insertion. The tower was also a fifteenth-century addition. Of the claustral buildings north of the church only the north range (the frater) remains standing to any extent.

LIMERICK

*** King John's Castle *(84)*, Castle Street, city center; open M-F, 10:00 A.M.-5:00 P.M.; Sa-Su, 10:30 A.M.-5:00 P.M.

Begun in 1200 and completed in 1207, this great Anglo-Norman keepless castle was originally five-sided and reinforced by four round corner towers, of which three survive, though lowered to provide platforms for heavy guns. The entrance is on the north side through a massive twin-towered gatehouse that still retains portcullis grooves. The houses inside the castle walls were built as barracks in the eighteenth century. Notwithstanding its formidable appearance, the castle surrendered three times in the seventeenth century: to the Confederate Catholics in 1641, to Cromwell's army under Henry Ireton in 1651, and to a Williamite army in 1691 just before the signing of the Treaty of Limerick.

Town Walls *(93)*, Old Clare and Lelia streets, city center

At the base of the angle between these two streets is a short stretch of the medieval town wall, recently excavated.

** Limerick Museum *(180, 192)*, St. John's Square, city center; open Tu-Sa, 10:00 A.M.-1:00 P.M., 2:15-5:00 P.M.

Here is a good collection of miscellany associated with the history of Limerick, the Shannon valley, and elsewhere in Ireland, from prehistoric times to the twentieth century. On the ground floor are samples of Limerick silver and lace, photos galore of the city in the late nineteenth century, memorabilia of the nineteenth-century Irish Nationalist movements (Fenians, etc.), and a very interesting exhibit pertaining to the War of Irish Independence and civil war, 1916–22. In the basement is a rare display of Irish Mesolithic flint cores, worked nodules, blades, scrapers, choppers, limpet hammers, and waste flakes from such widely separated areas as Counties Antrim, Clare, and Kerry. Also here are Neolithic axes and other flint implements, Neolithic and bronze-age pottery, flint arrowheads, iron-age tools and weapons, and Viking jewelry.

** St. John's Cathedral *(231)*, Cathedral Place

Designed by the English architect Philip C. Hardwick and built mostly between 1856 and 1861 (with later additions by the Limerick architect Maurice Hennessey), this is a splendid neo-Gothic edifice in the Early

English style with an ornate 280-foot spire, the highest of its kind in Ireland.

* St. Alphonsus Redemptorist Church *(231)*, Henry Street

Designed by Philip C. Hardwick of London and built between 1858 and 1862, this is a long apsed church (without transepts) in the Early English style, with an elaborate tympanum over the west doorway.

* Limerick Municipal Art Gallery *(222)*, Pery Square

Hanging here is a small collection of the works of sundry nineteenth- and twentieth-century Irish artists, including paintings by William Mulready, Daniel Maclise, Maurice Macgonigal, Sean Keating, Paul Henry, Walter Osborne, and Evie Hone.

*** St. Mary's Cathedral *(114, 128)*, Merchant's Quay, N of city center

This frequently modified and much restored Protestant (Church of Ireland) cathedral was built originally by Donal Mór O'Brien, king of Thomond, beginning in about 1180. Of the original church only the fine (restored) Romanesque west doorway and parts of the nave and chancel survive. The western tower was built early in the thirteenth century, when the choir and transepts were extended. In the fifteenth century ranges of chapels were added outside the nave on both sides, thus squaring off the ground plan of what was originally a cruciform church. At the same time Decorated windows were inserted throughout. A final great work of restoration took place in the nineteenth century. Inside, the most interesting features are the fifteenth-century misericords (unique in Ireland) and a fine array of medieval tombs.

Custom House *(191)*, Patrick Street, town center

Built in 1769 to the design of Davis Ducart (Daviso de Arcort), this is a typically neoclassical building with a rusticated ground floor and fluted Ionic pilasters.

Limerick Treaty Stone *(168)*, W of town center

This stone on which the Treaty of Limerick is believed to have been signed in 1691 rests on a pedestal at the west end of the Thomond Bridge.

*** Hunt Museum *(28, 173)*, 3 mi E; 1 mi N of N 7 (to Dublin) in Plassey House on grounds of NIHE (National Institute of Higher Education); not signposted; open Apr–Sept, daily, 10:00 A.M.–1:00 P.M., 1:45–5:00 P.M.

Here is one of the finest private collections of rare artifacts in the British Isles, many, though not all, of Irish provenance. The prehistoric exhibit contains numerous Neolithic tools and microliths, a rare bronze-age shield (one of two in Ireland), bronze ax heads, a bronze-age cauldron, a gold torc, pins and rings, several examples of bronze-age funerary pottery, and numerous iron-age brooches and pins. There is a small selection of Viking personal jewelry. Among the Early Christian items are the bronze "Cashel Bell," an eighth-century cross-shaped bronze mount from County Antrim, and several small eighth- and ninth-century bronze bells. Among the religious items of interest are three reliquary crosses and the seventeenth-century "Galway chalice." From the eighteenth century comes a beautiful array of Irish delftware; also some fine examples of Irish silver. Dated to the eighteenth and nineteenth centuries is a collection of Irish rosaries and so-called "penal crosses" (actually mementos of pilgrimages to Lough Derg).

* Carrigogunnell Castle *(83)*, 6 mi W; ½ mi N of N 69 (to Askeaton) from Clarina village; signposted; OS ½ 17R 50 55

This is a romantic ivy-covered ruin perched on a high volcanic rock overlooking the Shannon estuary. The original castle on this site was built by William de Burgh in the early thirteenth century. The present buildings date to the fifteenth and sixteenth. They consist of a four-storey tower house, a lower gabled tower adjoining it, and remnants of a high curtain wall. The stronghold surrendered to a Williamite army in 1691 and was later blown up by order of General Ginckel.

*** Lough Gur Interpretive Centre *(18, 26, 30, 38, 144, 155)*, 12 mi S; 2 mi E and N of R 512 (to Kilmallock) from Holy Cross village; signposted; OS ½ 18R 64 41

The settlement here dates back to at least 3000 B.C., that is, within the late Neolithic period. Remains of Neolithic and bronze-age stone huts have been excavated and served as the model for the two thatched houses that together form the interpretive center and museum. The latter contains a small selection of stone-age and bronze-age artifacts and offers at regular intervals a twenty-minute audiovisual show explaining the site. Guided walking tours are also scheduled regularly. Looking southward from the center is Bolin Island, originally a man-made bronze-age crannog. Just beyond are the ruins of Bourchier's Castle (fifteenth century), and beyond that Black Castle (probably thirteenth century). Numerous prehistoric monuments are to be found in the vicinity, of which the most worthy of inspection are:

Giant's Grave *(27)*, 1 mi S and W of Interpretive Center; S of road to Holycross village; signposted

This is a bronze-age wedge grave situated close to the road. It consists of a low gallery more than fifty feet long and about eleven feet wide, covered partially by capstones. The sides are formed of double walling with rubble in between, and the gallery is divided into two chambers by a septal slab.

*** The Grange (The Lios) *(30)*, 2 mi W of center; E of R 512 (to Limerick), ½ mi N of Holycross village; signposted

This early-bronze-age stone circle is the finest of its kind in Ireland. It is an embanked circular setting of more than a hundred boulders and cut stones enclosing an area 150 feet in diameter. The largest of the stones, a huge thick block, stands eight feet high. Two entrance stones flank a paved passageway that enters the circle from the east through the surrounding embankment. The site stands next to the road and close to the western shore of Lough Gur. It is unusually well tended, with explanatory signs in situ.

Newcastle West

* Glenquin Castle *(104)*, 7 mi SW; 3 mi S of N 21 (to Abbeyfeale) from Ballyconway village, on N side of R 515, 7 mi W of Broadford; not signposted but visible from road; OS ½ 17R 25 26; locked, and key not available

This is a fine seven-storey battlemented sixteenth-century square tower house, repaired and reroofed in the nineteenth century and again in the twentieth. According to tradition, it was built by the O'Hallinans, but its history is obscure.

Rathkeale

* Castle Matrix *(144, 155)*, N of town center; signposted; open 15 May–15 Sept, Sa–Tu, 1:00–5:00 P.M.

On the bank of the river Deel, this heavily restored eighty-foot-high, stepped-battlemented tower house was built originally in the fifteenth century by the earls of Desmond. After the failure of the Desmond rebellion of 1580, the castle came into the possession of Henry Billingsley, who later sold it to Sir John Dowdall. Eventually it went to the Southwell family, one of whose descendants, John Southwell Brown, added the two-storey residential quarters in the early nineteenth century. Restored again and filled with antiques in the 1970s, it now serves as headquarters of the Irish International Arts Centre and the Heraldry Society of Ireland.

TARBERT

* Glin Castle *(210)*, 5 mi E; S side of N 69 (to Askeaton); open 16 May–26 June, daily, 10:00 A.M.–noon, 2:00–4:00 P.M.; gatehouse shop open, April–Oct

Both castle and gatehouse are the handiwork of John Francis FitzGerald, twenty-fifth knight of Glin, who, in the second decade of the nineteenth century, rebuilt the ancient family stronghold into a Gothick fantasy. The castle's interior is distinguished for its fine plasterwork and eighteenth-century furnishings but is open to the public for only about a month during the early summer. The gatehouse has been converted into a restaurant and gift shop.

County Clare

BALLYVAUGHAN ·

** Gleninagh Castle *(103)*, 2 mi W; ¼ mi N of R 477 (coast road to Lisdoonvarna) at end of one-track road; not signposted but visible from main road; OS ½ 14M 19 10

Beautifully situated on the south shore of Galway Bay, this L-plan tower house was an O'Loughlin stronghold built in the fifteenth or sixteenth century. The small leg of the L is occupied by a spiral staircase that can still be climbed to the fourth storey. The entrance is in the reentrant angle of the L. High above is a machicolation, and the round corner turrets are also machicolated.

Newtown Castle *(103)*, 2½ mi SW; ½ mi W of N 67 (to Lisdoonvarna); signposted; OS ½ 14M 22 07

On the grounds of a farmhouse currently being restored for commercial use as lodgings, this sixteenth-century tower house rises to five storeys and can be climbed. The vaulted ceilings have especially clear marks of the wickerwork employed to hold the mortar in place during construction—a uniquely Irish building technique. The tower itself is unusual in being square at the base and round at the top.

Gleninsheen Wedge Tomb *(27)*, 4 mi S, E side of R 480 (to Corofin via Leamaneh Castle); signposted and visible from road; OS ½ 17M 24 03

This small wedge grave, one of many scattered about The Burren, consists of a single long capstone supported by three long, thin uprights. Some of the megaliths may be missing.

*** **Poulnabrone Dolmen** *(22)*, 5 mi S, E side of R 480 (to Corofin via Leamaneh Castle); signposted and visible from road; OS ½ 14M 24 00

In the midst of a typically Burren landscape of fissured limestone rocks, this is one of Ireland's most photographed Neolithic portal dolmens. More than most, it resembles a stone table (the literal meaning of the Breton word *dolmen*), for its capstone rests almost horizontally on two high, narrow side walls of stone. The two portals face south. Currently under repair, the monument is covered by ugly scaffolding that presumably will soon be removed.

Caherconnell Ringfort *(37)*, 6 mi S, W side of R 480 (to Corofin via Leamaneh Castle); signposted and visible from road; OS ½ 14R 24 99

This is a typical drystone ring-fort, about 120 feet in diameter, with walls as high as ten feet in places.

* **Cahermacnaghten Fort** *(37, 94)*, 6 mi S; 1 mi S of N 67 (to Ennistymon), W side of minor road to Kilfenora via Doonyvarden; signposted and visible from road; OS ½ 14M 19 00

This Early Christian or iron-age circular ring-fort about a hundred feet in diameter is unusual in that, owing to a long period of occupation, the interior ground level is almost flush with the surrounding drystone wall. On the east side are the remains of a medieval entranceway. Opposite this at the west end of the fort are the stone foundations of a house presumably connected with the Brehon law school that flourished here under the O'Davoren family until late in the seventeenth century.

** **Corcomroe Abbey** *(126)*, 5½ mi E; 1 mi S and E of N 67 (to Kinvara, County Galway) from Bell Harbor (Bealaclugga); not signposted; OS ½ 14M 29 09

These are the substantial ruins of a Cistercian monastery founded by Donal Mór O'Brien in 1194 or possibly by his son Donough Cairbreach. The cruciform church was built between 1210 and 1225. There is a triplet of Early English lancets, topped by a fourth, in the east wall; twin lancets in the west. The choir is rib-vaulted, and there are fine carved capitals supporting the choir arch and the chapel arches in both of the shallow transepts. The transverse wall across the nave is a fifteenth-century addition, doubtless installed so as to foreshorten the nave after the departure of the lay brothers following the Black Death. Inside the choir is a well-carved tomb and effigy, traditionally said to be of Conor O'Brien, grandson of the founder; also a sedilia and an altar stone. The claustral remains south of the church are fragmentary.

COROFIN

** Clare Heritage Centre *(214)*, village center

Housed in a deconsecrated Protestant (C of I) church is an interesting miscellany of scaled models and artifacts illustrating various aspects of nineteenth-century life in southwestern Ireland. Topics covered include land tenure, the Famine, elementary education, emigration, and native music. Also on view is the original of a rare Early Christian "Tau Cross" from nearby Killinaboy. In the Dr. George MacNamara Gallery are Neolithic stone ax heads, seventeenth-century chalices, watercolors by Frederick William Burton, and a list of male convicts transported from County Clare to Australia in 1831. Other genealogical records are also available.

*** Dysert O'Dea Church, Round Tower, and High Cross *(60, 63, 68)*, 3 mi S; 1 mi W of R 476 (to Ennis); signposted; OS ½ 14R 28 85

The ruined nave-and-chancel church is a seventeenth-century reconstruction of a twelfth- or thirteenth-century building. The three fine lancets in the east wall date probably to the thirteenth; the fine twelfth century Romanesque doorway was removed from its original position and inserted in the south wall. It has well-cut outward-pointing sawtooth chevrons and a complete semicircle of carved human and animal heads in the arch.

At the northeast corner of the church the remains of a Round Tower stand about fifty feet high. It probably dates to the twelfth century.

East of the church is a superbly carved High Cross, with the figure of a bishop on the east face surmounted by a smaller representation of the crucified Christ. The other faces are covered with geometric designs and interlace.

* Dysert O'Dea Castle and Archaeological Centre *(103, 256)*, 3 mi S; 1½ mi W of R 476 (to Ennis); signposted; also approachable by footpath northeast of Dysert O'Dea church; OS ½ 14R 29 85; open daily, 10:00 A.M.–8:00 P.M.

Here is a recently restored four-storey battlemented tower house built by the O'Deas in the late fifteenth century. The castle was taken and slighted by Cromwell's forces in 1651.

On the second floor is a small museum containing Neolithic stone ax heads, bronze-age spear and javelin heads, medieval and eighteenth-century swords, a rifle used in the 1916 Easter Rising, a German Mauser smuggled into Ireland at about the same time, and IRA weapons from the Irish civil war. On the floor below, a thirty-minute audiovisual presentation of local history and archaeology is shown regularly.

* Cahercommaun Hill-Fort *(37)*, 6 mi N, W of minor road to Carran and Bealaclugga, ½ mi by footpath from car park; signposted; OS ½ 14M 28 99

On the edge of a steep cliff, this is a trivallate (triple-walled) hill-fort with a circular drystone wall at the center and around it two D-shaped walls, each terminating at the cliff's edge. The inner walls rise to a height of about fifteen feet; those on the outside are shorter and more overgrown. The inner wall has three mural cells, and there is a souterrain leading from the interior to the outer face of the rampart. Excavations have fixed a ninth-century date for the habitation here, but an earlier iron-age provenance is possible.

The path to this place is steep and rocky, but the climb is worth it, especially for the glorious view of surrounding Burren landscape.

ENNIS

*** Ennis Friary *(124, 128)*, town center; open daytime hours; optional guided tour

Founded in about 1240 by Donough Cairbreach O'Brien for Franciscan friars, this is today one of Ireland's more handsome ecclesiastical ruins. The choir with its splendid five-lighted east window dates to the thirteenth or early fourteenth century. Most of the nave, the south wing, the west doorway, the tower, and the several Decorated windows, with switch-line or curvilinear tracery, are fifteenth-century additions. The claustral remains are fragmentary, with only one of the conventual buildings (either the chapter house or the sacristy) still complete. Noteworthy features are the windows, the fifteenth-century MacMahon tomb (taken over by the Creagh family in the nineteenth century), the canopy of the O'Brien tomb, and numerous wall carvings, including one of St. Francis with the stigmata showing in his right hand. The optional guided tour is very informative.

** Clare Abbey *(119, 127)*, 1 mi S; ½ mi E of N 18 (to Limerick) from Clarecastle; 200 yd by footpath from locked gate across railway track; signposted; OS ½ 17R 35 76

The substantial ruins of this Augustinian abbey, founded late in the twelfth century by Donal Mór O'Brien, king of Thomond, date mostly from a fifteenth-century rebuilding. They consist of a nave and choir with a battlemented central tower complete to the top. The claustral buildings stand fairly high. There is a fine Decorated window at the south end of the east range and a kitchen fireplace and chimney in the south range. Nothing is left of the west range except a wall.

* **Killone Abbey** *(119)*, 4 mi S; 2 mi S of N 18 (to Limerick) from Clarecastle; ½ mi W of R 473 (to Killadysert), ¼ mi by footpath past derelict cottage from locked gate; signposted from road; OS ½ 17R 32 73

These are the ruins of one of the few nunneries (for Augustinian canonesses) left standing in Ireland. Founded in the late twelfth century by Donal Mór O'Brien, king of Thomond, this was a small nave-and-chancel church with a cloister to the south. The east wall of the church retains its two fine round-headed narrow windows of twelfth- or thirteenth-century provenance, but the belfry and west wall were added in the fifteenth century, when the nave was shortened. Of the claustral buildings, the east and south ranges are fairly substantial. The site is situated on the shore of tiny Lough Killone—a secluded place of serene beauty.

Drumcliff Church and Round Tower *(60)*, 2 mi NE; 1¼ mi E of N 85 (to Ennistymon); church visible from road; OS ½ 17R 33 80

The ruined single-cell church here dates to the fifteenth century, though the round-headed west window was possibly part of a much earlier building. North of it lies the high (thirty-five-foot) stump of a Round Tower.

KILFENORA

** **Kilfenora Cathedral and Crosses** *(63, 68, 115)*, village center; signposted

Although the nave of this thirteenth-century church is still used for Church of Ireland services and is locked on weekdays, the ruined chancel has a good three-lighted east window, a triple sedilia in the north wall, and effigies of medieval bishops on the south side.

The best feature here, however, is the collection of Early Christian crosses on the premises. South of the church is the stem of a cross with interlace carvings. To the west behind the church is the Doorty Cross, with three men carved on the east face and on the west the figure of a man on horseback, possibly Christ entering Jerusalem. In the northwest corner of the graveyard is another cross (not ringed) with interlace designs. A hundred yards farther west, in a field outside the graveyard, is a very high ringed cross with the Crucifixion on the east face and interlace on the west.

* **Burren Display Center** *(27)*, village center

Here is a large topographical model of The Burren. Visitors are treated to a ten-minute film followed by a fifteen-minute lecture on the region's geology, botany, archaeology, and history. It is a good starting place for exploring the many archaeological sites nearby.

** **Leamaneh Castle** *(103, 154)*, 3 mi E; N side of R 476 (to Corofin); not signposted but clearly visible from road; OS ½ 14R 23 93

This is a late-fifteenth-century tower house to which a four-storey mansion was added in the seventeenth. It was an O'Brien residence. The tower house has a murder hole above the east entrance and a circular stairway that can be climbed to the top. The mansion is well fenestrated with many mullioned windows, some modern. It was erected in about 1643 by Conor O'Brien and his wife Máire Ni Mahon, about whom many legends accumulated, including one to the effect that in 1651 she denied entry into the castle of her husband's supposed corpse and later married one of Cromwell's soldiers to preserve the estate from confiscation.

** **Ballykinvarga Ringfort** *(37)*, 2 mi NE, by footpath S of minor road opposite two-storey farmhouse, past black-and-white striped pole and across stone fence; signposted; OS ½ 17M 19 95

Here is a large circular ring-fort with stone walls rising as high as ten feet. The most unusual feature of the site is the wide belt of sharply pointed rocks covering the approaches to the enclosure from three sides. This is known as a *chevaux de frise*, a rare species of primitive defense works designed to impede the advance of hostile forces on foot or on horseback. Visitors today who must pick their way cautiously through these jagged rocks can well understand how hard it would have been to storm this place.

KILKEE

* **Carrigaholt Castle** *(103)*, 6 mi SW; S end of R 488 in village center next to car park; signposted; OS ½ 17Q 85 51

Beautifully situated on the north bank of the Shannon estuary, this is a well-preserved late-fifteenth-century tower house built by the MacMahons, subsequently occupied by O'Briens, and captured in 1652 by the Cromwellian general Edmund Ludlow. It is five storeys high with a machicolation high above the main entrance, gunports on either side of it, a murder hole just inside, and another one at the northeast corner. A circular stairway goes to the top but is too insubstantial to be climbed safely. The bawn wall is in a good state of preservation.

KILLADYSERT

* Canon Island Abbey *(119)*, 3 mi E by boat; call Morgan McMahon in Killadysert, tel (065) 26313, or inquire at Irish Tourist Information Office in Ennis; OS ½ 17R 30 59

One of the foundations of Donal Mór O'Brien, king of Thomond, in the late twelfth century, this was a house of Augustinian canons regular. The simple nave-and-chancel church was built in the thirteenth century, but the tower south of the nave and the claustral buildings were added in the fifteenth. The ruins of the latter are fairly substantial, consisting of a sacristy and chapter house in the east range and a kitchen and refectory in the south. There is no west range.

KILLALOE

** Killaloe Cathedral *(66, 114)*, town center

Construction of this cruciform cathedral church was begun in the late twelfth century, and it is chiefly distinguished for its fine recessed Hiberno-Romanesque south doorway, a mélange of chevrons, zigzags, carved heads, foliage, and animals, probably inserted here after being removed from an earlier church built by Donal Mór O'Brien, king of Thomond. Most of the church is of thirteenth-century provenance, as indicated by the profusion of lancets throughout. Especially noteworthy is the east window, with its fine triplet of high lancets (the central one round-headed). Near the west end are two objects of still greater antiquity: a tenth- or eleventh-century Ogham stone that also bears a Scandinavian runic inscription, and a plain High Cross brought here from Kilfenora.

On the cathedral grounds St. Flannan's oratory is also of twelfth-century provenance and has a good, but simpler, Romanesque west doorway. It is locked, but the interior is visible through the grating.

St. Molua's Oratory *(49)*, W of town center on grounds of St. Flannan's (RC) Church

The roofless nave of this tiny building, with its flat-lintelled west doorway, was built before A.D. 1000; the choir with its steeply pitched roof was added later. The oratory formerly stood on Friar's Island in the river Shannon and was reconstructed on this site when the river was dammed and the island submerged.

KILRUSH

** Scattery Churches and Round Tower *(60)*, 2 mi SW; 20 minutes by boat from Cappa Pier; contact Gerald Griffen, tel (055) 51407; allow 2 hours for visit, including boat trip; OS ½ 17Q 97 52

On this Early Christian monastic site are the ruins of five churches plus a Round Tower about eighty feet high with a conical stone roof and a doorway at ground level—an unusual feature. The entrance is open, thus giving the visitor a view of the interior up to the top.

Of the churches the most interesting is the Romanesque cathedral lying east of the tower. It has a flat-lintelled west doorway and antae projecting from the west wall. The rest of the church dates from a rebuilding in the thirteenth or fourteenth century. Just north of the Round Tower is a small Romanesque nave-and-chancel church or oratory, mostly dated to the twelfth century, although the chancel was rebuilt in the nineteenth. Still farther north is Temple Senan, a medieval building, much ruined. In a field to the southwest of the cathedral and Round Tower are the scant remains of the Church of the Hill of the Angel, part Early Christian and part medieval. Finally, to the east, not far from the boat landing, is the Church of the Dead, a fourteenth- or fifteenth-century building measuring about seventy by twenty feet. The other more recent derelict buildings nearby are the deserted homes of the last of the island's inhabitants, who left this place within living memory.

QUIN

*** Quin Friary and Castle *(90, 96, 132)*, S of Quin village center; E side of R 469 (to Sixmilebridge); signposted and visible from road; OS ½ 17R 42 74

Here is an amalgam of castle and friary ruins not easily distinguished from each other. The castle was built in 1278–80 by Richard de Clare and overthrown by the O'Briens after their victory at Dysert O'Dea in 1318. In about 1433 a house for Observant Franciscan friars was built on the site of the ruins, incorporating the remains of the castle—a square keep with massive round towers at each of its corners and curtain walls eleven feet thick. Of the friary church, nave, chancel, central tower, and south transept walls stand fairly high. Inside are several fine tombs, the best being the carved MacNamara tomb niche (circa 1500) on the north side of the chancel beside the altar stone. The cloister, thirty-six feet by thirty-two feet, lies north of the church and is surrounded on three sides by an arcaded walk, probably the best of its kind in Ireland. Claustral buildings are in a fair state of preservation. North of the chancel is the sacristy from which a stairway leads up to the first-floor dormitory (now grassed over) above a vaulted undercroft.

St. Finghin's Church *(115)*, S of village center; E of R 469 (to Sixmilebridge); not signposted but clearly visible across stream from Quin Castle and Friary

This little ruined nave-and-chancel church dates to the fourth quarter of the thirteenth century, as indicated by the triple lancets in the east wall. The belfry at the west end is a later addition.

Moghane Hill-Fort *(35)*, 3 mi S on minor road; 300 yd by footpath through forest; signposted from Dromoland Wood picnic area car park; OS ½ 17R 41 70

Just short of the summit, to the left of the marked footpath, is a stone ring-fort about eighty-five feet in diameter and four to six feet high, with a single entrance on the southeast. Farther up the hill, marked by a stone pillar, are the barely discernible remains of the three concentric banks and ditches that make up the remains of probably the largest hill-fort in County Clare. From this point there is a splendid view in all directions, including the Fergus estuary to the southwest and the Shannon beyond it.

*** Knappogue Castle *(104)*, 2 mi S; ¾ mi NE of R 469 (to Sixmilebridge); signposted; OS 17R 44 72; open daily 9:30 A.M.–5:30 P.M.; medieval banquets twice nightly, 5:45 and 8:45 P.M.; tel (061) 61788

The original three-storey tower house on this site was built by the MacNamaras in 1467. Restored in the early nineteenth century by the Scotts of Cahircon, it subsequently came into the possession of Thomas F. Butler, Baron Dunboyne, who added elegant residential quarters to the ground floor. In the 1960s it was rerestored and refurnished by Mark Edwin Andrews of Houston, Texas.

Entering through the courtyard, today's visitor comes first to the Dalcassian Room, with a fifteenth-century carving of St. George. On the same floor is the hall where "medieval banquets" are served nightly, as well as the nineteenth-century drawing room and dining room. On the floor above are the Clancullen Room, with a fine Elizabethan fireplace, and a chapel. On the top floor is the great hall.

*** Craggaunowen Project *(38, 45, 104)*, 4 mi S; 1½ mi SW of R 469 (to Sixmilebridge); signposted; open daily, 10:00 A.M.–6:00 P.M.

On the grounds of Craggaunowen Castle, a mid-sixteenth-century MacNamara tower house, the late John Hunt (donor of the Hunt Collection in Limerick) established this unique outdoor museum consisting of a number of imaginatively reconstructed iron-age and Early Christian sites.

Only the ground floor of the restored castle is open, but in it is a small sampling of Hunt's fine collection of medieval antiquities. Footpaths lead from here to replicas of (1) an iron-age crannog (an artificial island connected by a wooden bridge to the shore and containing a thatched house and barn surrounded by a palisade); (2) a ring-fort enclosing circular thatched huts, a souterrain, and kilns; (3) an iron-age wooden track or *togher*, recovered from a bog; and (4) a *fulacht fiadh* or open-air cooking site where heated stones were used to boil water in a wooden trough.

Also on the site is the Brendan Exhibition, containing the leather-hulled curragh that Tim Severin and his crew of four sailed to North America in 1976, thereby demonstrating that St. Brendan could have made the same voyage in the same sort of craft and thus been the first to discover the New World.

Magh Adair *(57)*, 2¾ mi NE, N side of minor road; signposted from Quin but not at site itself (note historic marker standing on a slight elevation in field); OS ½ 17R 44 77

This flat-topped mound surrounded by a bank and ditch was the inauguration site of the Dál Cais kings of Thomond, including Brian Boru. In the field to the south, across a small stream, is a lone pillar that may have played some part in the inauguration rites.

SHANNON AIRPORT

*** **Bunratty Castle and Folk Park** *(96, 104, 216, 251)*, 6 mi SE; N side of N 18 (to Limerick); signposted; OS ½ 17R 45 61; castle open daily, 9:30 A.M.–5:30 P.M.; folk park open June–Aug, 9:30 A.M.–7:00 P.M.; medieval banquets twice nightly, 5:45 P.M., 8:45 P.M.; tel (061) 61511; allow 2–3 hours for visit to castle and folk park

The first castle on this site was a motte-and-bailey erected by Robert de Muscegros in about 1250. Late in the thirteenth century this was replaced by a stone castle built by Thomas de Clare. His son Richard de Clare was killed at the Battle of Dysert O'Dea in 1318, after which his widow set fire to the castle before leaving the area. Rebuilt in 1355 by Thomas de Rokeby, it was soon destroyed again. The oldest parts of the present castle date from the middle years of the fifteenth century, when the MacNamaras were in possession. By 1500 it had passed to the O'Briens. In 1543 its owner, Murrough O'Brien, was made first earl of Thomond by King Henry VIII. Late in the sixteenth century the fourth earl, Donough O'Brien, made considerable structural changes in the building and also greatly embellished its interior. During the mid-seventeenth-century civil war it was held for parliament by Admiral William Penn (father of the founder of

Pennsylvania) but surrendered to the Catholic confederates. Later it was owned by the Stoddert family before being bought by Lord Gort in 1956. It was he who financed its recent restoration by the Office of Public Works. Today a favorite tourist attraction here are the "medieval banquets" served twice nightly.

The "castle" is in fact a late medieval tower house, though larger and more elaborate in plan than most. It consists of a three-storey rectangular block with six-storey square towers on each corner. On both the north and south sides a high arch extends between the two towers, above which the exterior walls are flush with the faces of the towers, thus making space for more rooms in the top storey.

The modern entrance leads, underneath a murder hole, into the vaulted "Main Guard," on the first floor. This was originally the living quarters for servants and armed retainers. Below it in the basement are the dungeons for storage and presumably for the incarceration of prisoners. Above, on the second floor, is the Great Hall of the earls of Thomond, adjoined by a chapel and kitchen. On the floor above are bedrooms and solars (private apartments). Throughout, the rooms are furnished with authentic Jacobean pieces—perhaps the best collection of its kind in the British Isles.

In the folk park are numerous replicas of rural and urban houses typical of nineteenth-century Ireland. Included are a blacksmith's forge, a fisherman's house, several farmhouses and thatched cottages, a farm laborer's bothy (*bothán scóir*), a schoolhouse, numerous urban shops and houses, a post office, a horizontal mill for grinding grain, a gentleman's house, and the Talbot Collection of agricultural machinery and implements.

EAST CENTRAL IRELAND
Dublin City
SOUTH OF RIVER LIFFEY

(North to South; East to West)

Sweney's Chemist's Shop *(245)*, Lincoln Place

Complete with its original nameplate and shop front, this place was visited on 16 June 1904 by the fictional character Leopold Bloom in James Joyce's *Ulysses*.

St. Andrew's (RC) Church *(228, 245)*, Westland Row

Built in 1837 to the design of James Bolger, this handsome neoclassic building has a Doric facade and, inside, an altar screen of Corinthian pillars. This place, renamed "All Hallows," is the scene of one of Leopold Bloom's stops on his wanderings through Dublin, as depicted by James Joyce in *Ulysses*.

*** **Trinity College** *(138, 189, 221)*, College Green; grounds open daily, 10:00 A.M.–6:00 P.M.; optional 30-minute guided tour; chapel open during Sunday services; all other buildings, except Museum Building and Old Library, closed to public

Chartered by Queen Elizabeth I in 1592 for "the planting of learning, the increasing of civility, and the establishment of true religion [i.e., Protestantism] within the realm," the college was opened for students in 1594 as the "mother of a university," which up to that time Ireland lacked. None of the present buildings dates before the early eighteenth century. No longer denominational, the college now has over seven thousand students, fellows, and faculty.

The gateway from College Green, flanked by statues of Edmund Burke and Oliver Goldsmith, pierces the west front with its fine Palladian facade, built in 1752–60 to the design of either the London architects Henry Keene and John Sanderson or an amateur, Theodore Jacobsen. Ahead lies a long grass-covered green—Parliament Square as far as the campanile (1852) and Library Square between the campanile and the long, low red brick building called the Rubrics. This building is the oldest construction on the campus—put up in the early eighteenth century with funds provided by Queen Anne, though the Dutch-style gables are late-nineteenth-century additions. On the north (left) side of the two squares, proceeding from the entrance, are the Chapel, the Dining Hall, and the Graduate Memorial Building. The Chapel, now multidenominational with a Catholic oratory off the entrance hall, is neoclassical in the Greek style and was completed in 1798 to the design of Sir William Chambers. The fine interior plasterwork is by Michael Stapleton. The Dining Hall, designed by Hugh Darley, dates from the 1760s; the Graduate Memorial Building, by Sir Thomas Drew, from the late nineteenth century. Behind (north of) the latter are the tennis courts of "Botany Bay" (originally a kitchen garden), flanked by the Dining Hall and two undistinguished residential buildings. On the south (right) side of Parliament Square, directly opposite the Chapel, is its twin, the Public Theatre or Examination Hall, another neoclassic masterpiece by Sir William Chambers with elegant plasterwork by Michael Stapleton inside. East of it is the twentieth-century Reading Room and, still farther east, the Old Library (see below). South of this is the Fellows Square with two twentieth-century buildings, the Berkeley Library, and the Arts Building. To the west lies the Provost's House, another splendid neoclassic Palladian edifice built in the 1760s.

Beyond (east of) the Rubrics is the New Square, lined on the north and east by two undistinguished granite buildings designed by Frederick Darley in the 1830s and on the south by the Museum Building, designed by Deane and Woodward and erected in 1854—a High Victorian masterpiece in the Lombardo-Venetian style favored by John Ruskin. Nearby is the little neo-Tuscan temple called the Printing House, built in 1734-36 to the design of the famous Dublin architect Richard Castle. Finally, at the far eastern end of the college grounds, back of the New Square, are the Rugby Field and College Park, beyond which are modern science and engineering buildings.

*** Trinity College Library *(43, 46, 54, 99)*, College Green; open M-F, 10:00 A.M.-4:45 P.M.; Sa, 10:00 A.M.-12:45 P.M.

The original neoclassic building was designed by Thomas Burgh and modelled on Sir Christopher Wren's library at Trinity College, Cambridge. When finished in 1732, the main part of the ground floor consisted of an open arcade. This was walled up in 1891 to make space for books. Thirty-odd years previously the present barrel-vaulted ceiling had been installed to replace the original—again to accommodate the growing number of volumes. This expansion can be attributed in part to the British Copyright Act, which extended to Trinity College the right to claim one copy of each of its publications from every publisher in the British Isles. Subsequent growth in the library's holdings led to the building of the nearby 1937 Reading Room. Since independence, both British and Irish copyright acts have confirmed Trinity as a legal library of deposit for publications in both countries, thus requiring the construction of the adjacent Berkeley Library.

Of the manuscripts on exhibit in the Long Room, the most valued are *The Book of Kells*; *The Book of Durrow*; *The Book of Dimma* (with shrine); *The Book of Armagh* (which includes St. Patrick's *Confessio*, his "Letter to Coroticus," "lives" of the saint by Muirchu and Tirechan, and a "Life of St. Martin"); and *The Yellow Book of Lecan*, containing a version of the *Táin*. Another object of interest is "Brian Boru's Harp," a musical instrument of great beauty but no older than the year 1500, which is about five hundred years after Brian's death.

*** Bank of Ireland (Parliament House) *(183, 187, 188, 195, 204)*, College Green

The cornerstone for this noble building to house the Irish parliament was laid in 1728 while William Connolly was speaker. The original architect was Sir Edward Lovett Pearce, after whose death Arthur Dobbs supervised construction until the completion of the house of commons in 1739. Facing College Green, its facade is 147 feet long, with twenty-two Ionic pillars, most of them freestanding. The central portion was the commons chamber, a circle enclosed within square walls under an octagonal dome. In 1785 James Gandon added the imposing portico, whose Corinthian pillars face Westmoreland Street and which was linked to Pearce's main front by a curved curtain wall. In 1797 the Ionic portico on Foster Place was added by Robert Park. After passage of the Act of Union in 1800 the premises were sold to the Bank of Ireland, which still occupies them. Of the interior only the chamber of the house of lords has been preserved more or less intact.

* St. Stephen's Church *(224)*, Mount Street Crescent; closed except during Church of Ireland services

Designed by John Bowden and built in 1824–25, this is a fine neoclassic building with a portico of Ionic columns supporting a pediment above which rises a clock tower topped by a cupola of Corinthian columns supporting a small dome.

* Merrion Square *(186, 208)*

Laid out by John Ensor in the 1760s, the north, east, and south sides of this charming square are lined with tall red brick Georgian houses, notable especially for their classical doorways and lacy fanlights. Several have at one time or another been the residences of well-known figures, including Arthur Wellesley, duke of Wellington (birthplace); Robert Stewart, Lord Castlereagh; Daniel O'Connell; Oscar Wilde (birthplace); W. B. Yeats; and George Russell (AE).

*** National Gallery of Ireland *(190, 222, 268)*, Merrion Square, West; open M–W, F, Sa, 10:00 A.M.–6:00 P.M.; Th, 10:00 A.M.–9:00 P.M.; Su, 2:00–5:00 P.M.

A neoclassical building designed by Francis Fowke and opened in 1864, this is one of the great art galleries in the British Isles, arguably second only to the National Gallery in London. It has a superb and representative collection of most of the great European and British artists from the fifteenth century to the twentieth. The works of native Irish painters from the seventeenth to the twentieth centuries are to be found in Rooms 1 through 7. They include seventeenth- to nineteenth-century portraits by Garret Morphey, Charles Jervas, James Latham, Thomas Frye, Stephen Slaughter, Nathaniel Hone the elder, Philip Hussey, Robert Hunter, Hugh Douglas Hamilton, Thomas Robinson, and Nicholas J. Crowley; eighteenth- and nineteenth-century landscapes by George Barret, Thomas Roberts, Jonathan Fisher, Nathaniel Grogan, William Ashford, James Arthur O'Connnor, and Nathaniel Hone the younger; eighteenth-century cityscapes by William Sadler and James Malton; nineteenth-century genre paintings by John George Mulvany, Trevor Thomas Fowler,

Edwin Hayes, Joseph P. Haverty, Daniel Maclise, Matthew Lawless, Richard T. Moynan, and Walter Osborne; nineteenth- and twentieth-century paintings by John Butler Yeats, Sarah Purser, William Orpen, Paul Henry, John Lavery, Mainie Jellett, Evie Hone, and, arguably the greatest of all Irish artists, Jack B. Yeats.

* **Leinster House** *(187, 208)*, Merrion Square, West; entrance from Kildare Street; admission on application at guardhouse

Built in 1744–48 for the twentieth earl of Kildare (later first duke of Leinster) to the design of Richard Castle, this splendid Palladian town house was sold to the Royal Dublin Society in 1814. In 1922 it was turned over to the parliament (Oireachtas) of the Irish Free State (now the Republic of Ireland). During sessions of the legislature the public galleries of both the house of representatives (Dáil Éireann) and the senate (Seanad Éireann) are usually filled, but visitors without previous arrangements can sometimes be admitted.

*** **National Museum of Ireland** *(16, 19, 25, 28, 32, 35, 42, 52, 59, 222, 237, 256)*, Kildare Street; open Tu–Sa, 10:00 A.M.–5:00 P.M.; Su, 2:00–5:00 P.M.

This neoclassic building was designed by Sir Thomas Newenham Deane and his son Sir Thomas Manly Deane and constructed between 1884 and 1890. The collection of antiquities on the ground floor is the most complete of any in Ireland. The "Treasury" contains the museum's most prized possessions, including the Ardagh Chalice, the Tara Brooch, St. Patrick's Bell Shrine, the Cross of Cong, the Clonmacnoise Crosier, St. Lachtin's Arm Shrine, the Stowe Missal Shrine, and the recently discovered Derrynaflan Hoard of Early Christian relics. Nearby, in the Great Hall, is a spectacular collection of bronze-age and iron-age gold torcs, gorgets, *lunulae*, penannular brooches, and other personal ornaments of exquisite workmanship; bronze cauldrons, buckets, spears, ax heads, swords, etc. In the same area are important Viking finds from Dublin, prehistoric sculptured stones (including the iron-age Mullaghmast Stone), and the Aglish Ogham stones. Display cases on the circular terrace surrounding the Great Hall contain the best collection of Mesolithic microliths and "Bann flakes" in Ireland, as well as a great variety of Neolithic and bronze-age stone and flint implements and weapons, pottery, and other artifacts. Also on the ground floor is a room devoted to the Irish Nationalist movements of the nineteenth century and another to the War of Irish Independence and civil war (1916–22). Upstairs are displays of Irish lace, silver, pottery, and musical instruments, including a number of harps. (Current reconstruction work may involve resiting parts of the collection at a future date.)

* St. Ann's Church *(176)*, Dawson Street; open weekdays and for Church of Ireland services

Designed by Isaac Wills and built in 1707, this a typical neoclassical church with a rectangular nave, shallow chancel, and galleries resting on Ionic pillars around three sides. The stained glass is a nineteenth-century insertion.

* Royal Irish Academy *(46, 54, 55, 99, 189, 204, 247)*, 19 Dawson Street; open M, 9:30 A.M.-8:00 P.M.; Tu-Sa, 9:30 A.M.-5:30 P.M.

Founded in 1785 as a society for the encouragement of science and learning (with special emphasis on Irish archaeology and history), the academy has occupied these premises since 1852. Of the many important manuscripts housed here in the library, the most notable are *The Cathach* (the oldest Irish Psalter—circa A.D. 500-630), *The Stowe Missal* (circa A.D. 800), the *Lebor na hUidre* (*Book of the Dun Cow*—circa A.D. 1100), the *Leabhar Breac* (*The Speckled Book*, circa 1408-11), the *Leabhar Mór Leacain* (*Book of Lecan*, circa 1420), *The Book of Fermoy* (mainly fifteenth century), and the *Book of Ballymote* (fourteenth to fifteenth centuries). Normally these are on exhibit only one at a time, but it is possible to see facsimiles and to buy colored postcard copies.

In the academy's meeting chamber behind the library are chandeliers and some other furnishings from the Irish house of lords, moved here after parliament was abolished by the Act of Union in 1801. (See also **Bank of Ireland.**)

Mansion House *(186, 255)*, Dawson Street

Built by Joshua Dawson in 1710, this became shortly thereafter the official residence of the lord mayor of Dublin. It was the scene of the meeting of the first Dáil Éireann in January 1919. The plastered front disguises an original red brick facade.

Davey Byrne's Pub *(245)*, 21 Duke Street

This is the "moral pub" visited on 16 June 1904 by Leopold Bloom, one of the two principal characters in James Joyce's *Ulysses*.

Harcourt Street Station *(221)*, Harcourt Street

Neoclassical in style and built in 1859 to the design of G. Wilkinson, this was the Dublin terminus of the Dublin and Wicklow Railway. The waiting room now houses a branch of Barclay's Bank.

** St. Stephen's Green *(165, 221, 254)*, S of St. Stephen's Green, North

First enclosed in 1663, but not opened to the public (by Arthur Edward Guinness, Lord Ardilaun) until 1880, this is reputedly the largest city square in Europe. Notable features are the Memorial Arch at the northwest corner, dedicated to the Royal Dublin Fusiliers killed during the Boer War; statues of Robert Emmet, Lord Ardilaun, Theobald Wolfe Tone, and Jeremiah O'Donovan Rossa; Henry Moore's memorial to William Butler Yeats; and the bronze busts of James Clarence Mangan, Tom Kettle, and Countess Markievicz (who was in the thick of the action here during the Easter Rising of 1916). John van Nost's huge equestrian statue of King George II, once situated at the park's center, was blown up in the 1930s.

** University (Newman's) Church *(234)*, St. Stephen's Green, South

This little chapel was built in 1855 under the direction of John Henry Newman as rector of the Catholic University, which was housed next door in Number 86. The architect was John Hungerford Pollen. Contrary to the then-fashionable architectural canon of A. W. N. Pugin, Newman insisted on the interior's being decorated and furnished in the Byzantine style. In plan the church is a long narrow rectangle with a rounded apse. The walls are covered with gold leaf, and the panelled ceiling carries an intricate vine decoration. The pulpit extends from a side wall, and there is a gallery in the rear. At one side is a bust of Cardinal Newman.

Royal College of Surgeons *(221, 254)*, St. Stephen's Green, West

Built between 1825 and 1827 to the design of William Murray, this is a handsome neoclassic structure with ten Tuscan pilasters in front and a balustrade on the roofline. This was the scene of the last stand of the contingent of volunteers to which Countess Markievicz was attached during the Easter Rising of 1916.

* Shelbourne Hotel *(221)*, Stephen's Green, North

Still one of Dublin's more luxurious hotels and one of the city's landmarks, the Shelbourne was opened in 1867 by William Jury and two partners. It is an elegant red brick building with bands of stucco, a parapet along the top, and, in front, bronze statues of Nubian princesses and slave girls holding torch-shaped lamps.

* Powerscourt Townhouse Centre *(188, 208)*, South William Street

This fine Palladian mansion with interior plasterwork by Michael Stapleton has recently been converted to an elegant shopping center—a happy combination of historic preservation and commercial enterprise.

* Civic Museum *(207)*, South William Street; open M–Tu, Th–Sa, 10:00 A.M.–6:00 P.M.; Su, 11:00 A.M.–2:00 P.M.

This is an interesting, though somewhat chaotic, small repository of artifacts, prints, etc., pertaining to the history of Dublin city from medieval times to the present. Most of the items are connected with shipping and fire fighting in the nineteenth century. There is also a good collection of Malton prints. Here too are fragments of the Nelson Pillar (including the admiral's sculpted head), which stood at the foot of O'Connell Street until dynamiters destroyed it in 1966.

* Irish Genealogical Museum and Genealogical Office *(221, 474)*, 2 Kildare Street; open M–F, 10:00 A.M.–12:30 P.M., 2:00–4:30 P.M.

This red brick Venetian-style building was originally occupied by the Kildare Street Club and was erected in 1859 to the design of Deane and Woodward, with stone carvings by the O'Shea brothers and Charles W. Harrison. The museum, recently moved here from its original site on the grounds of Dublin Castle, is devoted chiefly to exhibits pertaining to Irish heraldry. The associated Genealogical Office contains, among other things, the Irish Register of Arms and Register of Pedigrees. A "preliminary consultancy service on ancestor tracing" will, for a fee, provide guidelines for genealogical research, if the office is contacted in writing. (The other half of the building is occupied by the Alliance Française.)

Royal College of Physicians *(221)*, Kildare Street

This handsome neoclassic building was erected in 1874 to the design of William G. Murray, Jr.

* National Library *(221)*, Kildare Street

Built in about 1890 to the design of Sir Thomas Manley Deane, this monumental neoclassic building houses major collections of books, manuscripts, prints, and archives relating mostly to Ireland and Irish history. It is the country's major repository of parish registers and other materials useful for genealogical research.

*** Dublin Castle *(86, 108, 147, 181, 196, 224, 254)*, between Cork Hill and Castle Street; signposted; State Apartments open M–F, 10:00 A.M.–12:15 P.M., 2:00–5:00 P.M.; Sa–Su, 2:00 P.M.–5:00 P.M.; mandatory 45-minute guided tours

In 1204 King John ordered a castle to be built on the present site of the Upper Yard; construction probably began a few years later under the justiciarship of John de Gray and was completed in about 1220 under that of Archbishop Henri de Londres. For roughly seven centuries it was to be the center of English rule in Ireland.

In 1534 the castle was besieged unsuccessfully by Thomas Fitzgerald, Lord Offaly ("Silken Thomas"), son of the ninth earl of Kildare. In 1591 Hugh Roe (Red Hugh) O'Donnell escaped from imprisonment (probably in the Record Tower), later to suffer self-exile in Spain. In 1684 fire broke out in the viceregal quarters, and some of the buildings had to be blown up to prevent its spread. In 1688 the castle was rebuilt. The next year it was occupied briefly by James II, who also stopped here for one night after his defeat at the Battle of the Boyne on 12 July 1690. In 1710 another fire destroyed most of the documents in the Record Tower. In the eighteenth century the Upper Yard, including the State Apartments, was reconstructed in the form in which it exists today. During the Easter Rising of 1916 there was some fighting in and around the castle grounds, and the wounded James Connolly was held here briefly before transfer to Kilmainham Jail and execution. On 16 January 1922 Dublin Castle was surrendered to members of the provisional government of Ireland.

Today's visitor enters the Upper Yard from Cork Hill near the northeast corner. On the right is the eighteenth-century Bedford Tower; ahead (at the northeast corner) is the Wardrobe Tower, the only substantial portion left of the original thirteenth-century building; abutting it to the east is the Church of the Holy Trinity (formerly the Chapel Royal), a neo-Gothic building of the early nineteenth century, designed by Francis Johnston; at the southwest corner of the yard is Bermingham's Tower, the battered base of which is of thirteenth-century construction, the rest an eighteenth-century rebuilding. Between the Record Tower and the Bermingham Tower, along the south side of the court, stretch the elegantly furnished eighteenth-century State Apartments, of which the most impressive are St. Patrick's Hall and the Throne Room. Also of interest here is the bedroom where James Connolly was temporarily lodged after his capture. The castle is the repository of Irish state papers, including police and criminal documents listing deported convicts and their crimes from the 1798 uprising through the greater part of the nineteenth century.

** City Hall *(188)*, Dame Street

Built originally (1769–79) as the Royal Exchange to the design of Thomas Cooley, this is a splendid neoclassical building with a spacious dome supported by twelve fluted columns of the Composite Order. The Adam-style plasterwork is by a Dublin alderman and later lord mayor, Charles Thorp.

** St. Werburgh's Church *(176)*, Werburgh Street; closed except for

Church of Ireland services, but key available from sexton at 8 Castle Street (around corner)

This is a handsome neoclassical church built in 1715 to the design of Thomas Burgh, surveyor general of Ireland. The exterior is unimpressive except for the broken-arch pedimented front doorway. The interior is splendid—a rectangular nave with narrow chancel, a rear gallery, and an organ loft. The elegant pulpit was designed by Francis Johnston and carved by Richard Stewart. Among the church's treasures is the font where Jonathan Swift was baptized.

*** Christ Church Cathedral *(62, 84, 107, 162, 168, 226)*, Christchurch Place and Winetavern Street

In 1162 Archbishop (later Saint) Laurence O'Toole invited Augustinian canons regular to form the chapter of the cathedral founded on this site in the eleventh century by Sitric, Norse king of Dublin. Sometime after the Anglo-Norman occupation of Dublin in 1170, work was begun on the east end of a new cathedral, but the nave was not completed until about 1240. In the sixteenth century the south wall of the nave collapsed and had to be rebuilt, along with much else on this side of the church. In 1872 a wealthy Dublin benefactor, Henry Roe, hired the London architect, George Edmund Street, to rebuild the entire church. Street retained as much of the early fabric as was feasible and scrupulously reproduced most of the rest. Hence the building, though mostly not much more than a century old, appears authentically medieval: Romanesque in the east end and Gothic (i.e., Early English) in the west.

Throughout most of the Middle Ages Christ Church shared "metropolitan" rank with St. Patrick's Cathedral, Dublin, although the archbishops were consecrated and enthroned in the former. In 1487 the boy pretender, Lambert Simnel, was crowned here as king of England and lord of Ireland. Since the Reformation it has been a Protestant house of worship, and since the disestablishment of the Church of Ireland in 1869 it has continued as the cathedral of the Protestant Diocese of Dublin and the metropolitan cathedral of the Southern Province.

Today the visitor enters the nave at the southwest corner after passing the ruins of the thirteenth-century chapter house on the right. Proceeding clockwise around the church, the following components are the most noteworthy: the north wall and windows of the nave from the capitals upward, which are pure Early English Gothic; the north and south transepts (especially the latter), which mostly retain the Romanesque character of the twelfth-century church; a reliquary containing the heart of St. Laurence O'Toole in the Chapel of St. Laud at the east end of the south aisle of the choir; the tomb of Archbishop John Comyn in one of the south transept chapels; the twelfth- to thirteenth-century underground crypt, entered (when open) from the east end of the south aisle of the nave; also in the south aisle, "Strongbow's Tomb," with a knightly effigy that is not authentic but probably that of a FitzOsbert of Drogheda, placed here after the original was destroyed by the collapse of the south wall in the sixteenth century.

* St. Audeon's (RC) Church *(228)*, High Street

Built in 1841 to the design of Patrick Byrne, this is a monumental neoclassic edifice with a gigantic Corinthian pedimented portico topped by three large statues. The barrel-vaulted interior is handsome, with a coffered flat ceiling, fine plasterwork, and a Corinthian altarpiece.

St. Audeon's (C of I) Church *(115)*, High Street; closed except during services

This is the sole surviving medieval church in Dublin. The round-arched doorway dates to the late twelfth century. Most of the thirteenth-century church is a roofless ruin. The high tower is a nineteenth-century restoration of a seventeenth-century structure. Protestant services are now held in the restored south aisles of the medieval nave and choir, which date from the fifteenth century, when they served as chapels (St. Anne's Chapel and the Portlester Chapel). Noteworthy in this part of the church are the twelfth-century font and the fifteenth- or sixteenth-century Perpendicular windows—a rarity in Ireland.

City Wall *(93)*, Cook Street

On the south side of this short street (running between Bridge and Winetavern streets) is a short section of the medieval wall. Behind St. Audeon's C of I Church is St. Audeon's Arch, the only remaining city gate.

Brazen Head Hotel *(206)*, Bridge Street

Now a down-at-the-heels bar, this inn was a favorite meeting place of seditious United Irishmen in the 1790s and again of Robert Emmet and his coconspirators in 1803. The oldest parts of the building date probably to the early eighteenth century.

Tailors' Hall *(174, 199)*, Back Lane

Recently restored and now the national headquarters of An Taisce, which rents the premises for miscellaneous social and official functions, this attractive red brick neoclassical building was erected as a guildhall in

1703-07. It was the meeting place of the Catholic Convention of 1792, which successfully petitioned King George III for Catholic relief. Also in the 1790s it was one of the headquarters of the Dublin Society of United Irishmen.

* St. Nicholas of Myra Church *(228)*, John Dillon Street

Built in the 1830s to the design of John Leeson, this neoclassic building has an Ionic portico topped by a clock tower, behind which is a copper dome. The gaudy interior is done in a peculiar mix of Georgian and Byzantine styles.

*** St. Patrick's Cathedral *(112, 178, 179, 225)*, Patrick Street

Archbishop John Comyn endowed St. Patrick's as a collegiate church in 1191, and his successor, Henri de Londres, had it raised to cathedral status in about 1220, at which time the present building was begun. Completed in 1254 in the Early English Gothic style, it has undergone many renovations and restorations, the most radical being in the nineteenth century under the direction of Sir Benjamin Lee Guinness, who essentially rebuilt the church, though adhering closely to the original plan.

Aisled and cruciform, it is the largest of Ireland's medieval cathedrals and now serves as a Protestant (Church of Ireland) house of worship. Of the original building, the following portions survive: the three eastern bays of the north aisle of the nave, the east wall and east aisle of the south transept, and the north and east walls of the choir. Noteworthy features of the interior include the massive and elaborate Boyle funeral monument erected in memory of his second wife by Richard Boyle, first earl of Cork (1566-1643); the brass tablets nearby, marking the graves of Jonathan Swift, dean of the cathedral from 1713 to 1745, and of his dear friend Esther Johnson, better known as "Stella"; a bust of Swift to the left of the adjacent door; miscellaneous Swift memorabilia in the north transept; also in the north transept a memorial book inscribed with the names of some fifty thousand Irishmen killed in World War I.

* Marsh's Library *(177, 179)*, St. Patrick's Close; open M, 2:00-4:00 P.M.; W-F, 10:30 A.M.-12:30 P.M., 2:00-4:00 P.M.; Sa, 10:30 A.M.-12:30 P.M.

Built by Archbishop Narcissus Marsh in 1701 to the design of Sir William Robinson, this is the oldest public library in Ireland. It contains about twenty-five thousand books printed in the sixteenth, seventeenth, and early eighteenth centuries, relating chiefly to theology, medicine, law, and travel. Marsh's own original contribution numbered about ten thousand items. The library contains two high-ceilinged galleries stacked with bookshelves—one barrel-vaulted, the other filled with readers' cages to which locks are fitted. On display are Dean Swift's death mask and other memorabilia.

Church of the Immaculate Conception (228), Merchant's Quay

Designed by Francis Byrne and built in 1830, this Franciscan house of worship is still known as "Adam and Eve's Church" after the tavern on the same site where Catholic services were held surreptitiously during penal times. It is neoclassical in style, with a facade of Doric and Corinthian pilasters and a little Doric temple on top to serve as a belfry. Inside it is quite attractive, with good plasterwork in the ceilings and a glassed dome over the crossing, where the nave, choir, and transepts intersect.

* Heuston (Kingsbridge) Station (221), Victoria Quay

Built between 1844 and 1848 to the design of Sancton Wood of Bath, this monumental Renaissance-style building with Corinthian pillars was the Dublin terminus of the Great Southern Railway. The train shed, with its blue-painted wood panelling and glass roof, is especially attractive.

St. Catherine's Church (176, 206), Thomas Street; closed except for special events

Designed by John Smyth and built in 1769, the Palladian granite front, pedimented and two-storeys high with giant Doric pilasters, is a handsome exercise in neoclassicism. The interior has been remodelled to serve as a concert hall. Robert Emmet was executed in September 1893 on a scaffold built in front of the church on the spot indicated by a bronze plaque attached to the railing.

* Guinness's Brewery (186, 220), St. James's Gate, James's Street

On this site is one of the world's largest and most famous breweries, begun in 1759, when Arthur Guinness leased an acre of ground and commenced producing ale and porter (porter only after 1799). Throughout the nineteenth century adjacent properties were purchased by the Guinnesses to form the present sixty-acre establishment. Guided tours through the plant are no longer conducted, but visitors are welcome in the interesting museum and audiovisual show.

* St. Patrick's (Swift's) Hospital (178, 179), James's Street and Steevens Lane

The original building here on the grounds of Dublin's leading facility for psychiatric care was erected in 1757 to the design of George Semple with funds provided by the bequest of Jonathan Swift for the founding of a hospital for "aged lunaticks and other diseased persons." Inside are to be found numerous Swift memorabilia, which are viewable on application.

** Royal Hospital, Kilmainham *(165)*, Military Road, west of city center; open July–Aug, Tu–Su, noon–5:00 P.M.; Sept–June, Sa, 2:00–5:00 P.M., Su, noon–5:00 P.M.; mandatory 45-minute guided tour

Built between 1680 and 1684 under the auspices of the first duke of Ormond and to a design by William Robinson, this splendid neoclassical building was the residence of retired soldiers of the British army's Irish regiments until 1922, when it was turned over to the Irish Free State government. It was inspired by Louis XIV's Les Invalides in Paris, to which it bears some resemblance. It is now a "National Centre for Culture and the Arts in Ireland" and is used mostly for concerts and art exhibits.

The fine neoclassical interior rooms are sparsely furnished, though the oak panelling and plasterwork are superb. Portraits of British monarchs, dukes of Ormond, archbishops of the Church of Ireland, et al., line the walls of the Great Hall. The best room is the chapel, a baroque masterpiece with a papier-mâché replica of the original plaster ceiling. The stained-glass windows date from 1840–41, though the rose window may possibly be the seventeenth-century original.

*** Kilmainham Jail *(206, 252, 254, 256)*, Inchicore Road; open Tu–Sa, 2:00–5:00 P.M.; Su, noon–5:00 P.M.; mandatory 30-minute guided tour on Sundays only

This grim building, the oldest parts of which date to 1796, has been converted into a shrine dedicated to Irish Nationalist heroes and martyrs. Prisoners from the 1798 uprising were jailed here, as well as Robert Emmet and his housekeeper Anne Devlin, who refused to buy her freedom by betraying him. On view in the 1916 corridor are the cells of Joseph Mary Plunkett, Countess Markievicz, Patrick and William Pearse, Tom McMillan, and other participants in the Easter uprising. In the main cell block is a fascinating museum with memorabilia of all the Nationalist rebellions, including weapons, ammunition, uniforms, photographs, books, etc.

In the courtyard outside is the execution place of five of the Fenian "Invincibles" convicted for participation in the Phoenix Park murders of 1882. The Deportation Yard was the mustering place of deportees to Australia. Nearby is Robert Emmet's exercise yard; also Erskine Childers' yacht *Asgard*, which brought German rifles to Ireland in 1914. Here too is the site of the execution of Irish republican prisoners by the pro-treaty government in 1922. In the Stonebreakers Yard is the execution place of the 1916 prisoners: Patrick Pearse, William Pearse, Thomas J. Clarke, Thomas MacDonagh, Joseph M. Plunkett, Edward Daly, Michael O'Hanrahan, John MacBride, Cornelius Colbert, Eamonn Ceannt, Michael Mallin, Sean Heuston, Sean MacDermott, and James Connolly.

NORTH OF RIVER LIFFEY

(South to North; East to West)

*** Custom House *(189)*, Custom House Quay

With its long facade of Portland stone and high copper dome, this is arguably Dublin's handsomest, and certainly its most visible, building. It was erected in the 1780s to the design of James Gandon, who was persuaded to leave England on the strength of this particular commission. The style is neoclassical; notable exterior features are the pedimented south portico supported by Doric columns and the keystones in the form of carved masks representing the principal rivers of Ireland, by the local sculptor Edward Smyth. The building was badly burned by soldiers of the IRA during the Irish civil war in 1921, was restored for the use of government offices, and is currently again under restoration.

* Abbey Theatre *(247)*, Lower Abbey Street

This building, completed in July 1966, stands on the site of the original theater of the same name that was purchased by Miss Annie Horniman in 1904 and turned over to the Irish National Theatre Society, founded by William Butler Yeats, Lady Augusta Gregory, and others. Here were staged the first performances of such noted plays as J. M. Synge's *Playboy of the Western World*, Sean O'Casey's *The Plough and the Stars*, and many others that together made Dublin one of the world's great theater capitals. On 17 July 1951 fire destroyed the original building, but the present theater contains a fine collection of portraits of the old abbey's founders, managers, actors, and playwrights. Included are likenesses of Lady Gregory, George Russell, and Annie Horniman by John Butler Yeats and of William Butler Yeats by Sean O'Sullivan.

Ormond Hotel *(245)*, 8 Upper Ormond Quay

Though much altered since 16 June 1904, when this place was patronized by Leopold Bloom (James Joyce's fictional character in *Ulysses*), the renovations more or less conform to the Edwardian decor of that date.

Tyrone House *(187, 208)*, Marlborough Street

This three-storey square granite house was built in 1740 for Sir Marcus Beresford, earl of Tyrone, to the design of Richard Castle. In the nineteenth century it became headquarters of the board of national education. Inside is plasterwork by the Francini brothers.

Connolly (Amiens Street) Station *(221)*, Amiens Street

Opened in 1844, this Italianate building designed by William Deane Butler was the Dublin terminus of the Dublin and Drogheda Railway.

O'Connell Monument *(237)*, O'Connell Street

Erected in 1854 to the design of the Irish sculptor John Henry Foley, this bronze statue of O'Connell looms over the street and bridge named in his honor. Around the base are the arms of the four Irish provinces and thirty figures, the central one representing Eire with a harp, holding in one hand a copy of the Catholic Emancipation Act of 1829. Seated around the monument are four winged figures representing courage, eloquence, fidelity, and patriotism.

** General Post Office *(209, 254)*, O'Connell Street

Built in 1815–17 to the design of Francis Johnston, this monumental neoclassic building is 223 feet wide and 150 feet deep, with an eighty-foot-long portico of fluted Ionic pillars supporting a pediment. The three statues on top by John Smith represent Hibernia, Mercury, and Fidelity. The building was taken over by Irish Volunteers on Easter Monday 1916, when Patrick Pearse read the Proclamation of the Irish Republic from the steps outside. Inside, in the main office, is Oliver Shepphard's bronze statue of the dying Cúchulainn with a raven perched on his shoulder. On the plinth beneath is reproduced the Proclamation of 1916 with the names of the signatories.

*** St. Mary's Pro-Cathedral *(226)*, Marlborough Street

Though somewhat crowded by adjacent buildings, this is a fine neoclassical church erected in 1816 to the design of John Sweetman, an amateur architect. The front portico with its six Doric columns was modelled on the Temple of Theseus in Athens. The basilical interior under its central dome is a thing of beauty. Noteworthy is the delicate Ascension in plaster relief over the altar.

* St. George's (C of I) Church *(224)*, Hardwicke Place; closed except during Church of Ireland services

Built in 1814–18 to the design of Francis Johnston, this is a fine example of early-nineteenth-century neoclassic style. The pedimented portico is supported by Ionic columns, and above it rises a tiered clock tower and high steeple. The church was perhaps modelled on James Gibbs's St. Martin's-in-the-Field, Trafalgar Square, London.

** **Rotunda Hospital** *(188, 196)*, Parnell Street (behind Ambassador Theatre); key to chapel from matron

This building was erected between 1751 and 1757 to the design of Richard Castle for the lying-in hospital founded in 1745 by Dr. Bartholomew Mosse (the oldest of its kind in the British Isles) and is still in service. Its most notable feature is the chapel, eighty-six feet high and thirty feet square, with marvelous baroque plasterwork by Bartholomew Cramillion, a French or Huguenot stuccodore.

** **Hugh Lane Municipal Gallery of Modern Art** *(188, 268)*, Parnell Square

Originally known as Charlemont House, this fine neoclassical building was erected between 1762 and 1765 for James Caulfield, first earl of Charlemont, to the design of Sir William Chambers. It now houses numerous paintings collected by Sir Hugh Lane, including works by Augustus John, Whistler, Burne-Jones, Corot, Millais, Renoir, Boudin, Degas, and Monet. Irish painting is represented by works of Roderic O'Conor, W. T. Leech, John Lavery, Walter Osborne, Paul Henry, Sean Keating, James Humbert Craig, and Jack B. Yeats. All are tastefully hung in the well-proportioned rooms of the original house.

Parnell Monument *(240)*, Parnell Street

At the top of O'Connell Street stands this bronze statue of Charles Stewart Parnell by Augustus St. Gaudens in front of a flame-topped stone obelisk pillar inscribed with a harp and an inscription taken from one of his speeches suggesting that his ambition for Ireland extended beyond Home Rule to national independence.

Belvedere College *(188, 209, 244)*, Great Denmark Street; admission by arrangement

Originally known as Belvedere House, this fine Georgian town house was built in about 1785 for George Rochford, Lord Belvedere, by Michael Stapleton, who also decorated the interior with elegant baroque plasterwork. In 1841 it was sold to the Society of Jesus and housed the school attended by James Joyce between 1893 and 1898.

The "Black Church" *(224)*, St. Mary's Place

This dark-hued building was erected in 1829–39 to the design of John Semple. It was a Protestant (Church of Ireland) chapel of ease but has since been deconsecrated.

* St. Saviour's Church *(231),* Lower Dominick Street

This is a lofty neo-Gothic Dominican church built between 1858 and 1861 to the design of James J. McCarthy. It has a lovely rose window in the west gable and a spacious aisled nave above which is a fine vaulted ceiling.

St. Mary's Abbey *(176),* Meetinghouse Lane (behind Capel Street); signposted; key from Mrs. K. Tyrrell, 35 Ormond Square

A solitary bolted doorway (not easily discerned in the surrounding complex of warehouses and office buildings) leads into the sunken chapter house of what was, in the Middle Ages, the richest Cistercian abbey in Ireland. The groin vaulting of the ceiling is a good example of thirteenth-century Gothic work.

Here, in 1534, Thomas FitzGerald, Lord of Offaly ("Silken Thomas"), renounced his allegiance to King Henry VIII, thus touching off an armed rebellion that took the English government more than a year to suppress. After the dissolution of the monasteries some of the abbey buildings were used as an armory, and the abbot's house was converted into a residence for the lord deputy, Leonard Grey.

* St. Mary's Church *(176),* Mary Street; closed except during Church of Ireland services

Designed by Thomas Burgh, surveyor general of Ireland, and built between 1697 and 1702, this church was probably modelled on one of those built by Sir Christopher Wren in London after the great fire of 1666. The exterior is undistinguished except for the west door, but the interior is handsome in the neoclassical manner. One of the first Protestant churches to be built in the eighteenth century, it is typically rectangular with a shallow chancel, a flat ceiling, and a gallery.

*** Four Courts *(183, 188, 189, 258),* Inns Quay

Incorporating an earlier building by Thomas Cooley, James Gandon designed and supervised the building of this magnificent neoclassical masterpiece between 1786 and 1802. It consists of two quadrangles with a double domed circular central hall in between. This handsome chamber is encircled by Corinthian columns. Corinthian columns also support the pedimented entrance portico, while those supporting the drum-shaped outer dome are of the Ionic order. The statues above the pediment (Moses and the Legal Virtues) are by Edward Smyth. The wing to the rear of Gandon's central building was added in about 1840. After the Irish civil war of 1922-23, when the building suffered heavily from exterior bombardment by the Irish provisional government and interior demolition by republican "irregulars" before their surrender, extensive restoration was required, but no great damage was done to Gandon's original handiwork. Although the Public Records Office suffered great destruction of important documents, it is still the major repository of materials useful for genealogical research.

* St. Paul's Church *(228)*, Arran Quay

Erected for Roman Catholic worship in 1837 to the design of Patrick Byrne, this is a typical early-nineteenth-century neoclassic building with an Ionic portico topped by a tall clock tower with a copper dome behind. Over the portico are statues of Saints Peter, Paul, and John.

Broadstone Station *(221)*, Prebend Street

Built in 1850 to the design of John S. Mulvany, this massive, rather ugly Graeco-Egyptianesque building was the Dublin terminus of the Midland Great Western Railway. It is now used as a bus station and freight depot.

* St. Michan's (C of I) Church *(165)*, Church Street; open daily; mandatory 20-minute guided tour

Built on the foundations of a medieval church, the present fabric dates mostly from 1686, although parts of the west tower may have belonged to the original building. The interior is somewhat shabby but contains a fine eighteenth-century organ that George Frederick Handel is believed to have played. Over the west doorway to the nave is a beautiful panel of musical instruments carved in wood. In the medieval crypt lie the mummified remains of several corpses, preserved over several centuries because of unusual climatic conditions.

*** King's Inns *(183, 188)*, Henrietta Street

Presently undergoing restoration, the central portion of this building is another of James Gandon's neoclassical masterpieces, built between 1794 and 1817. The two wings were added in the mid-nineteenth century. The statues in front, looking toward Constitution Hill, are by Edward Smyth. On deposit here is the Irish Registry of Deeds, an important source of historical information, especially useful for genealogical research.

** Blue Coat School (King's Hospital) *(188)*, Blackhall Place

Built between 1773 and 1783 to the design of Thomas Ivory, this fine neoclassical building originally housed a school for boys (uniformed in blue; hence the name). It now houses the offices and law school of the Incorporated Law Society of Ireland.

** Phoenix Park *(165)*, W of city center via Benburb and Parkgate streets

Originally designed and walled as a deer park in 1671 by the first duke of Ormond and opened to the public in 1747 by the lord lieutenant, Lord Chesterfield, this magnificent stretch of greenery covers 1,752 acres. Notable features (from east to west) are the People's Gardens, containing the Department of Defense's "Red House" designed by James Gandon; the **Wellington Monument** *(208)*, erected in 1817; the Dublin Zoo; Aras an Uachtarain (the official residence of the president of Ireland); the Phoenix Monument (1747); the American Ambassador's Residence; the Ordnance Survey Office; and the eighteenth-century Magazine Fort.

ENVIRONS

** Glasnevin Cemetery *(238, 240, 245)*, Finglas Road

First opened in 1832, primarily for the interment of Catholics, this lovely burial ground has since expanded from nine to a hundred acres. At the main entrance stands the ornate neo-Gothic mortuary chapel erected in 1879 to the design of James J. McCarthy. Nearby is a replica of a Round Tower standing above the crypt of Daniel O'Connell. Not far away are the tombs of Charles Stewart Parnell (a simple uncut boulder), Michael Collins (a plain cross), Jim Larkin, Eamon de Valera (another simple cross), Patrick Pearse, Robert Casement (a simple slab set in concrete), and Arthur Griffith (a column deliberately left unfinished until the day the six northern counties might be incorporated into the Republic of Ireland). Readers of James Joyce's *Ulysses* will remember this as the scene of Paddy Dignam's funeral, attended by Leopold Bloom.

** Pearse Museum *(253)*, St. Edna's School, Grange Road, Rathfarnham; signposted; open daily, 10:00 A.M.–noon, 2:00–8:00 P.M.

This eighteenth-century mansion (Hermitage House) was converted into a school by Patrick Pearse, Irish Nationalist and Gaelic revivalist, executed in 1916 after the Easter Rising. Throughout the well-furnished rooms are exhibits of Pearse's life and works: letters, publications, photgraphs, etc., arranged chronologically.

*** Casino Marino *(188)*, 3 mi N of city center in Marino village, W side of Malahide Road (R 107); entrance from Cherrymount Crescent; signposted; mandatory 20-minute guided tour; open daily, 10:00 A.M.–6:40 P.M.

Built between 1762 and 1777 as a garden house on the country estate of James Caulfield, first earl of Charlemont, to the design of Sir William Chambers, this neoclassical Roman-style temple is in the plan of a Greek cross. Three storeys high and encircled with Tuscan columns, it contains sixteen rooms with elaborate plaster ceilings and intricately patterned inlaid floors.

*** Malahide Castle and Garden *(190, 198, 269)*, S of Malahide village center; signposted; open M-F, 10:00 A.M.-12:45 P.M.; 2:00-5:00 P.M.; Sa, 11:00 A.M.-6:00 P.M.; Su, 2:00-6:00 P.M.

Set in a demesne of 270 acres, this is the ancestral home of the Talbot family, including the Jacobite Richard, earl of Tyrconnel, whose portrait hangs in the great hall. The core of the castle is of fifteenth-century provenance, but its present external appearance is mostly Gothick—the product of an eighteenth-century restoration. The property is now under the care of the Dublin and East Tourism Region and serves as Ireland's national portrait gallery, with a fine collection of paintings on loan from the National Gallery in Dublin. Among these are huge representations of the Battle of the Boyne by Jan Wyck and the Battle of Ballynahinch by Thomas Robinson; a fine hunting print, *The Ward Hunt,* by William Osborne; and numerous portraits and other Irish paintings by Nathaniel Hone the elder, James Latham, Hugh Douglas Hamilton, and William Ashford. The truly splendid twenty-acre garden, laid out by Lord Milo Talbot de Malahide between 1948 and 1973, contains a fine collection of over five thousand species of shrubs and trees.

** Dunsoghly Castle *(105)*, 6½ mi N of city center; E of N 2 (to Slane); signposted; OS ½ 13O 12 43; key at nearby #4 Newtown Cottages

Built in the mid-fifteenth century by Sir Thomas Plunkett, chief justice of the court of common pleas, this partially restored eighty-foot-high four-storey tower house consists of a rectangular block with a vaulted square tower at each corner. The wooden roof is original, though partially restored, and being the only one of its kind to have survived, it served as a model for restorations at Bunratty Castle and at Rothe House in Kilkenny. The stairs can be climbed to the top. The little chapel nearby was built in 1573 by Sir John Plunkett, chief justice of the queen's bench.

** Howth Castle Garden *(269)*, 7½ mi N of city center; W of Howth village, 1 mi S of Clontarf Road from Parsons factory through golf course to Deer Park Hotel, then by footpath behind hotel; signposted to Deer Park Hotel

This cliffside mass of rhododendrons is unmatched for floral splendor when in bloom. First plantings here took place in about 1850.

* St. Mary's, Howth *(126)*, 8 mi NE of city center; Church Street, Howth town center; not signposted; key from Mrs. McBride, 20 Church Street

Situated in what is known locally as the "Old Abbey Burial Ground," this well-preserved ruined church represents several periods of construction. The west end dates from the eleventh and thirteenth centuries, the east end from the late fourteenth or early fifteenth, the crenellated belfry tower at the west end of the south aisle from the fifteenth. In the chantry chapel, under a fine Decorated window, is the splendid carved tomb of the St. Lawrence family.

County Dublin

BRAY

Tully Church and Crosses *(50)*, 4½ mi N, 2 mi W of N 11 (to Dublin) through Cahinteely; poorly signposted; OS ½ 16O 23 23

This twelfth- or thirteenth-century ruined church is unusual in that the chancel, with two round-headed east windows, is wider than the nave. Several Early Christian grave slabs are to be found leaning against the north wall. On the roadside north of the church is an undecorated Early Christian granite ringed cross on a modern base. Across the road, over a stile and through a field, stands a tall, narrow cross with one arm missing. On one side are the eroded outlines of the figure of a bishop and on the other a face.

Rathmichael Grave Slabs *(40)*, 6 mi NW; 3 mi W of N 11 (to Dublin), ½ mi W of Rathmichael C of I Parish Church, up lane from Rathmichael Road back of parish church to ancient graveyard; signposted to church; OS ½ 16O 23 22

Built into the south wall of this much ruined sixteenth-century church are several badly eroded Early Christian grave slabs. At the southwest corner stands the low stump of a Round Tower.

CLONDALKIN

* Clondalkin Round Tower *(60)*, town center

This tower is eighty-four feet high and retains its original conical cap.

It also has an outside stone staircase (not original) leading to the doorway about ten feet above ground. There is no access to the base of the tower, currently under restoration, but it is clearly visible from the street.

DALKEY

* St. Begnet's Church *(49)*, Dalkey Island, ½ mi E by boat from Colliemore Harbor (no previous arrangements required); OS ½ 16O 28 26

This tiny (twenty- by 13.7-foot) roofless Early Christian church of mortared stone has antae on both east and west gable walls, a west doorway with inward-leaning jambs supporting a flat lintel, and thick (three-foot), slightly battered side walls, which stand to their full height on all four sides and are pierced with small round-headed windows.

* Dalkey Island Martello Tower *(207)*, ½ mi E by boat from Colliemore Harbor; boat trips easily arranged at harbor without advance notice; no entry to interior

On a rocky outcrop near the south shore of the island, and clearly visible from the mainland, is this fine martello tower, built in 1804 (along with fifteen others) to guard Dublin Bay against invasion by Napoleonic troops. It is of standard construction: round, three storeys high with a slightly convex roof, the entrance doorway elevated about ten feet above ground, gunports, and a circular track on top for training a twenty-four-pound cannon in all directions.

DUN LAOGHAIRE

*** Joyce's Tower *(207, 245)*, 1 mi E in Sandy Cove; open M–Sa, 10:00 A.M.–1:00 P.M., 2:00–5:15 P.M.

One of sixteen martello towers built in 1804 to protect Dublin Bay against the expected invasion by Napoleonic troops, this building stands about forty feet above the rocky outcrop on which it was built and commands a fine view of Dublin Bay across to Howth. With walls eight feet thick, the only visible defensive features today are the gunports on the landward side, the corbelled machicolation over the entrance door, and on the roof a central pivot and iron runner by which a twenty-four-pound cannon could be rotated to point in any direction.

This tower, as the name implies, is most famous for having been featured in the opening scene of James Joyce's *Ulysses*. It was in fact rented briefly by Joyce's friend Dr. Oliver St. John Gogarty (fictionalized as Buck Mulligan). Joyce himself lived here for only a few days in September 1904.

Today it houses an excellent collection of Joyceana, including first editions, copies of letters, articles of clothing, photographs, etc.

*** The National Maritime Museum *(17, 200)*, Haigh Terrace; open T–Su, 2:30–5:30 P.M.

Housed in the former "Mariners' Church" (built in 1837), this fine museum offers some five hundred exhibits relating to Ireland's nautical history. Included are the lens from the Baily Lighthouse, Howth; a long four-oared curragh from County Kerry; miniature boat and ship models, including a Dingle curragh, a Boyne coracle, the S.S. *Helga*, used by the Royal Navy to bombard rebel positions in Dublin during the 1916 Rising, and the S.S. *Great Eastern*, designed by Isambard Kingdom Brunel in 1859 and employed to lay the first Atlantic telegraph cables in the 1860s. Here also is a captured longboat from the French frigate *Resolue*, which participated in the abortive 1796 naval expedition to Bantry Bay, which Wolfe Tone persuaded the French Directory to undertake.

* St. Mary's Church, Monkstown *(225)*, 1 mi W; closed except for Church of Ireland services, but key available from custodian's office at back of church

Rebuilt by John Semple in the early nineteenth century, this large cruciform church with two vast galleried transepts and a long east end is an architectural oddity resembling the Gothic styles of Portugal more than any other known model.

LUSK

* Lusk Tower *(60, 129)*, village center; not signposted but visible from street

Here is a five-storey Round Tower, more than eighty feet high, still retaining its original conical roof. It is incorporated into one corner of a square fifteenth-century belfry tower with more or less matching towers at the other three corners. The attached church (no longer in use) is of nineteenth-century provenance.

NEWCASTLE

* Newcastle Church *(129)*, village center; locked except during Church of Ireland services; key from rectory, tel 288 231

Built in the fifteenth century, this nave-and-chancel church has a square three-storey tower at the west end. The choir has since been abandoned, and the nave now serves as the Protestant (Church of Ireland) parish church. The fine east window with its Decorated curvilinear tracery was removed from the choir and reinstalled in its present position in the east wall.

SWORDS

* Swords Round Tower *(60)*, town center

Standing in the grounds of the Church of Ireland parish church, this Early Christian tower stands to a height of almost eighty feet. The conical roof topped with a cross is modern. Owing to silting, the door is at ground level and may be entered.

** Newbridge House *(196)*, 4 mi NE; W of Donabate village, 1 mi W of N 1 (to Balbriggan); signposted; open M–F, 10:00 A.M.–12:45 P.M., 2:00–5:00 P.M.; Su, 2:00–5:30 P.M.; optional 40-minute guided tour

This handsome Georgian house was built sometime in the early eighteenth century for Charles Cobbe, bishop of Kildare, and enlarged and decorated for his son Thomas by the great Irish architect and stuccodore Robert West. Its outstanding interior feature is the plasterwork in the red drawing room. Also of interest are the museum of curiosities and, on the top floor, the doll collection. The spacious grounds are magnificent.

County Kildare

ATHY

Ardscull Motte *(83)*, 4 mi NE; W of N 78 (to Kilcullen); signposted; OS ½ 16S 73 98

Here are the remains of a twelfth-century Anglo-Norman motte-and-bailey castle—a thirty-five-foot-high round, tree-covered mound with a declivity in the center and surrounded by a ditch. The barely discernible bailey lies to the north. Fine views from here in all directions.

CASTLEDERMOT

* Castledermot Friary *(122)*, town center; entry barred but interior visible from street; key at house next door

This is the substantial ruin of a Franciscan friary church founded by Walter de Riddlesford in 1247. The lancet windows in the north and west walls attest to the building's thirteenth-century origin. In the fourteenth century the choir was extended eastward and the large north wing was added. In the windows of the latter is some fine switch-line tracery, perhaps the first appearance in Ireland of this early form of the Decorated Gothic style.

** Castledermot Crosses and Round Tower *(60, 61)*, E of town center

Here are two fine granite scriptural crosses and the stump of a third. Figured scenes cover the whole surface of the two highest. The west face of the south cross shows the Crucifixion, surrounded by numerous scenes not easy to identify, while the east face is given over to pure ornamentation. On the north cross the Fall of Adam and Eve is on one side and the Crucifixion on the other. Sundry other representations surround both figures.

The nearby Round Tower, about sixty-five feet high with a battlemented top (perhaps a medieval addition) has no door visible on the outside and can be entered only through the modern church to which it is attached.

** Moone Cross *(61)*, 5 mi N; ¼ mi W of N 9 (to Kilcullen) through stone piers from Moone village; signposted; OS ½ 16S 79 93

This fine granite cross, about seventeen feet high, dates to the ninth century and is among the earliest of Ireland's "scriptural crosses." The high pyramidal base is covered with carved biblical scenes about whose identity there is some dispute. A close scrutiny, however, will reveal the following representations: the Crucifixion, the Twelve Apostles (heads only), the Miracle of the Loaves and Fishes (loaves and fishes only), Adam and Eve, the Sacrifice of Isaac, Daniel in the Lions' Den, and Saints Paul and Anthony in the desert.

The nearby ruined church has antae, though it dates no earlier than the thirteenth century, which is quite late for this type of construction.

KILCULLEN

* Old Kilcullen Cross *(61)*, 2 mi S; W of N 9 (to Castledermot); not signposted; OS ½ 16N 83 07

On untended grounds is the shaft of a granite cross, on the south side of which is the representation of a man, possibly a bishop, below which is an interlace design. The east and west faces depict biblical scenes, badly eroded. The upper section, including the ring, is missing. Nearby is a much-ruined Round Tower, the upper portion of which was destroyed during the insurrection of 1798.

KILDARE

** St. Brigid's Cathedral and *** Kildare Round Tower *(60, 113, 226)*, on cathedral grounds, town center

Now serving as a Protestant (Church of Ireland) cathedral church, the original aisleless cruciform church on this site was built under the direction of Bishop Ralph of Bristol in the years following 1223. Portions of the south transept, the north and south walls of the nave, and half of the massive central tower are original. All the windows are lancets, and when the building was restored in 1875 by the English architect George Edmund Street its Early English Gothic character was largely retained. Noteworthy features of the interior include Bishop Wellesley's altar tomb, the early medieval font, and the tomb of Maurice FitzGerald (d. 1575).

Standing east of the cathedral, the Round Tower, more than a hundred feet high, has a Romanesque doorway and a battlemented roof that replaced the original conical top. The interior has been restored so that the tower can be climbed to the top, which affords a splendid view of the Wicklow Mountains to the east.

** Irish Horse Museum *(28, 32)*, 1 mi SE in Tully; open M–Sa, 10:30 A.M.–12:30 P.M., 2:00–5:00 P.M.; Su, 2:00–5:00 P.M.

On the grounds of the National Stud, this is a splendid modern museum devoted to the history of the horse in Ireland from the Bronze Age to the present. Well-written placards accompanying an interesting collection of artifacts make this a model of museumship. Next door are the attractive Japanese Gardens, also open to view.

MAYNOOTH

* Maynooth Castle *(83, 98, 107, 108, 156)*, town center, to right of entrance to Maynooth College; not signposted but visible from street; key at Mrs. Kelly's across street

This was the *caput* of the FitzGerald lords of Offaly and earls of Kildare from the early thirteenth century until it was abandoned in the mid-seventeenth. The high stone keep was begun in about 1203 by Gerald fitz Maurice (FitzGerald), baron of Offaly, and subsequently enlarged and modified by his successors, especially John, the sixth earl, in 1426. Another major restoration took place in the early seventeenth century at the hands of the earl of Cork, father-in-law of the fifteenth earl of Kildare. The ruined portions of these two additions lie east of the keep. Parts of the medieval curtain wall still stand, including the present main gatehouse, still used as the entrance to the castle grounds. From here Garret Mór FitzGerald, the eighth earl, in effect ruled Ireland from 1478 to 1513. Here also "Silken Thomas" FitzGerald, baron of Offaly, took his final stand against the English during the "Geraldine Rebellion" of 1534-35. The castle's surrender marked the beginning of the Tudor conquest of Ireland.

* Maynooth (C of I) Parish Church *(130)*, town center, to left of entrance to Maynooth College; locked except during Church of Ireland services

This building stands on the site of the collegiate church built in 1521 by Gerald Óg, ninth earl of Kildare. The tower and the west wall probably date to the original construction.

*** Maynooth (St. Patrick's) College *(174, 229)*, W of town center

Founded and endowed by the Irish parliament in 1795 as the Royal College of St. Patrick's for the education of Roman Catholic priests, this was the first Catholic seminary in post-Reformation Ireland. The original building (facing the entrance) is Stoyte House, built in the last decade of the eighteenth century and sold to the college at the time of its founding. Back of it is the Long Corridor, added as a dormitory for students in 1796-98 and subsequently enlarged. Behind (west of) this is St. Joseph's Square, flanked by Dunboyne House on the south, begun in 1814; New House on the north, begun in 1830 and later remodelled; and St. Patrick's House on the west, built in the nineteenth century to the design of the great Victorian Gothic Revival architect Augustus Welby Northmore Pugin. To the rear (west) of St. Patrick's House is St. Mary's Square (also known as the Pugin Quadrangle or the Gothic Quadrangle), with the Refectory and Russell Library on its south side and, on the north, the grandiose College Chapel, built in 1879 to the design of Pugin's disciple and the greatest of the Irish Gothic Revivalists, James J. McCarthy. To the south of the two quadrangles lie miscellaneous college buildings, including Riverstown Lodge, the oldest structure on the campus (1781), Loftus House, and the museum (see below). To the north stand the Senior Infirmary (also by J. J. McCarthy), the Aula Maxima, the John Paul II Library, and the new campus.

* Maynooth College Ecclesiological Museum *(173)*, south side of Pugin Quadrangle, near Loftus Hall; open Su, 3:00-6:00 P.M.; Tu, 2:30-5:30 P.M.; or by appointment with Father Casey at college

This small museum contains an interesting collection of Roman Catholic historical memorabilia, including chalices, vestments, rosaries, and, of particular interest, eighteenth-century penal crosses. One section is dedicated to the work of Dr. Nicholas Callan (1799-1864), professor of science at the college, pioneer in electrical research, and inventor of the induction coil.

* Taghadoe Round Tower *(60)*, 3 mi S; ½ mi W of R 406 (to Straffan); signposted; OS ½ 16N 96 26

This Early Christian round tower is sixty-five feet in height. A round-arched doorway stands about fifteen feet above ground, but there are only three windows, which may indicate that the building was never finished. The flat molding around the round-headed doorway topped by a carved head is an unusual embellishment to this type of monument. The adjacent odd-looking church ruin is a nineteenth-century building.

*** Castletown *(195)*, 4 mi S, in Cellbridge; open M–F, 10:00 A.M.–1:00 P.M., 2:00–5:00 P.M.; Sa, 11:00 A.M.–1:00 P.M.; Su, 2:00–6:00 P.M.; mandatory 30-minute guided tour

This is Ireland's grandest Palladian mansion. Begun in 1722 for Speaker William Conolly to the design of Allesandro Galilei and constructed mostly under the supervision of Sir Edward Lovett Pearce, the house consists of a huge three-storey central block connected to flanking pavilions by colonnades of Ionic columns. It was inherited in 1758 by the speaker's grandnephew Thomas Conolly, who hired the Francini brothers to install the elegant plasterwork on the walls of the great stairwell that encloses the fine cantilevered stone staircase added at about the same time. Thomas's wife, Louisa, was responsible for the Print Room and the Long Gallery. The house is now the headquarters of the Irish Georgian Society.

NAAS

** Jigginstown House *(159)*, ¾ mi W; S side of N 7 (to Kildare); not signposted but visible from road; OS ½ 16N 88 19; no entry

This splendid ruined mansion was built by Thomas Wentworth, earl of Strafford and lord deputy of Ireland, not long before his recall in 1640 to England, where he was attainted and executed. Built of stone and brick, it is 380 feet long, including its square projecting wings that flank the narrow rectangular central block. Striking to the eye are the large number of huge windows and the massive brick chimneys. Architecturally its most remarkable feature is the groined brick vaulting of the basement storey.

* Punchestown Standing Stones *(29)*, 3 mi SE; ¾ mi S of R 410 (to Blessington); adjacent to Punchestown Race Course; not signposted but visible from road; OS ½ 16N 92 17

On the east side of the road just north of the racecourse is the tallest single standing stone (*gallán*) in Ireland, measuring nineteen feet above ground and four feet underneath. The discovery of a bronze-age burial at its base indicates a date of about 2000 B.C. In a field across the road (not accessible) is another standing stone, slightly tilted.

* Oughterard Round Tower (60), 7 mi NE; 1½ mi N of N 7 (to Dublin) from 1 mi E of Kill, 100 yd to churchyard by footpath from iron gate S of white house; not signposted; OS ½ 16N 96 26

Here is a thirty-four-foot-high stump of an Early Christian tower with a round-arched doorway about ten feet above ground. Next to the tower are the ruins of an early-seventeenth-century church with a three-lighted cusped east window and a staircase built separately from the main body of the church. The grounds are unusually well tended.

NEWBRIDGE (DROICHEAD NUA)

Curragh Camp Military Museum (258), 2 mi W; 1 mi SE of N 7 (to Kildare); signposted; admission by appointment with commandant, Military College, tel (045) 41301

This small museum houses numerous weapons and some photos and newspaper clippings pertaining to the Easter Rising of 1916 and of the camp's 1922 takeover from the British by the Free State army. Also on the premises is the Chester Beatty collection of exotic swords.

ROBERTSTOWN

Grand Canal (185), village center

Here, and for several miles in either direction, is a good stretch of the canal that reached this point from Dublin in 1779. The abandoned red brick building opposite the locks was a hotel for canal boat passengers, opened in 1803.

County Offaly

BIRR

* Birr Castle and ***** Gardens** (210, 269), town center; castle closed to public; grounds open daily, 9:00 A.M.–1:00 P.M., 2:00–6:00 P.M.

Visible only from the outside, the castle is the product of an early-nineteenth-century Gothick remodelling of a seventeenth-century gatehouse keep built on the foundations of the medieval stronghold of the O'Carrolls. It was done under the direction of the architect John Johnston for Laurence Parsons, second earl of Rosse. The giant telescope and its housing were installed in 1845 by William Parsons, third earl.

The best features of the estate are the extensive gardens, laid out mostly in the twentieth century by the sixth earl. Crisscrossed by paths and well signposted, the demesne is a wonderland of box hedges, magnolias, azaleas, flowering fruit trees, exotic firs, water lilies, herbaceous borders, etc. Especially noteworthy are the river garden, the planted terraces close to the house, and the formal gardens on the far side of the grounds.

FERBANE

** Gallen Priory (50), ½ mi SE; on grounds of Gallen Priory Convent (entry signposted); OS ½ 15B 12 14

Here is one of the most important collections of Early Christian grave slabs in Ireland. They are embedded in two walls, reconstructed from the gables of the early priory church, and date from the eighth through the eleventh century. Between the two low walls is a single standing slab.

* Clonony Castle (105), 6 mi SW; N side of R 357 (to Ballinasloe), 3 mi W of Cloghan village; OS ½ 15N 05 20

Standing on the roadside here is the substantial ruin of a battlemented four-storey sixteenth-century tower house with a projecting wing. The stairs can be climbed for only a short distance as the interior is very ruinous and probably not safe. The attached bawn wall, also battlemented, is unusually well preserved.

*** Clonmacnoise Monastery (49, 50, 51, 60, 62, 63, 66, 86, 128), 12 mi NW; 6 mi W of N 62 (to Athlone); signposted; OS ½ 15N 01 31

This was one of the great centers of learning in the Early Christian era. Proceeding clockwise from the Visitors' Centre, the following points of special interest are to be observed:

1. Visitor's Centre: Here is a fine collection of Early Christian grave slabs, some inscribed with the formula OR DO ("a prayer for").

2. **The Cross of the Scriptures (West Cross)** (62): Arguably the most elaborate and therefore the most interesting of all Irish High Crosses. Its two arms tilt slightly upward, and the ring looks like a metal brooch with four bosses where it is attached to shaft and arms of the cross. On the west face is the Crucifixion, accompanied by New Testament scenes. On the east is

Christ sitting in judgment with the good souls on His right, the con-demned on His left. David adorns the south face, but the figures on the north face are hard to identify. On the base are hunters on horses, warriors in chariots, and numerous animals.

3. O'Rourke's Tower *(60)*: The remains of a tenth-century Round Tower.

4. Teampull Connor *(66)*: A restored church, the west doorway and south window of which date from the original early-twelfth-century construc-tion.

5. Teampull Finghin (St. Finghin's Church) *(66)*: Built in the twelfth century, the nave of this two-chambered church is reduced to its founda-tions, but most of the chancel remains standing. The chancel arch has some good Hiberno-Romanesque decoration (chevrons), and a small round-headed window is to be seen in the east gable wall. There is an attached high round belfry (now called "MacCarthy's Tower") with conical roof about fifty-six feet above ground.

6. Teampull Ciaráin (St. Ciaran's Church) *(49)*: The smallest building within the precinct, measuring only 12½ by eight feet, it is a partly col-lapsed single-chambered church or oratory of mortared stone with antae and is reputed to be the burial place of the monastery's founder.

7. The Nuns' Church *(66)*: About three hundred yards east of the monas-tery precincts (so as to avoid too-close contact with the monks), this is a fine nave-and-chancel church built in the twelfth century. The triple-arched west entry is deeply carved with outward-pointing sawtooth chev-rons, animals, and other typically Hiberno-Romanesque decorative fea-tures.

8. Teampull O'Kelly: A very ruinous twelfth-century church.

9. Teampull Rí *(66)*: A well-preserved twelfth-century ruin with fine lancet east windows.

10. Teampull Torpain and Teampull Doolin: Conjoined churches built in the seventeenth century on the ruins of an Early Christian church.

11. The Cathedral (Teampull Mór) *(128)*: Originally a single-chambered church with antae (possibly tenth-century), this, the largest building on the grounds, underwent several modifications. The twelfth-century Ro-manesque west doorway is an insertion, as are the fine fifteenth-century north doorway and vaulted chancel at the east end. The sacristy was added in the seventeenth century.

12. North Cross: A fragmentary shaft with carved animals on the south side and a curious humanoid figure on the north.

13. South Cross *(51)*: This is the earliest of the High Crosses on the site, dating perhaps to the ninth century. On the west face below the ring is a Crucifixion, but most of the surface is carved with interlacing interspersed with animals. There is a frieze of horses on the base.

14. Castle *(86)*: Finally, west of the monastic precincts lie the sparse ruins of the stone castle built by Archbishop Henri de Londres in about 1213 on the site of an earlier Anglo-Norman motte-and-bailey.

TULLAMORE

* Rahan Churches *(66)*, 6 mi W, in Rahan village; signposted; OS ½ 15N 26 25

The larger of the two churches here has been reroofed and somewhat unfortunately restored, but the chancel arch is a fine example of twelfth-century Hiberno-Romanesque stone carving, and most of the chancel behind it is also of twelfth-century date, including the unique round window high in the east gable. The north window is flanked by interesting animal carvings, probably of fifteenth-century provenance. The fragmentary ruins adjoining the church are parts of the original transepts when the building was cruciform. About a hundred yards to the east is the well-preserved ruin of a fifteenth- or sixteenth-century small church into which was inserted a fine Hiberno-Romanesque doorway, round arched and with good downward-pointing sawtooth chevrons.

** Durrow Abbey and High Cross(*50, 62*), 4 mi N; ¼ mi W of N 52 (to Kilbeggan), through iron-grille gates and down long avenue to derelict modern church; not signposted; OS ½ 15N 32 31

West of the church stands a well-preserved tenth-century High Cross with the following figural representations: east face (top to bottom)—Christ in glory, the Sacrifice of Isaac, and what appears to be David; west face—Crucifixion, the Mocking of Christ, soldiers at the tomb of Christ; south face—Cain and Abel, Adam and Eve. Nearby are five Early Christian grave slabs, two with the inscriptions OR DO, meaning "a prayer for."

County Meath

BALBRIGGAN

*** Fourknocks *(24)*, 7 mi W; 1 mi W of R 108 (to Drogheda) from 1 mi N of Naul village; signposted and visible from road; OS ½ 13O 11 62; key at Mrs. T. Connel's house (first house E of site)

Underneath this grass-covered mound (about sixty feet in diameter) is the ovoid chamber of an unusually large late Neolithic (circa 1800 B.C.) passage grave. The passageway faces northeast and is quite short; around the main burial chamber are three side niches; above it is a modern concrete domed roof pierced by light shafts. On the walls are incised decorations in the form of chevrons, spirals, diamonds, and concentric circles.

CEANNANAS (KELLS)

*** **Kells Monastery** *(49, 60, 61, 62)*, town center; signposted; OS ½ 13N 74 76

The buildings here were put up sometime after the resettlement in 804 of monks from St. Columba's monastery at Iona following repeated Viking attacks. The major remaining sites, located on the grounds of, or in the vicinity of, the Church of Ireland parish church, are:

1. **St. Columb's House** *(49)*: A single-chambered mortared stone church without antae, but still retaining its steeply pitched stone roof, beneath which is a typical Irish croft supported by a propping arch. The interior measures nineteen by 15½ feet; the walls are exceptionally thick; the window in the west wall is triangular-headed and that in the east round-headed. The existing ground-floor doorway in the south wall is an insertion owing to the subsidence of the ground level. The original western doorway has been walled in. The building is locked, but a key is available from Mrs. Carpenter, who lives at the bottom of the steep road leading up to the site.

2. **Kells Round Tower** *(60)*: The tower stands about a hundred feet high, with five windows (instead of the usual four) in the top storey and badly eroded heads carved on the doorway. It dates probably to the eleventh century.

3. **The South Cross (Cross of Saints Patrick and Columba)** *(61)*: A High Cross carved with the following scenes: west face—Crucifixion surmounted by a representation of Christ in glory; east face—Adam and Eve, Cain and Abel, the Three Children in the Fiery Furnace, Daniel in the Lions' Den, the Sacrifice of Isaac, and others not agreed upon.

4. **The East Cross** *(62)*: Built in the tenth century, the cross was unfinished, though the Crucifixion is carved clearly.

5. **The West Cross** *(62)*: Of ninth-century provenance, only the shaft survives. On its west side are Noah's Ark and Adam and Eve and on the east scenes from the life of Christ.

* **Kells Market Cross** *(60)*, town center at junction of Market, Cross, and Castle streets

This is probably not the original position of this finely carved cross. On the side facing Market Street is a representation of the Crucifixion, below which are New Testament scenes and an inscription carved in 1688. On the rear are Christ in the Tomb and Old Testament scenes, including Adam and Eve, Cain and Abel, and Daniel in the Lions' Den. Around the base are hunting and battle scenes.

* **Castle Keeran High Crosses and Ogham Stone** *(43)*, 4 mi W; 1½ mi NW of R 162 (to Oldcastle), across gate, field, and stile; signposted; OS ½ 13N 88 64

Here are three High Crosses, none with the usual figure carvings. Also on the grounds is a single Ogham stone with clear-cut incisions.

Robertstown Castle *(153)*, 7 mi NE; 4 mi NE of N 52 (to Ardee) from Carlanstown, through farmyard; not signposted; OS ½ 13N 79 84; building locked

This is a substantial ruin of a seventeenth-century gabled house with slit windows on the ground floor and mullioned windows in the upper storeys. Its most distinct features are the two corner turrets, corbelled in the Scottish fashion and probably designed by masons employed in building contemporary "planters' castles" in Ulster, many miles to the north.

NAVAN

** **Tara** *(24, 38, 201, 236)*, 6 mi SE; 1 mi SW of N 3 (to Dublin), by footpath through churchyard and over stile; signposted; OS ½ 13N 92 60

A sacred site since Neolithic times, Tara became in the Iron Age the inaugural place of the kings of Meath and, later still, in the Early Christian period, the royal seat of the high kings of Ireland. On first glance today it appears to be nothing more than a grass-covered hilltop covered with numerous embankments and distinguished chiefly by the splendid views in all directions. The lone, and somewhat inappropriate, stone statue is an anachronistic representation of St. Patrick, erected in the nineteenth century. Beside it is a pillar stone dedicated to the fallen heroes of the insurrection of 1798. The stone is thought to have served originally as the site of royal inaugurations.

Aside from these the most prominent feature is the Mound of the Hostages, underneath which lies a small Neolithic passage grave (circa

2100 B.C.). It lies near the north end of an ovoid enclosure demarked by an earthen bank, which may date from the Iron Age when Tara became the inauguration site of the kings of Meath. Near the middle of the enclosure stand two linked circular embankments of the type known as "ring-forts." South of here is another circular earthwork, known as the Fort of King Laoghaire, and to the north is still another called the Rath of the Synods. Still farther north is a long rectangular hollow area surrounded by banks that bears the name of Banqueting Hall. This, like the other names attached to the various earthworks at Tara, is purely fanciful.

There is a useful map of the premises at the entrance near the car park.

Skreen Church *(128)*, 6 mi SE; 2 mi SE of N 3 (to Dublin); obscurely signposted; OS ½ 13N 95 61

Here are the remains of a fourteenth-century nave-and-chancel parish church with a high west tower added in the fifteenth. Inside the tower is a baptismal font. Over the south door is a carving of a bishop. North of the church is a roughly carved medieval cross with an eroded Crucifixion on the west face.

* Killeen Church *(129)*, 10 mi SE; 1 mi SW of N 3 (to Dublin) from Berrillstown village; on grounds of Killeen Castle; not signposted; OS ½ 12N 93 55; entry to church barred, but interior visible through grilles

Here is the high-standing ruin of a nave-and-chancel church with square towers at each corner, built by Sir Christopher Plunkett between 1403 and 1405. Much of the original Decorated window tracery survives. In the south wall of the choir is a fine sedilia, and near the north wall a carved Plunkett tomb.

Killeen Castle *(210)*, 10 mi SE; 1 mi SW of N 3 (to Dublin) from Berrillstown village; not signposted; no entry

Viewable only from the outside, this huge, vacant, much battlemented house was remodelled in the Gothick style by Francis Johnston for the eighth earl of Fingall in the first decade of the nineteenth century. James Shiel added further embellishments for the ninth earl in the 1830s.

** Dunsany Church *(129)*, 10½ mi SE; 2½ mi SW of N 3 (to Dublin) from Ross Crossroads, on Dunsany Castle grounds, ¼ mi SE of Dunsany village; not signposted; OS ½ 13N 91 55; permission to visit obtainable at gate lodge

This is the well-preserved ruin of a nave-and-chancel church built in the mid–fifteenth century by Nicholas Plunkett, first Baron Dunsany. Like the nearby Killeen Church (above), the architectural style is fundamentally Late English Decorated, though sometimes identified as Perpendicular. The fine curvilinear tracery in the east window is a nineteenth-century insertion. At each corner of the building is a square tower. In the north wall is a double-effigy tomb, probably of Christopher, Lord Dunsany, and his wife, Anna FitzGerald. The contemporary baptismal font in the west end, carved with figures of the Crucifixion and the Twelve Apostles, is especially fine. Outside the north doorway is a fifteenth-century carved cross, also with representations of the apostles. The beauty of the ruin is enhanced by its location within the lovely parkland of the Dunsany estate.

* Donaghmore Round Tower *(60)*, 1½ mi NE; E side of N 51 (to Slane); not signposted but visible from road; OS ½ 13N 88 69

Next to the very ruinous fifteenth-century church is a well-preserved Round Tower with a restored conical top and a round-headed doorway above which is carved a Crucifixion and on either side of which are carved heads, probably a thirteenth- or fourteenth-century insertion.

* Rathmore Church *(129)*, 8 mi W; S of N 51 (to Athboy), in field past two gates; signposted; OS ½ 13N 75 67

Built in the mid–fifteenth century by Sir Thomas Plunkett, this is a nave-and-chancel church with corner towers and curvilinear Decorated windows. The building resembles two other Plunkett churches: Killeen and Dunsany (described earlier). Noteworthy are the crocketed sedilia, the fifteenth-century carved font, and the tomb of Sir Thomas and his wife.

OLDCASTLE

** Loughcrew (Slieve na Calliagh) Cemetery *(24)*, 4½ mi SE; ¾ mi N of R 154 (to Trim); signposted to car park; OS ½ 13N 57–60 77–78; key to tombs from Basil Balfe, first house on right after turnoff from R 154

Of the thirty or so tombs in this Neolithic cemetery, Carnbane East and Carnbane West are most worth close inspection. Carnbane East is easily accessible from the car park by crossing the stile and proceeding over the crest of the hill lying ahead and slightly to the left. It is a cruciform passage grave under a kerbed mound about 105 feet in diameter. The central chamber, off which lie three side niches, is corbelled to a height of about nine feet. Inside and out the stones are decorated liberally with incised chevrons, rayed circles, serpentine lines, spirals, etc. Carnbane West lies about four hundred yards to the west. It is also a kerbed mound about 120 feet in diameter built over an irregularly shaped central chamber with eight side chambers. Here too are numerous decorated stones.

SLANE

* Slane Castle *(197)*, 1 mi W; S of N 51 (to Navan); signposted; open Su, 2:00–6:00 P.M.; mandatory 30-minute guided tour of 4 rooms only

James Wyatt designed this house in 1785 for the second Baron Co-nyngham—the earliest known example of Gothick residential architecture in Ireland. In plan the building, though adorned with pointed arches and battlements, is too symmetrical to conform precisely to the new style made fashionable by Sir Horace Walpole at Strawberry Hill near London. The ballroom, however, with its fanciful tracery, is quintessentially Gothick. The furnishings are mostly Regency or Victorian. A good portion of the interior is taken up by a restaurant and nightclub.

** Slane Friary and College *(130)*, NW of village center; W of N 2 (to Ardee); signposted; OS ½ 13N 96 75

These substantial hilltop ruins are the remains of a sixteenth-century Franciscan friary and of a small contemporary collegiate foundation established by Sir Christopher Fleming and his wife for four priests, four clerks, and four choristers. Nave, chancel, and south wing of the friary church stand fairly high. The west gable displays a fine Decorated window, and the slender tower can be climbed to the top from which a marvelous view of the surrounding countryside can be obtained. There are no claustral remains. North of the church lies the ruined college—a multicompart-mented building with a turret (also climbable) at the southeast corner.

* Knowth *(24)*, 2 mi E; ½ mi S of N 61 (to Drogheda); signposted; OS ½ 13N 99 73

This is the westernmost of the three great Neolithic passage graves of the Bend of the Boyne Cemetery. The covering earthen mound is about forty feet high and 220 feet in diameter. A number of the kerbstones surrounding it are decorated with typical stone carvings of zigzags, spirals, etc. The site is currently undergoing thorough excavation, and the burial chambers underneath the mound are not open for inspection.

*** Newgrange *(23, 30)*, 3½ mi E; 1½ mi SE of N 61 (to Drogheda); signposted; OS ½ 13O 99 73; open daily, 10:00 A.M.–6:00 P.M; mandatory 20-minute guided tour

This well-preserved late Neolithic passage grave (circa 3100 B.C.) is among the best of its kind in Europe and is Ireland's most famous prehistoric monument. The covering mound is about 280 feet in diameter and nearly forty-five feet in height. A stone circle of about thirty-four tall boulders was set in place around the tomb during the Bronze Age, but only twelve of these stones are still standing. The mound itself is revetted by horizontal kerbstones, many of them bearing inscribed decorations. Of these the best known is the entrance stone with its triple spirals, double spirals, concentric semicircles, and lozenges.

Above the entrance is a decorated and slitted stone box through which rays from the rising sun at the winter solstice penetrate onto the floor of the inner chamber. The narrow passageway is sixty-two feet long, with walls decorated richly with triple spirals, zigzags, concentric circles, etc. It leads to a round corbelled chamber, twenty feet high, off which lie three side chambers. In each of the three are more decorated stones, as well as shallow stone basins, probably used to contain the bodies of the dead before cremation.

* Dowth *(23)*, 4 mi E; 3 mi SE of N 61 (to Drogheda); signposted; OS ½ 13O 02 74

Along with Newgrange and Knowth, this late Neolithic passage grave forms part of the great Bend of the Boyne Cemetery. The covering mound is about 280 feet in diameter and fifty feet high. Some of the kerbstones edging the mound are incised with primitive designs. At the northwest end of the mound is an Early Christian souterrain. There are two tombs underneath the mound at its western end. Formerly open for inspection, they are now and for the foreseeable future closed as unsafe.

Athlumney (Athcarne) Castle *(105)*, 8½ mi SE; 2 mi W of N 2 (to Dublin) from Balrath village, across from Castle View shop; signposted; OS ½ 13O 02 65

This is a ruined four-storey fifteenth-century tower house to which was appended in the late sixteenth century a residential mansion with mullioned windows.

* Duleek Abbey *(116)*, 9 mi SE, in Duleek village center; not signposted but visible from street; OS ½ 13O 04 69

This was originally a house of Augustinian canons regular founded by Hugh de Lacy in 1182. The earliest part of the church (the south arcade) probably dates to the thirteenth century, but the tower is a fifteenth-century addition. In the choir is a fifteenth-century Preston-Plunkett altar tomb. North of the adjacent modern church is a short ninth-century cross with figure carvings on the west side and incised decorations on the east.

TRIM

*** Trim Castle *(81, 85, 87)*, town center; not signposted but visible from street

The first castle here was a motte-and-bailey put up by Hugh de Lacy in 1172, promptly destroyed by king Rory O'Connor, and rebuilt about 1190. On the death of Hugh de Lacy it went to his son Walter and was taken from him by King John in 1210. In about 1220 William Peppard raised the present seventy-six-foot high rectangular keep. Richard II visited here in 1399 and left behind him the boy who later became King Henry V. Following the sack of Drogheda in 1649 the royalist garrison here promptly surrendered to the Cromwellians, after which the castle fell into disuse.

The keep was unique in Ireland in that from each side of the rectangle lesser towers projected outward, thus forming a twenty-sided ground plan. Around it stretches the curtain wall, with five remaining towers and two entranceways. The Dublin gate on the south side is a single tower pierced by an entrance passageway. In front of it lies a barbican spanning the moat over which stretched a drawbridge operated from an upper room of the barbican tower. Another gateway, with grooves for a portcullis, pierces the west wall. Of the four original towers in the keep, three remain.

The interior of the castle is poorly tended, and although the stairs can be climbed to the top, the exercise is somewhat risky.

Town Wall *(93)*, town center

On the north side of the river, opposite the castle, are fragments of the medieval town wall, including a much-ruined water gate and the two-storey Sheepgate.

St. Mary's Priory *(72)*, N of town center, across river

Known locally as the "Yellow Steeple," this 125-foot tower was built in the fourteenth century as the belfry of the priory church of the Augustinian canons regular who came here in about 1140, probably under the persuasion of St. Malachy. Nothing else remains of the establishment.

* Newtown Trim Priory and Cathedral Church *(113, 128)*, 1 mi E of town center; signposted; OS ½ 13N 81 57

Built in the early thirteenth century by Bishop Simon de Rochfort, today's ruins consist chiefly of the choir and nave, the latter foreshortened in the fifteenth century, when a new west wall was built. The cathedral chapter was made up of Augustinian canons regular, and the remains of their refectory still stand south of the church. So do remnants of the thirteenth-century doorway to the chapter house. East of the cathedral church are the ruins of a thirteenth-century parish church containing an interesting double-effigy sixteenth-century tomb of Sir Luke and Lady Dillon.

** **Bective Abbey** *(71, 127, 140)*, 4 mi NE; ½ mi E of R 161 (to Navan); signposted; OS ½ 13N 86 60

Founded in 1150 by Murchad O'Melaglin, king of Meath, this was the first of the Cistercian daughterhouses of Mellifont. No twelfth-century remains can be authenticated; the earliest work seems to be the high-standing south arcade of the nave and part of the south transept, rebuilt after 1274. To the south is the cloister, which, according to the architectural historian Roger Stalley, is "the most intimate and secluded" of any of the ruined Irish Cistercian houses. The vaulted ambulatories of the south and west ranges were built in the fifteenth century and are especially attractive. Of about the same date is the massive fortified tower in the south range, which, along with other parts of the abbey, was converted after the dissolution into a sprawling Tudor mansion by the new lessee, Thomas Agard.

* **Donore Castle** *(105)*, 8 mi SW; S side of R 161 (to Kinnegad); not signposted but visible from road; OS ½ 13N 70 50; key location not available

This plain three-storey ruined tower house with rounded corners conforms closely to the dimensions laid down by an act of Parliament of 1429 offering a ten-pound subsidy to residents of the Pale who would construct such a building within ten years. Although a number were actually built, this is the only survivor that can almost certainly be attributed to the statute.

County Westmeath

ATHLONE

** **Athlone Castle and Museum** *(86, 145, 166)*, town center; open M–Sa, 11:30 A.M.–1:00 P.M., 3:00–6:00 P.M.

The oldest part of the castle is the polygonal keep. It was probably built soon after the collapse of the first stone castle on this site, erected in 1210 by the justiciar John de Gray. The three-quarter-round flanking towers of the curtain wall were probably a mid-thirteenth-century addition. Other alterations were made in the 1570s, when Sir Edward Fitton was president of Connacht, and again during the Restoration period (1669–85). The place was badly damaged during the Williamite siege of Athlone. Substantial alterations ensued. Again in the nineteenth century the castle was much altered to accommodate heavy guns. The present entrance ramp is modern. The museum contains an interesting miscellany of items pertaining to the history and prehistory of Athlone: cannonballs from the 1691 siege, Early Christian grave slabs, a penal cross dated 1792, stone querns, various domestic implements and accoutrements, the recorded voice of the tenor John McCormack, etc.

CASTLEPOLLARD

** **Tullynally Castle** *(209)*, 1 mi NW; S of R 395 (to Granard); open 16 July–15 Aug, 2:30–6:00 P.M. 1430–1800; mandatory 45-minute guided tour

This is the ancestral home of the Pakenham family, renowned warriors and more recently distinguished for their literary prowess. Although the oldest parts of the building date to the mid–seventeenth century, its present appearance stems from a Gothick remodelling in the early nineteenth for the second earl of Longford by Francis Johnston plus later additions by James Shiel, and, for the third earl, two wings and a central tower added in 1840 by Richard Morrison. The most interesting features of the interior are the octagonal dining room, the basement laundry room, and the furnace room with its massive boiler providing central heating— allegedly the first of its kind in the British Isles.

The park and gardens (open throughout the summer months) were originally laid out in the eighteenth century but were modified drastically with the change of horticultural fashions in the mid-nineteenth. Included are a woodland garden, flower garden, kitchen garden, grotto, and artificial lake. The historian Thomas Pakenham now owns the property.

** **Fore Abbey** *(116, 127, 140)*, 4½ mi E; 1½ mi S of R 195 (to Oldcastle); signposted; OS ½ 13N 51 70

Here are the substantial ruins of one of the few surviving Benedictine abbeys in Ireland—founded by Hugh de Lacy in the late twelfth century or early thirteenth century. The three round-headed windows in the east wall of the rectangular church date from about the time of the foundation. The two towers, which give the place a military appearance, were added in the fifteenth century. Both can be climbed. The high-standing claustral buildings, probably also of fifteenth-century provenance, were rebuilt in the present century. Inside the cloister is a handsome segment of arcade. On the roadside just north of the abbey are the remains of a gate forming part of the medieval town wall. The property fell to the Nugent family at the time of the dissolution of the monasteries in the 1540s and was converted to residential use.

* St. Fechin's Church *(49)*, across road from Fore Abbey (preceding site); OS ½ 13N 51 70

This is an Early Christian mortared stone church with antae. The chancel was added to the originally single-chambered church in about 1200, its two east windows in the fifteenth century. The most notable feature here is the Greek cross within a circle carved in low relief on a stone panel above the lintel of the west doorway.

MULLINGAR

Mullingar Cathedral Museum *(173)*, city center, on second floor of cathedral church; admission obtainable at priests' residence, tel (044) 48378

Here are numerous vestments and religious objects, the most interesting of which is a good collection of eighteenth- and early-nineteenth century penal crosses.

Mullingar Military Museum *(202, 256)*, Columb Barracks, town center; open by arrangement, tel (044) 48391

Here is an interesting collection of military miscellany, including expended cannonballs from the storming of Birr Castle by Patrick Sarsfield in 1790; bayonets and pike heads from the 1798 insurrection; eighteenth-century swords; World War I rifles and pistols; artifacts made in the Ballykinlon Internment Camp by IRA prisoners in 1921; posters and clippings from the Irish War of Independence, 1919–21; and mementos from UN operations in Zaire and Cyprus.

* Belvedere House *(196)*, 4 mi S; W of N 52 (to Kilbeggan); open daily, noon–6:00 P.M.

This somewhat ungainly country house, possibly designed by Richard Castle, was built in the 1740s for Robert Rochfort, later first earl of Belvedere. The exterior design is remotely Palladian. The interior has been denuded of most of its original furniture, though the fine rococo plasterwork is still in place on the ground-floor ceilings. Outside is a curious folly, called the Jealous Wall, built in the eighteenth century to resemble a medieval ruin. The view over Lough Ennel is glorious, and the walled garden is superb.

* Taghmon (St. Munna's) Church *(129)*, 5 mi NE; 1 mi E of R 394 (to

Castlepollard) from Crookedwood village; signposted; OS ½ 12N 49 61; key at cottage west of church

The distinctive feature of this small restored fifteenth-century church is the battlemented four-storey square tower at the west end, which obviously served as the priest's residence. The ogee-headed, trefoil-cusped narrow windows are typically Decorated Gothic in style. The tower can be climbed to the roof.

County Longford

BALLYMAHON

Abbeyshrule Abbey *(119)*, 6 mi E; 3 mi NE of R 392 (to Mullingar); signposted; OS ½ 12N 22 59

Very little is left here of the Cistercian monastery founded in about 1200 by the O'Farrels. The tower probably dates to the original building, as does the choir, though the latter was much altered in the sixteenth century to form a separate chapel. The ruins are rank with ivy and other vegetation.

GRANARD

Granard Motte *(81, 85, 95)*, W of village center behind RC church; OS ½ 12N 33 81

This deeply ditched mound is the site of a motte-and-bailey castle raised by Richard de Tuit late in the twelfth century. It was taken by King John during his punitive expedition against Hugh de Lacy II in 1210. It was among the strongholds burned by Edward Bruce during his invasion of Ireland in 1315-18. The modern statue of St. Patrick is a twentieth-century intrusion.

Abbeylara Abbey *(118, 127)*, 2 mi SE; W of R 396 (to Coole); signposted; OS ½ 12N 37 79

The only surviving parts of this Cistercian abbey, founded in 1211 by Richard de Tuit, are fragments of the crossing of the thirteenth-century church, surmounted by a fifteenth-century tower.

LONGFORD

** Carriglas Manor *(197)*, 3 mi NE; S of R 194 (to Granard); open Th, Sa-Su, 2:00-6:00 P.M.; mandatory 60-minute guided tour by owner

Built in 1837 for Thomas Lefroy to the design of Daniel Robertson, this is a fine example of the early-nineteenth-century Gothic revival. The interior furnishings are mostly Regency and early Victorian. The most interesting feature of the establishment is the neoclassical stable yard, designed in 1790 by James Gandon. The house is still in the possession of the Lefroy family and has been partially converted into a guest house.

St. Mel's, Ardagh *(49)*, 7 mi SE; E of R 393 (to Mullingar via Carrickboy), in village center behind abandoned modern church; not signposted; OS ½ 12N 20 69

Here are the restored ruins of an Early Christian single-cell rectangular church with antae. It is unusually broad in plan. The walls stand about six feet high, and the west doorway is lintelled.

County Louth

CARLINGFORD

** **Carlingford (King John's) Castle** *(85, 97)*, N of village center; not signposted but visible from road; entry barred but interior visible through grating

Of the original castle, probably constructed by Hugh de Lacy II around the year 1200 and not by King John, who visited here in 1210, the semicircular western half survives; the dividing wall and the eastern half were built in 1261. It was among the castles ruined by the O'Neills in the late fourteenth century, but came under royal control again in the fifteenth. Whatever its original plan may have been, as modified this is a courtyard castle divided in half by a massive high wall. Enclosing the western part is a curving curtain wall, pierced by a gatehouse of twin rectangular towers of which only parts of the northern tower remain standing. To the south stands a smaller rectangular mural tower. East of the dividing wall stand the remains of a two-storey building that probably served as the great hall. The view from here of Carlingford Lough is spectacular.

* **"The Mint"** *(105)*, village center; signposted; entry barred but interior visible through grating

This well-preserved three-storey fifteenth-century tower house displays good ogee-headed windows and typically Irish stepped battlements. The origin of its name is unknown.

DROGHEDA

* St. Peter's (RC) Church *(165)*, West Street, town center

At the east end of the north aisle of this fine aisled church, begun in 1888, is the shrine and embalmed head of Saint Oliver Plunkett, executed in London at the time of the 1678 Popish Plot on false charges of conspiring with the French to effect an armed invasion of Ireland. Also on view is the door of his cell in Newgate prison.

* St. Laurence Gate *(93)*, juncture of Laurence Street and Chord Road, town center

This fine twin-towered thirteenth-century building astride the modern city street formerly served as the barbican guarding the easternmost of the city gates. The slots for the portcullis are still visible.

St. Mary's Priory *(122)*, Old Abbey Lane, town center

Known locally as "Old Abbey," this was a thirteenth-century house of Augustinian friars. All that remains are the ruined tower and the east gable arch.

** St. Peter's (C of I) Church *(177)*, Lower Magdalene Street, town center; open only for Church of Ireland services, but key obtainable at rectory NW of church

Built in 1753 on the site of the former church burned by Cromwell's soldiers, this is a fine neoclassical rectangular church with a west tower and spire added by Francis Johnston in the late eighteenth century. There are galleries on three sides supported on octagonal Corinthian pillars, a shallow chancel, and fine wall monuments lining the sides. The stained-glass east window is a nineteenth-century insertion. At one corner of the churchyard wall is an interesting medieval mortuary tomb with carvings representing decaying bodies.

Magdalene Tower *(128)*, Upper Magdalene Street, town center

This high belfry tower was built in the fifteenth century as an addition to the Dominican friary founded here by Archbishop Luke Netterville in 1224—the first house of this order in Ireland. The Decorated windows with cusped ogee heads attest to the date of construction.

Millmount *(82)*, Duleek Street, south of town center

This high conical-shaped mound is a typical Norman motte of the twelfth century. On top is a round fortress of the Napoleonic era, now housing the **Millmount Museum** *(161, 256)* (open Tu–Su, 3:00–6:00 P.M.; 40-minute mandatory guided tour). Here is an interesting collection of local memorabilia, including expended cannonballs from Cromwell's siege of Drogheda (1649) and items associated with the War of Irish Independence and civil war (1916–22).

** **Termonfeckin Castle** *(125)*, 4 mi NE; E of R 156 (to Clogherhead); signposted; OS ½ 13O 14 80; key from Patrick Duffin, across road

This three-storey fifteenth-century battlemented tower house was one of the episcopal palaces of the late medieval archbishops of Armagh who preferred living within the Pale to taking up residence at their archiepiscopal seat in the cathedral city of Armagh. (They maintained a second house in Drogheda.) A distinct, and possibly unique, feature is the circular corbelled ceiling. The tower can be climbed to the roof, from which there is a fine view of the Irish Sea to the east.

** **Mellifont** *(71, 127, 140)*, 5 mi NW; 2 mi W of R 168 (to Collon); signposted; OS ½ 13O 01 78

This is the earliest of the Cistercian abbeys in Ireland—founded by St. Malachy in 1142 on land granted by Donogh O'Carroll, king of Oriel. Remains of the original twelfth-century buildings are scanty. From the site office today's visitor first crosses through the north transept of the church, of which only the lower portions of walls and piers survive. These date mostly to thirteenth-, fourteenth-, and fifteenth-century rebuildings. Of the claustral buildings south of the church the most substantial remnant is the chapter house in the east range, with fine groined vaulting. Of the west range nothing remains except for foundation stones. The same is true of the south range, but here, in front of what was once the refectory (dining hall), is the unique octagonal stone lavabo, of which about half survives. Nearby are portions of the arcade that once surrounded the central yard (the garth) of the cloister. Next to the car park is the high-standing ruin of the monastic gatehouse. After the dissolution of the monastery in 1539 the property went to Sir William Brabazon and then to Sir Edward Moore, who built here the house where the earl of Tyrone and Lord Mountjoy signed the treaty ending the Nine Years' War.

*** **Monasterboice** *(60, 62)*, 7 mi N; ½ mi W of N 1 (to Dundalk); signposted; OS ½ 13O 04 92

Here are some of the best-preserved relics of any Early Christian monastery in Ireland, including:

1. **Cross of Muiredach (South Cross)** *(62)*: Eighteen feet high, this is

among the finest of the Irish High Crosses. It was probably built in the ninth century, and at the bottom of the shaft is the name of Muiredach, possibly an abbot here. On the west face is carved the Crucifixion, with scenes from the New Testament on the stem beneath; on the east, the Last Judgment with the Archangel Michael weighing the souls and beneath him scenes from the Old Testament. South and north sides are covered with human figures, animal interlace, geometric patterns, and vine scroll inhabited by animals; the base shows hunters, animals, and more interlace; on the top is a finial resembling a house shrine on which other biblical scenes are inscribed.

2. Tall Cross (West Cross) *(62)*: This cross is 21½ feet high. The east face shows, among other scenes, David Killing the Lion, the Sacrifice of Isaac, and the Three Children in the Fiery Furnace. On the west face are the Crucifixion and other scenes probably from the New Testament. North and south faces are also filled with carvings.

3. Round Tower *(60)*: This Round Tower, 110 feet high and well preserved, could be climbed to the top, but the location of the key to the door is not posted.

4. Cemetery: Two small churches, still another High Cross with a Crucifixion on one side, and an Early Christian grave slab lie in the nearby cemetery.

DUNDALK

Dún Dealgan Motte *(82, 85, 95)*, 1½ mi W; S of N 53 (to Castleblayney), over stile and up steep footpath; not signposted; OS ½ 9J 03 08

Here are the remains of a late-twelfth-century motte-and-bailey erected by Bertram de Verdun on land granted by King John. The site is alleged to be the birthplace of the legendary Cúchulainn. It was held by Hugh de Lacy II in 1210 and abandoned by him, probably after burning, to King John. It is also the scene of the Battle of Faughart, where Edward Bruce was killed in 1318. The building on top of the mound is an eighteenth-century folly.

* St. Mochta's House *(66)*, 7 mi SW in Louth village; not signposted but visible from road; OS ½ 9H 96 01

On the grounds of a ruined fourteenth- or fifteenth-century church is a small rectangular Early Christian oratory with a steeply sloped roof under which is a loft reachable by a modern ladder.

* Castleroche Castle *(88)*, 7 mi NW; 1½ mi SW of R 177 (to Newtownhamilton) through Drumbilla village; not signposted; OS ½ 9H 99 12

This is a mid-thirteenth-century keepless courtyard castle, built probably by John de Verdon. High curtain walls enclose a triangular courtyard. In the middle of the north side is the twin-towered gatehouse, now mostly ruined on the inside. At the southeast end of the enclosure is a roofless two-storey building that housed the great hall.

** Proleek Dolmen *(22)*, 4 mi NE; N of R 173 (to Carlingford), 1 mi E of junction with N 1 (to Newry) by footpath from behind Ballymascanlon Hotel; signposted; OS ½ 9J 09 11

This is a typical "tripod" portal dolmen, its massive forty-ton capstone resting on three uprights. The overall height is twelve feet. Close by are the remains of a bronze-age tomb.

DUNLEER

Greenmount Motte *(82)*, 3½ mi N; E of N 1 (to Belfast), behind White House bed-and-breakfast; not signposted; OS ½ 13O 06 03

An early-thirteenth-century Anglo-Norman motte-and-bailey castle stood on the site of this tall, grass-covered mound that has a declivity on the summit.

* Roodstown Castle *(105)*, 6 mi NW; 1¾ mi W of N 1 (to Belfast) through Stabannon village; not signposted; OS ½ 13N 00 93; key from Mr. MacMahon, fourth house to E across road

Built in the fifteenth century, this well-preserved four-storey tower house has a rectangular central block with square towers at diagonally opposite corners. In Scotland this would be called a Z-plan tower and is a fairly common variety, but this is the only known Irish example of the type from this period. There is a murder hole over the entrance passage; also trefoil-headed windows, and one mullioned window. The circular stairway in one of the corner towers can be climbed to the top.

Dromiskin Round Tower *(60)*, 7 mi N; 1 mi W of N 1 (to Belfast), through churchyard; not signposted; OS ½ 13O 05 98

Here is the fifty-five-foot-high stump of an Early Christian tower with a recessed round-arched door about fifteen feet above ground and a conical cap added in the nineteenth century. East of the tower is a remounted High Cross with a whorl carved at the crossing on the west face and hunting scenes on the east. Close by are the scant remains of a medieval parish church.

County Monaghan

CLONES

Clones Cross *(62)*, town center

This High Cross, probably of tenth-century date, is constructed out of portions of two separate crosses fitted together. The usual Crucifixion appears on the east face along with New Testament scenes, while on the west face, from bottom to top, are Adam and Eve, Cain and Abel, and Daniel in the Lions' Den.

Clones Round Tower *(60)*, SW of town center, through gateway from street; not signposted but visible from street; OS ½ 8H 50 26

The tower is about seventy-five feet high with square-headed door and windows. Nearby is St. Tighernach's shrine, in the shape of a house.

Clones Castle *(86)*, NW of town center, by footpath from street; signposted; OS ½ 8H 50 26

On this tree-covered mound was a motte-and-bailey castle, probably built by the justiciar John de Gray in the early years of the thirteenth century.

MONAGHAN

* Monaghan County Museum *(19)*, Court House, town center (behind Irish Tourist Information Office); open all year Tu–Sa, 10:00 A.M.–1:00 P.M., 2:00–5:00 P.M.; June–Aug, Su, 2:00–6:00 P.M.

Once reorganization is completed, this promises to be an excellent museum of local history and archaeology of a sort too seldom found in Ireland. Its holdings include a fine collection of prehistoric pottery, a Mesolithic flint blade (5500–4000 B.C.), bronze-age weapons, an iron-age cauldron, the Cross of Clogher (circa 1400), sundry nineteenth-century domestic furnishings, and paintings by local artists.

** St. MacCartan's Cathedral *(231)*, SE of city center

Begun in 1861 to the design of James J. McCarthy, this is a fine neo-Gothic cruciform church in the Decorated style. The nave is very high and covered with a hammerbeam roof; the transepts are shallow; the Victorian stained glass is of high quality, especially the rose window in the west gable, though from the inside it is somewhat obscured by the mighty organ with its many-colored pipes. Anomalous features are the Corinthian capitals of the columns and the starkly modernistic altar table, pulpit, and lectern.

County Cavan

BELTURBET

* Belturbet Parish Church *(152)*, town center; open daily and for Church of Ireland services

This is a pretty cruciform Jacobean-Gothic church with galleries at the back and in both transepts. The north transept doorway displays typically seventeenth-century pinnacles and battlements. Unlike most Protestant churches in Ireland, it is not locked during the week.

* Drumlane Round Tower and Church *(60)*, 4 mi SW; ½ mi E of R 201 (to Killeshandra); signposted; OS ½ 8H 34 12

This thirty-seven-foot-high stump of a Round Tower is distinguished for its carvings of two birds on the north face about six feet above ground. The nearby church dates probably to the thirteenth century, with alterations made in the fifteenth century, at which time the west door and some of the windows were embellished with interesting carved heads. The site is unusually well tended, and from here there are lovely views of the river Erne.

CAVAN

Kilmore (St. Feidhlimidh's) Cathedral *(66)*, 4 mi SW; E of R 199 (to Crossdoney); signposted; OS ½ 8H 38 04; locked except during Church of Ireland services

The north doorway of this otherwise undistinguished nineteenth-century cathedral church is a fine example of twelfth-century Hiberno-Romanesque design. It was inserted here incorrectly after being removed from its original site nearby. It is round-arched and recessed with both outward- and downward-pointing sawtooth chevrons.

COOTEHILL

* Cohaw Court Cairn *(20)*, 3 mi SE; N side of R 192 (to Shercock); poorly signposted but visible from road; OS ½ 8H 64 13

This is a Neolithic double-court cairn laid out on a north–south axis. Though somewhat tumbled and uncared for, the ground plan is clearly discernible: a semicircular open court at each end and a gallery of five burial chambers in between. Kerbstones encircle the tomb.

WEST CENTRAL IRELAND
County Roscommon
BOYLE

*** Boyle Abbey *(71)*, N of town center; E side of N 4 (to Sligo); signposted; OS ½ 7G 80 03

This is one of the largest and best preserved of Ireland's Cistercian abbeys. Founded in 1161, it was colonized from Mellifont. The ruined cruciform abbey church, built in the Transitional style, stands high. It is typically Cistercian in having a short, square choir and two chapels along the east face of both north and south transepts. Pointed and rounded arches are intermingled, as are round-headed windows and lancets, square and cylindrical pillars. The lower portions of the crossing tower date from the original construction. Corbels and capitals are finely carved. The east gable wall is pierced by high triple lancets. Over the west door is a single tall lancet under an arch decorated with chevrons. Except for the sacristy next to the south transept, the original claustral remains have all disappeared, the present ruins being of seventeenth- and eighteenth-century provenance.

* Ballinafad Castle *(145)*, 4 mi N, in County Sligo; W of N 4 (to Sligo); Signposted; OS ½ 7G 78 08

Built probably while Sir Richard Bingham was president of Connacht (about 1590), to stand guard over the Curlew Pass, this well-preserved ruin consists of a high central rectangular block with massive rounded towers at all four corners. It is more medieval in appearance than most contemporary tower houses.

CASTLEREA

** Clonalis House *(247)*, ½ mi N; N of N 60 (to Castlebar); signposted; open M–Sa, 11:00 A.M.–5:30 P.M.; Su, 2:00 P.M.–5:30 P.M.; mandatory 45-minute guided tour

Built in 1880 by Charles Owen O'Conor, this three-storey Italianate mansion, furnished in High Victorian style, houses a priceless collection of Gaelic-language manuscripts and books, mostly gathered and preserved in the late eighteenth century by Charles O'Conor of Ballingare. Also on display is the harp of the famous blind harpist Turlogh O'Carolan.

ROSCOMMON

**** Roscommon Castle** *(90, 97, 145)*, N of town center; signposted; OS ½ 12M 64 65

Built by the justiciar Robert de Ufford in 1269, the castle was rebuilt by him in about 1280 after having been thrown down by Aedh O'Connor, king of Connacht. In the following 3½ centuries it exchanged hands many times, though held for the greater part of the time by the O'Connors. The large number of mullioned windows were inserted in the sixteenth century by Sir Nicholas Malby, who carried out numerous other alterations. In 1652 it was captured and dismantled by the Cromwellian general, Sir John Reynolds.

This is a fine keepless courtyard castle, arguably the best example of this type in Ireland. Thick battlemented walls enclose a rectangular courtyard, entered through a high twin-round-towered gatehouse that pierces the east wall. At all four corners of the curtain are D-shaped mural towers. Opposite the main gatehouse is a second entrance flanked by rectangular towers.

*** Roscommon Friary** *(123)*, S of town center, on Galway Road behind Abbey Hotel; signposted; OS ½ 12M 88 64

Of the Dominican church built by order of Felim O'Connor in the mid–thirteenth century the only reminder is the row of five lancets in the south wall. The traceried windows were inserted in the fifteenth, as was the north wing. The best feature here is the fine effigy of the founder in the north wall. This was sculpted in the late thirteenth century and then placed on a fifteenth-century tomb carved with figures of eight armed and armored gallowglasses.

*** Castlestrange Stone** *(32)*, 5 mi SW; 2 mi N of N 63 (to Galway) from Athleague on road to Fuerty; signposted; OS ½ 12M 82 60

Here is a small rounded stone with incised curvilinear decorations typical of Celtic La Tène art. It probably dates from the third to first centuries B.C. and, like the more famous Turoe Stone, which it resembles, was in all likelihood a cult object.

** **Ballintober Castle** *(89)*, 12 mi NW; in Ballintober village; not signposted but visible from road: OS ½ 12M 73 75

Though occupied by the O'Connor kings of Connacht in the thirteenth century, and said to have been erected by them, the original building here was probably of Anglo-Norman construction. This was a typical moated keepless courtyard castle, though larger than most. The curtained courtyard is approximately square, with polygonal corner towers of which the two on the west side still stand quite high. A twin-towered gatehouse pierced the east curtain wall but is now reduced to a very ruinous condition.

STROKESTOWN

** **Strokestown Park House** *(196, 214)*, village center; open W–Su, noon–5:00 P.M.; mandatory 30-minute guided tour

This is an attractive Palladian mansion (an enlargement of an earlier house) built for Thomas Mahon in the 1730s to the design of Richard Castle. Especially interesting are the two wings, one containing a stable with neoclassical pillars, the other a galleried kitchen. Inside the main house, one room is devoted to memorabilia of Major Denis Mahon, who was murdered in 1847 for alleged maltreatment of his tenants. The town outside the demesne was the creation of Maurice Mahon, first Baron Hartland. It is a typical late-eighteenth/early-nineteenth-century landlord village.

Rath Croghan *(34)*, 8 mi W; S of N 5 (to French Park), 3 mi NW of Tulsk village; OS ½ 12M 80 84

This rather confusing complex of earthworks, about two square miles in area, is thought to be Cruachan, the royal site of the iron-age kingdom of Connacht, from which, according to the legend of the *Táin*, King Ailil and Queen Medb set forth to invade Ulster and capture the brown bull of Cooley.

County Galway

ATHENRY

* **Athenry Castle** *(80)*, town center; key from Mrs. Sheehan, Church Street

This three-storey battlemented keep was built by Meiler de Bermingham in about 1238, three years after Richard de Burgh's invasion of

Connacht. The high battlemented curtain wall is a later addition, but the one remaining corner turret is probably original.

* Town Wall *(93)*, town center

The town was first walled in 1211, and considerable fragments of the medieval wall survive, including the North Gate Tower, which spans a modern street.

* Athenry Friary *(123)*, town center; church barred but interior visible through grating

This ruined Dominican friary was founded in 1241 by Meiler de Bermingham. Only the north wall of the choir with its seven fine lancets (partially walled up) dates to the original thirteenth-century period of construction. The choir was extended in about 1324, at which time was inserted the fine Decorated Gothic east window with its switch-line tracery as well as the north arcade. The church was rebuilt in the fifteenth century, when the north wing with its elegant Decorated tracery in the north window was added. It was rebuilt again in the seventeenth century and was used as a barracks in the eighteenth. The cloister has disappeared.

BALLINASLOE

* Clontuskert Abbey *(72, 127)*, 4 mi S; ¼ mi E of R 395 (to Laurencetown), over gate and through field; not signposted; OS ½ 15M 86 26

On this site, sometime after 1140, a priory of Augustinian canons regular was founded, probably by the O'Kellys. The original church dates to the thirteenth century but was reconstructed in the fifteenth following a fire. The most attractive feature of the building is the fine western doorway inserted during the rebuilding. Over the door is a sculpted representation of St. Michael weighing the souls of the dead, while on the sides appear a pelican, a mermaid, two deers, and a dog biting its tail. There are no claustral remains.

** Kilconnell Friary *(131)*, 8 mi W; N of R 348 (to Athenry); signposted; OS ½ 15M 73 32

Here are the ruins of a Franciscan friary, founded in 1414 by William O'Kelly, lord of Uí Maine. The church consists of a narrow nave and chancel, a south wing, and a fine late-fifteenth-century tower (locked). In niches in the north wall are two splendid tombs, that in the choir belonging to the Daly family. A fair amount of Decorated tracery remains in place in some of the windows. North of the church are the substantial ruins of the cloister, including a fine segment of arcade.

*** Clonfert Cathedral *(67, 128)*, 14 mi SE; 1 mi N of Laurencetown–Banagher road from 5 mi E of Laurencetown; signposted; OS ½ 15M 96 21

The Hiberno-Romanesque west doorway here is probably the most photographed of its kind in Ireland and, in the words of Harold G. Leask, "quite breath-taking in beauty and highly individual in design." It is the largest among Irish examples, measuring over thirteen feet wide. It is recessed in six orders and is richly decorated with figure-eight interlace, zoomorphic interlace, chevrons, circles, beads, zigzags, animal masks, etc. Above it is a triangular tympanum, or false gable, filled with human masks, some with interlocking beards. Like the doorway, the red sandstone church behind it was built in the twelfth century. The east windows are original, though the chancel arch was inserted in the fifteenth century, as were the sacristy and the arches supporting the tower at the west end. Still in use as a Church of Ireland cathedral, it has been subjected to much interior restoration. The south transept is in ruins, and the north transept has been removed.

DUNMORE

* Dunmore Castle *(89)*, 3/4 mi NW of village center; signposted; OS ½ 11M 50 64

This ruined five-storey rectangular tower, probably built after 1315, replaced the original castle raised here by the de Berminghams in the early thirteenth century.

Dunmore Friary *(131)*, village center; signposted; OS ½ 11M 51 64

Founded by Walter de Bermingham, this ruined nave-and-chancel church is all that remains of a friary established in 1425 for Augustinian Eremites. The central tower stands high, and the west doorway displays interesting carvings.

GALWAY

*** St. Nicholas Church *(126, 129, 145)*, town center, Church Lane

Still used for Protestant (Church of Ireland) services, this is the second largest medieval parish church in Ireland (collegiate after 1484). Cruciform in plan, it was built originally in the fourteenth century, and to this period the present choir, as well as the chapels north and south of it, can be assigned. The rest is mostly the product of expansion and rebuilding during the two subsequent centuries: the tower and the west doorway in the fifteenth; the north and south aisles, the extension of the south transept, the south doorway, the chapel of the Blessed Sacrament, the west window, and the three-gabled west front in the sixteenth on the initiative of the Lynch family. The tall steeple above the stepped parapets was installed in 1783. Noteworthy features are the twelfth- or thirteenth-century "Crusader's Tomb," the Lynch and Joyce altar tombs (seventeenth and sixteenth centuries respectively), the War Memorial commemorating parishioners killed in World War I, and the freestanding holy water stoop.

Outside the church facing Market Street is a stone wall pierced by the "Lynch Memorial Window" under which is carved a skull and crossbones. This is traditionally thought to commemorate the sentencing and execution of Walter Lynch by order of his father, Mayor James Lynch, in 1493. (The story is apocryphal.)

Lynch's Castle *(145)*, town center, on corner of Shop Street and Upper Abbeygate

This much restored four-storey tower house, now occupied by the Allied Irish Bank, was built in the sixteenth century by a member of the city's Old English merchant aristocracy. Unusual features are the gargoyles and carved stone medallions on the exterior.

City Wall *(93, 145)*, Spanish Arch, behind Galway City Museum

Extending from the Spanish Arch is a substantial segment of the sixteenth-century city wall, currently under excavation.

* University College, Galway *(233)*, University road, N of city center

The original college is now used as the main administration building (first on the left from the entrance gate). It was designed by Joseph B. Keane and constructed between 1846 and 1849 for Queen's College, Galway, one of the three "godless colleges" founded by Sir Robert Peel. The style is neo-Tudor, and the building was modelled on Christ Church, Oxford, the clock tower being a good rendering of Tom Tower. The much expanded college grounds now serve a student body of more than three thousand.

* Drumacoo Church *(115)*, 12 mi SE; ¼ mi W of N 67 (to Kinvara); signposted to "Drum Muchada"; OS ½ 14M 40 17

This ruined church is of thirteenth-century construction but incorporates the remains of an Early Christian church in its south gable, including the flat-lintelled doorway. The two east windows are Early English lancets, contemporary with the finely carved south door. The north wing is a nineteenth-century addition.

** **Claregalway Friary** *(123, 128)*, 6 mi NE; W side of N17 (to Tuam); signposted and visible from road; OS ½ 14M 37 33

Here are the well-preserved ruins of a Franciscan friary founded before 1252 by John de Cogan. The choir, with its row of six wide lancets in each of the side walls, dates to the thirteenth century, but the switch-line tracery of the east window dates to the fifteenth. The west wall of the nave is missing, but the short wide lancets in the south wall also indicate a thirteenth-century date. The north aisle with its fine arcade, however, was added in the fourteenth century, and the central tower was added in the fifteenth. The cloister lies south of the church—an unusual location for a medieval friary. It is fairly substantial, especially the east and south ranges.

* **Annaghdown Priory** *(71)*, 12 mi N; 4½ mi W of N 84 (to Headford) from Cloonboo; 100 yd down lane W of modern cemetery; signposted to Annaghdown Pier; OS ½ 14M 29 38

Here on the shore of Lough Corrib are the remains of an Augustinian double monastery (that is, for both canons and canonesses), founded in about 1140 by Turlough O'Connor, king of Connacht, possibly at the instance of St. Malachy. The choir, with its round-headed windows, may date to the twelfth century; the nave is possibly later. To the south are the fairly substantial ruins of the cloister. A hundred yards to the east, in the grounds of a modern cemetery, stand (1) a fifteenth-century cathedral church with a fine Romanesque window and doorway, possibly borrowed from the original priory church; (2) the bare foundations of an Early Christian church (north of the cathedral); and (3) the remains of an undistinguished medieval church (still farther to the north).

*** **Aughnanure Castle** *(103)*, 17 mi NW; ½ mi N of N 69 (to Oughterard); signposted; open daily, 10:00 A.M.–6:00 P.M.; OS ½ 11M 15 42

Built by the O'Flahertys around the end of the fifteenth century, this is a fine six-storey, stepped-battlemented tower house, partially restored. Rectangular in plan, it has roof-high machicolations on all sides and projecting turrets at three corners. It stands inside a double bawn, the inner enclosure of which is mostly gone except for a rounded turret with a corbelled roof at the southwest corner. The outer bawn also has a turret and encloses a much-ruined "banqueting hall" built in the sixteenth century. The tower can be climbed to the roof, from which there is a splendid view of Lough Corrib.

GORT

** Kilmacduagh Churches and *****Round Tower** *(60, 113, 119, 128)*, 3 mi SW; W of R 460 (to Corofin); signposted; OS ½ 14M 40 00

Here are the remains of four medieval churches. The most interesting architecturally is O'Heyne's Church (a hundred yards northwest of car park; key at house across road). It was built for Augustinian canons regular in the early thirteenth century and has a handsome chancel arch and two nicely carved east windows. Closer to the road is the Glebe House, a two-storey building, probably the bishop's residence. Immediately south of it is the Church of St. John the Baptist, a Transitional building with both round-headed (Romanesque) and pointed (Gothic) windows in the nave. South of it is the cathedral, whose nave dates to the late twelfth century, though the west wall is probably older, while the two transepts, choir, west window, and south doorway were added in about 1500. Next to the cathedral is the fine Round Tower, the tallest in Ireland (about 120 feet), with a pronounced list like that of the Leaning Tower of Pisa. Finally, across the road, is St. Mary's Church, whose round-headed east window dates to about 1200, while the south doorway is of fifteenth-century provenance.

* Ardamullivan Castle *(103)*, 4 mi S; ½ mi W of N 18 (to Ennis), over red gate and across field; signposted; OS ½ 14R 44 95

Here is a well-preserved five-storey tower house built in the sixteenth century by the O'Shaughnessys. Interesting wickerwork marks are to be seen on the ground-floor vaulting. The mullioned windows and first-floor fireplace are later insertions.

** Coole Park *(246)*, 2½ mi N; W of N 18 (to Galway); signposted

This splendid nature preserve and wildlife park was once the estate of Lady Augusta Gregory, patroness of William Butler Yeats and countless other noted contemporary Irish literary and artistic figures. Lady Gregory's residence has been torn down, but the "autograph tree" still stands—a huge beech on which are carved the timeworn initials of many of her famous guests, including Yeats, George Russell (AE), and Sean O'Casey. One of the well-marked trails leads to the lake, still frequented by swans, as in Yeats's day, when he commemorated them in verse.

*** Thoor Ballylee *(266)*, 4 mi N; W of N 66 (to Loughrea); signposted; open daily, 10:00 A.M.–6:00 P.M.

This four-storey sixteenth-century tower house was bought by William Butler Yeats in 1915. After his marriage to Georgie Hyde-Lees in 1917 the couple took up residence here and devoted much time to making the place livable, which required extensive alterations both inside and out. It is now a Yeats museum containing numerous memorabilia and copies of his works. A tape-recorded room-by-room description is available at the front desk.

** Dunguaire (Dungory) Castle *(103)*, 9 mi NW; ½ mi NW of N 67 (to Ballinderreer) from Kinvara village; signposted and visible from road; "Medieval banquets," 15 May–30 September, 5:45 P.M. and 8:45 P.M. tel (069) 64264; OS ½ 14M 38 11

Now restored and under the care of the Shannon Free Airport Development Company, this fine three-storey battlemented tower house with its bawn wall intact was probably built by Edmond O'Heyne in about 1520. In the seventeenth century it passed to the Martyns of Galway city. In the present century the castle belonged successively to Edward Martyn, Oliver St. John Gogarty, and Christabel, Lady Ampthill, who was responsible for its restoration.

HEADFORD

*** Ross Errilly Friary *(131)*, 1½ mi NW; W of R 334 (to Cong); signposted; OS ½ 11M 25 48

This exceptionally large and very well-preserved Franciscan Observant friary was built in the latter part of the fifteenth century. To the usual nave-and-chancel ground plan was added a double south wing with a tiny chapel projecting eastward. The switch-line tracery in the windows of the church is in an excellent state of preservation. Especially noteworthy are the substantial remains of the domestic buildings, which extend north of the church around two separate courtyards. Immediately next to the church is the cloister proper with all four ambulatories extant. The outer courtyard is surrounded by the kitchen, the refectory, and the main dormitory. North of the kitchen is the mill. At the northeast corner are the latrines.

INISHMORE, ARAN ISLANDS

Access by plane (Aer Aran) from Galway Airport—M-F, 5 flights daily; Sa, 2 flights; by passenger ferry (no cars) from Galway, daily trips (approximately 3 hours); by motorboat from Rossaveal, daily trips (approximately 1 hour, not including coach trip from Galway); for schedules, inquire at Irish Tourist Information Office, Galway city. Note: adverse weather conditions occasionally require cancellation of scheduled flights or boat trips.

(East to West)

* Tighlagh Enda (Teillach Einde) *(63)*, in modern graveyard E of Cille Einde (Killeany) village; signposted; OS ½ 14L 89 06

Barely visible from the road because of its location in a hollow of the graveyard, this tenth-century single-chambered church of mortared stone has antae at the east end and a round-headed window and doorway on the north side, probably added later. The west end of the church was also probably a later addition, which explains why the building is longer than average for this period. Inside is the carved shaft of an Early Christian High Cross.

* Teampull Benen (Bheanáin) *(49)*, ¼ mi S of Cille Einde (Killeany) village by footpath, steep climb; signposted; OS ½ 14L 88 06

This is a very tiny Early Christian church or oratory, built of mortared stone but without antae. Internal dimensions of the single chamber are only eleven by seven feet. It is uniquely oriented north and south. Thus the tiny round-headed eastern window is in the side and not the gable end. The window is unusual also in that the round inner and outer heads are cut from a single stone.

** Dún Dúbh Cathair (Doocaher, The Black Fort) *(35)*, 1½ mi SW of Cille Einde (Killeany) village, by road and gravel footpath to south coast of island, then east along cliffside about 300 yd across rocky fields and over stone fences (a 35-minute climb); entrance on E side of fort through narrow gap between wall and edge of cliff (extreme caution mandatory); signposted; OS ½ 14L 87 07

This is a splendid cliffside iron-age promontory fort, once circular but, owing to its partial collapse into the sea, now consisting of a high stone wall semicircular in shape. On the outside is a band of jagged stone stakes constituting a *chevaux de frise*, which served as additional protection against attack from the landward side. Inside the terraced wall are the foundation stones of two or more houses. Though access to the fort is not easy, the view of Inishmore's south (Atlantic) coastline is alone worth the effort.

** Dún Eóchla (Oghil Fort) *(35)*, 1¾ mi W of Cill Rónán (Kilronan) village, at island's highest point just east of abandoned lighthouse, by footpath from road; 30-minute climb; not signposted; OS ½ 14L 87 11

This ovoid ring-fort has two concentric walls about twelve to fifteen feet high surrounding an area about eighty-one feet by sixty-nine feet in dimension. Inside is a circular stone platform, possibly the remains of a *clochán* (beehive hut). The view from here in all directions is truly spectacular.

Teampull MacDuagh *(63)*, S of Cill Mhuirbhigh (Kilmurvey) village, on grounds of Johnston Hernon's Kilmurvey Guest House; OS ½ 14L 83 03

This little roofless church of mortared stone, probably of tenth-century date, has antae at the west end. The east end, with its narrow round- and triangular-headed windows, is a later addition. An Early Christian cross pillar stands just west of the church.

*** Dún Aenghus *(35)*, ½ mi S of Cill Mhuirbhigh (Kilmurvey) village by footpath; 20-minute climb past Johnston Hernon's Kilmurvey Guest House; signposted (white arrows); OS ½ 14L 82 10

This iron-age promontory fort is one of Ireland's most spectacular man-made sights. It stands on the edge of a sheer cliff rising more than two hundred feet above the Atlantic. Two widely spaced stone walls form an arc around the semicircular citadel, and fragments of a third wall lie just outside. Landward of this is a broad band of upright stone stakes constituting a *chevaux de frise*, a sort of prehistoric tank trap. Considerable restoration work has taken place, including the exterior buttresses.

** Dún Eóganachta (Onaght) *(35)*, ½ mi S of Sruthán village, by road and footpath; 15-minute climb; not signposted; OS ½ 14L 81 11

Here is a partially restored iron-age ring-fort whose circular stone wall encloses an area about seventy-five feet in diameter. The wall is sixteen feet thick and is terraced inside, with flights of stone steps to the ramparts. The view across Galway Bay to the Connemara Mountains is breathtaking.

Loughrea

* Loughrea Friary *(123)*, town center, on grounds of modern monastery; not signposted but visible from street; OS ½ 14M 62 17; key available at monastic house

Heavily restored, this nave-and-chancel church was originally built in the late thirteenth century for Carmelite friars brought here by Richard de

Burgh, lord of Connacht and earl of Ulster. The five pairs of Early English lancets in the south wall of the choir date to the first period of construction, but the east window is a fifteenth-century insertion. To the latter period also can be assigned the tower, the south wing, and the small chapel south of the west end of the nave.

** St. Brendan's Cathedral *(248)*, town center

Built between 1897 and 1903, this is a typical late-nineteenth century-neo-Gothic (Decorated) cruciform church with a polygonal apse, distinguished chiefly for its stained glass and interior furnishings by artists of the "Celtic Revival." The mosaic Stations of the Cross are by Ethel Mary Rhind; the stained-glass windows are by Sarah Purser, A. E. Childe, Michael Healy, Hubert McGoldrick, Patrick Pye, and Evie Hone; the marble Madonna and child are by John Hughes; the sodality banners are by Jack B. Yeats; and the ironwork is by Michael Scott. On the grounds is the diocesan museum (open on request, M-F, 9:30 A.M.-4:30 P.M.; Sa, 3:00-5:00 P.M.) containing a good collection of vestments and some fine wood carvings dating from the late Middle Ages to the seventeenth century.

** Turoe Stone *(32)*, 4 mi N; ½ mi W of R 350 (to New Inn) from Bullaun village; signposted to "Tuar Ruadh Sculpted Stone"; OS ½ 14N 62 23

This is a domed cut granite boulder a little more than three feet high. The top half is carved in low relief with a profusion of curvilinear designs, chiefly spirals and trumpets, typical of the Celtic La Tène art style of the third to first centuries B.C. Moved here from a nearby ring-fort, it is thought to have been a cult object of some sort.

PORTUMNA

** Portumna Friary *(131)*, S of town center on grounds of Portumna Forest Park; signposted; OS ½ 15M 85 04

Although the choir of this ruined church dates to the thirteenth century, when it belonged to the Cistercians of Dunbrody Abbey, the rest of the building (nave, transepts, and sacristy) was constructed for Dominican friars brought here by the local O'Madden chieftain in the early fifteenth century. Noteworthy features of the church are the fine Decorated windows in the east and south walls and the thirteenth-century round-headed windows in the choir. The claustral buildings north of the church still stand fairly high, notably the refectory in the north range.

** Portumna Castle *(154, 158)*, S of town center in Portumna Forest Park, up footpath N of Portumna Friary; signposted; entry barred during repairs

Overlooking Lough Derg, this is a fine high-standing ruin of a four-storey Jacobean mansion built before 1618 by Richard Burke, earl of Clanrickard. The house is pierced liberally with mullioned windows and topped by a crenellated parapet with curvilinear gables; at the front is an elegant Renaissance-style doorway, with gunports on either side and a machicolation above. Here Lord Deputy Thomas Wentworth held court in 1635 for the purpose of sequestering the estates of the great Galway landowners, including those of the owner, Clanrickard.

* Terryglass (Old Court) Castle *(82)*, 6 mi S; W of Terryglass village center, County Tipperary, through wrought-iron gate to end of private avenue; OS ½ 15M 86 01

This picturesque ruined castle on the shore of Lough Derg was built probably by Theobald Walter early in the thirteenth century and remained in the hands of his Butler descendants until the mid-seventeenth. It was a square keep with rounded corner turrets, but only the bottom storey remains standing.

Lorrha Friary *(122)*, 6 mi E; 1 mi SE of R 489 (to Birr) in Lorrha village center, County Tipperary; OS ½ 15M 92 05

These high-standing ruins are those of a Dominican friary church founded by Walter de Burgh, earl of Ulster, in about 1269. Nave and chancel are of equal length. A row of five double-lancet windows in the south wall of the choir indicates a thirteenth-century date for the building.

** Pallas Castle *(103)*, 6 mi NW; 200 yd SW of minor road to Duniry, from polygonal house on north side of road, in back of private farmhouse (disregard "no trespassing" signs); not signposted; OS ½ 15M 76 08

This is one of the best-preserved tower houses in Ireland. It stands four storeys high with roof and floors still in place. Numerous gunslits and gunports pierce the lower stories, but mullioned windows adorn those above. The roof is not battlemented, but at two corners there are roof-high machicolations. The castle was built by the Burkes in about 1500. After Cromwell took it, it was given to the Nugents, who may have been responsible for the adjoining gabled house (seventeenth-century) of which only one wall remains. The high battlemented bawn wall is entered through a rectangular two-storey gatehouse and is further guarded by two round corner turrets with numerous gunports. Around three sides of the inner face of the bawn wall is a walkway built at a height to allow defenders to fire through the open spaces of the battlements.

** **Meelick Friary** *(131),* 12 mi NE; 3 mi SE of R 356 (Banagher-Eyrecourt) from 3½ mi N, W of Banagher, in Meelick village; signposted; OS ½ 15M 94 14

Overlooking the river Shannon, this tall barnlike building is one of the few medieval friary churches still in use for Roman Catholic services. It was built in the fifteenth century for Franciscan friars. Of the original building there remain the four walls, the west doorway, three arches in the south wall, the scant ruins of the south wing of the church, and the roofless ruins of the cloister to the north. The west window is a seventeenth-century insertion. The church has been very tastefully restored and the interior is exceptionally pretty.

ST. MACDARA'S ISLAND

* **St. MacDara's Church** *(49),* at mouth of Galway Bay, 2 mi offshore; access by boat from Carna Pier, tel Carna Osten Hotel, (095) 32255, or inquire at Irish Tourist Information Office, Galway city

This Early Christian church is single-chambered, quite small, with unusually thick mortared walls (note the plentiful spalls fitted between the larger stones). At the gable ends the remains of the roof can still be seen. The antae here are unique in that they continue up the gable slopes to the peak. The west doorway is lintelled; there is a round-headed east window and, in the south wall, a small lintelled window.

TUAM

* **Tuam Cathedral** *(67, 115, 225),* W of town center; locked except during services

This is a Church of Ireland cathedral, rebuilt in the nineteenth century to the design of Sir Thomas Deane, though retaining parts of the original thirteenth- or fourteenth-century choir. The only distinguished original feature here is the magnificent Hiberno-Romanesque chancel arch, nearly sixteen feet across, with deeply carved interlace, foliage, chevrons, and human masks with interlocking hair.

* **Tuam Market Cross** *(62),* town center

Fragments of High Crosses of probable twelfth-century date have been pieced together to form this composite monument. The base has figures of bishops on each side and on one an inscription reading "A prayer for

Turloch O'Conor . . . and for O Hessian by whom it was made." (Turlough O'Connor was king of Connacht from 1106 to 1156; Aed O'Oissin was archbishop of Tuam in the late twelfth century.) The shaft has interlace and Scandinavian-style beasts; there is a Crucifixion on one side of the head of the cross and the figure of an ecclesiastic, probably a bishop, on the other.

** **Knockmoy Abbey** *(119, 127)*, 10 mi SE; N of N 63 (Claregalway to Moylough) through Abbey Knockmoy village, by foot up gravelled lane across 4 stiles; not signposted but visible from road; OS ½ 11M 51 44; interior barred but accessible over stile at SW corner of nave

Here are the fairly substantial remains of a Cistercian monastery founded by King Cathal Crovderg O'Connor in 1190. The church is cruciform, with an unusually long nave of which only the western end survives to any considerable height. The reroofed choir is rib-vaulted, with three narrow round-headed windows surmounted by a lancet in the east wall. The partially collapsed central tower is probably a fifteenth-century insertion. Of the claustral buildings the chapter house in the east range is well preserved and lighted by Early English lancets. Remains of the night stair leading from the church to the monks' dorter are still extant. The south range with its refectory is also fairly high-standing, though not much is left of the west range.

County Leitrim

MANORHAMILTON

*** **Park's Castle** *(153)*, 8 mi SW; S side of road to Dromahair; signposted and visible from road; OS ½ 7G 78 35

Overlooking Lough Gill, this substantial ruin was built early in the seventeenth century at the time of the Ulster plantation. The rectangular three-storey house, well fenestrated with mullioned windows, is flanked by a four-storey rectangular tower and a smaller round turret. A five-sided battlemented and turreted bawn wall lies to the west of the castle, and on the lake side is a postern gate. Floodlights illuminate the grounds at night.

** **Creevelea Friary** *(131)*, 9 mi SW; N of Dromohair village center, by footbridge from Abbey Hotel and path downstream along south bank of river Banet; signposted; OS ½ 7G 80 31

Founded in 1508 by Owen O'Rourke, this is the last of the Franciscan friaries to have been established in Ireland before Henry VIII's suppression of the religious houses. It is a well-preserved, though poorly tended, ruin.

Nave, choir, central tower, and south wing all stand high. The traceried east and west windows (Decorated style) are in good condition, as is the west doorway. The claustral buildings north of the church stand high, and the freestanding claustral ambulatory is almost complete. In the center of the north range, opposite the refectory, are carved representations of Saint Francis. North of the cloister are the remains of a gatehouse.

County Sligo

BALLYMOTE

* **Ballymote Castle** *(91, 97)*, village center, on grounds of St. John of God's Nursing Home; not signposted but clearly visible from road; OS ½ 7G 66 15; entry barred but interior visible through grille

This large keepless courtyard castle was built by Richard de Burgh, the "Red Earl" of Ulster, in about the year 1300. Sometime after the death of his son, the "Brown Earl," in 1333, it fell into the hands of the Gaelic Irish. The square courtyard is enclosed by a massive curtain wall with three-quarter-round towers at each corner. A large twin-towered gatehouse pierced the north curtain wall but is now reduced to foundations. Midway along the west curtain wall a rounded mural tower is in a better state of preservation.

SLIGO

** **Sligo Museum and Art Gallery** *(254, 268)*, Stephen's Street, town center; open Tu-F, 10:30 A.M.–12:30 P.M., 2:30–4:30 P.M.

This fine small museum of local history contains, among other things, a few letters of William Butler Yeats and, most interesting of all, sundry memorabilia of Countess Markievicz, including the apron she wore while interned at Aylesbury Prison. Next door, in a former Congregational church, is the town library, with an art gallery upstairs that has the largest and finest extant collection of the paintings of Jack B. Yeats.

*** **Sligo Friary** *(122, 128)*, Abbey Street, SE of town center; key at 6 Charlotte Street around corner

Founded in 1253 by Maurice FitzGerald, second baron of Offaly, as a house for Dominican friars, this is one of the better preserved of Ireland's ecclesiastical ruins. The oldest parts are the thirteenth-century choir with its eight lancet windows and the sacristy and chapter house in the east range of the cloister north of the church. The east window of the choir, however, dates from a restoration following a disastrous fire in 1414. So do most of the nave, the beautifully carved altar, the partially reconstructed rood screen separating choir from nave, the tower over the crossing, and the claustral ambulatory and arcade. The south wing was built no earlier than the sixteenth century. Inside the church is an interesting collection of sixteenth- and seventeenth-century tombs and monuments.

* Drumcliffe Church, *** High Cross, and Round Tower *(62, 275)*, 4 mi N; E and W of N 15 (to Bundoran); signposted; OS ½ 7G 68 42

The modern church is attractive, though undistinguished except for its fine mural on the east wall. In the churchyard to the north is the simple headstone of the poet William Butler Yeats, with the inscription "Cast a Cold Eye/On Life, on Death/Horseman Pass By." On the path between church and road is a tenth-century High Cross. On the east face (top to bottom) are Christ in glory, David and Goliath, a lion (without Daniel), and Adam and Eve. On the west face is the Crucifixion and underneath it some unintelligible figure carving. Across the road is the stump of a Round Tower standing about thirty-five feet high.

*** Lissadell House *(211, 253)*, 8 mi NW; 4 mi W of N 15 (to Bundoran) from Drumcliffe; signposted; open M–Sa, 2:00–5:15 P.M.; mandatory 45-minute guided tour

Built in the 1830s by Francis Goodwin for Sir Robert Gore-Booth, this is a rather plain neoclassic two-storey house over a basement. The interior is more impressive than the outside. The entrance hall is lined with square Doric and round Ionic columns and a double staircase leading to a half landing with fireplace. The gallery, flanked by Ionic columns, reaches to the roof and is illuminated by a clerestory and skylight. Library and dining room are full of memorabilia of the Gore-Booth family, especially of the famous sisters Eva and Constance (Countess Markievicz)—much admired by William Butler Yeats, their great friend, who frequently visited here. Their double portrait by Sarah Purser hangs in the dining room.

Elegantly shabby in appearance, this place has an air of livability more pronounced than in the case of most "stately homes" open to the public—probably because it is still owned and occupied by a member of the Gore-Booth family.

*** Creevykeel Court Cairn *(20)*, 14 mi N; S side of N 15 (to Bundoran); signposted and visible from road; OS ½ 7G 72 54

Known locally as the "Giant's Grave," this is one of the best preserved, best tended, and most accessible of Ireland's Neolithic court graves. On a hillside overlooking the sea, the ovoid central court is entered through a passageway from the east. Behind it are two burial chambers. Near the narrow western end of the cairn are two side chambers.

** **Carrowmore** *(24)*, 4 mi SW; 1 mi W of N 4 (to Boyle); signposted and visible on both sides of road; OS ½ 7G 66 33

This is the largest prehistoric cemetery of megalithic graves in Ireland, though most of the extant cairns are small and modern gravel quarrying has destroyed much of the archaeological quality of the site. The ancient stones are scattered over a wide area and consist mostly of small denuded Neolithic passage graves, which have the appearance of dolmens, and of stone circles, which are in fact the exposed kerbstones that originally served as revetments surrounding the long-gone covering mounds.

** **Knocknarea (Queen Maeve's Grave)** *(24-25)*, 6 mi W; 2½ mi SE of Strandhill, by footpath from roadside; 50-minute steep climb; signposted; OS ½ 7G 63 35

This is a huge unopened cairn (thirty-five feet high and two hundred feet in diameter) underneath which is presumed to be a Neolithic passage grave. It is not the burial place of Medb (Maeve), legendary queen of Connacht, who figures so prominently in the *Taín*. For one thing the grave is far older than the events depicted in that epic; for another, Maeve was not a real person but an eheumerized Celtic goddess. The cairn stands out prominently on the summit of Knocknarea Mountain, from which the panoramic view is breathtaking. To the north and east lie Sligo Bay and Drumcliffe Bay, to the west the city of Sligo, and to the south Ballysadare Bay.

* **Carrowkeel** *(24)*, 19 mi SE; 4 mi SW of N 4 (to Boyle) from Castle Baldwin, 3 mi S of Castle Baldwin–Ballymote Road, by very treacherous unpaved mountain road through closed farm gate; obscurely signposted; OS ½ 7G 76 11

At least fourteen Neolithic passage graves are scattered here on the slopes of the Bricklieve Mountain, overlooking Lough Arrow to the east. Of these the most accessible (though not very!) are the four to be found along the path leading uphill south of the Irish Tourist Board explanatory marker, which is more or less at the center of the cemetery. The remainder are discoverable with some difficulty. Some are open but are considered unsafe to enter. Unlike contemporary tombs in the Boyne valley, these lack decorative stone markings. Given the extreme difficulty of reaching this place by car, only the most avid lovers of antiquities will find it worth the effort.

County Mayo

BALLINA

*** Rosserk Friary *(131)*, 7½ mi NE; 3 mi E of R 314 (to Killala); signposted; OS ½ 6G 25 25

Founded in the mid–fifteenth century for Franciscan Tertiaries, this is one of the best-preserved ruined friaries in Ireland, as well as being beautifully situated at the mouth of the river Moy. The church is of simple nave-and-chancel design with a south wing containing two small chapels. There is a slender tower over the center. The west door is a fine example of Decorated Gothic style, as are the windows in the east and south walls. In the choir is a double piscina, intricately carved. All three ranges of the cloister stand high, each with vaulted rooms on the ground floor and mural stairs leading upward. Sacristy and chapter house comprise most of the east range (with dormitories above); kitchen and refectory comprise the north range and a hall or dormitory the west. Curiously, there is no sign of an ambulatory around the cloister.

** Moyne Friary *(131)*, 8½ mi N; ½ mi SE of R 314 (to Killala), down farm lane, across gate and over fields; signposted; OS ½ 6G 33 97

Here on the west bank of the Moy estuary is an extensive and very well-preserved Franciscan friary ruin, founded in 1455 by one of the MacWilliam Burkes. The ground plan is unusual. On the south side of the nave is a wide L-shaped wing that is larger in dimensions than the nave itself. A chapel lies south of the choir. The claustral buildings north of the church are extensive. The east range includes both the sacristy and the chapter house; the refectory and kitchen comprise the north range, while the vaulted building in the west range was used for storage. Above the church rises a fine tower, and the cloister has a well-preserved integrated ambulatory.

* Killala Round Tower *(60)*, 8 mi N in Killala village (R 314); signposted; OS ½ 6G 20 30; key from caretaker next door

Standing on a plinth three feet high, this well-preserved Round Tower reaches a total height of eighty-four feet to its conical top. Its doorway is eleven feet above ground.

Breastagh Ogham Stone *(43)*, 11 mi N; 1½ mi N of R 314 (to Ballycastle) on W side of minor road, about 200 yd across field; signposted and visible from road; OS ½ 6G 18 34

Here is an eight-foot-high standing stone (possibly of bronze-age provenance) with Ogham cuttings on both sides.

* Rathfran Friary *(123),* 12 mi N; 2 mi N of R 314 (to Ballycastle); not signposted; OS ½ 6G 19 33

The nave and chancel of this Dominican friary, founded in 1274, date from the thirteenth century, as indicated by the double lancets in the south wall. The south wing, with its Decorated window, was added in the fifteenth century. To the north of the choir are the remains of the sacristy, which in the sixteenth century was converted into living quarters, probably by Thomas Exeter, to whom the suppressed friary was granted. In the low foundations to the north can be traced the original double cloister of which nothing else remains.

CASTLEBAR

*** Ballintubber Abbey *(119),* 8 mi S; 1 mi NE of N 8 (to Ballinrobe); signposted; OS ½ 11M 15 79

This beautifully restored abbey church was built originally in the early thirteenth century to serve Augustinian canons regular brought here by Cathal Crovderg O'Connor, king of Connacht. It is cruciform, with four round-headed Hiberno-Romanesque windows in the east end and ribbed vaulting in the choir. It now serves as a Roman Catholic house of worship. Of the claustral remains those of the chapter house are coeval with the church. Items of special interest include the restored thirteenth-century altar, the fifteenth-century abbot's tomb, the twelfth-century font in the south transept, and the thirteenth-century doorway to the chapter house.

* Turlough Round Tower *(60),* 4 mi E; N of N 5 (to Bellavary); not signposted but visible from road; OS ½ 11M 21 94

Here is a well-preserved Round Tower, about seventy-five feet high to its conical top. It is larger in diameter than most and therefore somewhat squat in appearance. The doorway is walled in. The adjacent church ruin is of eighteenth-century provenance.

* Strade Friary *(123),* 8½ mi NE; W of N 58 (to Ballina), in Straide village; signposted; OS ½ 11M 26 98

When originally founded in the early thirteenth century, this was a Franciscan friary, but by mid-century it was in the hands of Dominicans. The six lancets in the north wall of the choir date to a thirteenth-century construction, but the rest of the building appears to have been put up about two hundred years later. The best feature of the site is the splendid fifteenth-century carved-stone tomb with its fine flamboyant tracery, ogee-headed niches with carved crockets and finials, and crowned figures in the panels.

Michael Davitt Memorial Museum *(218)*, 8½ mi NE; W of N 58 (to Ballina) in Straide village

Here is a room full of miscellaneous mementos of the life and career of Michael Davitt, including an address from Land League sympathizers, books by and about Davitt, newspaper clippings, letters, etc.

Ballylahan Castle *(89)*, 10 mi NE; junction of N 58 (to Ballina) and R 321 (to Knock); signposted; OS ½ 11M 27 99

These scattered ruins are those of a thirteenth-century castle built by Jordan of Exeter. It was a polygonal courtyard castle with a twin-towered gatehouse, of which the remains of only one tower are still to be seen.

* Meelick Round Tower *(60)*, 14 mi E; 2 mi NE of N 5 (to Swinford); not signposted but visible from road; OS ½ 11M 01 79

Close to seventy feet high, but lacking its conical cap, this is a fine Round Tower with a round-headed doorway and flat-headed and pointed windows.

CONG

Ashford Castle *(220)*, E of village center; admission to building or grounds barred except for overnight guests at hotel

Built in 1870 to the design of Joseph Franklin Fuller for Arthur Edward Guinness, Lord Ardilaun, this much-castellated, machicolated, and many-bartizaned sprawling mansion represents the apogee of Victorian neo-Gothicism in Ireland. It is now the country's best-known (and possibly most expensive) luxury hotel.

* Cong Abbey *(71)*, W of village center, beside exit from Ashford Castle; not signposted but visible from street; OS ½ 11M 14 55

The abbey was founded as a house for Augustinian canons regular in about 1140 by Turlough O'Connor, king of Connacht, possibly under the influence of St. Malachy. To Turlough's son and successor, Rory O'Connor, is credited the first building of the church. Not much remains of it except for the three tall lancets in the east gable and the fine Romanesque doorway of about 1200, rebuilt and inserted in the north wall. The ruins of the cloister to the south are in a better state of preservation. Especially noteworthy are the segments of the ambulatory arcade and the fine Transitional carved doorway leading to the chapter house.

Aghalard Castle *(103)*, 2 mi N; E of abandoned farmhouse at end of lane; not signposted; OS ½ 11M 14 57

Built in the fifteenth century by the gallowglass family of MacDonnells, this is a much ruined three-storey tower house standing within a polygonal bawn.

KNOCK

* Knock Shrine and Folk Museum *(229)*, village center

This is a pilgrimage center for worship and devotional exercises on the site of the apparition of the Virgin Mary and Saints Joseph and John the Evangelist, claimed to have been seen by a group of villagers in August 1879. Behind the parish church where the reported miracle took place are the glass-enclosed statues of the Virgin and the two saints. On the grounds are a High Cross erected at the time of the visit of Pope John Paul in 1979 and a huge basilica built in the years 1974 and following. The Folk Museum is devoted mostly to the history of the shrine, although it also contains sundry items connected with local crafts and village life. Among other items are the pope's chair used by John Paul and a collection of newspaper clippings concerning Monsignor James Horan, who promoted the papal visit and the construction of the local airport, which has so enhanced the accessibility of this otherwise remote village.

NEWPORT

* Burrishoole Friary *(131)*, 2 mi W; S of N 59 (to Achill Sound); signposted; OS ½ 11L 97 96

Here are the ruins of a Dominican friary founded in 1486 by Richard Burke and consisting of nave, choir, south wing, stubby tower, and part of the eastern wall of the cloister. The site is beautifully located overlooking an estuary of Newport Bay.

** Rockfleet (Carrigahowley) Castle *(103)*, 5 mi W; ¼ mi S of N 59 (to Achill Sound); signposted to Carrigahowley Castle; OS ½ 6L 93 95; key at nearby garage

Overlooking an inlet of Clew Bay, here is an exceptionally well-preserved fifteenth- or sixteenth-century four-storey tower house with machicolated turrets at three corners but no battlements on the roof. After 1583 it was occupied by the colorful Grace O'Malley, who used this place as headquarters for her far-flung maritime enterprises and occasional piracies. When remnants of the Spanish Armada appeared in Clew Bay in 1588, she is believed to have pillaged the ships before destroying them and executing their crews.

WESTPORT

*** **Westport House** (196, 202), 1½ mi W; N of R 335 (to Louisburgh); open daily, 2:00–6:00 P.M.

The original section of this more-or-less Palladian mansion—the east front—was built in the 1730s to the design of Richard Castle for John Browne, afterward first earl of Altamont. In 1778 three sides were added, probably by Thomas Ivory, and still later the central court thus created was roofed in. These changes somewhat distorted the exterior proportions of the building, but the interior is splendid, owing chiefly to redecoration by James Wyatt, hired by the third earl (later first marquess of Sligo). Especially attractive is the large dining room with its fine plasterwork. Family portraits (two by Sir Joshua Reynolds) adorn the walls, as do several good landscapes by the Irish painter James Arthur O'Connor (1792–1841). In the small dining room is the "Mayo Legion Flag" brought from France by General Humbert when he landed at Killala Bay in 1798. For better or worse, the Westport estate has recently been converted into a holiday center with apartments for visitors, a caravan park, playground and zoo for children, boating facilities, etc. Most of this activity goes on, however, out of sight and hearing of the house itself.

Aghagower Round Tower (60), 5 mi S; 2 mi S of R 330 (to Ballinrobe); signposted; OS ½ 11M 03 80

In an untended graveyard near the scant ruins of a fifteenth-century church this Early Christian tower stands four storeys high with round-headed doorway about twelve feet above ground and a modern entrance at ground level.

* **Murrisk Friary** (131), 7 mi W; N of R 338 (to Louisburgh); signposted; OS ½ 11L 92 83

Beautifully situated on the shore of Westport Bay and under the shadow of Croagh Patrick, these are the ruins of an Augustinian friary founded by Hugh O'Malley in 1457. Surviving are the nave-and-chancel church with unusual battlemented walls, fine switch-line tracery in the east window, and portions of the east range of the cloister.

NORTHWESTERN IRELAND
County Donegal

BUNCRANA

* Fahan Mura Cross-slab *(50)*, 4 mi S; W of R 238 (to Derry); by footpath to untended graveyard S of church; signposted; OS ½ 1C 34 26

In the cemetery behind the modern church is a fine Early Christian standing grave slab carved in low relief with an intricate interlace on both faces. In the outside wall of the cemetery, beside the gate, is another grave slab, incised with a ringed cross inside a square, also of Early Christian date.

*** Fort Dunree and Military Museum *(257)*, 6 mi N; on unnumbered coastal road; signposted; open Tu–Sa, 9:30 A.M.–6:00 P.M.; Su, noon–6:00 P.M.

Following the capture of Wolfe Tone aboard the French frigate *La Hoche* in November 1798, a small fort was erected on this site to guard against a possible return of a French invasion fleet. In the late nineteenth century the fort was enlarged and modernized, and in the First World War it stood guard for a while over Admiral Lord Jellicoe's Grand Fleet, which had moved here from Scapa Flow. Like the two other British naval installations at Queenstown (Cobh) and Bearhaven, Dunree was transferred to Eire in 1938. During the Second World War, Irish forces were based here to prevent the warships of belligerent nations from violating the country's neutrality.

The fort has recently been converted into a first-rate military museum, with an audiovisual show and demonstrations of the workings of a twentieth-century coast artillery installation.

CARNDONAGH

* Carndonagh Cross and Pillars *(50)*, 1 mi N; S side of R 244 (to Buncrana); signposted and visible from road; OS ½ 1C 47 45

Standing tall at the corner of the Church of Ireland churchyard facing the road is this Early Christian sculpted cross, flanked by two stubby carved pillars. The cross is decorated with interlace and human figures, two of which (one on each side) are probably representations of Christ. The identity of the figures on the pillars is undetermined. In front of the church door is a lintel stone of fifteenth-century date showing carved figures of bishops. In the graveyard is a tall pillar, probably of Early Christian provenance, with a Crucifixion on one side.

Carrowmore Crosses *(51)*, 6½ mi SE, 200 yd S on minor road from R 238 (to Moville); signposted; OS ½ 2C 52 45

On each side of the road is a plain Early Christian cross standing in a field. That on the east is the more complete—a slab carved roughly in the shape of a cross; that on the west has truncated arms. Close to the latter is a boulder with a cross inside a circle inscribed on the face.

CARRICKART

*** Doe Castle *(102)*, 5 mi SW; ½ mi W of R 245; signposted; OS ½ 1C 08 32

On the shore of Sheephaven Bay, inside a battlemented bawn, this substantial ruin of a well-fenestrated two-storey residence is reinforced by a four-storey square tower at one end and a shorter round tower at the other. Gunports abound in both castle and bawn walls. In the sixteenth century, when it was first built, this was a MacSweeney stronghold and served as a refuge for shipwrecked sailors from the Spanish Armada in 1588. During the following century it was captured and recaptured many times by both Irish and English until peace came to County Donegal in the eighteenth century, when the fortress was converted into a country residence. Magnificent views of the western Donegal coastline.

DONEGAL

*** Donegal Castle *(102, 153)*, town center; signposted

Here are the substantial and high-standing ruins of a tower house built probably in the fifteenth century by Aedh Rua O'Donnell. It was the residence of Hugh Roe O'Donnell, earl of Tyrconnell, until his self-imposed exile to Spain, where he died in 1602. About twenty years later the property was granted to Sir Basil Brooke, who fenestrated the tower with mullioned windows and installed the splendid carved fireplace. Later he added the adjacent three-storey gabled residence with its many mullioned windows and the fine Jacobean doorway on the first floor, as well as the gatehouse and bawn wall.

* Donegal Friary *(131)*, at foot of town dock; signposted

Here, overlooking the headwaters of Donegal Bay, are the scant ruins of a Franciscan Observant house, founded in 1473 or 1474 by Red Hugh O'Donnell, his wife, and his mother. The site, unusually well tended, includes the roofless choir, the north wall of the nave, the west gable of the south wing, and the north and east walls of the cloister lying north of the church.

* **Donegal Historical Society Museum** *(19, 173, 202, 256)*, in Franciscan Friary, Rossnowlagh, 11 mi SE; 4 mi SE of N 18 from Ballintra; signposted to "Friary"

This small local museum houses Neolithic axes and flint arrowheads; penal crosses and other memorabilia of Catholic persecution during the eighteenth century; mementos of the 1798 uprising, including a proclamation issued by Napper Tandy prior to his abortive landing near here and a bayonet carried by a French officer aboard the *Hoche* when it was captured off Lough Swilly; memorabilia of the War of Irish Independence and civil war, 1916–23; etc.

GLENCOLUMBKILLE

*** **Glencolumbkille Folk Museum** *(214, 215, 220)*, village center; signposted; mandatory 30-minute guided tour

Here are three model thatched cottages built and furnished in styles appropriate to 1800, 1850, and 1900 respectively. Together they are meant to indicate the extent of material progress among the common people of Donegal in the nineteenth century. On the "village" grounds also are a nineteenth-century schoolhouse, a shebeen (an illegal private drinking house), and a large iron cauldron purporting to be a "famine pot" from which soup was served during the Famine of 1845–49.

* **Glencolumbkille Cross-Slabs, Pillar, and Souterrain** *(50)*, C of I parish church, village center

At the east end of the churchyard are two small sculpted Early Christian grave slabs. A ten-foot-tall pillar, inscribed with crosses on both faces, stands near the roadside about fifty yards west of the church. This is one of the "stations" along a 3½ mile pilgrimage. Just in front of the church door is a large souterrain now covered with sheet metal.

Farranmacbride (Mannernamortee) Court Cairn *(20)*, 1 mi N of C of I parish church; signposted "Mannernamortee Megalithic Tomb"; OS ½ 3G 54 86

This tumbled ruin was a Neolithic court grave of the "central court" variety. The scattered stones are difficult to interpret, especially since the central court is now cut by a stone wall.

* Malin More Portal Dolmens *(22)*, 1½ mi SW of village center, ½ mi E of Glenbay Hotel, behind farmhouses on S side of minor road running east; OS ½ 3G 53 83

Here is a row of six badly tumbled portal dolmens. The two at either end are in better condition than the rest.

* Cloghanmore (Malin More) Court Cairn *(20)*, 2 mi SW of village center; ½ mi SE of Glenbay Hotel, on S side of minor road running west, up cement footpath from small car park; signposted "Glen Malin Court Cairn" and visible from road; OS ½ 3G 52 82

This is a very large restored Neolithic court cairn with an enormous forecourt facing east and a small lintelled burial chamber at the west end.

LETTERKENNY

*** Glenveagh Castle, Gardens, and National Park *(217, 269)*, 13 mi NW; 3½ mi NW of R 251 (to Bunbeg) from Church Hill; signposted; mandatory 30-minute guided tour of castle

This splendid Scottish baronial house was built between 1870 and 1873 for John Adair, who had previously become notorious for his eviction of forty-seven families from the estate. It was enlarged by his widow. A later owner, Henry McIlhenny, was responsible for most of the present furnishings as well as for the splendid gardens and for embellishing the surrounding park begun by Mrs. Adair. The spectacularly scenic park, now owned and managed by the Forest and Wildlife Service, consists of 23,875 acres and includes beautiful Lough Veagh and the peaks of the two highest mountains in County Donegal, Errigal and Slieve Snaght. The Visitors' Centre at the entrance to the park offers a twenty-minute audiovisual show describing the area's geological history, flora and fauna, etc.

*** Grianan of Ailech *(39, 464)*, 18 mi NE; 2 mi S of N 13, 6 mi W of Derry; signposted; OS ½ 1C 37 20

On a high hill overlooking Lough Foyle, Lough Swilly, and the city of Derry, this is one of the finest stone ring-forts in Ireland, though much of it is the product of a nineteenth-century restoration. It consists primarily of a high, massive drystone circular wall surrounding an area seventy-seven feet in diameter. Inside the wall are three mural chambers, and on the inner face stone steps rise to the ramparts. Below this, surrounding the hilltop, are three low concentric ramparts, probably of earlier construction than the stone fort. This place was the royal seat of the Uí Néill kings of

Donegal. The date of its foundation is uncertain, though probably no earlier than the fifth century A.D.

MOVILLE

Greencastle (Northburgh Castle) *(90, 95, 97)*, 4 mi NE; E side of R 238 (to Inishowen Head); not signposted but visible from road; OS ½ 2C 65 40

Beautifully situated on a point overlooking the mouth of the river Foyle, this castle was built in the late thirteenth century by Richard de Burgh, the "Red Earl" of Ulster. It was captured and held briefly by Edward Bruce in 1315–18, returned to the earl of Ulster, then taken over by the O'Dohertys after the murder of William de Burgh, the "Brown Earl," in 1333. Sir Arthur Chichester owned the property in the late seventeenth century.

Badly neglected and untended, the ruins are difficult to decipher. They appear to consist of a rectangular keep incorporated into the north curtain wall and a twin-towered gatehouse piercing the west wall.

Greencastle Martello Tower *(207)*, 4 mi NE; E side of R 238 (to Inishowen Head); not signposted; no entry into interior

Situated on the grounds of holiday homes just north of the ruined castle, the tower was built in 1812 to guard the mouth of Lough Foyle against a Napoleonic invasion. (It is matched on the east bank by a similar fortalice at Magilligan Point.) Ovaloid in plan, it is more than thirty feet high, with walls eight feet thick and a door about ten feet above ground.

RATHMULLAN

* Rathmullan Friary *(132, 151)*, town center; not signposted but visible from road; OS ½ 1C 29 28

Overlooking Lough Swilly, these are the scant ruins of an early-sixteenth-century Carmelite friary founded by Owen Roe MacSweeney, a century later converted into an episcopal residence by the Protestant bishop Andrew Knox. Only the choir at the east end of the church was kept intact; the nave and south wing were extended during the conversion, at which time new windows and a door (dated 1617) were inserted and a pair of Scottish-style turrets added to the east end of the nave. The grounds are untended and the ruins difficult to decipher, but the view of Lough Swilly is superb. Across the road from here on 7 September 1607 Hugh O'Neill, Hugh Maguire, and Rory O'Donnell, with their families and followers, took ship for the Continent—an episode known to history as "The Flight of the Earls."

Northern Ireland

County Down

ARDGLASS

* **Jordan's Castle** *(102)*, town center, between Kildare and Quay streets; signposted; open weekdays only

Restored and partially furnished, this is a fifteenth-century tower house, one of several put up in what was then a busy port. In plan it is U-shaped with two corner towers projecting from a rectangular central block. These are connected by a high machicolated arch over the doorway in the north face of the tower. At right angles is still another smaller machicolation. The ground plan is rare in Ireland, except for County Down, and was probably based on Scottish models.

** **St. John's Point Church** *(49)*, 6 mi S, 2 mi S of Killough; signposted; OS 21J 142 604

This tiny Early Christian ruined church is beautifully situated close to St. John's Point Light, with a view of the sea on one side and the Mourne Mountains on the other. Still standing to some height are the two sides of the church and the west gable wall with a lintelled doorway and inward-leaning jambs. Antae rise to the height of the door on either side, and a portion of the south window also survives.

BANBRIDGE

* **First Presbyterian Church** *(181)*, E of town center; open for services only; key at manse (minister's house) next door

This is a very pretty neoclassical eighteenth-century church with a front porch supported by Ionic pillars, a central pulpit facing elegant galleries on three sides, and a fine panelled wood ceiling.

CASTLEWELLAN

* Clough Castle *(81)*, 4½ mi E, in Clough village center; E of A 24 (to Ballynahinch); not signposted but visible from road; OS 21J 409 403

Here are the remains of a high-standing Anglo-Norman motte separated by a ditch from its irregular-shaped bailey to the south. The small rectangular stone keep, above which now flies the Union Jack, was installed late in the thirteenth century. Dundrum Bay is visible to the southeast and the Mourne Mountains to the west.

*** Legananny Dolmen *(22)*, 8 mi NW on minor roads; signposted; OS 20J 288 434

Though not the easiest to find, this is one of the best of Ireland's tripod dolmens. Its capstone rests almost horizontally on three tall uprights, thus conforming to the "tabletop" tradition of this species of Neolithic tombs. The two portal stones face southward toward the magnificent Mourne Mountains.

CLOGHY

White House of Ballyspurge *(153)*, 1 mi S, through caravan park to end of road; not signposted; OS 21J 643 550

This is a moderately sized ruined stone house probably built in the 1640s by Patrick Savage. The gable ends stand high, the side walls less so. Gunports pierce the building at ground level, and there are fragmentary remains of a bawn wall. Good views of the Scottish coast to the east.

* Kirkiston Castle *(153)*, 1¼ mi N; W of A 2 (to Ballywater) from Ringboy; not signposted; OS 21J 646 580; no entry

Locked and untended, but visible through the gates, is this fine ruined three-storey towerhouse overlooking the North Channel, probably built in about 1622 by Roland Savage. It is three storeys high, well fenestrated, and machicolated on the entrance side. The elegant front portal was added in about 1800 and the massive buttresses flanking it somewhat later in the nineteenth century.

COMBER

* Nendrum Monastery *(47)*, 8 mi SE by a series of minor roads and causeways signposted to Island Mahee; OS 21J 524 637

Three concentric stone walls comprise the *vallum* of a monastery founded on the shore of Strangford Lough in the seventh century or earlier. The innermost of the enclosures contains the partially reconstructed church (probably tenth- or eleventh-century) and the stump of a Round Tower, about twelve feet high and also partially restored. In the site museum (the Display Centre) are a few Early Christian cross slabs found on the premises, as well as a series of good explanatory placards.

DOWNPATRICK

* Downpatrick Mound (Mound of Down) *(80)*, N of city center; ¼ mi N of Holy Trinity Cathedral, N of English Street; car park; signposted

Built by John de Courcy in about 1177, this crescent-shaped motte lies inside an iron-age hill-fort, both ditched. Best viewed by following the outer ditch to the steep footpath at the west end, then to the top of the grass-covered mound. Good views of Mourne Mountains and Quoile Marsh.

* Holy Trinity Cathedral *(177)*, English Street, town center; open only for Church of Ireland services

Very little is left here of the twelfth-century church founded by John de Courcy on the site of which this Georgian neo-Gothic building was erected in the 1790s. The most interesting interior features are the fine eighteenth-century organ, the early nineteenth-century box pews, and the eleventh-century "Celtic" font.

** Inch Abbey *(116, 126)*, 1 mi N; ½ mi W of A 7 (to Saintfield); signposted; OS 21J 477 455

These are the remains of a Cistercian monastery founded by John de Courcy in the 1180s and colonized from Furness Abbey in Lancashire. The nave is a scant ruin with not much left besides the foundations of walls and piers. The choir was enlarged and the nave shortened in the fifteenth century by the insertion of a transverse wall at about the midpoint of the nave. Seven tall lancets survive in the east wall, six complete to the arch. Both transepts of the cruciform church survive in part, though the opening from the choir to the north transept is blocked. The claustral remains south of the church are fragmentary. Overlooking the river Quoile, the well-tended site is a thing of quiet beauty.

** Ballynoe Stone Circle *(31)*, 3 mi S; ¼ mi by marked footpath W of Ballynoe Road from N end of Ballynoe village; OS 21J 481 404

Here is fine large stone circle of early bronze-age (or even late Neolithic) date measuring 108 feet in diameter. It is composed of fifty-five stones, cut and uncut, the highest rising to about six feet above ground. In the center is a mound kerbed with low-lying boulders. The entrance appears to be in the north quadrant. Outside the circle are two or three outlying standing stones of unknown significance.

DROMORE

** Dromore Mound *(81)*, E of town center; S side of Mount Street; obscurely signposted but visible from street

Probably the best-preserved Anglo-Norman motte in Ulster, this deeply ditched mound rises abruptly to a height of about thirty-six feet. It is easily climbed by way of the spiral path leading to the top. South of it is a lower, squarish mound, also ditched—the site of the palisaded bailey.

GREYABBEY

*** Grey Abbey *(117, 140)*, E of village center; S side of B 5 (to Ballywalter); signposted; OS 21J 583 682; custodian on duty

Here is one of the finest and best-preserved ruined Cistercian abbeys in Ireland. Founded in 1193 by Affreca, daughter of the king of Man and wife of John de Courcy, the buildings date mostly to the thirteenth century. The church is cruciform, with a partially restored recessed west doorway, an aisleless nave, transepts with two chapels in each, a tower over the crossing, and a shallow choir with a fine triple lancet in the east wall and single lancets in the side walls. Of the claustral buildings south of the church the most distinguished feature is the refectory in the south range, extending south of the cloister in the manner peculiar to the Cistercians. It stands fairly high, with three tall lancets in the south gable and a raised reader's pulpit in the west wall. The chapter house in the east range is more ruined, though the foundations of six piers are still in position. The west range has disappeared. The monastery was dissolved in 1541, and Queen Mary later granted some of its lands to Gerald FitzGerald, earl of Kildare. In the early seventeenth century the property fell into the hands of Sir Hugh Montgomery, who restored the nave for the use of the local Church of Ireland parish. Toward the end of the eighteenth century it was abandoned again, though it has been partially restored since.

HILLSBOROUGH

*** St. Malachy's Church *(161, 177)*, town center; open daily and for Church of Ireland services

This is one of the loveliest parish churches in Ireland, situated in one of the island's prettiest villages. Facing a long expanse of well-tended lawn, the cruciform building has a high tower and spire at the west end and lower square towers at the end of each transept. Inside and out, the church reflects the Gothick style popular in the 1760s and 1770s, when it was drastically remodelled by Wills Hill, earl of Hillsborough. The earliest part of the building, however, dates to the 1660s, when it was begun by Sir Arthur Hill on the site of an earlier church burned down during the uprising of 1641.

** **Hillsborough Fort** (161), town center, by footpath from north side of St. Malachy's Church; not signposted

Built by Colonel Arthur Hill in about 1650, this is a square enclosure surrounded by ramparts of earth and stone, 270 feet long on each side. Following the fashion of seventeenth-century military architecture, at each corner is an arrowhead bastion. The rectangular gatehouse in the north wall was remodelled in the eighteenth century, when the corner towers, battlements, and pointed doors and windows were also added. The Gothick gazebo in the center of the east wall was installed at about the same time.

Duneight Motte and Bailey (81), 3 mi NE; 2 mi E of A 1 (to Lisburn) through Ravenet; signposted; OS 20J 278 608

The Anglo-Norman motte is represented by a triangular grass-covered ditched mound. East of it lies a lower oval-shaped mound where stood the bailey.

HILLTOWN

* **Goward (The Cloughmore) Dolmen** (22), 2½ mi NE, ½ mi S of B 8 (to Castlewellan) at end of one-track gravel lane; signposted; OS 29J 244 310

The huge boulderlike capstone of this Neolithic portal dolmen has slipped sidways from its original position above the rectangular burial chamber. Entrance to the tomb through the two upright portals is blocked by a third upright.

KILKEEL

*** **Greencastle** (90, 95, 97, 146), 6 mi SW; by minor roads; signposted and visible from road; OS 29J 247 119; custodian on duty

Overlooking Carlingford Lough, the original castle on this site was built in the thirteenth century, taken by Irish "insurgents" in 1260, cap-

tured again by Edward Bruce in 1316, ruined by the O'Neills late in the
fourteenth century, and subsequently occupied by the Magennises. It was
recovered for the English Crown early in the sixteenth century by Sir
Nicholas Bagenal, governor of Newry.

The high rectangular battlemented keep has square towers at each
corner, added probably in the fifteenth century. The curtain wall originally contained D-shaped turrets at each corner, but only one of these (at
the northwest corner) survives to any height. The foundations of the
southwest wall turret can be seen from the upper storeys of the keep. The
west curtain wall has been incorporated into a modern farmhouse adjacent
to the site.

NEWCASTLE

*** **Dundrum Castle** *(85, 146)*, 4 mi N; W side of A 2 (to Ballynahinch);
signposted; OS 21J 404 369; custodian on duty

The original construction of this important stronghold may have been
begun by John de Courcy but more likely by Hugh de Lacy II after 1205.
The castle was taken by King John in 1210; was restored to the earldom of
Ulster in 1227; then, after the murder of William de Burgh ("the Brown
Earl"), it passed into the hands of the Magennises, from whom it was seized
by Lord Deputy Leonard Grey during the reign of Henry VIII. In the
seventeenth century the property was owned by the Blundell family, which
built the dwelling house in the lower ward.

The twin square-towered gatehouse is of late-thirteenth-century construction. It leads into the upper ward surrounded by a curtain wall, parts
of which belong to the original early-thirteenth-century castle. So does the
splendid ruin of the four-storey round keep, though the present entrance to
it is a fifteenth-century intrusion. The lower ward is a later addition of
uncertain date. Fine views of the Mourne Mountains, Dundrum Bay, and
the North Channel.

NEWRY

** **Narrow Water Castle** *(146)*, 5 mi SE; W side of A 2 (to Warrenpoint);
signposted and visible from road; OS 29J 127 193

This partially restored towerhouse and bawn was built in the 1560s to
control passage up the river Newry from Carlingford Lough. There are
three storeys (climbable), a corbelled machicolation above the main doorway with a murder hole inside, and typically Irish wickerwork markings on
the ground-floor barrel-vaulted ceiling as well as in the window casings of

the top storey. The bawn wall is in good condition, and the well-tended grounds have been beautified by a small garden.

* **Killevy Churches** *(50)*, 5½ mi SW, in County Armagh; 3 mi S of A 25 (to Newtonhamilton) from Camlough; obscurely signposted; OS 29J 040 220

On the site of one of Ireland's earliest nunneries are the ruins of two churches, back to back, with a stone wall dividing them. The older of the two is the west church, with a huge lintel over the west doorway, indicating a possible tenth-century date, although the round-headed east window is no earlier than the twelfth. The east church has a fifteenth-century Decorated east window. Leaning against the dividing wall is an Early Christian grave slab with an incised cross inside a circle.

* **Kilnasaggart Stone** *(50)*, 7½ mi S, in County Armagh, 1½ mi SW of N 1 (to Dundalk) through Jonesborough; by footpath over two stiles; signposted; OS 29J 063 150

Within a fenced enclosure, this eight-foot Early Christian pillar stone has carved crosses enclosed in disks on both sides and on the southeast face a long Irish inscription indicating a late-seventh- or early-eighth-century date for the monument.

* **Moyry Castle** *(148)*, 7½ mi SW, in County Armagh; 2 mi SW of N 1 (to Dundalk) through Jonesborough; signposted and visible from road; OS 29J 057 146

Built in 1601 to guard Moyry's Pass during Mountjoy's Ulster campaign, this small rectangular tower with rounded corners and numerous gunports survives to its full height of three storeys. Only a portion of the original bawn wall remains standing.

NEWTOWNARDS

*** **Mount Stewart** *(209, 269)*, 5 mi SE; E side of A 20 (to Portaferry); National Trust of Northern Ireland (NTNI); open May–June, W–Su, 2:00–6:00 P.M.; July–Aug, Tu–Su, noon–8:00 P.M.; 1-hour mandatory guided tour

This is among the finest of the stately homes in the British Isles. Construction of the house was commenced in 1804 by Robert Stewart, first marquess of Londonderry, under the architectural direction of George Dance of London, who built the west wing with its handsome balustraded staircase, the "Castlereagh Room" (originally a dining room), the elegant music room, and "Lady Londonderry's Sitting Room" (originally the library). Most of the present building was completed in the late 1830s during the ownership of Charles Stewart, third marquess, with the assistance of the eminent Irish Greek Revival architect William Vitruvius Morrison, who was responsible for the magnificent domed octagonal Great Hall, the Black and White Hall, the Drawing Room, and the Dining Room.

The best-known occupant of Mount Stewart was Robert Stewart, second marquess, better known as Lord Castlereagh, the title he held before his father's death. As British foreign secretary during the final years of the Napoleonic Wars, he was, along with Austria's Prince Clemens von Metternich, the leading statesman at the Congress of Vienna (1815), which wrote the peace treaty and redrew the map of Europe. Among the many Castlereagh mementos are the chairs used by the delegates to the congress (later embroidered with their personal arms and those of the countries they represented). Most of the present interior decoration was completed under the direction of the seventh marchioness, whose husband served in the British cabinet under both Ramsey MacDonald and Stanley Baldwin in the 1930s. But perhaps the most prized of all the house's many possessions is the large painting by George Stubbs of the racehorse Hambletonian, which hangs in the landing of the grand staircase.

Mount Stewart's exquisite gardens are also mostly the handiwork of the seventh marchioness and of her daughter, Lady Mairie Bury. The formal gardens—the Italian Garden, the Dodo Terrace, the Spanish Garden, the Peace Garden, and the Lily Wood—lie south and west of the house. To the east lies the Mairie Garden and to the west the Shamrock Garden. The extensive grounds north of the house contain woodland gardens. Still farther to the northwest, and approached by a separate driveway from the A 20, stands the Temple of the Winds, a neoclassic masterpiece built in 1782–85 by James "Athenian" Stuart—a two-storey hexagonal temple derived from the Temple of the Winds in Athens and meant to serve as a banqueting house.

PORTAFERRY

Derry Churches *(49)*, 1½ mi NE; E of A 2 (to Cloghy), by fenced footpath; not signposted; OS 21 J 613 524

Of the two tiny ruined churches on this untended site the smaller and southernmost is the older, possibly built as early as the tenth century. Its most distinguished feature is the pair of antae on both east and west ends. The north church is probably medieval in date.

ROSTREVOR

* **Kilfeaghan Dolmen** *(22)*, 5 mi SE, ½ mi N of A 2 (to Kilkeel), by footpath through two turnstiles and iron gate; signposted; OS 29J 232 154

This odd-looking portal dolmen, overlooking Carlingford Lough, consists of a huge rounded capstone propped up at its front end by two low uprights. The burial chamber is in the hollow underneath.

SAINTFIELD

** **Rowallane Gardens** *(269)*, 1 mi S; W side of A 7 (to Downpatrick); signposted; NTNI; open M-F, 9:00 A.M.-9:00 P.M.; Sa-Su, 2:00-9:00 P.M.

This fine woodland garden is the headquarters of the National Trust for Northern Ireland. In addition to extensive plantings of rhododendrons, azaleas, and conifers, there are two walled gardens, one with roses, herbaceous plants, and flowering shrubs, the other featuring hydrangeas, late summer flowers, and dwarf rhododendrons. Also noteworthy is the rock garden.

STRANGFORD

* **Kilclief Castle** *(102)*, 3 mi S; W side of A 2 (to Ardglass); signposted and visible from road; OS 21J 597 457; no entry to interior

This typical U-plan County Down tower house was probably built in 1413-41 by John Sely, bishop of Down. Two corner towers project forward from a rectangular block, and between them, high over the doorway, is an arched machicolation. Fine view of the sea.

*** **Castle Ward** *(198)*, 2 mi W; ¾ mi N of A 25 (to Downpatrick); signposted; NTNI; open May-June, W-Su, 2:00-6:00 P.M.; July-Aug, W-M, noon-8:00 P.M.; mandatory 1-hour guided tour

This very handsome and palatial country house was built about 1767 by Sir Bernard Ward, subsequently Viscount Bangor. It is architecturally unique in being split almost equally between two distinct styles: neoclassic in the southwest half; Gothick in the northeast. The contrast is apparent not only in the exterior architecture of the two facades but in the interior decoration and furnishings as well. The disparity is owed to radical differences in taste between the builder and his wife, Lady Anne: he preferred the conventional Palladian style of the mid-eighteenth century, she the new Gothick fashion popularized by Sir Horace Walpole at Strawberry Hill near London.

The effect is somewhat startling as the visitor moves from the chaste entrance hall with its broken-arched doorway, Doric columns, and symmetrical plasterwork, up the Grand Staircase with its Venetian window and then abruptly into Lady Anne's Boudoir, with its fan-vaulted ceiling and ogival windows, and on to the Saloon and Morning Room decorated in the same manner. Finally the visitor returns to the symmetry of the Augustan Age in the Dining Room and then outside to the neoclassical temple at the head of a long, rectangular, artificial lake called Temple Water.

** **Audleystown Cairn** (20), 4½ mi W; 1½ mi NE of A 25 (to Downpatrick); signposted; OS 21J 562 504

Overlooking Strangford Lough, this is a Neolithic double-court cairn with crescent-shaped forecourts at each end, both leading to galleries of four segmented burial chambers. The cairn is now grass-covered and revetted by drystone walling. It has the distinction of having yielded to excavators the largest number of corpses (thirty-four unburned skeletons) of any megalithic tomb in Ireland.

** **Audley's Castle** (102), 5 mi W; 2 mi NE of A 25 (to Downpatrick); signposted; OS 21J 578 506

Overlooking the narrow mouth of Strangford Lough, this fifteenth-century tower house consists of a rectangular central block with two square corner towers projecting forward. Between these two stretches a machicolated arch high above the main doorway. This is a typical County Down U-plan tower, modelled probably on Scottish prototypes. To the south lies Castle Ward's Temple Water—laid out in the eighteenth century so as to capture the reflection of this romantic ruin. Fine views in all directions.

County Armagh

ARMAGH

* **St. Patrick's (C of I) Cathedral** (58, 225), Cathedral Close and Abbey Street, open weekdays and for services

This much restored medieval church is believed to be the site of St. Patrick's original episcopal foundation. It is an aisled cruciform building of red sandstone with a square chancel and a rather stubby square central tower without spire. Except for the thirteenth-century crypt (closed), not much was left of the original church after its restoration in the nineteenth century at the hands of the English architect Lewis Cottingham.

There is a much-worn Early Christian cross in the north aisle and several pieces of sculpture from the medieval church in the chapter house in the north transept. In the south transept is the chapel of the Royal Irish Fusiliers. Outside, in the wall of the north transept, a bronze plaque marks the reputed burial site of King Brian Boru.

** **Armagh County Museum** *(19, 173, 286)*, the Mall, Armagh; open M-Sa, 10:00 A.M.-1:00 P.M., 2:00-5:00 P.M.

This is a very well-organized local museum and art gallery, the latter including paintings by George Russell (AE). The prehistoric gallery has a fine collection of Neolithic and bronze-age axes, bronze-age knives, daggers, palstaves, horse trappings, pins, brooches, swords, and "crotals" (small, hollow pear-shaped metal objects with pebbles inside). There is a good array of "penal crosses" from the eighteenth century and from the nineteenth exhibits of pottery, china, lace, and household utensils. There is also a costume gallery and a section devoted to natural history.

Armagh Public Library *(42, 178)*, Abbey Street, diagonally across from St. Patrick's (C of I) Cathedral; open weekdays, 2:00-4:00 P.M.

Built by Archbishop Robinson in 1771 and modelled on Marsh's Library, Dublin, this is a fine small neoclassic building with an equally elegant interior housing a priceless collection of sixteenth-, seventeenth-, and eighteenth-century publications, many superbly bound. In the basement is the Drumconwell Ogham Stone, oddly shaped and with very clear Ogham markings as well as a Christian cross inside a circle.

* **Royal Irish Fusiliers Museum** *(208)*, the Mall, city center

This is a very well-organized military museum containing mementos of two regiments of the British army (the 87th or Prince of Wales's Irish Regiment and the 89th Foot) and three regiments of Irish militia raised in 1793. Here are excellent exhibits of uniforms, weapons, paintings, etc., illustrating the participation of these units in the Peninsular War of 1811-14, the Crimean War, the Boer War, and the First and Second World Wars.

*** **St. Patrick's (RC) Cathedral** *(231)*, Cathedral Road, N of town center

Designed by James J. McCarthy and built between 1848 and 1872, this is perhaps the masterpiece of that most prolific of nineteenth-century neo-Gothic architects. Lofty twin spires tower above the west doorway, flanked by statues of St. Malachy and St. Patrick. The style is Curvilinear Decorated. The church is cruciform and aisled, with a square chancel, soaring columns, and high walls adorned with fine mosaics. It is altogether a fitting seat for the Catholic primate of Ireland.

Orange Order Museum *(175)*, 5 mi NE; on NW side of B 77 (to Portadown) in Loughgall village center; not signposted; key at house next door

In this house the "Orange Institution" was founded in 1795 following the "Battle of the Diamond," two miles northeast of here on the Portadown Road. The contents of the tiny museum include Orange Order sashes, proclamations, handbills, and other memorabilia of this militant Protestant society.

**Navan Fort *(34, 98)*, 2½ mi W; ½ mi N of A 28 (to Caledon) from Navan village; signposted; OS 19H 847 452

This is the Emain Macha of the *Táin* and other legends of the Ulster Cycle, where Conchobar mac Nessa, king of Ulster, presided over the warriors of the Ulaid (Ulstermen), including the great Cúchulainn. All that remains today is a large bowl-shaped grassy mound, about 140 feet in diameter and eighteen feet high, inside an earthen bank with an interior ditch. Underneath the mound archaeologists have discovered the remains of a large circular wooden building that must have served as some kind of assembly hall. It was later filled with stones, ritually burned, and finally covered with earth. To the southeast stands another, smaller mound, probably the site of the house built here in the late fourteenth century by Nial O'Neill for the entertainment of scholars and poets. In spite of the proximity of a huge stone quarry, the views from this place are impressive.

CROSSMAGLEN

** Annaghmare Cairn *(20)*, 3 mi N; ¾ mi W of B 135 (to Newtonhamilton), 200 yd by marked footpath through 2 gates and into low forest plantation; signposted; OS 28H 905 178

A semicircle of high stones facing southwest forms the forecourt of this Neolithic court cairn. Behind the court lie three burial chambers in a row. At the northeast end are two smaller chambers, one on each side, probably later intrusions. Most of the rocky cairn material is still in place. The site is untended but fenced.

* Ballykeel Dolmen *(22)*, 8 mi NE; ½ mi S of B 30 (to Newry); signposted; OS 28H 995 214

This is a fine tripod dolmen with three uprights and a capstone slanting slightly to the rear. The two portal stones with a blocker in between face south. The site is untended but fenced.

PORTADOWN

** **Ardress House** *(197)*, 7 mi W; S side of B 28 (to Moy); signposted; NTNI; open June, F–M, 2:00–6:00 P.M.; July–Aug, M, W–Sa, 2:00–6:00 P.M.; Su, 2:00–5:00 P.M.; mandatory 30-minute guided tour

This rather plain country mansion is an eighteenth-century enlargement by the English architect George Ensor of an earlier house built by his wife's family. Numerous decorative classical features adorn the facade. At the back of the house are well-preserved stables, byres, a smithy, and a harness room. The interior is furnished elegantly with eighteenth-century pieces, and the plasterwork on ceilings and walls by Michael Stapleton is superb.

County Tyrone

BALLYGAWLEY

* **Grant Ancestral House & Simpson Farm** *(193)*, 5 mi E; 2 mi S of A 4 (to Dungannon); signposted

This is the homestead of John Simpson, President Ulysses S. Grant's maternal grandfather, who left here in 1768 to settle in Ohio. There is a vistors' center with explanatory placards, a two-roomed furnished thatched cottage, a byre, a pigsty (with pig), and a storeroom with farm implements. The surrounding fields are part of a working farm.

BENBURB

Benburb Castle *(153)*, town center, on grounds of Benburb Priory; poorly signposted

This is an unusual planter's castle, built by Sir Richard Wingfield in about 1615. It consists of a rectangular enclosure surrounded by high bawn walls, well defended with gun-loops and with high rectangular towers at the northeast and northwest corners. Another tower (circular) stands at the south end of the wall. No contemporary residential quarters are attached (the house inside the wall is a privately owned nineteenth-century building).

CLOGHER

* **Clogher Cathedral** *(51, 177)*, S side of A 4 (to Ballygawley) in village center; closed except for Church of Ireland services; key at Fannin's Grocery, 100 yd E and across road

This attractive small eighteenth-century church has a good Venetian window at the east end and neoclassic round-arched windows elsewhere. In the foyer is the Clogher Cross, about five feet high—a roughly hewn grave slab of the seventh or eighth century with interlace carved on both sides. Behind the church is the Rathmore hill-fort, reputed to have been sacred to the kings of Airgialla.

** **Knockmany Passage Grave** (25), 3½ mi N; 1 mi N of B 83 (to Omagh) through Knockmany Forest to Cairn Carpark, then by marked footpath, ½ mi to summit; OS 18H 547 559; no entry to interior

Overlooking the broad Clogher valley, this is a Neolithic tomb now covered by a modern superstructure. Though it is technically a "passage grave," the usual passage is missing. The burial tomb is spacious and is distinguished for the numerous stone carvings within: concentric circles, spirals, zigzags, etc. Though entry into the interior is barred, the decorated stones are clearly visible through an open grille. The view is breathtaking.

COAGH

*** **Arboe Cross** (62), 5½ mi E; S of B 73 through Moortown village (not through Arboe village on B 161); signposted at site but not from B 73; OS 14H 966 756

Overlooking Lough Neagh, this is the finest of Ulster's Early Christian High Crosses. It probably dates to the ninth century, and the iconography is unusually clear-cut. On the east side (top to bottom) are Christ in glory, the Second Coming of Christ, the Children of Israel in the Fiery Furnace, Daniel in the Lions' Den, and Adam and Eve. On the west are the Crucifixion, the Arrest of Christ, the Entry to Jerusalem, the Miracle of the Loaves and Fishes, the Miracle at Cana, and the Visit of the Magi. On the south are the hermit saints, Paul and Anthony, in the desert, David and Goliath, David and the Lion, and Cain and Abel. The north side is difficult to interpret.

North of the cross are the insubstantial ruins of a medieval abbey, and to the east is the more substantial ruin of a small seventeenth-century church.

COALISLAND

* **Mountjoy Castle** (149), 4 mi E; ¼ mi N of B 161; signposted; OS 18H 901 687

There is some doubt as to whether this small "campaign fortress" was built in 1602 or 1605, but in either case it is named after Lord Mountjoy, the English conqueror of Ulster, and its purpose was to guard the western shore of Lough Neagh, which it overlooks. The substantial ruin consists of a central keep of stone and brick, with only two of the original four corner towers still standing to any height. Gunports are numerous, especially at the ground level.

COOKSTOWN

Tullaghoge *(39, 147, 149)*, 2½ mi S; E of B 162 (to Stewartstown), by single-track cement lane from car park to hilltop, then by marked footpath; signposted; OS 13H 825 743

This is a large tree-covered earthen ring separated by a ditch from an interior polygonal earthwork. It was the inauguration site of the Cenél nEógain (the Tyrone O'Neills) as early as the eleventh century and very probably before. The great Hugh O'Neill was inaugurated here as late as 1595. The sacred stone chair on which he and others of his clan were installed was broken by order of Lord Mountjoy in 1602 on the eve of the collapse of the earldom of Tyrone. In the Middle Ages the site belonged to the O'Hagans, whose burial place is the circular walled graveyard to the southwest.

*** Wellbrook Beetling Mill *(192)*, 5 mi W; ½ mi N of A 505 (to Omagh); signposted; NTNI; open M, W–Sa, 2:00–6:00 P.M.; Su, 2:00–7:00 P.M.; mandatory 20-minute guided tour

Restored by the National Trust in Northern Ireland, this water-powered mill was established in 1764 for finishing linen cloth. Around the walls are placards explaining the processes by which flax was converted into linen. The intricate machinery and the exterior wheel by which it is activated are still in place and in working order. The short walk along the millrace and millstream is not to be missed.

** Springhill *(197)*, 6 mi NE, in County Londonderry; ½ mi S of Moneymore, W of B 18 (to Coagh); signposted; NTNI; open June, W–M, 2:00–6:00 P.M.; July-Aug, M, W–Sa, 2:00–6:00 P.M.; Su 2:00–7:00 P.M.; mandatory 30-minute guided tour

The central block of this charming country house dates to the late seventeenth century, when it was built by "Good" Will Conyngham, a royalist soldier during the War of the Two Kings. The two side wings were constructed in the eighteenth, probably by his grand-nephew William Conyngham, who died in 1784; the dining room is from the nineteenth.

The furnishings are mostly eighteenth- and nineteenth century. Of special interest are the gun room, the nursery, and the costume collection in the laundry room. Outside lies a lovely walled garden at one end of which is a fortified seventeenth-century barn, the oldest building on the property.

*** **Beaghmore** *(30)*, 8½ mi NW; 2¾ mi N of A 505 (to Omagh) through Dunnamore village; signposted; OS 13H 685 842

Here are seven stone circles arranged in three pairs plus one large circle, called the Dragon's Teeth because it is packed with sharp close-set stones. Also in the vicinity are a number of small cairns and stone alignments. Three of the stone rows are oriented to the point on the horizon where the sun rises at the summer solstice, but the others have no observable astronomical significance.

DUNGANNON

* **Castle Caulfield** *(153)*, 2 mi W, in Castlecaulfield village center; OS 19H 755 626

These are the substantial remains of a fortified manor house built between 1611 and 1619 by Sir Toby Caulfield, whose family crest is carved above the gatehouse door. The three-storey house is well fenestrated but lacks defensive features. The gatehouse, built earlier, is well supplied with murder holes and gun-loops. The attached bawn wall has all but disappeared. During the uprising of 1641 the castle was burned by the O'Donnellys but was later repaired and reoccupied by the Caulfields.

** **Donaghmore Cross** *(62)*, 2½ mi NW in C of I churchyard, W of Donaghmore village center, at junction of B 43 (to Pomeroy) and road to Castlecaulfield; visible from road; OS 19H 768 654

This is a composite of two Early Christian crosses joined together at the middle. The carving is quite clear-cut. On the east side facing the road are (top to bottom) the Crucifixion, the Arrest of Christ, the Miracle of the Loaves and Fishes, the Miracle at Cana, the Adoration of the Magi, and the Annunciation to the Shepherds. On the west face are the Sacrifice of Isaac, Cain and Abel, and Adam and Eve.

MOY

* **The Argory** *(211)*, 4 mi NE, in County Armagh; N of Derrycaw Road; signposted; NTNI; mandatory 50-minute guided tour

Architecturally undistinguished, this is a neoclassic building consisting of a main block with a north wing ending in an octagonal pavilion. It was built between 1829 and 1834 by the brothers Arthur and John Williamson for Walter McGeogh, who later changed his name to Bond. The interior furnishings, however, are mostly of a later date, reflecting the tastes of the High Victorian era. The most interesting items are the cast-iron stove, the early-nineteenth-century Colza oil lamp, and the huge cabinet barrel organ.

NEWTOWNSTEWART

** Harry Avery's Castle *(97)*, ¾ mi SW; W of minor road to Rakelly; signposted; OS 12H 392 852

This pair of high round towers backed by the low remains of a curtain wall looks like an early medieval keepless courtyard castle but isn't. There is no entranceway between the towers, and the only approach to the courtyard is by a stairway leading into one of them. The place was built in the fourteenth or fifteenth century by Henry Aemreidh (Harry Avery) O'Neill of the Clandeboy branch of that family and is the only stone castle in the North known to have had a Gaelic Irish builder. Actually it is less formidable than it looks, which suggests that it may have been built as much for show as for defensibility.

OMAGH

*** Ulster-American Folk Park *(193)*, 5 mi N; E of A 5 (to Newtownstewart); signposted; open M–Sa, 11:00 A.M.–6:30 P.M.; Su, 11:30 A.M.–7:00 P.M.; allow 2 hours for visit

These extensive grounds and their exhibits are laid out in two sections. On the Ulster side are the exhibition hall, with life-sized models of America-bound emigrants; a model shop; a forge with live demonstration; a weaver's cottage where an informative talk is given about the domestic textile industry; a T-plan Protestant meetinghouse; the home of Thomas Mellon, grandfather of the American financier Andrew Mellon; the Hughes cottage, home of John Hughes, first Catholic archbishop of New York; a thatched one-room nineteenth-century schoolhouse; and the "Emigration Gallery," with reproductions of an Ulster dockside scene, an emigrant ship, and the American arrival port. On the American side are reproductions of a log cabin, a Pennsylvania log barn with a Conestoga wagon inside, a smokehouse, a spring house, a henhouse, a two-storey Pennsylvania log farmhouse, and a camp meeting site. Map provided.

POMEROY

** **Creggandevesky Court Grave** *(20)*, 3½ mi NW, 2½ mi NW of B 4 (to Carrickmore), W of minor road to Creggan and Gorton; not signposted but easily found by following south shore of Lough Mallon to its west end; OS 13H 643 750

This is a fine and well-preserved Neolithic court grave. The semicircular forecourt faces southeast, and behind it is a three-chambered tomb. Although the capstones are gone, the revetted cairn stands high.

County Fermanagh

BELLEEK

*** **Belleek Pottery** *(219)*, village center; mandatory 20-minute guided tour

Built between 1857 and 1860 on the initiative of John Caldwell Bloomfield and David McBirny, the factory first went into full production in 1863 to become one of the few successful industrial enterprises in nineteenth-century Ireland outside of brewing, distilling, linen manufacture, and shipbuilding. It first specialized in general earthenware, stoneware, patented toilet bowls, and wall tiles, and not until about 1884 did it begin to concentrate on the fancy ceramic ware for which it is now world-famous.

The guided tour enables the visitor to witness at close quarters the successive stages in the production of this ware, including the painstaking craftsmanship involved in shaping and hand-painting various items. Products of the pottery can be purchased at the visitors' center.

ENNISKILLEN

*** **Fermanagh County Museum, Enniskillen Castle** *(19, 42, 102, 147, 153, 208)*, Castle Street; open M–Sa, 10:00 A.M.–12:30 P.M., 2:00–5:00 P.M.

Only the lower portion of the keep of this impressive castle on the bank of the river Erne can be dated to the fifteenth century, when it was erected by Hugh Maguire. It changed hands several times during the Nine Years' War (1594–1601) between Irish and English, finally falling to the latter. Beginning in 1607, the English constable remodelled the main keep and added the fine water gate with its pair of corbelled pepper-pot bartizans—best seen from the path along the river. The military barracks are of eighteenth- and nineteenth-century provenance.

The county museum has a well-organized display of Neolithic arrowheads and stone axes; bronze-age palstaves, pottery, and personal ornaments; and iron-age weapons and pottery. Along with this collection of prehistoric artifacts is a three-dimensional model of a Neolithic court-cairn burial. Here also are a small Ogham stone, Early Christian relics, and miscellaneous medieval artifacts.

On the floor above, an audiovisual show describes various aspects of the history of the town of Enniskillen and of the Maguire kings of Fermanagh.

The top floor contains two rooms full of uniforms, badges, regimental silver, weapons, etc., belonging to the Royal Inniskilling Fusiliers.

*** Castle Coole *(197)*, 2 mi S; N of A 4 (to Dungannon); signposted; NTNI

This is James Wyatt's Palladian masterpiece designed in 1790, though built by other hands, for Armar Lowry Corry, later earl of Belmore. Made of imported Portland stone, the house is 280 feet long, including the pavilions flanking the central block and the connecting colonnades. Ionic porticos front and back, Venetian windows, and Doric colonnades are all within the Palladian tradition. The interior stuccowork is by Joseph Rose, the scagliola pillars in the hall by Dominic Bartoli, the magnificent chimneypieces by Richard Westmacott. The most impressive rooms are the entrance hall, the oval saloon, the library, the dining room, the large first-floor lobby, and the state bedroom. The furnishings are predominantly Regency.

** Florence Court *(197, 239)*, 8½ mi S; 3 mi S of A 4 (to Sligo); signposted; NTNI; open W–M, noon–6:00 P.M.; mandatory 30-minute guided tour

The central portion of this fine Palladian mansion was built in about 1760 by John Cole, Baron Mount Florence; the pavilions and their connecting arcades were added in about 1770 by his son William, later first earl of Enniskillen. The Dublin stuccodore, Robert West, is probably responsible for the elaborate rococo plasterwork. The present interior is the product of a thorough restoration after a devastating fire in 1955. One of the few furnishings left after the fire is a chamber pot with William Gladstone's portrait on the inside bottom—a reminder of the strong anti–Home Rule sentiment among the Ulster gentry.

*** Devenish Churches and Round Tower *(60, 72)*, 2½ mi NW on Devenish Island in Lower Lough Erne; excursion boat *Kestrel* leaves twice daily from Round "O" Jetty, town center, allowing 30 minutes on island before returning; or 5 mi N by way of ferry from Trory Point W of junction of B 82 (to Kesh) and A 32 (to Ballinamallard)

On this Early Christian monastic site the following ruins are open to inspection (in the order of their proximity to the boat landing):

1. **Teampull Mor:** a small single-celled thirteenth-century church with a molded round-headed south window.

2. **St. Molaise's House:** A tiny twelfth-century rectangular cell with a doorway but no visible windows.

3. **Round Tower** *(60)*: A twelfth-century Round Tower eighty-one feet high with a conical top. To climb the tower, procure the key at the site museum.

4. **St. Mary's Priory** *(72)*: A fifteenth- or sixteenth-century church built on the site of a twelfth-century foundation for canons regular of the Order of St. Augustine. Still standing are the choir, the lower parts of the nave, and a high square central tower. An elaborately carved doorway leads from the choir into the cloister to the north, where parts of the claustral buildings survive. In the graveyard stands a fine fifteenth-century carved stone cross.

5. **Site Museum:** Provides ample information concerning the history and architecture of the island.

*** Monea Castle *(152)*, 7 mi NW; 1 mi E of B 81; 3½ mi SE of Derrygonnelly; signposted; OS 17H 164 493

Here is the high-standing, well-preserved, and well-tended ruin of a plantation castle built in 1618–19 by Malcolm Hamilton. Round twin towers at the entrance front are capped by square chambers with crow-stepped gables—a Scottish architectural feature found at Claypotts in Angus County but nowhere else in Ireland. Gun-loops cover the entrance to the rectangular tower and the bawn. Notwithstanding the defensive features, the tower is well fenestrated. The bawn wall is in a more ruinous condition than the castle itself, although the latter is bereft of flooring, vaults, or stairways.

*** Tully Castle *(152)*, 11½ mi NW; 3 mi N of Derrygonnelly; ¾ mi E of A 46 (to Belleek); signposted; OS 17H 126 566

Standing on a hill overlooking Lough Erne, this well-preserved ruined fortified house and bawn were built in 1618 by the Scottish planter Sir John Hume. It is three storeys high, with square turrets at the four corners. A modern stairway leads to the first floor above the barrel-vaulted ground floor. Bawn walls still stand fairly high, with square corner towers at each end of the east wall. A formal garden has recently been planted inside the bawn. The castle was abandoned by its owners during the Ulster uprising of 1641, when it was taken by Rory Maguire and burned.

KESH

* Old Castle Archdale *(153)*, 3 mi S; E of B 82 (to Enniskillen) in Castle Archdale Forest Park; signposted; OS 17H 186 599

Here are the scant remains of a planter's castle built in the early seventeenth century by John Archdale, an English planter. The partially restored ruins are those of a gabled house, a three-storey tower with a number of gun-loops, and the adjacent bawn wall.

** Drumskinny Stone Circle *(31)*, 4½ mi N, 100 yd E of minor road to Castlederg, County Tyrone; signposted; OS 12H 201 707

Standing within a sturdy wooden fence is this circle of thirty-nine stones, the highest rising to about five feet. The diameter of the circle is about forty feet. Tangential to it is a stone alignment of twenty-four stones pointing south.

LISNASKEA

* Castle Balfour *(152)*, W of village center on grounds of C of I parish church; signposted

This is a much restored, though still ruinous, plantation castle built in 1618 by the Scottish settler Sir James Balfour of Fife. The original bawn wall is missing. It is a T-plan building with a vaulted ground floor and a modern stairway leading to the first floor above.

County Antrim

ANTRIM

** Antrim Round Tower *(60)*, NW of town center; E side of A 26 (to Ballymena); signposted and visible from road

This eleventh- or twelfth-century Round Tower stands about ninety feet high. It is all original, except for the conical cap, which is a restoration. An unusual feature is the ringed cross carved in the lintel above the door, which itself is in the usual place about ten feet above ground.

* Shane's Castle *(209)*, 2 mi W; S of A 6 (to Randalstown); signposted

Within this extensive parkland overlooking Lough Neagh are a ruined sixteenth-century tower house incorporated into a castellated palatial residence, with a conservatory (the Camellia House) designed by John Nash and added in 1815. To the east of the castle lies the O'Neill family grave-yard, containing a vault built in 1722. A miniature railway runs from the visitors' center to the site, although the distance can also be covered on foot over the path bordering the track.

BALLYCASTLE

Holy Trinity Church *(177)*, the Diamond, town center; open only for Church of Ireland services

Built in 1756 at the instance of Hugh Boyd, this is a typical Irish eighteenth-century "landlord church." It is a plain-looking rectangular building with a classical pedimented west doorway surmounted by tower and steeple.

** Bonamargy Friary *(132)*, ½ mi E; S side of A 2 (to Cushendun), on Ballycastle golf course; signposted and visible from road; OS 5D 126 408

Here are the substantial ruins of a Franciscan Third Order (Tertiary) friary, founded in about 1500 by Rory MacQuillan. The approach is through the high-standing precinct gatehouse, and the remains consist of the roofless nave-and-chancel church with a Flamboyant Decorated win-dow in the east wall and part of the east range of claustral buildings, including the sacristy, dayroom, and friars' dormitory above. South of the church is the restored seventeenth-century burial vault of the MacDonnell earls of Antrim.

* Kinbane Castle *(146)*, 2½ mi NW; N of B 15 (to Ballintoy), down steep footpath from car park and across rocky headland (treacherous walking); signposted; OS 5D 112 026

This badly ruined tower house, hugging the rocky north Antrim coast, was a MacDonnell stronghold built in the mid–sixteenth century. Here is a spectacular view, with Rathlin Island and even the Mull of Kintyre (Scotland) visible on a clear day.

BALLYMENA

* Harryville Motte and Bailey *(81)*, E of town center; N of Larne Road to top of Casement Street, in public park; not signposted

Here are the substantial remains of an Anglo-Norman motte-and-bailey. The steep tree-covered mound surrounded by a deep ditch is the motte; the lower ditched mound is the bailey.

BALLYMONEY

** Dooey's Cairn *(21)*, 7 mi SE; ¾ mi SE of Dunloy, 200 yd W of B 93 (to Glarryford); signposted; OS 8D 021 182

This is a very well-preserved court grave dated to about 3000 B.C. The semicircular court opens to the southwest; behind it is a narrow passage containing a cremation chamber, and behind that is a burial chamber. The cairn is revetted with kerbstones.

BELFAST

** Custom House *(223)*, Queen Square

Commanding a fine view of the river, this monumental neoclassic building was designed by Charles Lanyon and built in 1857. Constructed of golden stone, it is essentially Palladian in design.

** Sinclair Seamen's Church *(226)*, Corporation Square; closed except during services but key available from minister, tel 776 985 or 757 730

Built in 1857 to the design of Charles Lanyon, this neo-Gothic brick Presbyterian church with a high Lombardic tower is distinguished chiefly for its collection of nautical artifacts and furnishings. The high corner pulpit incorporates the bow, bowsprit, and figurehead of a sailing vessel; the organ is decorated with port and starboard running lights; the ship's bell of the HMS *Hood* is rung to announce the beginning of services. Indeed the church is a sort of nautical museum, in keeping with its original mission to serve the spiritual needs of seamen "frequenting the port of Belfast."

Royal Ulster Rifle Regimental Museum *(208)*, Waring Street; open M–F, 10:00 A.M.–4:00 P.M. by appointment, tel (0232) 232 086

Situated at the rear of the Northern Ireland War Memorial building, this is a small but well-maintained museum featuring mostly medals, honors, uniforms, a few weapons, and other memorabilia of the regiment.

* Belfast Bank *(223)*, Waring Street

Remodelled in 1895 by Charles Lanyon to resemble an Italian palazzo, this is a fine example of the High Victorian Renaissance Revival.

** Ulster Bank *(223)*, Waring Street

Completed in 1860 to the design of James Hamilton of Glasgow, this is a splendid Victorian Italianate building, both inside and out. At the front is a double portico of Tuscan pillars below and Corinthian above. Under a glass-domed ceiling the interior is a mélange of intricate stucco carvings, mosaics, stained glass, etc.

May Street Presbyterian Church *(226)*, May Street; closed except during services

Built in 1829 to the design of William Smith, this is a Palladian-style building of brick and stucco with Ionic columns and pilasters.

*** St. Malachy's Church *(229)*, Alfred Street

Built in 1841–44 to the design of Thomas Jackson, this Roman Catholic house of worship is a Victorian masterpiece in the Tudor Gothic or Perpendicular style. The interior, modelled after Henry VII's chapel in Westminster Abbey, is extraordinarily pretty, with its fan-vaulted ceiling, lacey plasterwork, and Italianate altar, reredos, and pulpit.

* St. George's Church *(224)*, High Street; open daily and for Church of Ireland services

Designed by John Bowden and built in 1816, this would be an architecturally undistinguished church but for the fine Corinthian portico, which was brought here from the earl/bishop of Derry's mansion in Ballyscullion and affixed to the front. The interior consists of a rectangular nave with a square chancel and a gallery around three sides. The Victorian stained glass does nothing to improve its appearance.

** City Hall *(250, 270, 271)*, Donegall Square; visitors' entrance on south side; open daily (rotunda only); guided tours through rest of building W, 10:30 A.M.

Designed by the London architect Alfred Brumwell Thomas, and built between 1907 and 1913, this is an enormous neoclassic building ranged around a central courtyard. It is three hundred feet wide, and the central Ionic dome is 173 feet high. Underneath the latter is a rotunda topped by a great red glass eye. The interior is full of marble and rococo plasterwork. "No building," writes the architectural historian C. E. B. Brett, "could better have symbolized the pretension of the Edwardian city." Here, in December 1912, took place the signing of Ulster's "solemn league and covenant" pledging the signatories to unconditional resistance to Home Rule. Here too, in June 1921, King George V formally opened the Northern Ireland parliament following the passage of the Government of Ireland Act of 1920.

Linen Hall Library *(191)*, 15–18 Donegall Square, North

In this building, originally a warehouse completed in 1864, is deposited the collection of books originally owned by the Belfast Reading Society and housed in the White Linen Hall, built in 1785 but demolished in 1898 to make way for the present city hall.

Richardson Sons and Owden Warehouse *(223)*, 1 Donegall Square, North

Built as a linen warehouse in 1860 to the design of W. H. Lynn and recently restored, this brownstone building is a good example of the Venetian style of Victorian architecture made fashionable by the art historian John Ruskin.

St. Patrick's Church *(231)*, Donegall Street

Completed in 1877 to designs by Timothy Hevey and Mortimer Thompson, this is a large red sandstone Roman Catholic church, neo-Romanesque in design and of no great beauty. Inside are a rectangular aisled nave with galleries above, a shallow rounded apse, and a handsome and ornate neo-Gothic altar.

** St. Anne's Cathedral *(271)*, Donegall Street; open daily and for Church of Ireland services

Begun in the first years of the twentieth century but not completed until 1927, this is a magnificent building, neo-Romanesque in style, with a large aisled nave, a deep chancel ending in a rounded apse, heavy round pillars and round-arched windows. The west front, dedicated as a post–World War I memorial, is a curious mix of neo-Gothic and neoclassical styles.

** First Presbyterian Church *(181)*, Rosemary Street; open for services only but key obtainable from caretaker's lodgings next door

This handsome red brick oval building, completed in 1783 to the design of Roger Mullholland, initially housed Belfast's first "nonsubscribing" Presbyterian congregation and is now Unitarian in doctrinal affiliation. The rectangular portico in front is a nineteenth-century addition. The interior is also oval, with a fine chaste classical plastered ceiling, curving galleries around all sides but the front, box pews, and a high centrally placed carved-oak pulpit. Upstairs is a small session room with portraits of past ministers.

* Clifton House *(191)*, North Queen Street

Erected in the 1770s by the Belfast Charitable Society on ground donated by Arthur Chichester, fifth earl and first marquess of Donegall, this handsome red brick building was originally a "Poor House and Infirmary for the Benefit of the Poor Sick of the Town and Parish of Belfast." The present wings were added during the nineteenth century. Clifton House is now home to over a hundred "aged men and women of good character who are natives of, or residents for some time in, Belfast."

General Assembly Hall *(271)*, Great Victoria Street

This soot-blackened neo-Tudor building, with its open-crown spire (copied after St. Giles Church, Edinburgh) is the headquarters of the Presbyterian Church in Northern Ireland.

** Crown Liquor Saloon *(220)*, Great Victoria Street; NTNI

Built in 1895 and recently restored by the National Trust for Northern Ireland, this is, in the words of the city's architectural historian C. E. B. Brett, "one of the finest High Victorian buildings in Belfast." The interior especially is a fantasy of gaudy Victoriana: a ceiling of red and yellow arabesques, Corinthian capitals on hexagonal wooden pillars, a long marble-top bar, the conventional brass rail, patterned mirror glass, brass pipes leading from huge casks, panelled snuggeries for semiprivacy, etc. A delightful spot for nostalgic drinkers or for anyone wanting a good quick lunch.

** Queen's University *(233)*, University Road

Opened in 1849 as one of Sir Robert Peel's three "godless colleges," the original building, designed by Charles Lanyon, is a splendid red brick Victorian creation in the neo-Tudor or Perpendicular style. The tower is modelled on Founder's Tower at Magdalen College, Oxford. Subsequent building on the grounds has been extensive, to accommodate a growing student body now numbering over seven thousand.

*** Ulster Museum *(19, 20, 25, 28, 32, 147, 190, 222, 268, 269)*, Stranmillis Road; open M-F, 10:00 A.M.-5:00 P.M.; Sa, 1:00-5:00 P.M.; Su, 2:00-5:00 P.M.

This neoclassical building was erected in 1924 and much enlarged in 1965-71. It is Northern Ireland's "national" museum *cum* art gallery and vies with Dublin's for the quality of its museumship, though taking a close second place with respect to the value of its holdings.

To the left of the main entrance is a reconstructed Neolithic court cairn brought here from Ballintaggart, County Armagh.

Starting at the top floor and proceeding downward by way of a spiral ramp, the museum's splendid collections can be inspected in the following order: (1) the best display of Irish paintings outside of Dublin, including

works by Sir John Lavery, Sarah Purser, Francis Wheatley, Andrew Ni-
choll, George Petrie, Jack B. Yeats, Paul Henry, Sir William Orpen, Joseph
Peacock, James Glen Wilson, William Conor, John (Sean) Keating,
Charles Lamb, W. J. Leech, Mainie Jellett, Hugh Douglas Hamilton,
Thomas Robinson, Strickland Lowry, James Arthur O'Connor, Joseph
Wilson, Philip Hussey, Nathaniel Hone the younger, John Michael
Wright, Robert Hunter, Thomas Bates, and Susannah Drury; (2) Waterford,
Dublin, and Belfast glassware, Georgian silver from Dublin, Belleek ware;
(3) Irish natural history and geology; (4) the Girona Treasure, salvaged
from a galleass of the Spanish Armada, which sank in 1588 off Port na
Spaniagh near the Giant's Causeway; (5) the Inauguration Chair of the
O'Neills of Clandeboy; (6) copies of Early Christian treasures, such as the
Book of Kells, Book of Durrow, Book of Armagh, the Cross of Cong, and
the Ardagh Chalice, plus contemporary brooches, pins, etc.; (7) medieval
pottery; (8) a great variety of prehistoric artifacts, including Neolithic
pottery, scrapers, axheads, etc., bronze-age gold articles, weapons, and
implements, and iron-age scabbards, pins, horse gear, etc., plus copies of
the Broughter hoard; (9) items pertaining to Northern Ireland's resistance
to Home Rule, including uniforms, photographs, weapons, etc.; (10) memorabilia of eighteenth-century Irish Nationalists; (11) items pertaining to
Northern Ireland's linen industry; (12) memorabilia of eighteenth- and
nineteenth-century emigration from Northern Ireland; and (13) one floor,
at the bottom, devoted entirely to industrial machinery: looms, warp and
weft winding machines, spinning reels, etc.

St. Peter's Pro-Cathedral *(232)*, Derby Street

Situated near the shabby, impoverished, and strife-ridden Catholic
enclave of Falls Road, this neo-Gothic building was completed in 1866 to
designs by Father Jeremiah McCauly and John O'Neill. The interior is
dark and gloomy.

** Witham Street Depot (Belfast Transport Museum) *(220)*, Newtownards
Road

Here is a fine, though somewhat overcrowded, display of Irish locomotives (both steam- and diesel-powered), coaches, tram cars (horse-drawn
and electric), trolley buses, etc. Both the nineteenth and twentieth centuries
are represented.

** Giant's Ring *(29)*, 4 mi S, in Ballynahatty, County Down; 1 mi S of A
55 (to Ballylesson) from Shaw's Bridge; signposted; OS 15J 327 678

This is a circular earthen rampart about six hundred feet in diameter
and averaging fifteen feet in height. It was built in the early Bronze Age by

Beaker People on the site of a Neolithic dolmen that stands at its center.

** **Stormont** *(271, 273)*, 5 mi E, in County Down; N of A 20 (to Dundonald); closed, but access and a conducted tour obtainable on request at custodian's office

Here stands the Northern Ireland Parliament Building, a huge neoclassical pile in the Greek manner, built between 1928 and 1932 to house the provincial legislature of Northern Ireland, which ceased to exist in 1972. The interior is furnished elegantly and ornately, the most interesting features being the central hall, the grand staircase, and the chambers of the two houses, senate and commons. Among other items on display is a register of civilians killed in Northern Ireland by German bombardments in World War II. In front of the building is an enormous bronze statue of Edward Carson, and to the side is the tomb of the longtime prime minister Sir James Craig (later Lord Craigavon).

*** **Ulster Folk and Transport Museum** *(216, 223)*, 8 mi E of city center on A 2 (to Bangor) in Cultra Manor, Holywood, County Down

This is the most authentic of Ireland's open-air folk museums, all the buildings having been brought here from their original sites and reerected. They include rural cottages and farmhouses, urban houses from Belfast and Dromore, a weaver's house from Ballydugan, a flax-scutching mill from Gortin, a forge from Lisrace, a spade mill from Coalisland, a schoolhouse from Ballycastle, and a late-eighteenth-century church from Kilmore. Across the main road is the Transport Museum, with a large collection of bicycles, carriages, automobiles, aircraft, etc.

* **Belfast Castle** *(223)*, Cave Hill, 3 mi N of city center; grounds open to general public; interior closed except for private parties

Situated in the center of handsome gardens, this massive pseudo-Gothic Scottish baronial pile was built in the 1870s for the third marquess of Donegall to the design of the Belfast architectural firm of Lanyon and Lynn. The exterior staircase was added in 1894.

BUSHMILLS

** **Old Bushmills Distillery** *(219)*, S of town center; mandatory 30-minute guided tour

The first license to distill whiskey here was granted in 1608, although the distillery claims a lineage going back to 1276. The very modern plant standing today produces three brands of malt whiskey. The well-conducted guided tour takes the visitor through the whole process from "mashing" the grist, to fermentation of the "wort," to distillation, to maturing in oak casks, to blending, and finally to bottling. A free drink is offered at the shop at the end of the guided tour.

*** **Dunluce Castle** *(90, 97, 146, 154)*, 3 mi W; N of A 2 (to Portrush); signposted; OS 5C 904 414

One of Northern Ireland's more spectacular sights, this castle may have been owned by Richard de Burgh, the "Red Earl" of Ulster, before it fell into the hands of the MacQuillans, probably after the murder of William de Burgh, the "Brown Earl," in 1333. In the sixteenth century it was occupied, and largely rebuilt, by Sorley Boy MacDonnell and his son Randall, who became the first earl of Antrim in 1620.

The mainland court, through which today's visitor enters the grounds, dates to about 1600. From it a footbridge leads across a chasm to the castle proper. The gatehouse was erected by the MacDonnells in the sixteenth century. To the right of it is the south wall, ending in the southeast tower. These constitute the oldest (early-fourteenth-century) part of the complex. The palatial great hall dominating the upper yards dates from the early seventeenth century. Behind it are the contemporary northeast tower, buttery, and kitchen. Beyond the kitchen is the lower yard, with various domestic buildings. In 1639 a substantial portion of this area fell into the sea, after which the castle was abandoned as a residence. Splendid views of the Antrim coast.

CARRICKFERGUS

*** **Carrickfergus Castle** *(81, 85, 95, 97, 172, 208)*, town center; E of A 2 (to Belfast)

John de Courcy began work on this great stone castle overlooking Belfast Lough probably in about 1180. It was captured by King John in 1210, enlarged by Hugh de Lacy between 1228 and 1242, taken after a long siege by Edward Bruce in 1316, then reoccupied by the English after his defeat and death in 1318. In 1690 General Schomberg took it for King William III; in 1760 it was briefly occupied by the French admiral, François Thurot. From the eighteenth century until the twentieth it was used as a prison, armory, and air-raid shelter (1939–45).

The twin-towered gatehouse and the outer ward onto which it opens date originally to the second quarter of the thirteenth century but have been altered considerably. Leading from the east end of the middle ward is a postern gate (sally port) next to a double latrine. The four-storey rectangular keep belongs to the earliest period of construction. Today it houses the museums of the Fifth Royal Iniskilling Dragoon Guards and the Queen's Royal Irish Hussars. The inner ward, enclosed by a high curtain wall, was the original bailey of the Anglo-Norman castle. Both gatehouse and keep are pierced by slitted windows (arrow-loops) and the exterior walls of the outer ward by gunports inserted in the sixteenth century and later. Marvelous views of Belfast Lough.

* Town Walls (93, 152), N of town center

About half of the remaining stone wall, built from 1611 by Sir Arthur Chichester, is still visible. The best-preserved portions are in Shaftsbury Park, the North Gate at the end of North Street, and the base of the Irish Gate at the foot of West Street.

*** St. Nicholas Church (152), town center; open daily and for Church of Ireland services

The original building on this site may date to the late twelfth century, when John de Courcy founded the town of Carrickfergus. Of the early medieval church only the nave with its round Romanesque pillars and arches and part of the chancel survive. In 1614 the building underwent heavy reconstruction by order of Sir Arthur Chichester, whose ornate neoclassical marble tomb stands in the Chichester or Donegall Aisle. The present steeple and spire were erected in 1778; the porch and vestries in 1787, and the war memorial bell tower in 1962.

* Andrew Jackson Centre (193), 1 mi E, in Boneybefore; S of A 2 (to Larne); signposted; open daily, 10:00 A.M.–1:00 P.M., 2:00–5:00 P.M., 6:00–8:00 P.M.

This small whitewashed thatched cottage museum, close to the reputed home of President Andrew Jackson's emigrant parents, offers an audiovisual show of about twenty minutes on the subject of Scotch-Irish emigration from Ulster to America in the late eighteenth and early nineteenth centuries.

CULLYBACKEY

* Arthur Ancestral Home (194), ½ mi W; ¼ mi N of B 96 (to Portglenone); signposted; open M–F, 2:00–6:00 P.M.

The home of President Chester Arthur's father, this is a whitewashed thatched furnished stone cottage consisting of two rooms and a loft. Behind is the barn, containing a variety of farm implements.

CUSHENDALL

* Layd Church *(115)*, 1 mi NE; E of coast road to Cushendun, 100 yd from car park; signposted; OS 5D 245 289

These are the ruins of a thirteenth-century parish church—single-celled and rectangular with a round-headed doorway on the south side and a low barrel-vaulted room leading off the west end. At some point a brick wall was installed to separate the east and west ends of the nave. The site lies close to the Antrim coast with a view of Scotland on a clear day.

* Ossian's Grave *(21)*, 1¾ mi NW; ½ mi W of A 2 (to Cushendun), ¼-mi steep climb by footpath; signposted; OS 5D 213 284

Here on a high hilltop overlooking the North Channel and the nearby coast of Scotland are the scanty remains of a Neolithic court grave. The forecourt faces eastward, with two burial chambers behind it. Nearby are outlying stones of unknown significance. The historic marker indicating this to be a stone circle is in error.

LARNE

* Ballylumford Dolmen *(22)*, 2 mi E in Island Magee; E side of B 90, 1 mi S of Larne ferry landing (regular trips from Larne harbor); obscurely signposted but visible from road; OS 9D 431 016

Standing in the front yard of a private house, this is a moderately sized megalithic tomb, probably a Neolithic portal dolmen, known locally as the "Druid's Altar." It consists of four uprights and a capstone about eight feet above ground.

LISBURN

** Lisburn Museum *(180, 192)*, Market Square; open Tu–Sa, 11:00 A.M.–1:00 P.M., 1:45–4:45 P.M.

Housed in the town's seventeenth-century market house, this is a well-organized small museum, specializing in the local linen industry and the Huguenot colony founded by Louis Crommelin in 1698. The display includes sundry linen spinning wheels and looms, French Bibles, Psalters, devotional books, etc., and miscellaneous materials pertaining to the Crommelin, La Cherois, and Dubourdieu families.

RANDALSTOWN

** First Presbyterian Church *(181)*, W of town center; open for services only but key obtainable from grounds keeper

This handsome church, erected in 1790, is oval in shape, with a polygonal porch added later to the front. Curved galleries (added in about 1829) face the centrally located high pulpit, behind which a door leads into the minister's study. The row of oculus (round) windows above the gallery was added in 1929, when the roof was raised.

County Londonderry

COLERAINE

** Downhill *(178)*, 7 mi NW; N of A2 to Limauady through stone gate signposted to picnic area; NTNI

This spectacularly sited ruin is that of the palatial mansion built in the late eighteenth century to the design of Michael Shanahan of Cork by Frederick Augustus Hervey, bishop of Derry and fourth earl of Bristol. It was burned and rebuilt in the mid–nineteenth century, turned over to the RAF in World War II, and then abandoned. It is a huge neoclassic building fronted on the seaward side by a medievallike double-gated gatehouse flanked by battlemented bastions. Northeast of here on the edge of a steep cliff plunging to the sea is ** Mussenden Temple *(000)*, a neoclassic masterpiece. It is a round domed building girded with engaged columns of the Composite order, allegedly modelled on the Temple of Vesta at Tivoli. South of the house is another neoclassical monument, this one in the Ionic style—a mausoleum dedicated to the bishop's brother.

DERRY (LONDONDERRY)

** City Wall *(152, 167)*, town center

Pedestrians can walk about three-fourths of the way around this high wall built between 1613 and 1618 to guard the new Protestant settlement of the "Irish Society" of London. The four original gates have been remodelled, including Bishop's Gate, which was closed against a Jacobite army in 1688 by the prompt action of a group of apprentice-boys. It was this wall that made it possible for the city's defenders to withstand the ensuing siege of 105 days. The best point of entry today is by way of steps leading up from

Shipquay Street or from behind St. Columb's Cathedral (see following site). The wall is battlemented and crowded with gunports. Facing the Guildhall are seventeenth- and eighteenth-century cannons pointing toward the river Foyle.

*** **St. Columb's Cathedral** *(152, 167)*, town center, St. Columb's Court; open daily and for Church of Ireland services

Built between 1628 and 1633 in the contemporary Jacobean-Gothic fashion (with later modifications to the tower and east end), this is an aisled rectangular church with a battlemented exterior and windows more or less Decorated in style. The wooden ceiling of the nave is particularly fine. Of special interest is the chapter house (a separate room at the northwest end of the church), with memorabilia, including spent cannon-balls, from the siege of Derry.

* **St. Eugene's Cathedral** *(321)*, Great James Street

Begun in 1853 and completed some twenty years later, this is a hand-some Roman Catholic neo-Gothic church in the Decorated style. The architect was James J. MacCarthy. A particularly good feature is the east window with fine Victorian stained glass.

DUNGIVEN

* **Dungiven Priory** *(72)*, 1 mi SE; W of A 6 (to Maghera); OS 7C 692 083

Here is the ruined church of an Augustinian priory founded after 1138 by the O'Cahans. It is two-chambered, with a rectangular twelfth-century nave and a thirteenth-century square choir, slightly narrower than the nave and pierced with a twin-lancet east window. Inside the chancel is an elaborately carved fifteenth-century tomb, probably that of Cooey-na-Gall O'Cahan. Some remodelling of the church was done in the seventeenth century by the planter Sir Edward Doddington, who also built the adjacent much ruined house.

* **Banagher Church** *(64)*, 2 mi SW; 1 mi E of B 74 (to Feeny); OS 7C 676 066

The nave of this two-celled church ruin dates probably to the early or mid–twelfth century, as does the west doorway. The square choir, with its molded south window and blocked sedilia, was added in the thirteenth century and enlarged in the fifteenth. The tiny stone mortuary house to the southwest is traditionally believed to be the burial place of the founder of the Early Christian monastery on this site, St. Muredach.

* Brackfield House and Bawn *(153)*, 11½ mi W; N side of A 6 (to Derry), 2½ mi W of Claudy village, on grounds of Cumber Presbyterian Church; signposted and visible from road; OS 7C 435 167

This is a planter's castle, built in the early seventeenth century on land granted to the Skinners' Company. The ruins of the house are scanty; those of the bawn wall, including one wall turret, are substantial.

LIMAVADY

* Magilligan Martello Tower *(207)*, 11½ mi N; at end of B 202, 4 mi NW of A 2 (to Coleraine) from Magilligan Bridge, past rifle range; no entry to interior

This squat round red sandstone tower was built in 1812, together with a matching building at Greencastle on the opposite Donegal coast, to guard the mouth of Lough Foyle against a Napoleonic invasion. The doorway is on the landward side, and a modern staircase leads up to it. Though locked, the interior is visible through an iron grille. Above the entry is a corbelled machicolation with three gunports. The view across to the Inishowen peninsula is magnificent.

MAGHERA

** Maghera Old Church *(64)*, E of town center; S of A 42 (to Portglenone); key at nearby Recreation Centre; OS 8C 855 002

The fragmentary nave of this ruined church may date to the tenth century. For about a hundred years after 1150 it was a cathedral church, during which time the most interesting feature of the site—the intricately carved lintel above the west door (now covered by the tower added in the seventeenth century)—was added. Here is a busy Crucifixion scene with Christ flanked by other figures, perhaps his disciples. In the graveyard west of the church is an Early Christian pillar stone carved with a ringed cross.

STRABANE

* "President Wilson's House" *(194)*, 2 mi SE; S of Dergalt Road; signposted; open daily; call at farmhouse next door

This whitewashed two-storey thatched farmhouse was the home of President Woodrow Wilson's emigrant grandfather. It still belongs to members of the Wilson family, who farm the property. In addition to some of the original furniture there are interesting Wilson records, photographs, and other memorabilia.

Appendix A

The Best of Ireland

THREE-STAR SITES

Prehistoric Sites

Beaghmore *(447)*, nr. Cookstown, Co. Tyrone
Browneshill Dolmen *(289)*, nr. Carlow, Co. Carlow
Creevykeel Court Cairn *(418)*, nr. Sligo, Co. Sligo
Drombeg *(324)*, nr. Ross Carbery, Co. Cork
Dún Aenghus *(412)*, Inishmore, Aran Islands, Co. Galway
Dunbeg *(329)*, nr. Dingle, Co. Kerry
Fourknocks *(383)*, nr. Balbriggan, Co. Meath
Grianan of Ailech *(428)*, nr. Letterkenny, Co. Donegal
Legananny Dolmen *(433)*, nr. Castlewellan, Co. Down
Lough Gur Interpretive Centre *(339)*, nr. Limerick, Co. Limerick
Newgrange *(388)*, nr. Slane, Co. Meath
Poulnabrone Dolmen *(342)*, nr. Ballyvaughan, Co. Clare
Staigue Fort *(333)*, nr. Sneem, Co. Kerry
The Grange (The Lios) *(340)*, nr. Limerick, Co. Limerick

Early Christian Sites

Ahenny Crosses *(300)*, nr. Carrick-on-Suir, Co. Tipperary
Arboe Cross *(445)*, nr. Coagh, Co. Tyrone
Ardmore Round Tower *(326)*, Co. Waterford, nr. Youghal, Co. Cork
Cashel (St. Patrick's) Rock *(301)*, Cashel, Co. Tipperary
Clonmacnoise Monastery *(381)*, nr. Ferbane, Co. Offaly
Devenish Churches and Round Tower *(450)*, nr. Enniskillen, Co.
    Fermanagh
Drumcliffe High Cross *(418)*, nr. Sligo, Co. Sligo
Dunloe Ogham Stones *(332)*, nr. Killarney, Co. Kerry
Dysert O'Dea High Cross and Round Tower *(343)*, nr. Corofin, Co. Clare
Gallarus Oratory *(329)*, nr. Dingle, Co. Kerry

Glendalough *(310)*, nr. Rathdrum, Co. Wicklow
Kells Monastery *(384)*, Ceannanas (Kells), Co. Meath
Kildare Round Tower *(377)*, Kildare, Co. Kildare
Kilkeeran Crosses *(300)*, Co. Kilkenny, nr. Carrick-on-Suir, Co.
   Tipperary
Kilkenny Round Tower *(295)*, Kilkenny, Co. Kilkenny
Kilmacduagh Round Tower *(409)*, nr. Gort, Co. Galway
Monasterboice *(397)*, nr. Drogheda, Co. Louth
Skellig Michael *(333)*, Skellig Islands, Co. Kerry

Ecclesiastical Ruins (Medieval)

Ardfert Cathedral *(326)*, Ardfert, Co. Kerry
Ardmore Cathedral *(326)*, Co. Waterford, nr. Youghal, Co. Cork
Askeaton Friary *(335)*, Askeaton, Co. Limerick
Boyle Abbey *(402)*, Boyle, Co. Roscommon
Dunbrody Abbey *(280)*, nr. Ballyhack, Co. Wexford
Dysert O'Dea Church *(343)*, nr. Corofin, Co. Clare
Ennis Friary *(344)*, Ennis, Co. Clare
Grey Abbey *(435)*, Greyabbey, Co. Down
Jerpoint Abbey *(297)*, nr. Thomastown, Co. Kilkenny
Muckross Friary *(332)*, nr. Killarney, Co. Kerry
Quin Friary and Castle *(348)*, Quin, Co. Clare
Ross Errilly Priory *(410)*, nr. Headford, Co. Galway
Rosserk Friary *(420)*, nr. Ballina, Co. Mayo
Sligo Friary *(417)*, Sligo, Co. Sligo

Churches

Ballintubber Abbey *(421)*, nr. Castlebar, Co. Mayo
Christ Church Cathedral *(360)*, Dublin
Clonfert Cathedral *(406)*, nr. Ballinasloe, Co. Galway
Holy Cross Abbey *(307)*, nr. Thurles, Co. Tipperary
Holy Trinity Cathedral *(286)*, Waterford, Co. Waterford
St. Canice's (C of I) Cathedral, *(295)*, Kilkenny, Co. Kilkenny
St. Columb's Cathedral *(464)*, Derry, Co. Londonderry
St. Malachy's Church *(455)*, Belfast, Co. Antrim
St. Malachy's Church *(435)*, Hillsborough, Co. Down
St. Mary's Cathedral *(331)*, Killarney, Co. Kerry
St. Mary's Cathedral *(338)*, Limerick, Co. Limerick

St. Mary's Church *(325)*, Youghal, Co. Cork
St. Mary's Pro-Cathedral *(226)*, Dublin
St. Multose Church *(322)*, Kinsale, Co. Cork
St. Nicholas Church *(461)*, Carrickfergus, Co. Antrim
St. Nicholas Church *(406)*, Galway, Co. Galway
St. Patrick's Cathedral *(362)*, Dublin
St. Patrick's (RC) Cathedral *(442)*, Armagh, Co. Armagh

Ruined Castles and Tower Houses

Aughnanure Castle *(408)*, nr. Galway, Co. Galway
Blarney Castle *(319)*, nr. Cork, Co. Cork
Doe Castle *(426)*, nr. Carrickart, Co. Donegal
Donegal Castle *(426)*, Donegal, Co. Donegal
Dundrum Castle *(437)*, nr. Newcastle, Co. Down
Dunluce Castle *(460)*, nr. Bushmills, Co. Antrim
Greencastle *(436)*, nr. Kilkeel, Co. Down
Monea Castle *(451)*, nr. Enniskillen, Co. Fermanagh
Park's Castle *(416)*, nr. Manorhamilton, Co. Leitrim
Roscrea Heritage Centre *(305)*, Roscrea, Co. Tipperary
Trim Castle *(390)*, Trim, Co. Meath
Tully Castle *(451)*, nr. Enniskillen, Co. Fermanagh

Furnished Castles and Tower Houses

(See also Stately Homes)

Bunratty Castle *(350)*, nr. Shannon Airport, Co. Clare
Cahir Castle *(298)*, Cahir, Co. Tipperary
Carrickfergus Castle *(460)*, Carrickfergus, Co. Antrim
Dublin Castle *(358)*, Dublin
King John's Castle *(331)*, Limerick, Co. Limerick
Knappogue Castle *(349)*, nr. Quin, Co. Clare
Ormond Castle *(299)*, Carrick-on-Suir, Co. Tipperary

Fortifications

Charles Fort *(323)*, Kinsale, Co. Cork
Fort Dunree and Military Museum *(425)*, nr. Buncrana, Co. Donegal

Stately Homes

Bantry House *(315)*, Bantry, Co. Cork ✓
Casino Marino *(370)*, nr. Dublin
Castle Coole *(450)*, nr. Enniskillen, Co. Fermanagh
Castle Ward *(440)*, nr. Strangford, Co. Down
Castletown *(379)*, nr. Maynooth, Co. Kildare ✓
Derrynane, *(328)*, nr. Caherdaniel, Co. Kerry ✓
Fota House *(320)*, nr. Cork, Co. Cork ✓
Glenveagh Castle *(428)*, nr. Letterkenney, Co. Donegal
Lissadell House *(418)*, nr. Sligo, Co. Sligo
Mount Stewart *(438)*, nr. Newtownards, Co. Down
Muckross House *(331)*, nr. Killarney, Co. Kerry ✓
Russborough *(309)*, nr. Blessington, Co. Wicklow ✓
Westport House *(424)*, Westport, Co. Mayo

Gardens

Anne's Grove *(321)*, nr. Fermoy, Co. Cork ✓
Birr Castle Gardens *(380)*, Birr, Co. Offaly
Glenveagh Castle Gardens and National Park *(428)*, nr. Letterkenney,
    Co. Donegal
Malahide Castle Gardens *(371)*, nr. Dublin
Mount Stewart Gardens *(438)*, nr. Newtownards, Co. Down
Powerscourt Estate and Gardens *(309)*, nr. Enniskerry, Co. Wicklow ✓

Public Buildings

Bank of Ireland *(353)*, Dublin ✓
Custom House *(365)*, Dublin ✓
Four Courts *(368)*, Dublin ✓
King's Inns *(369)*, Dublin

Educational Institutions

Maynooth (St. Patrick's) College *(378)*, Maynooth, Co. Kildare
Trinity College and Library *(352, 353)*, Dublin ✓

Industrial Sites

Belleek Pottery *(219)*, Belleek, Co. Fermanagh
Waterford Glass Factory *(287)*, nr. Waterford, Co. Waterford
Wellbrook Beetling Mill *(446)*, nr. Cookstown, Co. Tyrone

Museums and Galleries

Bunratty Folk Park *(351)*, nr. Shannon Airport, Co. Clare
Cork Public Museum *(318)*, Cork, Co. Cork
Craggaunowen Project *(349)*, nr. Quin, Co. Clare
Fermanagh County Museum, Enniskillen Castle *(449)*, Enniskillen, Co.
  Fermanagh
Glencolumbkille Folk Museum *(427)*, Glencolumbkille, Co. Donegal
Hunt Museum *(338)*, nr. Limerick, Co. Limerick
Johnstown Castle and Agricultural Museum *(283)*, nr. Wexford, Co.
  Wexford
Joyce's Tower (James Joyce Museum) *(373)*, nr. Dalkey, Co. Dublin
Kilmainham Jail *(364)*, Dublin
Malahide Castle (Portrait Gallery) *(371)*, nr. Dublin
National Gallery of Ireland *(354)*, Dublin
National Maritime Museum *(374)*, Dun Laoghaire, Co. Dublin
National Museum of Ireland *(355)*, Dublin
Reginald's Tower and Waterford Civic Museum *(285)*, Waterford, Co.
  Waterford
Rothe House *(294)*, Kilkenny, Co. Kilkenny
Thoor Ballylee (W. B. Yeats Museum) *(410)*, nr. Gort, Co. Galway
Ulster-American Folk Park *(448)*, nr. Omagh, Co. Tyrone
Ulster Folk and Transport Museum *(459)*, Co. Down, nr. Belfast, Co.
  Antrim
Ulster Museum *(457)*, Belfast, Co. Antrim

Appendix B
Genealogical Research

Genealogical research is a growth industry in Ireland, the chief market for its product being third-, fourth-, fifth-, or sixth-generation Irish-Americans. Such people have an advantage over Americans of older stock in that fewer years are likely to have elapsed since the arrival of their immigrant ancestors and therefore the traces of their origins are usually less faint. They also have an advantage over ethnic groups of non-British origin in that the source materials they must use to discover their roots are written in English. Their major disadvantage is that, historically, Irish record keeping, both public and private, has been very lax. Even more unfortunate has been the wholesale obliteration of large caches of important documents, most notably resulting from the destruction of the Record Tower in Dublin Castle in 1710 and the even more disastrous burning of the Public Records Office in the Four Courts building during the Irish Civil War in 1922. To the ardent genealogist, however, these mishaps serve only to make the task more challenging.

The key to the problem facing the descendant of Irish immigrants is to establish the identity of his or her immigrant ancestor or ancestors. Identity in this context means not only the exact name but also, if possible, place of origin, religious affiliation, and dates of birth, death, and departure from Ireland. By place of origin is meant the county, barony, townland, and/or parish from which he or she came. (The townland is the smallest administrative division of land in Ireland, with an average area of 350 acres; a barony is comprised of multiples of townlands; a parish can be either civil or ecclesiastical and, if the latter, either Catholic or Church of Ireland.) Also useful to know are the names of the immigrant's children, especially his eldest son, who, according to Irish custom, was normally named after his paternal grandfather. For it is the identification of this person, the immigrant's father, that is the essential entry point into the Irish records from which the family tree is to be constructed.

Obviously the information above can be obtained only in America. The most likely places to look for it are in family records (if any), American parish records, graveyards, local libraries, local historical societies, state archives, the local history and genealogy section of the Library of Congress, and the National Archives in Washington, D.C. Major sources include family traditions (often unreliable), gravestones, census returns, passenger lists, naturalization proceedings, registers of enlistment in the U.S. or Confederate armies, land entry files, county histories, city directories, and published family histories. In any case, *American research must come first*, before undertaking to tackle the Irish archives themselves.

The major Irish respositories in which useful genealogical information can be obtained are in Dublin and Belfast, although there is a growing number of smaller centers throughout the country (that is, the Republic). These are all listed below, with brief descriptions of their major holdings of interest to genealogists.

Dublin

National Library of Ireland *(358)*, Kildare Street: Contains most of the Roman Catholic parish registers, 1845–80; a list of surviving Church of Ireland parish registers; a list of householders in each Irish county (1850–60), called *Griffith's Valuation*; street trade directories, mostly for eighteenth- and nineteenth-century Dublin; seventeenth- to twentieth-century newspaper files; estate papers; and Ordnance Survey maps (six inches to the mile). Also available at the main desk is a two-page pamphlet describing the contents of other repositories—very helpful to the beginner.

Irish Genealogical Office *(358)*, 2 Kildare Street: Contains the Register of Arms of all patented Irish coats of arms and the Register of Pedigrees (a record of all Irish noblemen and their issue). Also, the office maintains a "preliminary consultancy service on ancestry tracing," which, for a small fee, provides subscribers a packet outlining the basic information needed to get started on an ancestor hunt. (Write to the Chief Herald and Genealogical Office Director.)

Public Records Office, Four Courts *(368)*, Upper Ormond Quay: In spite of the conflagration of 1922, the Irish PRO still contains a scattering of census returns for 1821, 1831, 1841, and 1851 and complete returns for 1901 (including Northern Ireland) and 1911. Information contained in these later records includes, inter alia, the name, age, religion, occupation, and marital status of almost the entire adult population. Other important sources of information are the *Tithe Allotment Books* for the first half of the nineteenth century; a large collection of testamentary records, numbering more than twenty thousand items; and microfilm copies of many Church of Ireland parochial registers.

Office of the Registrar-General, 8–11 Lombard Street East: Contains registers of all births, marriages, and deaths from 1 January 1864, and of all marriages other than Roman Catholic since 1845.

Registry of Deeds, **King's Inns** *(369)*, Henrietta Street: Contains records of deeds, leases, business transactions, marriage articles, and wills since 1708, with two volumes of indexes; difficult to use and not recommended for the beginner, although rich in genealogical information.

State Papers, **Dublin Castle** *(358)*: These contain police and criminal documents listing deported convicts and their crimes. They are of primary interest to Australian-Irish researchers; less so to Irish-Americans, only a tiny fraction of whom are descended from prosecuted (or persecuted) nineteenth-century Fenians. (Family traditions to the contrary should be viewed with suspicion.)

Belfast

Public Record Office of Northern Ireland, 66 Balmoral Avenue: Contains wills, land records, deeds, leases, marriage settlements, and other official records from government departments relating to Northern Ireland from about 1830; *Tithe Allotment Books* for Ulster; microfilm copies of all surviving Church of Ireland parish registers for the six northeastern counties; parish registers for some Roman Catholic churches; and a large collection of private papers, including records of major landed estates.

Ulster Historical Foundation, 66 Balmoral Avenue: Provides a genealogical search service on a fee-paying basis, of interest especially to the descendants of Presbyterian emigrants who left Ulster in the eighteenth and early nineteenth centuries.

Registrar-General's Office, Northern Ireland, Oxford House, Chichester Street: Contains records of births, marriages, and deaths from 1864 and of Protestant marriages from 1845 (Northern Ireland only).

At Large

The recently founded National Genealogical Project administered by the Irish Family History Cooperative is in the process of organizing a vast computerized genealogical record to which access can be had on application at any of the Family History Research Centres throughout the Republic. Below is a partial list of those establishments now in operation:

Carlow County Heritage Society, Athy Road, Carlow
Cavan Heritage & Genealogical Centre, Cavan Library, Cavan
Clare Heritage Centre (343), Corofin, County Clare
Mallow Heritage Centre, Parish Centre, Mallow, County Cork
Cork Heritage Centre, Bandon, County Cork

Donegal County Library, Letterkenny, County Donegal

St. Audeon's Heritage Centre, High Street, Dublin

Fingall Heritage Group, 10 North Street, Swords, County Dublin

County Galway Family History Society, 4 New Docks, Galway

Woodford Heritage Centre, Woodford, County Galway

Kerry Diocesan Genealogy Centre, Killarney, County Kerry

County Library, Newbridge, County Kildare

Laois/Offaly Family History Research Centre, Tullamore, County Offaly

Leitrim Heritage Centre, Ballinamore, County Leitrim

Mid-West Archives, The Granary, Michael Street, Limerick, County Limerick

Mayo North Family History Research Centre, Enniscoe, Ballina, County Mayo

South Mayo Family History & Heritage Research Centre, Crossboyne (Ballinrobe), County Mayo

Meath Heritage Centre, Trim, County Meath

County Roscommon Heritage & Genealogy Centre, Strokestown, County Roscommon

County Sligo Heritage & Genealogy Centre, Stephen's Street, County Sligo

Nenagh District Heritage Society, Governor's House, Nenagh, County Tipperary

Bru Boru Heritage Centre, Cashel, County Tipperary

Waterford Heritage Survey, St. John's College, Waterford, County Waterford

Athlone Heritage Centre, County Library, Mullingar, County Westmeath

Tapgoat Community Development Company, Tapgoat, County Wexford

Wicklow County Heritage Centre, County Buildings, Wicklow, County Wicklow

A word should be said also in behalf of hiring a professional genealogist, who normally can complete the necessary research in a mere fraction of the time required of the amateur. Fees vary and of course depend in large part on the number of hours spent on the job. The Dublin and Belfast newspapers and telephone directories are replete with the names and addresses of these practitioners. A quick way to identify reputable genealogists is to apply for the approved lists issued by both the National Library of Ireland and the Genealogical Office in Dublin and by the Public Records Office of Northern Ireland in Belfast. An alternative is to write to either or both of the following two tourist-oriented journals for their recommendations: *Ireland of the Welcomes*, Customer Relations, Baggot Street Bridge, Dublin 2; *Inside Ireland*, Rookwood, Stocking Lane, Ballyboden, Dublin 16. (An application for a subscription to either will guarantee results and, besides, provide pleasurable reading throughout the year.)

Finally, there is no substitute for informal inquiries in the neighborhood(s) from which one's immigrant ancestor(s) came (if this is known in advance). A half hour's visit with a parish priest or rector, or the local minister, or the village postmistress, or even the cabdriver who meets the train can sometimes produce more clues to family history (or even introductions to unknown relatives) than hours of labor in the archives of Dublin or Belfast. And nothing can be more exciting than the unexpected discovery of a lichen-covered gravestone recording the name of one's great-great-grandfather. It is moments like this that make the often tiresome search for family roots more than worth the effort.

Appendix C

Selected Readings

Guidebooks

Appletree Press. *Irish Touring Guide*. Belfast: The Appletree Press Ltd., 1986.

Brett, C. E. B. *Buildings of Belfast: 1700–1914*. Rev. ed. Belfast: Friar's Bush Press, 1985.

Department of the Environment for Northern Ireland. *Historic Monuments of Northern Ireland*. Belfast: Her Majesty's Stationery Office, 1983.

Gallagher, Lyn, and Dick Rogers. *Castle, Coast and Cottage: The National Trust in Northern Ireland*. Belfast and Wolfeboro, N.H.: The Blackstaff Press, 1986.

Harbison, Peter. *Guide to the National Monuments of the Republic of Ireland*. Dublin: Gill and Macmillan, 1970.

Irish Tourist Board (Bord Failte). *Ireland Guide*. Dublin: Irish Tourist Board—Bord Failte, 1982.

Jacobs, Michael, and Paul Stirton. *The Knopf Traveler's Guides to Art: Britain and Ireland*. New York: Alfred A. Knopf, 1984.

Killanin, Lord, and M. V. Duignan. *The Shell Guide to Ireland*. Revised and updated by Peter Harbison. Dublin: Gill and Macmillan, 1989.

Lehane, Brendan. *The Companion Guide to Ireland*. Rev. ed. Englewood Cliffs, N.J.: Prentice-Hall, Inc., 1985.

MacLoughlin, Adrian. *Guide to Historic Dublin*. Dublin: Gill and Macmillan, 1979.

Murphy, Marese. *Travellers' Guide to Ireland*. London: Thornton Cox Ltd., 1977.

Nicholson, Robert. *Guide to Ireland*. London: Robert Nicholson Publications, Ltd., 1973.

——. *The Ulysses Guide: Tours Through Joyce's Dublin*. London: Methuen London, Ltd., 1988.

Popplewell, Sean. *The Irish Museums Guide*. Dublin: Ward River Press, 1983.

Robertson, Ian, ed. *Blue Guide, Ireland*. Chicago, New York, San Francisco: Rand McNally & Company, 1979.

Sandford, Ernest. *Discover Northern Ireland*. Belfast: Northern Irish Tourist Board, 1976.

Somerville-Large, Peter. *The Grand Irish Tour*. London: Hamish Hamilton, 1982.

Trevor, William. *A Writer's Ireland*. London: Thames and Hudson, Ltd., 1984.

General Histories

Beckett, James C. *The Anglo-Irish Tradition*. Ithaca, N.Y.: Cornell University Press, 1976.

Bottigheimer, Karl S. *Ireland and the Irish: A Short History*. New York: Columbia University Press, 1982.

Colum, Padraic, ed. *A Treasury of Irish Folklore*. New York: Crown Publishers, Inc., 1967.

Cullen, Louis M. *Life in Ireland*, London and New York: Batsford, Putnam, 1968.

Curtis, Edmund. *A History of Ireland*. London: Methuen & Company, Ltd., 1936.

Cusack, M. F. *Compendium of Irish History*. Boston: Patrick Donahoe, 1971.

de Breffny, Brian, ed. *The Irish World*. London: Thames and Hudson, 1977.

de Paor, Liam. *Portrait of Ireland*. Wicklow: Rainbow Publications, Ltd., 1985.

————. *Milestones in Irish History*. Cork, Dublin: The Mercier Press, 1986.

————. *The Peoples of Ireland*. South Bend, Ind.: University of Notre Dame Press, 1986.

Edwards, Ruth Dudley. *An Atlas of Irish History*. London, New York: Methuen and Co., 1981.

Evans, Emryn Estyn. *The Personality of Ireland: Habitat, Heritage and History*. Cambridge: At the University Press, 1973.

Foster, R. F. *Modern Ireland: 1600–1972*. London: Allen Lane, The Penguin Press, 1988.

Kee, Robert. *Ireland, A History*. London: Weidenfield and Nicolson, 1980.

Moody, T. W., and F. X. Martin, eds. *The Course of Irish History*. Cork: The Mercier Press, 1967.

Neill, Kenneth. *An Illustrated History of the Irish People*. Dublin: Gill and Macmillan, 1979.

Nolan, William, ed. *The Shaping of Ireland: The Geographic Perspective*. Cork and Dublin: The Mercier Press, 1986.

O'Brien, Conor Cruise, ed. *The Shaping of Modern Ireland*. Toronto: University of Toronto Press, 1960.

O'Brien, Maire and Conor Cruise. *A Concise History of Ireland*. Rev. ed. London: Thames and Hudson, 1985.

O'Faolain, Sean. *The Story of the Irish People*. New York: Avenal Books, 1959.

———. *The Irish*. Harmondsworth, Middlesex: Penguin Books, 1980.

Orel, Harold, ed. *Irish History and Culture*. Lawrence, Manhattan, Wichita, Kan.: The University Press of Kansas, 1976.

Stewart, A.T.Q. *The Narrow Ground: Patterns of Ulster History*. Belfast: Pretani Press, 1986.

Uris, Jill and Leon. *Ireland: A Terrible Beauty*. Toronto, New York, London: Bantam Books, 1978.

White, Terence de Vere. *Ireland*. London: Thames and Hudson, 1968.

Topical Studies

Arnold, Bruce. *A Concise History of Irish Art*. Rev. ed. New York and Toronto: Oxford University Press, 1977.

Begley, Donal F. *Irish Genealogy: A Record Finder*. Dublin: Heraldic Artists Ltd., 1981.

———, ed. *Handbook on Irish Genealogy*. 6th edition. Dublin: Heraldic Artists Ltd., 1984.

Brady, Anne M., and Brian Cleeve. *A Biographical Dictionary of Irish Writers*. Mullingar: The Lilliput Press, 1985.

Corish, Patrick. *The Irish Catholic Experience: A Historical Survey*. Dublin: Gill and Macmillan, 1985.

Craig, Maurice. *The Architecture of Ireland: from the Earliest Times to 1880*. London: B. T. Batsford, Ltd.; Dublin: Eason and Son, Ltd., 1982.

Crotty, R. D. *Irish Agricultural Production: Its Volume and Structure*. Cork: University College, Cork University Press, 1966.

Cullen, Louis M. *An Economic History of Ireland Since 1660*. London: David and Charles, 1972.

de Breffny, Brian, and Rosemary Ffolliott, *The Houses of Ireland*. London: Thames and Hudson, 1984.

Deane, Seamus. *A Short History of Irish Literature*. London: Hutchinson & Co., 1986.

Donoghue, Denis. *We Irish: Essays on Irish Literature and Society*. New York: Alfred A. Knopf, 1986.

Forde-Johnston, J. *Castles and Fortifications of Britain and Ireland*. London, Toronto, Melbourne: J. M. Dent & Sons, Ltd., 1977.

George, Michael, and Patrick Bowe. *The Gardens of Ireland*. London: Hutchinson, Ltd., 1986.

Harbison, Peter, Homan Potterton, and Jeanne Sheehy. *Irish Art and*

Architecture: From Prehistory to the Present. London: Thames and Hudson, 1978.

Hayes-McCoy, G. A. *Irish Battles.* London and Harlow: Longmans, Green and Co., Ltd., 1969.

Heslinga, M. W. *The Irish Border as a Cultural Divide.* Sociaal Geografische Studies, Nr. 6, Assen, The Netherlands: Royal Van Gorcum Ltd., 1962.

Larkin, Emmet. *The Historical Dimensions of Irish Catholicism.* Washington, D.C.: The Catholic University of America Press, 1984.

Mills, John FitzMaurice. *The Noble Dwellings of Ireland.* London: Thames and Hudson, 1987.

Mitchell, G. Frank, Peter Harbison, Liam de Paor, Maire de Paor, Robert A. Stalley. *Treasures of Irish Art: 1500 B.C.–1500 A.D.* New York: The Metropolitan Museum and Alfred A. Knopf, 1977.

Somerville-Large, Peter. *Dublin.* London, Toronto, Sydney, New York: Granada Publishing, Ltd., 1981.

Prehistoric and Early Christian Ireland

(Chapters One and Two)

Brown, Peter, ed. *The Book of Kells.* London: Thames and Hudson, 1980.

Byrne, Francis John. *Irish Kings and High-Kings.* New York: St. Martin's Press, 1973.

de Paor, Maire and Liam. *Early Christian Ireland.* New York: Frederick A. Praeger, 1958.

Dillon, Myles. *Early Irish Literature.* Chicago: The University of Chicago Press, 1948.

Dillon, Myles, and Nora K. Chadwick. *The Celtic Realms.* London: Weidenfeld and Nicolson, 1967.

Evans, John G. *The Environment of Early Man in the British Isles.* Berkeley and Los Angeles: University of California Press, 1975.

Forde-Johnston, J. *Prehistoric Britain and Ireland.* London: J. M. Dent & Sons, Ltd., 1976.

Hanson, R. P. C. *The Life and Writings of the Historical Saint Patrick.* New York: The Seabury Press, 1983.

Harbison, Peter. *Pre-Christian Ireland: From the First Settlers to the Early Celts.* London: Thames and Hudson, 1988.

Henry, Françoise. *Irish Art in the Early Christian Period (to 800 A.D.).* Ithaca, N.Y.: Cornell University Press, 1965.

———. *Irish Art During the Viking Invasions (800–1020 A.D.).* Ithaca, N.Y.: Cornell University Press, 1967.

——. *Irish Art in the Romanesque Period (1020–1170 A.D.).* Ithaca, N.Y.: Cornell University Press, 1970.

——. *Irish High Crosses.* Dublin: Cultural Relations Committee of Ireland, At the Three Candles, 1964.

——. *Early Christian Irish Art.* Cork: The Mercier Press, 1979.

Herity, Michael. *Irish Passage Graves: Neolithic Builders in Ireland and Britain, 2500 B.C.* Dublin: Irish University Press, 1974.

Herity, Michael, and George Eogan. *Ireland in Prehistory.* London: Henley and Boston, Routledge & Kegal Paul, 1977.

Hughes, Kathleen. *The Church in Early Irish Society.* London: Methuen & Co., Ltd., 1966.

——. *The Early Celtic Idea of History and the Modern Historian.* An Inaugural Lecture. Cambridge, London, New York, Melbourne: Cambridge University Press, 1977.

Hughes, Kathleen, and Ann Hamlin. *The Modern Traveller to the Early Irish Church.* London: Society for the Propagation of Christian Knowledge, 1977.

Jackson, Kenneth H. *The Oldest Irish Tradition: A Window on the Iron Age.* Cambridge: At the University Press, 1964.

Laing, Lloyd. *The Archaeology of Late Celtic Britain and Ireland, c. 400–1200 A.D.* London: Methuen & Co., Ltd., 1975.

Leask, Harold G. *Irish Churches and Monastic Buildings, Vol. I: The First Phases and the Romanesque.* Dundalk: Dundalgan Press (W. Tempest) Ltd., 1977.

Mac Niocaill, Gearóid. *Ireland Before the Vikings.* The Gill History of Ireland, Vol. 1. Dublin: Gill and Macmillan, 1972.

McNally, Kenneth. *Standing Stones and Other Monuments of Early Ireland.* Belfast: The Appletree Press, Ltd., 1984.

Moore, Donald, ed. *The Irish Sea Province in Archaeology and History.* Cardiff: Cambrian Archaeological Association, 1970.

Corráin, Donncha. *Ireland Before the Normans.* The Gill History of Ireland, Vol. 2. Dublin: Gill and Macmillan, 1972.

O'Rahilly, Thomas F. *Early Irish History and Mythology.* Dublin: Dublin Institute for Advanced Studies, 1971.

O'Riordain, Sean P. *Antiquities of the Irish Countryside.* 5th ed. London and New York: Methuen & Co., Ltd., 1979.

Raftery, Joseph. *The Celts.* Cork: The Mercier Press, 1964.

Ryan, Michael, ed., *The Treasures of Ireland.* Dublin: The Royal Academy, 1983.

Thomas, Charles. *The Iron Age in the Irish Sea Province.* London: Council for British Archaeology, 1972.

Woodman, Peter C. *The Mesolithic in Ireland: Hunter-Gatherers in an Insular Environment.* BAR British Series 58, Oxford: B.A.R., 1978.

Medieval and Tudor Ireland

(Chapters Three, Four, and Five [first half])

Bradshaw, Brendan. *The Dissolution of the Religious Orders Under Henry VIII*. Cambridge: Cambridge University Press, 1974.

——. *The Irish Constitutional Revolution of the Sixteenth Century*. Cambridge, London, New York, Melbourne: Cambridge University Press, 1979.

Brady, Ciaran, and Raymond Gillespie, eds. *Natives and Newcomers*. Dublin: Irish Academic Press, Ltd., 1986.

Canny, Nicholas P. *The Elizabethan Conquest of Ireland: A Pattern Established, 1565-76*. New York: Barnes & Noble Books, 1976.

——. *From Reformation to Restoration: Ireland, 1534-1660*. Dublin: Helicon Limited, 1987.

Collins, M. E. *Ireland 1478-1610*. Dublin: The Educational Company of Ireland, Ltd., 1980.

Cosgrove, Art. *Later Medieval Ireland, 1370-1541*. Dublin: Helicon Limited, 1981.

Curtis, Edmund. *A History of Medieval Ireland*. 2nd ed. London: Methuen & Co., Ltd., 1938.

de Breffny, Brian. *Castles of Ireland*. London: Thames and Hudson, 1985.

de Breffny, Brian, and George Mott. *The Churches and Abbeys of Ireland*. London: Thames and Hudson, 1976.

Dolley, Michael. *Anglo-Norman Ireland*. Gill History of Ireland, Vol. 3. Dublin: Gill and Macmillan, 1972.

Ellis, Steven G. *Tudor Ireland*. London and New York: Longman, 1985.

Falls, Cyril. *Elizabeth's Irish Wars*. London: Methuen & Co., Ltd., 1950.

Frame, Robin. *Colonial Ireland, 1169-1369*. Dublin: Helicon Limited, 1981.

Gwynn, Aubrey, and R. Neville Hadcock. *Medieval Religious Houses: Ireland*. London: Longman, 1970.

Jones, Frederick M. *Mountjoy, 1563-1606: The Last Elizabethan Deputy*. Dublin: Clonmore and Reynolds Ltd.; London: Burns Oates & Washbourne Ltd., 1958.

Leask, Harold G. *Irish Castles and Castellated Houses*. Dundalk: Dundalgan Press (W. Tempest) Ltd., 1986.

——. *Irish Churches and Monastic Buildings, Vol. II: Gothic Architecture to A.D. 1400*. Dundalk: Dundalgan Press (W. Tempest) Ltd., 1966.

——. *Irish Churches and Monastic Buildings, Vol. III: Medieval Gothic: the Last Phases*. Dundalk: Dundalgan Press (W. Tempest) Ltd., 1985.

Lydon, J. F. *The Lordship of Ireland in the Middle Ages*. Dublin: Gill and Macmillan, 1972.

——. *Ireland in the Later Middle Ages*. Gill History of Ireland, Vol. 6. Dublin: Gill and Macmillan, 1973.

MacCarthy-Morrogh, Michael. *The Munster Plantation: English Migration to Southern Ireland, 1583-1641.* Oxford: The Clarendon Press, 1986.

MacCurtain, Margaret. *Tudor and Stuart Ireland.* The Gill History of Ireland, Vol. 7. Dublin: Gill and Macmillan, 1972.

Martin, F. X., F. J. Byrne, W. E. Vaughan, Art Cosgrove, and J. R. Hill, eds. *A New History of Ireland.* Vol. II. Oxford: The Clarendon Press, 1987.

Moody, Theodore W., F. X. Martin, F. J. Byrne, eds. *A New History of Ireland.* Vol. III. Oxford: The Clarendon Press, 1976.

Nicholls, Kenneth. *Gaelic and Gaelicised Ireland in the Middle Ages.* The Gill History of Ireland, Vol. 4. Dublin: Gill and Macmillan, 1972.

Otway-Ruthven, A.J.A. *A History of Medieval Ireland.* London and New York: Barnes & Noble, 1968.

Scott, A. B., and F. X. Martin, eds. *Expugnatio Hibernica (The Conquest of Ireland) by Giraldus Cambrensis.* Dublin: Royal Irish Academy, 1978.

Stalley, Roger A. *Architecture and Sculpture in Ireland, 1150-1350.* Dublin: Gill and Macmillan, 1971.

——. *The Cistercian Monasteries of Ireland.* London, New Haven: Yale University Press, 1987.

Watt, John A. *The Church and the Two Nations in Medieval Ireland.* Cambridge: At the University Press, 1970.

——. *The Church in Medieval Ireland.* The Gill History of Ireland, Vol. 5. Dublin: Gill and Macmillan, 1972.

The Seventeenth and Eighteenth Centuries

(Chapters Five [Second Half] and Six)

Beckett, James C. *Protestant Dissent in Ireland, 1697-1780.* London: Faber and Faber Ltd., 1948.

——. *The Making of Modern Ireland, 1603-1923.* London, Boston: Faber and Faber, 1981.

Bottigheimer, Karl. *English Money and Irish Land.* New York: Oxford University Press, 1971.

Canny, Nicholas P. *The Upstart Earl: A Study of the Social and Mental World of Richard Boyle, First Earl of Cork, 1566-1643.* Cambridge, London, New York, New Rochelle, Melbourne, Sydney: Cambridge University Press, 1982.

Clarke, Aidan *The Old English in Ireland, 1625-42.* London: MacGibbon & Kee, Ltd., 1966.

Corish, Patrick J. *The Catholic Community in the Seventeenth and Eighteenth Centuries.* Dublin: Helicon Limited, 1981.

Cullen, Louis M. *An Economic History of Ireland Since 1660*. London: B. T. Batsford Ltd., 1987.

————. *The Emergence of Modern Ireland: 1600–1900*, Dublin: Gill and Macmillan, 1983.

Dickson, David. *New Foundations: Ireland 1600–1800*. Dublin: Helicon Limited, 1987.

Dickson, R. J. *Ulster Emigration to Colonial America, 1718–1775*. London: Routledge and Kegal Paul, 1966.

Johnston, Edith Mary. *Ireland in the Eighteenth Century*. The Gill History of Ireland, Vol. 8. Dublin: Gill and Macmillan, 1974.

Kearney, Hugh F. *Strafford in Ireland, 1733–41*. Manchester: Manchester University Press, 1959.

Kee, Robert. *A Most Distressful Country*. Vol. One of *The Green Flag* (3 vols.) London, Melbourne, New York: Quartet Books, Ltd., 1976.

Maxwell, Constantia, ed. *Arthur Young: A Tour in Ireland*. Belfast: The Blackstaff Press, Ltd., 1983.

McDowell, Robert Brendan. *Ireland in the Age of Imperialism and Revolution: 1760–1801*. Oxford: The Clarendon Press, 1979.

Miller, Kerby A. *Emigrants and Exiles: Ireland and the Irish Exodus to North America*. New York, Oxford: Oxford University Press, 1985.

Moody, T. W., and W. E. Vaughan, eds. *A New History of Ireland*. Vol. IV. Oxford: Clarendon Press, 1986.

Pakenham, Thomas, *The Year of Liberty: The Story of the Great Irish Rebellion of 1798*. Englewood Cliffs, N.J.: Prentice-Hall Inc., 1969.

Robinson, Philip S. *The Plantation of Ulster*. Dublin: Gill and Macmillan; New York: St. Martin's Press, 1984.

Simms, John G. *The Williamite Confiscation in Ireland, 1690–1703*. London: Faber and Faber Ltd., 1956.

The Nineteenth and Early Twentieth Centuries

(Chapters Seven and Eight)

Beckett, James C. *The Making of Modern Ireland, 1603–1623*. London, Boston: Faber and Faber, 1981.

Brown, Terence. *Ireland: A Social and Cultural History, 1922 to the Present*. Ithaca and London: Cornell University Press, 1985.

Buckland, Patrick. *A History of Northern Ireland*. Dublin: Gill and Macmillan, 1981.

Connolly, Sean. *Religion and Society in Nineteenth Century Ireland*. No. 3 in Studies in Irish Economic and Social History. Dundalk: Dundalgan Press, 1985.

Corish, Patrick J., ed. *A History of Irish Catholicism*. Vol. 5. Dublin: Gill and Macmillan, 1971.

Cullen, Louis M. *The Emergence of Modern Ireland: 1600–1900*. Dublin: Gill and Macmillan, 1983.

———. *An Economic History of Ireland Since 1660*. 2d ed. London: B. T. Batsford, Ltd., 1987.

Daly, Mary E. *Social and Economic History of Ireland Since 1800*. Dublin: The Educational Company of Ireland, Ltd., 1981.

———. *The Famine in Ireland*. Dundalk: Dublin Historical Association, Dundalgan Press, 1986.

Doyle, Oliver, and Stephen Hirsch. *Railways in Ireland: 1834–1984*. Dublin: Signal Press, 1983.

Edwards, R. D., and T. D. Williams, eds. *The Great Famine*. Dublin: Browne and Nolan, Ltd., 1956.

Ellman, Richard. *Yeats: The Man and the Masks*. London: Penguin Books, 1987.

———. *James Joyce*. New York: Oxford University Press, 1982.

Fanning, Ronan. *Independent Ireland*. Dublin: Helicon Limited, 1983.

Fitzpatrick, D. *Irish Emigration, 1801–1921*. No. 1 in Studies in Irish Economic and Social History. Dundalk, Dundalgan Press, Ltd., 1984.

Harkness, David. *Northern Ireland Since 1920*. Dublin: Helicon Limited, 1983.

Hoppen, K. Theodore. *Elections, Politics, and Society in Ireland, 1832–1885*. Oxford: The Clarendon Press, 1984.

Hull, Roger H. *The Irish Triangle: Conflict in Northern Ireland*. Princeton, N.J.: Princeton University Press, 1976.

Johnson, David. *The Interwar Economy in Ireland*. No. 4 in Studies in Irish Economic and Social History. Dundalk: Dundalgan Press, 1985.

Johnston, Joseph. *Irish Agriculture in Transition*. Dublin: Hodges Figgish and Co., Ltd.; Oxford; Basil Blackwell, 1951.

Kee, Robert. *The Bold Fenian Men*. Vol. II in *The Green Flag*. London: Quartet Books Limited, 1976.

———. *Ourselves Alone*. Vol. III in *The Green Flag*. London: Quartet Books Limited, 1976.

Lee, Joseph. *The Modernisation of Irish Society: 1848–1918*. The Gill History of Ireland, Vol. 10. Dublin: Gill and Macmillan, 1975.

Lyons, F.S.L. *Ireland Since the Famine*. London: Collins/Fontana, 1973.

Macdonagh, Oliver. *Ireland: The Union and Its Aftermath*. London: George Allen & Unwin, 1977.

———. *States of Mind: A Study of Anglo-Irish Conflict, 1780–1980*. London: George Allen & Unwin, 1983.

McCartney, Donal. *The Dawning of Democracy: Ireland 1800–1870*. Dublin: Helicon Limited, 1987.

Miller, Kerby A. *Emigrants and Exiles: Ireland and the Irish Exodus to North America*. New York, Oxford: Oxford University Press, 1985.

Murphy, John A. *Ireland in the Twentieth Century*. The Gill History of Ireland, Vol. 11. Dublin: Gill and Macmillan, 1975.

Nowlan, Kevin B., and T. Desmond Williams, eds. *Ireland in the War Years and After: 1939–1951*. South Bend, Ind.: University of Notre Dame Press, 1970.

O'Connor, Ulick. *Celtic Dawn: A Portrait of the Irish Literary Renaissance*. London: Black Swan, 1985.

Gróda, Cormac. *Ireland Before and After the Famine*. Manchester: Manchester University Press, 1988.

Tuathaigh, Gearóid. *Ireland Before the Famine, 1798–1848*. The Gill History of Ireland, Vol. 9. Dublin: Gill and Macmillan, 1972.

Solow, Barbara Lewis. *The Land Question and the Irish Economy, 1870–1903*. Cambridge, Mass.: Harvard University Press, 1971.

Vaughan, W. E. *Sin, Sheep and Scotsmen: John George Adair and the Derryveagh Evictions, 1861*. Belfast: The Appletree Press and the Ulster Society for Irish Historical Studies, 1983.

———. *Landlords and Tenants in Ireland, 1848–1904*. No. 2 in Studies in Irish Economic and Social History. Dundalk: Dundalgan Press Ltd., 1984.

Whyte, J. H. *Church and State in Modern Ireland, 1923–1979*. 2d ed. Totowa, N.J.: Gill and Macmillan, Barnes & Noble Books, 1980.

Woodham-Smith, Cecil. *The Great Hunger*, New York: Dutton. 1962.

Index

Page numbers in **bold type** refer to Gazetteer

About the Author

Philip A. Crowl was born in Dayton, Ohio, in 1914. After graduating from Oakwood High School in that city, he was educated at Swarthmore College (A.B. with Highest Honors in History, 1936), the University of Iowa (M.A. in History, 1939), and the Johns Hopkins University (Ph.D. in History, 1942). He has taught history and related subjects at Princeton University, the U.S. Naval Academy, Swarthmore College, the University of Nebraska, Stanford University, and the U.S. Naval War College. Between 1942 and 1945 he served as an officer in the U.S. Navy, mostly in the Pacific, and between 1957 and 1967 as an intelligence officer in the Department of State in Washington. His publications include *Maryland During and After the American Revolution* (1943), *The U.S. Marines and Amphibious War* (with J. A. Isely—1951), *Seizure of the Gilberts and Marshalls* (with E. G. Love—1955), *Campaign in the Marianas* (1960), and three historic guidebooks: *The Intelligent Traveller's Guide to Historic Britain* (1983), *The Intelligent Traveller's Guide to Historic Scotland* (1986), and the present volume, which completes the trilogy.